Communications in Computer and Information Science 2789

Rationale

The CCIS series is devoted to the publication of proceedings of computer science conferences. Its aim is to efficiently disseminate original research results in informatics in printed and electronic form. While the focus is on publication of peer-reviewed full papers presenting mature work, inclusion of reviewed short papers reporting on work in progress is welcome, too. Besides globally relevant meetings with internationally representative program committees guaranteeing a strict peer-reviewing and paper selection process, conferences run by societies or of high regional or national relevance are also considered for publication.

Topics

The topical scope of CCIS spans the entire spectrum of informatics ranging from foundational topics in the theory of computing to information and communications science and technology and a broad variety of interdisciplinary application fields.

Information for Volume Editors and Authors

Publication in CCIS is free of charge. No royalties are paid, however, we offer registered conference participants temporary free access to the online version of the conference proceedings on SpringerLink (http://link.springer.com) by means of an http referrer from the conference website and/or a number of complimentary printed copies, as specified in the official acceptance email of the event.

CCIS proceedings can be published in time for distribution at conferences or as post-proceedings, and delivered in the form of printed books and/or electronically as USBs and/or e-content licenses for accessing proceedings at SpringerLink. Furthermore, CCIS proceedings are included in the CCIS electronic book series hosted in the SpringerLink digital library at http://link.springer.com/bookseries/7899. Conferences publishing in CCIS are allowed to use Online Conference Service (OCS) for managing the whole proceedings lifecycle (from submission and reviewing to preparing for publication) free of charge.

Publication process

The language of publication is exclusively English. Authors publishing in CCIS have to sign the Springer CCIS copyright transfer form, however, they are free to use their material published in CCIS for substantially changed, more elaborate subsequent publications elsewhere. For the preparation of the camera-ready papers/files, authors have to strictly adhere to the Springer CCIS Authors' Instructions and are strongly encouraged to use the CCIS LaTeX style files or templates.

Abstracting/Indexing

CCIS is abstracted/indexed in DBLP, Google Scholar, EI-Compendex, Mathematical Reviews, SCImago, Scopus. CCIS volumes are also submitted for the inclusion in ISI Proceedings.

How to start

To start the evaluation of your proposal for inclusion in the CCIS series, please send an e-mail to ccis@springer.com

Teresa Guarda · Filipe Portela ·
Maria Fernanda Augusto ·
Jairo R. Coronado-Hernández
Editors

Advanced Research in Technologies, Information, Innovation and Sustainability

5th International Conference, ARTIIS 2025
Cartagena de Indias, Colombia, October 21–23, 2025
Revised Selected Papers, Part II

Editors
Teresa Guarda
Universidad Estatal Peninsula
Santa Elena, Ecuador

Maria Fernanda Augusto
BITrum Research Group
León, Spain

Filipe Portela
Algoritmi Research Centre Universidade do Minho
Guimarães, Portugal

Jairo R. Coronado-Hernández
Universidad de la Costa
Atlántico, Colombia

ISSN 1865-0929 ISSN 1865-0937 (electronic)
Communications in Computer and Information Science
ISBN 978-3-032-16757-6 ISBN 978-3-032-16758-3 (eBook)
https://doi.org/10.1007/978-3-032-16758-3

This Springer imprint is published by the registered company Springer Nature Switzerland AG
The registered company address is: Gewerbestrasse 11, 6330 Cham, Switzerland

Preface

The need for a greener and more digital world leads academia, governments, industry and citizens to look for emerging, sustainable, intelligent solutions and trends.

These new solutions and ideas must promote communication and ubiquitous computing between society agents, i.e., citizens, industry, organizations, net-worked machines and physical objects, and provide a promising vision of the future integrating the real world of knowledge agents and things with the virtual world of information. The emerging approaches in study or development can address several dimensions with a technological focus like Information, Innovation, Sustainability and topics such as Computing Solutions, Data Intelligence, Ethics, Security, Privacy and Sustainability.

These topics are closely related to the field of Information Systems (IS) because all of them involve the use and management of technology and data to achieve specific purposes or goals. Computing Solutions are a crucial aspect of information systems as they provide the technical infrastructure and tools for organizations to manage and process data. Data Intelligence is also a key area of information systems as it involves the collection, analysis and interpretation of data to support decision-making and problem-solving. Sustainability is becoming an increasingly important aspect of information systems as organizations are recognizing the impact of technology on the environment and are looking for ways to reduce their carbon footprint. Ethics, Security and Privacy are also essential aspects of information systems as they involve the responsible and secure use of technology and data to protect individuals and organizations from potential harm.

The change observed in society modifies the landscape of human activity, particularly regarding knowledge acquisition and production, offering new possibilities and challenges that need to be explored, assessed and disseminated.

ARTIIS is an international forum for researchers and practitioners to present and discuss the most recent innovations, trends, results, experiences and concerns from several perspectives of Technologies, Information, Innovation and Sustainability.

The conference was held in a hybrid format, with some participants present in person, in Cartagena de Indias, Colombia. We enabled virtual participation for those who were unable to attend the event, due to logistical, political, economic or other types of issues, by adopting the infrastructure of the Microsoft Teams platform.

These three volumes (CCIS volumes 2788–2789–2790) consist of the peer-reviewed papers from the 2025 International Conference on Advanced Research in Technologies, Information, Innovation and Sustainability (ARTIIS 2025), which took place during October 21–23, 2025. In addition, the peer-reviewed papers of the 15 Workshops, the Workshops proceedings, are published in a separate set consisting of two volumes (CCIS 2791–2792).

The first volume of the book (CCIS volume 2788) contains all the papers on the topic Computing Solutions: it addresses the development of applications and platforms involving computing that relates to some area of knowledge or society. It includes topics like networks, pervasive computing, gamification and software engineering.

The second volume (CCIS volume 2789) contains all the papers on the topic Data Intelligence: it focuses on data (e.g., text, images) acquisition and processing using smart techniques or tools. It includes topics such as computing intelligence, Artificial Intelligence, Data Science and Computer Vision.

The third volume (CCIS volume 2790) contains all the papers on the topics Sustainability, Ethics, Security and Privacy. Sustainability explores a new type of computing, more green, connected, efficient and sustainable. Topics like Immersive Tech, Smart Cities and Sustainable Infrastructures are part of this topic. Ethics, Security and Privacy show a more strict and secure area of Information Systems where the end-user is the main concern. Vulnerabilities, Data Privacy and cybersecurity are the main subjects of this topic.

The fifth edition of ARTIIS, realized in 2025, received 443 contributions from 46 countries worldwide. The acceptance rate was 38%, 150 regular papers and 18 short papers. We accepted 91 full papers and 10 short papers from 266 submissions to the Main Conference. For the 15 workshops we accepted 59 full papers and 8 short papers from 177 submissions.

The papers accepted to ARTIIS 2025 are published by the Communications in Computer and Information Science series (Springer CCIS). It is indexed in DBLP, Google Scholar, EI-Compendex, SCImago and Scopus. CCIS volumes are also submitted for inclusion in ISI Proceedings.

ARTIIS 2025 had the support of Universidad Estatal Península de Santa Elena, Ecuador; the Algoritmi Research Center of the University of Minho, Portugal; Universidad de la Costa, Colombia; and Corporación Universitaria Rafael Núñez, Colombia.

The Program Committee was composed of a multidisciplinary group of more than 453 experts from 61 countries, with the responsibility for evaluating, in a 'double-blind review' process, the papers received for each of the main themes proposed for the conference and workshops. Submissions to the main conference received three reviews each on average.

The success of the ARTIIS conference series, and especially ARTIIS 2025, reinforces our commitment to continuing this valuable work. We extend our sincere gratitude to everyone who contributed to this achievement: Authors, Presenters, Participants, Keynote Speakers, Workshop chairs, Session chairs, Organizing committee members, Student volunteers, General Chairs, Program Committee members, Steering Committee members, Communication Chair and Reviewers.

We also wish to thank our publisher, Springer, for their agreement to publish the proceedings, and for their kind and professional assistance.

We cordially invite you to visit the ARTIIS website https://artiis.org.

November 2025

Teresa Guarda
Filipe Portela
Maria Fernanda Augusto
Jairo R. Coronado-Hernández

Organization

General Chairs

Teresa Guarda	Universidad Estatal Península de Santa Elena, Ecuador University of Minho, Portugal
Filipe Portela	University of Minho, Portugal

Program Committee Chairs

Teresa Guarda	Universidad Estatal Península de Santa Elena, Ecuador
Filipe Portela	University of Minho, Portugal
Jairo Coronado-Hernández	Universidad de la Costa, Colombia

Local Organizing Committee Chairs

Jairo Coronado-Hernández	Universidad de la Costa, Colombia
Ivan Portnoy	Universidad de la Costa, Colombia
Jairo Acosta Solano	Corporación Universitaria Rafael Núñez, Colombia
Miguel Caro	Corporación Universitaria Rafael Núñez, Colombia
Gustavo Gatica	Universidad Andrés Bello, Chile

Steering Committee

Beatriz De La Iglesia	University of East Anglia, UK
Bruno Sousa	University of Coimbra, Portugal
Modestos Stavrakis	University of the Aegean, Greece
Ricardo Vardasca	ISLA Santarém, Portugal
Simon Rogerson	De Montfort University, UK
Wolfgang Hofkirchner	Technische Universität Wien, Austria

Special Sessions Chairs

Abrar Ullah	Heriot-Watt University, Dubai, UAE
Teresa Guarda	Universidad Estatal Península de Santa Elena, Ecuador

Communication Chair

Maria Fernanda Augusto	BITrum Research Group, Spain

Program Committee

A. Manuela Gonçalves	University of Minho, Portugal
Abbas Aljuboori	Al Zahra College for Women, Oman
Alberto Simões	Instituto Politécnico do Cávado e do Ave, Portugal
Alejandro Rodriguez	Universidad Politécnica de Madrid, Spain
Aleksandra Djordjevic	University of Belgrade, Serbia
Alfredo Cuzzocrea	University of Calabria, Italy
Alfredo Milani	University of Perugia, Italy
Ana Azevedo	Polytechnic of Porto, Portugal
Ana Cláudia Campos	University of Algarve, Portugal
Ana Paula Teixeira	Universidade de Trás-os-Montes e Alto Douro, Portugal
Ana Pereira	Polytechnic Institute of Bragança, Portugal
Ana Ramires	Universidade Europeia, Portugal
Anacleto Correia	CINAV/Escola Naval, Portugal
Andreas Fricke	University of Potsdam, Germany
Andrei Tchernykh	CICESE Research Center, Mexico
Angel Dacal-Nieto	CTAG Centro Tecnologico de Automocion de Galicia, Spain
Anisha Kumari	National Institute of Technology Rourkela, India
Antonio Dourado	University of Coimbra, Portugal
António Fernandes	Instituto Politécnico de Bragança, Portugal
Antonio Jesús Muñoz-Montoro	Universidad de Málaga, Spain
Antonio Silva Sprock	Universidad Central de Venezuela, Venezuela
António Trigo	Instituto Politécnico de Coimbra, ISCAC, Portugal
Arnulfo Alanis Garza	Instituto Tecnológico de Tijuana, Mexico
Asma Patel	Staffordshire University, UK
Attila Körei	University of Miskolc, Hungary

Babar Shah	Zayed University, United Arab Emirates
Barna Iantovics	University of Medicine, Pharmacy, Science, and Technology of Targu Mures, Romania
Beatriz De La Iglesia	University of East Anglia, UK
Benedetto Barabino	Università degli Studi di Brescia, Italy
Bertil P. Marques	Instituto Superior de Engenharia do Porto, Portugal
Biswajeeban Mishra	University of Szeged, Hungary
Bruno Sousa	University of Coimbra, Portugal
Camille Salinesi	CRI, Université de Paris1 Panthéon-Sorbonne, France
Carina Pimentel	University of Aveiro, Portugal
Carina Silva	Escola Superior de Tecnologia da Saúde de Lisboa, Portugal
Carla Cavallo	University of Naples Federico II, Italy
Carlos Balsa	Instituto Politécnico de Bragança, Portugal
Carlos Costa	Universidade de Lisboa, Portugal
Carlos Fajardo	Fundación Universitaria Konrad Lorenz, Colombia
Carlos H. F. Alves	Federal Center of Technological Education, Brazil
Carlos Lopezosa	Universitat Pompeu Fabra Barcelona, Spain
Carlos R. Cunha	Instituto Politécnico de Bragança, Portugal
Carmen Guida	Università degli Studi di Napoli Federico II, Italy
Cecilia Avila	Fundación Universitaria Konrad Lorenz, Colombia
Cecilia Castro	Universidade do Minho, Portugal
Celia Ramos	University of the Algarve, Portugal
Chien-Sing Lee	Sunway University, Malaysia
Christian Grévisse	University of Luxembourg, Luxembourg
Christoph Schütz	Johannes Kepler University Linz, Austria
Christos Anagnostopoulos	University of Glasgow, UK
Clara Bento Vaz	Instituto Politécnico de Bragança, Portugal
Clarice Maraschin	Universidade Federal do Rio Grande do Sul, Brazil
Claudia Seabra	University of Coimbra, Portugal
Corrado Rindone	Università degli studi Mediterranea di Reggio Calabria, Italy
Daniele Granata	Università della Campania "Luigi Vanvitelli", Italy
Dasa Munkova	Constantine the Philosopher University in Nitra, Slovakia
Dimos Pantazis	Technological Education Institution of Athens, Greece

Elena Cantatore	Politecnico di Bari, Italy
Elena Cocuzza	University of Catania, Italy
Elisabetta Ronchieri	INFN CNAF, Italy
Elisete Mourão	Universidade de Trás-os-Montes e Alto Douro, Portugal
Emmanuel Okewu	University of Lagos, Nigeria
Enrique Carrera	Universidad de las Fuerzas Armadas, Ecuador
Erica Isa Mosca	Politecnico di Milano, Italy
Ester Scotto di Perta	University of Naples Federico II, Italy
Estrella Diaz	Castilla-La Mancha University, Spain
Eugen Rusu	Dunărea de Jos University of Galați, Romania
Fabio Alberto Schreiber	Politecnico di Milano, Italy
Fabio Rocha	Universidade Tiradentes, Brazil
Fabio Silveira	Federal University of São Paulo, Brazil
Fakhri Alam Khan	King Fahd University of Petroleum & Minerals, Saudi Arabia
Federica Gaglione	Università degli Studi del Sannio, Italy
Felipe S. Semaan	Fluminense Federal University, Brazil
Felix Härer	University of Fribourg, Switzerland
Fernanda A. Ferreira	Polytechnic Institute of Porto, Portugal
Fezile Ozdamli	Near East University, Turkey
Filipe Mota Pinto	Polytechnic Institute of Leiria, Portugal
Filipe Portela	University of Minho, Portugal
Flavia Marzano	Link Campus University, Italy
Flora Ferreira	University of Minho, Portugal
Florin Pop	University Politehnica of Bucharest, Romania
Francesco Mercaldo	University of Sannio, Italy
Francesco Palmieri	University of Salerno, Italy
Francesco Santini	Università di Perugia, Italy
Francisco Alvarez	Universidad Autónoma de Aguascalientes, Mexico
Frederico Branco	Universidade de Trás-os-Montes e Alto Douro, Portugal
Frederico Lopes	Universidade Federal do Rio Grande do Norte, Brazil
Gabriel Hornink	Federal University of Alfenas, Brazil
Geert Poels	Ghent University, Belgium
George Stalidis	Alexander Technological Educational Institute of Thessaloniki, Greece
Georgios Georgiadis	Aristotle University of Thessaloniki, Greece
Gerardo Carpentieri	University of Naples Federico II, Italy
Gianni D'Angelo	University of Salerno, Italy

Giovanni Paragliola	ICAR-CNR, Italy
Guillermo Rodriguez	ISISTAN-UNICEN, Argentina
Gustavo Gatica	Universidad Andrés Bello, Chile
Héctor Bedón	Universidad a Distancia de Madrid, Spain
Helia Guerra	University of the Azores, Portugal
Henrique Vicente	Universidade de Évora, Portugal
Hugo Peixoto	University of Minho, Portugal
Humberto Rocha	Universidade de Coimbra, Portugal
Ilaria Matteucci	IIT-CNR, Italy
Inna Skarga-Bandurova	Oxford Brookes University, UK
Ioan Ciumasu	Université de Versailles Saint-Quentin, France
Ioannis Politis	Aristotle University of Thessaloniki, Greece
Ioannis Vrellis	University of Ioannina, Greece
Iqbal H. Sarker	Edith Cowan University, Australia
Isabel Lopes	Instituto Politécnico de Bragança, Portugal
J. Luis Luviano-Ortiz	University of Guanajuato, Mexico
Jakub Swacha	University of Szczecin, Poland
Joanna Kolodziej	NASK Warsaw and Cracow University of Technology, Poland
Jordi Vallverdú	Universitat Autònoma de Barcelona, Spain
Jorge Buele	Universidad Tecnológica Indoamerica, Ecuador
Jorge Herrera-Tapia	Universidad Laica Eloy Alfaro de Manabí, Ecuador
Jorge Luis Bacca Acosta	University of Girona, Spain
Jorge Oliveira e Sá	University of Minho, Portugal
José Carlos Paiva	University of Porto, Portugal
Jose Guillermo Guarnizo Marin	Santo Tomás University, Colombia
José Machado	University of Minho, Portugal
José María Díaz-Nafría	Madrid Open University, Spain
José Méndez Reboredo	University of Vigo, Spain
José Rufino	Polytechnic Institute of Bragança, Portugal
Juan-Ignacio Latorre-Biel	Public University of Navarre, Spain
Kalinka Kaloyanova	University of Sofia, Bulgaria
Kanchana Rajaram	SSN College of Engineering, India
Karine Ferreira	Instituto Nacional de Pesquisas Espaciais, Brazil
Kazuaki Tanaka	Kyushu Institute of Technology, Japan
Laura Verde	Università della Campania Luigi Vanvitelli, Italy
Lelio Campanile	Università degli studi della Campania Luigi Vanvitelli, Italy
Leonardo Soto-Sumuano	Universidad de Guadalajara, Mexico
Leticia Vaca-Cardenas	Universidad Técnica de Manabí, Ecuador

Ľubomír Benko	Constantine the Philosopher University in Nitra, Slovakia
Luigi Piero Di Bonito	University of Campania Luigi Vanvitelli, Italy
Luis Gomes	Universidade dos Açores, Portugal
Luís Matos	Universidade do Minho, Portugal
Luiza de Macedo Mourelle	State University of Rio de Janeiro, Brazil
M. Filomena Teodoro	Portuguese Naval Academy, Portugal
Manuela Cañizares Espada	Universidad a Distancia de Madrid, Spain
Manuele Kirsch-Pinheiro	Université Paris 1 Panthéon-Sorbonne, France
Marcelo Fajardo-Pruna	Escuela Superior Politécnica del Litoral, Ecuador
Marcelo Leon	Universidad Tecnológica Empresarial de Guayaquil, Ecuador
Marcin Woźniak	Silesian University of Technology, Poland
Marco Gribaudo	Politecnico di Milano, Italy
Marco Zucca	University of Cagliari, Italy
Marco Cabezas González	Universidad de Salamanca, Spain
Margherita Lasorella	Polytechnic University of Bari, Italy
Maria Isabel Ribeiro	Instituto Politécnico Bragança, Portugal
Maria João Fernandes Polidoro	Politécnico do Porto, Portugal
Maria João Rodrigues	Universidade do Porto, Portugal
Maria José Abreu	Universidade do Minho, Portugal
Maria Macchiaroli	University of Salerno, Italy
Maria Sousa	Universidade do Algarve, Portugal
Maria Stella de Biase	Università degli Studi della Campania Luigi Vanvitelli, Italy
Mariapia Raimondo	Università degli Studi della Campania Luigi Vanvitelli, Italy
Marílio Cardoso	Instituto Superior de Engenharia do Porto, Portugal
Marilisa Botte	University of Naples Federico II, Italy
Marina Alexandra Andrade	ISCTE Instituto Universitário de Lisboa, Portugal
Mario Pérez-Montoro	University of Barcelona, Spain
Mario Pinto	Politécnico do Porto, Portugal
Maritza Placencia	Universidad Nacional Mayor de San Marco, Peru
Martinha Piteira	Instituto Politécnico de Setúbal, Portugal
Mauro Iacono	Università degli Studi della Campania Luigi Vanvitelli, Italy
Michal Baczynski	University of Silesia in Katowice, Poland
Michal Munk	Constantine the Philosopher University in Nitra, Slovakia
Michel Soares	Universidade Federal de Sergipe, Brazil
Michele Mastroianni	University of Salerno, Italy
Mirka Mobilia	University of Salerno, Italy

Modestos Stavrakis	University of the Aegean, Greece
Mohamad Molaei Qelichi	University of Tehran, Iran
Mohammadsadegh Mohagheghi	Vali-e-Asr University of Rafsanjan, Iran
Mónica Pinto	Universidad de Málaga, Spain
Muhammad Younas	Oxford Brookes University, UK
Naveed Abbas	Islamia College, Peshawar, Malaysia
Naveenbalaji Gowthaman	University of KwaZulu-Natal, South Africa
Neelam Gohar	Shaheed Benazir Bhutto Women University, Pakistan
Nguyen D. Thanh	Banking University of Ho Chi Minh City, Vietnam
Nikolaos Matsatsinis	Technical University of Crete, Greece
Nishu Gupta	Norwegian University of Science and Technology in Gjøvik, Norway
Nuno C. Marques	Universidade Nova de Lisboa, Portugal
Nuno Pombo	University of Beira Interior, Portugal
Olivier Parisot	Luxembourg Institute of Science and Technology, Luxembourg
Omar Castellanos	Universidad Estatal Península de Santa Elena, Ecuador
Omid Fatahi Valilai	Jacobs University Bremen gGmbH, Germany
Oscar Dias	University of Minho, Portugal
Pankaj Mishra	G. B. Pant University of Agriculture and Technology, India
Paola Britos	Universidad Nacional de Río Negro - Sede Andina/Atlántica, Argentina
Paolino Di Felice	University of L'Aquila, Italy
Patricia Cano-Olivos	Universidad Popular Autónoma del Estado de Puebla, Mexico
Paula Amaral	Universidade Nova de Lisboa, Portugal
Paula Odete Fernandes	UNIAG; Instituto Politécnico de Bragança, Portugal
Paulo Piloto	Polytechnic Institute of Bragança, Portugal
Paulo Vasconcelos	University of Porto, Portugal
Pedro Gago	Polytechnic Institute of Leiria, Portugal
Piedade Carvalho	Instituto Superior de Engenharia do Porto, Portugal
Rafal Scherer	Częstochowa University of Technology, Poland
Raphael Gomes	Instituto Federal de Goiás, Brazil
Ricardo Cajo	Escuela Superior Politécnica del Litoral, Ecuador
Ricardo Correia	Instituto Politécnico de Bragança, Portugal
Ricardo Queirós	Politécnico do Porto, Portugal
Ricardo Vardasca	ISLA Santarém, Portugal
Robertas Damasevicius	Silesian University of Technology, Poland

Roberto Andrade	Escuela Politécnica Nacional, Ecuador
Roberto Nardone	University of Naples “Parthenope”, Italy
Roman Chertovskih	University of Porto, Portugal
Ronan Guivarch	Université de Toulouse, France
Rosa Reis	Instituto Superior de Engenharia do Porto, Portugal
Rytis Maskeliunas, Kaunas	University of Technology, Lithuania
S. B. Kulkarni	SDMCET, India
Said Broumi	Hassan II University Mohammedia-Casablanca, Morocco
Samson Oruma	Østfold University College, Norway
Sanjay Misra	Østfold University, Norway
Sanket Mishra	BITS Pilani Hyderabad Campus, India
Sara Paiva	Instituto Politécnico de Viana do Castelo, Portugal
Sergio Cappucci	ENEA, Italy
Sergio Ilarri	University of Zaragoza, Spain
Shelly Sachdeva	National Institute of Technology Delhi, India
Sherali Zeadally	University of Kentucky, USA
Shuhei Kimura	Tottori University, Japan
Silvia Araújo	University of Minho, Portugal
Silvia Rossetti	Università degli Studi di Parma, Italy
Simone Belli	Universidad Complutense de Madrid, Spain
Simone Corrado	Università degli Studi della Basilicata, Italy
Smriti Agrawal	Chaitanya Bharathi Institute of Technology, India
Socrates Basbas	Aristotle University of Thessaloniki, Greece
Sofia Almeida	Universidade Europeia, Portugal
Sonia Casillas Martín	Universidad de Salamanca, Spain
Spyros Panagiotakis	Hellenic Mediterranean University, Greece
Stefania Regalbuto	Ca’ Foscari University of Venice, Italy
Stefano Falcinelli	University of Perugia, Italy
Stephan Scheele	Fraunhofer IIS, Germany
Sumit Babu	Harcourt Butler Technical University, India
Syeda Sumbul Hossain	Daffodil International University, Bangladesh
Sylwia Krzysztofik	Lodz University of Technology, Poland
Tapiwa Gundu	Sol Plaatje University, South Africa
Telmo Pinto	University of Minho, Portugal
Tengku Adil Tengku Izhar	Universiti Teknologi MARA, Malaysia
Teresa Guarda	Universidad Estatal Península de Santa Elena, Ecuador
Tetiana Biloborodova	Volodymyr Dahl East Ukraine National University, Ukraine
Tiziana Campisi	University of Enna KORE, Italy

Ugo Fiore	University of Naples Federico II, Italy
Ulises Ruiz	Instituto Nacional de Astrofisica Optica y Electronica, Mexico
Vanda Lourenco	NOVA University of Lisbon, Portugal
Vasileios Gkioulos	Norwegian University of Science and Technology, Norway
Vicente F. De Lucena Jr	Federal University of Amazonas, Brazil
Victor Alves	University of Minho, Portugal
Victor Darriba	Universidade de Vigo, Spain
Virginie Felizardo	Universidade da Beira Interior, Portugal
Vitor Monteiro	University of Minho, Portugal
Vladimir Tcheverda	Institute of Petroleum Geology and Geophysics, Russia
Milliam Maxime Zekeng Ndadji	University of Dschang, Cameroon

Workshops

Applications of Computational Mathematics to Simulation and Data Analysis (ACMaSDA 2025)
Business, Technology and Digital Transformation (BTDT 2025)
Challenges and the Impact of Communication and Information Technologies on Education (CICITE 2025)
Cybersecurity in Information and Communication Technologies (CICT 2025)
Emerging Technologies in Communications and Networking (ET-CN 2025)
Workshop on Gamification Application and Technologies (GAT 2025)
Mapping the information understanding (glossaLAB 2025)
Innovation in Information Security (IIS 2025)
Intelligent Systems for Health and Medical Care (ISHMC 2025)
International Symposium on Technological Innovations for Industry and Society (ISTIIS 2025)
International Workshop on Electronic and Telecommunications (IWET 2025)
International Workshop on Next-Generation Software Engineering (NEXT-SOFT 2025)
Smart Tourism and Information Systems (SMARTTIS 2025)
Technological Strategies on Digital Communication and Marketing (TechDiComM 2025)
Workshop on IoT Networks and Wireless for Sustainability (WIN-WIN-4S 2025)

Sponsoring Organizations

Universidad Estatal Península de Santa Elena, Ecuador
Universidad de la Costa, Barranquilla, Colombia

Corporación Universitaria Rafael Núñez, Colombia
Universidade do Minho, Portugal
International Association for Technologies, Information, Innovation and Sustainability, Portugal
Institute for a Global Sustainable Information Society GSIS, Austria

Plenary Lectures

The Usage of Imaging and AI Methods in Aiding Skin Cancer Identification

Ricardo Vardasca

ISLA Santarém – Instituto Politécnico, Portugal

Abstract. Skin cancer can appear in two forms: melanoma and non-melanoma. Every year there are an estimated 331,000 new cases of melanoma and 1,234,000 new cases of non-melanoma skin cancer per year and both incidences are growing exponentially year by year. Both types of skin cancer cause around 17.6% and 5.6% death rates per year for melanoma and non-melanoma skin cancer respectively. Its early identification is difficult due to a shortage of specialists and lack of specific technology. Different imaging modalities can be used to collect data from people showing early signs of skin cancer; that data can be classified using Artificial Intelligence methods such as Machine Learning and Deep Learning.

It is the aim of this research to present the most recent developments in the area and disclose how they could be effectively implemented to cope with the wide need for early identification of skin cancer.

The overall accuracy in diagnosis of skin cancer by an experienced dermatologist is 59.2% in diagnosing melanoma skin cancer and for an assistant the value drops to 40.8%. The diagnosis can be aided using dermatoscopic images using the A, B, C, D and E method, considering the asymmetry, border, color and diameter of the lesion and its evolution between visits. Other imaging modalities such as near infrared, and ultraviolet thermography can be used to provide complementary information.

The existing freely available skin cancer imaging datasets are scarce and small. Techniques such as Gray-level Co-occurrence Matrix along with concatenation of simple Histogram of Oriented Gradients with a Support Vector Machines classification model achieved an accuracy of 97.8% for dermatoscopic images. Using a deep learning model composed of 40 neurons with infrared thermographic images achieved an accuracy of 92% in distinguishing melanoma from non-melanoma skin cancer. A mobile phone application consisting of a deep learning model trained with the HAM100000 dataset of dermatoscopic images achieved an accuracy of 91.10%; the model was DenseNet169 for two classes.

Despite the availability of proven imaging modalities that can act as complimentary diagnostic methods, which can be used with automated machine learning and deep learning technologies, their wide adoption is still failing due to lack of standardization and acceptance by medical professionals. For the standardization, stacking deep and machine learning methods combining different imaging methods, historical and social demographic information is required. AI Models in a clinical setting can help to cope with the shortage of health professionals and aid in reducing the waiting time for a specific consultation to address skin cancer identification. Although no electronic tool can replace the clinical judgement of diagnosis, it can provide prognosis insights to support decision making.

The Rise of Agentic Learning: Gamified AI for Personalized and Inclusive Classrooms

Ricardo Queirós

Polytechnic Institute of Porto, Portugal

Abstract. The rapid evolution of Artificial Intelligence (AI) is reshaping the landscape of education, introducing new opportunities for personalization, inclusivity, and learner engagement. This keynote examines the emergence of Agentic Learning, a paradigm in which autonomous AI agents actively collaborate with learners to co-construct learning trajectories. Unlike traditional AI-driven educational tools, agentic systems leverage reasoning, planning, and context persistence to deliver highly adaptive learning experiences that evolve over time. These systems are supported by modern frameworks and standards such as the Model Context Protocol (MCP), agent-to-agent (A2A) communication, and dynamically adaptive user interfaces, enabling multi-agent collaboration that aligns with learners' goals, behaviors, and developmental needs.

Gamification plays a complementary role by providing motivational structures that foster autonomy, mastery, and sustained engagement. Game-thinking mechanics, such as levels, quests, reward systems, and adaptive challenges, are enhanced by AI's ability to generate dynamic content, monitor engagement, and deliver personalized feedback loops. Together, agentic AI and gamification form a powerful ecosystem capable of addressing many long-standing challenges in education, including the diversity of student backgrounds, the increasing complexity of curriculum content, the limited time available to teachers, and persistent inequalities in access to high-quality learning support.

This keynote also highlights the evolving role of educators within this new landscape. Rather than being replaced, teachers are empowered to act as designers and orchestrators of AI-mediated learning experiences, focusing on mentorship, creativity, ethical guidance, and the development of human-centered learning environments.

Finally, it presents practical implementations that demonstrate the real-world potential of gamified agentic learning. These include the Framework for Gamified Programming Education (FGPE) [1], an integrated ecosystem for motivation-aware programming instruction; the Digital Hub, a centralized environment for interactive digital learning; and Gamibot [2], a gamified AI chatbot for Moodle that enhances student participation and feedback. Collectively, these examples illustrate how agentic AI, combined with game-thinking principles, can support the development of more personalized, equitable, and engaging classrooms.

1. Swacha, J., Queirós, R., Paiva, J.C., Leal, J.P., Kosta, S., Montella, R.: A roadmap to gamify programming education. In: Queirós, R., Portela, F., Pinto, M., Simões, A. (eds.) First International Computer Programming Education Conference (ICPEC

2020), pp. 26:1–26:7. Schloss Dagstuhl – Leibniz-Zentrum für Informatik (2020). https://doi.org/10.4230/OASIcs.ICPEC.2020.26

2. Moreira, M., Paiva, J., Pinto, M., Queirós, R.: GAMIBOT: Um chatbot educativo gamificado com integração no Moodle para suporte personalizado à aprendizagem. P.PIC – Conferência de Inovação Pedagógica do Porto, 8(3) (2025). https://doi.org/10.34630/pel.v8i3.6372

The Need to Break Disciplinary Walls: Co-creating Transdisciplinary Knowledge

José María Díaz-Nafría

Madrid Open University, Spain

Abstract. Interdisciplinary research is frequently presented as essential for addressing contemporary challenges, yet the rationale behind this claim is not always explicit. Why is disciplinary research insufficient in certain contexts? What historical and methodological factors shaped disciplinary boundaries, and what limitations do they impose? The modern organization of knowledge—deeply influenced by the tree-like structures of classification that emerged from Aristotle through Enlightenment science and reached its peak in positisim—has been extraordinarily successful in enabling specialization. However, these same structures constrain our ability to deal with the complex, interconnected problems characteristic of socio-technical and ecological systems. As parts of reality are strongly interconnected, so its understanding has to be. As scientific domains have multiplied and differentiated, the distance between conceptual frameworks has grown, making integrative understanding increasingly difficult. The distinction between multidisciplinarity and interdisciplinarity is therefore fundamental: whereas the former juxtaposes disciplinary contributions, the latter seeks bridges among them. Yet even interdisciplinarity can fall short when incompatible assumptions, methods, or conceptual vocabularies prevent meaningful synthesis. At what point are neither multidisciplinarity nor interdisciplinarity adequate, and what does it mean to move beyond them toward genuine knowledge integration?

In this keynote, Díaz Nafría examines these questions through the lens of knowledge networks, showing how both cognitive development and scientific practice rely on relational structures rather than hierarchical classifications. He traces the historical movement from tree-based representations of knowledge to network-based approaches that better reflect the complexity of contemporary research landscapes. Drawing on work in semantic networks, concept interaction, and the dynamics of knowledge agents, he argues that transdisciplinarity offers a pathway toward shared understanding by enabling the co-construction of concepts, categories, and frameworks across scientific communities.

A central part of the keynote is devoted to the collective effort embodied in glossaLAB, a platform designed to support transdisciplinary collaboration. glossaLAB provides tools for mapping, clarifying, and connecting conceptual structures across knowledge domains, allowing users to create networked glossaries, annotate content semantically, and observe how conceptual systems evolve when multiple knowledge domains merge. The platform also plays a key role in revitalizing and integrating the extensive work of some encyclopaedic endeavours that have lasted several decades and can play a significant role in the development of transdisciplinary science.

Díaz Nafría outlines ongoing developments within glossaLAB aimed at enhancing coherence and discovering epistemic emergence: automatic semantic annotation of large corpora, federated systems of interdisciplinary glossaries in subsidiarity relations, and tools for tracking structural changes in conceptual networks as transdisciplinary dialogue unfolds. Together, these efforts seek to strengthen the foundations for knowledge integration and foster environments in which disciplinary boundaries become permeable—not by erasing differences, but by enabling collaborative meaning-making. Ultimately, the keynote argues that transdisciplinarity is not merely an academic ideal but a practical necessity for addressing the complexity of the challenges faced by contemporary societies.

Contents

Data Intelligence

Data Intelligence

Improving Public Sector Efficiency Through Rapid Machine Learning-Based Product Classification

David Ruete[2], Nicolás Caselli[1](✉), Omar Salinas[2], Alejandro Caroca[2], Carla Taramasco[3], Marcelo Reyes[2], Diego Mellado[2], Jean Paul Maidana[2,3], Carlos Segura[2], and Mauricio Hernandez[2]

[1] Universidad Andres Bello, Concepción, Chile
nicolas.caselli@unab.cl
[2] Universidad Andres Bello, Viña del Mar, Chile
[3] Instituto de Tecnología para la Innovación en Salud y Bienestar, Universidad Andrés Bello, Viña del Mar, Chile

Abstract. This paper evaluates the use of machine learning models for text classification as a means to reduce the time required to construct the Coverage Indicator in the Technical Products Department of the Superintendency of Electricity and Fuels (SEC) in Chile. The current manual process to identify whether imported electrical products are certified is time consuming and limits national inspection capacity.

The proposed solution uses supervised machine learning models implemented in Python, including Support Vector Machines, Random Forest, Logistic Regression, and others, to automatically classify textual descriptions of imported products. The results of a pilot study demonstrate that the classification time can be reduced by more than 90%, with an accuracy rate that exceeds 99% using SVM models. In addition, the application of these models led to a significant improvement in the coverage indicator and enabled a wider coverage of inspection at the national level.

The study confirms the hypothesis that artificial intelligence techniques can substantially optimize regulatory processes, reduce operational times, and enhance public safety through faster detection of non-compliant products.

Keywords: Machine Learning · Text Classification · Regulatory Compliance · Operational Efficiency · Public Sector · Automation · Coverage Indicator · Supervised Learning

1 Introduction

The growing digitalization of processes in both public and private organizations leads to an exponential increase in the volume and diversity of available data. This reality presents a technical and strategic challenge: transforming such data

T. Guarda et al. (Eds.): ARTIIS 2025, CCIS 2789, pp. 3–15, 2026.
https://doi.org/10.1007/978-3-032-16758-3_1

into useful, timely, and actionable knowledge. In this context, Machine Learning (ML)—a branch of Artificial Intelligence (AI)—emerges as a key tool for automating processes, enhancing operational efficiency, and supporting informed decision-making in complex and dynamic environments [11,16,30].

The Superintendency of Electricity and Fuels (SEC) of Chile, whose institutional mandate is to ensure that energy products and services comply with quality and safety standards, faces a structural challenge in its certification process for imported products. The manual processing of records provided by Chilean Customs (ADUANAS DE CHILE)—which exceed one million units annually—results in lengthy classification times and delays in generating the coverage indicator. This situation compromises not only the efficiency of the process but also the critical response times required for the preventive inspection of products that may pose a risk to the public.

To address this problem, the present study proposes the incorporation of machine learning systems for the classification of customs records, aiming to reduce processing times, lessen the operational burden on inspectors, and enhance the institution's capacity for oversight and coverage. The central hypothesis posits that the use of supervised machine learning models significantly outperforms the manual process in terms of accuracy, speed, and scalability.

Numerous studies validate the use of supervised learning models for automatic text classification tasks in institutional and operational contexts. Algorithms such as Support Vector Machines (SVM), Naïve Bayes, Random Forest, and Logistic Regression prove effective in handling multiclass classification and imbalanced datasets, both of which are common in scenarios like that of the SEC [19,32,40]. These models can be enhanced through natural language processing (NLP) techniques—such as TF–IDF, Word2Vec, or pretrained language models like BERT—which improve the semantic representation of text and, consequently, the quality of classification [7,39].[1]

Moreover, at the international level, various government agencies have begun adopting AI-based solutions to modernize their processes. For instance, the United Kingdom government implements intelligent systems to analyze social benefit applications; Canada develops predictive models to detect tax fraud; and Singapore integrates machine learning into its border control systems to automatically classify high-risk cargo [27,37].

From a strategic perspective, the adoption of machine learning-based solutions provides not only greater efficiency, but also enhanced resilience, traceability, and adaptability to scenarios involving growing demand. These attributes are critical in the current context, where regulatory complexity, product diversity, and the speed of imports demand agile, data-driven responses [10,32].

[1] **Terminology at first mention:** *TF–IDF (Term Frequency–Inverse Document Frequency)* weights terms by their importance across documents; *Word2Vec* denotes shallow neural embedding models that learn dense vectors from local co-occurrence contexts; *BERT (Bidirectional Encoder Representations from Transformers)* is a pretrained bidirectional Transformer yielding contextualized token embeddings.

This research aims not only to demonstrate the technical feasibility of implementing machine learning models in the classification process of imported products managed by the SEC, but also to contribute to the academic and practical discourse on the role of artificial intelligence in the modernization of the public sector. Through the development of a pilot project, the study empirically evaluates the performance of various algorithms applied to historical SEC data, measuring key metrics such as accuracy, recall, F1-score, and response time, with the objective of delivering a replicable and scalable solution.

2 Context and Related Works

2.1 Context

Currently, the use of technologies based on data science and artificial intelligence (AI) has proven to be a key tool for optimizing critical processes in public institutions [5,27]. One of the most significant challenges in this domain is the automated processing of large volumes of unstructured textual information, particularly in tasks that involve classification or prioritization to support operational decision-making [39].

In the Chilean context, the Superintendency of Electricity and Fuels (SEC) must review a massive daily flow of customs records for imported products in order to determine whether such products require certification prior to being commercialized.

This task, currently carried out manually by the inspection team of the Technical Department of Products, presents several limitations. The high operational workload, the sustained growth in data volume, and the linguistic variability in the records (including typographical errors, abbreviations, and semantic ambiguity) have caused considerable delays in the generation of the coverage indicator, a key metric used to prioritize inspection efforts at the national level. Because this indicator relies on timely and accurate product classification, it is directly affected by the time-consuming nature of manual analysis, thereby compromising the institution's preventive oversight capacity.

This scenario reveals a critical gap between operational needs and institutional response capacity. Unlike structured processes, where traditional automation systems operate under fixed rules, the SEC's case demands a solution capable of understanding and adapting to the natural language used in customs product descriptions. In this context, Machine Learning (ML) techniques—particularly supervised models—emerge as an effective methodological alternative [16,19]. These models enable algorithms to be trained on historical data to automatically classify new records, even when those records exhibit high textual variability.

The international literature has extensively documented the effectiveness of ML in similar tasks across both public and private sectors, reporting improvements in efficiency, coverage, traceability, and adaptability [11,37]. The application of these techniques not only delivers value in terms of speed and accuracy, but also aligns with public sector modernization strategies aimed at strengthening smart regulatory oversight through the adoption of emerging technologies [4,27].

Building on this context, the present article proposes to evaluate various automatic classification techniques applied to real-world data provided by the SEC, with the objective of designing a model that automates the categorization process of imported products. The expected outcomes include reduced processing times, improved quality of the coverage indicator, and enhanced institutional capacity to operate effectively in an increasingly dynamic environment.

2.2 Related Works

Semantic Enrichment and Linguistic Cleaning in Administrative Texts. Recent literature highlights the importance of text normalization and entity disambiguation techniques as critical steps for improving the performance of classification models. Studies such as Atienza et al. (2022) propose specialized linguistic pipelines to address the ambiguity of technical terms in regulatory domains, emphasizing the need for adaptive approaches to texts with a high degree of domain-specific semantics [25]. Similarly, the work of Rodríguez et al. (2023) advocates the use of specialized embeddings trained on normative corpora, demonstrating significant improvements in multi-criteria categorization tasks [8].

Lightweight Models and Transfer Learning in Institutional Contexts. While Transformer-based models have demonstrated high levels of accuracy, their deployment in institutional environments with limited computational resources has driven the development of more lightweight variants. Models such as DistilBERT, ALBERT, and TinyBERT have been evaluated in document classification tasks within European public agencies, achieving competitive results with significantly lower computational costs [15,21]. Furthermore, transfer learning and domain adaptation techniques enable the effective use of general pretrained models, allowing them to be efficiently adapted to specific contexts such as customs reports, contracts, or regulatory forms [13].

Custom Taxonomies and Hierarchical Classification. An emerging trend is the use of hierarchical classification schemes and custom taxonomies, which enable a more structured representation of the semantic diversity present in administrative records. Studies such as [1] have explored hierarchical neural network architectures that incorporate ontological relationships among categories, allowing documents to be classified across multiple levels of specificity with greater accuracy and consistency. This approach proves particularly valuable in cases like the SEC, where records may simultaneously belong to different product families based on technical and regulatory attributes.

Data Quality and Human Feedback Mechanisms. Another key aspect identified in the literature is the need for strategies that ensure the quality of data used to train machine learning models. In governmental contexts, where the availability of labeled data may be limited or noisy, approaches such as active learning and human-in-the-loop have been proposed. These methods enable the integration of expert knowledge during the model training process, thereby enhancing both the accuracy and the institutional acceptance of the system [29,38].

Impact Evaluation and Management-Oriented Metrics. Finally, several authors propose evaluation frameworks that go beyond traditional metrics such as accuracy or F1-score, incorporating operational indicators relevant to institutional environments—such as response time, avoided human error rate, and contribution to key performance indicators (KPIs). Examples of such evaluations can be found in recent experiences in Brazil and Estonia, where the impact of intelligent systems on regulatory, administrative, and oversight processes has been well documented [24,27].

3 Methodology

The **CRISP–DM (Cross-Industry Standard Process for Data Mining)** methodology was selected due to its proven effectiveness and flexibility in structuring machine learning projects across diverse domains, facilitating clarity in complex workflows and ensuring quality assurance throughout the project's lifecycle. Recent studies demonstrate its wide adoption and success across various sectors such as manufacturing [2,23,36], fintech [5], healthcare [3], education [22], and anomaly detection [28]. Particularly, Bokrantz et al. (2024) highlight CRISP–DM's strength in providing a comprehensive lifecycle model with clear stages, including operation and maintenance, crucial for ongoing model management in manufacturing environments [2]. Similarly, Cheng (2023) emphasizes its robust framework for classifying financial risks in fintech, supporting systematic analysis and enhanced predictive capabilities [5]. Furthermore, its adaptability is demonstrated by studies integrating domain-specific knowledge to improve decision-making accuracy, such as in manufacturing processes [23], and addressing complex issues like responsibility decisions for production non-conformities [41]. Therefore, adopting CRISP–DM ensures a structured, adaptable, and thoroughly validated approach, critical to the success and scalability of this machine learning project at the SEC.

3.1 Process Framework

The end-to-end workflow follows the CRISP-DM standard (Fig. 1). First, business requirements were elicited with SEC domain experts, defining the binary objective *certifiable* vs. *non-certifiable*. Second, historical data were extracted from the SEC data warehouse (Sect. 3.2). Data preparation comprised linguistic cleaning, rule-based exclusions and feature extraction. Third, five candidate algorithms were selected based on literature prevalence in high-dimensional sparse text spaces [19]. Hyper-parameter optimisation used **nested stratified five-fold cross-validation**. Finally, models were evaluated on a **held-out test set** and the best model integrated into a prototype decision-support tool.

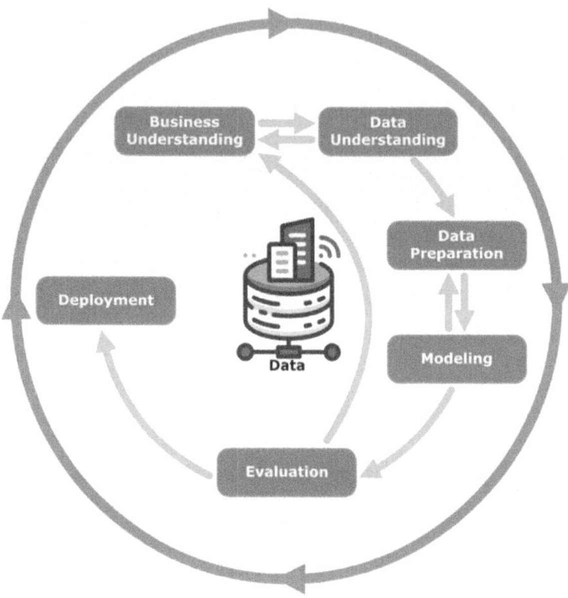

Fig. 1. CRISP-DM stages applied to the SEC case.

3.2 Data Acquisition and Pre-Processing

The raw corpus consists of **736 369** declarations for fiscal year 2017. Each record includes a free-text field with up to 250 characters, numeric quantities and metadata. A rule-based filter—developed with SEC engineers—removed obviously irrelevant entries (e.g., quantities < 5, veterinary equipment, incomplete tax identifiers), yielding **387 057** candidate records (Table 1).

Text normalization comprised **lowercasing**, accent removal, punctuation stripping, and heuristic correction of 214 frequent misspellings (e.g., *herbidor*→*hervidor*). **Spanish stopword removal** was applied using a standard stopword list prior to vectorization. Tokens that occurred in fewer than five documents were discarded. The final vector space of 21 134 terms was weighted using **sublinear TF–IDF**.

Table 1. Dataset composition after successive filtering steps.

Stage	Records	Retention (%)
Raw ADUANA stream	736 369	100.0
Rule-based exclusions	387 057	52.6
Train–validation split (75%)	290 292	–
Test split (25%)	96 765	–

3.3 Model Selection and Hyper-parameters

The selection of machine learning algorithms for text classification in this study is based on their proven efficiency in handling sparse, high-dimensional textual data and their broad application in similar contexts. Specifically, Support Vector Machines (SVM), Logistic Regression (LR), Random Forest (RF), Stochastic Gradient Descent (SGD), and Multinomial Naïve Bayes (MNB) were considered due to their distinct computational advantages and demonstrated effectiveness.

SVM is extensively recognized for its robustness and accuracy in classifying text data, particularly effective with linear kernels in high-dimensional spaces [6,26]. Logistic Regression, chosen for its simplicity and interpretability, effectively handles large-scale datasets while maintaining high classification accuracy [20]. The Random Forest model was selected for its capacity to manage feature interactions and inherent resistance to overfitting, proving valuable in complex text classification tasks [17].

Stochastic Gradient Descent was adopted due to its scalability and computational efficiency in handling extensive datasets, showing substantial efficacy when dealing with sparse text features [33,35]. Lastly, Multinomial Naïve Bayes was utilized because of its proven simplicity, computational efficiency, and effectiveness in managing text classification problems with sparse data [9,12].

For hyper-parameter optimization, a grid search method was implemented to methodically examine parameter combinations pivotal for model performance. The SVM and LR models explored regularization parameters $C \in \{0.1, 1, 10\}$, addressing the trade-off between model complexity and generalization ability [14]. The RF model utilized 500 trees, assessing maximal depths of {None,30}, providing a balance between complexity and prediction accuracy. The SGD classifier, characterized by the hinge loss function, explored alpha values of $\alpha \in \{10^{-4}, 10^{-5}\}$, optimizing performance in high-dimensional spaces [31]. Finally, the MNB model investigated smoothing parameters $\alpha \in [10^{-3}, 10^{-1}]$, effectively addressing the issue of zero-frequency features [18,34].

Grid search aimed to minimize macro-averaged cross-entropy on validation folds, ensuring that selected hyper-parameters enhance the models' generalization capabilities.

- **Support Vector Machine (SVM):** linear kernel; $C \in \{0.1, 1, 10\}$.
- **Logistic Regression (LR):** L2 penalty; $C \in \{0.1, 1, 10\}$.
- **Random Forest (RF):** 500 trees; max_depth $\in \{\text{None}, 30\}$.

- **Stochastic Gradient Descent (SGD):** hinge loss; $\alpha \in \{10^{-4}, 10^{-5}\}$.
- **Multinomial Naïve Bayes (MNB):** additive smoothing $\alpha \in [10^{-3}, 10^{-1}]$.

Grid search minimised macro-averaged cross-entropy on the validation folds.

3.4 Evaluation Metrics

Following regulatory requirements, priority was given to *Recall* for the minority class (certifiable) to minimize false negatives. **Therefore, we report** Accuracy, macro-averaged Precision, Recall, F1 and Matthews correlation coefficient (MCC). Execution time per 100 k records was measured on an Intel Xeon Silver 4214 CPU.

4 Experimental Results

Table 2 summarises the test-set performance of the evaluated models. The linear SVM consistently outperformed other models, achieving a macro-F1 score of 99.19% and exhibiting the lowest false-negative rate, underscoring its superior discriminative capability. The Random Forest model provided competitive performance, although its computational cost was notably higher.

Table 2. Performance on the held-out test set (96 765 records).

Model	Accuracy	Precision	Recall	F1	Time [s]
SVM	**0.9926**	0.9924	**0.9913**	**0.9919**	3.4
LR	0.9875	0.9877	0.9868	0.9872	2.9
RF	0.9794	0.9781	0.9803	0.9792	45.1
SGD	0.9763	0.9749	0.9756	0.9752	**1.8**
MNB	0.9586	0.9558	0.9571	0.9564	2.0

To provide a more balanced evaluation of classifier performance, particularly under class imbalance conditions typical in regulatory datasets, we report the F1 score for each model. The F1 score is the harmonic mean of precision and recall, defined as:

$$\text{F1} = 2 \cdot \frac{\text{Precision} \cdot \text{Recall}}{\text{Precision} + \text{Recall}}. \tag{1}$$

This metric is especially relevant in our context, where false negatives can have significant safety implications by omitting certifiable products from regulatory scrutiny. Unlike accuracy, which may be misleading when class distributions are skewed, the F1 score accounts for both over-prediction and under-prediction of the positive class, offering a more informative assessment (Table 3).

Table 3. F1 score computed from precision and recall for each model tested on the held-out set.

Model	Precision	Recall	F1 Score
Logistic Regression	0.9838	0.9835	0.9836
Stochastic Gradient Descent	0.9776	0.9745	0.9760
Support Vector Machine	0.9856	0.9867	**0.9861**
Random Forest	0.9848	0.9824	0.9836
Naïve Bayes	0.9571	0.9571	0.9571

Table 4. Confusion matrices per learner (counts in thousands). Rows: *True class* (Positive/Negative). Columns: *Predicted class.* Notation: (+) = predicted positive (certifiable), (−) = predicted negative (non-certifiable). Abbreviations: LR, SGD, SVM, RF, MNB.

	LR		SGD		SVM		RF		MNB	
	(+)	(−)	(+)	(−)	(+)	(−)	(+)	(−)	(+)	(−)
Positive	83.728	1.402	83.710	1.283	83.591	1.443	84.062	1.071	81.133	4.099
Negative	1.535	10.100	2.641	9.131	1.373	10.358	1.892	9.740	1.169	10.364

To further assess model effectiveness, Table 4 presents the **confusion matrices for all evaluated learners**. These matrices illustrate each model's behavior on positive (certifiable) and negative (non-certifiable) classes.

Figure 2 visually compares the accuracy and error rates of the evaluated models. The Support Vector Machine (SVM) achieved the highest precision of 97.09%, outperforming the other algorithms evaluated. Logistic Regression and Random Forest also provided competitive precision, while Stochastic Gradient Descent showed moderate performance.

Upon deployment on the full 2022 dataset comprising approximately 1.02 million records, the SVM model classified all entries in merely **7.6 s**, significantly faster than the previous manual process, which required approximately **45 days** of cumulative analyst time. This performance translates to a remarkable efficiency improvement of approximately **5 300-fold**.

5 Discussion

The proposed machine learning pipeline effectively balances high classification accuracy and minimal operational latency, critical for enhancing regulatory processes within the SEC. Utilizing lightweight TF–IDF vectors in conjunction with linear models such as the Support Vector Machine (SVM), the implemented solution achieves a remarkable macro-F1 score of 99.19%, significantly reducing computational overhead compared to resource-intensive transformer-based models. This optimization results in near-real-time performance, enabling daily updates of the coverage indicator, a notable improvement over the previous quarterly

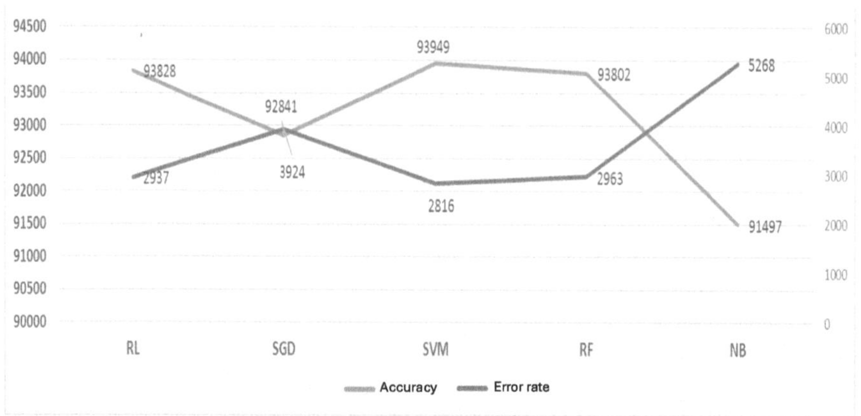

Fig. 2. Comparison of model *accuracy* (orange line) and *error rate* (blue line) across evaluated learners (LR, SGD, SVM, RF, MNB). (Color figure online)

computations. Consequently, this approach facilitates proactive inspections and significantly enhances the institution's preventive capabilities.

An operational analysis underscores the practical benefits, where the deployment of the SVM model on a dataset comprising over 1.02 million records resulted in a substantial reduction in processing time—from approximately 45 days of manual analysis to merely 7.6 s. Such efficiency improvement translates directly into operational expansion, with the potential to increase the geographical scope of audits from a mere 2.2% to an estimated 10.9% of the national territory, aligning closely with strategic targets established by the SEC.

Detailed error analysis identified that most classification errors originated from ambiguous or vague product descriptions, as well as linguistic code-switching between Spanish and English. These findings suggest that future model iterations could significantly benefit from advanced natural language processing techniques, including contextual embeddings like BETO, and human-in-the-loop methodologies such as active learning. These enhancements promise iterative refinement of model precision, particularly addressing linguistic and semantic complexities, thereby further strengthening both accuracy and operational reliability.

6 Conclusion and Future Work

This study has conclusively demonstrated the substantial benefits of adopting carefully designed classical supervised machine learning models to enhance regulatory processes within resource-constrained public agencies. The proposed linear SVM-based solution significantly reduced processing time—from manual workloads spanning weeks down to mere seconds—while maintaining a robust macro-F1 accuracy exceeding 99%, meeting stringent regulatory standards. These advancements highlight the potential for considerable operational efficiency improvements in the SEC's certification workflow.

Future research directions include further integrating advanced methodologies and technologies to enhance model robustness and usability. Specifically, ongoing initiatives involve: (i) developing a human-in-the-loop interface to refine model predictions **continuously**, thus leveraging inspector expertise; (ii) expanding the classification taxonomy to address a more granular categorization across the 31 regulated subclasses, enabling more precise and actionable decisions; and (iii) conducting comparative analyses with advanced multilingual Transformer-based models, ensuring that future improvements capitalize on emerging computational resources and natural language processing capabilities. These developments will ensure sustained accuracy improvements and greater adaptability of the solution to increasingly complex operational scenarios.

Acknowledgements. We thank the Technical Products Department of the SEC for providing the anonymised dataset and valuable domain expertise, as well as the Universidad Andrés Bello for computing support.

References

1. Araya-Campos, P., Fillottrani, P.: Multi-class document classification using lexical ontology-based BERT architecture. Appl. Sci. **13**(10), 6139 (2023). https://doi.org/10.3390/app13106139
2. Bokrantz, J., Subramaniyan, M., Skoogh, A.: Realising the promises of artificial intelligence in manufacturing by enhancing CRISP-DM. Prod. Plann. Control **35**(16), 2234–2254 (2024). https://doi.org/10.1080/09537287.2023.2234882
3. Caetano, N., Cortez, P., Laureano, R.M.S.: Using data mining for prediction of hospital length of stay: an application of the CRISP-DM methodology. In: Cordeiro, J., Hammoudi, S., Maciaszek, L., Camp, O., Filipe, J. (eds.) ICEIS 2014. LNBIP, vol. 227, pp. 149–166. Springer, Cham (2015). https://doi.org/10.1007/978-3-319-22348-3_9
4. Caminero, A., García-Sánchez, F., Martínez, A.: Machine learning for public procurement contract classification: a study in Spain. Expert Syst. Appl. **208** (2023). https://doi.org/10.1016/j.eswa.2022.119912
5. Cheng, A.: Evaluating fintech industry's risks: a preliminary analysis based on CRISP-DM framework. Financ. Res. Lett. **55**, 103966 (2023). https://doi.org/10.1016/j.frl.2023.103966
6. Dansalan, J.F., Diaz, J., Ostia, C.J.: Short-term load demand forecasting using multinomial naive bayes with support vector machine. In: 16th International Conference on Computer and Automation Engineering, ICCAE 2024, pp. 158–162 (2024). https://doi.org/10.1109/ICCAE59995.2024.10569950
7. Devlin, J., Chang, M., Lee, K., Toutanova, K.: BERT: pre-training of deep bidirectional transformers for language understanding. In: Proceedings of the 2019 Conference of the North American Chapter of the Association for Computational Linguistics: Human Language Technologies (NAACL-HLT), pp. 4171–4186 (2019)
8. Fragkogiannis, P., Forster, M., Lee, G.E., Zhang, D.: Context-aware classification of legal document pages. arXiv preprint arXiv:2304.02787 (2023)

9. Gan, S., Shao, S., Chen, L., Yu, L., Jiang, L.: Adapting hidden naive bayes for text classification. Mathematics **9**(19) (2021). https://doi.org/10.3390/math9192378
10. Álvarez González, E.M.: La función normativa y la técnica legislativa en españa: una nueva herramienta – la inteligencia artificial. Revista de Administración Pública (221), 321–327 (2023)
11. Goodfellow, I., Bengio, Y., Courville, A.: Deep Learning. MIT Press (2016). www.deeplearningbook.org
12. Harzevili, N.S., Alizadeh, S.H.: Mixture of latent multinomial naive bayes classifier. Appl. Soft Comput. **69**, 516–527 (2018). https://doi.org/10.1016/j.asoc.2018.04.020
13. Howard, J., Ruder, S.: Universal language model fine-tuning for text classification. In: Proceedings of the 56th Annual Meeting of the Association for Computational Linguistics (Volume 1: Long Papers), pp. 328–339. Association for Computational Linguistics, Melbourne, Australia (2018). https://doi.org/10.18653/v1/P18-1031, https://aclanthology.org/P18-1031/
14. Jiang, W., Siddiqui, S.: Hyper-parameter optimization for support vector machines using stochastic gradient descent and dual coordinate descent. EURO J. Comput. Optim. **8**(1), 85–101 (2020). https://doi.org/10.1007/s13675-019-00115-7
15. Jiao, X., et al.: TinyBERT: distilling BERT for natural language understanding. In: Findings of the Association for Computational Linguistics: EMNLP 2020, pp. 4163–4174 (2020)
16. Jordan, M.I., Mitchell, T.M.: Machine learning: trends, perspectives, and prospects. Science **349**(6245), 255–260 (2015)
17. Kalcheva, N.A., Karova, M.N.: A comparison of machine learning classification algorithms and methods for English author's works and their translations into Bulgarian. In: 2022 57th International Scientific Conference on Information, Communication and Energy Systems and Technologies (ICEST), pp. 164–167 (2022). https://doi.org/10.1109/ICEST55168.2022.9828579
18. Kim, S., Rim, H., Kim, J.: Topic document model approach for naive bayes text classification. IEICE Trans. Inf. Syst. **E88D**(5), 1091–1094 (2005). https://doi.org/10.1093/ietisy/e88-d.5.1091
19. Kowsari, K., Jafari Meimandi, K., Heidarysafa, M., Mendu, S., Barnes, L.E., Brown, D.E.: Text classification algorithms: a survey. Information **10**(4), 150 (2019)
20. Kumar, S., Sharma, A., Reddy, B.K., Sachan, S., Jain, V., Singh, J.: An intelligent model based on integrated inverse document frequency and multinomial naive bayes for current affairs news categorisation. Int. J. Syst. Assur. Eng. Manage. **13**(3), 1341–1355 (2022). https://doi.org/10.1007/s13198-021-01471-7
21. Lan, Z., Chen, M., Goodman, S., Gimpel, K., Sharma, P., Soricut, R.: AlBERT: a lite BERT for self-supervised learning of language representations. In: International Conference on Learning Representations (ICLR) 2020. OpenReview.net (2020). https://openreview.net/forum?id=H1eA7AEtvS
22. Lebkiri, N., Daoudi, M., Abidli, Z., et al.: Using machine learning for prediction students failure in Morocco: an application of the crisp-dm methodology. Int. J. Educ. Inf. Technol. **15**, 344–352 (2021). https://doi.org/10.46300/9109.2021.15.36
23. Lundén, N., Bekar, E.T., Skoogh, A., Bokrantz, J.: Domain knowledge in CRISP-DM: an application case in manufacturing. In: IFAC PapersOnline, vol. 56, pp. 7603–7608 (2023). https://doi.org/10.1016/j.ifacol.2023.10.1156
24. Madan, R., Ashok, M.: AI adoption and diffusion in public administration: a systematic literature review and future research agenda. Govern. Inf. Q. **40** (2023). https://doi.org/10.1016/j.giq.2022.101774

25. Maier, F., Müller, S., Becker, A.: Semantic normalisation of administrative texts using domain-adaptive NLP pipelines. In: Proceedings of the 30th European Conference on Artificial Intelligence (ECAI 2022), pp. 3345–3353 (2022). https://doi.org/10.3233/ECAI220094, https://ecai2022.org/papers/3345.pdf
26. Mocherla, S., Danehy, A., Impey, C.: Evaluation of naive bayes and support vector machines for Wikipedia. Appl. Artif. Intell. **31**(9-10), 733–744 (2017). https://doi.org/10.1080/08839514.2018.1440907
27. Organisation for Economic Co-operation and Development (OECD): Governing with artificial intelligence: Are governments ready? OECD policy report, OECD Publishing (2024). https://www.oecd.org/en/publications/governing-with-artificial-intelligence_26324bc2-en.htm. Accessed 21 June 2025
28. Schwenzfeier, N., Gruhn, V.: Towards a practical process model for anomaly detection systems. In: IEEE/ACM 1st International Workshop on Software Engineering for Cognitive Services, pp. 41–44 (2018). https://doi.org/10.1145/3195555.3195568
29. Settles, B.: Active Learning. Synthesis Lectures on Artificial Intelligence and Machine Learning, vol. 6. Morgan & Claypool (2012)
30. Shalev-Shwartz, S., Ben-David, S.: Understanding Machine Learning: From Theory to Algorithms. Cambridge University Press (2014)
31. Sharma, S., Rastogi, R.: Stochastic conjugate gradient descent twin support vector machine for large scale pattern classification. In: Mitrovic, T., Xue, B., Li, X. (eds.) AI 2018. LNCS (LNAI), vol. 11320, pp. 590–602. Springer, Cham (2018). https://doi.org/10.1007/978-3-030-03991-2_54
32. Sun, C., Qiu, X., Xu, Y., Huang, X.: How to fine-tune BERT for text classification? In: Sun, M., Huang, X., Ji, H., Liu, Z., Liu, Y. (eds.) CCL 2019. LNCS (LNAI), vol. 11856, pp. 194–206. Springer, Cham (2019). https://doi.org/10.1007/978-3-030-32381-3_16
33. Tao, H., Wu, B., Lin, X.: Budgeted mini-batch parallel gradient descent for support vector machines on spark. In: 2014 20th IEEE International Conference on Parallel and Distributed Systems (ICPADS), pp. 945–950 (2014). https://doi.org/10.1109/PADSW.2014.7097906
34. Wang, S., Jiang, L., Li, C.: Adapting naive bayes tree for text classification. Knowl. Inf. Syst. **44**(1), 77–89 (2015). https://doi.org/10.1007/s10115-014-0746-y
35. Wang, Z., Shao, Y.H., Bai, L., Li, C.N., Liu, L.M., Deng, N.Y.: Insensitive stochastic gradient twin support vector machines for large scale problems. Inf. Sci. **462**, 114–131 (2018). https://doi.org/10.1016/j.ins.2018.06.007
36. Wiemer, H., Drowatzky, L., Ihlenfeldt, S.: Data mining methodology for engineering applications (DMME)–a holistic extension to the CRISP-DM model. Appl. Sci. **9**(12), 2407 (2019). https://doi.org/10.3390/app9122407
37. Wirtz, B.W., Weyerer, J.C., Geyer, C.: Artificial intelligence and the public sector: applications and challenges. Int. J. Public Adm. **42**(7), 596–615 (2019). https://doi.org/10.1080/01900692.2018.1498103
38. Wu, X., Xiao, L., Sun, Y., Zhang, J., Ma, T., He, L.: A survey of human-in-the-loop for machine learning. arXiv preprint (2021). arxiv.org/abs/2108.00941
39. Young, T., Hazarika, D., Poria, S., Cambria, E.: Recent trends in deep learning based natural language processing. IEEE Comput. Intell. Mag. **13**(3), 55–75 (2018)
40. Zhang, L., Wang, S., Liu, B.: Deep learning for sentiment analysis: a survey. Wiley Interdiscip. Rev.: Data Min. Knowl. Discov. **8**(4), e1253 (2018). https://doi.org/10.1002/widm.1253, https://onlinelibrary.wiley.com/doi/10.1002/widm.1253
41. Ziv, B., Parmet, Y.: Improving nonconformity responsibility decisions: a semi-automated model based on CRISP-DM. Int. J. Syst. Assur. Eng. Manage. **13**(2), 657–667 (2022). https://doi.org/10.1007/s13198-021-01318-1

Image-Based Search and Data Collection: An Integrated Approach Using Machine Learning and Web Scraping

Diogo Pereira(✉), Sílvia Ferrão, Rosa Matias, and Paulo Valente da Cruz

ESTG, Polytechnic University of Leiria, Leiria, Portugal
diogo.raimundo.pereira@gmail.com, {silvia.ferrao, rosa.matias}@ipleiria.pt

Abstract. Visual search technologies have become pivotal in enhancing online shopping experiences, particularly in second-hand markets, where accurate text descriptions are often limited or inconsistent. The proposed system, Snap & Shop, is a web-based platform designed to enable users to find similar products across three popular online marketplaces serving the Portuguese market. The motivation arose from the absence of integrated solutions combining image-based search with aggregated, relevant results tailored to the Portuguese second-hand sector. To achieve this, the system employs machine learning models alongside web scraping techniques for dynamic data collection.

At its core, the system utilizes a multimodal Large Language Model (LLM) with a custom prompt for product identification, coupled with a classification model that extracts visual features from images, which are then compared to assess their similarity. Data acquisition is performed via web scraping, using simulated browser behavior through undocumented yet publicly available platform-specific endpoints to bypass restrictions without requiring a dedicated database. This method allows real-time retrieval of relevant product listings from multiple marketplaces.

Experimental results demonstrate the system's effectiveness in retrieving highly relevant, visually similar products, highlighting the potential of visual search within the Portuguese used goods market. The integration of advanced machine learning models with web scraping techniques proves to be a scalable and efficient approach to enhance product discovery. This research establishes a foundation for future developments, including improved search precision, platform interoperability, and sophisticated marketplace functionalities, ultimately contributing to a richer, more accessible online second-hand shopping experience.

Keywords: Image-Based Search · Machine Learning · Web Scraping

1 Introduction

1.1 Background

The adoption of e-commerce platforms has experienced a significant increase, driven by greater technological accessibility across different populations and regions, coupled with a general rise in digital literacy. Concurrently, advances in artificial intelligence

T. Guarda et al. (Eds.): ARTIIS 2025, CCIS 2789, pp. 16–26, 2026.
https://doi.org/10.1007/978-3-032-16758-3_2

(AI) have positioned it as a fundamental technology for enhancing the user experience in online shopping.

One of the most promising developments in this area is visual search, which enables users to find products by uploading images instead of entering text. This capability is particularly valuable when users have an image of the desired product but are unaware of its exact name, brand, or product features. Visual search functionalities serve as differentiating features across various e-commerce platforms; for instance, solutions like Pinterest's "Shop The Look" [1] demonstrate the added value of such functionalities.

This project is centered on developing a web application that, based on an image uploaded by the user, retrieves the most similar products available across multiple e-commerce platforms. The aim is to explore the potential of visual search technologies and demonstrate their practical usability in real-world product retrieval scenarios.

1.2 Problem Statement

The main challenge this work addresses is the difficulty users encounter when searching for products without knowing their specific names, compounded by the lack of platforms that combine visual similarity search with relevant result aggregation. Currently, several platforms aggregate search results from various online stores, some supporting image uploads; however, these often lack reliable relevance or do not offer effective visual search features. For example, platforms such as Google Lens [2] can identify products corresponding to an image but do not provide functionalities like filtering or extensive results, especially second-hand products, and tend to return limited relevant results.

Additionally, there are no dedicated Portuguese aggregators focusing on used goods with effective visual search capabilities. The proposed system seeks to address these gaps by offering a tailored, scalable solution that enhances visual product search and result aggregation within the Portuguese context.

1.3 Objectives

The primary goal of this project is to develop a web application acting as both an aggregator for product listings from various e-commerce sites and an accurate visual identifier for user-uploaded images. The system will source data from used goods marketplaces serving the Portuguese market, offering functionalities such as filtering results by platform, sorting based on different criteria, and filtering by price to enhance the user experience.

Technically, the system leverages machine learning models for image captioning and visual feature extraction, combined with web scraping techniques using undocumented yet public endpoints. This approach allows dynamic retrieval of relevant product listings, effectively overcoming current limitations and providing a specialized, effective visual search tool tailored for Portugal's second-hand products market.

2 Background and Related Work

Although applications for image-based search have existed for over two decades, their significance has grown substantially with advances in AI and computer vision. Additionally, there is an increasing user demand for faster search results that do not rely on elaborate textual descriptions. This section highlights some relevant applications within this domain.

The Like.com platform, launched in 2006, was the first to implement the concept of image-based product search. It functioned as a visual search engine for products, equipped with a feature capable of analyzing visual characteristics by comparing mathematical representations of images to identify similar items [3]. In 2010, it was acquired by Google to enhance services such as Google's product search engine, now known as Google Shopping [4].

Currently, one of the most widely used applications in this field is Google Lens, which conducts over 20 billion visual searches per month [5]. It enables users to identify objects, plants, and animals, translate text, recognize locations, and search for products online based on photographs taken by the user [2]. The latter functionality holds significant economic potential, as Google has established partnerships with numerous retailers to display their products [6]. Google Lens is not a standalone app; it is integrated into the Google ecosystem and embedded within its search bar.

Pinterest's Shop the Look exemplifies a visual shopping system that allows users to discover and purchase products depicted within images. It employs scene decomposition via object detection and candidate retrieval using visual embeddings, providing a seamless shopping experience from images to purchasable items [1].

Among recent market solutions, Perplexity AI stands out as a search engine utilizing an LLM. It distinguishes itself through its focus on delivering high-quality responses to user queries, leveraging web sources and citing links within answers [7]. Recently, Perplexity AI introduced a "snap-to-shop" feature, integrated with e-commerce platforms like Shopify. This allows users to identify products within images and, after retrieval, communicate with the system to obtain more refined results aligned with their preferences [8]. For example, if initial suggestions do not match users' expectations or if they seek products with specific characteristics, this integration enables users to query the system further. The use of an LLM enhances various functionalities, including product recommendations and discount inquiries. A distinctive feature of Perplexity AI is its "one-click checkout", which facilitates purchasing directly through their platform without redirecting users to the retailer's website [9].

Another AI-powered search engine capable of product identification and suggestion generation is ChatGPT. While sharing many features with Perplexity AI - both being applications of LLMs - there are key differences. Notably, Perplexity AI offers a "one-click checkout" functionality, available to Pro users [9], whereas ChatGPT directs users to the original product listing pages without direct purchase options.

Furthermore, ChatGPT requests additional information to improve results, whereas Perplexity AI does not but still provide reliable outcomes. Comparing the two, each presents advantages and limitations. For instance, ChatGPT suffers from lower result reliability regarding discounts, often providing fictitious offers that do not exist in the corresponding online stores. However, a major advantage of ChatGPT is that it tends to show products from well-known stores relevant to the user's location. In contrast, Perplexity AI offers accurate discount information, but it tends to feature lesser-known stores less relevant to local consumers. Despite this, Perplexity AI also offers additional features such as a FAQ chat section and higher data reliability evidenced by verified discounts.

3 Method

Software development methodologies are structured approaches that guide the entire cycle of creating, maintaining, and delivering systems, aiming for increased efficiency, predictability, and quality. Among these, traditional and agile models are prominent.

The Linear Model, such as Waterfall, is characterized by a sequence of distinct phases: requirements, design, implementation, testing, and maintenance, which occur in a linear, non-overlapping manner. This approach provides comprehensive documentation and a clear structure but has limitations, since it is constrained by restricted adaptability to change and extended delivery timelines. [10, 11].

Agile Models, on the other hand, focus on iterative and adaptable development. Scrum is a methodology that breaks the project into short cycles called sprints, with well-defined roles (Product Owner, Scrum Master, and Development Team), daily stand-up meetings, and continuous deliveries. Its primary goal is to facilitate adaptation to changing requirements, promote transparency, and involve the client throughout the process [12]. While advantageous, Scrum requires experienced teams and places less emphasis on extensive documentation [10].

Another agile technique, Kanban, utilizes visual boards with columns representing different workflow stages (e.g., "To Do", "In Progress", "Done"). Its simplicity and focus on limiting work in progress enhance flow transparency, efficiency, and continuous improvement. Kanban is particularly suitable for smaller projects or maintenance workflows, although the lack of fixed deadlines can pose risks of delays [13, 14].

In summary, selecting the appropriate methodology depends on the project characteristics: traditional models offer detailed planning and control, while agile approaches provide greater flexibility, rapid delivery, and responsiveness to change [10–13].

After evaluating the advantages and disadvantages of various software development methodologies, a Kanban-based agile approach was elected. This choice was motivated by the flexibility it offers, as initial requirements do not need to be fully defined upfront, thereby facilitating iterative development. Additionally, this methodology enables continuous refinement of the platform's interface design, allowing for regular demonstrations to the client and the incorporation of feedback to enhance both usability and functionality throughout the development process.

This approach leveraged the principles of Kanban to support the academic and research-focused nature of the project. Kanban's visual workflow management enabled continuous monitoring and iterative adjustment of project objectives throughout its development cycle. Regular review meetings - conducted weekly or biweekly - facilitated the validation and prioritization of tasks, ensuring that implemented functionalities aligned with ongoing research outcomes and emerging insights. This iterative process allowed for flexible adaptation to new data and evolving project requirements.

4 Snap and Shop Platform Development

The project implementation began with the objective of delivering a seamless user experience for consumers searching for second-hand products online. The Snap & Shop platform is designed to aggregate listings from multiple used goods marketplaces and facilitate visual search functionality. By enabling users to upload an image as a query input, the system employs machine learning models and web scraping to retrieve relevant results. This approach enhances user interaction by providing an intuitive, responsive interface that requires no prior technical knowledge.

4.1 The Platform Architecture

As previously stated, Snap & Shop is a search engine developed to assist users in locating specific items within used goods marketplaces through both image-based and text-based queries. To support the Snap & Shop platform, the system architecture follows a layered design consisting of a React-based frontend, a FastAPI backend, and integrations with external services. While the codebase itself is organized into two main layers—frontend and backend—the backend integrates multiple responsibilities, including handling requests, running a machine learning model, performing web scraping, and interacting with an external API, into a single service. This results in a monolithic backend architecture, optimized for simplicity and rapid development and deployment. The system can therefore be described in terms of the following three layers:

- **Frontend:** A responsive and intuitive single-page application that users access through web browsers. It supports image upload and text-based search queries, handles user input, renders search results, and manages client-side state to provide a seamless experience. Implemented using React, leveraging its component-based architecture for dynamic UI updates and efficient state management.
- **Backend:** An asynchronous server-side application that orchestrates system operations. It processes incoming requests, coordinates communication with external services, and consolidates responses. The backend runs a locally hosted machine learning model for image feature extraction, generating high-dimensional embeddings from uploaded images. It also manages web scraping, external API interactions, and image downloads efficiently. Built with FastAPI [15] in Python, utilizing async/await for asynchronous programming. The httpx [16] library is employed for non-blocking HTTP requests to optimize I/O-bound tasks.
- **External services**: the backend integrates with various third-party services to extend the platform's capabilities and improve overall performance:

  - **Google Gemini API** [17]**:** generates semantic descriptions for user-uploaded images, which are then used to guide product search queries.
  - **Online marketplaces:** the platform accesses multiple third-party used goods marketplaces as primary data sources. These sources are queried through automated web scraping processes that extract real-time product listings.

This layered design enables Snap & Shop to deliver an intuitive visual search experience across heterogeneous data sources. The application was designed using a component-based architecture to promote reusability (see Fig. 1).

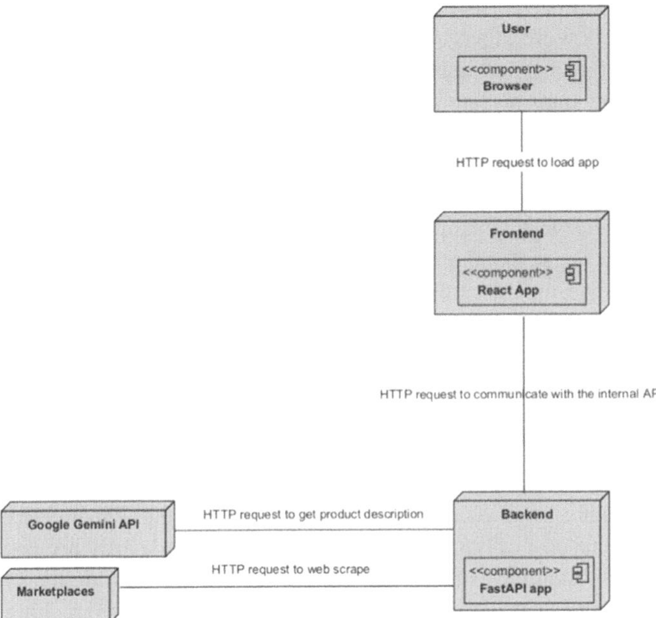

Fig. 1. The Snap & Shop Component-Oriented Architecture.

4.2 Implementation

The development of the Snap & Shop platform originated with a focused emphasis on image feature extraction methodologies, initially prototyped utilizing the ResNet50 architecture [18]. While effective, this classification model was later replaced with MobileNetV3-Large [19], which provided comparable performance at significantly higher speed, offering a more favorable trade-off between efficiency and accuracy. This foundational approach enabled the encoding of uploaded images into high-dimensional feature vectors, facilitating comparison via cosine similarity to evaluate their visual relevance. This proof-of-concept established the core visual search functionality underpinning subsequent system enhancements. Following the establishment of the feature extraction and comparison framework, the next development phase involves integrating web scraping capabilities across various online marketplaces. The system exploited publicly accessible, though undocumented, backend APIs - endpoints typically employed internally within sites utilizing Client-Side Rendering (CSR). In CSR architectures, servers serve minimal HTML shells while JavaScript orchestrates page hydration and dynamically fetches listing data through these hidden APIs. Access to these endpoints allowed the backend to reliably retrieve structured product data, with scraper implementations emulating genuine user interactions through carefully configured HTTP headers to mitigate detection and blocking risks. While the image embeddings facilitated effective visual similarity assessments between user-uploaded images and marketplace listings, they were insufficient for generating textual search queries - an essential component for targeted data retrieval, since the marketplaces must first be queried with text before relevant listings can be retrieved for visual comparison. To address this, preliminary experiments involved using pre-trained image classification models to generate high-level labels; however, these models often produced imprecise or contextually irrelevant labels that undermined search accuracy. Similarly, vision-language models were explored; however, their narrative-style captions tended to be excessively verbose and unsuitable for concise search queries. These limitations underscored the necessity for alternative approaches to enhance textual representation fidelity. To overcome these challenges, Google Gemini API was integrated into the platform, specifically leveraging the newly released preview version of the Gemini 2.5 Flash-Lite model due to its optimal balance of speed, low latency, and reliability. This model demonstrated strong performance in generating concise, meaningful textual descriptions across multiple languages, including Portuguese (pt-PT), thereby aligning with the platform's target user demographic. By converting visual inputs into accurate textual descriptions, Gemini enabled the generation of valid textual queries required to access marketplace endpoints, thereby bridging the gap between image-based inputs and the text-based search mechanisms necessary for web scraping.

It is important to note that the visual feature extraction and comparison - which users can enable or disable - significantly increases processing time. This delay is partly due to the computational cost of running inference on images, and partly because the system needs to download the images from marketplaces before performing the visual feature extraction and comparison. The increased processing time motivated making this feature optional for users.

Initially designed for desktop deployment, the user interface was subsequently adapted for mobile responsiveness through Tailwind CSS, ensuring a consistent and fluid experience across devices. Layout refinements were informed by internal usability testing, aimed at optimizing key interactions such as marketplace selection, result filtering, and price constraints, to enhance accessibility and intuitiveness (Fig. 2).

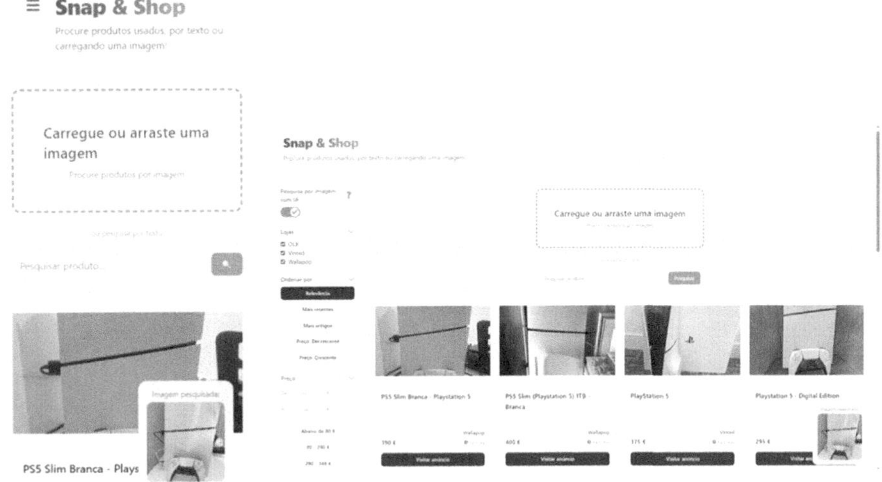

Fig. 2. The Snap & Shop Layout: (i) on the left for mobile-sized devices, and; (ii) on the right for desktop-sized devices.

Throughout the development process, performance optimization was a priority. The backend leveraged FastAPI's asynchronous programming model (via async/await), enabling concurrent operations, such as scraping across multiple marketplaces and simultaneous interactions with the Gemini API. The httpx library was employed in lieu of traditional blocking HTTP requests, further enhancing I/O efficiency and system throughput. Ultimately, the evolved platform provides end users with the following core functionalities:

- **Uploading an image**: which is immediately processed by the Gemini API to generate a concise textual description used as a search query across multiple marketplaces.
- **Visual feature comparison (optional)**: which involves extracting feature embeddings from both the uploaded image and the images of the resulting listings, followed by embedding comparison to deliver more visually pertinent search results.
- **Filtering options:** including marketplace selection, price ranges, and result sorting.
- **Mobile-Optimizes:** a seamless, mobile-optimized interface powered by React and Tailwind CSS, facilitating dynamic and responsive interactions.

This incremental development approach transformed the Snap & Shop platform from a basic prototype focused on feature extraction and comparison into a sophisticated, highly interactive search engine that leverages cutting-edge computer vision and web scraping.

5 Usability Testing

User interaction with the Snap & Shop platform was evaluated through a usability study involving nine volunteers, each guided through a series of predefined tasks. These tasks were designed to assess the platform's core functionalities, including image-based searches (both with and without feature extraction and comparison), text-based searches, and the use of various filtering and sorting options.

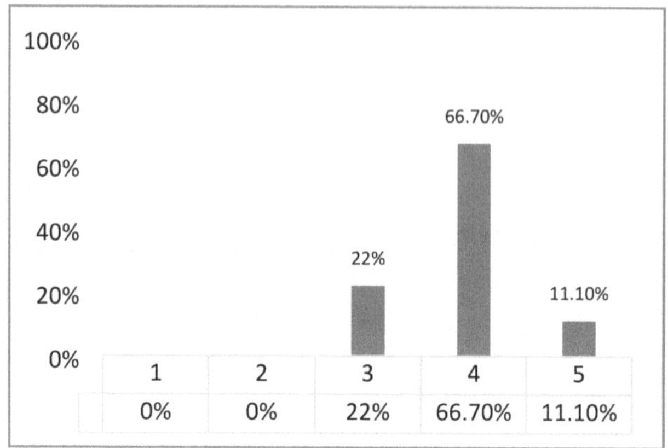

Fig. 3. Participants approval in having image feature extraction and comparison enabled.

Participants were instructed to perform product searches by uploading an image - initially without enabling image feature extraction and comparison, and subsequently with the feature activated. Most users expressed a preference for having the image feature extraction and comparison enabled, as it significantly improved result relevance, despite increasing search times. This preference was clearly reflected in the survey results, where most participants rated the feature highly, indicating strong user approval (see Fig. 3). Additionally, participants experimented with filtering results by selecting preferred stores, adjusted sorting options (relevance, date ascending or descending, price ascending or descending), and tested price range filtering both via text input and dynamically generated percentile range buttons.

Throughout the process, participants provided feedback after each task, rating its ease of use and commenting on how well the results met their expectations. At the end of the session, a SUS (System Usability Scale) questionnaire was administered for a more general assessment of the platform's usability.

The results indicated that most participants rated the system very highly and were able to easily complete the given tasks. The option to extract and compare visual characteristics was widely seen as a valuable enhancement, improving search relevance despite the increased processing time.

6 Conclusion and Future Work

The development of the Snap & Shop application was driven by a dual objective: firstly, to address a market gap, given the absence of a platform that aggregates products from used goods marketplaces with relevance at a national level; and secondly, to create a platform that implements an image-based search functionality. This solution not only allows for the identification of products from uploaded images and conducts corresponding searches but also processes the results to present the most similar products to the provided image. Accordingly, the aim is to offer a more efficient search experience aligned with user needs, enhancing the overall utility of the tool.

The work incorporates a range of technological solutions, notably machine learning models and web scraping techniques. Regarding machine learning, these models enable both product identification within the uploaded image - using the "gemini-2.5-flash-lite-preview-06–17" model accessed via an external API - and the comparison of search results with the original image, employing the locally hosted "MobileNetV3-Large" model to ensure fast and accurate similarity assessments.

Web scraping capitalized on Client-side Rendering (CSR) present in used goods websites, utilizing their public endpoints originally intended for page hydration. Employing an asynchronous HTTP request library, a method was developed to obtain product listing data by mimicking browser behavior, thus avoiding blocks or bans. This approach addressed various challenges such as cookie validation, with requests constructed to return search-specific parameters - including query text, price ranges, and product quantity – to retrieve the relevant data.

The image feature extraction and comparison solution can be integrated into existing applications, enabling users to retrieve visually similar results, in this case, analogous products. As for the image captioning solution, it served to circumvent the absence of an indexed database; however, this limits its interest to applications lacking their own database.

Regarding limitations, although the solution is functional and effective within current contexts, scalability in high-demand enterprise environments presents challenges. Heavy reliance on web scraping of public endpoints may encounter restrictions such as rate limits, frequent response structure changes, or IP blocking, which may intensify with increasing user traffic. Mitigating strategies include the use of rotating proxies or IP pools to ensure data access continuity. Additionally, the system is currently deployed as a monolithic and shared deployment environment that, whilst suitable for testing and moderate loads, could become a bottleneck at scale. In a production environment, distributing the workload across multiple servers, utilizing asynchronous processing, microservices, and GPU acceleration for inference would be advisable.

Finally, given that part of the pipeline depends on Gemini, an externally accessible API, factors such as system availability, latency, and potential API usage costs remain factors affecting eventual deployment. Future work may encompass implementing architectural enhancements for production-scale deployment and advancing web scraping robustness, including techniques capable of handling more protected platforms such as Facebook Marketplace.

Another critical issue for future research involves legal and ethical considerations, emphasizing the importance of integrating compliance and responsible practices into subsequent investigations and applications. This approach is essential to ensure that data collection is carried out in a manner that is both ethically sound and in full accordance with legal regulations [20].

References

1. Shiau, R., et al.: Shop the look: building a large scale visual shopping system. In: KDD'20: Proceedings of the 26th ACM SIGKDD International Conference on Knowledge Discovery & Data Mining. New York: Association for Computing Machinery, United States (2020). https://arxiv.org/abs/2006.10866. Accessed 13 Mar 2025
2. Google LLC. Google Lens (2018). https://play.google.com/store/apps/details?id=com.google.ar.lens&hl=en_US. Accessed 10 Mar 2025
3. Arrington, M.: Riya's Like.com Is First True Visual Image Search (2006). https://techcrunch.com/2006/11/08/riyas-likecom-is-first-true-visual-image-search/. Accessed 9 Mar 2025
4. Perez, J.C.: Google buys Like.com, visual shopping engine for retail products (2010). https://www.infoworld.com/article/2290898/google-buys-like-com-visual-shopping-engine-for-retail-products.html. Accessed 23 Mar 2025
5. Goode, L.: Google's Visual Search Can Now Answer Even More Complex Questions (2024). https://www.wired.com/story/google-lens-multimodal-search/. Accessed 10 Mar 2025
6. Weatherbed, J.: Google Lens will now help you decide what to buy in-store (2024). https://www.theverge.com/2024/11/19/24300424/google-lens-shopping-feature-stock-availability-reviews. Accessed 10 Mar 2025
7. Singh, S.: Perplexity AI raises $73.6M in funding round led by Nvidia, Bezos, now valued at $522M (2024). https://www.businesstoday.in/entrepreneurship/start-up/story/perplexity-ai-raises-736m-in-funding-round-led-by-nvidia-bezos-now-valued-at-522m-412130-2024-01-06. Accessed 06 Mar 2025
8. Perplexity Team. (2024, November 18). Shop like a Pro: Perplexity's new AI-powered shopping assistant (2024). https://www.perplexity.ai/hub/blog/shop-like-a-pro. Accessed 12 Mar 2025
9. Rijo, L.: Perplexity launches AI-powered shopping assistant with one-click checkout feature (2024). https://ppc.land/perplexity-launches-ai-powered-shopping-assistant-with-one-click-checkout-feature/. Accessed 15 Mar 2025
10. Nikitin, V.: Software development methodologies: types, selection criteria & stats. (itransition) (n.d.). https://www.itransition.com/software-development/methodologies. Accessed 9 Mar 2025
11. Laoyan, S.: Tudo o que é preciso saber sobre a gestão de projetos em cascata. (asana) (2024). https://asana.com/pt/resources/waterfall-project-management-methodology. Accessed 9 Mar 2025
12. Gomes, M.: O que é o Agile e porque deveria usar esta metodologia? (cegid Jasmin) (2024). https://www.jasminsoftware.pt/blog/metodologia-agile/. Accessed 11 Mar 2025
13. Radigan, D.: Como a metodologia Kanban é aplicada ao desenvolvimento de software. (Atlassian) (n.d.). https://www.atlassian.com/br/agile/kanban. Accessed 11 Mar 2025
14. Naydenov, P.: O que é Kanban? Um Guia Simples para Melhorar a Eficiência. (businessmap) (n.d.). https://businessmap.io/pt/recursos-kanban/primeiros-passos/o-que-e-kanban. Accessed 11 Mar 2025
15. FastAPI. (n.d.). FastAPI. https://fastapi.tiangolo.com. Accessed 22 June 2025
16. HTTPX. (n.d.). HTTPX. https://www.python-httpx.org/. Accessed 22 June 2025
17. Google. (n.d.). Gemini API. https://console.cloud.google.com/apis/library/generativelanguage.googleapis.com. Accessed 22 June 2025
18. He, K., Zhang, X., Ren, S., Sun, J.: Deep Residual Learning for Image Recognition (2015). https://arxiv.org/abs/1512.03385. Accessed 22 June 2025
19. Howard, A., et al.: Searching for MobileNetV3 (2019). de https://arxiv.org/abs/1905.02244. Accessed 18 Aug 2025
20. Khder, M.A.: Web scraping or web crawling: state of art, techniques, approaches and applications. Int. J. Adv. Soft Comput. Appl. **13**(3) (2021). https://doi.org/10.15849/IJASCA.211128.11

Tokenization and Search of Postal Addresses

David Ruete[1], Jorge Ruíz-Chávez[1], Alejandro Caroca[1], Carla Taramasco[1,2], Nicolás Caselli[1], Marcelo Reyes[1], Omar Salinas[1], Danilo Leal Moraga[1], Jean Paul Maidana[1,2], and Diego Mellado[1,2(✉)]

[1] Universidad Andres Bello, Viña del Mar, Chile
diego.mellado@unab.cl

[2] Instituto de Tecnología para la Innovación en Salud y Bienestar, Universidad Andrés Bello, Quillota 980, Viña del Mar, Chile

Abstract. Accurate and structured postal address data is essential for logistics, geolocation services, and public administration. In countries like Chile, companies such as Correos de Chile and Starken frequently encounter delivery failures due to informal or incomplete address records in their databases. This paper presents a token-based retrieval model for Spanish-language postal addresses, designed to support normalization tasks in georeferenced information systems. The model employs lexical tokenization and a similarity scoring function to identify structured address records that match informal or partial user queries. Using a standardized Chilean address database, we implemented a retrieval pipeline in R and evaluated it through two experiments involving incomplete and reordered input forms. Results show that the model robustly retrieves semantically consistent entries across executions and shows token order invariance. Our proposed approach offers a lightweight, interpretable, and language-specific solution for address normalization, suitable for integration into postal or spatial data systems in resource-constrained or linguistically diverse environments.

Keywords: Natural Language Processing · Postal Address Normalization · Data Quality in Logistics

1 Introduction

The growing demand for automatic systems capable of processing large volumes of textual information motivates the development of Natural Language Processing (NLP) techniques aimed at structuring and retrieving unnormalized data. In particular, the extraction and retrieval of postal addresses from free-form text represents a significant challenge due to linguistic ambiguity, morphosyntactic diversity, and the informal manner in which such data are commonly written. This issue arises not only in administrative and public service contexts but also directly affects the efficiency of logistical, census, and georeferencing processes on digital platforms [2].

T. Guarda et al. (Eds.): ARTIIS 2025, CCIS 2789, pp. 27–38, 2026.
https://doi.org/10.1007/978-3-032-16758-3_3

Postal addresses exhibit unique characteristics that hinder their automatic identification and normalization: they often contain abbreviations, regional variations, spelling errors, and non-standard syntactic structures. In response to this challenge, the specific tokenization of addresses—that is, the process of segmenting a text into minimal meaningful units related to geographic or postal components—constitutes a critical stage for any system aiming to automate the search, classification, or geolocation of such information.

The work of [8] proposes an approach that combines linguistically adapted rules for Spanish with information retrieval techniques to address the search for addresses in unstructured texts. This proposal aligns with a line of research aimed at improving the recognition of spatial entities, contributing to the advancement of intelligent systems applied to territorial databases, land registries, and citizen service platforms.

At the international level, initiatives such as GeoNames and the OpenCage project demonstrate significant advances in semantic geolocation; however, substantial gaps persist in processing Spanishlanguage texts, particularly those involving highly informal address formats or local idiomatic expressions [14]. In this context, the tokenization and search model proposed by Ruiz aligns with current trends in multilingual and contextualized natural language processing (NLP), representing a methodological contribution that can be integrated into relational database systems, search engines, and urban mapping platforms.

This research aims not only to validate the effectiveness of the proposed model but also to explore its potential as a component of a broader geospatial analysis system, in line with the growing need to develop interoperable and accessible territorial data infrastructures [7]. Ultimately, the study helps bridge the gap between linguistic processing and geographic information systems (GIS), thereby strengthening the link between natural language and spatial data in real-world environments.

2 Context and Related Works

2.1 Context

In the era of digital transformation, the ability to automatically process large volumes of unstructured textual data is essential across various strategic domains, including urban logistics, territorial cadastres, postal services, and geospatial planning. Within this context, Natural Language Processing (NLP) emerges as a critical tool for extracting, classifying, and normalizing information from texts characterized by highly variable morphosyntactic structures [9].

One of the most complex challenges in this domain lies in the identification and retrieval of postal addresses from free-form text. Unlike other named entities, addresses exhibit a high degree of semantic ambiguity, frequent use of abbreviations, spelling errors, local idiomatic variations, and non-standard syntactic structures [15]. These difficulties directly impact the effectiveness of tasks such as automated georeferencing, urban mapping, and census segmentation—especially in Spanish-speaking contexts, where informality in address writing is more pronounced [16].

Although notable international initiatives exist—such as GeoNames, OpenStreetMap, and the OpenCage geocoding engine—their performance decreases significantly when processing unstructured Spanish textual inputs, highlighting a technological gap in the multilingual handling of spatial data [12]. Consequently, the development of specialized tokenization and search models becomes a priority, enabling the segmentation of addresses into minimal semantic units and linking them to spatial components recognizable by Geographic Information Systems (GIS).

Recent studies propose hybrid solutions that combine linguistic rules, machine learning, and information retrieval to enhance the normalization of postal addresses [5]. However, methodological challenges remain regarding the interoperability of these solutions with territorial databases, the scalability of processing, and the generalization across diverse urban and rural environments.

This work presents a lightweight address retrieval model based on token overlap similarity, designed for integration into postal services, and validates it using Chilean address data. This system was designed to address the challenges posed by informal or incomplete address inputs commonly found in operational postal databases, especially in contexts where standardization procedures are either absent or loosely enforced. By relying on token-level representations, the model enables flexible and interpretable matching of partial queries against structure records, without the need for deep linguistic annotation or external ontologies. The proposed approach also contributes to the broader challenge of linguistic normalization in territorial data, supporting the integration of spatial identifiers into relational and georeferenced information systems.

2.2 Related Works

The automatic extraction and normalization of postal addresses from unstructured text presents a multidimensional challenge within Natural Language Processing (NLP), particularly in languages with high morphological variability such as Spanish. Unlike standard named entities (e.g., persons or organizations), addresses exhibit irregular syntactic patterns, frequent use of abbreviations, spelling errors, and substantial regional linguistic variation. These characteristics render their identification a complex task, especially when addresses are embedded in informal or noisy textual environments such as citizen reports, administrative forms, or social media entries [11].

Address Parsing and Geocoding Systems. International initiatives such as GeoNames, OpenCage, and Google Geocoding API provide general-purpose geolocation services. However, these systems perform poorly with informal or non-standard address formats, especially in Latin American contexts [3]. This performance gap has prompted the development of specialized tools for parsing postal addresses. For example, Libpostal, a language-agnostic parsing engine, has achieved substantial accuracy in English but still struggles with the morphosyntactic nuances of Spanish. Moreover, its rule-based architecture limits adaptation to informal expressions common in Latin American data sources [1].

Hybrid and Linguistic Rule-Based Models. [13] proposes a hybrid system that combines manually crafted linguistic rules adapted to Spanish with basic Information Retrieval (IR) techniques. This model addresses issues such as abbreviation expansion and regional name disambiguation, demonstrating high precision in controlled datasets. Similar approaches have been explored in urban address modeling, where regular expressions are employed to identify elements such as street types, numbers, and locality markers [5]. Nonetheless, the scalability of these solutions remains limited when applied to heterogeneous corpora or multilingual environments.

Advances in Multilingual NLP and Geospatial Text Processing. Recent studies have focused on integrating geospatial intelligence into natural language processing (NLP) pipelines. Multilingual transformer models (e.g., mBERT, XLM-R) have been fine-tuned to extract spatial entities from text and align them with geographic coordinates using gazetteers [10]. However, these models require large annotated corpora for training and tend to underperform in informal domains lacking structural consistency. To mitigate these challenges, some researchers incorporate syntactic features and contextual embeddings to improve the disambiguation of place names and address fragments [6].

Research Gaps and Motivation. While these approaches have contributed valuable insights to the task of address normalization, significant gaps remain. Particularly in handling informal, unstructured, and multilingual textual data typical of Latin American contexts. Rule-based systems, although precise in narrow domains, lack flexibility and scalability. Meanwhile, transformer-based models require substantial annotated corpora and often underperform when exposed to noisy, real-world inputs.

These limitations highlight the need for hybrid strategies that combine linguistic knowledge, contextual embeddings, and adaptive learning mechanisms. In response, this study proposes a lightweight yet robust framework for Spanish address normalization, designed to perform reliably across diverse sources, including citizen complaints, social media, and administrative texts. By integrating syntactic cues, domain-specific heuristics, and pretrained language models, the proposed approach aims to enhance recall and precision while maintaining operational feasibility in real-world systems.

3 Methodology

The proposed pipeline is described in the following section. This method operates on an standardized database of addresses and proceedes in three main steps, as described. A normalization stage to ensure consistency across all records. Followed by a word-level tokenization process using standard NLP utilities, yielding structured sequences of each entry. And finally, a query processing stage, where the input is tokenized and compared against all database entries using a similarity score.

3.1 Database

We used the "Streets Master Database 2018" provided by the Chilean National Institute of Statistics (INE) as the primary source of data for our experiments. This dataset compiles all registered street name records across all regions and municipalities in the country, compiled by the "Ejes viales de IDE Chile" work group. It includes a total of 395480 entries corresponding to a unique street name, by region and city. To explore the lexical composition of the dataset, we applied basic text-mining techniques to extract the most frequent terms present in the dataset. Using an n-gram analysis, we identified the top 10 most common unigrams, as shown in Fig. 1. The most frequent term was "pasaje" (alley), followed by "calle" (street). Other commonplace terms were articles and prepositions in Spanish, such as "los", "las".

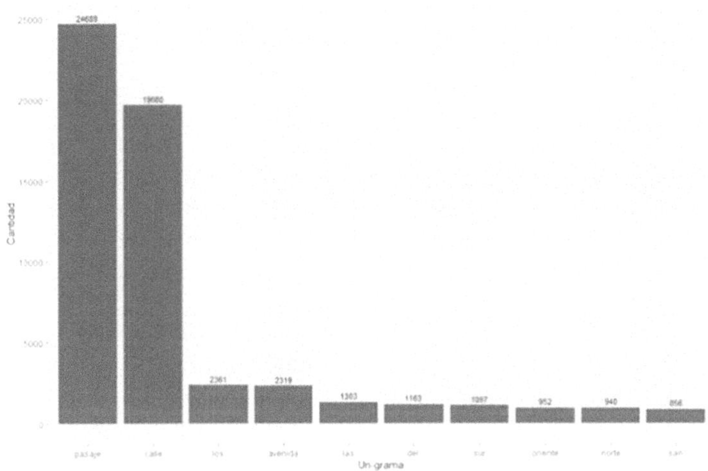

Fig. 1. Bar plot of top 10 most common words within the Chilean street names dataset

We then extended this analysis to include bi-gram representations to observe common co-occurrence patterns. As shown in Fig. 2, the top-ranking bigram predominantly featured combinations of "pasaje" or "calle" with a definite article. (i.e. "pasaje los").

This initial lexical analysis informed our choice for the tokenization process. For this purpose, we used functions from the Keras library in R [4], which provides utilities commonly employed in both machine learning and natural language processing tasks.

3.2 Data Processing

All records provided in the dataset were used for our processing pipeline. Our procedure is detailed as follows: Initially, the dataset was loaded in its raw CSV

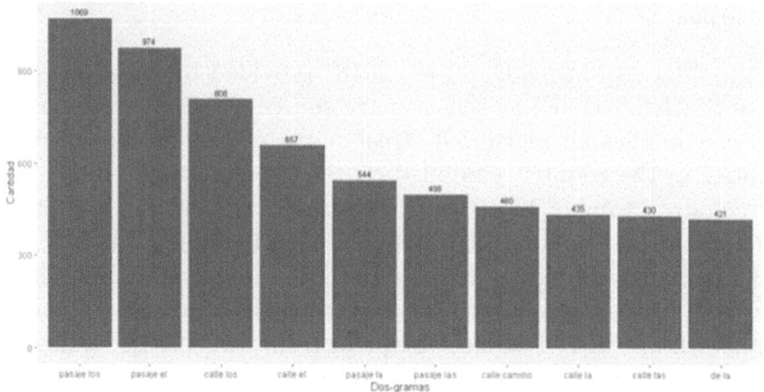

Fig. 2. Bar plot of the top 10 most common bi-gram representations within the Chilean street names dataset.

format, and only the variables relevant to the address text were imported for further processing.

The first stage involved a data cleaning process. Each entry corresponding to a street name was converted to lowercase to ensure uniformity. Punctuation marks and special characters, such as accent marks, were removed. And all records with missing or duplicated values were discarded. Ensuring that text variations due to casing or orthography differences would not impact on our matching process in subsequent stages.

Following this cleaning stage, each street name was converted to a standard character format. A vocabulary list was compiled, containing all unique tokens present in the cleaned address entries. Subsequently, we applied a word-level tokenization process using the `text_tokenizer()` and `fit_text_tokenizer()` functions provided by the Keras Library in R. Generating structured token sequences for each address.

3.3 Experiment

To test our proposed model using sample texts, we applied two experiments, as detailed below.

Experiment 1. The first experiment was designed to evaluate the effectiveness of a token-based similarity model for retrieving relevant address records from a reference database. The goal is to assess whether the system could return relevant matches when provided with incomplete or partially accurate input queries.

This similarity score was computed as the ratio of shared tokens between the query and each address record, normalized by the total number of tokens in the address (Eq. 1. This approach ensures higher scores for more concise and lexically aligned results.

$$\text{Similarity}(q, r) = \frac{|\text{Tokens}(q) \cap \text{Tokens}(r)|}{|\text{Tokens}(r)|} \tag{1}$$

Initially, a query string was tokenized using a custom function implemented in R. The resulting tokens were compared against all tokenized records in the database, as represented in Fig. 3. For each record, a similarity score was calculated as the ratio of matching tokens between the query and the registered addresses. All records were then sorted by this similarity score in descending order, retaining only those with non-zero values as candidate results.

Several test cases were used to evaluate the model's behavior. These included a common surname found in Chilean street names (*almeyda*), an ordinal term commonly used in street designations (*segunda*), and a name pair to test order invariance (*varas antonio* and *antonio varas*).

On each query, our pipeline returned a set of addresses with shared terms with the input string. The similarity score provided an interpretable metric for ranking matches, enabling the retrieval of relevant results regardless of position or order of tokens within the full address.

NOMBRE_MAESTRO	NOMBRE_MAESTRO_TOKENIZADO
avenida 10 de julio huamachuco	c(1795, 3, 5414, 8925, 8170)
avenida alameda libertador bernardo ohiggins	c(1795, 648, 9593, 2374, 12145)
avenida alcalde carlos valdovinos	c(1795, 720, 3494, 16915)
avenida almirante blanco encalada	c(1795, 912, 2487, 6068)
avenida beaucheff	c(1795, 2206)
avenida brasil	c(1795, 2734)
avenida cardenal jose maria caro	c(1795, 3448, 8870, 10562, 3515)
avenida viel	c(1795, 17172)
avenida centenario	c(1795, 3833)
avenida club hipico	c(1795, 4472, 8001)
avenida corredor santa rosa	c(1795, 4961, 15099, 14759)
avenida diego portales	c(1795, 5589, 13552)
avenida matucana	c(1795, 10753)
avenida ejercito libertador	c(1795, 5958, 9593)
avenida el mirador	c(1795, 5963, 11169)
avenida el parque	c(1795, 5963, 12703)
avenida general rondizzoni	c(1795, 7216, 14746)
avenida españa	c(1795, 6261)
avenida exposicion	c(1795, 6468)

Fig. 3. example of tokenization of street names, resulting in the codification of each word to a corresponding value.

Experiment 2. To evaluate the consistency and robustness of the proposed retrieval pipeline, we conducted the following experiment from a clean state. This was done to ensure that no residual memory, preprocessing artifacts, or cached elements from previous experiments did not influence the system's behavior. To test the model's ability to provide consistent results when executed independently.

Initially, we re-imported the original dataset without any formatting or prior preprocessing. We then applied our preprocessing pipeline, which included normalizing each entry to a standardized form, removing punctuation and special characters, and filtering out duplicates and blank entries. Producing a clean set of addresses ready for tokenization.

Once preprocessing was completed, we input our query string and proceeded to tokenize it using our custom tokenizer. The query tokens were then compared against the tokenized address records. For each record, the similarity score to the query was estimated and ranked. Selecting the top-ranked results.

As with the previous experiment, we manually inspected the returned addresses to determine if they were matches. For instance, when using the term *antonio varas*, we expected results such as *avenida antonio varas*, *pasaje antonio varas norte*, and similar to be retrieved and positioned appropriately within the ranking.

4 Results

4.1 Experiment 1

This experiment allowed us to demonstrate the model's capacity to retrieve semantically relevant results from partial or reordered queries. Table 1 presents a summary of the top results obtained for each input case. The retrieved matches demonstrate that the model can identify relevant entries even when the input is incomplete or presented in a non-canonical order.

Table 1. Top-ranked matches and corresponding similarity scores for a selection of test queries using the proposed token-based retrieval method

Query	Top Match	Similarity Score
almeyda	*calle cayetano almeyda*	0.333
segunda	*avenida segunda*	0.500
antonio varas	*calle antonio varas*	0.667
varas antonio	*calle antonio varas*	0.667

In the case of the query *almeyda*, the top-ranked addresses contained the target term as part of compound names. As shown in Fig. 4, the model favored shorter results such as *calle cayetano almeyda* over longer expressions such as *calle diego de almeyda*, which, although still relevant, achieved a lower similarity score due to token dilution.

In the case of the queries *antonio varas* and *varas antonio*, the results were nearly identical, confirming that the model is invariant to token order. As shown in Fig. 5, the highest-ranked entries contained both terms with minimal modifiers. In contrast, longer variants, such as *calle juan antonio varas*, received lower scores despite being semantically plausible, due to the presence of additional tokens that reduce the matching ratio.

NOMBRE_MAESTRO	NOMBRE_MAESTRO_TOKENIZADO	VARIABLE_INPUT_TOKENIZADO	VALIDACION_TOKENIZADO	PONDERACION_PROBABLE
calle cayetano almeyda	c(3123, 3741, 909)	909	c(FALSE, FALSE, TRUE)	0.3333333
calle puerto almeyda	c(3123, 13773, 909)	909	c(FALSE, FALSE, TRUE)	0.3333333
pasaje puerto almeyda	c(12732, 13773, 909)	909	c(FALSE, FALSE, TRUE)	0.3333333
calle duble almeyda	c(3123, 5795, 909)	909	c(FALSE, FALSE, TRUE)	0.3333333
pasaje duble almeyda	c(12732, 5795, 909)	909	c(FALSE, FALSE, TRUE)	0.3333333
avenida duble almeyda	c(1795, 5795, 909)	909	c(FALSE, FALSE, TRUE)	0.3333333
calle cruz almeyda	c(3123, 5142, 909)	909	c(FALSE, FALSE, TRUE)	0.3333333
pasaje cruz almeyda	c(12732, 5142, 909)	909	c(FALSE, FALSE, TRUE)	0.3333333
calle diego de almeyda	c(3123, 5589, 5414, 909)	909	c(FALSE, FALSE, FALSE, TRUE)	0.2500000
calle diego duble almeyda	c(3123, 5589, 5795, 909)	909	c(FALSE, FALSE, FALSE, TRUE)	0.2500000
pasaje diego de almeyda	c(12732, 5589, 5414, 909)	909	c(FALSE, FALSE, FALSE, TRUE)	0.2500000
pasaje diego duble almeyda	c(12732, 5589, 5795, 909)	909	c(FALSE, FALSE, FALSE, TRUE)	0.2500000
calle luis cruz almeyda	c(3123, 10059, 5142, 909)	909	c(FALSE, FALSE, FALSE, TRUE)	0.2500000
calle doctor alfredo almeyda de saa	c(3123, 5676, 823, 909, 5414, 14911)	909	c(FALSE, FALSE, FALSE, TRUE, FALSE, FALSE)	0.1666667

Fig. 4. Top address matches resulted from query *almeyda* using our method. The model favors entries with fewer non-matching tokens.

NOMBRE_MAESTRO	NOMBRE_MAESTRO_TOKENIZADO	VARIABLE_INPUT_TOKENIZADO	VALIDACION_TOKENIZADO	PONDERACION_PROBABLE
calle antonio varas	c(3123, 1294, 16968)	c(16968, 1294)	c(FALSE, TRUE, TRUE)	0.6666667
avenida antonio varas	c(1795, 1294, 16968)	c(16968, 1294)	c(FALSE, TRUE, TRUE)	0.6666667
pasaje antonio varas	c(12732, 1294, 16968)	c(16968, 1294)	c(FALSE, TRUE, TRUE)	0.6666667
pasaje antonio	c(12732, 1294)	c(16968, 1294)	c(FALSE, TRUE)	0.5000000
calle juan antonio varas	c(3123, 8898, 1294, 16968)	c(16968, 1294)	c(FALSE, FALSE, TRUE, TRUE)	0.5000000
calle ministro antonio varas	c(3123, 11156, 1294, 16968)	c(16968, 1294)	c(FALSE, FALSE, TRUE, TRUE)	0.5000000
avenida avenida antonio varas	c(1795, 1795, 1294, 16968)	c(16968, 1294)	c(FALSE, FALSE, TRUE, TRUE)	0.5000000
pasaje antonio varas interior	c(12732, 1294, 16968, 8596)	c(16968, 1294)	c(FALSE, TRUE, TRUE, FALSE)	0.5000000
pasaje varas	c(12732, 16968)	c(16968, 1294)	c(FALSE, TRUE)	0.5000000
calle varas	c(3123, 16968)	c(16968, 1294)	c(FALSE, TRUE)	0.5000000
avenida san antonio	c(1795, 15062, 1294)	c(16968, 1294)	c(FALSE, FALSE, TRUE)	0.3333333
calle antonio ricaurte	c(3123, 1294, 14547)	c(16968, 1294)	c(FALSE, TRUE, FALSE)	0.3333333
calle san antonio	c(3123, 15062, 1294)	c(16968, 1294)	c(FALSE, FALSE, TRUE)	0.3333333
pasaje antonio ricaurte	c(12732, 1294, 14547)	c(16968, 1294)	c(FALSE, TRUE, FALSE)	0.3333333
calle antonio garrido	c(3123, 1294, 7139)	c(16968, 1294)	c(FALSE, TRUE, FALSE)	0.3333333
calle antonio quezada	c(3123, 1294, 13967)	c(16968, 1294)	c(FALSE, TRUE, FALSE)	0.3333333

Fig. 5. Search results for the query *varas antonio* using our method. Identical top matches were retrieved in the case of *antonio varas*, indicating order invariance.

4.2 Experiment 2

To evaluate the robustness and consistency of the retrieval model, a second experiment was conducted from a clean initialization. As with Experiment 1, four test queries were used, and the resulting outputs were manually reviewed to assess the reproducibility of the system's behavior.

For the query *almeyda*, as shown in Fig. 3, the retrieved results closely resemble those from the first experiment. However, the ranking order differs: In this run, longer compound names, such as *calle diego de almeyda*, were prioritized over shorter alternatives, like calle cayetano almeyda. This variation reflects the model's sensitivity to minor fluctuations in token distribution, while also confirming its ability to identify semantically consistent matches (Fig. 6).

For the queries *antonio varas* and *varas antonio*, the outputs were once again nearly identical, confirming that the models maintain order invariance. As shown

NOMBRE_MAESTRO	NOMBRE_MAESTRO_TOKENIZADO	VARIABLE_INPUT_TOKENIZADO	VALIDACION_TOKENIZADO	PONDERACION_PROBABLE
calle diego de almeyda	c(3123, 5589, 5414, 909)	909	TRUE	1
calle diego duble almeyda	c(3123, 5589, 5795, 909)	909	TRUE	1
pasaje diego de almeyda	c(12732, 5589, 5414, 909)	909	TRUE	1
pasaje diego duble almeyda	c(12732, 5589, 5795, 909)	909	TRUE	1
calle cayetano almeyda	c(3123, 3741, 909)	909	TRUE	1

Fig. 6. Top ranked result for the query *almeyda* in Experiment 2. All returned entries were also present in the previous experiment, though their order of appearance varied.

in Fig. 7, entries containing both query terms in sequence were ranked highest, followed by partial matches that preserved semantic proximity.

NOMBRE_MAESTRO	NOMBRE_MAESTRO_TOKENIZADO	VARIABLE_INPUT_TOKENIZADO	VALIDACION_TOKENIZADO	PONDERACION_PROBABLE
calle antonio varas	c(3123, 1294, 16968)	c(16968, 1294)	c(TRUE, TRUE)	1
avenida antonio varas	c(1795, 1294, 16968)	c(16968, 1294)	c(TRUE, TRUE)	1
pasaje antonio varas	c(12732, 1294, 16968)	c(16968, 1294)	c(TRUE, TRUE)	1
calle juan antonio varas	c(3123, 8898, 1294, 16968)	c(16968, 1294)	c(TRUE, TRUE)	1
calle ministro antonio varas	c(3123, 11156, 1294, 16968)	c(16968, 1294)	c(TRUE, TRUE)	1

Fig. 7. Top matches for the query *varas antonio*. The returned entries replicate the structure and composition of those in Experiment 1, reinforcing the system's order-invariant behavior.

In the case of query *segunda*, the retrieved entries, as shown in Fig. 8, prioritize concise address forms with high lexical overlap, such as *avenida segunda*, over results like *calle segunda oriente*. These results are consistent with the expected behavior, confirming that the model favors short, token-aligned matches when dealing with high-frequency terms.

NOMBRE_MAESTRO	NOMBRE_MAESTRO_TOKENIZADO	VARIABLE_INPUT_TOKENIZADO	VALIDACION_TOKENIZADO	PONDERACION_PROBABLE
avenida segunda	c(1795, 15260)	15260	TRUE	1
calle segunda	c(3123, 15260)	15260	TRUE	1
pasaje segunda	c(12732, 15260)	15260	TRUE	1
calle segunda longitudinal	c(3123, 15260, 9952)	15260	TRUE	1
calle segunda transversal	c(3123, 15260, 16518)	15260	TRUE	1
avenida segunda transversal	c(1795, 15260, 16518)	15260	TRUE	1
pasaje segunda sinfonia	c(12732, 15260, 15460)	15260	TRUE	1
pasaje segunda transversal	c(12732, 15260, 16518)	15260	TRUE	1
calle segunda avenida	c(3123, 15260, 1795)	15260	TRUE	1

Fig. 8. Top matches for the query *segunda*. Results show a higher match to expressions with more common terms.

Overall, the model exhibited stable and interpretable behavior across independent executions. While minor variations in ranking may occur, the retrieved entries remain lexically and semantically aligned to the input queries, confirming the system's robustness in practical retrieval tasks.

5 Discussion

The results obtained from both experiments provide empirical support for our hypothesis that token-based similarity retrieval can serve as a reliable method for identifying incomplete or irregular postal addresses within a structured database. The consistent recovery of relevant entries across independent executions of our model confirms the robustness of the model and its potential for integration into real-world workflows.

In this case, our approach demonstrated sensitivity to lexical structure and token ordering, yet remained tolerant to variations in input format. This property is valuable in an operational context where address data may be entered inconsistently by the user. These invariances, as observed in the *antonio varas*/*varas antonio* cases, are a key advantage over more rigid rule-based parsers, which often fail to generalize under such permutations.

However, these results highlight several limitations to our model. First and foremost, our choice of similarity metric does not account for semantic equivalence between tokens. For example, terms such as *avenida* and its abbreviation *av.*. Or when minor spelling variants are present (i.e., *almeyda* and *almeida* would not be matched unless explicitly included as similar within our set rules. This restricts the system's applicability in cases involving the correction of abbreviations or typographical errors.

Second, while the retrieval process is interpretable and computationally light, it does not leverage contextual or morphological information that more advanced NLP models typically exploit. As such, our system may underperform in cases involving ambiguous or highly localized expressions that cannot be resolved solely through token matching.

Despite these limitations, our proposed method offers a viable baseline for addressing normalization tasks on a Spanish-language dataset. Making it suitable for integration into pre-validation stages of postal or georeferencing systems, especially in settings with limited resources or domain-specific constraints.

Future work may address current limitations by incorporating phonetic similarity measures, fuzzy token matching, or embedding-based approaches.

6 Conclusions

This work presented a token-based approach to postal address retrieval for Spanish-language data. The system demonstrated robust performance across two independent experiments, showing tolerance to incomplete or reordered input queries. While limited in handling semantic variation or abbreviations, the method provides a transparent and computationally efficient solution for integration into practical data quality pipelines. Future work includes the integration of fuzzy matching techniques and phonetic similarity metrics.

References

1. Beauchemin, D., Yassine, M.: Deepparse: an extendable, and fine-tunable state-of-the-art library for parsing multinational street addresses. arXiv preprint arXiv:2311.11846 (2023)
2. Camacho-Collados, J., Pilehvar, M.T.: From word to sense embeddings: a survey on vector representations of meaning. J. Artif. Intell. Res. **63**, 743–788 (2018)
3. Chen, H., Dan, L., Lu, Y., Chen, M., Zhang, J.: An improved data augmentation approach and its application in medical named entity recognition. BMC Med. Inform. Decis. Making **24**(1), 221 (2024)
4. Chollet, F., et al.: Keras (2015). https://keras.io
5. Cruz, P., Vanneschi, L., Painho, M., Rita, P.: Automatic identification of addresses: a systematic literature review. ISPRS Int. J. Geo Inf. **11**(1), 11 (2021)
6. Esmaail, N., Omar, N., Mohd, M., Fauzi, F., Mansur, Z.: Named entity recognition in user-generated text (English twitter): a systematic literature review. IEEE Access (2024)
7. Freddi, F., et al.: Innovations in earthquake risk reduction for resilience: recent advances and challenges. Int. J. Disaster Risk Reduction **60**, 102267 (2021)
8. Hu, X., et al.: Location reference recognition from texts: a survey and comparison. ACM Comput. Surv. **56**(5), 1–37 (2023)
9. Jurafsky, D., Martin, J.H.: Speech and Language Processing: An Introduction to Natural Language Processing, Computational Linguistics, and Speech Recognition with Language Models, 3rd edn. (2025). https://web.stanford.edu/~jurafsky/slp3/, online manuscript released January 12, 2025
10. Kopanov, K.: Comparative performance of advanced NLP models and LLMs in multilingual geo-entity detection. In: Proceedings of the Cognitive Models and Artificial Intelligence Conference, pp. 106–110 (2024)
11. Liu, W., Cui, X.: Improving named entity recognition for social media with data augmentation. Appl. Sci. **13**(9), 5360 (2023)
12. Orgoványi, P., Hammer, T., Karches, T.: Geocoding applications for enhancing urban water supply network analysis. Urban Sci. **9**(2), 51 (2025)
13. Plensack, G., Finardi, P.: Normalizador neural de datas e endereços (2020). https://arxiv.org/abs/2007.04300
14. Serere, H.N., Resch, B., Havas, C.R.: Enhanced geocoding precision for location inference of tweet text using spacy, nominatim and google maps. a comparative analysis of the influence of data selection. Plos One **18**(3), e0282942 (2023)
15. Wang, C., Dong, Q., Wang, X., Sui, Z.: Statistical dataset evaluation: a case study on named entity recognition. Nat. Lang. Process. **31**(1), 90–110 (2025)
16. Yin, Z., et al.: Toward building next-generation geocoding systems: a systematic review. arXiv preprint arXiv:2503.18888 (2025)

Human - AI Collaboration in Organisational Decision-Making

Insights from Public and Private Sectors

Milan Bokan, Adam Jacobson, and Niki Chatzipanagiotou(✉)

Department of Informatics, Lund University, Lund, Sweden
niki.chatzipanagiotou@ics.lu.se

Abstract. The research study examines how employees in private and public sector organisations utilize AI-powered tools in organisational decision-making, focusing on the perceived benefits and challenges of their use. It further examines how such tools can enhance decision quality. A qualitative research design was employed, involving interviews with purposively selected employees from organisations in Sweden. Thematic analysis of the data resulted in six key findings. Interpreted through a theoretical lens incorporating sensemaking theory, the results show that AI-powered tools are increasingly applied in operational and tactical decisions, particularly through secure, in-house generative AI systems. Private sector organisations demonstrate rapid integration, driven by efficiency and competitive advantage, whereas public sector counterparts adopt a more cautious approach, emphasizing compliance, data protection, and accountability. In both sectors, AI is primarily seen as a supportive aid rather than an autonomous decision-maker, with human oversight remaining critical. Benefits include increased speed, consistency, and enhanced collaboration, while challenges relate to transparency, potential over-reliance, and regulatory limitations. The study offers theoretical and practical contributions by highlighting conditions for responsible AI integration, stressing the importance of contextual adaptation, user competence, and alignment with organisational goals.

Keywords: Artificial Intelligence · AI-Powered Systems · AI-Powered Tools · Decision-Making · Private organisations · Public organisations · Sweden · European Union · Sensemaking

1 Introduction

The growing integration of digital technologies into modern society has transformed the way individuals and organisations operate, communicate, and make decisions. Among these technologies, Artificial Intelligence (AI) has emerged as a pivotal force, enabling the extraction of actionable insights from vast data sources and redefining decision-making processes across sectors. By enhancing human analytical capabilities, AI not only supports but reshapes how information from data is interpreted and how decisions are made.

T. Guarda et al. (Eds.): ARTIIS 2025, CCIS 2789, pp. 39–53, 2026.
https://doi.org/10.1007/978-3-032-16758-3_4

AI however is more than an automation tool; it is a transformative technology that augments human intelligence and facilitates new forms of human-machine collaboration. As such, its increasing use raises fundamental questions about its role in supporting decision-making and the evolving relationship between humans and AI systems. Existing research presents two primary perspectives: AI as a cognitive amplifier that enhances decision quality [39, 48], and AI as an autonomous agent capable of executing tasks independently. These perspectives represent a spectrum of human-AI collaboration, ranging from task delegation to cooperative problem-solving.

Across both private and public organisations, AI-powered systems have gained prominence for improving decision-making and operational efficiency. In the private sector, they are widely used in strategic planning, customer service, fraud detection, and market analysis [6, 10, 48]. In the public sector, AI supports mainly policymaking, healthcare resource management, public safety, and service delivery [39]. Despite differences in objectives and regulatory environments, organisations across sectors face similar challenges in ensuring that AI-driven decisions are transparent, accountable, and effectively integrated with human oversight.

Organisational decision-making is inherently complex and collaborative, involving stakeholders, departments, and information systems [23, 29, 45, 47]. The introduction of AI-powered tools into these contexts introduces new dynamics that warrant closer examination. These systems raise important questions about how they influence collaboration, distribute responsibility, and support collaborative decision-making in organisational settings.

Prior studies have examined AI's potential to support strategic decisions under uncertainty [48], the implications for security and ethics [7], and the unintended organisational impacts of AI systems [30]. Other previous studies have called for interdisciplinary approaches, explainable AI, and closer scrutiny of the social dynamics affecting AI adoption [10, 39]. Despite this growing body of work, there remains limited understanding of how employees perceive and engage with AI-powered systems as collaborative tools for decision-making. Key questions remain around how these tools can be effectively integrated, what barriers hinder their use, and how they affect roles and responsibilities in organisations.

To address this gap, this study explores how employees in private and public sector organisations interact with AI-powered tools in decision-making contexts. It examines the conditions under which AI systems can function as collaborative agents, the benefits they bring to decision-making processes, and the challenges that arise from their use. Consequently, the research offers actionable recommendations to leverage AI-powered tools to support effective, collaborative decision-making. By examining these dynamics, the study contributes to the broader discourse in information systems (IS) research, offering insights into the socio-technical transformation triggered by AI adoption and integration.

Following this introduction, the rest of the paper is structured as follows. Section two includes the theoretical framework of the research. The methodological choices of the research are described in section three. In section four, the findings are presented followed by a discussion in section five. The paper concludes with section six where the conclusions of this research are presented.

2 Theoretical Background

2.1 Decision Making

Decision making involves selecting from available alternatives, yet this seemingly straightforward process incorporates complex cognitive, contextual, and social dimensions. Drawing from multiple disciplines - economics, psychology, organisational theory - scholars such as Simon [45] and Harrison [23], have developed diverse frameworks to understand decision behavior in organisations.

Harrison [23] identifies six sequential functions in the decision process: setting objectives, searching for alternatives, evaluating options, making a choice, implementing, and conducting follow-up. He also outlines four decision-making models: rational (focused on optimization through analysis), organisational (satisficing within cognitive constraints), political (driven by negotiation and compromise), and process (sequential and objective-driven). These models guide different types of decisions, from routine operational tasks to complex strategic planning [20].

Operational decisions are structured, rule-based, and often automated due to their repetitive nature [29]. Tactical decisions, by contrast, bridge strategy and operations. They are flexible, time-sensitive, and responsive to dynamic contexts [18]. Unlike operational decisions, tactical decision-making requires contextual judgment and adaptability to real-time conditions. Strategic decisions on the other hand focus on long-term direction, typically addressing complex, high-impact issues such as market entry or innovation investments [14]. These decisions, made under uncertainty, often rely on judgment and scenario planning rather than solely on data.

In organisations, the decision-making context differs due to delayed feedback and the influence of broader systemic factors [42]. Feedback loops are less direct, and decision outcomes are harder to trace, increasing reliance on models that acknowledge informational limitations [23]. Hammond et al. [22] highlight common decision failures, such as poor data collection and undefined alternatives, further illustrating why satisficing often replaces strict rationality.

2.2 Artificial Intelligence in Organisational Decision Making

AI is a rapidly evolving field with wide-ranging applications across organisational domains [43]. The OECD [19] defines AI systems as machine-based entities that generate outputs such as predictions, decisions, or recommendations based on input data. These systems differ in autonomy and adaptability and are increasingly central to decision processes.

A key branch of AI is Machine Learning (ML), which develops models that learn from data to solve problems without explicit programming [25]. ML models are particularly useful for predictive tasks and data-driven decisions [39, 44]. However, their "black box" nature raises concerns about transparency. Explainable AI (XAI) aims to address this by making ML outputs interpretable to human users, enhancing trust and accountability in decision-making contexts [44]. Natural Language Processing (NLP), a subfield of ML, enables machines to understand and interact using human language [3]. NLP underpins the functionality of Large Language Models (LLMs) like ChatGPT, facilitating natural interaction and content generation [41]. Generative AI, an emerging focus area, differentiates itself by creating original content - text, images, code - based on user inputs [34]. These models, powered by deep learning, simulate aspects of human cognition and are foundational to LLMs [5].

The integration of Artificial Intelligence (AI) into organisational decision-making has accelerated due to advances in computing power and the growing availability of high-quality data [35]. Many organisations report increased productivity and improved decision-making through AI-powered tools [8, 35]. More specifically, AI facilitates complex decision-making by analysing large datasets and uncovering patterns [32], echoing early visions of decision support [31]. Effective data visualization helps reduce overload and aids stakeholder interpretation [21, 37]. Further, AI enhances efficiency by automating repetitive tasks and accelerating data analysis [8, 39]. It also supports creative processes, acting as a collaborative agent [21, 27]. Integration varies between sectors. Private firms, driven by competition and customer expectations, move faster toward AI integration [16]. In contrast, public organisations face budget constraints and limited expertise [36]. Initiatives like Estonia's reusable AI components and Sweden's AI [2] aim to address these gaps.

Despite these benefits, integration remains complex and presents several challenges [15]. The challenges include over-reliance, bias from flawed data, and hallucinations, where AI generates plausible but false information [4, 26]. Security and data privacy are key concerns, especially when sensitive information is used [33]. Prompt engineering has emerged as a way to improve input quality and tool effectiveness.

Thus, effective use of AI depends on balanced human - AI collaboration. Users must avoid both blind trust and excessive skepticism. Adaptive systems that provide uncertainty indicators and interactive outputs help align AI insights with human judgment [12, 46].

2.3 Sensemaking Theory in Organisational Decision-Making

Sensemaking theory, pioneered by Karl E. Weick [50], provides a framework for understanding how individuals actively construct meaning when confronted with complexity, ambiguity, or unexpected events. Rather than passively processing information, people interpret their environments through a dynamic, social, and reflective process. At its essence, sensemaking is about creating coherence in uncertain or unfamiliar situations.

According to Weick [50], sensemaking involves connecting abstract understanding, such as general insights about technology integration, with real-time experiences, and it unfolds as an ongoing, iterative process. The theory is particularly useful in organisational settings where ambiguity is common, and it highlights the following seven interrelated properties:

Identity Construction: Individuals' self-perceptions shape how they interpret events, meaning that different people might derive distinct meanings from the same situation.

Retrospection: Sensemaking often occurs in hindsight, as people reinterpret events after they have occurred, influencing future actions through reflective learning.

Enactment: People actively shape their environments through decisions and actions, thus creating the very context in which sensemaking takes place.

Social Context: The process is inherently social, as meaning is co-constructed within groups, influenced by interpersonal interactions and shared values.

Ongoing Nature: Sensemaking is not static; it is continuous and adapts as new information and experiences emerge.

Cues Extraction: Individuals selectively pick up clues from their environment to form a coherent narrative, though this process is influenced by their prior experiences and identities.

Plausibility Over Accuracy: Emphasis is placed on what seems reasonable or believable rather than on objective correctness, allowing for multiple interpretations of the same event.

In organisational contexts, sensemaking is crucial for interpreting new technologies and managing change. It helps teams and individuals negotiate uncertainty, coordinate actions, and adjust practices as technology, such as AI-powered decision tools, is integrated into daily workflows. Thus, sensemaking theory is especially pertinent to this research as it explains how employees in both private and public sector organisations interpret and respond to AI-driven decision support. Individuals do not simply accept data-driven outputs as factual; they filter and reinterpret these outputs through the lenses of their own roles, experiences, and the prevailing organisational culture [50]. For example, identity construction may lead some employees to view AI systems as valuable enhancements, while others might perceive these tools as threats to their expertise. Social context further reinforces these interpretations through cross-departmental interactions and shared practices. Moreover, retrospective evaluations of AI performance, where past successes or failures influence current trust, highlight the dynamic and context-dependent nature of sensemaking. By applying the seven properties of sensemaking, this research examines not only which decisions are made using AI-powered tools, but also how meaning around AI-generated recommendations is constructed within organisations. This approach provides deeper insight into the factors that lead employees to embrace or resist AI integration, thereby shaping both organisational hierarchies and decision outcomes.

The theoretical framework of this study is thus built upon the integration of sensemaking theory [50] with existing literature on organisational decision-making and AI adoption. This framework underpins the analysis of how AI-powered tools affect decision-making in varying contexts, providing a lens to interpret the research findings in light of both technological affordances and human cognitive and social dynamics.

3 Methodology and Methods

3.1 Research Approach

The study employed a qualitative research design to explore how employees in public and private sector organisations perceive and engage with AI-powered tools in decision-making. A qualitative approach is well suited to uncovering nuanced insights into experiences, attitudes, and contextual factors that quantitative methods might overlook [38]. Following Patton's guidance [38], we aimed to capture rich, in-depth perspectives that reflect the complex and situated nature of human - AI collaboration.

3.2 Empirical Setting and Participants

The empirical setting included medium to large-sized organisations based in the Skåne region of Sweden, operating under the European Union's AI governance and data protection framework. The choice of setting was motivated by Sweden's advanced digital infrastructure and active engagement with responsible AI integration, making it a relevant context for exploring organisational decision-making with AI tools.

Purposive sampling was used to recruit information-rich cases [38]. Eligibility criteria required participants to (1) work in either the public or private sector, (2) have a minimum of three years of experience with AI-supported decision-making processes, and (3) hold a role involving operational or tactical decision tasks. While gender and age were not selection criteria, an effort was made to ensure a balanced and diverse sample. A total of eight participants were interviewed. Table 1 provides an overview of their role, and interview details:

Table 1. Research Participants Overview

Participants	Role	Interview	Date and Place
Participant 1	Engineering Analyst	47 min	2025-04-10 Online
Participant 2	Data Engineer	27 min	2025-04-11 Online
Participant 3	Data Annotation Lead	48 min	2025-04-15 In person
Participant 4	AI Strategist	46 min	2025-04-16 Online
Participant 5	Service Owner Microsoft 365	44 min	2025-04-17 Online
Participant 6	Digitalisation Unit Head	42 min	2025-04-17 Online
Participant 7	Solution Architect	49 min	2025-04-17 In person
Participant 8	IT Business Architect	41 min	2025-04-22 Online

This sample provides a cross-sectoral snapshot of AI-powered tool use in decision-making. While the small number of participants limits generalizability, the depth and diversity of roles support analytical insights into sectoral differences, tool integration, and human - AI collaboration dynamics. The findings are not meant to be statistically representative but rather transferable to similar organisational contexts facing similar challenges and decisions.

3.3 Data Collection

Data were collected through semi-structured, in-depth interviews, which allowed for a balance between thematic consistency and conversational flexibility [28]. An interview guide was developed based on key themes identified in the literature review, such as AI usage contexts, trust, decision-making processes, and organisational culture. This guide ensured comparability across interviews while allowing participants to elaborate on issues most relevant to their roles and organisational settings.

Interviews were conducted between February and April 2025 using secure online video conferencing platforms. Each session lasted between 45 and 70 min and was audio-recorded with participant consent. Ethical considerations were addressed in line with the ACM Code of Ethics [1], including informed consent, anonymity, and the right to withdraw at any point.

3.4 Data Analysis

All interview recordings were transcribed using Microsoft Teams' built-in transcription tool, with manual correction to ensure accuracy. Transcripts were then subjected to thematic analysis following Braun and Clarke's [11] six-step process. Thematic analysis is widely used to identify and interpret patterns in qualitative data, providing insights into participants' experiences. The analysis began with familiarization through thorough reading of interview transcripts. Next, initial coding segmented the data, which were then refined into broader themes representing core ideas. Codes were derived inductively from the data and iteratively refined during analysis to reflect the emergent themes. The analysis emphasized participants' lived experiences, organisational contexts, and interpretations of AI's role in decision-making. The interpretive lens was shaped by sensemaking theory [50], enabling us to explore how meaning was constructed around AI-powered systems in everyday work practices. Themes were reviewed collaboratively by the authors to ensure consistency and reliability in coding. This approach ensured rigor and depth in analysis.

4 Empirical Findings

4.1 Theme 1: Types and Roles of AI-Powered Systems in Organisational Decision-Making

All participants used AI tools, mostly generative chatbots, either in-house or integrated into internal systems for secure handling of sensitive data. P1 valued internal models for minimizing "data leaks," while P5 noted their "better control." Usage varied: some organisations were piloting tools (P3, P5, P6, P8), while others had broader deployment (P1, P2, P4, P7). P8 emphasized strict access policies and warned, "Sometimes it gives wrong answers. You still need to think for yourself."

Tools embedded in everyday software improved accessibility (e.g., Excel, email), while external tools were used for non-sensitive tasks or cross-checking outputs. P2 used multiple tools for comparison; P5 noted offloading tasks to preserve system capacity. Specialized tools also supported legal checks, permit evaluations, and media creation (P3, P4, P5). P4 said, "It helps us reach colleagues who prefer watching or listening." Across all cases, AI supported, not replaced, human oversight. Tool selection depended on task and data sensitivity.

AI-powered tools were widely used in operational decision-making, aiding in coding, transcription, summarization, and data validation. P4 likened it to mentoring junior staff; P8 used AI to interpret code. For tactical decision-making, AI-powered tools were used more cautiously. P3 said outputs were "often generic," and P1 noted difficulties in handling "complex business contexts." Still, AI supported planning and brainstorming (P5, P7), filtered alternatives (P7), and acted as a "sounding board" (P2). Operational and tactical boundaries sometimes blurred; as P3 put it, "AI can handle short-term tasks that touch on both sides." Overall, AI was a support tool, with humans making final decisions, particularly in tactical areas.

4.2 Theme 2: Sectoral Patterns in the Use of AI-Powered Tools

The use of AI-powered tools in decision-making varied between the public and private sectors, shaped by organisational goals, regulatory frameworks, and cultural attitudes toward innovation and risk. While both sectors recognised the value of AI in enhancing operational efficiency and decision quality, their adoption paths and integration strategies reflected different logics.

4.2.1 Private Sector: Speed, Experimentation, and ROI Focus

Private-sector participants reported a pragmatic and iterative approach to AI adoption. Tools were often introduced through bottom-up initiatives, driven by teams seeking to solve concrete problems or improve workflows. P1 said: *"If a tool can do that, we try it."* The decision to adopt new tools was typically based on quick return on investment (ROI), time savings, or creative enhancement. P2 noted: *"The licence costs less than the man-hours it replaces,"* highlighting the emphasis on efficiency.

AI tools were used across functions; from customer insights and campaign planning (P3) to debugging and reporting (P7). Organisations frequently experimented with multiple tools, comparing results to identify the most effective solutions. AI was described as a *"sounding board"* for brainstorming and a co-pilot for tasks requiring high-volume or repetitive input. Despite this openness, human oversight remained central. As P2 emphasized: *"Stay critical, compare outputs, never copy-paste blindly."* This sectoral culture supported rapid scaling and layering of tools into daily work, often without formal approval processes. Adoption was accelerated by competition and customer expectations, especially in marketing and software development domains.

4.2.2 Public Sector: Caution, Control, and Compliance

In contrast, *public-sector* organisations followed a more deliberate and risk-averse path to AI integration. The emphasis was on legality, accountability, and the ethical implications of AI use. Participants described tight control mechanisms, including on-premises systems, no-cloud policies, and formal governance structures such as AI Councils and internal guidelines.

P6 stressed the political dimensions of decision-making: *"AI helps collect facts but choosing what to do with them is still politics."* Tools were primarily deployed in operational contexts, such as document summarisation, fact-checking, and internal knowledge retrieval (P4, P5). Tactical use was limited and closely monitored, with human authority firmly preserved. P8 noted, *"It supports, but it doesn't decide for me."*

Budget constraints and long procurement cycles further slowed adoption. As P4 explained: *"We don't have the funds to test everything."* Nonetheless, the public sector recognised the potential of AI to improve consistency and reduce costs in service delivery. For example, AI-generated uniform responses for permit decisions saved significant staff time (P5). Participants highlighted a desire to innovate, but within the bounds of institutional trust and legal safeguards. Public-sector staff viewed themselves as guardians of compliance, privacy, and citizen accountability, which shaped a more cautious posture toward AI integration.

4.2.3 Comparing Sectoral Logics

The contrast between sectors can be understood through differing institutional logics and operational priorities. Private-sector actors prioritised agility, competitive advantage, and experimentation, resulting in faster and broader adoption of AI-powered tools. In contrast, the public sector emphasised fairness, transparency, and legal defensibility, leading to controlled and selective deployment.

These differences were not only structural but also cultural. Private-sector employees often framed AI as an enabler of innovation and productivity, whereas their public-sector counterparts viewed it as a tool requiring ethical stewardship. While both groups valued the benefits of AI, such as speed, consistency, and support for complex tasks, their underlying motivations, constraints, and integration strategies diverged significantly.

4.3 Theme 3: Benefits and Challenges of AI-Powered Tools in Organisational Decision-Making

Participants highlighted five key *benefits*: faster data access, consistency, inclusiveness, time efficiency, and improved reasoning. AI saved time on routine tasks, enabling deeper analysis and discussion. P1 said, "It doesn't decide for me, but it supports the process." P4 noted that discrepancies in records could be flagged quickly. Consistency improved through automation; P5 saw uniform decisions in permit applications. Writing tools helped standardize quality across users (P7). AI made analysis more inclusive, non-experts could contribute. P8 used tools to understand code logic, while P3 said campaign planning became more accessible. AI use also fostered clearer thinking. P2 described a "learning curve" that sharpened how problems were framed. AI-powered tools were viewed as collaborators. P4 said, "I make many decisions myself with the support of AI." P7 used AI to explore product alternatives. In all cases, AI supported rather than replaced human decision-making.

Participants identified five main *challenges*: lack of transparency, security risks, over-reliance, prompt engineering complexity, and regulatory concerns. AI's "black box" nature limited trust. P3 questioned how outputs were generated; P6 believed traceability should become standard. Still, P3 noted that even transparent models may remain too complex for non-experts. Security was a major concern, especially with cloud-based tools. P4 worried about data leaks: "We don't want to send our source code to the cloud." On-premises tools offered more control and comfort for experimentation. Participants also feared user over-reliance. Without critical thinking, users might accept AI outputs uncritically, particularly in areas where subject knowledge is lacking. These challenges underscored the need for cautious integration, strong governance, and continuous human oversight to ensure responsible use of AI in decision-making.

4.4 Theme 4: Recommendations for Leveraging AI-Powered Tools

Participants across sectors advocated for a cautious, *step-by-step approach* to AI usage, recommending organisations "start small" with clear, well-defined business cases. As P4 advised: "Start by testing on a small scale...where you can see concrete benefits." This iterative process allows early learning and gradual scaling, as P7 put it: "Put the tools in the hands of employees... the earlier you start testing, the faster you'll see results." *Collaboration* was another key recommendation. Participants (e.g., P4, P5) emphasized inter-organisational cooperation to share resources and accelerate progress. P5 suggested: "Neighbouring municipalities...could share costs and co-develop." *Individual experimentation* was also encouraged. P2 noted: "Use the tools! It's actually really fun to work with," pointing to tasks like web scraping and API integration as accessible entry points. Despite enthusiasm, participants stressed maintaining *human oversight*. P3 warned: "Trust your own human judgment...You need to find your own voice," while R8 urged critical evaluation of data sources and platform ownership. Concerns about *data availability* also surfaced. As P4 observed: "We have too little data to train on." Overall, participants highlighted the importance of deliberate, collaborative, and critically informed strategies when adopting AI tools in organisational settings.

5 Discussion

Private sector organisations adopt AI pragmatically, layering tools to support, not replacing human decisions [16, 20, 23, 45]. AI-powered tools' use varies by task and decision level, with experienced staff retaining final authority. Three AI-powered tool types emerged: (1) internal chatbots for sensitive data, (2) public chatbots for non-sensitive tasks, and (3) task-specific tools for routine processes like permit triage [25, 36]. AI supported operational (routine checks) and tactical (debugging, campaigns) decisions [18, 29] but was rarely used strategically due to its limited contextual understanding [14]. It assisted early decision stages, such as data gathering, option generation, and drafting, filling gaps and narrowing choices [22, 32]. Final decisions remained human-led, supporting AI's role as an exploratory aid [37]. Prompt engineering was crucial to output quality [21]. The focus was augmentation over automation, with careful use strategies like prompt logging, output comparison, and pilot tests to maintain oversight and adaptive trust [46]. Integration was driven by pragmatic aims such as reducing effort, boosting creativity, and improving efficiency [16], reinforcing AI's role in enhancing speed and consistency under human control [42].

Public sector organisations prioritize legality and fairness, reflecting institutional accountability [23]. Data governance was central; public-cloud AI was avoided in favor of internal or EU-hosted systems compliant with GDPR and the principle of public access to official documents [17, 40]. AI-powered tools supported operational and limited tactical decisions, such as content generation, comparisons, and fact collection, but final authority remained with humans, especially for citizen-facing decisions [18, 29, 37]. Oversight was formalized via AI Councils, usage guidelines, and no-cloud policies to calibrate trust [46]. Budget constraints shaped AI deployment, which had to demonstrate cost and service benefits [16, 36]. In short, public organisations adopted a compliance-first AI approach rooted in legal safeguards and institutional oversight, contrasting with the more experimental private-sector logic.

Both private and public sector organisations value the use of AI-powered tools for data analysis but *differ in integration* due to private-sector responsiveness versus public-sector accountability. Budgeting differs; private firms fund AI operationally for faster uptake, while public agencies need capital budget approval, causing delays [36]. AI-powered tool diversity is higher in private firms, with multiple assistants used; public bodies rely on vetted, domain-specific tools.

Governance contrasts sharply: private firms use cloud services with vendor controls, whereas public organisations keep data in-house for legal compliance [40, 36]. Financial aims also diverge. Private firms seek cost efficiency; public agencies look for staffing ROI. *Risk tolerance and pace* differ; private firms test and scale rapidly; public bodies adopt cautiously, awaiting regulatory clarity. These differences stem from tool variety, governance, finances, risk culture, and infrastructure—defining sector-specific AI integration paths.

AI enhances decision-making by processing large datasets and extracting insights, enabling data-driven decisions [8, 15, 39, 44]. Visualizations aid in reducing cognitive overload and spotting patterns [37]. AI also supports brainstorming and scenario planning, acting as a "sounding board" [21, 27], albeit always within GDPR-compliant advisory roles [17]. However, AI's opacity (the "black-box" problem) challenges transparency [44]. Over-reliance may reduce critical thinking [4, 8], necessitating domain expertise to interpret outputs. AI hallucinations, that is, confident inaccuracies, pose risks [4, 26]. AI also struggles with context-rich or ambiguous decisions, reinforcing the need for human-in-the-loop systems [48, 49]. Security concerns include sensitive data leaks via commercial tools [8, 33]. In-house systems offer safer alternatives. Prompt engineering is essential; poor prompts yield poor results [21].

The OECD [36] identifies key public-sector barriers: limited resources, data, funding, and skills. Our findings expand this, showing how municipalities collaborate to share resources and reduce duplication. Pilot projects build trust and momentum. High-quality, frequently updated datasets remain essential for effective AI training [31].

Applying sensemaking theory [50] to the findings offers a framework to understand how employees in both sectors interpret and engage with AI-powered tools in decision-making. Mapping the seven properties of sensemaking [50] onto the findings provides a conceptual foundation for the study's conclusions.

Identity construction shaped how employees interpreted AI. Public sector staff, identifying as protectors of compliance and public trust, used AI cautiously. Private sector employees, viewing themselves as innovators, embraced experimentation. These identity-driven perspectives framed AI as either a risk to control or a tool to optimize. *Retrospection* informed how past experiences shaped current comfort with AI. Public employees recalled compliance failures and were more hesitant, while private-sector counterparts pointed to productivity gains, viewing AI as part of ongoing tech evolution. *Enactment* was evident in how users embedded AI into daily tasks, such as using Copilot in secure environments. These choices actively shaped how AI was perceived and normalized in workflows, particularly in operational settings. *Social context* played a central role. In public organisations, formal norms and governance shaped AI use, while private organisations leaned on peer learning and informal trials. This illustrates the socially embedded nature of sensemaking. *Ongoing sensemaking* was evident in evolving attitudes. Improvements in AI outputs led to shifting perceptions, and the line between tactical and operational decision-making continued to blur, showing that understanding is fluid and negotiated over time. *Cues* such as output speed, interface usability, and regulatory signals informed how employees judged AI's reliability. Positive cues fostered trust (e.g., helpful outputs), while concerns about AI's opacity triggered caution. These cues helped build plausible stories to guide action. *Plausibility over accuracy* was key. Employees used AI when outputs seemed useful, even if exact correctness was unverifiable. AI was seen as a "sounding board", with risks like hallucinations managed via oversight and peer checks. Usefulness outweighed full transparency.

Concluding, AI-powered tools' use for decision-making is shaped more by employees' interpretations of roles, norms, and responsibilities than by the technology itself. Identity and organisational culture dictate what AI is allowed to do. Sensemaking is a social, evolving process, where tools gain meaning through interaction, trust, and contextual embedding. Employees use selective cues to form narratives about AI's role, aligning with broader IS research [9, 13, 24]. Effective AI integration depends on not only technical infrastructure but also shared reflection and dialogue that support sensemaking within organisations.

6 Conclusion

The study explored the use of AI-powered tools in organisational decision-making within the Swedish private and public sectors. The research findings provide insights into how the AI-powered tools, approached as AI collaborative agents, can be leveraged to support better organisational decision-making based on the needs of these organisations. The findings show that while AI-powered tools are widely used to enhance operational and tactical decisions, they function primarily as supportive aids, not autonomous agents. Human oversight remains essential, and the integration process is shaped more by organisational culture, roles, and sectoral norms than by the technology itself. The research demonstrates that AI adoption is context-dependent: private-sector organisations tend to move quickly, driven by efficiency and competitive pressure, while public-sector bodies proceed cautiously due to regulatory, ethical, and governance considerations. These sectoral logics shape not only the pace of adoption but also the purposes and constraints surrounding AI-powered tools use.

To translate these insights into practical value, we propose the following sector-specific recommendations:

For Private Sector Organisations

1. Train employees in prompt engineering and critical evaluation to maximize the value of AI outputs while minimizing over-reliance.
2. Encourage internal experimentation and iterative scaling, starting with pilot use cases that demonstrate tangible value in everyday workflows.
3. Establish multidisciplinary AI oversight teams, combining technical, legal, and operational perspectives to guide responsible integration.

4. Adopt a layered tool strategy, combining public, internal, and domain-specific tools, tailored to different data sensitivity and task complexity levels.

For Public Sector Organisations

1. Invest in secure, on-premises AI systems to align with GDPR and public data governance principles.
2. Develop and disseminate AI usage guidelines and decision protocols, ensuring that transparency, traceability, and fairness are embedded into workflows.
3. Leverage inter-organisational collaborations (e.g., municipalities, public agencies) to pool resources, reduce costs, and share best practices.
4. Incorporate AI literacy and ethical awareness into public administration training, empowering staff to engage critically with AI tools.

This research advances the IS field by deepening theoretical and practical insights into AI-powered tools in organisational decision-making. It extends sensemaking theory by showing how employees interpret AI as collaborative agents, shaped by sector-specific values, efficiency and innovation in the private sector, compliance and trust in the public sector. Practically, it offers guidance for responsible AI use, emphasizing that AI should augment, not replace, human judgment. Key recommendations include piloting, cultural alignment, user training, and ongoing human oversight, with cross-sector collaboration encouraged to ensure ethical and effective integration.

Future research could use longitudinal approaches to track evolving sensemaking, examine leadership's role in adoption, compare cross-cultural and regulatory contexts, and explore training and prompt engineering to boost user capability and trust in AI.

References

1. ACM Code of Ethics and Professional Conduct, Code of Ethics (acm.org)
2. AI Sweden. (2025). AI Sweden – Sveriges nationella center för tillämpad artificiell intelligens
3. Agarwal, M., Saxena, A.: An overview of natural language processing. Int. J. Res. Appl. Sci. Eng. Technol. (IJRASET) **7**(5), 2810–2813 (2019)
4. Akinwale, O.E., Kuye, O.L., Doddanavar, I.: Scourge of replacing contemporary work environment with artificial intelligence (AI-dark-side): the role of capacity development in quality of work-life and organisational performance. J. Syst. Inf. Technol. **27**(1), 116–145 (2024)
5. Banh, L., Strobel, G.: Generative artificial intelligence. Electron. Mark. **33**(64), 1–17 (2023)
6. Benbya, H., Pachidi, S., Jarvenpaa, S.: Special issue editorial: artificial intelligence in organisations: Implications for information systems research. J. Assoc. Inf. Syst. **22**(2), 10 (2021)
7. Bhattacharya, P.: Guarding the intelligent enterprise: securing artificial intelligence in making business decisions. In: 2020 6th International Conference on Information Management (ICIM) Proceedings, IEEE, pp. 235–238 (2020)
8. Bisht, R., Uniyal, A.K.: Smart workspaces: integrating IoT and AI to foster work-life balance. In: Proceedings of the 2024 1st International Conference on Advances in Computing, Communication and Networking (ICAC2N), IEEE, pp. 1224–1229 (2024)
9. Bitilis, P., Chatzipanagiotou, N.: Digitalizing the football experience: a study on electronic performance and tracking systems (EPTS) from the perspective of football athletes and training staff. In: New Trends in HCI and Sports Workshop (NTSPORT 2022) Proceedings, Vancouver, 1 October 2022, vol. 3267, CEUR-WS (2022)

10. Booyse, D., Scheepers, C.B.: Barriers to adopting automated organisational decision-making through the use of artificial intelligence. Manag. Res. Rev. **47**(1), 64–85 (2023)
11. Braun, V., Clarke, V.: Thematic analysis. J. Posit. Psychol. **12**(3), 297–298 (2016)
12. Cao, S., Gomez, C., Huang, C.-M.: How time pressure in different phases of decision-making influences human-AI collaboration. Proc. ACM Hum.-Comput. Interact. CSCW2 **7**(277) (2023)
13. Chatzipanagiotou, N.: Managers' Cooperative Work Practices in Computational Artefacts-Supported Library Systems, PhD thesis, Linnaeus University Press (2021)
14. Csaszar, F.A., Ketkar, H., Kim, H.: Artificial intelligence and strategic decision-making: evidence from entrepreneurs and investors. Strategy Science **9**(1), 1–20 (2024)
15. Eager, J., Whittle, M., Smit, J., Cacciaguerra, G., Lale-Demoz, E.: Opportunities of artificial intelligence, Study for the Committee on Industry, Research and Energy (ITRE), Policy Department for Economic, Scientific and Quality of Life Policies, European Parliament, Luxembourg: European Union (2020)
16. Enholm, I.M., Papagiannidis, E., Mikalef, P., Krogstie, J.: Artificial intelligence and business value: a literature review. J. Bus. Res. (2021)
17. European Commission. (2024). Are there restrictions on the use of automated decision-making? https://commission.europa.eu/law/law-topic/data-protection/rules-business-and-organisations/dealing-citizens/are-there-restrictions-use-automated-decision-making_en
18. Evertsz, R., Thangarajah, J., Yadav, N., Ly, T.C.: Agent oriented modelling of tactical decision making. In: Bordini, R.H., Elkind, E., Weiss, G., Yolum, P. (eds.), Proceedings of the 14th International Conference on Autonomous Agents and Multiagent Systems (AAMAS 2015), Istanbul, Turkey, 4–8 May, International Foundation for Autonomous Agents and Multiagent Systems, pp. 1051–1060 (2015)
19. Grobelnik, M., Perset, K., Russell, S.: What is AI? Can you make a clear distinction between AI and non-AI systems? OECD.AI. (2024)
20. Habiba, U., Asghar, S.: A survey on multi-criteria decision making approaches. In: International Conference on Emerging Technologies, 2009 Proceedings, pp. 321–325 (2009)
21. Hamza, M., Siemon, D., Akbar, M.A., Rahman, T.: Human-AI collaboration in software engineering: lessons learned from a hands-on workshop. In: Proceedings of the 2024 ACM/IEEE International Workshop on Software-intensive Business (IWSiB'24), Lisbon, Portugal, 16 April 2024. ACM, New York, NY, pp. 1–8 (2024)
22. Hammond, J.S., Keeney, R.L., Raiffa, H.: The hidden traps in decision making. Harv. Bus. Rev. **76**(5), 47–58 (1998)
23. Harrison, E.F.: Interdisciplinary models of decision making. Manag. Decis. **31**(8), 27–33 (1993)
24. Hughes, J.M., Henning, R.A., Robertson, M.M.: Emergent properties of organizational sense-making systems: a grounded theory assessment of the HITEC project. Hum. Factors **65**(2), 289–304 (2023)
25. Jordan, M.I., Mitchell, T.M.: Machine learning: trends, perspectives, and prospects. Science **349**(6245), 255–260 (2015)
26. Kaate, I., et al.: "You Always Get an Answer": analyzing users' interaction with AI-generated personas given unanswerable questions and risk of hallucination. In: Proceedings of the 30th International Conference on Intelligent User Interfaces (IUI)'25), Cagliari, Italy, 24–27 March 2025. ACM, New York (2025)
27. Karolinska Institutet. (2023). AI an available sounding board for the researcher 24/7, 18 December. https://news.ki.se/ai-an-available-sounding-board-for-the-researcher-247
28. Klein, H.K., Myers, M.D.: A set of principles for conducting and evaluating interpretive field studies in information systems. MIS Q. **23**(1), 67–93 (1999)
29. Leewis, K., van der Waa, J., van Diggelen, J., Neerincx, M.: Decision discovery: a framework for modelling operational decisions in AI contexts. Decis. Support Syst. **174**(114086) (2024)

30. Mayer, A.S., Strich, F., Fiedler, M.: Unintended consequences of introducing AI systems for decision making. MIS Q. Exec. **19**(4) (2020)
31. Meredith, R., O'Donnell, P., Arnott, D.: Databases and data warehouses for decision support. In: Burstein, F., Holsapple, C.W. (eds.), Handbook on Decision Support Systems 1, International Handbooks Information System. Springer, Berlin, Heidelberg (2008). https://doi.org/10.1007/978-3-540-48713-5_11
32. Molina, D.A., Kharlov, V., Chen, J.-S.: Towards effective human-AI collaboration in decision-making: a comprehensive review and conceptual framework. In: 2024 Portland International Conference on Management of Engineering and Technology (PICMET) Proceedings (2023)
33. Moslemi, S.: Examining the dimensions of big data privacy (block chain solution for privacy protection). Int. J. Innov. Manag. Econ. Soc. Sci. **1**(4), 10–16 (2021)
34. Nhavkar, K.V., Goel, K.D.S.: Impact of generative AI on IT professionals. Int. J. Res. Appl. Sci. Eng. Technol. (IJRASET) **11**(7) (2023)
35. Nicodeme, C.: Build confidence and acceptance of AI-based decision support systems – explainable and liable AI. In: 2020 13th International Conference on Human System Interaction (HSI) Proceedings, Tokyo, Japan, 6–8 June 2020
36. OECD. (2024). Governing with artificial intelligence: Are governments ready? OECD Artificial Intelligence Papers, no. 20, June 2024. Paris: OECD Publishing
37. Oral, E., Chawla, R., Wijkstra, M., Mahyar, N., Dimara, E.: From information to choice: a critical inquiry into visualization tools for decision making (2023)
38. Patton, M.Q.: Qualitative Research & Evaluation Methods: Integrating Theory and Practice, 4th edn. SAGE, Thousand Oaks, CA (2015)
39. Ramachandran, K.K., Semwal, A., Singh, S.P., Al-Hilali, A.A., Alazzam, M.B.: AI-powered decision making in management: a review and future directions. In: 2023 3rd International Conference on Advance Computing and Innovative Technologies in Engineering (ICACITE) Proceedings, IEEE, pp. 82–86 (2023)
40. Regeringskansliet. (2015). Offentlighetsprincipen. https://www.regeringen.se/sa-styrs-sverige/grundlagar-och-demokratiskt-deltagande/offentlighetsprincipen/
41. Roumeliotis, K.I., Tselikas, N.D.: ChatGPT and Open-AI models: a preliminary review. Future Internet **15**(6) (2023)
42. Rousseau, D.M.: Making evidence-based organizational decisions in an uncertain world. Organ. Dyn. **47**(2), 135–146 (2018)
43. Russell, S., Norvig, P.: Artificial Intelligence: A modern approach, 4th edn. Prentice Hall, Upper Saddle River, NJ (2021)
44. Shah, T., Shekokar, K., Barve, A., Khandare, P.: An analytical review: explainable AI for decision making in finance using machine learning. In: 2024 15th International Conference on Computing Communication and Networking Technologies (ICCCNT) Proceedings (2024)
45. Simon, H.A.: The New Science of Management Decision. Prentice-Hall, Englewood Cliffs, NJ (1977)
46. Swaroop, S., Gajos, K.Z., Buçinca, Z., Doshi-Velez, F.: Personalising AI assistance based on overreliance rate in AI-assisted decision making. In: Proceedings of the 30th International Conference on Intelligent User Interfaces (IUI'25), 24–27 March 2025, Cagliari, Italy. ACM, New York, NY (2025)
47. Szukits, Á., Móricz, P.: Towards data-driven decision making: the role of analytical culture and centralization efforts. RMS **18**, 2849–2887 (2024)
48. Trunk, A., Birkel, H., Hartmann, E.: On the current state of combining human and artificial intelligence for strategic organizational decision making. Bus. Res. **13**(3), 875–919 (2020)
49. Wang, Y., Yu, Z., Liu, S., Zhou, Z., Guo, B.: Genie in the model: automatic generation of human-in-the-loop deep neural networks for mobile applications. Proc. ACM Interact. Mob. Wearable Ubiquitous Technol. **7**(36), 1–29 (2023)
50. Weick, K.E.: Sensemaking in Organisations. SAGE, Thousand Oaks, CA (1995)

Synthetic Sales Data Generation for Chilean SMEs Using GANs

David Ruete[1], Marcia Durán-Riveros[1], Sebastián Maldonado-Durán[1], Alejandro Caroca[1], Carla Taramasco[1], Danilo Leal[1], Nicolás Caselli[2], Marcelo Reyes[1], Omar Salinas[1], Diego Mellado[1,3], and Jean Paul Maidana[1,3](✉)

[1] Universidad Andres Bello, Viña del Mar, Chile
jean.maidana@unab.cl

[2] Universidad Andres Bello, Concepción, Chile

[3] Instituto de Tecnología para la Innovación en Salud y Bienestar, Universidad Andres Bello, Viña del Mar, Chile

Abstract. The synthetic generation of data using artificial intelligence has emerged as a strategic response to data scarcity, confidentiality, and imbalance. This study explores whether a Generative Adversarial Network (GAN) can generate synthetic daily sales data for Chilean SMEs that preserves statistical distributions and temporal patterns for sales forecasting. The methodology trains a tailored GAN on anonymized datasets and evaluates the generated data using distributional similarity, Dynamic Time Warping (DTW), and regression-based predictive performance. Results show that combining real and synthetic data improves forecasting accuracy while maintaining privacy. The study contributes to AI-driven data augmentation by adapting GANs to a local context with limited data availability, with a systematic evaluation framework, and by demonstrating the potential of synthetic datasets to support inclusive financing and digital transformation in underrepresented Latin American ecosystems.

Keywords: Synthetic Data · Generative Adversarial Networks · Small and Medium Enterprises (SMEs)

1 Introduction

The scarcity, confidentiality, and imbalance of real-world datasets remain major barriers to the development of artificial intelligence (AI) applications across various domains. In this context, synthetic data generation has emerged as a strategic solution, as it allows the creation of artificial datasets that preserve the statistical properties of the original data while reducing privacy risks [1]. Among the available approaches, Generative Adversarial Networks (GANs), introduced by Goodfellow in [2], have demonstrated remarkable effectiveness in generating realistic synthetic data for images, text, and, more recently, tabular and sequential

T. Guarda et al. (Eds.): ARTIIS 2025, CCIS 2789, pp. 54–68, 2026.
https://doi.org/10.1007/978-3-032-16758-3_5

data. GANs operate through the competitive training of two neural networks—generator and discriminator—enabling the former to approximate complex distributions and replicate the underlying characteristics of real datasets.

The application of GANs to tabular data has advanced significantly [3] proposed CTGAN, a model capable of handling nonlinear relationships and multimodal distributions in mixed-type data, outperforming classical synthesis methods. For sequential data, such as time series, preserving temporal dependencies becomes critical. In [4] addressed this challenge with TimeGAN, a hybrid model combining recurrent networks and self-attention to capture both marginal distributions and temporal dynamics, proving effective in domains such as demand forecasting and finance.

In Chile, the Fintech ecosystem has experienced sustained growth, driven by the demand for solutions in credit assessment, sales planning, and business automation [5]. However, small and medium-sized enterprises (SMEs) still face barriers to adopting these technologies, particularly due to the scarcity of digitized historical data and the absence of models adapted to their operational realities [6]. This gap limits the development of inclusive AI solutions for financing and business management, creating a favorable scenario for the use of synthetic data as a strategic input.

Based on this context, the present study addresses the following research question: Can a Generative Adversarial Network generate synthetic daily sales data for Chilean SMEs that preserves statistical distributions and temporal patterns, making it suitable for sales forecasting? To answer this, we propose a tailored GAN architecture trained on anonymized transactional data, evaluated through statistical similarity, Dynamic Time Warping (DTW), and regression-based predictive performance.

The contributions of this study are threefold. First, it adapts GAN architectures to a local context characterized by limited data availability. Second, it provides a systematic framework for evaluating synthetic data quality, combining statistical, temporal, and predictive metrics. Third, it demonstrates the potential of synthetic datasets to improve forecasting accuracy when integrated with real data. In doing so, the study contributes to AI-driven data augmentation and supports technological solutions for SME financing, fostering digital inclusion in underrepresented Latin American contexts.

To situate this proposal within the broader scientific landscape, it is essential to examine the advances in synthetic data generation. Generative models, particularly Generative Adversarial Networks (GANs), provide the conceptual and methodological foundation for this study.

2 Context and Related Works

2.1 Context

Synthetic data generation is gaining prominence in the field of artificial intelligence, particularly in environments where access to real data is limited, regulated, or costly. By 2025, this approach has evolved from an experimental practice into a strategic tool in regulated sectors such as healthcare, finance, and technology, helping to overcome challenges related to privacy constraints, data inequality, and operational cost burdens [7].

GANs have emerged as one of the most powerful solutions for this task. Since their introduction by [8], GANs have evolved rapidly, expanding from image generation to the synthesis of sequential and tabular data. Their ability to learn complex distributions and generate statistically coherent artificial data has been widely documented.

A notable case is the application of GANs in generating daily sales data for SMEs. A recent study focused on a Chilean Fintech demonstrated that a tailored GAN architecture produced synthetic time series with strong temporal coherence and increased the volume of synthesizable data by 10%, without compromising the privacy of real customers [9].

In addition, the exponential growth of the generative intelligence industry worldwide, with projections reaching USD 71 billion by 2025 and an expected increase to USD 890 billion by 2032, further underscores the relevance and commercial impact of this type of technology [10].

For SMEs, particularly in countries like Chile, these advancements represent a significant opportunity. Many businesses face a lack of digitized data and difficulties in training predictive models. The generation of synthetic sales data involves replicating temporal, seasonal, and behavioral patterns, enabling the strengthening of risk, demand, and financing models without requiring large volumes of real data.

This scientific context, grounded in the global transformations of artificial intelligence, the evolution of GANs, and local application cases involving SMEs, positions this research at the forefront of leveraging synthetic data as analytical infrastructure for small businesses in emerging economies, demonstrating its potential to drive inclusive financing and accelerate the digitalization of the sector.

2.2 Related Works

Recent developments in synthetic tabular data generation have led to a unified taxonomy that incorporates traditional methods, diffusion-based techniques, and large language models (LLMs) [11]. Representative approaches include GANs (e.g., CTGAN), diffusion models (e.g., TabDDPM, TABDIFF), and zero-shot LLMs like GPT-4o. This convergence addresses challenges such as data heterogeneity, privacy concerns, and the preservation of intricate inter-variable dependencies.

Since their introduction in 2014, GANs have evolved into specialized architectures for tabular synthesis [2]. IT-GAN integrates reversible networks and density regularization to enhance fidelity and privacy [12]. CasTGAN (2023) employs a cascaded structure to better capture variable relationships [13], while TAEGAN, presented at ICLR 2025, leverages masked autoencoder pretraining to improve results in low-data contexts [14]. These advances collectively offer more robust and efficient solutions.

For time series, preserving temporal structure is key. TimeGAN (2019) combines autoencoders with recurrent supervision to retain sequential dependencies [15]. Industrial-grade tools like YData Fabric (2025) improve scalability [16], while domain-specific models address privacy and robustness in sensitive areas like healthcare and finance [17].

LLMs like GPT-4o achieve competitive zero-shot performance in synthetic tabular data generation without fine-tuning, highlighting their value in low-resource and specialized domains [18]. Simultaneously, diffusion models like Tab-DDPM reconstruct data through noise reversal, effectively handling tabular heterogeneity [19]. Together, these models mark a shift toward adaptable, domain-agnostic, and minimally supervised generative frameworks.

Evaluation methods for synthetic tabular data rest on four pillars. Statistical fidelity is assessed using metrics like Maximum Information Discrepancy and multivariate correlations. Temporal coherence relies on measures such as Dynamic Time Warping (DTW) [20]. Practical utility is validated using training-transfer schemes (e.g., TSTR), while privacy is examined through membership inference and adversarial attacks [19]. Recent contributions, such as those in Nature (2024), propose AutoML-based pipelines for scalable quality, utility, and privacy assessments [21].

Despite evidence of impact in retail [22] and e-commerce [23], the application of synthetic data in SMEs, especially in Latin America, is still emerging [24]. This study explores GAN-based synthesis of daily sales data from Chilean SMEs, offering one of the first detailed analyses on temporal coherence, distributional fidelity, and predictive utility in such settings.

Several key challenges remain. Balancing fidelity with privacy remains difficult [19], and generating rare events or outliers, vital for financial modeling, poses risks [7]. Traditional metrics often fall short in capturing the semantic and contextual relevance of synthetic data, especially in regulated sectors [25,26]. Finally, the lack of interpretability in deep generative models continues to hinder broader institutional adoption [7].

Building on these advances, the present study develops a tailored GAN framework designed to generate synthetic sales data under local constraints. The following section details the proposed methodology.

3 Methods

3.1 Research Design and Data Preprocessing

This study adopts a quantitative experimental design to evaluate the performance of a GAN for synthesizing time-series data that reflect daily sales from Chilean SMEs. The proposed approach is grounded in an image-based transformation strategy that enables temporal dynamics to be processed spatially through convolutional architectures [4,27,28]. The dataset used in this study was provided by Fintech Dank and comprises daily sales data exhibiting typical SME behaviors, such as seasonality, long-term trends, and periods of high volatility.

Each time-series was normalized to the range $[-1, 1]$ using min–max scaling to ensure numerical consistency and stable convergence during model training. Following normalization, the sequences were converted into two-dimensional images via the Gramian Angular Field (GAF) transformation, a method that encodes temporal dependencies in a symmetric matrix using polar coordinates. Specifically, for a time-series vector $x = [x_1, \ldots, x_n]$, the angular projection is defined as $\phi_i = \arccos(x_i)$ and the matrix is computed as $G_{i,j} = \cos(\phi_i + \phi_j)$. The resulting $n \times n$ matrix represents a grayscale image that captures correlation structures over time [28]. GAF has proven effective in previous studies for preserving both magnitude and temporal relationships, supporting global pattern extraction through convolutional representation learning [29]

3.2 GAN Architecture and Experimental Setup

The model architecture is based on the Deep Convolutional GAN (DCGAN) framework and consists of a generator and a discriminator trained adversarially. The generator receives a 100-dimensional noise vector $z \sim \mathcal{N}(0, I)$, which is passed through a dense layer and reshaped into a $7 \times 7 \times 128$ feature tensor. This is then progressively upsampled through four ConvTranspose2D layers that double the spatial dimensions at each stage. Batch Normalization and ReLU activations are applied throughout, with a final tanh activation producing the output image of size 28×28 pixels.

The discriminator processes grayscale images through multiple Conv2D layers with 4×4 filters and stride 2, using LeakyReLU activations (slope $= 0.2$) and Batch Normalization. The final output layer is a fully connected unit with a sigmoid activation, estimating the probability of the input being real. Loss functions follow the original GAN formulation [2].

$$L_D = -\mathbb{E}[\log D(x)] - \mathbb{E}[\log(1 - D(G(z)))]$$
$$L_G = -\mathbb{E}[\log D(G(z))]$$

Training is performed using the Adam optimizer [30] with learning rate $\alpha = 0.0002$ and momentum parameter $\beta_1 = 0.5$. Four main experimental configurations were tested to evaluate model robustness. These varied in terms of training epochs (500, 750, 1000), batch sizes (32, 64, 128), and learning rates (0.0001, 0.0002), with the latent space dimension fixed at 100, following standard practice.

3.3 Evaluation Criteria and Baseline Comparison

Model performance was assessed using a combination of quantitative and qualitative metrics, in both image and time-series domains. The Fréchet Inception Distance (FID) was used to evaluate the distance between the distributions of real and synthetic GAF images [31], while Dynamic Time Warping (DTW) was applied to the reconstructed time-series sequences derived from the synthetic images, enabling precise comparison of shape and dynamics against the original data. In addition to quantitative metrics, a manual visual inspection was performed to assess the structural realism and temporal coherence of the GAF images.

To contextualize the results, the TimeGAN model [4] was trained as a competitive baseline. This hybrid model incorporates adversarial loss with supervised reconstruction loss and has demonstrated state-of-the-art performance in sequence generation tasks. The same data splits and preprocessing pipeline were applied to ensure a fair comparison.

3.4 Experimental Procedure

The full experimental pipeline proceeded as follows. First, the raw time-series were normalized and transformed into GAF images. GAN models were then trained under the four experimental settings described above, alongside the TimeGAN baseline. After training, synthetic datasets were generated, and their quality was evaluated using FID in the image domain and DTW in the time-series domain. Finally, qualitative visual assessments were performed to evaluate realism and structural fidelity, and the best-performing configuration was selected based on the combined outcomes of these analyses.

Once the model was trained, its performance was assessed through this multi-level evaluation strategy. The results of these assessments are presented below.

4 Results

A set of four experimental configurations were explored to assess the impact of key hyperparameters on the quality of synthetic time-series generated by the GAN model. The first experiment employed a baseline architecture and revealed limited representativeness, as synthetic series tended to cluster around low sales averages. The second experiment increased the number of training epochs, but this led to overfitting and degradation in performance. The fourth experiment reduced the training duration too aggressively, yielding data that, while similar in mean values, misrepresented the distribution of days with no sales.

The third configuration proved to be the most effective. With a balanced number of epochs, the synthetic images displayed greater visual diversity and intensity. As shown in Fig. 1, the distribution of average sales in the synthetic series more closely aligned with that of the real data, exhibiting a well-formed structure and dispersion across the domain of interest.

These findings highlight the potential of synthetic data to approximate the statistical and temporal behavior of real sales series. However, beyond numerical validation, it is necessary to analyze their implications for SMEs, particularly in relation to decision-making, forecasting, and inclusion in the digital economy.

This result suggests that moderating the number of training iterations prevented mode collapse and allowed the generator to better capture the diversity inherent in the real dataset.

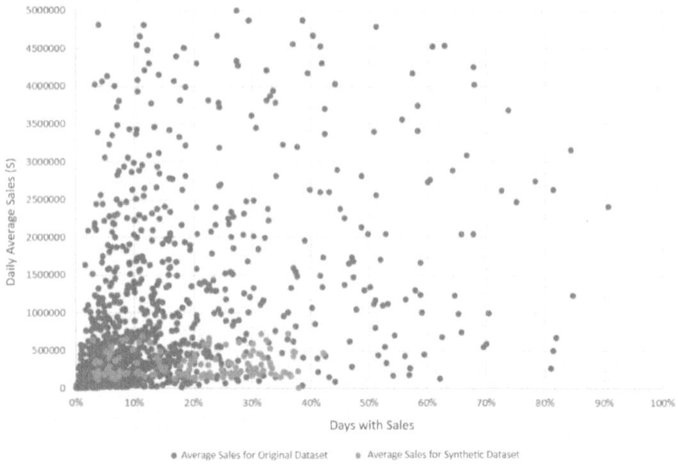

Fig. 1. Average sales comparison between real and synthetic series (third experiment). This bar chart shows the frequency distribution of average sales per series for three groups: real data, synthetic data generated by the GAN model, and real-synthetic pairwise comparisons. The alignment of the synthetic and real series across most intervals demonstrates the model's ability to replicate the distributional structure of average sales, especially within the central range. The figure supports the selection of the third experimental configuration as the most balanced in terms of representativeness and diversity.

4.1 DTW Evaluation

To quantify the similarity between synthetic and real sequences, Dynamic Time Warping (DTW) was used. Table 1 summarizes the maximum, minimum, mean, and standard deviation of DTW distances across three comparisons: real-to-real, synthetic-to-synthetic, and synthetic-to-real.

The synthetic data exhibited lower variance in intra-group distances, indicating that while structurally coherent, the generator may have underrepresented outlier patterns. Nonetheless, the real-to-synthetic distance metrics are aligned with those of real-to-real, evidencing satisfactory generative performance.

Figure 2 depicts the normalized DTW distances, binned into regular intervals. The synthetic data tend to cluster in the middle range (0.4–0.9), whereas real data distances show a more uniform distribution across the full interval.

4.2 Fréchet Distance Evaluation

In addition to DTW, the Fréchet distance was calculated to further evaluate sequence alignment. Summary statistics for the three comparisons are presented in Table 2. The maximum Fréchet distance occurred within the real data, suggesting that no synthetic sequence lies outside the real data's variability range.

Table 1. DTW summary statistics across different series pairings. This table presents the minimum, maximum, mean, and standard deviation of Dynamic Time Warping (DTW) distances computed between pairs of real, synthetic, and mixed series. The similar average distances between real–real and real–synthetic comparisons, along with a lower variance in synthetic–synthetic distances, indicate that the GAN model effectively captures the overall temporal structure, though with slightly reduced variability in synthetic sequences.

Comparison	Min	Max	Mean	SD
Real vs. Real	2.31	6.23	3.88	1.11
Synthetic vs. Synthetic	2.18	5.04	3.26	0.84
Real vs. Synthetic	2.33	5.87	3.65	0.97

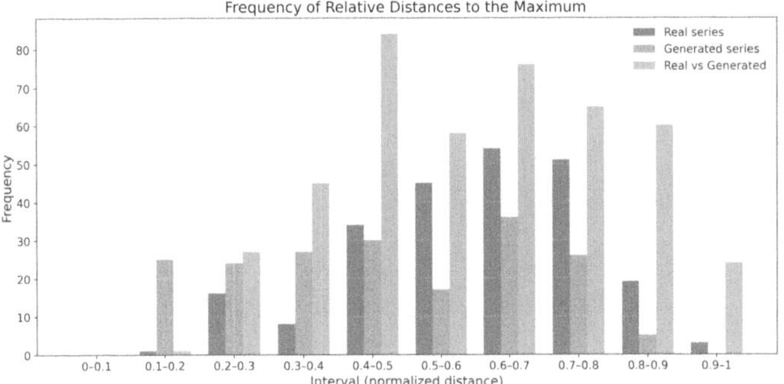

Fig. 2. Normalized DTW distance distribution. This histogram displays the distribution of normalized DTW distances between time-series sequences for three comparisons: real–real, synthetic–synthetic, and real–synthetic. The concentration of synthetic data in the mid-range (0.4–0.9) suggests that the generated series preserve general temporal dynamics but may underrepresent extreme or outlier patterns present in the real data.

Figure 3 shows the normalized Fréchet distance distribution. Similar to the DTW pattern, the synthetic data display a central concentration between 0.2 and 0.6, reinforcing the observation of reduced variance.

4.3 Global Synthesis and Scaling

To evaluate the scalability and practical utility of the model, a generation test was performed aiming to augment the dataset by 10%. Figure 4 shows the graphical comparison between the 1,495 real series and the 150 synthetic series generated under the optimal configuration. Both sets appear analogously distributed.

This confirms that the model generalizes beyond training samples and produces plausible data under controlled scaling.

Table 3 shows that the model-generated expansion aligns with target expectations for data augmentation (10%).

Table 2. Fréchet distance summary statistics across series pairings. This table reports descriptive statistics for Fréchet distances, which quantify geometric similarity between time-series curves. The slightly lower average and standard deviation for synthetic data reflect a more homogeneous generation process, while the maximum value for real–real confirms that synthetic sequences remain within the natural variability of the real dataset.

Comparison	Min	Max	Mean	SD
Real vs. Real	3.45	8.74	5.91	1.32
Synthetic vs. Synthetic	3.22	7.35	5.12	1.05
Real vs. Synthetic	3.44	8.01	5.46	1.19

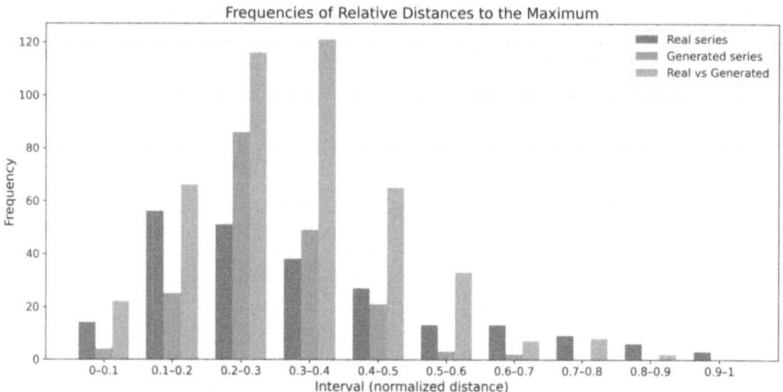

Fig. 3. Normalized Fréchet distance distribution. This figure visualizes the distribution of normalized Fréchet distances for real–real, synthetic–synthetic, and real–synthetic series comparisons. The central concentration of synthetic sequences reinforces the observation of reduced dispersion in generated data, while the overlap with the real distribution indicates successful modeling of global structural patterns.

Finally, Table 4 synthesizes the generative performance across the two main distance metrics. The consistency of these results consolidates the third configuration as the most reliable in this experimental framework.

5 Discussion

The results obtained in this study highlight the capacity of GAN-based models to learn and replicate complex temporal structures inherent to small and medium enterprise (SME) datasets, particularly in low-resource environments such as those found in emerging economies. The low Fréchet Inception Distance (FID) and Dynamic Time Warping (DTW) scores, along with the successful reproduction of stylized facts, such as volatility clustering and heavy-tailed distributions, demonstrate that the model captured both low-level statistics and higher-order dynamics. This degree of fidelity indicates that the generator did not merely memorize sequences but internalized generalizable rules of behavior,

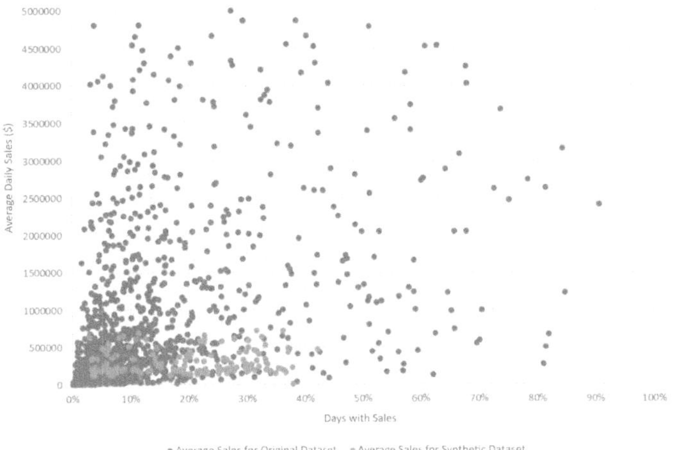

Fig. 4. Distribution of real and synthetic time-series. This figure illustrates the overall distribution of time-series in the real dataset (1,495 sequences) and the synthetic dataset (150 sequences generated under the optimal GAN configuration). The similarity in shape and density across both sets confirms that the generator generalizes effectively, producing realistic sequences at scale suitable for data augmentation purposes.

Table 3. Sample size validation after augmentation. This table verifies that the synthetic generation process achieved the intended 10% increase in the number of time-series. The total count after augmentation (1,645) confirms that the model scales in a controlled and consistent manner.

Dataset	Number of Series
Original	1495
Generated	150
Total	1645

Table 4. Summary of DTW and Fréchet evaluations. This summary table presents the mean and standard deviation values for DTW and Fréchet distances across real–real and real–synthetic comparisons. The closeness of these values confirms that the GAN model produces synthetic sequences with similar structural and dynamic characteristics to those of the real data, supporting its potential for realistic data simulation.

Metric	Mean	Standard Deviation
DTW Real–Real	3.88	1.11
DTW Real–Synthetic	3.65	0.97
Fréchet Real–Real	5.91	1.32
Fréchet Real–Synthetic	5.46	1.19

a result that aligns with broader research on generative models for time-series data [32,33].

A particularly notable outcome was the preservation of stylized statistical features characteristic of economic time-series. The synthetic data exhibited significant autocorrelation in squared returns and elevated kurtosis values, both of which mirror empirical patterns described in foundational econometric literature [34]. These results suggest that the GAN did not only replicate data visually or through proximity metrics, but also learned the deeper probabilistic structure that governs SME behavior in real markets. This finding is especially relevant when synthetic data is used to simulate policy or market scenarios, where fidelity to structural properties is more important than superficial similarity.

The use of Gramian Angular Fields (GAF) for time-series encoding represents a methodological innovation that played a central role in the model's performance. By transforming time-series into visual representations, the generator was able to exploit convolutional layers designed for images, thus facilitating learning of patterns that would be harder to capture in raw temporal form [28]. Moreover, the application of FID, originally intended for image generation quality assessment, was adapted to the time-series domain using Time-Inception embeddings, which have been shown to correlate with human-perceived similarity [32]. These methodological choices position this work within the growing field of hybrid generative learning, where insights from one domain (computer vision) can meaningfully improve performance in another (temporal modeling).

From a practical perspective, the use of synthetic data generated by this model had a tangible impact on downstream machine learning tasks. The classifier trained exclusively on synthetic data achieved over 83% accuracy when tested on real data, and models trained on a combination of real and synthetic samples reached nearly 90% accuracy. These figures not only validate the realism of the generated data but also suggest that synthetic augmentation can enhance predictive performanc, particularly in data-scarce environments, a scenario well documented in SME contexts in Latin America [3]. The ability to simulate data that supports model generalization is key for democratizing access to machine learning technologies among small enterprises, who often lack historical records or the technical infrastructure for data curation.

The model's performance is also competitive with recent state-of-the-art approaches. For instance, compared to TimeGAN [4] and QuantGAN [35] which rely on recurrent and autoregressive modules, the architecture presented in this work achieved similar generalization results while using a simpler convolutional structure. The synthetic data also preserved latent cluster structures in a manner comparable to more complex generative pipelines, as evidenced by the minimal divergence in K-means partitioning of statistical features. This supports the growing understanding that well-structured representation, such as GAF or recurrence plots, can enable convolutional GANs to compete with recurrent architectures, especially when data is limited.

Nonetheless, several limitations must be acknowledged. The model was trained on a relatively small dataset, which, although sufficient for capturing macro-patterns, may limit its ability to generalize to rare or outlier behaviors. Furthermore, the absence of exogenous covariates, such as macroeconomic indicators or seasonal variables, constrains the interpretability and applicability of the synthetic data in real-world forecasting scenarios. Future work should consider the incorporation of conditional GANs or multimodal frameworks that jointly model external drivers and endogenous dynamics. Additionally, while performance metrics such as FID and TSTR provide valuable insights, they do not fully assess privacy risks or memorization. More rigorous tests, such as membership inference attacks [36], should be used to ensure that synthetic data does not leak sensitive information, particularly when working with real business datasets.

Finally, ethical and regulatory dimensions must be addressed. The growing use of synthetic data, especially in decision, making contexts, raises questions about traceability, transparency, and accountability. If synthetic samples are indistinguishable from real ones, they may inadvertently be used in critical systems without adequate disclosure. Organizations such as the UK Information Commissioner's Office (2022) [37] have recommended that synthetic data pipelines include disclosure mechanisms and audit trails to ensure ethical compliance. In emerging economies, where data regulation is still developing, establishing best practices for synthetic data generation and usage will be crucial for ensuring trust, fairness, and data sovereignty.

In light of these insights, the study underscores the feasibility of applying GAN-based models to SMEs sales data. The following conclusions synthesize the main contributions, practical implications, and future research directions.

6 Conclusion

This study demonstrated that GANs combined with GAF encoding can generate realistic sales time-series for Chilean SMEs. The model captured essential statistical traits, including volatility and kurtosis—suggesting structural rather than superficial fidelity.

Convolutional architectures benefited from visual encoding, offering efficient learning without relying on recurrent networks. Evaluation via FID, DTW, and classification tasks confirmed the generated data's high utility and realism.

The research underscores synthetic data's potential to mitigate data scarcity among SMEs. By enabling access to predictive modeling tools without compromising privacy, synthetic datasets become a practical asset for digital inclusion.

Nonetheless, concerns remain regarding overfitting, privacy leakage, and ethical deployment. Future work should integrate conditional inputs, expand to diverse datasets, and apply robust privacy audits.

Overall, the study offers a scalable, interpretable approach to synthetic time-series generation, with applications extending to other data-scarce domains in finance, healthcare, and policy.

References

1. OECD. Going Digital to Advance Data Governance for Growth and Well-Being. OECD Publishing, Paris (2022). https://doi.org/10.1787/e3d783b0-en
2. Goodfellow, I., et al.: Generative adversarial nets. In: Advances in Neural Information Processing Systems (NeurIPS 27), pp. 2672–2680 (2014)
3. Xu, L., Skoularidou, M., Cuesta-Infante, A., Veeramachaneni, K.: Modeling tabular data using conditional GAN. In: Advances in Neural Information Processing Systems (NeurIPS 32), pp. 7335–7345 (2019)
4. Yoon, J., Jarrett, D., van der Schaar, M.: Time-series generative adversarial networks. In: Advances in Neural Information Processing Systems (NeurIPS 32), pp. 5508–5518 (2019)
5. OECD: Making digital transformation work for all in Chile. OECD Publishing, Paris (2021). https://doi.org/10.1787/6b1a524c-en
6. APEC: Building a FinTech ecosystem for the recovery of the MSME sector. APEC Publications, Singapore (2024). https://www.apec.org/publications/2024/09/building-a-fintech-ecosystem-for-the-recovery-of-the-msme-sector
7. Nikolenko, S.I.: Synthetic Data for Deep Learning, vol. 174. Springer, Cham (2021)
8. Alqahtani, H., Kavakli-Thorne, M., Kumar, G.: Applications of generative adversarial networks (GANs): an updated review. Arch. Comput. Methods Eng. **28**(2), 525–552 (2021)
9. Lopez, F.A., et al.: Evaluation of a FinTech sales synthetic data generation model using a generative adversarial network. In: International Conference on Computational Science and Its Applications (ICCSA 2024). LNCS, pp. 56–70. Springer, Cham (2024)
10. MarketsandMarkets.: Generative AI market size, trends, & technology roadmap.(2025). https://www.marketsandmarkets.com/Market-Reports/generative-ai-market-142870584.html. Accessed 25 Oct 2023
11. Nadăs, M., Diosan, L., Tomescu, A.: Synthetic data generation using large language models: advances in text and code. IEEE Access (2025)
12. Lee, J., Hyeong, J., Jeon, J., Park, N., Cho, J.: Invertible tabular GANs: killing two birds with one stone for tabular data synthesis. In: Advances in Neural Information Processing Systems (NeurIPS 34), pp. 4263–4273 (2021)
13. Alshantti, A., Varagnolo, D., Rasheed, A., Rahmati, A., Westad, F.: CasTGAN: cascaded GAN for realistic tabular data. arXiv preprint arXiv:2301.12345 (2023)
14. Li, J., Zhao, Z., Yee, K., Javaid, U., Sikdar, B.: TAEGAN: generating synthetic tabular data for data augmentation. arXiv preprint arXiv:2410.01933 (2024)
15. EkandariNasab, M.: Supervised generative adversarial networks for time series generation in embedding space. arXiv preprint (2024, to appear)
16. Tasmurzayev, N., Amangeldy, B., Smagulova, G., Baigarayeva, Z., Imash, A.: A low-cost IoT sensor and preliminary machine-learning feasibility study for monitoring in-cabin air quality: a pilot case from Almaty. Sensors **25**(14), 4521 (2025)
17. Hyrup, T., Lautrup, A.D., Zimek, A., Schneider-Kamp, P.: A systematic review of privacy-preserving techniques for synthetic tabular health data. Discover Data **3**(1), 5 (2025)
18. Barr, A.A., Rozman, R., Guo, E.: Generative adversarial networks vs large language models: a comparative study on synthetic tabular data generation. arXiv preprint arXiv:2502.09876 (2025)
19. Kotelnikov, A., Baranchuk, D., Rubachev, I., Babenko, A.: TabDDPM: modelling tabular data with diffusion models. In: Proceedings of the International Conference

on Machine Learning (ICML 2023). Proceedings of Machine Learning Research, vol. 202, pp. 17564–17579. PMLR (2023)
20. Stübinger, J., Walter, D.: Using multi-dimensional dynamic time warping to identify time-varying lead-lag relationships. Sensors **22**(18), 6884 (2022)
21. Rashidi, H.H., Albahra, S., Rubin, B.P., Hu, B.: A novel and fully automated platform for synthetic tabular data generation and validation. Sci. Rep. **14**(1), 23312 (2024)
22. Lautrup, A.D., Hyrup, T., Zimek, A., Schneider-Kamp, P.: Syntheval: a framework for detailed utility and privacy evaluation of tabular synthetic data. Data Min. Knowl. Discov. **39**(1), 6 (2025)
23. Gabryel, M., Kocić, E., Kocić, M., Patora-Wysocka, Z., Xiao, M., Pawlak, M.: Accelerating user profiling in e-commerce using conditional GAN networks for synthetic data generation. J. Artif. Intell. Soft Comput. Res. **14**(4), 309–319 (2024)
24. Álava, W.L.S., Rodríguez, A.R., Cornelio, O.M., Fonseca, B.B.: El papel de la inteligencia artificial en la transformación digital de las empresas. Tono, Rev. Téc. Empresa Telecomun. Cuba SA **19**(1), 23–42 (2023)
25. Pezoulas, V.C., et al.: Synthetic data generation methods in healthcare: a review on open-source tools and methods. Comput. Struct. Biotechnol. J. **23**, 2892–2910 (2024)
26. Fragkouli, S.C., et al.: An ELIXIR scoping review on domain-specific evaluation metrics for synthetic data in life sciences. arXiv preprint arXiv:2506.14508 (2025)
27. Huang, T., Chakraborty, P., Sharma, A.: Deep convolutional generative adversarial networks for traffic data imputation encoding time series as images. Int. J. Transp. Sci. Technol. **12**(1), 1–18 (2023)
28. Wang, Z., Oates, T.: Encoding time series as images for visual inspection and classification using tiled convolutional neural networks. In: Workshops at the Twenty-Ninth AAAI Conference on Artificial Intelligence, vol. 1, pp. 1–7 (2015)
29. Sidike, P., Reyes, A.A., Kasaragod, A., Oommen, T.: GAF-NAU: gramian angular field encoded neighborhood attention U-Net for pixel-wise hyperspectral image classification. In: Proceedings of the IEEE/CVF Conference on Computer Vision and Pattern Recognition Workshops (CVPRW), pp. 408–416 (2022)
30. Kingma, D., Ba, J.: Adam: a method for stochastic optimization. In: Proceedings of the 3rd International Conference on Learning Representations (ICLR) (2015)
31. Heusel, M., Ramsauer, H., Unterthiner, T., Nessler, B., Hochreiter, S.: GANs trained by a two time-scale update rule converge to a local Nash equilibrium. In: Advances in Neural Information Processing Systems (NeurIPS 30), pp. 6626–6637 (2017)
32. Brophy, E., Wang, Z., She, Q., Ward, T.: Generative adversarial networks in time series: a systematic literature review. ACM Comput. Surv. **55**(10), 199:1–199:31 (2023)
33. Esteban, C., Hyland, S.L., Rätsch, G.: Real-valued (medical) time series generation with recurrent conditional GANs. arXiv preprint arXiv:1706.02633 (2017)
34. Cont, R.: Empirical properties of asset returns: stylized facts and statistical issues. Quant. Finance **1**(2), 223–236 (2001)
35. Wiese, M., Knobloch, R., Korn, R., Kretschmer, P.: Quant GANs: deep generation of financial time series. Quant. Finance **20**(9), 1419–1440 (2020)

36. Hayes, J., Melis, L., Danezis, G., De Cristofaro, E.: LOGAN: membership inference attacks against generative models. Proc. Privacy Enhancing Technol. **1**, 133–152 (2019)
37. Information Commissioner's Office. How to use AI and personal data appropriately and lawfully (Version 1.0) (2022). https://ico.org.uk/media2/migrated/4022261/how-to-use-ai-and-personal-data.pdf

Facial Emotion Recognition Through Graph-Based Analysis of Face Mesh Landmarks in Real Time

Oscar Loyola-Valenzuela[1(✉)], Diana Suarez[2], and Marvin Molina[3]

[1] Grupo de Investigación Aplicada en Robotica e Industria 4.0, Facultad de Ingeniería, Universidad Autónoma de Chile, Santiago, Chile
oscar.author@uautonoma.cl

[2] Grupo de Investigación AGLAIA, Facultad de Ingeniería, Corporación Universitaria Americana, Barranquilla, Colombia
dsuarez@americana.edu.co

[3] Grupo de Investigación AGLAIA, Facultad de Ingeniería, Corporación Universitaria Americana, Barranquilla, Colombia
marvin.molinac@unilibre.edu.co

Abstract. This paper presents a hybrid approach to facial emotion recognition that combines visual texture analysis via convolutional neural networks with structural features extracted from MediaPipe's facial landmark mesh. Instead of applying trainable Graph Neural Networks, we define a graph-inspired representation where a subset of 30 expressive landmarks is encoded through geometric descriptors—specifically radial distances and angular orientations relative to the facial centroid. These features, concatenated with deep visual embeddings, enable robust and interpretable emotion classification across seven categories. The model operates in real time with average inference latency below 65ms per frame, requiring only standard CPU and webcam input. Experimental results on the FER2013 dataset demonstrate that incorporating graph-based descriptors improves class separability—particularly for high-arousal emotions—and enhances resilience to noise, occlusion, and head pose variation. This work offers an efficient and deployable alternative to full GNNs while preserving the benefits of topological facial reasoning.

Keywords: Facial expression recognition · Computer vision · Graph theory · Feature extraction · Deep learning · Real-time systems

1 Introduction

Facial expression recognition (FER) is an active research area with applications in human-computer interaction, mental health assessment, and affective computing. Classical approaches often rely on convolutional neural networks (CNNs) that require high computational power and large annotated datasets. More

T. Guarda et al. (Eds.): ARTIIS 2025, CCIS 2789, pp. 69–80, 2026.
https://doi.org/10.1007/978-3-032-16758-3_6

lightweight methods employ handcrafted features, such as distances between facial landmarks, but often lack robustness and adaptability.

Facial expressions play a crucial role in social interactions by revealing internal emotions and intentions of an individual. The primary objective of FER systems is to accurately categorize these expressions into discrete emotion classes. However, local feature-based methods may struggle when different facial regions produce similar gradient-based responses such as edges or corners [8].

Over the past two decades, advancements in artificial intelligence and computer vision have fueled sustained interest in FER, especially in efforts to facilitate seamless communication between humans and machines. FER aims to infer emotional states by analyzing involuntary facial muscle movements [9]. Its applications are increasingly diverse, spanning online education, healthcare, driver monitoring, and interactive robotics. For example, in some countries FER is used in classrooms to monitor students' mood fluctuations and in transportation systems to assess driver fatigue [1].

Ekman and Friesen [2] identified six universal facial expressions—happiness, anger, sadness, surprise, fear, and disgust—that remain foundational for FER systems. However, these basic emotions may not fully capture the complexity and nuance of real-world affective communication [3]. Non-verbal cues like micro-expressions and facial dynamics demand more flexible and structurally informed representations.

Recent efforts in facial affect analysis (FAA) emphasize the need for robust preprocessing, meaningful affective representation, and task-specific adaptation [4]. Dense landmark detection has become a central tool in this pipeline, enabling virtual reenactment, monitoring, and expression tracking under unconstrained conditions [5].

In this context, facial landmarks coupled with mesh structures provide a powerful alternative to purely appearance-based models. MediaPipe—developed by Google—offers real-time extraction of 468 high-resolution landmarks across the face. While most existing works treat these points as isolated or pairwise measures, recent studies have begun to explore graph-based modeling as a means to capture structural relationships [7]. For example, [6] employed a custom facial mesh to train a graph convolutional network (GCN) with weighted loss, showing promising results in classifying expressions from facial geometry.

In our previous work [13], we investigated CNNs and Dynamic Mode Decomposition (DMD) for FER on FER2013. CNNs yielded higher classification accuracy, while DMD captured temporal patterns, though both lacked explicit modeling of facial structure.

This study extends that line of inquiry by proposing a hybrid approach that fuses visual features from CNNs with graph-inspired geometric descriptors derived from MediaPipe landmarks. Our model achieves real-time performance using a lightweight architecture that avoids the overhead of full GNN training while preserving the structural advantages of topological encoding.

Related literature further illustrates the breadth of current FER research. In [15], a multimodal fusion model combined facial images with textual data using BERT and CNNs, enhancing emotion inference in context-sensitive tasks. EA-Net [16] integrated EfficientNetB0 and InceptionV3 with spatial attention to improve low-resolution FER. The dataset FER24-CK+ [17] was proposed to overcome label noise and demographic bias.

Other efforts [18,19] explored physiological signal fusion and privacy-preserving learning frameworks. In [20], federated learning and differential privacy were employed to ensure ethical deployment of FER in surveillance settings.

In summary, the field is advancing along three key directions: (1) multimodal learning for richer affective modeling, (2) neural architecture optimization for performance in the wild, and (3) privacy-aware system design. Our work contributes to this landscape by offering a structurally grounded, computationally efficient FER framework designed for real-time operation on conventional hardware.

2 Methodology

2.1 Face Mesh as a Graph

We define a facial representation as a geometric graph $G = (V, E)$, where each node $v_i \in V$ corresponds to a landmark extracted using MediaPipe FaceMesh. The complete mesh provides $|V| = 468$ landmarks per face. The edge set E is implicitly derived from the anatomical connections provided by MediaPipe's tessellation, encoding topological adjacency between semantically related regions (e.g., eye contours, lip border, eyebrows). Each node v_i is associated with a 2D coordinate vector $\mathbf{p}_i = [x_i, y_i]^\top \in \mathbb{R}^2$.

2.2 Feature Extraction

From the full graph G, we extract a subgraph $G' = (V', E')$ by selecting a subset $V' \subset V$ of $n = 30$ key landmarks covering high-expressivity regions. For each node $v_i \in V'$, we compute:

- **Radial distance:** $r_i = \|\mathbf{p}_i - \mathbf{p}_c\|_2$, where $\mathbf{p}_c = \frac{1}{n}\sum_{i=1}^{n} \mathbf{p}_i$ is the centroid of the landmark set.
- **Angular orientation:** $\theta_i = \text{atan2}(y_i - y_c, x_i - x_c)$.

Each node v_i is thus represented by a local feature vector $\mathbf{x}_i = [r_i, \theta_i]^\top \in \mathbb{R}^2$, and the graph signal is encoded as a matrix $\mathbf{X} \in \mathbb{R}^{n \times 2}$. The complete descriptor $\mathbf{g} \in \mathbb{R}^{2n}$ is obtained by flattening and concatenating all node features. Prior to training, $\mathbf{g}$ is standardized via z-score normalization.

To reduce computational complexity while retaining the most expressive facial dynamics, we selected a subset of 30 key landmarks from the full MediaPipe mesh. These landmarks are located on regions known to exhibit strong motion and deformation during facial expressions, such as the mouth corners, eyebrows, eyes, nose, and jawline. The selected indices are summarized in Table 1, and follow the standard MediaPipe FaceMesh indexing convention.

Table 1. Subset of 30 facial landmarks used for geometric descriptor computation. Indices follow the MediaPipe FaceMesh specification.

Facial Region	Landmark Indices
Mouth (outer and corners)	61, 146, 91, 181, 84, 17, 314, 405, 321, 375
Eyebrows (inner and outer ends)	70, 63, 105, 66, 107, 336, 296, 334, 293, 300
Eyes (corners and center)	33, 133, 159, 145, 362, 263, 386, 374
Nose ridge and tip	1, 6, 197, 195
Jaw (chin center)	152

2.3 Affective Modeling via Russell's Circumplex Structure

To introduce a psychologically meaningful representation of emotion, we project the geometric descriptor $\mathbf{g}$ into Russell's Circumplex Model of Affect [12], where each emotional state is represented by a point $(v, a) \in [-1, 1]^2$ corresponding to valence and arousal. We define a linear mapping from the feature vector to this affective space:

$$v = \mathbf{w}_v^\top \mathbf{g}, \quad a = \mathbf{w}_a^\top \mathbf{g} \tag{1}$$

where $\mathbf{w}_v, \mathbf{w}_a \in \mathbb{R}^{2n}$ are weight vectors encoding the contribution of each topological descriptor to valence and arousal, respectively. These weights can be heuristically defined or learned via regression.

The quadrant-based classification is defined as:

- $(v > \delta_v, a > \delta_a)$: Happiness
- $(v < -\delta_v, a > \delta_a)$: Anger
- $(v < -\delta_v, a < -\delta_a)$: Sadness
- $(v > \delta_v, a < -\delta_a)$: Calmness

with $\delta_v, \delta_a \in (0, 1)$ as thresholds calibrated on the training set. This mapping enhances the model's interpretability and allows capturing transitional or mixed affective states.

Table 2. Heuristic mapping of emotions onto the valence-arousal space (v, a) based on geometric feature combinations.

Emotion	Valence v	Arousal a	Dominant Features
Happiness	$v > 0.5$	$a > 0.5$	Lip corner elevation, cheek lift
Anger	$v < -0.5$	$a > 0.5$	Eyebrow frown, jaw tension, eye widening
Sadness	$v < -0.5$	$a < -0.5$	Inner eyebrow raise, lip corner depression
Calmness	$v > 0.5$	$a < -0.5$	Relaxed features, slight smile, neutral gaze
Fear	$v < 0$	$a > 0.5$	Eye widening, mouth opening, raised eyebrows
Surprise	$v \approx 0$	$a > 0.7$	Raised eyebrows, open mouth
Disgust	$v < -0.5$	$a > 0.3$	Nose wrinkle, upper lip raise
Neutral	$\|v\| < 0.2$	$\|a\| < 0.2$	Minimal muscular activity

Table 2 summarizes the heuristic projection of common emotional categories into the valence-arousal space (v, a), using combinations of normalized geometric features extracted from the facial landmark graph. The signs and magnitudes of these values reflect the intensity and polarity of affective states as inferred from facial deformation patterns.

2.4 Emotion Classification via Graph-Based CNN Architecture

Rather than implementing a trainable Graph Neural Network, we adopt a hybrid model that fuses image-based texture analysis and graph-based structural encoding. The architecture is composed of two parallel branches:

- A **CNN branch**, which processes the grayscale image $I \in \mathbb{R}^{48\times48}$ through a series of convolutional layers:

$$\mathbf{v}_{\text{CNN}} = \text{Flatten}\left(\text{Conv}_2\left(\text{MaxPool}(\text{Conv}_1(I))\right)\right) \tag{2}$$

- A **geometric branch**, which receives the descriptor $\mathbf{g} \in \mathbb{R}^{2n}$ as input.

The outputs of both branches are concatenated:

$$\mathbf{z} = [\mathbf{v}_{\text{CNN}}; \mathbf{g}] \tag{3}$$

and passed through a fully connected layer $\mathbf{h} = \phi(\mathbf{W}_h\mathbf{z} + \mathbf{b}_h)$ with ReLU activation $\phi(\cdot)$ and dropout regularization. The final output is a softmax layer over $C = 7$ emotion classes:

$$\hat{\mathbf{y}} = \text{softmax}(\mathbf{W}_o\mathbf{h} + \mathbf{b}_o) \tag{4}$$

The model is trained to minimize the categorical cross-entropy loss:

$$\mathcal{L} = -\sum_{k=1}^{C} y_k \log(\hat{y}_k) \tag{5}$$

where y_k is the one-hot encoded ground truth label (Fig. 1).

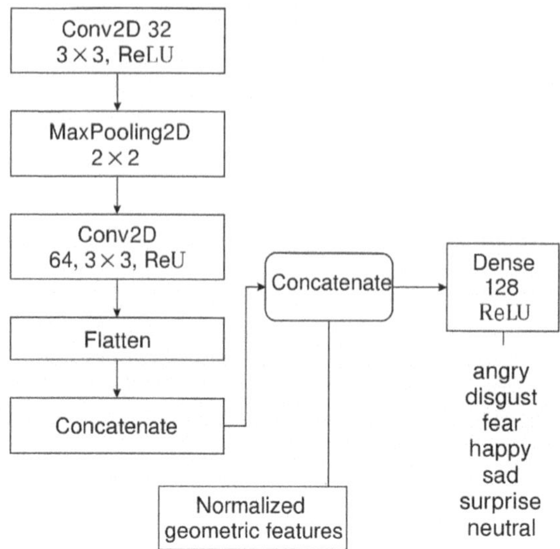

Fig. 1. Hybrid architecture combining a convolutional branch for visual features and a graph-based branch for geometric descriptors derived from the facial landmark mesh.

This formulation exploits the facial mesh's spatial topology through efficient, interpretable features, enabling real-time performance and competitive classification accuracy without requiring a full GNN pipeline.

3 Experimental Setup

3.1 Hardware and Software Environment

All experiments were conducted on a workstation equipped with an AMD Ryzen 5 5600H CPU at 3.30 GHz, 32 GB RAM, and an NVIDIA GeForce RTX 3050 GPU with 4 GB VRAM. Real-time facial video input was obtained using a Logitech C920 webcam capturing at 30 FPS. The implementation stack included:

- Python 3.10
- OpenCV 4.7.0 for video capture and image preprocessing
- MediaPipe 0.10.9 for facial landmark detection (FaceMesh)
- TensorFlow/Keras 2.13 for CNN model implementation and training
- Scikit-learn and Matplotlib for evaluation and visualization

3.2 Graph-Based Real-Time Pipeline

The proposed emotion recognition pipeline was implemented for real-time performance, achieving an average inference latency below 65 ms per frame. It operates through the following stages:

1. **Facial landmark extraction:** Each video frame is processed using MediaPipe FaceMesh, which yields 468 high-resolution facial landmarks.
2. **Geometric feature computation:** From a predefined subset of 30 expressive landmarks, we compute:
   - Normalized 2D coordinates
   - Radial distances to the facial centroid
   - Angular orientations

   These are concatenated into a 60-dimensional geometric descriptor $\mathbf{g} \in \mathbb{R}^{60}$ that encodes structural deformation.
3. **Visual feature extraction:** The preprocessed grayscale frame is passed through a convolutional encoder to produce a latent visual representation $\mathbf{v}_{\text{CNN}}$.
4. **Multimodal fusion and classification:** The vectors $\mathbf{g}$ and $\mathbf{v}_{\text{CNN}}$ are concatenated and input to a fully connected neural classifier that outputs class probabilities via softmax.
5. **Real-time inference and display:** The predicted emotion label is rendered live on screen. Optionally, a projection onto the valenceâĂŞarousal plane is computed using a weighted linear transformation of $\mathbf{g}$.

The architecture supports two operational modes: (1) softmax-based classification over discrete emotion categories, and (2) continuous affect mapping based on the Circumplex Model of Affect.

3.3 Training and Evaluation Protocol

The hybrid CNN+geometry model was trained using the FER2013 dataset, partitioned into 80% training and 20% validation. Precomputed geometric descriptors were normalized using z-score transformation. Key training parameters:

- Optimizer: Adam, learning rate $= 10^{-3}$
- Batch size: 64
- Epochs: 30 (with early stopping, patience = 5)
- Loss function: Categorical cross-entropy
- Dropout: 0.3 on the dense layer after fusion

Evaluation metrics included accuracy, confusion matrix, and ROC curves per class. All experiments were repeated with fixed seeds for reproducibility.

4 Results and Discussion

4.1 Quantitative Evaluation

The hybrid CNN+geometric model achieved an overall accuracy of 52.5% on the FER2013 validation split. Per-class AUC values (Fig. 3) demonstrate strong discriminative performance in emotions such as *Surprise* (AUC = 0.94), *Happy* (AUC = 0.93), and *Disgust* (AUC = 0.93), while *Fear* remains the most challenging (AUC = 0.76).

Figure 3 shows the ROC curves for each class. High-arousal emotions such as *Surprise* and *Happy* achieved superior separability, likely due to distinct geometric signatures (e.g., mouth openness, raised eyebrows) captured in the landmark topology.

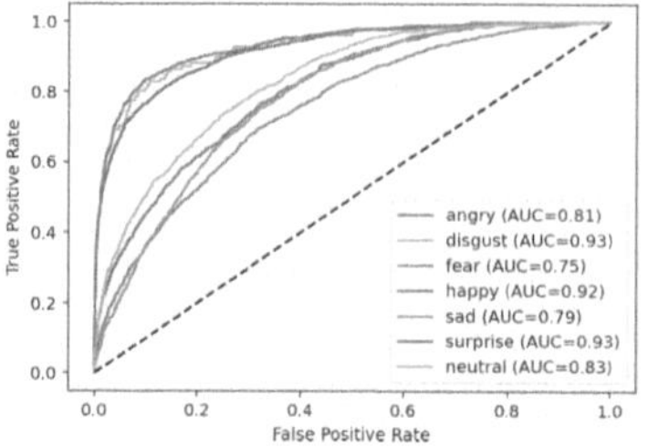

Fig. 2. ROC curves per class for the CNN-only model.

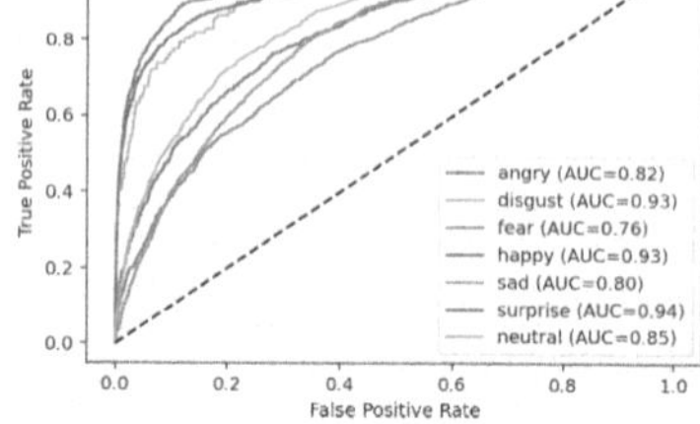

Fig. 3. ROC curves per class for the hybrid model.

4.2 Confusion Analysis

Figure 4 presents the normalized confusion matrix for the hybrid model. The most frequent misclassifications occurred between *Fear* and *Sad*, and between *Neutral* and *Angry*, which are known to exhibit overlapping facial features in unconstrained settings. The inclusion of geometric features contributed to improved recognition of *Surprise* and *Happy*, where spatial deformation is more pronounced.

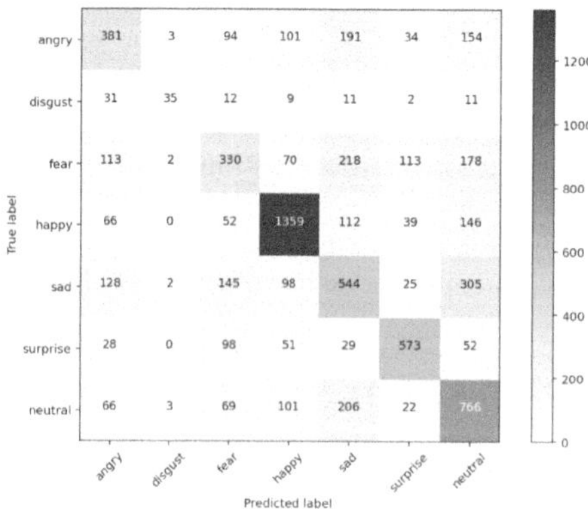

Fig. 4. Confusion matrix of the proposed hybrid model.

4.3 Comparison with CNN-Only Baseline

To quantify the contribution of structural descriptors, we trained a baseline model using the same CNN backbone as the hybrid system, but without the geometric input branch. The CNN-only model achieved an overall accuracy of 47.3% on the FER2013 test set, compared to 52.5% obtained by the proposed hybrid model—an absolute improvement of 5.2% points.

Figure 2 shows the ROC curves for each emotion class under the CNN-only configuration. While high-arousal classes such as *Disgust*, *Happy*, and *Surprise* still achieve AUC values above 0.90, the class *Fear* remains the most challenging, with an AUC of 0.75. Compared to the hybrid model, slight improvements in separability were observed across most classes, particularly for *Angry* (+0.01), *Sad* (+0.01), and *Neutral* (+0.02).

The confusion matrix in Fig. 5 further reveals that the CNN-only model exhibits higher misclassification between *Neutral* and *Angry*, and between *Fear* and *Sad*. These findings support the hypothesis that introducing graph-inspired topological encodings enhances the discriminative capacity of CNNs, especially in ambiguous or subtly differentiated expressions (Table 3).

Table 3. Comparison between CNN-only and Hybrid CNN + Geometric models on FER2013.

Metric	CNN-only	Hybrid (Ours)
Accuracy (%)	47.3	52.5
Average AUC	0.85	0.89
Best AUC	0.93 (Surprise)	0.94 (Surprise)
Worst AUC	0.75 (Fear)	0.76 (Fear)

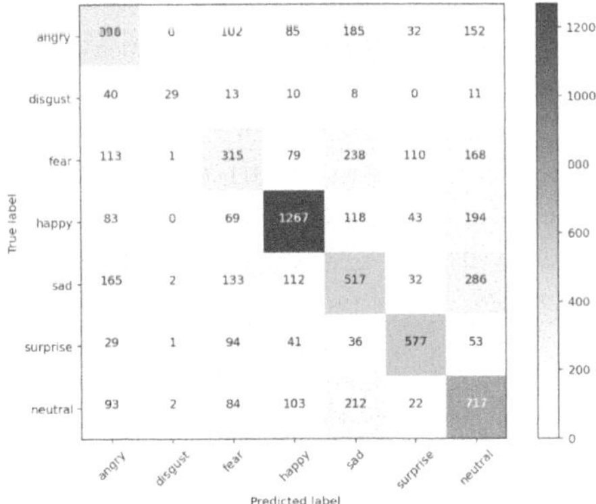

Fig. 5. Confusion matrix of the CNN-only baseline model on FER2013.

4.4 Qualitative Insights

The combination of visual and graph-derived features improved the system's robustness under varying lighting, head pose, and partial occlusion. Geometric encodings captured expressive regions (e.g., eyebrows, lips) more distinctly than CNN alone. In comparison to the CNN-only baseline, the hybrid model achieved a 5.2% point increase in classification accuracy and higher AUC scores across most emotion classes. These results indicate that incorporating structural information not only enhances quantitative performance, but also provides interpretability through spatially grounded descriptors.

This structurally enriched formulation is especially valuable for real-world emotion-aware systems, such as human-robot interaction or driver monitoring, where transparent decision-making and generalization are critical.

4.5 Comparison with State-of-the-Art Methods and Limitations

The proposed approach was compared with recent FER alternatives based on lightweight CNNs, classical geometric descriptors, and models with trainable Graph Neural Networks (GNNs). On FER2013, our hybrid method (CNN + geometry (r, θ)) achieved a +5.2% accuracy gain over the CNN baseline with a CPU latency below 65 ms, placing it within the range of real-time methods. Unlike GNNs operating on the full facial mesh, our radialâĂŞangular representation captures structural relationships while maintaining a significantly lower computational cost. This balance makes it particularly suitable for resource-constrained environments, where GNN-based or heavier architectures are not feasible.

However, the model presents relevant limitations. Because it depends on accurate landmark detection, its performance may degrade in the presence of partial occlusions, lighting variations, or significant morphological differences (e.g., age, ethnicity, facial hair). Moreover, as it was mainly validated on FER2013, further studies on generalization to more diverse datasets (e.g., RAF-DB or AffectNet) are needed to estimate its robustness in real-world scenarios. As future work, we plan to (i) incorporate a lightweight GNN module on top of the geometric encoding to improve adaptability, (ii) explore temporal information integration to better handle microexpressions, and (iii) establish cross-dataset validation protocols. These actions, together with calibration and rejection mechanisms for uncertain predictions, will help mitigate the identified risks and expand the applicability of the system.

5 Conclusion and Future Work

This work presented a hybrid architecture for facial emotion recognition that integrates convolutional visual processing with graph-based geometric features extracted from facial landmarks. By leveraging the topological structure of the face mesh provided by MediaPipe, we enriched the input representation with interpretable descriptors such as radial distances and angular orientations. This approach improves both classification performance and structural robustness, particularly in distinguishing high-arousal emotional states.

The proposed method demonstrates that explicit graph-based encoding—without requiring a full Graph Neural Network—can significantly enhance traditional CNN pipelines. The resulting system is lightweight, real-time capable, and suitable for deployment in constrained environments, such as mobile or embedded platforms.

Future research directions include:

- **Incorporation of trainable GNN layers**: We plan to integrate Graph Convolutional Networks (GCNs) that operate directly on the adjacency matrix of the face mesh to further capture relational dependencies among landmarks.
- **Dataset expansion and cross-dataset validation**: Beyond FER2013, we will experiment with AffectNet and RAF-DB to assess generalization across demographic and expressive variability.
- **Spatiotemporal modeling**: We aim to incorporate temporal dynamics through recurrent or temporal GNN architectures to recognize evolving expressions and micro-expressions in continuous video streams.
- **Development of a dedicated facial expression dataset**: We intend to build a custom dataset featuring high-resolution images and annotated facial landmarks under controlled and real-world conditions. This will allow fine-grained geometric calibration and support training of topology-aware models tailored to local context and cultural variability.

Overall, this study underscores the importance of combining visual and structural modalities for more accurate and explainable emotion recognition systems. Future work will explore deeper integration of graph learning and temporal dynamics, enabling more adaptive and socially aware applications in embedded and mobile contexts.

References

1. Farkhod, A., Abdusalomov, A.B., Mukhiddinov, M., Cho, Y.-I.: Development of real-time landmark-based emotion recognition CNN for masked faces. Sensors. **22**(22), 8704 (2022). https://doi.org/10.3390/s22228704
2. Ekman, P., Friesen, W.V.: Constants across cultures in the face and emotion. J. Personal. Soc. Psychol. **17**(2), 124 (1971)
3. Ekman, P., Friesen, W.V.: Nonverbal behavior and psychopathology. The psychology of depression: contemporary theory and research, pp. 3–31 (1974)
4. Liu, Y., Zhang, X., Li, Y., Zhou, J., Li, X., Zhao, G.: Graph-based facial affect analysis: a review. IEEE Trans. Affect. Comput. **14**(4), 2657–2677. IEEE (2023). https://doi.org/10.1109/TAFFC.2022.3215918
5. Khabarlak, K., Koriashkina, L.: Fast facial landmark detection and applications: a survey. J. Comput. Sci. Technol. **22**(1), e02 (2022). https://doi.org/10.24215/16666038.22.e02

6. Arabian, H., Abdulbaki Alshirbaji, T., Chase, J.G., Moeller, K.: Emotion recognition beyond pixels: leveraging facial point landmark meshes. Appl. Sci. **14**(8), 3358 (2024)
7. Quinonez, Y., Lizarraga, C., Aguayo, R..: Machine learning solutions with MediaPipe. In: 11th International Conference On Software Process Improvement (CIMPS) on Proceedings, pp. 212–215. Publisher, Acapulco, Guerrero, Mexico (2022). https://doi.org/10.1109/CIMPS57786.2022.10035706
8. Kartheek, M.N., Prasad, M.V.N.K., Bhukya, R.: Radial mesh pattern: a handcrafted feature descriptor for facial expression recognition. J. Ambient Intell. Hum. Comput. **14**, 1619–1631 (2023). https://doi.org/10.1007/s12652-021-03384-6
9. Ekundayo, O.S., Viriri, S.: Facial expression recognition: a review of trends and techniques. IEEE Access **9**, 136944–136973 (2021). https://doi.org/10.1109/ACCESS.2021.3113464
10. Sariyanidi, E., Gunes, H., Cavallaro, A.: Automatic analysis of facial affect: a survey of registration, representation, and recognition. IEEE Trans. Pattern Anal. Mach. Intell. **37**(6), 1113–1133 (2015)
11. Goodfellow, I., Bengio, Y., Courville, A.: Deep Learning. MIT Press, Cambridge (2016)
12. Russell, J.A.: A circumplex model of affect. J. Pers. Soc. Psychol. **39**(6), 1161–1178 (1980)
13. Loyola, O., Suarez, D., Salazar, G.: Advancements in AI-driven emotion recognition: a study on CNN and DMD methodologies. In: Figueroa-García, J.C., Hernández, G., Suero Pérez, D.F., Gaona García, E.E. (eds.) Applied Computer Sciences in Engineering. WEA 2024. CCIS, vol. 14603, pp. 138–150. Springer, Cham (2024). https://doi.org/10.1007/978-3-031-74595-9_13
14. MediaPipe Face Mesh. https://google.github.io/mediapipe/solutions/face_mesh.html. Accessed 9 Apr 2025
15. Boitel, E., Mohasseb, A., Haig, E.: MIST: multimodal emotion recognition using DeBERTa for text, Semi-CNN for speech, ResNet-50 for facial, and 3D-CNN for motion analysis. Expert Syst. Appl. **270**, 126236 (2025). abr. https://doi.org/10.1016/j.eswa.2024.126236
16. Khan, T., Yasir, M., Choi, C.: Attention-enhanced optimized deep ensemble network for effective facial emotion recognition. Alex. Eng. J. **119**, 111–123 (2025). abr. https://doi.org/10.1016/j.aej.2025.01.078
17. Rehman, A., Mujahid, M., Elyassih, A., AlGhofaily, B., Bahaj, S.A.O.: Comprehensive review and analysis on facial emotion recognition: performance insights into deep and traditional learning with current updates and challenges. Comput. Mater. Contin. **82**(1), 41–72 (2025). https://doi.org/10.32604/cmc.2024.058036
18. Yalcin, N., Alisawi, M.: Introducing a novel dataset for facial emotion recognition and demonstrating significant enhancements in deep learning performance through pre-processing techniques. Heliyon **10**(20), e38913 (2024). https://doi.org/10.1016/j.heliyon.2024.e38913
19. Tao, X., et al.: Facial video-based non-contact emotion recognition: a multi-view features expression and fusion method. Biomed. Signal Process. Control **96**, 106608 (2024). https://doi.org/10.1016/j.bspc.2024.106608
20. Vyas, H., Torrens, P.M.: Tackling, "leaky" facial and object recognition operations over federated learning. In: 2024 4th Interdisciplinary Conference on Electrics and Computer (INTCEC), Chicago, IL, USA, IEEE, jun. 2024, pp. 1–5 (2024). https://doi.org/10.1109/INTCEC61833.2024.10603278

Automatic Prediction of Liver Cancer

Ivan Marcelo Quimi Ramirez(✉) and Maricela Pinargote-Ortega

Universidad Técnica de Manabí, Portoviejo, Manabí, Ecuador
{iquimi4702,maricela.pinargote}@utm.edu.ec

Abstract. Cancer remains one of the major global health challenges, with a significant impact on morbidity and mortality worldwide, making early detection crucial for improving survival rates through more timely interventions and treatments. However, the early diagnosis of liver cancer presents complexities and often relies on technologies and methods with inherent limitations. This study aims to develop an early detection model for liver cancer from abdominal Computed Tomography scan images, applying an experimental methodology based on the phases of the CRISP-DM process. Analysis of results demonstrates that the model achieved 95% accuracy in validation tests. In a real-world evaluation, it assigned a cancer probability $\geq$ 80% to 77.7% of cases, reflecting high confidence in detecting high-risk lesions and suggesting that this approach could accelerate oncological diagnosis, benefit more patients, and optimize clinical resources. Subsequent phases could involve expanding the dataset, exploring additional artificial intelligence algorithms, and implementing advanced segmentation techniques using masks and multi-label classification to optimize the precise delineation of tumor areas.

Keywords: Liver Cancer · Early Detection · Machine Learning

1 Introduction

Hepatic cancer stands as one of the leading causes of oncological mortality worldwide, affecting millions of people each year [1–3]. Early detection of this disease is crucial for improving survival rates, as it allows for more effective interventions and timely treatments. However, early diagnosis of hepatic cancer presents significant challenges, often relying on technologies and methods that have inherent limitations. In the field of oncological detection, various challenges are faced regarding the accuracy of tests. For instance, in the context of prostate cancer, the current screening test, prostate-specific antigen (PSA), shows high sensitivity but low specificity for high-risk and clinically significant prostate cancer, leading to overdiagnosis and overtreatment of cases that are not clinically significant [4]. This situation is similar in hepatic cancer, where current detection tools may not effectively differentiate between benign and malignant lesions, leading to inaccurate diagnoses and potentially unnecessary treatments [5].

In recent years, artificial intelligence has emerged as a transformative tool in medicine, particularly in the analysis of medical images. Artificial intelligence has the

T. Guarda et al. (Eds.): ARTIIS 2025, CCIS 2789, pp. 81–95, 2026.
https://doi.org/10.1007/978-3-032-16758-3_7

potential to revolutionize cancer detection and diagnosis through the analysis of computed tomography (CT) scans and other imaging modalities. A notable example is the hybrid VER-Net model, which has proven effective in detecting lung cancer through tomography images, emphasizing the potential of artificial intelligence to identify malignant nodules with high precision [6]. A previous study explores the early detection of tumors through convolutional neural networks (CNNs) and convolutional autoencoders [7]. The study's framework provides a solid foundation for detecting cancers in other parts of the body, such as the liver, while illustrating how deep learning techniques can enhance diagnostic accuracy [8].

This strategy underscores the utility of these techniques in improving early diagnosis by analyzing magnetic resonance images. The ability of these models to identify tumors with high precision suggests that similar approaches could be applied to detect other types of cancer, such as liver cancer, in CT images. A broader analysis of the use of artificial intelligence in the diagnosis of hepatocellular carcinoma reveals how machine learning-based diagnostic paradigms can overcome the limitations of traditional methods [9].

Although international research on artificial intelligence applied to oncological diagnosis has led to relevant advancements, gaps remain in its practical implementation. For example, the algorithms developed are often optimized for high-tech contexts in developed countries, while their applications in local healthcare systems are limited due to a lack of adaptation to specific conditions. In the case of liver cancer, segmentation and analysis of medical images using artificial intelligence have shown high accuracy in controlled studies. However, these models face challenges when integrated into real clinical workflows, such as the need for high-quality data and interoperability with existing medical systems [10].

Despite these advancements, the adoption of artificial intelligence models in healthcare systems, particularly in developing regions such as Latin America, faces significant barriers, including technological limitations, lack of medical staff training, and uneven infrastructure between urban and rural areas [10].

In Ecuador, hospitals like SOLCA Manabí are exploring innovative technologies to optimize medical care, underscoring the opportunity to integrate artificial intelligence into diagnostic processes, specifically for liver cancer. In this regard, the purpose of this research is to develop an early detection model for liver cancer using abdominal CT scan images. The main contribution of this work is the implementation of an artificial intelligence model designed considering the clinical characteristics of local images, with SOLCA Manabí serving as an initial reference for system adaptation. This model will be validated through functional and performance tests and is intended to serve as a reference for future research and potential applications in regional oncology centers.

This article is structured as follows: Sect. 2 describes the related works used; Sect. 3 presents the methodology; Sect. 4 details the results obtained and includes a critical analysis of them. Finally, Sect. 5 presents the conclusions and future work directions.

2 Related Works

Various studies have explored the use of artificial intelligence to support oncological diagnosis. At Jinan University of Science and Technology, they developed a transfer learning model called VER-Net, which successfully detected lung cancer in computed tomography (CT) scans with an accuracy of 91% [11]. Similarly, at Case Western Reserve University, artificial intelligence was applied to the management of gliomas, improving diagnoses and treatments by combining imaging, genomic, and clinical data. However, this approach faced ethical challenges related to the lack of demographic representation [12].

In another initiative, the University of Calgary, in collaboration with Nanostics Inc., presented ClarityDX, an artificial intelligence platform that achieved a sensitivity of 95% and a specificity of 35% for predicting significant prostate cancer (csPCa), avoiding up to 35% of unnecessary biopsies [13]. In parallel, at the University of Jinan and the Yantai Institute of Science and Technology, the ResUNet model was implemented to segment liver tumors in CT images, using the MSD Task03 Liver dataset. This model achieved a coefficient of 0.98 for detection and 0.87 for segmentation, demonstrating high precision in tumor identification [14].

On the other hand, between Albany Medical College, United States, and Gachon University, South Korea, a CNN-based approach was developed to differentiate between healthy and cancerous liver tissue using TCGA images, achieving a 90% accuracy in validation [15]. At the hospitals in Fujian and Jiangxi, the use of contrast-enhanced ultrasound (CEUS) for early liver cancer detection was analyzed, supporting its effectiveness in leading hospitals, although barriers to its adoption in secondary hospitals were identified [16].

In a similar oncological context, the University of Turkey and other international institutions conducted a comparative analysis of deep learning methods for the early detection and segmentation of lung cancer from CT images. Using pre-trained CNNs such as MobileNetV2, ResNet152V2, InceptionResNetV2, Xception, VGG-19, and InceptionV3, the researchers achieved a detection accuracy of 98.5% with the InceptionResNetV2 model. For tumor segmentation, models such as UNet, SegNet, and InceptionUNet were employed, with UNet achieving the best segmentation score, with a Jaccard index of 95.3% [17].

Another study has explored the use of high-frequency reconstruction kernels in CT to enhance the radiomic characterization of hepatic metastases through deep neural networks. Using a simulation pipeline, 10,000 virtual metastases were generated, demonstrating that these kernels better preserve radiomic information under controlled conditions, which emphasizes their potential for more accurate clinical analysis [18].

At the School of Public Health of Southeast University, glucose-6-phosphate dehydrogenase (G6PD) was identified as a key biomarker due to its overexpression in tumor tissues compared to normal tissues. Using public databases such as TCGA, ICGC, and GEO, and combining bioinformatics analysis with cell experiments, it was demonstrated that G6PD significantly contributes to the development of hepatocellular carcinoma (LIHC). Furthermore, its inhibition reduces tumor cell proliferation, migration, and invasion. This study also integrated machine learning algorithms to predict the prognosis of

LIHC patients, with the Decision Tree C5.0 standing out for its superior classification accuracy [19].

Finally, at the Polytechnic University of Madrid, a systematic review was conducted on the use of statistical methods and machine learning (ML) in cancer research and clinical practice. The analysis revealed that statistical methods and linear ML models were the most commonly used, while nonlinear approaches were less common. Despite the advancements, only a small percentage of the studies showed a low risk of bias, and many did not report data quality assessment procedures. The review also highlighted a shift toward combined approaches of computational biology and data analysis in more recent studies (2021–2023), emphasizing the importance of systematic procedures to ensure the clinical validity of ML-based interventions in the field of cancer [20].

3 Methodology

This study implements the Cross-Industry Standard Process for Data Mining (CRISP-DM) methodology, adapted from [21, 22]. The details are as follows:

3.1 Phase 1. Problem Understanding and Data Collection

Problem Definition. Development of a machine learning model for the early detection of liver cancer.

Image Collection. A dataset consisting of clinical, genomic, and pathological data related to liver cancer, specifically The Cancer Genome Atlas Liver Hepatocellular Carcinoma Collection (TCGA-LIHC), was used.

3.2 Phase 2. Data Preparation

Preprocessing. Advanced image processing techniques were applied, such as image segmentation through body part filtering and pixel normalization before training, to enhance the quality and standardize the collected images, optimizing their use in artificial intelligence models.

3.3 Phase 3. Modeling

Model Development. Design and training of a model using CNN with preprocessed images, applying data augmentation techniques and image scaling.

3.4 Phase 4. Evaluation

Model Validation. The model was evaluated using key metrics such as accuracy, applying an independent test dataset.

4 Results and Discussion

In this section, the results for each phase of CRISP-DM are presented.

4.1 Phase 1. Problem Understanding and Data Collection

The TCGA-LIHC dataset was used, consisting of 125397 images in DICOM format, with a total of 56.38 GB of data. The images covered various modalities, including CT and magnetic resonance (MR). To focus the study on the detection of liver cancer, the images were filtered, excluding those of magnetic resonance and those corresponding to other parts of the body, such as the chest and pelvis, using a metadata file in.csv format (Fig. 1).

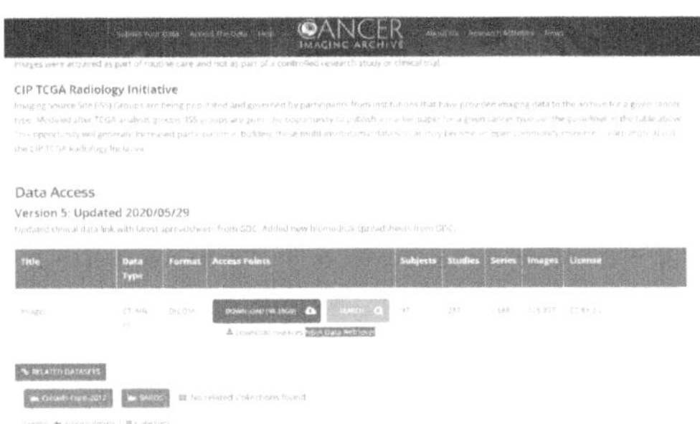

Fig. 1. Image from the cancer imaging archive portal with the TCGA-LIHC dataset.

Additionally, to ensure the suitability of the image dataset for the artificial intelligence model, the MicroDicom software was used to visualize and verify the DICOM images (Fig. 2).

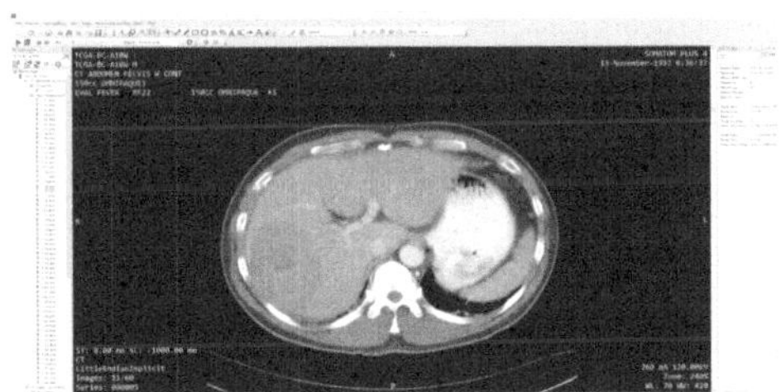

Fig. 2. Image of the MicroDicom Software Image Viewer.

4.2 Phase 2. Data Preparation

In this phase, the images were selected and filtered to train the artificial intelligence model. From the dataset, two main categories were created "with cancer" and "without cancer." For the "with cancer" images, the following filters were applied:

Cancerous. Body Part Examined IN (LIVER) AND Cancer Type IN (Liver Hepatocellular Carcinoma) AND Modality IN (Computed Tomography) (Fig. 3).

Non_Cancerous. Body Part Examined IN (ABDOMEN) AND Cancer Type IN (Non-Cancer) AND Modality IN (Computed Tomography) (Fig. 4).

After filtering, the images were downloaded using the tool s5cmd_2.3.0, which streamlined the process through a download script executed from the terminal.

Once the data was downloaded, the selection of the information to be used proceeded, with the initial dataset containing a total of 161,296 images and a total size of 83.5 GB.

After the download, they ensured that the number of images was balanced between the "with cancer" and "without cancer" categories, adjusting the total number of images to 67,523 per category, resulting in a total of 135046 images, following Table 1 gives a summary of collected data.

Fig. 3. Selection of Data from Portal.Imaging.Datacommons.Cancer.gov with Graph of Patients with Cancer.

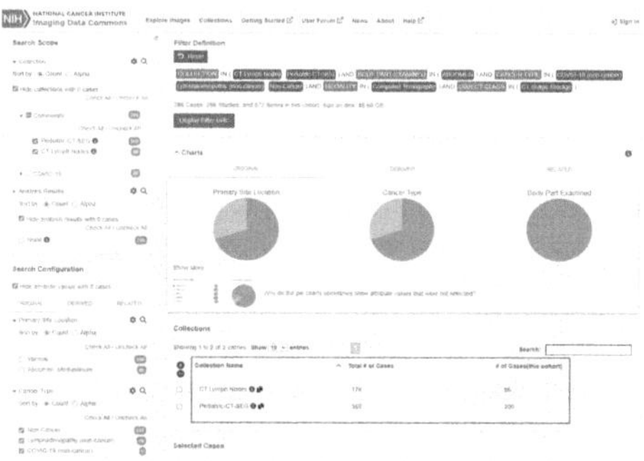

Fig. 4. Selection of Data from Portal.Imaging.Datacommons.Cancer.gov with Graph of Patients without Cancer.

Table 1. Summary of collected data.

Category	Collection	No. of Images	Weight (GB)	Link
Cancerous	TCGA-LIHC	67,523	34.8 GB	Link
Non_Cancerous	Pediatric-CT-SEG	39,175	21.6 GB	Link
	CT Lymph Nodes	54,598	27 GB	

The data was obtained from public sources and preprocessed to ensure compatibility with the analysis.

4.3 Phase 3. Modeling

The CT images were labeled to optimize the classification process and the training of the machine learning model, subsequently converting them into numerical matrices. In Fig. 6, image (a) has a diagnostic label of cancer associated with probability values of 0.00, while image (b) shows a non-cancer label with values of 0.99, demonstrating the probabilistic distribution used in the classification.

For the classification of medical images, CNN was used. The architecture of the network was structured as follows (Fig. 5).

- *Convolutional Layer (Conv2D).* To extract relevant features from the images.
- *MaxPooling Layer.* To reduce the dimensionality of the images and highlight the most important features.
- *Additional Convolutional Layer.* To extract more complex features.
- *Another MaxPooling Layer.* To continue reducing dimensionality.
- *Flatten Layer.* To convert feature matrices into one-dimensional vectors.
- *Dense Layer.* Fully connected neural network layer with 64 neurons and ReLU activation.
- *Output Layer.* With sigmoid activation to classify between "with cancer" and "without cancer."

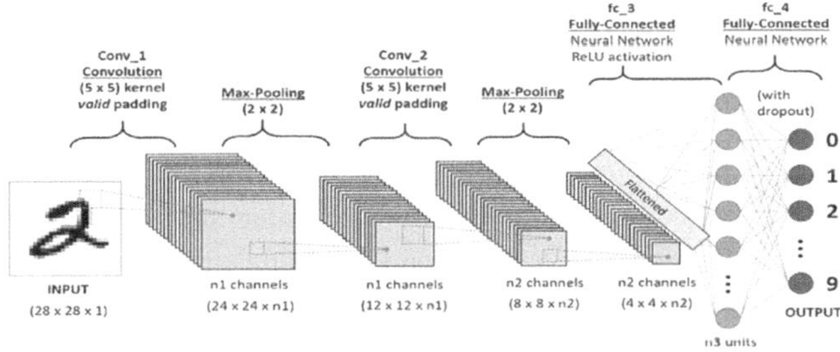

Fig. 5. Visualization of the convolutional neural network architecture, adapted from [23].

During the model training, several techniques were implemented to improve its performance:

- *Image scaling.* Pixel values were normalized between 0 and 1.
- *Data Augmentation.* Random transformations such as rotations, zooms, and horizontal reflections were applied.
- *Image Size.* All images were resized to 224 × 224 pixels.

The model training additionally incorporated L2 regularization techniques (0.001) and a Dropout layer (0.5) to prevent overfitting.

- *Batch size. 32 images per iteration.*
- *Number of epochs. 30.*
- *RAM usage. Approximately 64,361.83 MB.*
- *Optimizer. Adam.*
- *Loss function. Binary_crossentropy.*
- *Evaluation metric. Accuracy.*

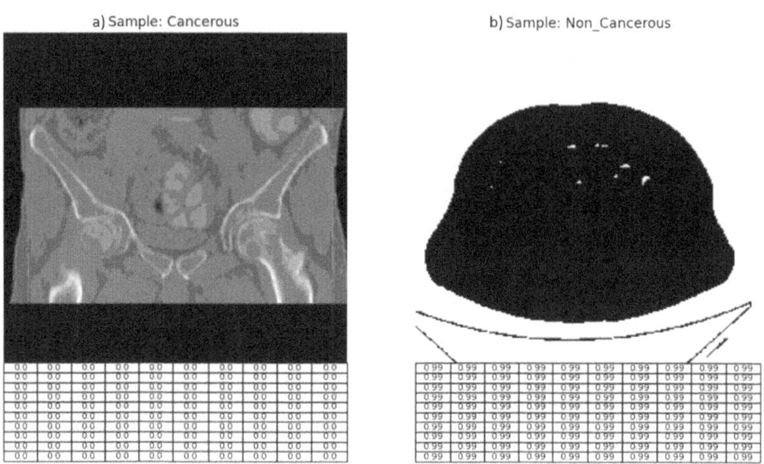

Fig. 6. Sample (a) Cancerous, 0.00 and (b) Non-cancerous, 0.99.

During the model training, a batch size of 32 was used, meaning that 32 images were processed at a time in each iteration before updating the parameters, optimizing the training process and reducing memory usage. The term "epoch" refers to a complete iteration through the training dataset, and in this case, the model passed through all images 30 times to adjust its parameters. For optimization, the Adam (Adaptive Moment Estimation) algorithm was implemented, combining the methods of Adagrad and RMSProp, adjusting the gradients using first- and second-order moments. This optimizer is highly effective for training deep neural networks due to its ability to efficiently adapt to the characteristics of the problem and gradient behavior. Additionally, callbacks such as ModelCheckpoint were used, which saves the model with the best accuracy, and Early Stopping, which stops the training if the loss stops improving.

4.4 Phase 4. Evaluation

The results obtained during the training were as follows:

Accuracy. Progressively increased as the epochs progressed, reaching values close to 0.99 in the last epoch (Fig. 7).

Loss. The loss gradually decreased during training, stabilizing around 0.004 and 0.005 in the last epoch (Fig. 7).

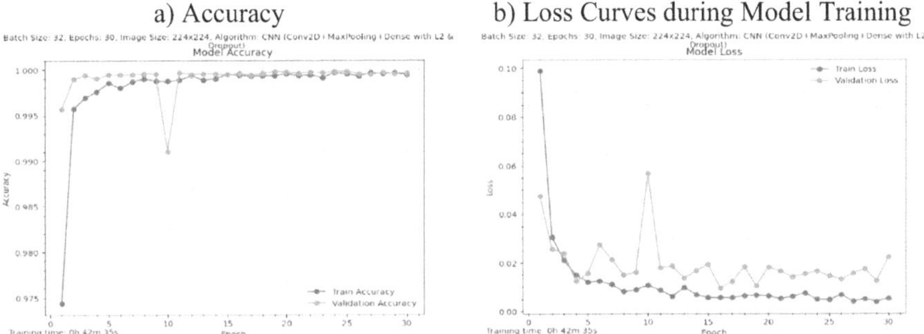

Fig. 7. Sample of the a) Accuracy and b) Loss Curves during Model Training.

The results demonstrate effective model optimization through training, with a progressive improvement in accuracy (99.96% training / 99.95% validation) and a consistent reduction in loss (Table 2). Although temporary overfitting was detected at epoch 10 (a + 0.15 increase in validation loss), the system achieved optimal stability at epoch 29 with minimal variations (Δ accuracy < 0.01%, σ loss < 0.02), demonstrating a balance between adaptability to complex patterns and generalization capability, validating the effectiveness of the parametric tuning process.

Table 2. Summary of accuray and loss data from training.

Epoch	Accuracy	Loss	Val_Accuracy	Val_Loss
1	0,9744	0,0990	0,9957	0,0475
2	0,9957	0,0307	0,9990	0,0257
3	0,9969	0,0210	0,9994	0,0238
4	0,9976	0,0151	0,9990	0,0124
5	0,9985	0,0121	0,9994	0,0156
6	0,9980	0,0124	0,9994	0,0274
7	0,9986	0,0111	0,9994	0,0214
8	0,9990	0,0081	0,9995	0,0150
9	0,9987	0,0089	0,9995	0,0161

(continued)

Table 2. (*continued*)

Epoch	Accuracy	Loss	Val_Accuracy	Val_Loss
10	0,9987	0,0107	0,9910	0,0569
11	0,9988	0,0087	0,9997	0,0179
12	0,9994	0,0062	0,9995	0,0186
13	0,9988	0,0098	0,9995	0,0137
14	0,9990	0,0069	0,9995	0,0167
15	0,9995	0,0057	0,9994	0,0193
16	0,9994	0,0057	0,9996	0,0097
17	0,9993	0,0057	0,9994	0,0123
18	0,9993	0,0065	0,9996	0,0184
19	0,9993	0,0067	0,9998	0,0105
20	0,9995	0,0063	0,9997	0,0182
21	0,9993	0,0052	0,9996	0,0166
22	0,9994	0,0062	0,9997	0,0142
23	0,9991	0,0076	0,9997	0,0154
24	0,9996	0,0049	0,9998	0,0165
25	0,9995	0,0048	0,9998	0,0146
26	0,9993	0,0068	0,9995	0,0132
27	0,9996	0,0041	0,9994	0,0157
28	0,9995	0,0051	0,9997	0,0175
29	**0,9996**	**0,0040**	**0,9995**	**0,0125**
30	0,9994	0,0054	0,9996	0,0222

4.5 Early Prediction Prototype for Liver Cancer

A prototype web interface was implemented to facilitate result visualization and the automatic recording of diagnoses. The solution was developed in Python using TensorFlow GPU for model training, along with libraries such as NumPy for data handling and processing. A specialized module was incorporated to convert DICOM-format images to PNG, ensuring compatibility with the analysis model.

The development followed agile methodologies, allowing the prototype to be adjusted based on feedback from usability testing. Additionally, basic logging and real-time monitoring mechanisms were integrated, enabling event tracking during image processing and early incident detection. The platform prototype interface allows the user to upload images, monitor the training progress, and perform classification by selecting the desired image (Fig. 8).

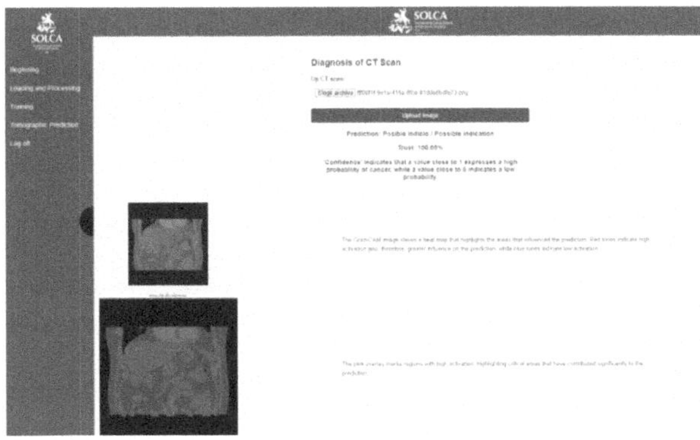

Fig. 8. Web interface prototype for system visualization and operation.

To evaluate the model's interpretability, the Grad-CAM technique was applied. This methodology generated images that combine a heatmap with a pink overlay, accurately highlighting critical areas in the prediction. In the heatmap, red tones indicate high activation and, therefore, greater influence on the prediction, while blue tones represent low activation. The pink overlay specifically emphasizes the regions that have significantly contributed to the outcome. These visual findings confirm the model's capability for early liver cancer detection (Fig. 9).

(a) Pink overlay indicating critical regions

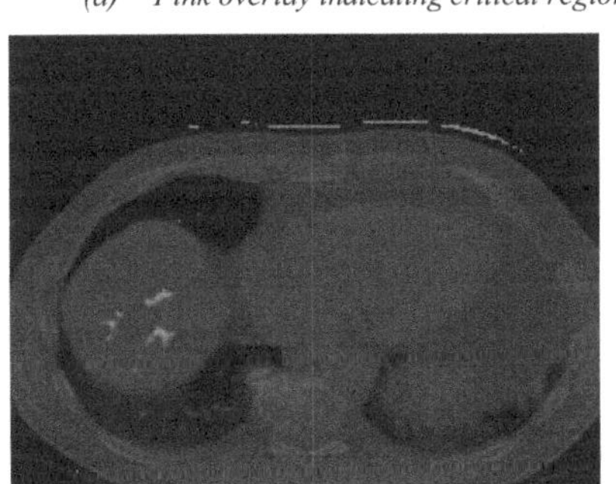

(b) *Heatmap* indicating activation levels

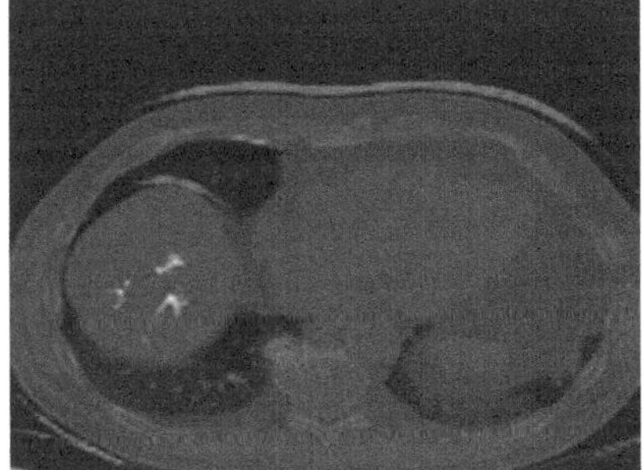

Fig. 9. Sample (a) Pink overlay indicating critical regions and (b) Heatmap indicating activation levels for early detection of hepatic cancer.

The validation is illustrated with a graph showing the distribution of false positives and false negatives in the classification:

Among the 20 images, without cancer, 18 were correctly classified, while 2 were incorrectly identified as cancer (Fig. 10).

Among the 20 images, with cancer, all were correctly classified (20/20) (Fig. 10).

For the manual evaluation of tomography images, the accuracy metric was used to analyze the quality of the model's predictions regarding cancer or non-cancer classification:

$$Overall\,Accuracy = \frac{\mathrm{TP} + \mathrm{TN}}{\mathrm{TP} + TN + FP + FN} \quad (1)$$

where:

TP. True Positives
TN. True Negatives
FP. False Positives
FN. False Negatives

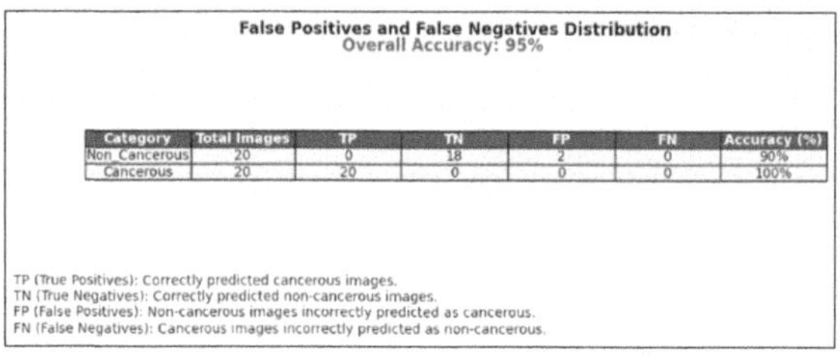

False Positives and False Negatives Distribution
Overall Accuracy: 95%

Category	Total Images	TP	TN	FP	FN	Accuracy (%)
Non_Cancerous	20	0	18	2	0	90%
Cancerous	20	20	0	0	0	100%

TP (True Positives): Correctly predicted cancerous images.
TN (True Negatives): Correctly predicted non-cancerous images.
FP (False Positives): Non-cancerous images incorrectly predicted as cancerous.
FN (False Negatives): Cancerous images incorrectly predicted as non-cancerous.

Fig. 10. Test-derived chart showing FP and FN distribution.

In summary, by correctly classifying at least 38 of the 40 images, making a maximum of 2 errors, an accurate score of 95% was achieved.

4.6 DICOM Image Acquisition, Management, and Validation in the Developed Platform

A repository of thousands of CT scans acquired from 2015 to 2025 at SOLCA Manabí Oncology Hospital was analyzed. From this archive, a cohort of 20 patients suspected of cancer was selected, and their abdominal series were isolated for detailed study. Each CT session could yield up to 150 images; after filtering metadata (e.g., StudyDate, SeriesDescription) and converting DICOMs into 224 $\times$ 224 px PNGs, the platform produced 632 images for validation. Using the CNN and Grad-CAM heatmaps, 491 out of 632 images (77.7%) registered a cancer probability $\geq$ 80%, while 141 (22.3%) fell below that threshold. These findings illustrate the platform's ability to confidently identify high-risk cases, underscoring its promise as an effective screening and diagnostic support tool (Fig. 11).

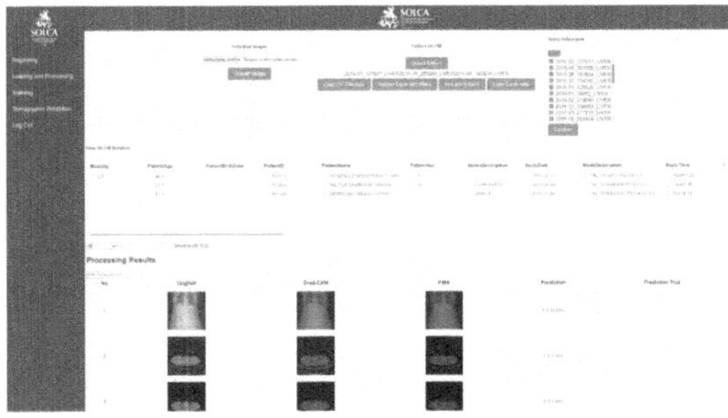

Fig. 11. Web interface prototype validated on SOLCA clinical DICOM datasets for large-scale data management and filtering.

In comparison to previous works, the results obtained in this study align with the achievements made by other researchers in the field of AI-assisted oncology diagnosis. For example, the VER-Net model developed by the University of Jinan Science and Technology achieved 91% accuracy in detecting lung cancer using CT scans, a result comparable to the 95% accuracy reached in this study in classifying liver cancer images [11]. However, this study stands out due to its focus on a specific type of cancer, hepatocellular carcinoma, while the VER-Net approach focused on lung cancer, thus broadening the scope of AI's utility in diagnosing various types of cancer.

Similarly, research from the University of Jinan and the Yantai Institute of Science and Technology, which implemented the ResUNet model for liver tumor segmentation, demonstrated high accuracy in cancer detection, achieving a coefficient of 0.98 [14]. In this study, a differently structured CNN was used but with similar goals, reinforcing the potential of neural networks in improving medical diagnosis through imaging.

On the other hand, the approach used by the University of Calgary and Nanostics Inc. in prostate cancer prediction achieved a sensitivity of 95%, reflecting the ability of AI models not only to detect the presence of cancer but also to avoid unnecessary diagnoses [13]. Although the models developed in this study were not specifically designed to prevent unnecessary biopsies, the high accuracy in classifying "with cancer" and "without cancer" is equally crucial in reducing false negatives, a common challenge in the early detection of oncological diseases.

Related works on the use of artificial intelligence in liver cancer diagnosis also resonate with the results obtained in this study. The combination of high-quality imaging with AI models has proven effective in improving diagnostic accuracy. The comparative analysis of methodologies employed in liver tumor detection and segmentation, such as those conducted by Albany Medical College and Gachon University, has shown that CNN-based approaches perform highly in classifying cancerous tissues [15], reinforcing the effectiveness of CNNs in the context of this study.

Although the results obtained in this study are promising, it is important to consider the challenges presented by [12] The successful implementation of AI models in hospital settings relies on the proper training of medical staff and efficient integration with existing systems. Furthermore, the literature has emphasized the importance of model validation across different datasets and clinical contexts, which remains a key area for continuous improvement of the accuracy and reliability of the system developed in this study.

5 Conclusions

The study achieved 95% accuracy in validation tests for liver cancer detection using convolutional neural networks (CNN), a performance comparable to leading models such as VER-Net (91% accuracy in lung cancer) and ResUNet (Dice coefficient of 0.98). In a real-world validation on SOLCA Manabí data, 77.7% of the 632 test images registered a cancer probability $\geq$ 80%, demonstrating the model's strong confidence in identifying high-risk cases.

Access to images from SOLCA Manabí enabled model tuning to the regional clinical context; however, reliance on a single center dataset requires inclusion of scans from other Ecuadorian oncology hospitals to strengthen and generalize the findings. Since validation assessed only the CNN's standalone performance, ongoing expert oversight will be essential to ensure accurate CT interpretation and adherence to diagnostic protocols.

Future perspectives include the development of hybrid architectures combining CNNs with transformers to improve result interpretability, along with the implementation of advanced segmentation techniques using masks and multi-label classification to optimize the precise delineation of tumor areas. In addition, it is proposed to validate the model in real operational environments through multicenter studies to assess its impact on reducing diagnostic times and unnecessary invasive procedures. These actions would be complemented by specialized medical training programs in artificial intelligence to facilitate their effective implementation in healthcare systems with limited resources, ensuring a smooth transition from the experimental phase to practical clinical applications.

References

1. Shen, Y., Huang, J., Jia, L., Zhang, C., Xu, J.: Bioinformatics and machine learning driven key genes screening for hepatocellular carcinoma. Biochem Biophys Rep. **37**, 101587 (2024). https://doi.org/10.1016/j.bbrep.2023.101587
2. Wu, G., Bajestani, N., Pracha, N., Chen, C., Makary, M.S.: hepatocellular carcinoma surveillance strategies: major guidelines and screening advances. Cancers (Basel). **16**, 3933 (2024). https://doi.org/10.3390/cancers16233933
3. Brasen, C.L., et al.: Machine learning in diagnostic support in medical emergency departments. Sci. Rep. **14**, 17889 (2024). https://doi.org/10.1038/s41598-024-66837-w
4. Hyndman, M.E., et al.: Development of an effective predictive screening tool for prostate cancer using the ClarityDX machine learning platform. npj Digit. Med. 7(1), 1–11 (2024). https://doi.org/10.1038/s41746-024-01167-9
5. Castilho, R.M., Castilho, L.S., Palomares, B.H., Squarize, C.H.: Determinants of chromatin organization in aging and cancer—emerging opportunities for epigenetic therapies and AI technology. Genes (Basel). **15**, 710 (2024). https://doi.org/10.3390/genes15060710
6. Brasen, C.L., et al.: Machine learning in diagnostic support in medical emergency departments. Sci. Rep. 14(1), 1–10 (2024). https://doi.org/10.1038/s41598-024-66837-w
7. Anil, B.C., Gowdru, A.K., Prithviraja, D., Kundur, N.C., Ramadoss, B.: Identifying liver cancer cells using cascaded convolutional neural network and gray level co-occurrence matrix techniques. IAES Int. J. Artif. Intell. (IJ-AI), **13**, 3083–3091 (2024). https://doi.org/10.11591/ijai.v13.i3.pp3083-3091

8. Lumamba, K.D., Wells, G., Naicker, D., Naidoo, T., Steyn, A.J.C., Gwetu, M.: Computer vision applications for the detection or analysis of tuberculosis using digitised human lung tissue images - a systematic review. BMC Med. Imaging **24**, 298 (2024). https://doi.org/10.1186/S12880-024-01443-W/TABLES/4
9. Addissouky, T.A., et al.: Latest advances in hepatocellular carcinoma management and prevention through advanced technologies. Egypt. Liver J. **14**(1), 1–18 (2024). https://doi.org/10.1186/S43066-023-00306-3
10. Arevalo-Herrera, M., et al.: Malaria in selected non-Amazonian countries of Latin America. Acta Trop. **121**, 303–314 (2012). https://doi.org/10.1016/J.ACTATROPICA.2011.06.008
11. Saha, A., Ganie, S.M., Pramanik, P.K.D., Yadav, R.K., Mallik, S., Zhao, Z.: VER-Net: a hybrid transfer learning model for lung cancer detection using CT scan images. BMC Med. Imaging **24**, 120 (2024). https://doi.org/10.1186/s12880-024-01238-z
12. Khalighi, S., Reddy, K., Midya, A., Pandav, K.B., Madabhushi, A., Abedalthagafi, M.: Artificial intelligence in neuro-oncology: advances and challenges in brain tumor diagnosis, prognosis, and precision treatment. NPJ Precis Oncol. **8**, 80 (2024). https://doi.org/10.1038/s41698-024-00575-0
13. Hyndman, M.E., et al.: Development of an effective predictive screening tool for prostate cancer using the ClarityDX machine learning platform. NPJ Digit Med. **7**, 163 (2024). https://doi.org/10.1038/s41746-024-01167-9
14. Muhammad, S., Zhang, J.: Segmentation of liver tumors by Monai and PyTorch in CT images with deep learning techniques. Appl. Sci. (Switzerland). **14**, 5144 (2024). https://doi.org/10.3390/app14125144
15. Asif, A., et al.: Machine learning based diagnostic paradigm in viral and non-viral hepatocellular carcinoma. IEEE Access. **12**, 37557–37571 (2024). https://doi.org/10.1109/ACCESS.2024.3369491
16. Wu, S., Zheng, Y., Wang, L., Liu, W.: Differences in influencing mechanism of clinicians' adoption behavior for liver cancer screening technology between the leading and subordinate hospitals within medical consortiums. BMC Cancer **24**, 514 (2024). https://doi.org/10.1186/s12885-024-12281-y
17. Kalkan, M., Guzel, M.S., Ekinci, F., Akcapinar Sezer, E., Asuroglu, T.: Comparative analysis of deep learning methods on CT images for lung cancer specification. Cancers (Basel). **16**, 3321 (2024). https://doi.org/10.3390/cancers16193321
18. Wiedeman, C., et al.: Simulated deep CT characterization of liver metastases with high-resolution filtered back projection reconstruction. Vis Comput Ind Biomed Art. **7**, 13 (2024). https://doi.org/10.1186/s42492-024-00161-y
19. Li, F., Wang, B., Li, H., Kong, L., Zhu, B.: G6PD and machine learning algorithms as prognostic and diagnostic indicators of liver hepatocellular carcinoma. BMC Cancer **24**, 157 (2024). https://doi.org/10.1186/s12885-024-11887-6
20. Lopez-Perez, L., et al.: Statistical and machine learning methods for cancer research and clinical practice: a systematic review. Biomed. Signal Process. Control **92**, 106067 (2024). https://doi.org/10.1016/j.bspc.2024.106067
21. Andrade-Arenas, L., Rubio-Paucar, I., Yactayo-Arias, C.: Data mining for predictive analysis in gynecology: a focus on cervical health. Int. J. Electr. Comput. Eng. (IJECE). **14**, 2822–2833 (2024). https://doi.org/10.11591/ijece.v14i3.pp2822-2833
22. Rosas-Lara, M., Mendoza-Tello, J.C., Flores, A., Zumba-Acosta, G.: A convolutional neural network-based web prototype to support melanoma skin cancer detection. In: Proceedings - 3rd International Conference on Information Systems and Software Technologies, ICI2ST 2022, pp. 1–7 (2022). https://doi.org/10.1109/ICI2ST57350.2022.00008
23. Karpathy, A.: A comprehensive guide to convolutional neural networks — the ELI5 way. Towards Data Sci. (2017)

Implementation of Convolutional Neural Networks for Object Detection in Robotic Pick-and-Place Processes

Renato Villazón[1], Andrea Pilco[2], Alvaro Javier Prado[3], Viviana Moya[4], Fernando Chicaiza[5], and Juan Pablo Vásconez[6(✉)]

[1] Faculty of Engineering, Universidad Andres Bello, 7500735 Santiago, Chile
r.villaznmartnez@uandresbello.edu

[2] Facultad de Ciencias Técnicas, Universidad Internacional del Ecuador UIDE, Quito 170411, Ecuador
anpilcoat@uide.edu.ec

[3] Departamento de Ingeniería de Sistemas y Computación, Universidad Católica del Norte, 1249004 Antofagasta, Chile
alvaro.prado@ucn.cl

[4] Dep. Automatización y Control Ind., Escuela Politécnica Nacional, Quito, Ecuador
viviana.moya@epn.edu.ec

[5] Centro de Investigación en Mecatrónica y Sistemas Interactivos, Universidad Tecnológica Indoamérica, Ambato 180103, Ecuador
fachicaiza@indoamerica.edu.ec

[6] Energy Transformation Center, Faculty of Engineering, Universidad Andres Bello, 7500971 Santiago, Chile
juan.vasconez@unab.cl

Abstract. Pick-and-place (P&P) tasks in robotic applications have attracted considerable interest for several years. As these are repetitive tasks that are performed continuously and uninterruptedly, any slight improvement in the efficiency of this process results in a significant increase of productivity. In this work, we propose improving a pick-and-place task performed by two Dobot Magician educational manipulator robots alongside a conveyor belt. This system natively incorporates a hardware-based color sensor that allows the robot to identify and classify objects on a conveyor belt, organizing and palletizing them in specific columns according to their color characteristics. However, the robot spends time picking up the objects, placing them on the sensor, and then beginning palletization. In this work, we propose using the Faster R-CNN object detection model with ResNet-50 for feature extraction as an external and independent vision system to streamline and reduce the time losses associated with the hardware-based color sensor tasks. The implemented model achieved a mean Average Precision (mAP) of 68.0% during validation and 65.32% in real-world operation. The system accurately detects all key components involved in the task, including robotic arms, end effectors, the conveyor belt, the color sensor, and the colored blocks (red, green, and blue). When compared to the hardware-based color sensor method, the proposed approach reduced the total processing time from 249.31 s to 196.65 s, representing an improvement

T. Guarda et al. (Eds.): ARTIIS 2025, CCIS 2789, pp. 96–110, 2026.
https://doi.org/10.1007/978-3-032-16758-3_8

of 52.66 s, or approximately 21.12% in overall efficiency. This demonstrates the potential and promising results of using deep learning models in pick-and-place-related applications.

Keywords: Object Detection · Convolutional Neural Networks · Robotic manipulator · Pick-and-Place · Conveyor belt · Task efficiency

1 Introduction

Manipulator robots have played a pivotal role in transforming industry and the workforce by enhancing productivity and improving safety in environments that involve heavy, hazardous, or repetitive tasks [5,16,28]. They can work faster and more efficiently than humans and can perform dangerous or monotonous tasks. Robotic arms perform various tasks in collaboration with humans, especially in industrial settings [27]. Collaborative robotics refers not only to human-robot interaction, but also applies when two or more robots work simultaneously and coordinate to perform joint tasks [27]. This collaboration occurs in activities such as welding, part assembly, packaging, handling hazardous materials, quality inspection, assisted surgeries, and logistics [25].

In the logistics sector, activities such as product selection, sorting, palletizing, and packaging—collectively known as pick-and-place operations—are critical yet often lack ergonomic design across the production chain. These repetitive, high-frequency tasks can lead to physical and mental strain on workers, driving the demand for automation solutions to enhance worker well-being and operational efficiency. The development of faster and more efficient sensors is pivotal in optimizing these processes, as even minor reductions in task duration can significantly boost overall efficiency due to the repetitive, in-line nature of P&P operations. For instance, shaving seconds off each cycle in a high-volume production line can lead to substantial time and cost savings over time. Robotic arms, widely adopted for P&P tasks, rely on object detection and visual features such as shape, size, weight, color, and spatial position to manipulate objects effectively [23]. Once an object's visual characteristics are processed, the robotic system can categorize and handle it accordingly.

To detect objects in robotic systems, a combination of sensors is often used, including infrared sensors [8], color sensors [19], load cells [22], and proximity sensors [21]. However, recent trends replace this hardware with a camera and computer vision techniques to achieve visual object recognition [11]. Visual attribute of color can be detected using various methods and techniques such as image processing algorithms [7,17], machine learning (ML) [3,13], and deep learning (DL) [20]. In this work, we propose an external vision system to improve the robotic pick and place tasks based on object color detection. To this end, a Faster Region-Based Convolutional Neural Network (Faster R-CNN) with a Residual Network of 50 layers (ResNet-50) is used for this task. In the following section, we present a brief state-of-the-art related to techniques used for object detection in vision-based robotic systems.

1.1 State of the Art

Object detection is one of the popular applications of computer vision (CV), which comprises the process of finding and classifying objects with common features or relationships [9,12]. With the advancement of artificial intelligence (AI), particularly in the fields of computer vision (CV), machine learning (ML), and deep learning (DL), several authors have applied numerous techniques for color detection [26]. The study in [24] developed CV techniques for an object classification and collection system using a robotic arm controlled by color-based image recognition. A Dobot Magician robotic arm was used. Color segmentation was performed using the Hue, Saturation, and Value (HSV) color space. Experimental results demonstrated that the system correctly classified three-color objects into random sequences, achieving 100% accuracy in ten consecutive tests. Similarly, the study in [7] proposed an image processing system capable of real-time detection of red, blue, and yellow colors, as well as the identification of object shapes such as triangles, squares, and rectangles. The HSV color space and a median filter were used for color detection. For shape recognition, a contour detection technique based on the modified boundary fill method was used, followed by the Douglas-Peucker algorithm to extract the geometric form from the identified contours. The system then used a robotic arm to automatically sort the objects based on the recognized features. In [2], an automated system was presented, focused on improving efficiency, precision, and productivity in industrial environments. The system enabled the identification and classification of objects based on their color, highlighting its potential to reduce the need for human intervention in repetitive tasks and streamline material handling processes.

Convolutional neural networks (CNN) stand for one of the most representative neural networks in the field of deep learning, achieving numerous advances in object detection [4]. For object color recognition in robotic systems, CNNs can be used with sundry results. In [18], a 6-Degree-of-Freedom (DOF) Ufactory Lite 6 industrial robot was used with a camera installed on the effector arm, and a CNN was used for color detection between red, green, and blue, achieving an accuracy of 92%. Furthermore, with the integration of the You Only Look Once (YOLO) algorithm, the study in [20] employed YOLOv5s for real-time color recognition and offers the flexibility of automatic operation and remote control. The system detected three ball colors: red, white, and yellow. Once the color was detected, a 3DoF arm picked up the ball and placed it in the corresponding color position. The model achieved an accuracy of 87%. The study [1] designed a framework composed by an intelligent robotic camera. Pre-trained deep learning models, Single Shot MultiBox Detector (SSD) and YOLO, were used for object detection and localization. Furthermore, the detection models were combined with different tracking algorithms. The detection models achieved a maximum true detection rate of 90% to 93%. To extract visual features of an object, improvements in CNNs have also been implemented. One of them is the Faster Region-based Convolutional Neural Network (Faster R-CNN). The study [26] implemented a system where a robot was capable of real-time recognizing the visual attributes of objects (shape, size, and color) and perform the collection of an object while operating a robotic arm. The authors created their dataset of 6,558 images of monochromatic objects with three colors and five shapes on a white background. For color detection, it was used HSV, whereas for object detection, it was used the YOLOv4 model. The physical prototype implemented on a Raspberry Pi 4B achieved 80.7% accuracy in shape recognition and 81.07% in color recognition. This work highlights the combination of implementing image processing and a machine learning model for the detection of objects and their visual characteristics.

The aforementioned methods have mostly focused on traditional image processing techniques, which are widely used in object detection due to their simplicity and low computational cost. However, these approaches present several limitations. They are often sensitive to environmental conditions, variations in viewing angles, and background clutter, all of which can significantly affect the system's accuracy and robustness [29]. In response to these limitations, the use of DL are a potential solution for a high-performance vision system. These models can learn from data, extract relevant features, and adapt to different contexts, thereby improving accuracy in object detection.

1.2 Main Contributions

This study presents a novel approach to enhancing the efficiency of pick-and-place (P&P) tasks by integrating a deep learning-based vision system to overcome the limitations of the native hardware-based color sensor of this system. Specifically, we propose a system using two Dobot Magician educational manipulator robots operating alongside a conveyor belt, where objects are picked, identified by color, and palletized. The conventional process, reliant on a hardware-based color sensor, incurs time losses due to sequential object handling and sensing. To address this, we implement a Faster Region-Based Convolutional Neural Network (Faster R-CNN) with ResNet-50 for feature extraction as an external vision system, enabling real-time object detection and color classification while objects are in motion on the conveyor belt. The key contributions of this work include:

- Development of an RGB image dataset comprising red, green, and blue blocks, derived from process videos captured from multiple angles of the two Dobot Magician educational manipulator robots with the conveyor belt.
- Implementation of the high-performance object detection algorithm Faster R-CNN with ResNet-50 feature extraction (backbone), achieving a mean Average Precision (mAP) of 68.0% during validation and 65.32% in real-world operation.
- Integration of the object detection approach with the two Dobot Magician educational manipulator robots and conveyor belt setup. This eliminates the need for the native hardware-based color sensor and reduces the total processing time by 21.12% (from 249.31 s to 196.65 s), thereby demonstrating significant improvements in efficiency for repetitive, in-line P&P tasks.

The proposed approach not only streamlines the P&P process but also highlights the potential of deep learning to enhance productivity in automated manipulator robotic systems.

2 Materials and Methods

The proposed methodology for enhancing the pick-and-place (P&P) process is illustrated in Fig. 1, which outlines the system's architecture and workflow. This figure compares the traditional method, where a robotic arm picks up a block, places it on a conveyor for travel, and a second arm transfers it to a hardware-based color sensor for identification before palletizing. The proposed approach integrates a Faster R-CNN with ResNet-50 for real-time object detection and feature extraction, allowing for streamlined detection while the object is in motion on the conveyor belt, which allows for increasing process efficiency.

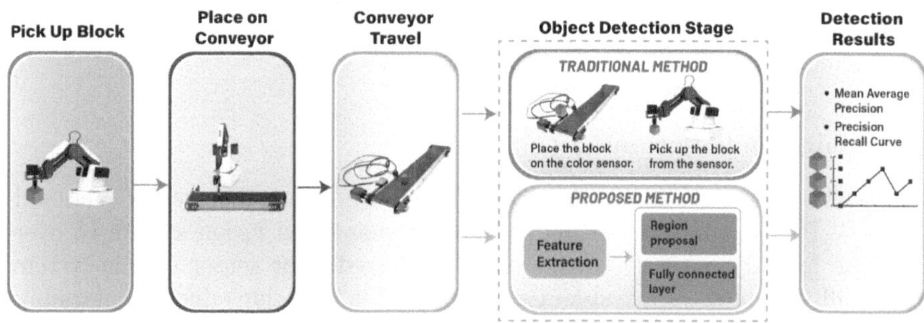

Fig. 1. Methodology and workflow of the proposed pick-and-place robotic system with traditional and the proposed approach.

2.1 Pick-and-Place Robotic System

The pick-and-place robotic system is composed of two Dobot Magician educational manipulator robots operating in tandem with a conveyor belt. In this setup, disordered blocks are sequentially placed onto the conveyor belt, where the first robot picks up each block and positions it on a hardware-based color sensor. This sensor, while effective, introduces a delay as it processes and identifies the block's color. Subsequently, the second robot retrieves the block and palletizes it, organizing and grouping the blocks into columns based on their color. To enhance this process, we propose an external RGB camera system to detect the robots, the conveyor belt, and the colored blocks (red, green, and blue) in real time. This approach eliminates the reliance on the hardware-based color sensor, significantly reducing the time spent on color recognition and optimizing the overall palletizing efficiency. The complete setup of the system is illustrated in Fig. 2.

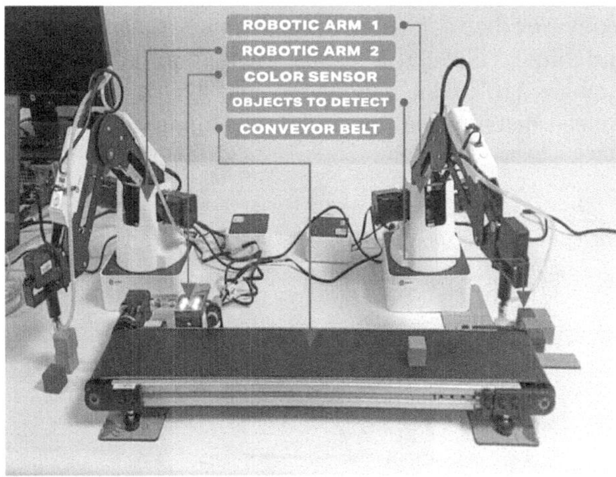

Fig. 2. Pick-and-place robotic System - Dobot Magician educational arms with conveyor belt.

2.2 Object Detection Faster R-CNN and ResNet-50

To detect and classify blocks by color, a deep learning-based object detection and feature extraction system was implemented. In the proposed methodology, a camera connected to the computer running the algorithm captures images of the blocks as they move along the conveyor belt. The model—built on ResNet-50 and Faster R-CNN—processes each image in real time on the operator's workstation. It classifies each block into one of three color categories: green, red, or blue. The model was trained using a custom dataset, which we explains below.

Dataset Acquisition: To generate the dataset for this study, images were extracted from recordings of a traditional pick-and-place process in operation. Data acquisition was performed using a Samsung A71 smartphone mounted on a tripod, ensuring stable and consistent capture from an angle that allowed us to detect the two robotic arms and the conveyor belt process. Three complete traditional P&P processes were recorded in an initial 4K resolution. These videos were subsequently converted into image sequences using a custom script designed to extract 3 frames per second, resulting in approximately 500 high-quality images per video. With a total of three videos, this yielded a dataset of 1500 images, all downscaled to a standardized resolution of 800×600 pixels and aligned in the same orientation, providing a robust foundation for subsequent analysis and model training.

Data Labeling: A dataset of 1500 images was collected and manually labeled using MATLAB's Image Labeler tool to support the Faster R-CNN object detection model. The labeled categories, illustrated in Fig. 3, include the robot arm, end effector, conveyor belt, hardware-based color sensor, and colored blocks (green, red, and blue). The dataset was divided into 1200 images (80%) for training, 150 images (10%) for validation, and 150 images (10%) for testing, ensuring a balanced distribution for model development and evaluation.

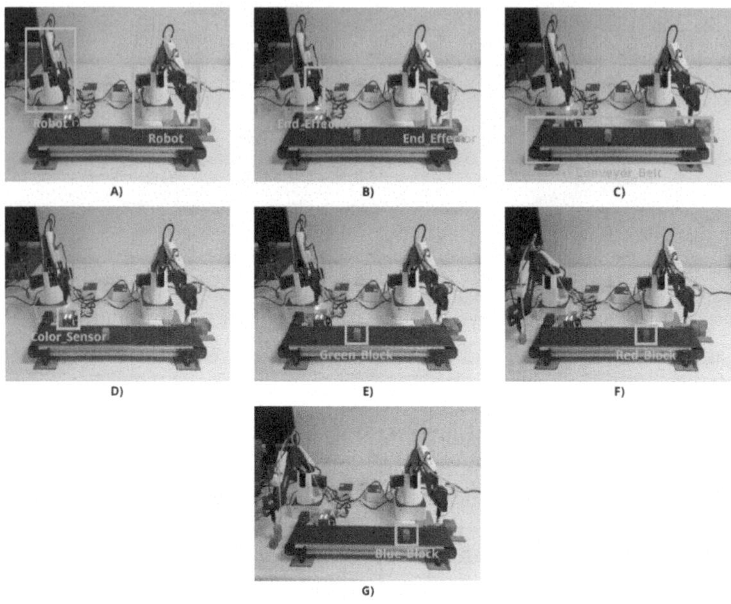

Fig. 3. Labeled Dataset categories for the Faster R-CNN object detection method. a) Robot arm, b) Robot end effector, c) Conveyor belt, d) Hardware-based color sensor, e) green block, f) red block, g) blue block. (Color figure online)

Faster R-CNN and ResNet-50 Arquitecture: In this study, the Faster R-CNN architecture was implemented, with ResNet-50 acting as the feature extractor (backbone) for the input images. The structure of the model used in this research is illustrated in Fig. 4. The Faster R-CNN architecture consists of three stages. First, the deep convolutional network ResNet-50, which performs convolutional operations on the input. ResNet is a 50-layer deep neural network composed of convolutional layers and four residual blocks [14]. As a feature extractor, ResNet-50 is used without its final classification layer, leveraging intermediate outputs as feature vectors containing visual information, forming the backbone of the detection pipeline. In the second stage, the extracted feature maps are passed to a Region Proposal Network (RPN), which generates candidate regions (object proposals) by sliding over the feature map using anchors of different sizes and aspect ratios. These proposed regions are refined by a Region of Interest (RoI) Align module, which standardizes their size to enable uniform processing [15]. In the third stage, each region passes through fully connected layers that perform object classification (including the background class) and bounding box regression, generating a final output of a list of detected objects with their respective classes, coordinates, and confidence levels.

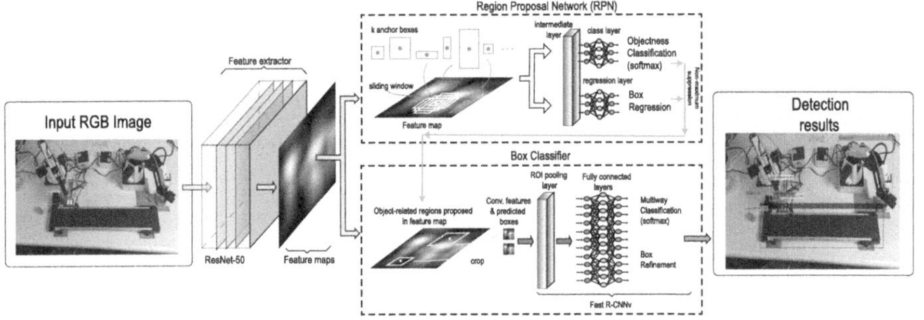

Fig. 4. Architecture of the Faster R-CNN model.

Training Procedure: Once the datasets were correctly defined and labeled, a training environment was implemented. The training environment utilized a computer equipped with an AMD Ryzen processor, 32 GB of RAM, and an NVIDIA GeForce RTX 4060 graphics card.

In this research, the Faster R-CNN model was trained in MATLAB using the trainFasterRCNNObjectDetector function, which requires three inputs: the datastore (ds), the layer graph (lgraph), and the training options. The input ds contains the images along with their corresponding class labels and bounding box annotations. The input lgraph is the layer graph in which ResNet-50 was selected as the base network and customized for object detection through the following steps:

1. The original classification fully connected layers of ResNet-50 for 1000 categories were removed.
2. New classification layers were added, adjusted for the proposed 7 target classes.
3. Specific layers for Region of Interest (ROI) handling were integrated, such as the ROI Max Pooling layer and the ROI Input layer.
4. All layers were connected to enable object classification and bounding box prediction.

The training configuration parameters defined using the training options function are presented in Table 1. The hyperparameters were selected through an iterative trial-and-error process, guided by domain knowledge and preliminary testing. Adjustments were made progressively, evaluating the impact of each change on the model's behavior, such as training consistency, prediction accuracy, and general responsiveness.

Table 1. Training parameters

Parameter	Value
Dataset	1500 images
Model Size	Faster R-CNN
Epochs	10
	12
Optimizer	Stochastic Gradient Descent with Momentum (SGDM)
	Adaptive Moment Estimation (Adam)
	Root Mean Squared Propagation (RMSprop)
Batch Size	10
Number of Classes	7
Learning Rate	0.001
	0.005
	0.0001

Performance Metrics: This section presents the evaluation metrics used to assess the performance of the Faster R-CNN object detection model with a ResNet-50 backbone, designed to detect elements involved in the pick-and-place task, such as robotic arms, end effectors, conveyor belt, color blocks, and a hardware-based color sensor. Two metrics were employed: the precision-recall (PR) curve and the mean average precision (mAP). The PR curve illustrates the trade-off between precision and recall across different threshold settings for each detected class [6], making it suitable for object detection tasks with imbalanced datasets, where true positives are significantly fewer than true negatives. The mAP summarizes performance across all classes and thresholds by averaging the Average Precision (AP) values for each class. The formula for AP is provided in Eq. (1), and the computation of mAP is given in Eq. (2) [10].

$$AP = \sum_{n} (R_n - R_{n-1}) P_n \tag{1}$$

where P_n and R_n represent the precision and recall at the n-th threshold, respectively.

$$mAP = \frac{1}{N} \sum_{i=1}^{N} AP_i \tag{2}$$

where N is the number of classes.

3 Results

This section presents the validation results, testing outcomes, and performance improvements of the pick-and-place process achieved using the proposed Faster R-CNN method.

Validation Results: To optimize the model during training, a validation dataset consisting of 150 images was employed. Table 2 summarizes the configurations and performance metrics for each of the seven tests conducted, where variations were made to the number of epochs, learning rate, and optimization algorithm. The best performance was achieved in Test 7, which utilized 12 epochs, a learning rate of 0.0001, and the Adam optimizer, resulting in a mean Average Precision (mAP) of 68%. The Precision–Recall (PR) curves corresponding to this configuration are shown in Fig. 5, detailing the model's performance across the seven classes involved in the pick-and-place task: End Effector, Robot, Red Block, Blue Block, Green Block, Hardware-based Color Sensor, and Conveyor Belt.

Table 2. Validation results.

Test	Epochs	Learning Rate	Optimizer	mAP
1	8	0.001	SGDM	24%
2	8	0.001	RMSprop	55%
3	8	0.001	Adam	20%
4	8	0.005	SGDM	27%
5	8	0.005	RMSprop	35%
6	8	0.005	Adam	30%
7	12	0.0001	Adam	68%

Testing Results: Figure 6 displays the Precision–Recall (PR) curves obtained under two different testing scenarios. In Fig. 6a, the Average Precision (AP) per class is shown for a test conducted under *constant lighting conditions and a fixed camera position*, with the addition of a *slight angular variation.* Although the environment remained mostly stable, certain objects were not consistently detected in every frame. This inconsistency is not critical for the objectives of this research, as the system's primary requirement is the **accurate identification of block colors at the moment of pickup**. However, the angular shift in the camera's perspective adversely affected the detection accuracy of several components, leading to a **reduced mean Average Precision (mAP) of 55.23%**. In contrast, Fig. 6b shows results from a scenario where a *frontal and stable camera perspective* was maintained. Under these conditions, the object detection performance improved significantly. The classes with the highest AP values

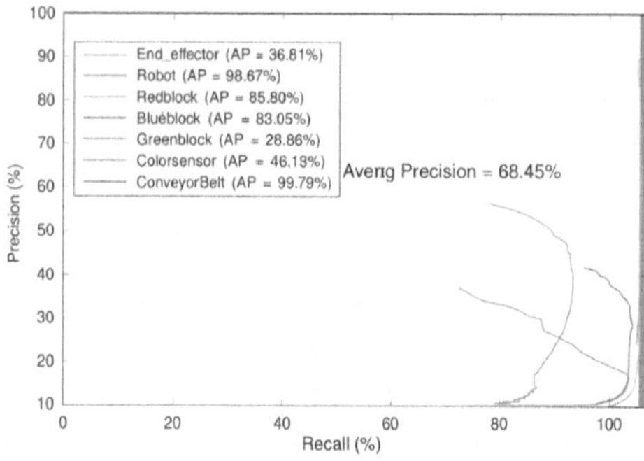

Fig. 5. Validation results. PR Curve for Test 7 – mAP 68%.

were **Conveyor Belt (99.77%)**, **Red Block (86.27%)**, and **Blue Block (82.30%)**. The overall **mAP** across the seven evaluated classes was **65.32%**. Finally, Fig. 7 presents an example illustrating the practical performance of the trained model, as obtained during the training and validation phases.

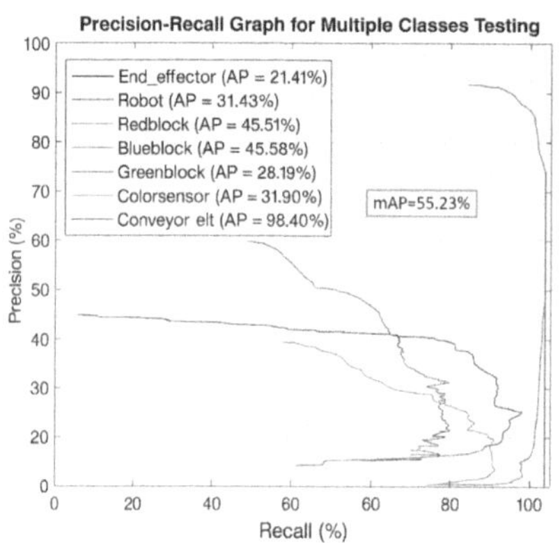

(a) Test results: mAP 55.23%. Slight angular variation in camera position.

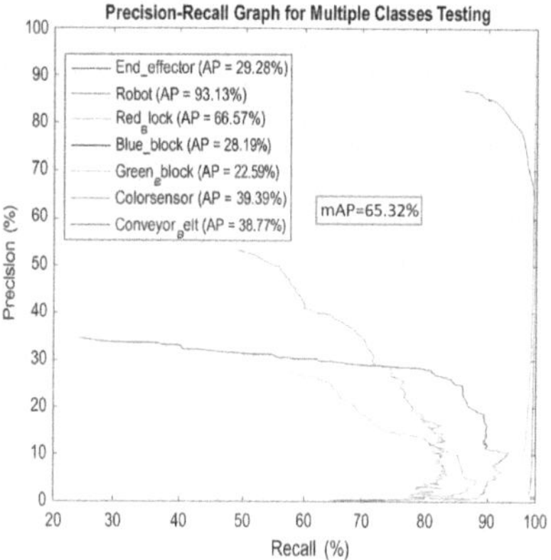

(b) Test results: mAP 65.32%. Stable frontal camera perspective.

Fig. 6. Comparison of precision–recall curves under two test configurations during the testing procedure. a) Slight angular variation in camera position. b) Stable frontal camera perspective.

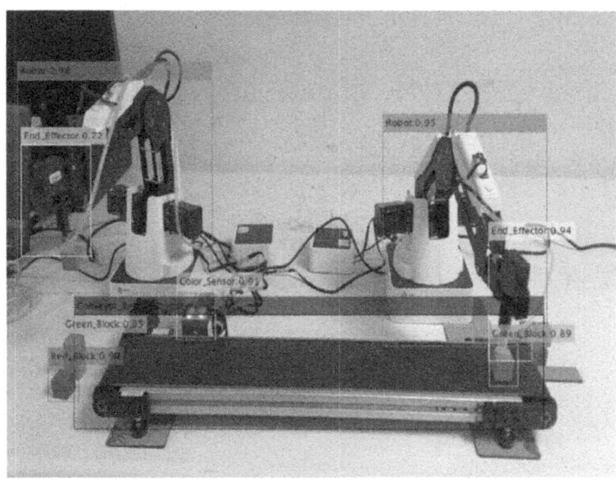

Fig. 7. Object detection results for Faster R-CNN with ResNet-50 for the pick-and-place process.

Pick-and-Place Performing Results: Table 3 provides a step-by-step breakdown of the pick-and-place process, detailing the time consumed for each step in seconds (s). The process begins with the robotic arm picking up the object and placing it onto the conveyor belt (*Pick & Place on Conveyor*). The object then moves along the belt (*Conveyor Travel*), followed by the *Place on Sensor* step. In the traditional method, this step requires the robotic arm positioned at the opposite end of the belt to pick up the object, place it onto a hardware-based color sensor, wait for color detection, and finally execute the appropriate palletizing action based on the identified color. In contrast, the proposed method eliminates the *Place on Sensor* step by employing a ResNet-50 backbone with a Faster R-CNN model for real-time object detection while the object is still in motion on the conveyor belt. This enhancement streamlines the process and reduces unnecessary handling. A total of nine tests were conducted using nine colored blocks, and the time taken for each step was recorded. The traditional process required a total of **249.31** s, whereas the proposed method completed the same task in only **196.65** s, resulting in a time reduction of approximately **21.12%**. This demonstrates the increased efficiency and practicality of the proposed system.

Table 3. Processing Times per Block: Traditional vs. Proposed Method.

Block	Block Pick & Place on Conveyor	Conveyor Travel	Place on Sensor		Palletizing Action
			Traditional	Proposed	
1	7.10	9.22	6.79	0.00	5.01
2	7.05	9.99	5.20	0.00	5.00
3	7.21	9.86	5.82	0.00	5.00
4	7.12	9.85	5.48	0.00	5.00
5	7.18	9.89	5.45	0.00	5.00
6	7.06	9.71	6.12	0.00	5.00
7	7.09	9.34	6.35	0.00	5.00
8	7.11	9.83	5.66	0.00	5.00
9	7.14	9.89	5.79	0.00	5.00
Total time (s)	**64.06**	**87.58**	**52.66**	**0.00**	**45.01**
Total processing time (9 blocks)					
Traditional process				**249.31** s	
Proposed process				**196.65** s	

4 Conclusions

This work demonstrated the effectiveness of a deep learning-based vision system, employing Faster R-CNN with a ResNet-50 backbone, to optimize the pick-and-place (P&P) process in alignment with the Industry 5.0 paradigm of human-centered automation. By integrating real-time object detection, the proposed system eliminates the need for a hardware-based color sensor, allowing for seamless identification of red, green, and blue blocks while in motion on the conveyor belt. The object detection model reliably identified all key components of the P&P system—including robotic arms, end effectors, the conveyor belt, and colored blocks—achieving a mean Average Precision (mAP) of **68.0%** during validation and **65.32%** under real-world conditions. In addition to detection performance, the proposed approach significantly improved operational efficiency by reducing the total P&P cycle time by **21.12%**, from **249.31 s** using the traditional hardware-based method to **196.65 s** with the vision-based system. This gain in efficiency results from removing the *Place on Sensor* step, streamlining the workflow and showcasing the potential of computer vision to enhance repetitive industrial tasks. By decreasing processing time and improving system flexibility, the proposed method supports more scalable, adaptable, and efficient P&P operations—contributing to the broader adoption of intelligent automation in Industry 5.0 environments.

Future work will explore further optimization of the detection model under variable environmental conditions and the integration of natural language interfaces to enrich human-robot interaction, as demonstrated in related studies.

Acknowledgments. This work has been supported by ANID (National Research and Development Agency of Chile) under Fondecyt Iniciación 2024 Grant 11240105 and Grant 11230962.

References

1. Ahmed, I., Din, S., Jeon, G., Piccialli, F., Fortino, G.: Towards collaborative robotics in top view surveillance: a framework for multiple object tracking by detection using deep learning. IEEE/CAA J. Automatica Sinica **8**(7), 1253–1270 (2021). https://doi.org/10.1109/JAS.2020.1003453
2. Ambatkar, D.: AI based robotic arm for color sorting object. Int. J. Sci. Res. Eng. Manage. **09**, 1–9 (2025). https://doi.org/10.55041/IJSREM46455
3. Awotunde, J.B., Misra, S., Obagwu, D., Florez, H.: Multiple colour detection of RGB images using machine learning algorithm. In: International Conference on Applied Informatics, pp. 60–74. Springer, Cham (2022)
4. Bai, Q., Li, S., Yang, J., Song, Q., Li, Z., Zhang, X.: Object detection recognition and robot grasping based on machine learning: a survey. IEEE Access **8**, 181855–181879 (2020). https://doi.org/10.1109/ACCESS.2020.3028740
5. Chico, A., et al.: Hand gesture recognition and tracking control for a virtual UR5 robot manipulator. In: 2021 IEEE Fifth Ecuador Technical Chapters Meeting (ETCM), pp. 1–6. IEEE (2021)
6. Cook, J., Ramadas, V.: When to consult precision-recall curves. Stand Genomic Sci. **20**(1), 131–148 (2020)
7. Fernandes, L., Shivakumar, B.: Identification and sorting of objects based on shape and colour using robotic arm. In: 2020 Fourth International Conference on Inventive Systems and Control (ICISC), pp. 866–871 (2020). https://doi.org/10.1109/ICISC47916.2020.9171196
8. Gao, S., Zhang, Z., Zhao, Z., Jamali, M.M.: Vision and infra-red sensor based fire fighting robot. In: 2018 IEEE 61st International Midwest Symposium on Circuits and Systems (MWSCAS), pp. 873–876. IEEE (2018)
9. García Cadena, A.A., Menéndez Granizo, O.A., Córdova, E.P., Prado Romo, A.J.: Clasificación de calidad de manzana para monitoreo de cosechabilidad utilizando visión por computador y algoritmos de aprendizaje profundo. Ingeniare. Revista chilena de ingeniería **31** (2023)
10. Hirsch, T., Hofer, B.: The map metric in information retrieval fault localization. In: 2023 38th IEEE/ACM International Conference on Automated Software Engineering (ASE), pp. 1480–1491. IEEE (2023)
11. Intisar, M., Khan, M., Islam, M., Masud, M.: Computer vision based robotic arm controlled using interactive GUI. Intell. Autom. Soft Comput. **27**, 533–550 (2021). https://doi.org/10.32604/iasc.2021.015482
12. Kaymak, C., Ucar, A.: Implementation of object detection and recognition algorithms on a robotic arm platform using Raspberry Pi. In: 2018 International Conference on Artificial Intelligence and Data Processing (IDAP), pp. 1–8 (2018). https://doi.org/10.1109/IDAP.2018.8620916
13. Kiruba, R., Sneha, V., Anuragha, S., Vardhini, S.K., Vismaya, V.: Object color identification and classification using CNN algorithm and machine learning technique. In: 2024 4th International Conference on Pervasive Computing and Social Networking (ICPCSN), pp. 18–24 (2024). https://doi.org/10.1109/ICPCSN62568.2024.00011

14. Li, B., Lima, D.: Facial expression recognition via resnet-50. Int. J. Cogn. Comput. Eng. **2** (2021). https://doi.org/10.1016/j.ijcce.2021.02.002
15. Maity, M., Banerjee, S., Sinha Chaudhuri, S.: Faster R-CNN and yolo based vehicle detection: a survey. In: 2021 5th International Conference on Computing Methodologies and Communication (ICCMC), pp. 1442–1447 (2021). https://doi.org/10.1109/ICCMC51019.2021.9418274
16. Moya, V., Maldonado, M., Vásconez, J.P., Abedrabbo, F., Pozo-Espin, D., Moya, M.: Automated assembly line with 2D cartesian robot and conveyor belt. Int. J. Technol. **16**(3), 914–932 (2025)
17. Noman, A., Eva, A., Yeahyea, T., Khan, R.: Computer vision-based robotic arm for object color, shape, and size detection. J. Robot. Control (JRC) **3**, 180–186 (2022). https://doi.org/10.18196/jrc.v3i2.13906
18. Ong, Z.C., Ho, K.H., Chua, W.S.: Towards industry 4.0: color-based object sorting using a robot arm and real-time object detection. Industr. Manage. Adv. **1**(1) (2023)
19. Panie, G.I.E., Mutiara, A.B.: Development of robotic arm for color based goods sorter in factory using tcs3200 sensor with a web-based monitoring system. In: 2018 Third International Conference on Informatics and Computing (ICIC), pp. 1–6. IEEE (2018)
20. Peña, S., Moreano, D., Buele, F., Moya, V., Pilco, A., Quito, A.: Color classification using a 3-DoF robotic arm based on the yolov5 model. In: 2024 IEEE Eighth Ecuador Technical Chapters Meeting (ETCM), pp. 1–6 (2024). https://doi.org/10.1109/ETCM63562.2024.10746227
21. Popov, D., Klimchik, A., Mavridis, N.: Collision detection, localization & classification for industrial robots with joint torque sensors. In: 2017 26th IEEE International Symposium on Robot and Human Interactive Communication (RO-MAN), pp. 838–843. IEEE (2017)
22. Prewthaisong, K.: Automatic weight classifying machine of objects with load cell. Adv. Mater. Res. **945**, 1565–1568 (2014)
23. Shaikat, A., Akter, S., Salma, U.: Computer vision based industrial robotic arm for sorting objects by color and height. J. Eng. Advancements **01**, 116–122 (2020). https://doi.org/10.38032/jea.2020.04.002
24. Sidehabi, S., Azis, M., Asbar, M.: Development of a color-based image recognition system for robotic sorting and picking. INTEK: Jurnal Penelitian **11** (2024). https://doi.org/10.31963/intek.v11i2.5009
25. Surati, S., Hedaoo, S., Rotti, T., Ahuja, V., Patel, N.: Pick and place robotic arm: a review paper. Int. Res. J. Eng. Technol **8**(2), 2121–2129 (2021)
26. Titu, M.F., Haque, S., Islam, R., Hossain, A., Qayum, M., Khan, R.: Experiments with cooperative robots that can detect object's shape, color and size to perform tasks in industrial workplaces. Int. J. Intell. Robot. Appl. **8**, 1–14 (2023). https://doi.org/10.1007/s41315-023-00305-y
27. Vasconez, J.P., Kantor, G.A., Cheein, F.A.A.: Human-robot interaction in agriculture: a survey and current challenges. Biosys. Eng. **179**, 35–48 (2019)
28. Vásconez, J.P., et al.: Joint angle estimation for an industrial manipulator robot via convolutional object detection and k-means clustering. In: International Conference on Advanced Research in Technologies, Information, Innovation and Sustainability, pp. 290–305. Springer, Cham (2024)
29. Ward, I.R., Laga, H., Bennamoun, M.: RGB-D image-based object detection: from traditional methods to deep learning techniques. In: Rosin, P.L., Lai, Y.-K., Shao, L., Liu, Y. (eds.) RGB-D Image Analysis and Processing. ACVPR, pp. 169–201. Springer, Cham (2019). https://doi.org/10.1007/978-3-030-28603-3_8

Complexity Measures of Time Series: A Theoretic-Information Approach

O. Castellanos[1(✉)], J. A. Mier[2], and J. M. Lopez[3]

[1] Facultad de Sistemas y Telecomunicaciones, Universidad Estatal Península de Santa Elena, La Libertad, Ecuador
ocastellanos@upse.edu.ec

[2] Departamento de Física Aplicada, Universidad de Cantabria, E-39005 Santander, Spain

[3] Instituto de Física de Cantabria (IFCA), CSIC–UC, E-39005 Santander, Spain

Abstract. A methodology based on permutation entropy and Lempel-Ziv complexity to characterize plasma fluctuations from the Santander Linear Plasma Machine is presented. These information-theoretic and symbolic dynamics tools are used to analyze temporal records and quantify randomness and structural complexity. The analysis reveals that the signals analyzed consistently occupy an intermediate region in the entropy-complexity plane, indicating low-dimensional chaotic behavior. This is supported by comparisons with synthetic signals, including white noise, periodic sequences, and outputs from chaotic maps. The pipeline involves preprocessing, symbolic encoding, and statistical validation, and is implemented using open-source tools in Python and MATLAB. The framework enables effective regime classification and anomaly detection in experimental plasma data, even under limited data conditions.

Keywords: Permutation entropy · Lempel-Ziv complexity · Plasma dynamics · Plasma turbulence · Time series analysis · Entropy-complexity plane

1 Introduction

Understanding the complex and often chaotic behavior of physical systems [1] is a central challenge in contemporary science and engineering. Plasma–an ionized gas governed by collective interactions and electromagnetic forces–is one such system exhibiting rich spatiotemporal dynamics such as turbulence, intermittency, and nonlinear coupling [2]. Analyzing time series from such systems provides valuable insights into their internal organization and enables the classification of regimes that might otherwise remain hidden.

Over the past decades, tools from information theory, symbolic dynamics, and complexity science have been successfully applied to characterize stochastic, periodic, and chaotic behavior in both simulated and empirical data [3–5]. Entropy-based metrics such as Shannon entropy [3], permutation entropy [5], and

T. Guarda et al. (Eds.): ARTIIS 2025, CCIS 2789, pp. 111–122, 2026.
https://doi.org/10.1007/978-3-032-16758-3_9

algorithmic complexity provide compact yet insightful descriptions of temporal organization [1]. When combined with symbolic representations and techniques such as mutual information and forbidden pattern analysis, these methods help reveal hidden structures and correlations in nonlinear systems.

In this study, we apply these methodologies to experimental data from the Santander Linear Plasma Machine (SLPM), which offers a controlled setting for investigating magnetized plasma behavior. Using high-resolution time series of fluctuation-driven plasma flux, we perform symbolic transformations and compute permutation entropy (H_{perm}) and Lempel-Ziv complexity (C_{LZ}), to distinguish between ordered, chaotic, and stochastic regimes. To contextualize the observed dynamics, we compare SLPM data with synthetic benchmarks, including white noise, periodic sequences, and outputs from chaotic maps.

Driven by the increasing demand for interpretable tools in plasma diagnostics and control–particularly in the context of fusion energy research [6,7]–this work presents a reproducible framework built on open-source computational tools developed in Python [8] and MATLAB [9]. The symbolic approach improves robustness to noise and short signal durations, which are common in experimental plasma measurements.

The broader goal of this work is to bridge theoretical concepts from dynamical systems and information theory with the practical analysis of time series in complex environments. We propose a scalable methodology applicable not only to plasma physics but also to fields such as neuroscience, finance, and environmental science. This approach integrates principles from self-organized criticality [10], symbolic dynamics [11], and entropy-complexity quantification [1,12].

The remainder of the article is organized as follows: in Sect. 2, the experimental arrangements are described, and the main plasma parameters are given. In Sect. 3, the analytical pipeline, which is based on symbolic dynamics and information-theoretic measures, is described. In Sect. 4, the computed permutation entropy and Lempel-Ziv complexity across radial positions in the SLPM, supported by comparative analysis with synthetic benchmarks, is presented. Finally, Sect. 5 outlines the key findings, methodological implications, and future research directions, including multivariate extensions and real-time anomaly detection in plasma environments.

2 Experimental Setup

The SLPM consists of a cylindrical glass vacuum chamber (0.07 m in diameter, 1 m in length) housed within a circular waveguide (0.08 m in diameter). Magnetized plasma is generated by longitudinal injection of 2.45 GHz electromagnetic radiation at input power levels ranging from 0.6 to 6 kW. A stable axial magnetic field (0.05–0.15 T) is produced using six water-cooled solenoid coils. The measurements analyzed in this work were carried out under helium and neon discharge conditions, with a fixed magnetic field strength of $B_0 = 0.12$ T.

Plasma diagnostics are performed using an array of Langmuir probes mounted on a radially movable support system, enabling spatially resolved measurements of local parameters such as electron density (n_e), temperature (T_e), and floating potential (ϕ). Each probe consists of a tungsten wire (0.5 mm in diameter, 2 mm in length) arranged in a square lattice configuration with a 2 mm pitch. Triple probe configurations are employed to estimate ion saturation current and potential fluctuations across the plasma column.

Time-resolved measurements of the $\mathbf{E} \times \mathbf{B}$ drift flux $\Gamma_{\mathbf{E}\times\mathbf{B}}$ were recorded at different radial positions ranging from $r = 0.20$ to 2.80 cm. Stationarity was confirmed by verifying the temporal invariance of the absolute flux probability density function. Each dataset contains 2×10^5 samples, acquired at a sampling interval of 1 μs, corresponding to a total recording duration of 0.2 s per run. These durations significantly exceed the typical autocorrelation time of the system ($\tau_c \sim 1$–6 μs), ensuring statistically robust estimation across spatial locations.

The drift flux is defined as:

$$\Gamma(t) = \tilde{n}(t)\tilde{v}_r(t) = \frac{1}{B}\tilde{n}(t)\tilde{E}_\theta(t), \tag{1}$$

where $\tilde{n}(t)$ denotes normalized plasma density fluctuations, $\tilde{v}_r(t)$ is the radial velocity induced by the $\mathbf{E} \times \mathbf{B}$ drift, B is the magnetic field strength, and $\tilde{E}_\theta(t)$ represents poloidal electric field fluctuations. All fluctuating components are assumed to have zero mean, i.e., $\langle\tilde{n}(t)\rangle = \langle\tilde{v}_r(t)\rangle = \langle\tilde{E}_\theta(t)\rangle = 0$.

3 Methodology

This study employs a data-driven analytical framework grounded in information theory and symbolic dynamics to investigate time series data acquired from the SLPM. The methodology is structured into several phases: data acquisition and preprocessing, entropy and complexity quantification, symbolic representation and binary encoding, and comparative analysis with synthetic dynamical benchmarks.

3.1 Data Acquisition and Preprocessing

Fluctuation flux data were extracted from files `flujo1054` to `flujo1068`, following quality control procedures. Although thirteen files were originally available, some could not be retrieved due to data integrity issues. The preprocessing pipeline consisted of the following steps:

i) Compute basic descriptive statistics: mean (μ_x), standard deviation (σ_x), and minimum and maximum values.
ii) Standardize the data using the z-score: $x'_i = (x_i - \mu_x)/\sigma_x$, where each value is rescaled to reflect its deviation from the mean in units of standard deviation. This step ensures that signals are centered and normalized relative to their local statistical properties.
iii) Shift the signal to ensure non-negativity: $x''_i = x'_i + |x'_{\min}|$.
iv) Round values to two decimal places to improve numerical stability and reduce floating-point errors during symbolic transformation. This ensures consistent representation while preserving sufficient precision for meaningful complexity estimation.

v) Convert values to integer format by scaling with 10^2, enabling binary encoding and string-based complexity analysis.

These preprocessing steps preserve essential dynamic characteristics of the signals while ensuring compatibility with discrete symbolic processing requirements.

3.2 Entropy and Complexity Quantification

To characterize the temporal structure of the SLPM-generated signals, we employed two foundational tools from information theory: permutation entropy (H_{perm}) and Lempel-Ziv complexity (C_{LZ}). These metrics provide complementary insights into the degree of randomness, structural richness, and algorithmic content of the underlying dynamics, enabling a refined distinction between stochastic, chaotic, and ordered regimes.

Permutation Entropy. Permutation entropy quantifies the uncertainty associated with the sequential ordering of a time series, offering a robust estimator of its predictability or disorder. In this work, H_{perm} was computed based on the distribution of ordinal patterns derived from the signal [5]. Formally, it is given by:

$$H_{\text{perm}}(X) = -\sum p(\pi) \log p(\pi), \tag{2}$$

where $p(\pi)$ denotes the empirical frequency of each unique ordinal pattern π. This formulation effectively captures the diversity and recurrence of short-term temporal structures within the signal. Higher entropy values reflect a greater degree of local unpredictability and signal irregularity.

All computed entropy values were normalized to the unit interval $[0, 1]$ by dividing each result by the maximum possible entropy $\log(n!)$, where n is the embedding dimension. This normalization ensures comparability across different radial positions and experimental conditions, enabling consistent interpretation. It also facilitates benchmarking against synthetic signals such as white noise, periodic sequences, and outputs from chaotic maps like the logistic equation.

Lempel-Ziv Complexity. Algorithmic complexity was quantified using the Lempel-Ziv complexity (LZC) [1], a metric that evaluates the number of distinct substrings required to reconstruct a sequence as it evolves. This measure provides a robust proxy for the sequence's information content and redundancy structure.

Binary strings were generated by thresholding each time series at its mean value:

$$b_i = \begin{cases} 1 & \text{if } x_i > \mu_x, \\ 0 & \text{otherwise.} \end{cases} \tag{3}$$

To preserve amplitude resolution and increase sensitivity to fine-scale structure, complexity was also computed directly on integer-valued symbolic sequences derived from the normalized flux data.

Because the raw LZC is inherently dependent on the sequence length, we applied the standard normalization based on Ziv's theorem [1]:

$$\mathrm{LZC}_{\mathrm{norm}}(n) = \frac{\mathrm{LZC}(n) \cdot \log_A(n)}{n}, \quad (4)$$

where n is the sequence length and A is the size of the symbol alphabet (here, $A = 100$). This normalized version ensures comparability across sequences of different lengths and allows interpretation in terms of entropy rates: in the limit $n \to \infty$, $\mathrm{LZC}_{\mathrm{norm}}$ converges to the Kolmogorov-Sinai entropy for deterministic systems or to Shannon entropy for stochastic processes.

Both raw and normalized LZC values were computed to ensure robustness in the characterization of SLPM time series and benchmark signals, especially under finite-size constraints.

3.3 Symbolic Representation and Binary Encoding

Symbolic dynamics was applied to transform continuous time series into interpretable symbolic sequences, enhancing both computational efficiency and interpretability. Three primary strategies were implemented:

- **Binary encoding**: Each sample was compared to the global mean, yielding a binary symbol (1 if above mean, 0 otherwise).
- **Integer rounding and scaling**: Normalized signals were discretized into integer sequences to facilitate direct application of complexity measures.
- **String concatenation**: Symbolic representations were combined into extended character sequences to facilitate the identification of recurring patterns and long-range structural dependencies within the time series.

This approach ensures computational tractability while maintaining resilience to measurement noise and suitability for short or nonstationary datasets [1,12].

3.4 Comparative Analysis with Synthetic Signals

To contextualize the observed behavior within known dynamical classes, we compared SLPM signals against synthetic reference systems exhibiting well-defined dynamics:

- **Uniform random noise**, representing fully stochastic processes.
- **Deterministic periodic sequences**, exemplified by repeated digit patterns such as `1234567890`.
- **Chaotic sequences** generated by the logistic map at supercritical parameter values.
- **Fractal-like sequences** derived from irrational numbers such as π, characterized by low algorithmic compressibility.

This comparative framework allows for reliable classification of SLPM dynamics within the broader landscape of nonlinear time series, aligning with widely accepted practices in the field [13].

3.5 Computational Implementation

All analyses were performed using Python-based open-source libraries:

- `numpy` and `pandas` for numerical operations and data structuring.
- `matplotlib` for visualization and graphical representation.
- `antropy`, a Python library for time series analysis, used for efficient computation of entropy and complexity metrics such as permutation entropy, and Lempel-Ziv complexity.
- Custom-developed routines for symbolic string manipulation and advanced complexity estimation.

The implementation prioritizes computational efficiency and cross-platform reproducibility, making it accessible even in environments with limited hardware resources.

3.6 Statistical Validation and Interpretation

To assess the statistical significance and reliability of our findings, we employed:

- **Surrogate data testing** and **bootstrap resampling** to evaluate deviations from null models.
- **Recurrence plots**, **phase-space reconstructions**, and **entropy complexity maps** for visual validation and regime transition detection.

These techniques facilitate discrimination between genuine dynamical features and stochastic artifacts, revealing qualitative shifts in the system's behavior across radial positions [10].

4 Results and Discussion

The application of entropy and complexity-based metrics to time series data offers a powerful lens through which to assess the intrinsic structure and dynamics of physical systems. In this work, we analyze magnetic flux signals acquired from the SLPM, a well-established experimental platform for studying nonlinear behavior and turbulence in magnetized, weakly ionized plasmas. The SLPM provides a controlled setting where plasma fluctuations can be systematically probed across multiple radial positions, enabling spatially resolved dynamical characterization.

4.1 Permutation Entropy: Quantifying Randomness and Temporal Structure

One of the tools for characterizing local randomness and predictability in time series is permutation entropy H_{perm}, defined as:

$$H_{\text{perm}} = -\sum_{i=1}^{m!} p_i \log p_i, \tag{5}$$

where p_i denotes the relative frequency of ordinal patterns of length m. This measure has proven particularly sensitive to changes in temporal structure within both stochastic and chaotic signals [5], making it well-suited for detecting phase transitions and intermittent dynamics.

In our analysis of SLPM data, we observed a clear correlation between H_{perm} values and the nature of the underlying plasma dynamics. During turbulent phases, characterized by high levels of fluctuation and instability, H_{perm} increased significantly, reflecting enhanced unpredictability. Conversely, during more coherent or quasi-periodic intervals, H_{perm} decreased, indicating reduced diversity in ordinal motifs and greater structural regularity. These observations align closely with results reported in analogous nonlinear systems under controlled conditions [?], reinforcing the reliability of permutation entropy as an indicator of disorder and dynamical variability in real-world environments.

Using ordinal pattern distributions derived from sequences with embedding dimension $m = 5$ and time delay $\tau = 1$, normalized H_{perm} values ranged from 0.71 to 0.94 across different radial positions within the plasma column. For instance, a representative signal from the intermediate region yielded $H_{\text{perm}} = 0.89$, suggesting a significant degree of irregularity—though still distinguishable from fully random processes such as white noise ($H_{\text{perm}} \approx 1.0$).

4.2 Lempel-Ziv Complexity: Measuring Pattern Generation Rate

Complementing the entropy-based perspective, Lempel-Ziv complexity C_{LZ} as a powerful estimator of the rate at which novel patterns emerge over time. Formally defined as:

$$C_{\text{LZ}} = \frac{\text{number of unique substrings discovered during compression}}{\text{total sequence length}}. \tag{6}$$

This measure can be interpreted as an empirical approximation of the Kolmogorov Sinai entropy [1]. While periodic sequences yield low values close to zero, fully random sequences approach unity.

To compute C_{LZ}, we first binarized each time series by thresholding at the mean value, see Eq. (3). A representative turbulent signal returned $C_{\text{LZ}}^{\text{tur}} = 0.73$, markedly higher than that of periodic signals, $C_{\text{LZ}}^{\text{per}} \sim 0.2$, but below the maximum value associated with white noise, $C_{\text{LZ}}^{\text{whn}} \sim 1.0$. This suggests that while the SLPM-generated signals exhibit rich and evolving structures, they retain a degree of algorithmic redundancy inconsistent with pure randomness.

4.3 Entropy-Complexity Plane and Regime Classification

To gain deeper insight into the nature of the observed dynamics, we mapped the SLPM signals onto the entropy-complexity plane—a two-dimensional representation where permutation entropy H_{perm} defines the horizontal axis and Lempel-Ziv complexity C_{LZ} the vertical one. We observe that this visualization is particularly useful in classifying dynamical regimes based on their information-theoretic signatures:

- Stochastic Regime: High entropy, $H_{\text{perm}}^{\text{sto}} > 0.9$, high complexity, $C_{\text{LZ}}^{\text{sto}} > 0.8$.
- Deterministic Chaos: Intermediate entropy, $0.7 < H_{\text{perm}}^{\text{cha}} < 0.9$, moderate complexity, $0.5 < C_{\text{LZ}}^{\text{cha}} < 0.8$.
- Periodic: Low entropy, $H_{\text{perm}}^{\text{per}} < 0.6$, low complexity $C_{\text{LZ}}^{\text{per}} < 0.4$.

The distribution of SLPM data points across the entropy-complexity plane reveals a predominant concentration within the intermediate region, a signature consistent with deterministic chaos embedded in turbulent fluctuations. This pattern aligns with earlier observations from similar experimental setups [2,14], lending further support to the hypothesis that what appears as stochastic turbulence may, in fact, originate from low-dimensional dynamical attractors rather than purely random processes.

4.4 Comparison with Synthetic Benchmarks

To contextualize the observed behavior, we compared SLPM signals against well-known synthetic benchmarks:

- White Noise: $H_{\text{perm}}^{\text{whn}} \approx 0.99$, $C_{\text{LZ}}^{\text{whn}} \approx 1.00$.
- Logistic Map: $(r = 3.99)$: $H_{\text{perm}}^{\text{log}} \approx 0.85$, $C_{\text{LZ}}^{\text{log}} \approx 0.70$.
- Periodic Signal: $H_{\text{perm}}^{\text{per}} \approx 0.00$–$0.30$, $C_{\text{LZ}}^{\text{per}} \approx 0.10$–$0.30$.

Notably, the SLPM data aligned most closely with the logistic map, suggesting a comparable balance between structural richness and algorithmic novelty. This agreement reinforces the utility of symbolic and information-theoretic metrics for the robust characterization of plasma dynamics under experimental constraints.

4.5 Summary and Outlook

In summary, the integration of permutation entropy and Lempel-Ziv complexity, provides a comprehensive toolkit for analyzing the informational and structural properties of time series in nonlinear systems. Applied to the SLPM dataset, this methodology successfully distinguishes between ordered, chaotic, and stochastic regimes, offering a promising path for future studies in nonlinear dynamics and experimental signal analysis.

The observed results confirm that time series obtained from the SLPM display features characteristic of chaotic yet organized dynamics. These findings align with previous studies on turbulence and transport mechanisms in linear plasma devices, reinforcing the hypothesis that such systems may exhibit low-dimensional deterministic structures despite their apparent stochasticity. Furthermore, the analytical framework proposed demonstrates robustness in distinguishing between dynamical regimes, even when confronted with short, noisy datasets–conditions frequently encountered in experimental plasma diagnostics.

By situating SLPM signals within a clearly defined information-theoretic landscape, this work enables new avenues for real-time regime identification, anomaly detection, and model verification in fusion-related environments. Importantly, these outcomes underscore the broader utility of entropy and complexity based tools in constructing interpretable, data-driven decision support systems applicable to diverse temporal datasets beyond plasma physics, including biological, environmental, and financial domains.

Future work will explore multivariate extensions, multiscale entropy, and machine learning integration to further improve predictive capabilities and uncover hidden dependencies in higher-dimensional diagnostics.

5 Conclusion

This study shows the effectiveness of entropy and complexity measures in characterizing the nonlinear dynamics of magnetized plasma using time series data from the SLPM. By integrating symbolic dynamics with information-theoretic tools–specifically permutation entropy H_{perm} and Lempel-Ziv complexity C_{LZ}–we have successfully identified and differentiated between ordered, chaotic, and stochastic dynamical regimes based on their distinct informational signatures.

The analysis revealed that SLPM signals predominantly occupy an intermediate region in the entropy-complexity plane, consistent with deterministic chaos embedded within turbulent fluctuations. This observation aligns with previous experimental findings using different techniques for the SLPM time series analysis [13–16], reinforcing the hypothesis that magnetized plasmas exhibit low-dimensional structures despite their apparent randomness. Notably, the placement of SLPM data points closely resembles that of synthetic chaotic systems such as the logistic map, while clearly diverging from both white noise and periodic sequences. This distinction underscores the structured nature of the observed turbulence, suggesting a potential for predictability and control.

Table 1. Normalized permutation entropy and Lempel-Ziv complexity for representative signals across different radial positions in the SLPM and for benchmark synthetic signals.

Signal Type/Position	H_{perm}	C_{LZ}
SLPM (Inner region: $r = 6$ mm)	0.86	0.55
SLPM (Intermediate region: $r = 20$ mm)	0.91	0.55
SLPM (Outer region: $r = 28$ mm)	0.99	0.87
White Noise	0.99	1.00
Logistic Map ($r = 3.99$)	0.85	0.70
Periodic Sequence	0.25	0.15

One of the principal contributions of this study is the development of a unified framework that integrates entropy estimation and complexity quantification into a systematic and reproducible pipeline. This approach demonstrates particular resilience when applied to datasets characterized by limited length and high noise levels—common features in experimental plasma diagnostics—where traditional methods may struggle to extract meaningful information. By incorporating optimal partitioning strategies that explicitly account for temporal dependencies, the methodology enhances the symbolic encoding process, leading to more accurate and interpretable representations of the underlying dynamics. These symbolic transformations not only improve sensitivity to subtle changes in system behavior but also serve as an effective interface between raw signal acquisition and higher-order dynamical classification, enabling robust regime identification even under challenging observational conditions.

To illustrate these findings, Table 1 presents normalized values of H_{perm} and C_{LZ} across representative radial positions in the SLPM, alongside benchmark signals. Figure 1 further visualizes the distribution of these signals in the entropy-complexity plane, offering a clear separation between different dynamical classes.

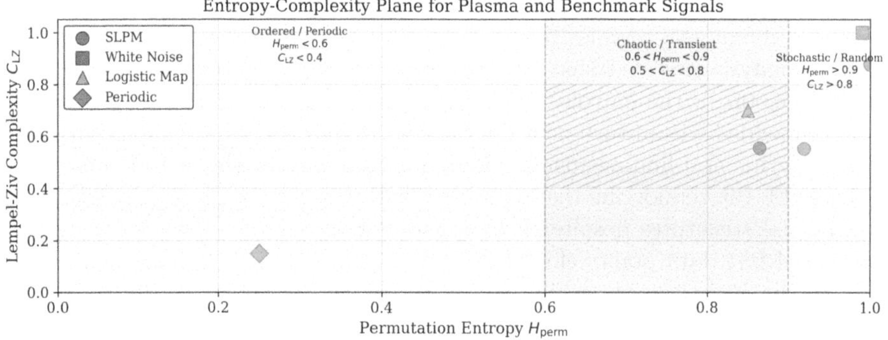

Fig. 1. Complexity-entropy plane showing SLPM time series (blue), white noise (red), periodic sequences (green), and logistic map outputs (orange). (Color figure online)

The results presented here open new perspectives for real-time monitoring, anomaly detection, and model validation in fusion-oriented plasma devices. The entropy-complexity framework offers a compact yet informative representation of system behavior, enabling robust classification of dynamical regimes and supporting the design of adaptive feedback strategies that respond to evolving plasma conditions.

Future work will focus on extending this approach to multivariate contexts through the integration of multiscale entropy, transfer entropy, and machine learning techniques. These additions are expected to reveal latent interdependencies among measured variables and enhance predictive performance–particularly in high-dimensional diagnostic settings where traditional methods may lack sensitivity. Furthermore, deploying these tools within online data acquisition systems could pave the way toward intelligent control architectures tailored for advanced fusion experiments.

In conclusion, this work reaffirms the theoretical soundness and practical utility of entropy and complexity-based methods in the empirical analysis of nonlinear systems [1, 12]. Their adaptability, computational efficiency, and strong theoretical foundation position them as essential components for building intelligent, data-driven frameworks across diverse scientific and engineering domains, from plasma physics to complex network analysis and beyond.

Acknowledgments. OC thanks Facultad de Sistemas y Telecomunicaciones (FACSISTEL) and the Instituto de Investigación Científica y Desarrollo de Tecnologías (INCYT) at the Universidad Estatal Península de Santa Elena (UPSE) for their institutional support. We also acknowledge Universidad de Cantabria and, in particular, the Department of Applied Physics, (Faculty of Science), for hosting a research stay and providing access to the laboratory and data from the SLPM. JML acknowledges financial support from Spanish Government MCIN/AEI/10.13039/501100011033/ through Project No. PID2021-125543NB-I00 by and by ERDF "A way of making Europe" by the European Union.

Disclosure of Interests. The authors declare no competing interests related to this work.

References

1. Lindgren, K.: Information Theory for Complex Systems. Chalmers University of Technology (2014)
2. Chen, F.F.: Introduction to Plasma Physics and Controlled Fusion, 2nd edn. Springer, Cham (2016)
3. Shannon, C. E., Weaver, W.: The Mathematical Theory of Communication. University of Illinois Press, Champaign (1964)
4. Ihara, S.: Information Theory for Continuous Systems. World Scientific, Singapore (1993)
5. Bandt, C., Pompe, B.: Permutation entropy: a natural complexity measure for time series. Phys. Rev. Lett. **88**, 174102 (2002)
6. Lawson, J. D.: Some criteria for a power producing thermonuclear reactor. Proc. Phys. Soc. **70** (1957)
7. Geng, S.: An overview of the ITER project. J. Phys. Conf. Ser. **2386** (2022)
8. León, I.: Teoría de la información aplicada a sistemas complejos: una aplicación para el estudio de plasmas. Universidad de Cantabria (2024). https://hdl.handle.net/10902/34138
9. Martínez, A.: Predicción no paramétrica de señales en plasmas de fusión nuclear. Universidad de Alcalá (2022). https://ebuah.uah.es/dspace/handle/10017/52692
10. Jensen, H.J.: Self-Organized Criticality: Emergent Complex Behavior in Physical and Biological Systems. Cambridge University Press, Cambridge (1998)
11. Mayers R. A. Mathematics of Complexity and Dynamical Systems. Springer, New York (2011)
12. Amigó, J.: Permutation Complexity in Dynamical Systems. Springer, Heidelberg (2010)
13. Mier, J.A., et al.: Tracer particle transport dynamics in the diffusive sandpile cellular automaton. Chaos, Solitons Fractals **140**, 110 (2020)

14. Castellanos, O.F., et al.: Parallel flows and turbulence in a linear plasma machine. Plasma Phys. Control. Fusion **47**(12), 2067–2074 (2005)
15. Mier, J.A., et al.: Avalanche statistics of fluctuation-induced fluxes from the SLPM and the W7-AS stellarator. Plasma Phys. Control. Fusion **66**, 065015 (2024)
16. Castellanos O.F. et al.: Intermittency, avalanche statistics and long-term correlations in a turbulent plasma. J. Stat. Mech. **04022** (2013)

High-Resolution Wind Downscaling in Southern Chile Using LightGBM Models

Benjamin Higuera[1](✉), Walter Gómez[2], Ana María Córdova[3,4], Jorge Arévalo[3,4], and Pablo Andrade[3]

[1] Magister en Ciencias de la Ingenieria, Universidad de la Frontera, Temuco, Chile
b.higuera01@ufromail.cl

[2] Departamento de Ingeniería Matemática, Universidad de la Frontera, Temuco, Chile

[3] Departamento de Meteorología, Universidad de Valparaiso, Valparaiso, Chile

[4] Centro de Investigación y Gestión de Recursos Naturales (CIGREN), Universidad de Valparaiso, Valparaiso, Chile

Abstract. The complex topography of southern Chile causes high spatial variability in near-surface winds, challenging the resolution limits of current operational weather models. To address this, we propose a machine learning–based downscaling approach using gradient boosting (LightGBM) to generate high-resolution (333 m) wind forecasts from 3 km WRF outputs. The models incorporate meteorological, topographic, and wind–terrain interaction variables. Trained on 16 WRF cases and tested on 965 hourly maps, the approach achieved R^2 values of approximately 0.88 ($U10$) and 0.93 ($V10$), outperforming previous methods. The framework offers a lightweight and operationally viable solution that can be transferred to similar applications. Enabling near real-time forecasts for maritime and aquaculture planning.

Keywords: Wind Downscaling · Machine Learning · LightGBM

1 Introduction

The southern zone of Chile has a characteristic topography mostly made up of islands, channels and gulfs with sizes varying from hundreds to thousands of meters. This complex topography generates a high spatial variability over the wind. [3,4,7], This means that there may be different weather conditions in nearby sectors. In turn, as a result of this topography, most of the productive activities are carried out by sea [6]. Since the safe performance of these activities is closely linked to weather conditions and mainly to the near-surface wind, it is necessary to have forecasts that can reflect the high variability of the wind in the area. In order to contribute to improving the quality of life of the inhabitants of the area and to achieve better planning of the activities.

T. Guarda et al. (Eds.): ARTIIS 2025, CCIS 2789, pp. 123–135, 2026.
https://doi.org/10.1007/978-3-032-16758-3_10

Currently, the Chilean National Weather Service and Chilean Navy Weather Service generate their weather forecasts with numerical Weather Research and Forecasting (WRF) models to forecast the weather [18]. However, currently implemented models reach a maximum resolution of 4 and 3 km [18]. Resolutions incapable of reflecting the effects of complex topography such as occurs in the austral zone. Bringing these models to the necessary orders (hundreds of meters) in an operational way requires high computational resources [10], which are beyond the current reach of meteorological services, making it unfeasible to emulate the dynamic downscaling performed by WRF. In this context, a machine learning model is implemented that enables downscaling to obtain high-resolution results (on the order of hundreds of meters), capable of predicting wind data in the southern region with sufficient accuracy.

This study addresses the challenge of downscaling near-surface wind fields in complex terrain, where conventional models often fail to capture fine-scale variability. The specific research objective is to evaluate the capacity of LightGBM for wind downscaling in southern Chile's complex topography.

2 Related Work

Numerical weather prediction is a forecasting methodology that employs the set of equations that describe the flow of fluids in the atmosphere [5]. This translates into a wide variety of models that are approached computationally.

In this context, the Global Forecast System (GFS) from National Centers for Environmental Prediction (NCEP) from the National Oceanic and Atmospheric Administration (NOAA) of the US and the Integrated Forecast System (IFS) models of the European Centre for Medium-Range Weather Forecasts (ECMWF) are the best known and most widely used worldwide.

In the case of GFS, the data are openly available and the models are under continuous improvement. Both models have global coverage and are usually used for the prediction of key variables such as temperature, precipitation, and winds [14,22]. The data available from the Chilean Navy Weather Service includes information from GFS models with resolutions of approximately 25 km and WRF models with resolutions of 27 km, 9 km and 3 km for different areas. GFS does not reach resolutions finer enough to capture local weather patterns.

The Weather Research & Forecast (WRF) is an open source regional model that allows users to choose between different physical parameterization schemes, domain nesting, and initialization for the prediction of weather phenomena, climate studies, air quality, etc. [1]. Because of this, WRF allows setting up smaller simulation domains with higher resolutions, typically between 300 m and 30 km [19]. While *WRF* can generate high-resolution weather forecasts (up to 300 m), the computational cost precludes its continuous operational availability. Simulations for a full day require 30 min of computation at 3 km resolution, while at 300 m they require 12 h of processing.

To address the limitations of large-scale model resolutions, downscaling techniques have been developed. These techniques fall into two main categories: statistical downscaling, which establishes statistical relationships between large-scale and local variables [21] and dynamic downscaling, which uses high-resolution limited-area models nested in global models [23].

As an alternative to traditional downscaling methods, the use of machine learning models has been positioned, given their ability to understand nonlinear relationships between input and output variables [11].

Although the training of these models maintains execution times similar to traditional methods (in the order of hours), the prediction they generate can be in the order of seconds [8]. These times are much shorter than the minutes or hours of simple models or even the days that complex models such as WRF can reach.

One class of relevant machine learning models to consider is Gradient Boosting. These models are very intuitive and easy-to-explain tools [13] and have proven useful for meteorological downscaling tasks [2]. A noteworthy advantage of Gradient Boosting type models is that they provide variable importance measures that can help to understand the relationships between predictor variables and the response variable [11]. Python machine learning libraries such as scikit-learn (https://scikit-learn.org/stable/modules/ensemble.html) can be used to implement Boosting methods.

Complementing this approach, [9]'s research presents a methodology that consists of constructing wind-topography interaction variables that would help machine learning models capture the spatial variability produced by complex topographies.

This work shows that Gradient Boosting models are a suitable tool to obtain wind downscaling at scales of hundreds of meters with sufficient accuracy, even for complex geographies.

3 Methodology

3.1 Preparation of Model Input Data

The objective of the models to be implemented is to be able to receive low resolution inputs and deliver high resolution outputs of the wind components ($U10$ and $V10$), where $U10$ and $V10$ represent the zonal (west-east) and meridional (north-south) components of the wind vector at 10 m above ground. For this purpose, the information is extracted directly from a WRF model.

The WRF model simulates several domains at different resolutions. For the problem to be addressed, we will work with domains 03 (3 km) and 05 (333 m), treating them as the coarse (low resolution) and fine (high resolution) domains, respectively.

Since the domains come from different sizes and scales, the coarse domain spatially contains the fine domain, although the fine domain contains many more points in the common area. To align the information, the coarse domain was cropped to the size of the fine domain and then interpolated to match in size and number of points with the fine domain. Then a division was made into 156 square patches of 32·32 points. This gives a total of $156 \cdot 32 \cdot 32 = 159,744$ points per map.

The bilinear technique was used for interpolation, which allowed the maps to be matched. The Kriging technique (based on *PyKrige*) was also tested, but the results were unsatisfactory.

To form the algorithm input from the WRF model, 8 meteorological variables $U10$, $V10$, $PSFC$, slp, $wspd10$, $wdir10$, $rh2$, $T2$ were selected in coarse scale; likewise, 4 topographic variables HGT, $Slope$, $Aspect$, $XLAND$ were selected in fine scale. The topographic variables are of the static type, so they are available at all times in both coarse and fine scale, while the meteorological variables are of the dynamic type, so only the daily calculation of the coarse scale is available, given the computational cost of obtaining them in fine scale.

Based on these, wind and topography interactions were calculated according to the variables described in the article by WindTopo, according to the following formulas described in the set of Eqs. 1:

$$\begin{aligned} E_{\max} &= \max\{\sin(\alpha), 0\} & \Delta u_{\tan} &= (\cos(\beta) - 1)u_c - \sin(\beta)v_c \\ E_{\min} &= \min\{\sin(\alpha), 0\} & \Delta v_{\tan} &= \sin(\beta)u_c + (\cos(\beta) - 1)v_c \\ E_{\max_u} &= E_{\max} \cdot U10 & E_{\max_v} &= E_{\max} \cdot V10 \\ E_{\min_u} &= E_{\min} \cdot U10 & E_{\min_v} &= E_{\min} \cdot V10 \end{aligned} \tag{1}$$

where

$$\begin{cases} \alpha = \arctan(\tan(slope)\cos(\delta)) \\ \beta = \left(\frac{\pi}{2} - |\delta|\right)\operatorname{sign}(\delta) \\ \delta = \arctan 2\,(-v,\, -u) - \text{aspect} \in]-\pi, \pi] \end{cases} \tag{2}$$

This resulted in the set of variables that will receive the models. The variables appear in the Table 1, separated according to their origin:

In order for the boosting models to receive the information from the maps, we chose to build windows around the points, i.e., for a point i, the model receives a flattened 3 array containing the point i together with its 8 neighboring elements. This process was performed for the 20 variables that the model receives, so that for each point in the map there are 180 associated features as explanatory variables to predict the wind at the point. We trained two separate boosting models, one to predict the $V10$ component and another to predict the $U10$ component.

3.2 Input Data

Data is available from a different study, where daily mean wind patterns were grouped in 8 clusters for the period 2016–2023. Retrospective 5-day (120-hours) forecasts for 4 dates within each cluster were available with hourly output. From the 32 simulations, 2 for each cluster were selected for training, other for validation, and the last for testing (totaling 16*120, 8*120, 8*120 hourly outputs). Hence, the cases include a large portion of the natural variability of real wind. With this, the training set consists of 1920 maps, the validation set consists of 960 maps, and the test set consists of 960 maps. Converting these simulations to

Table 1. Variables summary

Variable	Description	Units
U10	Zonal wind component at 10 m	ms^{-1}
V10	Meridional wind component at 10 m	ms^{-1}
PSFC	Surface pressure	hPa
slp	Sea level pressure	hPa
T2	Temperature at 2 m	K
wspd10	Wind speed at 10 m	ms^{-1}
wdir10	Wind direction at 10 m	$^{\circ}$
rh2	Relative humidity at 2 m	%
XLAND	Land mask (1=land, 2=water)	dimensionless
HGT	Terrain height	m
Slope	Terrain slope	$^{\circ}$
Aspect	Maximum slope orientation	$^{\circ}$
E_{max}	$\max\{\sin(\alpha), 0\}$ (positive topographic influence)	dimensionless
E_{min}	$\min\{\sin(\alpha), 0\}$ (negative topographic influence)	dimensionless
E_{max_u}	$E_{\text{max}} \times U10$	ms^{-1}
E_{min_u}	$E_{\text{min}} \times U10$	ms^{-1}
E_{max_v}	$E_{\text{max}} \times V10$	ms^{-1}
E_{min_v}	$E_{\text{min}} \times V10$	ms^{-1}
Δu_{tan}	Tangential perturbation of zonal wind component	ms^{-1}
Δv_{tan}	Tangential perturbation of meridional wind component	ms^{-1}

the X input sets described above, the training, validation and test sets have a weight of 232, 103 and 103 GB, respectively. Given the RAM requirements, the vectors were saved and worked as numpy memmaps, since this way they can be handled for future loading and edits without the need to load the entire file into memory [16].

In order to determine the best way to represent the spatial environment of each point, four different configurations for constructing the input windows were tested. These configurations were: (i) full window $(3 \cdot 3)$, which includes the central point and its eight adjacent neighbors; (ii) x-shape, consisting of the central point and its diagonal neighbors (corners); (iii) cross shape, which considers only the central point together with its neighbors in the cardinal directions (north, south, west and east); and (iv) only the central point, without spatial context. To perform a quick comparison between window configurations, each one was initially tested using a single case from the train set and evaluated performance on the full validation set, in order to guide the design of the input representation. The same hyperparameters were used for all models: `learning_rate` = 0.05, `num_boost_round` = 150, `max_depth` = 15 and `num_leaves` = 40. The results of this exploratory evaluation are summarized in Table 2.

Table 2. Error comparison according to window configurations

Window	U10				V10			
	MSE	MAE	RMSE	R^2	MSE	MAE	RMSE	R^2
Full	4.8463	1.4408	2.2014	0.7084	2.5982	1.0566	1.6119	0.8217
X	5.2263	1.5110	2.2861	0.6855	2.5820	1.0527	1.6069	0.8229
Point	6.1130	1.6634	2.4725	0.6322	2.6880	1.0910	1.6395	0.8156
Cross	4.8150	1.4363	2.1943	0.7103	2.6073	1.0595	1.6147	0.8211

Due to the similar performance observed between the full window and cross configurations, it was decided to continue the work with both structures: cross and full window. For this stage, the models were trained using the 16 cases of the training set and evaluated on the 8 cases of the validation set. On this occasion, the hyperparameter configuration was more ambitious: `learning_rate` = 0.05, `max_depth` = 15, `num_leaves` = 40 and `num_boost_round` = 500. The results of this evaluation are presented in Table 3. A Leave-One-Feature-Out (LOFO) experiment was conducted to evaluate the relative contribution of each predictor by training models while systematically excluding one variable at a time and comparing the performance against the full-feature baseline. As shown in Fig. 1, the omission of any variable consistently increased the prediction error for both $U10$ and $V10$, with the strongest effects observed for topographic features such as terrain height (HGT), slope, and aspect, as well as the meteorological variable surface pressure ($PSFC$). These results highlight that all features provide meaningful information to the models, either directly or through their interactions, and therefore none were excluded from the final configuration, which retained the complete predictor set.

Table 3. Performance of models with full-window and cross-window configurations, trained with the 16 cases.

Window	U10				V10			
	MSE	MAE	RMSE	R^2	MSE	MAE	RMSE	R^2
Full	1.3138	0.7516	1.1462	0.8846	1.5862	0.8068	1.2594	0.9358
Cross	1.4889	0.7847	1.2202	0.8886	1.8183	0.8604	1.3484	0.9361

To assess the influence of topography on model performance, the study area was divided according to terrain complexity. Specifically, several topographic complexity indices were used to determine a separation of the study area. In particular, the Terrain Ruggedness Index (TRI), the Terrain Diversity Index (TDI), and the Topographic Position Index (TPI) were employed to capture variations in terrain heterogeneity, morphological diversity, and relative elevation, respectively [11,17,20]. As shown in Fig. 2, two regions arose: a first one extending up

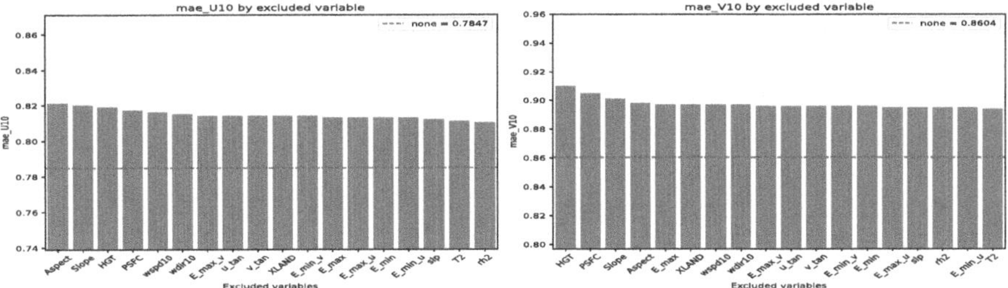

Fig. 1. Mean Absolute Error (MAE) obtained in the LOFO experiment. The red dashed line represents the baseline performance when all features are included. (Color figure online)

to the horizontal component 320 (representing a more regular topography) and a second with the remaining section of the map (representing complex terrain).

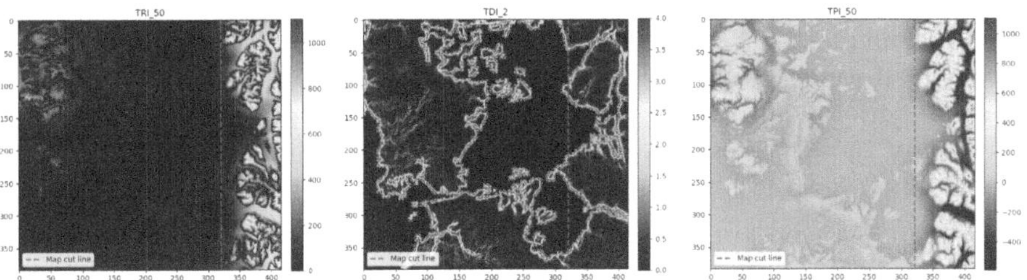

Fig. 2. Subdivision of the study area into regular and complex topographic domains. The notation **50-2-50** indicates the pixel radius used: 50 for TRI, 2 for TDI, and 50 for TPI.

Separate models were trained for each of the two subdomains. Table 4 presents the results when each model was trained and tested on its corresponding domain. Compared to the baseline model (Table 6), the differences are minor, suggesting that domain-specific training does not provide a substantial performance gain.

To examine the generalization ability of the models, cross-domain experiments were performed. In this setup, the model trained on the western domain was tested on the eastern domain, and vice versa. The results are summarized in Table 5. The errors are not drastically different from those obtained when models were trained and tested within the same domain (Table 4), which can be interpreted as indications of generalization ability. In practice, this indicates that the models can provide reliable preliminary predictions even in regions not directly included in the training set.

As an alternative to spatial subdivision of the domain, topographic complexity indices were directly included as input variables for the model. Specifically, the Terrain Ruggedness Index (TRI 50), the Terrain Diversity Index (TDI 2),

Table 4. Performance metrics for wind components when models were trained and tested on the same domain.

Test Domain	Model Domain	U10			V10		
		MAE	RMSE	R^2	MAE	RMSE	R^2
East	East	0.6249	0.9500	0.9308	0.6682	1.0013	0.9678
West	West	1.3176	1.8927	0.7483	1.4823	2.1248	0.7661

Table 5. Validation metrics for cross-domain evaluation, where models were trained on one domain and tested on the other.

Test Domain	Model Domain	U10			V10		
		MAE	RMSE	R^2	MAE	RMSE	R^2
East	West	0.8166	1.1475	0.8991	0.9098	1.2668	0.9485
West	East	1.4574	2.1279	0.6818	1.5903	2.3332	0.7180

and the Topographic Position Index (TPI 50) were incorporated to account for terrain heterogeneity without explicitly splitting the study area. Table 6 summarizes the performance metrics obtained under this approach, showing that the inclusion of these indices does not lead to significant differences with respect to the baseline.

Table 6. Performance metrics for wind components in the baseline model and when including topographic complexity indices (TRI 50, TDI 2, TPI 50) as input variables.

Domain	Configuration	U10			V10		
Train and Test		MAE	RMSE	R^2	MAE	RMSE	R^2
East	Baseline	0.636	0.957	0.929	0.682	1.016	0.966
	Baseline + Indices	0.642	0.971	0.927	0.691	1.025	0.966
West	Baseline	1.321	1.909	0.743	1.477	2.150	0.760
	Baseline + Indices	1.377	2.000	0.718	1.522	2.212	0.746

When comparing the three approaches—spatial subdivision of the domain (Table 4), inclusion of topographic complexity indices (Table 6), and the baseline model (Table 6) it becomes evident that splitting the domain into eastern and western regions yields only marginal benefits.

The eastern subdomain shows slightly better performance in terms of error reduction ($MAE = 0.62$–0.67 and $R^2 \approx 0.93$–0.97), Table 4), however the western domain consistently exhibits lower predictive skill ($MAE = 1.32$–1.48 and $R^2 = 0.74$–0.77, Table 4)). Importantly, cross-domain validation indicates that the models retain a reasonable degree of generalization capacity: when trained in one domain and tested in the other, performance drops moderately (R^2 decreases to 0.68–0.90, Table 5) but does not collapse, suggesting that the learned relationships are transferable across topographic contexts to a certain extent. In contrast, incorporating topographic indices directly into the baseline configuration produces results statistically indistinguishable from the domain-splitting strategy (Table 6). For instance, the differences between baseline and index-augmented models are below 0.02 in R^2 and within 0.05 in MAE across both components, confirming that topographic complexity can be effectively captured by predictor variables, without the need to train and maintain multiple region-specific models. From a methodological perspective, these findings suggest that spatial subdivision adds unnecessary complexity while offering no clear advantage. Therefore, the study proceeded with a unified modeling framework, as this configuration balances accuracy, generalizability, and parsimony.

3.3 Final Modeling

Considering the similarity in performance between the full and cross window configurations, together with the significant advantage that the latter almost halves the size of the data sets, it was decided to continue the work using exclusively the cross window configuration. Accordingly, the *LGBM* models were trained using the same configuration employed in the final stage of the previous experiments. Since we are looking to predict both wind components ($U10$ and $V10$) a model was trained for each component using the same input sets, but changing their target to the corresponding wind component. This generated the final predictions on the test set. A summary of the methodology presented, from the extraction and preparation of variables from the *WRF* model, can be seen in Fig. 3.

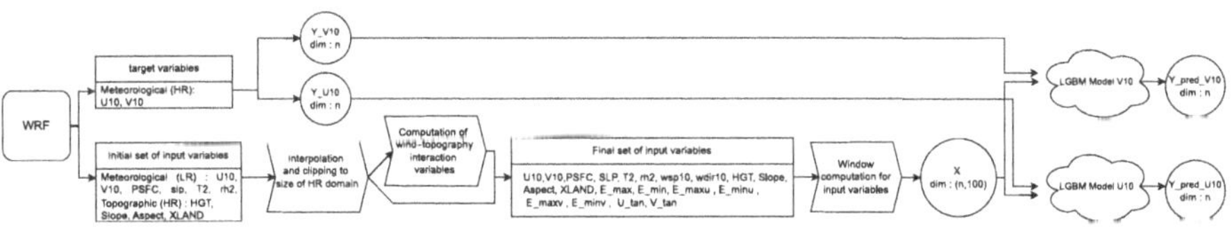

Fig. 3. Methodology flowchart.

4 Results and Discussion

Table 7 shows the errors made by the final models in their predictions on the test cases (8 cases; 965 maps).

The LightGBM models achieved strong predictive skill for near-surface winds across southern Chile with values of R^2 greater than 0.85 indicate an acceptable fit [15] and this value is higher than that seen in other works with similar problems, such as those of [12] and [11].

Table 7. Prediction errors on the test set

Model	Variable	MSE	MAE	RMSE	R^2
Final	U10	1.3954	0.7708	1.1813	0.8757
Final	V10	1.7666	0.8628	1.3291	0.9271

Figure 4 shows the average absolute and quadratic errors per map for the test set. It is observed that the errors are concentrated in the western area of the maps; this is consistent with the terrestrial topography present in this site, given its complexity. For the quadratic errors, the 95th percentile was taken as the maximum value for the color scale to improve the visualization, since there are errors that are too high and ruin the visualization.

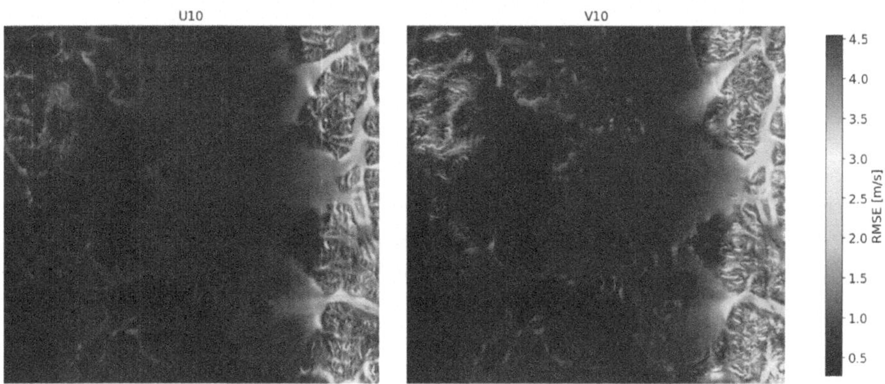

Fig. 4. mean rmse map.

Feature importance analysis confirmed that both meteorological and topographic variables contribute substantially to prediction accuracy. Excluding key predictors such as elevation, slope, aspect, or surface pressure systematically degraded results, indicating that a comprehensive predictor set is required to represent wind–terrain interactions. In exploring domain subdivision, only marginal improvements were observed when training separate models for eastern and western regions, and cross-domain validation showed limited performance degradation (R^2 between 0.68–0.90). This suggests that the models maintain a reasonable level of generalization across contrasting topographies. Incorporating topographic complexity indices (TRI, TDI, TPI) directly into the feature set produced results statistically equivalent to domain splitting, confirming that heterogeneity can be captured within a unified modeling framework.

Overall, these findings show that LightGBM is a robust and efficient tool for high-resolution wind downscaling in complex terrain. However, higher errors persist in the western domain, reflecting the challenges posed by complex topography, and the $V10$ component proves consistently harder to predict than $U10$, suggesting greater sensitivity to local effects. These patterns highlight both the strengths and current limitations of the approach.

5 Conclusion

In [11], downscaling was performed on wind speed from weather station data in areas presenting complex topography using XGBoost models, obtaining an $RMSE$ of 2.05 m/s. In this study, wind speed at each sample was derived by taking the Euclidean norm of the $U10$ and $V10$ components both for the true values and the model predictions, and the $RMSE$ between these computed wind speeds and the reference wind speeds on the test set was found to be 1.238 m/s. With this, the cross-window configuration delivers performance equivalent to the full-window method while using almost half the data volume and requiring substantially lower computational resources while the estimated RMSE remains comparable to values reported in the literature.

Regarding the quality of the accuracies, the implementation of LGBM based models proved to be able to perform wind downscaling in the southern zone of Chile with high accuracy. The results show that the models achieved an R-squared of 0.8757 and 0.9271 for the $U10$ and $V10$ components, respectively, providing evidence of the capability of the models built to capture the wind variability in the pilot area.

Regarding error characterization, the largest errors were concentrated in the western area of the maps, which coincides with the presence of more complex topography. This result highlights the importance of considering topographic interactions and opens the possibility of exploring more advanced methodologies or architectures in future implementations.

Finally, the framework developed here demonstrates clear practical value: it is computationally efficient, generates predictions within minutes, and can therefore support near-real-time maritime and aquaculture planning in the austral zone. Moreover, given its modular design, the system has potential for extension to other geographic regions and variables, broadening its applicability beyond the local context.

Acknowledgments. This work was financed by ANID, IDeA I+D Fondef Contest ID22I10206 and partially funded by Direción de Investigación, Universidad de La Frontera, Apoyo PP24-0014.

Disclosure of Interests. The authors have no competing interests to declare that are relevant to the content of this article.

References

1. Anacona, H.V., Mattar, C., de Linaje, N.G.A., Sepúlveda, H.H., Crisóstomo, J.: Wind simulations over western patagonia using the weather research and forecasting model and reanalysis. Atmosphere **14** (2023). https://doi.org/10.3390/atmos14071062

2. Arthur, D.F.: Classificacao de series temporais por meio de random forest para previsao em curto prazo de fenomenos de sobreirradiancia em natal-rn. Anais do XVI Congresso Brasileiro de Inteligência Computacional (2023)
3. Bernardoni, F., Guzman, M., Leonardi, S.: Implications of complex terrain topography on the performance of a real wind farm. J. Phys. Conf. Ser. **2505** (2023). https://doi.org/10.1088/1742-6596/2505/1/012052
4. Berri, G., Carruthers, D., Dalu, G., Hanna, S.: Atmospheric processes over complex terrain (1990). https://www.researchgate.net/publication/261005909
5. Bravo-Méndez, J.H.: Comparación del pronóstico de precipitación del modelo wrf usando datos iniciales de dos modelos globales/regionales diferentes precipitation forecast comparison using wrf model with data from two different models global/regional. Digital Ciencia@UAQRO 12, 2395–8847 (2019)
6. Cancino, R.: Diagnóstico transversal y estudio linea de base macro zona sur austral (2021)
7. Correa, M., Zuluaga, C., Palacio, C., Pérez, J., Jiménez, J.: Antioquia, colombia surface wind coupling from free atmosphere winds to local winds in a tropical region within complex terrain. case of study: Aburra valley antioquia, colombia. Año 76, 17–27 (2009)
8. Davy, R.J., Woods, M.J., Russell, C.J., Coppin, P.A.: Statistical downscaling of wind variability from meteorological fields. Bound.- Layer Meteorol. **135**, 161–175 (2010). https://doi.org/10.1007/s10546-009-9462-7
9. Dujardin, J., Lehning, M.: Wind-topo: downscaling near-surface wind fields to high-resolution topography in highly complex terrain with deep learning. Q. J. R. Meteorol. Soc. **148**(744), 1368–1388 (2022). https://doi.org/10.1002/qj.4265, https://rmets.onlinelibrary.wiley.com/doi/abs/10.1002/qj.4265
10. Hidalgo, A., et al.: Variabilidad y predictibilidad del viento a escala regional: Modelos dinÁmico y estadÍstico sobre terreno complejo (2010)
11. Hu, W., Scholz, Y., Yeligeti, M., von Bremen, L., Deng, Y.: Downscaling era5 wind speed data: a machine learning approach considering topographic influences. Environ. Res. Lett. **18** (2023). https://doi.org/10.1088/1748-9326/aceb0a
12. Li, L.: Geographically weighted machine learning and downscaling for high-resolution spatiotemporal estimations of wind speed. Remote Sens. **11** (2019). https://doi.org/10.3390/rs11111378
13. Miguel, T.A.: Estudio de idoneidad de la tecnica Random Forest para la regionalizacion estadística de proyecciones de cambio climatico. Tesis de máster, Universidad de Cantabria (2019). disponible en https://repositorio.unican.es/xmlui/bitstream/handle/10902/16905/2019_TFM_MiguelTraspuesto.pdf?sequence=1
14. Molteni, F., Buizza, R., Palmer, T.N., Petroliagis, T.: The ECMWF ensemble prediction system: methodology and validation. Q. J. R. Meteorol. Soc. **122**(529), 73–119 (1996). https://doi.org/10.1002/qj.49712252905
15. Nakagawa, S., Schielzeth, H.: A general and simple method for obtaining r2 from generalized linear mixed-effects models. Methods Ecol. Evol. **4**(2), 133–142 (2013). https://doi.org/10.1111/j.2041-210x.2012.00261.x, https://besjournals.onlinelibrary.wiley.com/doi/abs/10.1111/j.2041-210x.2012.00261.x
16. NumPy: NumPy Documentation: numpy.memmap. https://numpy.org/doc/stable/reference/generated/numpy.memmap.html. fecha de acceso: 2024–12-31
17. Riley, S., Degloria, S., Elliot, S.: A terrain ruggedness index that quantifies topographic heterogeneity. Int. J. Sci. **5**, 23–27 (1999)
18. Servicio Meteorológico de la Armada de Chile: Servicio meteorolÓgico de la armada (2024). disponible en: https://web.directemar.cl/met/jturno/indice/index.htm (Fecha de acceso: 2024–12-10)

19. Skamarock, W.C., et al.: A Description of the Advanced Research WRF Version 3 (2008). https://doi.org/10.5065/D68S4MVH
20. Wang, X., et al.: Terrain gradient response of landscape ecological environment to land use and land cover change in the hilly watershed in south China. Ecol. Ind. **146**, 109797 (2023). https://doi.org/10.1016/j.ecolind.2022.109797, https://www.sciencedirect.com/science/article/pii/S1470160X22012705
21. Wilby, R.L., et al.: Statistical downscaling of general circulation model output: a comparison of methods. Water Resour. Res. **34**, 2995–3008 (1998). https://doi.org/10.1029/98WR02577
22. Wilks, D.S., Hamill, T.M.: Comparison of ensemble-mos methods using GFS reforecasts. Monthly Weather Rev. **135**, 2379–2390 (2007). https://doi.org/10.1175/MWR3402.1
23. Xu, Z., Han, Y., Yang, Z.: Dynamical downscaling of regional climate: a review of methods and limitations. Sci. China Earth Sci. **62**, 365–375 (2019). https://doi.org/10.1007/s11430-018-9261-5

Generative AI in Education: Impacts on Student Autonomy, Critical Thinking, and Epistemic Justice

Teresa Guarda[1,2,3(✉)]

[1] Universidad Estatal Península de Santa Elena, La Libertad, Ecuador
tguarda@gmail.com
[2] BiTrum Research Group, Leon, Spain
[3] Algoritmi Centre, Minho University, Guimarães, Portugal

Abstract. This paper is a critical review of how generative AI affects the way students engage with complex information in education. These tools make content easier to access and give personalized help. However, they also bring serious risks. Students may become too dependent on AI, lose the habit of thinking for themselves, and only see ideas that the system repeats most often. This review looks at sixteen peer-reviewed studies published between 2020 and 2025. It focuses on three main questions. First, how AI changes how students understand what they read and manage their own learning. Second, how these systems influence which types of knowledge are shown and how they are judged. Third, what these effects mean for teaching, especially for student voice, inclusion, and classroom decisions. The findings show that AI is not just a tool to help students. It changes how they reach, trust, and understand information. This creates new responsibilities for teachers and schools. There is a clear need for AI literacy programs that build critical thinking, ethical awareness, and fair access to knowledge. Schools must help students use AI in ways that support learning while keeping their autonomy and fairness.

Keywords: Generative AI · Student Autonomy · Critical Thinking · AI Literacy · Epistemic Justice · Inclusive Education · Teaching Practices

1 Introduction

The use of generative AI in education has grown quickly, changing how students find and work with information. These tools can make learning more accessible and personal, but they also raise hard questions about how students think for themselves, stay involved, and understand who controls knowledge. Tools such as large language models (LLMs) are capable of producing fluent and plausible responses to user prompts; however, they often do so without ensuring epistemic reliability [1]. The gap between how smooth AI outputs sound and how accurate they are creates real problems for teaching and learning. Studies in education have shown growing concern that students may rely too much on AI, skipping the effort needed to think deeply or reflect [2, 3]. When students accept

T. Guarda et al. (Eds.): ARTIIS 2025, CCIS 2789, pp. 136–147, 2026.
https://doi.org/10.1007/978-3-032-16758-3_11

what AI says without question, especially because it sounds confident and clear, they may slowly lose their own voice and judgment, especially in tasks that ask for careful thinking and intellectual responsibility. As [4] points out, this shows a bigger shift: the power to make meaning is moving from students to machines. These transformations raise fundamental questions not only about what students learn, but also about how they come to know, and under whose influence.

At the same time, scholars emphasize the need for critical and creative AI literacies that go beyond technical skills. Atenas et al. (2025) argue that teaching should help students think about both the ethical and knowledge-related sides of AI [5].

They propose teaching approaches that emphasize fairness in how data is used, combined with encouraging students to reflect critically on the ethical and knowledge-related dimensions of AI. In the same line, Biagini (2025) stresses that AI education should go beyond technical skills, helping students question who holds power, how meanings are shaped, and what social impacts these systems produce [6]. Roshanaei (2024) further warns that ignoring AI bias, especially in universities, risks deepening educational inequalities and limiting fair access to learning [7].

Given these developments, there is a pressing need to examine how AI influences students' engagement with complex content, not only at the level of usability, but also at the levels of cognition, epistemology, and pedagogy.

This paper responds to that need by reviewing sixteen peer-reviewed studies published between 2020 and 2025. Unlike reviews that only describe or map topics, a critical review looks deeper. It brings ideas together, points out tensions, and offers careful judgement based on theory [8, 9].

The findings show that students need more than technical skills to work with AI. Schools should teach them to think critically, understand ethical problems, and make sure AI is used in a fair and inclusive way in the classroom.

The paper has five parts. The second section gives an overview of studies on how AI is changing student engagement. The third looks at how AI affects thinking, knowledge, and teaching. The fourth connects these ideas to wider discussions in education. The last section explains why schools need to use AI in ways that are fair, ethical, and focused on people.

This review shows that generative AI does more than give students access to information. It changes how they understand it, how much they trust it, and how they use that knowledge. These changes create new responsibilities for teachers, who must help students stay in control of their own learning. It is also important to make sure that AI does not exclude different ways of thinking. Because of this, schools should create AI literacy programs that teach students to think critically, understand ethical issues, and use AI in a fair and responsible way.

2 Reviewed Studies

This section brings together sixteen studies that look at how generative AI affects student engagement with complex content. These studies were selected based on their relevance to the cognitive, epistemological, and pedagogical dimensions of AI in education, and were all published between 2020 and 2025. It starts with Floridi and Chiriatti (2020), who warn that GPT-3 can sound convincing while still giving false or misleading information [1]. Burns (2025) shares this concern, noting that while AI can help with simple thinking tasks, it does not support deeper learning and does not match the top levels of Bloom's taxonomy [3].

Wu et al. (2023) found that students using AI often put in less effort to interpret content, which shows a risk of relying too much on the system and thinking less critically [2]. Lee et al. (2024) link this to weaker self-regulated learning when students use AI without proper guidance [10]. Hong and Guo (2025) also note that although AI tools can lower mental effort and boost motivation, they might reduce student independence if teachers are not there to guide the process [11].

At the level of knowledge and meaning, Miragoli (2024) argues that generative AI can reinforce dominant views while ignoring knowledge from less represented groups [12]. Coeckelbergh (2025) builds on this idea by showing how AI becomes part of a wider system that shifts the power to decide what counts as knowledge from people to machines. Yoo (2024) adds that AI is also changing how research is shared and judged, especially in academic publishing.

From an ethical and teaching point of view, Atenas et al. (2025) and Biagini (2025) say that students need to learn more than just how to use AI [5, 6]. Students also need to learn how power works inside these systems and how to question the way they are built. Gouseti et al. (2025) focus on schools and suggest setting clear rules for how AI should be used with children [13]. Terrazas-Arellanes et al. (2025) explore how AI affects students' ability to make choices and stay in control of their learning, especially in science classes [14].

Other researchers focus on fairness. Viberg et al. (2024), Roshanaei (2024), and Vučković and Sikimić (2024) show that AI can make digital gaps worse if it is not designed with everyone in mind [7, 15, 16]. Wang et al. (2024) add that for AI to support learning fairly, it must be built from the start with care for people and teaching in real classrooms [17].

Taken together, these studies show that AI does more than support learning. It changes how knowledge is defined, how students connect to it, and which ways of thinking are included or left out.

A comparative overview of these studies is provided in Table 1. Collectively, these studies affirm that generative AI is not a neutral tool. It alters how students access, interpret, and construct knowledge, raising urgent pedagogical and ethical responsibilities for educators.

Table 1. Comparative Overview of Reviewed Studies (2020–2025).

Authors	Focus Area	Key Findings
(Floridi & Chiriatti, 2020)	Epistemology	GPT-3's fluency can mislead users into trusting inaccurate content
(Burns, 2025)	Bloom's Taxonomy / Critical Thinking	AI supports surface-level learning but not deep cognitive development

(continued)

Table 1. *(continued)*

Authors	Focus Area	Key Findings
(Wu, Lee, Chai, & Tsai, 2023)	Student Agency / Interpretation	Students reduce interpretive effort and rely heavily on AI guidance
(Lee, Chen, Wang, Huang, & Wu, 2024)	Higher-order Thinking	Guided AI use supports self-regulated learning and higher-order skills
(Hong & Guo, 2025)	Cognitive Load	AI systems ease cognitive effort but risk reducing learner autonomy
(Miragoli, 2024)	Epistemic Injustice	AI reinforces dominant knowledge systems, excluding marginalized voices
(Coeckelbergh, 2025)	Epistemic Infrastructure	AI reshapes belief systems and shifts cognitive control from humans to machines
(Yoo, 2024)	Scholarly Knowledge Dissemination	Generative AI is altering the structure and gatekeeping of academic publishing
(Atenas, Havemann, & Nerantzi, 2025)	AI Literacy & Data Justice	Emphasizes critical and ethical AI/data literacy pedagogies
(Biagini, 2025)	AI Literacy (Review)	Synthesizes global efforts to define and implement AI literacy in education
(Gouseti, James, Fallin, & Burden, 2025)	AI Ethics in K–12	Urges responsible AI use in early education through clear ethical guidelines
(Terrazas-Arellanes, Strycker, Alvez, Miller, & Vargas, 2025)	Student Agency	AI can both support and undermine agency depending on implementation
(Viberg, Kizilcec, Wise, Jivet, & Nixon, 2024)	AI Equity/Inclusion	Equity must be central to AI-EDSS design or disparities will widen
(Vučković & Sikimić, 2024)	Justice & Inclusion	AI in education must be governed by epistemic and ethical pluralism
(Roshanaei, 2024)	Implicit Bias in AI	Unaddressed bias in AI undermines equity and inclusion in higher education

(continued)

Table 1. (*continued*)

Authors	Focus Area	Key Findings
(Wang, et al., 2024)	Human-centered AI in Education	Recommends institution-wide frameworks for ethical, inclusive AI adoption

3 Critical Analysis

In the studies reviewed, one clear tension appears. AI makes learning easier to access, but it also brings risks to how students think and make ethical choices. Floridi and Chiriatti (2020) and Yoo (2024) both point out that because AI sounds fluent and automatic, it can seem more trustworthy than it really is. This can make students overlook the deeper problems behind the information it gives.

Students are prone to accepting AI outputs uncritically, particularly when the interface mimics human expertise, as Wu et al. (2023) and Burns (2025) indicate. These overlapping concerns: cognitive, epistemic, and pedagogical, are illustrated in Fig. 1. The Venn diagram highlights the three core dimensions identified in the literature, cognitive effect, epistemic risk, and pedagogical challenge, and their overlapping consequences on student engagement with complex content.

Table 1 gives a side-by-side look at what each study focused on. Together, the studies make it clear that generative AI is not a neutral tool. It alters how students access, interpret, and construct knowledge, raising urgent pedagogical and ethical responsibilities for educators.

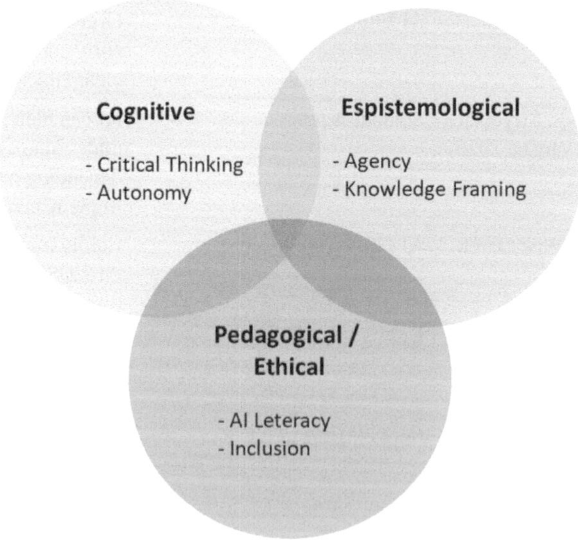

Fig. 1. Interconnected Dimensions of AI-Driven Educational Impact.

This overreliance leads to reduced interpretative effort, weakening students' ability to question, analyze, and reframe information. Lee et al. (2024) highlight how scaffolding mechanisms, such as prompts, instructor-led reflection, or peer discussion—are necessary to avoid these effects and promote higher-order learning [10]. Without these, as Hong and Guo (2025) warn, AI may act as a cognitive crutch, increasing dependency rather than fostering autonomy [11].

From an epistemological standpoint, Miragoli (2024) and Coeckelbergh (2025) raise concerns about the systemic exclusion of alternative knowledge forms. The algorithms underlying generative AI are trained on dominant language patterns, making it more likely to reproduce mainstream perspectives and marginalize others [4, 12]. This is especially problematic in educational settings, where the purpose is not just to transfer knowledge but also to cultivate critical, diverse, and inclusive worldviews.

The studies also underscore the need for rethinking AI literacy. Atenas et al. (2025) and Biagini (2025) advocate for pedagogies that teach students not only how to use AI tools, but also how to question their outputs, understand their construction, and evaluate their limitations [5, 6]. Gouseti et al. (2025) add that ethical education is necessary from the earliest stages of schooling if we are to develop students capable of navigating AI environments responsibly [13]. These interconnected components of critical AI literacy are summarized in Fig. 2.

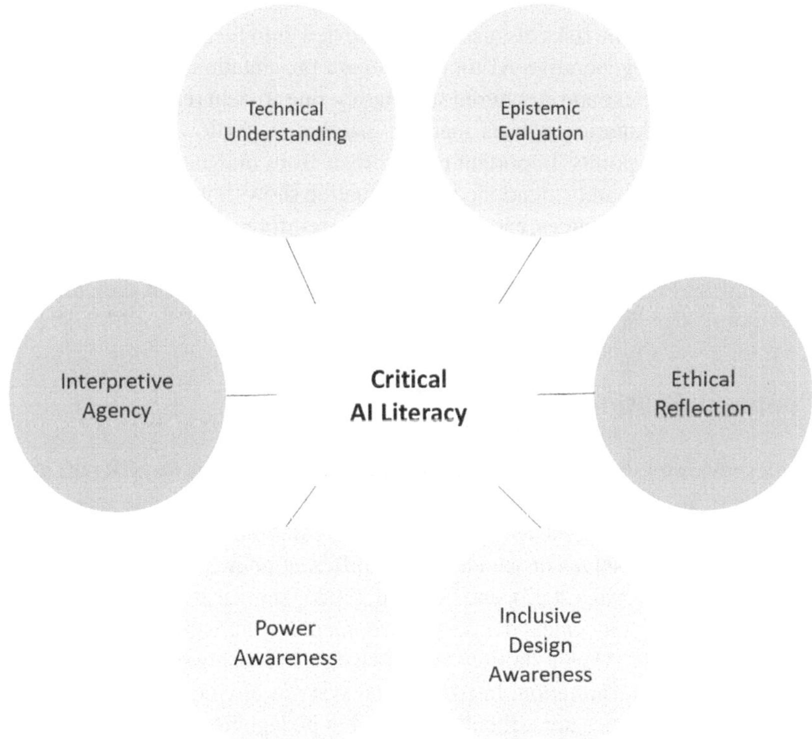

Fig. 2. Conceptual Map of Critical AI Literacy.

This figure shows six key parts of what it means to understand AI in a critical way. These include knowing how it works, thinking about how we judge information, asking ethical questions, keeping control over how we use it, seeing who holds power in these systems, and making sure they include everyone. These ideas, taken together, point to a fair and careful way to use AI in education.

Viberg et al. (2024), Roshanaei (2024), and Vučković stress that fairness must be part of every plan for using AI in schools [7, 15, 16]. If AI tools are not built and used with all types of students in mind, they can make inequality worse. The tools themselves are not biased by nature, but the data they use, how they are built, and where they are used often are. That is why these systems need to be looked at with care and thought.

The papers reviewed in this work show useful perspectives on how AI affects learning, but they often separate topics that, in practice, happen together. When students use AI, the cognitive effort, the way knowledge is presented, and ethical concerns are not isolated effects. They overlap. However, most studies do not offer solutions on how to support students in keeping their role as active learners when AI is involved. This is especially important for students from groups that already face barriers in education. Another point that appears is that much of the research focuses on reducing the negative effects of AI, but less attention is given to how teachers and students can develop critical views about these systems. For that, AI literacy should not stay at the technical level. It should also help students reflect on power, meaning, and fairness in the use of AI in the classroom.

To bring the epistemic risks discussed in this review into focus, consider a classroom where students use a generative AI tool to prepare presentations on historical topics. While many receive clear and structured summaries, one student researching indigenous resistance in Latin America notices that the material is shallow and framed mainly through colonial viewpoints. Important perspectives from indigenous scholars and oral traditions are absent or barely mentioned. This situation shows how generative AI, shaped by dominant knowledge sources, can unintentionally reinforce epistemic injustice, giving space to certain voices while overlooking others. It reminds us why teaching must go beyond using AI tools, helping students to question both the content they receive and the assumptions that shape it.

4 Contextualization

The studies reviewed show that AI is changing education in deeper ways. It puts pressure on old ways of teaching and learning. While many see AI as a way to make learning faster, more engaging, and easier to access, these gains may also reduce how much students think for themselves or see ideas from different points of view.

Burns (2025), Wu et al. (2023), and Lee et al. (2024) show that AI tends to encourage passive learning behaviors unless deliberately countered by human instruction [2, 3, 10]. Students may perceive AI as a shortcut to knowledge, bypassing the effort required for deep reflection and interpretation. In educational systems already pressured by metrics and speed, such tendencies are difficult to resist, but pedagogically dangerous.

Coeckelbergh (2025) and Yoo (2024) explain that AI changes more than just what information we can find. It also shapes how knowledge is made and shared [4, 18]. When students or researchers use AI to write, check, or explain ideas, they are dealing with choices made by the system that are often hidden but still very important. These tools don't just help, they also decide which meanings are shown or left out.

Because of this, teachers are being asked to guide students in how they use AI. Atenas et al. (2025) and Biagini (2025) say that this goes beyond teaching technical skills [5, 6]. It means helping students think about what AI gives them, where it comes from, and what it might miss. AI outputs should be read not just as answers, but as shaped by culture, values, and ideas.

This shift also raises policy and infrastructure challenges. Viberg et al. (2024) and Wang et al. (2024) emphasize the need for institutional frameworks that support ethical AI use, from data governance to professional development. Inclusion must be a core principle, not an afterthought, particularly given the disproportionate impact AI systems can have on marginalized learners [15, 17].

Figure 3 summarizes the main educational benefits and risks of AI identified across the reviewed literature.

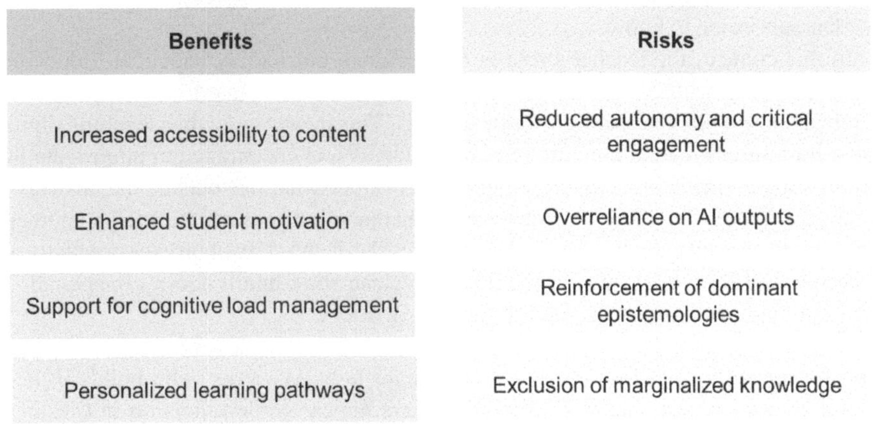

Fig. 3. Educational Benefits and Risks of AI.

This figure contrasts key pedagogical opportunities offered by AI—such as personalization and cognitive support, with major concerns related to student autonomy, critical capacity, and epistemic fairness.

5 Conclusions

Generative AI is becoming part of everyday educational settings, and its advantages are immediately apparent. It makes information easier to reach and helps with completing routine tasks. For some learners, this kind of support can reduce mental effort and make it easier to stay focused. But as shown in the studies examined here, these gains are not without trade-offs. Some of the most significant concerns are less visible at first, yet they touch the core of the learning process. When AI is used without careful framing, there's a real risk that students begin to lose independence in how they think, relying more on the system than on their own reasoning [1–3].

AI-generated outputs often sound fluent, confident, and complete. This surface-level credibility can cause students to treat them as authoritative, particularly when there is no obvious error. Over time, this may reduce students' willingness to question what they read, investigate alternative perspectives, or develop original interpretations. The very ease that makes these tools attractive can also make them epistemically dangerous. And crucially, these risks do not emerge because students are making mistakes, they emerge because the systems are designed to present partial knowledge in a polished and persuasive way.

More than simply delivering content, these systems shape what content is seen and how it is framed. They filter knowledge through datasets and algorithms that reflect dominant discourses, often-omitting voices, experiences, and frameworks that fall outside mainstream patterns. The studies reviewed highlight how this mechanism can reinforce epistemic injustice, especially when marginalized perspectives are excluded not by intent, but by omission [4, 7]. In educational settings, where exposure to difference is central to growth, this is not a small concern; it is a structural problem that influences how learners come to know.

In this context, the teacher's role is not optional, nor merely technical. Educators are not just responsible for introducing tools; they are responsible for helping students sustain agency while interacting with those tools. This means more than teaching digital skills. It requires creating conditions where students feel encouraged to interrogate the system's logic, question its assumptions, and consider what lies outside the answers it generates. Figure 4, in a way, captures something that often goes unnoticed, that moment when a student stops just taking in what AI gives them and starts, however gradually, to make sense of it on their own terms. It's not a clean shift, and it doesn't happen all at once, but that's precisely why teacher guidance matters.

The implications for AI literacy are significant. Teaching students how to use AI is no longer sufficient. They must also be taught how AI works, who builds it, how its outputs are shaped, and why certain answers appear while others do not. Ethical awareness, fairness, and epistemic sensitivity must be integrated into this literacy. This isn't something to be left for advanced students or treated as an optional extra. If we want AI to be used fairly and responsibly in education, then these issues need to be part of the core learning experience [5, 6].

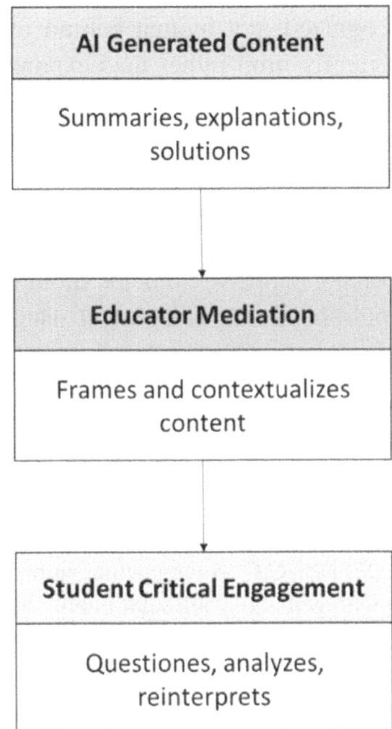

Fig. 4. Stages of Educator Mediation in AI-Supported Learning.

The flowchart shows how teachers support students as they interact with content generated by AI. It follows the movement from automatic responses to more thoughtful learning and points to the teacher's role in guiding how students read and interpret what the system presents.

The review also makes one thing clear: if we're going to teach AI, it needs to be more than technical. Students should be able to ask where these systems come from, who builds them, and what they leave out. Ethics, fairness, and understanding how knowledge is shaped must be part of that work. Teaching like this keeps education close to what it's meant to be, not just passing on facts, but helping people think, question, and take part in how meaning is made.

The implications for AI literacy are significant. Teaching students how to use AI is no longer sufficient. They must also be taught how AI works, who builds it, how its outputs are shaped, and why certain answers appear while others do not. Ethical awareness, fairness, and epistemic sensitivity must be integrated into this literacy.This isn't something to be left for advanced students or treated as an optional extra. If we want AI to be used fairly and responsibly in education, then these issues need to be part of the core learning experience.

One thing that stands out across this review is that generative AI doesn't simply assist, it alters the way knowledge moves, and shifts influence over who gets to define what counts as relevant, or even valid.

That power must be recognized, not hidden behind technical proficiency. If left unexamined, AI may inadvertently limit rather than expand the epistemic horizons of students.

Education is not just about delivering answers or accelerating output. Its purpose is to support learners in becoming critical, reflective, and active participants in the world. If AI is going to have a place in learning that actually means something, it has to fit the process, not sit above it. Learning still needs doubt, effort, moments where things don't come easily. That's where thinking happens. Students shouldn't just walk away knowing how to use the tool; they should be able to stop, ask if what it gave them makes sense, and keep working through ideas that go beyond what the system offers.

References

1. Floridi, L., Chiriatti, M.: GPT-3: its nature, scope, limits, and consequences. Minds Mach. **30**(4), 681–694 (2020). 30(4), 681–694. https://doi.org/10.1007/s11023-020-09548-1
2. Wu, J.Y., Lee, Y.H., Chai, C.S., Tsai, C.C.: Strengthening human epistemic agency in the symbiotic learning partnership with generative artificial intelligence. Educ. Res. (2023). https://doi.org/10.3102/0013189X251333628
3. Burns, L.R.: Beyond problem-solving: the future of learning in an AI-driven world. Creat. Educ. **16**(4), 520–534 (2025). https://doi.org/10.4236/ce.2025.164031
4. Coeckelbergh, M.: AI and epistemic agency: how AI influences belief revision and its normative implications. Soc. Epistemol. 1–13 (2025). https://doi.org/10.1080/02691728.2025.2466164
5. Atenas, J., Havemann, L., Nerantzi, C.: Critical and creative pedagogies for artificial intelligence and data literacy: an epistemic data justice approach for academic practice. Res. Learn. Technol. **32**, 1–16 (2025). https://doi.org/10.25304/rlt.v32.3296
6. Biagini, G.: Towards an AI-Literate Future: a systematic literature review exploring education, ethics, and applications. Int. J. Artif. Intell. Educ. 1–51 (2025). https://doi.org/10.1007/s40593-025-00466-w
7. Roshanaei, M.: Towards best practices for mitigating artificial intelligence implicit bias in shaping diversity, inclusion and equity in higher education. Educ. Inf. Technol. **29**(14), 18959–18984 (2024). https://doi.org/10.1007/s10639-024-12605-2
8. Grant, M.J., Booth, A.: A typology of reviews: an analysis of 14 review types and associated methodologies. Health Inf. Libr. J. **26**(2), 91–108 (2009). https://doi.org/10.1111/j.1471-1842.2009.00848.x
9. Snyder, H.: Literature review as a research methodology: an overview and guidelines. J. Bus. Res. **104**, 333–339 (2019). https://doi.org/10.1016/j.jbusres.2019.07.039
10. Lee, H.Y., Chen, P.H., Wang, W.S., Huang, Y.M., Wu, T.T.: Empowering ChatGPT with guidance mechanism in blended learning: Effect of self-regulated learning, higher-order thinking skills, and knowledge construction. J. Educ. Technol. High. Educ. **21**(1), 16, 1–28 (2024). https://doi.org/10.1186/s41239-024-00447-4
11. Hong, X., Guo, L.: Effects of AI-enhanced multi-display language teaching systems on learning motivation, cognitive load management, and learner autonomy. Educ. Inf. Technol. 1–35 (2025). https://doi.org/10.1007/s10639-025-13472-1
12. Miragoli, M.: Conformism, ignorance & injustice: AI as a tool of epistemic oppression. Episteme 1–19 (2024). https://doi.org/10.1017/epi.2024.11
13. Gouseti, A., James, F., Fallin, L., Burden, K.: The ethics of using AI in K-12 education: a systematic literature review. Technol. Pedagog. Educ. **34**(2), 161–182 (2025). https://doi.org/10.1080/1475939X.2024.2428601

14. Terrazas-Arellanes, F.E., Strycker, L., Alvez, G.G., Miller, B., Vargas, K.: Promoting agency among upper elementary school teachers and students with an artificial intelligence machine learning system to score performance-based science assessments. Educ. Sci. **15**(1), 1–21 (2025). https://doi.org/10.3390/educsci15010054
15. Viberg, O., Kizilcec, R.F., Wise, A.F., Jivet, I., Nixon, N.: Advancing equity and inclusion in educational practices with AI-powered educational decision support systems (AI-EDSS). Br. J. Edu. Technol. **55**(5), 1974–1981 (2024). https://doi.org/10.1111/bjet.13507
16. Vučković, A., Sikimić, V.: Global justice and the use of AI in education: ethical and epistemic aspects. AI & Soc. **40**, 3087–3104 (2024). https://doi.org/10.1007/s00146-024-02076-x
17. Wang, S., Wang, F., Zhu, Z., Wang, J., Tran, T., Du, Z.: Artificial intelligence in education: a systematic literature review. Expert Syst. Appl. **252**, 1–19 (2024). https://doi.org/10.1016/j.eswa.2024.124167
18. Yoo, Y.: Evolving epistemic infrastructure: the role of scientific journals in the age of generative AI. J. Assoc. Inf. Syst. **25**(1), 137–144 (2024). https://doi.org/10.17705/1jais.00870

Analysis the Effect of Title Expression Forms on Content Selection for Japanese UGC Educational Videos

Tomohiro Kawata[1(✉)], Takumi Kato[2], and Kazuhiko Tsuda[1]

[1] University of Tsukuba, 1-1-1 Tennodai, Tsukuba, Ibaraki, Japan
s1745002@u.tsukuba.ac.jp

[2] Meiji University, 1-1 Kanda-Surugadai, Chiyoda-Ku, Tokyo, Japan

Abstract. Video titles are critical for the discoverability of educational User-Generated Content (UGC) on YouTube, particularly in Japanese, where multiple script systems allow for various keyword notations. This study empirically investigates how different title notations for "Microsoft Excel"—specifically alphabetical ("Excel"), Katakana phonetic ("エクセル"), and uppercase alphabetical ("EXCEL")—impact view counts of Japanese Excel tutorial videos. We analyzed 10,048 videos (published 2010–2023), categorizing them by the keyword notation used in titles and statistically comparing their log-transformed view counts. Results indicate that using "Excel" alone was associated with significantly higher view counts than using "エクセル" alone or "EXCEL" alone. The combination of "Excel" and "エクセル" did not outperform "Excel" used solitarily. Notably, the combination of Katakana "エクセル" and uppercase "EXCEL" yielded the highest average view counts among the analyzed categories. We conclude that the choice of keyword notation in Japanese YouTube titles significantly and complexly influences video viewership, offering practical insights for content creators to optimize visibility.

Keywords: Video-sharing platform · Title · Keyword · Viewing behavior · synonym · UGC · Japanese language

1 Introduction

The rapid development of the internet and digital technologies has fundamentally changed the ways in which information is produced, distributed, and consumed. In particular, the proliferation of User-Generated Content (UGC) has significantly transformed the traditional mass media-centric information dissemination model, creating an environment where individuals can actively function as information providers [1].

At the forefront of this change is the video-sharing platform YouTube. Since its establishment in 2005, YouTube has grown to become the world's largest video platform, and in Japan, with over 70 million monthly users, it has achieved significant societal influence [2].

T. Guarda et al. (Eds.): ARTIIS 2025, CCIS 2789, pp. 148–159, 2026.
https://doi.org/10.1007/978-3-032-16758-3_12

While YouTube content was initially entertainment-focused, the proportion of educational content has rapidly increased in recent years. The surge in demand for online learning, especially due to the COVID-19 pandemic, further accelerated this trend.

However, with a vast amount of video content being uploaded to YouTube daily, it is not easy for individual content to be discovered by viewers. In fact, the phenomenon of "long-tail distribution," where the majority of total views on YouTube are concentrated on a very small percentage of channels, has also been pointed out [3].

In such a situation, video titles are a crucial element that determines the viewer's first impression, influences top ranking in search results and click-through rates, and also impacts YouTube's recommendation algorithm [4, 5].

Japanese has a linguistic characteristic of using multiple script systems concurrently: Kanji, Hiragana, Katakana, and the Roman alphabet. This characteristic allows for multiple notation methods for the same concept or product name. For example, the software "Microsoft Excel" can be written as "Excel" (alphabetical), "エクセル" (Katakana), or "EXCEL" (uppercase alphabetical). Previous research [6] pointed out the possibility that the diversity of character types in Japanese YouTube videos could affect the visual characteristics of titles, but the specific impact of different notation forms for the same concept on viewing behavior had not been sufficiently examined.

The primary purpose of this study is to quantitatively analyze how different keyword notation forms for the same concept in the titles of Japanese educational UGC indirectly affect viewers' cognitive processes, as inferred from view count data, and what effects these notation forms have on content discoverability, viewers' selection behavior, and ultimately, their initial interest in and receptivity to the content (operationally defined in this study as the impact on view counts). Specifically, focusing on tutorial videos related to Microsoft Excel, this study analyzes how the main notation forms—"Excel" (alphabetical), "エクセル" (Katakana), and "EXCEL" (uppercase alphabetical)—lead to differences in the behavioral indicator of view counts, through factors such as the ease of viewers' instantaneous recognition and the impressions evoked (e.g., professionalism, familiarity).

The structure of this paper is as follows. Section 2 reviews existing research and presents the hypotheses. Section 3 describes the verification method. Section 4 presents the verification results and discussion based on them. Finally, Sect. 5 states the conclusions of this research and future prospects.

2 Literature Review and Hypothesis Development

2.1 Cognitive Psychological Foundations and Character Recognition Processes

Human information processing is said to involve two processes: an automatic "System 1" and a controlled "System 2" [7, 8]. In high-speed browsing environments like viewing YouTube titles, it is thought that instantaneous cognitive processes, mainly by System 1, are at play.

Empirical research on Japanese character recognition, such as the work by Shibasaki (2010) which investigated the readability of Kanji and Hiragana orthography by measuring reaction times in sentence correctness decision tasks, has shown that processing speed and cognitive load can differ depending on the character type and word familiarity. For instance, Shibasaki found that for low-frequency/difficult Kanji words (e.g., level 8 and 9 of the Japanese Kanji Aptitude Test), Hiragana renditions took longer to process (were more difficult) than their Kanji counterparts, whereas for high-frequency/easy Kanji words (e.g., level 1), Kanji renditions required more processing time than Hiragana.

While this study focused on Kanji and Hiragana, it underscores the principle that different script representations of the same lexical item can lead to varied cognitive processing demands. This suggests that the cognitive processes for alphabetical and Katakana notations, particularly for loanwords like "Excel," may also differ, potentially influenced by factors such as familiarity with the term in each script, and the typical script used in the specific context (e.g., IT-related terms). This implies that for viewers familiar with IT-related terms, alphabetical notation might be recognized more quickly if it is the more conventional or frequently encountered form.

2.2 Visual Salience Theory and Cognitive Load Theory

Visual salience theory [10] explains how human attention mechanisms are drawn to specific visual features. Uppercase alphabetical notations like "EXCEL" may have the effect of being visually prominent in a typical list of titles, but excessive prominence also carries the risk of reducing readability. On the other hand, Cognitive Load Theory [11] explains the limits of human working memory and learning efficiency. The mixed use of multiple character types or redundant information in titles can increase extraneous cognitive load, potentially hindering instantaneous comprehension.

2.3 Linguistic Foundations and YouTube's System

Japanese has a complex mixed-script system employing Kanji, Hiragana, Katakana, and the Roman alphabet. This characteristic creates diversity in the notation of loanwords and technical terms. Katakana can give an impression of "foreignness" or "novelty," while alphabetical notation, especially for IT terms, may convey "professionalism" or "internationality." The choice of notation can affect comprehension speed and memory retention [12, 13]. YouTube's search and recommendation systems use video titles as important information [14], and the match between search queries and title notation affects discoverability [15].

2.4 The Impact of Video Titles and the Conception of This Study

Previous research [6] focused on structural characteristics of video titles (length, word count) as factors influencing view counts and pointed out the significant impact of visual information (character count). However, the effects of Japan's unique notation system, particularly the choice of different keyword expression forms for the same concept, remained largely unexplored.

Therefore, this study addresses this issue based on the aforementioned cognitive psychological findings and linguistic background. For instance, differences in cognitive processing speed due to character type suggest that notation forms such as "Excel" (alphabetical), "エクセル" (Katakana), and "EXCEL" (uppercase alphabetical) for IT terms originating from foreign languages, like Microsoft Excel, can have different effects on the speed and ease of viewers' instantaneous cognitive processing. As [xxx] research indicates, these notations are also thought to create differences in evoked impressions (e.g., professionalism, familiarity). Furthermore, from the perspective of search engine optimization (SEO), the degree of match between the notation in user search queries and the notation in video titles is an important point to consider for video discoverability [14, 15].

On the other hand, while a strategy of using different notations for the same concept in combination may correspond to a wider range of search queries, it also carries the risk of reducing viewers' information processing efficiency and hindering instantaneous content understanding by increasing information redundancy within the title [15–17].

Thus, the choice of keyword notation form in Japanese titles is thought to affect both viewers' cognitive processes (processing speed, impression, load) and search behavior, consequently leading to differences in video discoverability, click selection, and ultimately, view counts. This is the fundamental concept of this research.

Therefore, this study derived the following hypotheses:

- H1: Differences in keyword expression forms for the same concept affect video view counts. Specifically, videos using the official notation "Excel" in the title tend to acquire more view counts compared to videos using other standalone notations such as Katakana "エクセル" or uppercase alphabetical "EXCEL".
- H2: Using multiple keyword expression forms for the same concept in combination within a title (e.g., "Excel" and "エクセル") has a different impact on video view counts compared to using only a single expression form. Certain combinations may lead to an increase in view counts.

3 Methodology

3.1 Data Acquisition

The dataset utilized in this study was originally compiled by Kawata et al. (2024) and comprises Japanese educational YouTube content. For the present research, we focused on videos published over a period spanning from January 2010 to November 2023.

The initial data collection process by Kawata et al. (2024) involved identifying relevant Japanese YouTube channels through keyword "Excel". Subsequently, metadata for videos from these channels were retrieved using the official YouTube Data API v3.

The focus on Japanese educational content was ensured through initial channel selection criteria and language filtering based on title and description content in the original data acquisition phase.

This study re-analyzes a subset of this comprehensive dataset, specifically focusing on videos pertinent to Microsoft Excel tutorials and the keyword notations within their titles.

3.2 Data Cleansing

To analyze the effects of keywords more rigorously, Japanese expressions were normalized after morphological analysis, and the data was limited to videos containing at least one of the keywords “Excel,” “エクセル,” or “EXCEL” in their titles. Consistent with previous research, the analysis was restricted to long-form videos (excluding Shorts), Japanese language videos, and videos primarily about Excel. As a result, 10,048 data points were obtained. This dataset includes information such as video titles, view counts, publication dates, channel subscriber counts, and video duration.

3.3 View Count Processing and Analytical Framework

As YouTube view counts typically show a skewed distribution, a log transformation was applied to enhance the normality of the distribution. The core of the analytical framework is the categorization of videos based on the presence and combination of specific keyword expressions (“Excel,” “エクセル,” “EXCEL”) in their titles. Specifically, mutually exclusive categories such as “Excel only,” “エクセル only,” “EXCEL only,” “Excel and エクセル,” “Excel and EXCEL,” “エクセル and EXCEL,” and “All included” were established, and view counts were compared across these categories.

4 Results and Discussion

4.1 Descriptive Statistics and Overall Trends

Table 1shows the occurrence of the keywords “Excel,” “エクセル,” and “EXCEL” in the video titles. “Excel” was the most frequent, followed by “エクセル,” and then “EXCEL.”

Table 1. Presence of Excel expressions.

Expression	Count
Excel	6,630
エクセル	4,253
EXCEL	9,38

Figure 1 presents a box plot comparing the log-transformed view counts of videos containing these primary standalone notations. The “Excel” notation (N = 6,630) shows the highest median value, followed by “エクセル” (N = 4,253), and then “EXCEL” (N = 938). The “EXCEL” notation exhibits a distribution of view counts clearly lower than the other two.

Figure 2 shows the probability density distribution of log-transformed view counts for the same three keyword notation categories. Videos containing “Excel” (blue line) show a relatively broad distribution, with higher density in the high view count range (log value 8–10) compared to other notations. The “エクセル” notation (orange line) shows a similar distribution shape to “Excel,” but its peak is located in a slightly lower view count range. The “EXCEL” notation (green line) shows a distribution skewed to the left (low view count range), with a sharp peak around log value 5–6, and markedly

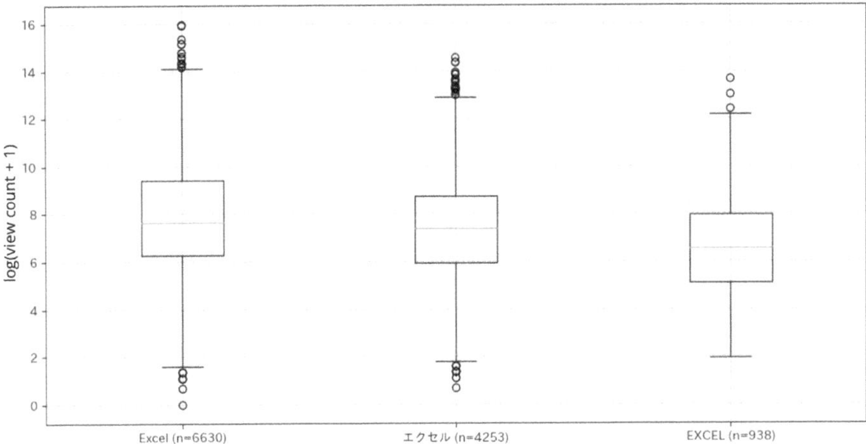

Fig. 1. Comparison of View Counts by Excel Expression Type in Title.

lower density in the high view count range compared to the other two notations. These trends support the hypothesized superiority of the official notation.

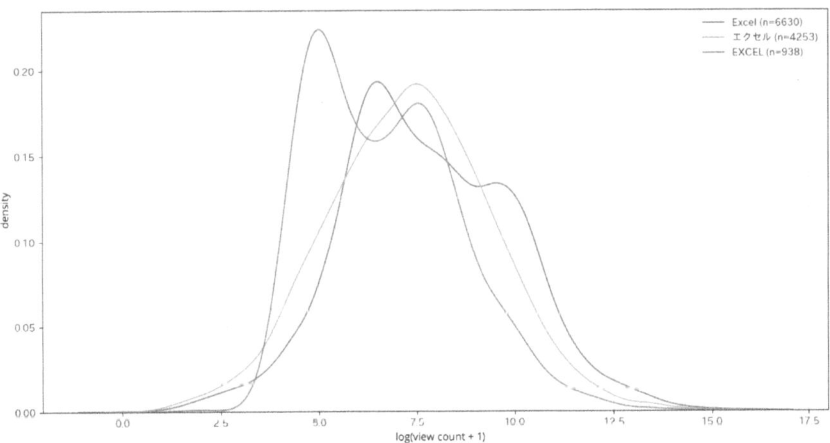

Fig. 2. Distribution of View Counts for Excel Expression Type in Title

4.2 Regression Analysis Results

To quantitatively evaluate the effect of standalone keyword notations, a linear regression model was estimated with dummy variables indicating the presence of the three main notation forms ("Excel," "エクセル," "EXCEL") as explanatory variables and log-transformed view counts as the dependent variable. The reference category was videos that did not contain any of these three keyword expressions in their titles. The results are shown in Table 2.

Table 2. Regression Analysis: Single Keyword Expression Effects

var	coef	std err	t-value	p-value	95 Confidence Interval
(const)	7.5624	0.074	102.486	< 0.001	[7.418, 7.707]
Excel	0.2713	0.069	3.908	< 0.001	[0.135, 0.407]
エクセル	-0.2578	0.060	-4.329	< 0.001	[-0.375, -0.141]
EXCEL	-0.7481	0.090	-8.269	< 0.001	[-0.925, -0.571]

The coefficient for the "Excel" dummy was 0.2713 ($p < 0.001$), positive and significant, indicating an effect of increasing log view counts by approximately 0.27 points compared to the reference category. In contrast, the coefficients for the "エクセル" dummy (–0.2578, $p < 0.001$) and the "EXCEL" dummy (–0.7481, $p < 0.001$) were both negative and significant, indicating effects of decreasing log view counts by approximately 0.26 and 0.75 points, respectively, compared to the reference category. Comparing these coefficients suggests that the "Excel" notation has a more positive impact (or the least negative impact) on view counts than the other two standalone notations, strongly supporting H1.

4.3 Analysis of Expression Occurrence Patterns

Next, we analyzed the impact of "occurrence patterns" of keyword expressions on view counts by comparing mutually exclusive categories. Table 3 shows the number of videos corresponding to each keyword expression pattern category.

Table 3. Count by Expression Combination Category.

Var	coef	std err	t-value	p-value	95 Confidence Interval
(const)	7.5624	0.074	102.486	< 0.001	[7.418, 7.707]
Excel	0.2713	0.069	3.908	< 0.001	[0.135, 0.407]
エクセル	-0.2578	0.060	-4.329	< 0.001	[-0.375, -0.141]
EXCEL	-0.7481	0.090	-8.269	< 0.001	[-0.925, -0.571]

The distribution of log-transformed view counts for these main categories was visualized using violin plots in Fig. 3.

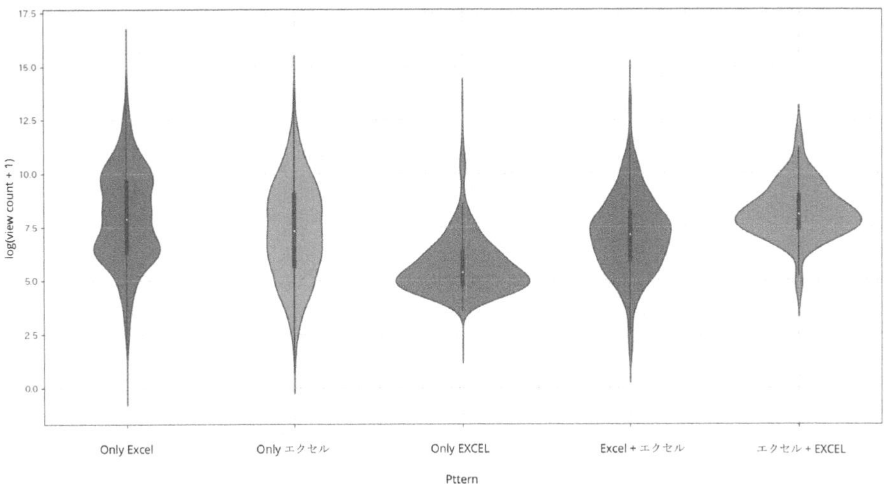

Fig. 3. Distribution of View Counts by Excel Expression Category

Table 4. Regression Analysis: Single Keyword Expression Effects.

Comparison Gr.1	Comparison Gr.2	Mean Difference (Gr.1-Gr.2)	t-value	p-value
Only "Excel"	Only "エクセル"	0.65	11.76	< 0.0001
Only "Excel"	Only "EXCEL"	2.23	33.12	< 0.0001
Only "エクセル"	Only "EXCEL"	1.59	21.06	< 0.0001
Only "Excel"	Only "エクセル"	0.65	11.76	< 0.0001

Table 5. Regression Analysis: Single Keyword Expression Effects

Comparison Gr.1	Comparison Gr.2	Mean Difference (Gr.1-Gr.2)	t-value	p-value
"Excel"+"エクセル"	Only "Excel"	-0.82	-13.94	< 0.0001
"Excel"+"エクセル"	Only "エクセル"	-0.17	-2.51	0.0121
"エクセル"+"EXCEL"	Only "Excel"	0.24	3.26	0.0012
"エクセル"+"EXCEL"	Only "エクセル"	0.88	11	< 0.0001
"エクセル"+"EXCEL"	Only "EXCEL"	2.47	27.66	< 0.0001
"エクセル"+"EXCEL"	"Excel"+"エクセル"	1.05	12.72	< 0.0001

Figure 3 visually confirms differences in view count distributions across categories. "Excel only" (blue) is relatively high, while "EXCEL only" (green) is markedly low. Interestingly, the combination of "エクセル and EXCEL" (purple) extends into a view count range similar to or partially exceeding that of "Excel only." To statistically verify these visual trends, t-tests were conducted on the mean differences in log-transformed view counts between major categories, with results shown in Table 4 and Table 5.

The results in Table 4 clearly show that when used alone, the official notation "Excel" is most associated with view acquisition, followed by the Katakana notation "エクセル," and then the uppercase alphabetical notation "EXCEL," strongly supporting H1.

From Table 5, the "Excel and エクセル only" category showed significantly lower view counts compared to both the "Excel only" category and the "エクセル only" category. This result indicates that the combination of "Excel" and "エクセル" did not improve view counts compared to their solitary use, and thus, the potential for increased view counts with this specific combination, as anticipated in H2, was not supported.

However, an unexpected and noteworthy finding in this study was that the "エクセル and EXCEL only" category (N = 377, mean log view count 8.19) showed statistically significantly higher view counts than many other categories analyzed (Table 5). This outstanding performance of the "エクセル and EXCEL" combination could be attributed to several factors, such as its appeal to a niche audience seeking specialized or advanced content, or the visual differentiation and emphasis created by combining the familiar Katakana "エクセル" with the uppercase "EXCEL."

4.4 Overall Discussion Based on Results

The analytical results of this study reveal that the choice of keyword "expression form" in the titles of Japanese educational UGC has a significant and complex impact on view counts.

As predicted in H1, the official notation "Excel" was associated with the highest view counts when used as a standalone term. This may reflect viewers' demand for reliability and accuracy in educational content, as well as the tendency for official names to be prioritized in general search behavior. Furthermore, the superior cognitive processing speed for alphabetical scripts might be particularly pronounced for IT-related terms.

On the other hand, the expected increase in view counts from combining "Excel" and "エクセル" (H2) was not observed; rather, performance was lower than their solitary use (especially "Excel only"). This could be due to information redundancy creating cognitive load [11] as semantically overlapping keywords are listed, or because it tends to exceed the optimal title length [6].

The most intriguing finding of this study is that the combination of "エクセル and EXCEL" was associated with significantly higher average view counts than many other categories, including "Excel only." This was not anticipated by the initial hypotheses. Factors for this could include effective appeal to a niche audience, or the combination of the common Katakana "エクセル" with the visually prominent uppercase "EXCEL" creating unique attention and prompting clicks within title listings. However, the smaller number of videos in this category compared to other main categories calls for cautious interpretation regarding the generalizability of this result.

These findings reaffirm the importance of information density [16] and title length optimization [6] in relation to view counts. Moreover, they highlight a unique challenge in languages with multiple script systems like Japanese: the choice of keyword "notation form" is not merely an SEO issue but is also deeply related to viewers' cognitive processes and receptivity.

5 Conclusion

This study aimed to quantitatively analyze how differences in major keyword expression forms ("Excel," "エクセル," "EXCEL") in the titles of Japanese educational UGC indirectly affect viewers' cognitive processes, as inferred from view count data, and what effects they have on content discoverability, viewers' selection behavior, and ultimately, initial interest in and receptivity to the content. An analysis of 10,048 Japanese Excel tutorial videos yielded the following key findings.

First, for standalone keyword expressions, the official notation "Excel" was associated with statistically significantly higher view counts compared to the Katakana notation "エクセル" or the uppercase notation "EXCEL." Second, the combination of "Excel" and "エクセル" tended to have lower view counts than their solitary use. Third, an unexpected finding was that the combination of "エクセル" and "EXCEL" showed the highest average view counts among the analyzed categories.

From these results, it is concluded that the choice of keyword "expression form" in the titles of Japanese educational UGC has a significant and complex impact on view counts. While a certain superiority of the official notation is suggested, keyword combination strategies are not straightforward, and unexpected effects may arise depending on the context and specific expression combinations. The findings of this study are expected to serve as a reference for content creators in designing more effective titles, considering their target audience and content characteristics.

This study provided certain insights into the effects of keyword expressions in titles within Japanese educational UGC, but several limitations are acknowledged. The limitation of the target domain to "Microsoft Excel" related tutorial videos means that generalizing these findings to other educational fields or different UGC genres requires careful consideration. Also, due to language dependency, these results, focusing on Japanese keyword expressions, may not apply to content in other language systems. The non-consideration of factors other than titles, such as thumbnail design, description content, and tag settings, which all complexly influence view counts, means their interaction effects were not sufficiently analyzed. Furthermore, this study demonstrates statistical associations between keyword expressions and view counts, not direct causal relationships, and the impact of temporal changes in YouTube's search and recommendation algorithms could not be fully controlled. The smaller sample size for certain categories (e.g., "エクセル and EXCEL only") compared to other main categories should also be noted in interpreting the results.

Considering these limitations, future prospects include, first, further in-depth investigation, using qualitative and quantitative approaches, into why the "エクセル and EXCEL" keyword combination performed highly, examining the specific genres or channel characteristics where it is particularly effective, and the underlying viewer cognitive mechanisms and search behaviors.

Second, it is important to verify the generalizability of these findings by applying this research framework to other educational fields (e.g., programming, language learning, design software) and different types of UGC (e.g., review videos, news commentary videos).

Furthermore, clarifying the combined effects and interactions of title keyword expressions with other metadata, such as the visual elements of thumbnails (colors, presence of people, text information), the structure and information volume of descriptions, and strategic tag utilization, is essential for building more comprehensive UGC optimization strategies.

Additionally, research directly capturing users' actual search behaviors and "instantaneous recognition" processes for different keyword expressions, using methods like search query log analysis or eye-tracking experiments, would be beneficial for deepening understanding in this field.

In the future, it is hoped that these multifaceted research outcomes will be integrated to develop more precise guidelines for proposing optimal title expressions according to content characteristics and objectives, and to develop machine learning-based title optimization support tools.

References

1. Hakuhodo, D.Y.: Media Partners Media Environment Research Institute: "Media Fixed-Point Survey 2023", 2023. https://mekanken.com/projects/media-survey/. (in Japanese)
2. Nielsen Digital Co., Ltd.: "TOPS OF 2023: DIGITAL IN JAPAN", 2023. https://www.netratings.co.jp/news_release/2023/12/Newsrelease20231220.html
3. Bärtl, M.: YouTube channels, uploads and views: a statistical analysis of the past 10 years. Convergence **24**(1), 16–32 (2018). https://doi.org/10.1177/1354856517736979
4. HP: "Service Features YouTube Search". https://support.google.com/youtube/answer/16090438. Accessed 17 May 2025
5. HP: "4 Responsibilities: Remove Violation Content". https://youtube-jp.googleblog.com/2019/09/4-responsibility-remove.html. Accessed 17 May 2025
6. Kawata, T., Kato, T., Tsuda, K.: Effect of title length and word count on views: evidence from Microsoft excel videos on YouTube. EAI Endorsed Trans. Scalable Inf. Syst. **12**(1) (2024). https://doi.org/10.4108/eetsis.7779
7. Kahneman, D.: Thinking, fast and slow. Farrar, Straus and Giroux (2011)
8. Sweller, J.: Cognitive load theory and individual differences. Learn. Individ. Differ. **110**, 102423 (2024). https://doi.org/10.1016/j.lindif.2024.102423
9. Shibasaki, H.: Difference at cognitive processing speed of sentences by character-types: basic study for development of the readability scale of Japanese texts. Res. Exp. Phonetics Linguist. **2**, 18–31 (2010)
10. Itti, L., Koch, C., Niebur, E.: A model of saliency-based visual attention for rapid scene analysis. IEEE Trans. Pattern Anal. Mach. Intell. **20**(11), 1254–1259 (1998)
11. Sweller, J.: Cognitive Load Theory (2011). https://doi.org/10.1007/978-1-4419-8126-4
12. Yamada, J., Leong, C.: Differential reading, naming, and transcribing speeds of Japanese Romaji and Hiragana. Read. Writ. **18**(4), 303–323 (2005). https://doi.org/10.1007/s11145-005-3356-y
13. Tamaoka, K., Miyaoka, Y.: The cognitive processing of Japanese loanwords in Katakana. Jpn. Psychol. Res. **45**(2), 69–79 (2003). https://doi.org/10.1111/1468-5884.t01-1-00035
14. Choudhari, K., Bhalla, V.K.: Video search engine optimization using keyword and feature analysis. Procedia Comput. Sci. **58**, 691–697 (2015)

15. Velho, R.M., Mendes, A.M.F., Azevedo, C.L.N.: "Communicating science with YouTube videos: how nine factors relate to and affect video". Front. Commun. **5** (2020)
16. Tafesse, W.: YouTube marketing: how marketers' video optimization practices influence video views. Internet Res. **30**(6), 1689–1707 (2020)
17. Figueiredo, F., Almeida, J.M., Gonçalves, M.A., Benevenuto, F.: TrendLearner: early prediction of popularity trends of user generated content. Inf. Sci. **349**, 172–187 (2016)
18. Borghol, Y., Ardon, S., Carlsson, N., Eager, D., Mahanti, A.: "The untold story of the clones: content-agnostic factors that impact youtube video popularity". In: Proceedings of the 18th ACM SIGKDD International Conference on Knowledge Discovery and Data Mining, pp. 1186–1194. (2012)
19. Debove, S., Füchslin, T., Louis, T., Masselot, P.: French science communication on YouTube: a survey of individual and institutional communicators and their channel characteristics. Front. Commun. **6** (2021)
20. Yoo, W., Kim, T., Lee, S.: Predictors of viewing YouTube videos on Incheon Chinatown tourism in South Korea: engagement and network structure factors. Sustainability **13**(22), 12534 (2021)
21. Kavitha, K.M., Shetty, A., Abreo, B., D'Souza, A., Kondana, A.: Analysis and classification of user comments on YouTube videos. Procedia Comput. Sci. **177**, 593–598 (2020)
22. Jang, H.E., Kim, S.H., Jeon, J.S., Oh, J.H.: Visual attributes of thumbnails in predicting YouTube brand channel views in the marketing digitalization era. IEEE Trans. Comput. Soc. Syst. 1–9 (2023)
23. Mohamed, F., Shoufan, A.: Choosing YouTube videos for self-directed learning. IEEE Access **10**, 51155–51166 (2022)
24. Yoon, S.-H., Lee, S.-H.: "What Likeability attributes attract people to watch online video advertisements?" Electronics **11**(13), 1960 (2022)
25. Shen, Z., Tan, S., Pritchard, M.J.: Understanding the effects of visual cueing on social media engagement with YouTube educational videos. IEEE Trans. Prof. Commun. **65**(2), 337–350 (2022)

A Brief Bibliometric Review on Marketing Trends Mediated by Artificial Intelligence

Mauricio Santamaría-Ruiz[1(✉)], Alexander Troncoso-Palacio[1(✉)], Gabriel País-Cerna[2], Isabella Serrano-Mesa[1], and Daniela Correa-Jaraba[1]

[1] Department of Business Sciences, Universidad de la Costa, Barranquilla, Colombia
{msantama,atroncos1}@cuc.edu.co
[2] Universidad Andrés Bello, Santiago de Chile, Chile

Abstract. This study provides a comprehensive analysis of the multifaceted role of artificial intelligence in contemporary marketing, emphasizing its function as a catalyst for innovation through automation, personalized consumer engagement, and data-driven decision-making. Focusing on sectors such as health and tourism, AI has progressed from an emerging technology to an essential operational tool that enhances profitability and strengthens consumer-brand relationships by integrating emotional engagement with advanced technology. However, the adoption of AI also introduces significant ethical challenges concerning privacy, transparency, and trust, requiring a balanced approach that maximizes AI's transformative potential while safeguarding consumer rights and promoting responsible marketing practices. Drawing on research spanning 2016 to 2025, this study identifies a shift toward a hybrid paradigm in AI-driven marketing, where operational efficiency, emotional personalization, and digital governance intersect signaling a strategic evolution from tactical implementations toward comprehensive value creation. Ultimately, AI represents a transformative force in modern marketing, uniting technological innovation, consumer-centric strategies, and social responsibility to shape the future direction of this field.

Keywords: Artificial Intelligence · Business Trends · Marketing · Machine Learning

1 Introduction

Marketing has established itself as an important discipline that acts as a tool that helps organizations position themselves in a market and retain their potential customers. It is responsible for maintaining profitability in a more intelligent and effective way that allows building strategies with the aim of achieving the goals of an organization, since from an orderly series of processes it manages to identify the needs and desires of customers, allowing the company to have profitable growth.

The evolution of marketing has been guided by the constant updating and emergence of new technological tools, with artificial intelligence (AI) being the trend par excellence in all marketing disciplines in 2016. AI has gone from being a futuristic idea

T. Guarda et al. (Eds.): ARTIIS 2025, CCIS 2789, pp. 160–172, 2026.
https://doi.org/10.1007/978-3-032-16758-3_13

and an emerging trend to becoming a driving force behind marketing transformations. According to [1]. Projections indicate that by 2025, the application of AI in marketing will continue its rapid expansion, further impacting the disciplinary areas and strategies of marketing and sales in organizations.

The integration of AI in marketing and tourism is rapidly reshaping organizational strategies, particularly through personalization, predictive analytics, and user experience enhancement. According to [2]., generative AI is becoming a cornerstone in the hospitality industry, enabling real-time content creation and customer interaction management. This aligns with [3], who emphasize AI's strategic value in transforming operational processes and service innovation within tourism and hospitality domains.

The emotional resonance of AI tools is also gaining scholarly attention. [4] evidence that anthropomorphic AI significantly influences purchase intention, especially when trust mediates the interaction. Similarly, [5] finds that anthropomorphic chatbots enhance customer loyalty by simulating human-like engagement, a factor that improves long-term consumer-brand relationships, on the customer interaction front, [6] offer a systematic review indicating that digital engagement driven by AI is critical to modern marketing strategies, allowing brands to build adaptive and data-informed experiences. This is reinforced by [7], who show that personalized advertising content, powered by AI, increases consumer engagement and relevance perception.

In the tourism sector, [8] highlights the role of augmented reality, integrated with AI, as a tool for improving user interaction and service delivery through immersive technologies. However, ethical considerations are not overlooked. [9] discuss the darker sides of AI in advertising, warning that misuse may lead to issues of data privacy, manipulation, and consumer distrust concerns echoed in broader ethical debates, from a predictive marketing standpoint, [10] propose an ethical framework that guides the use of AI tools to anticipate consumer behavior while maintaining transparency and managerial responsibility. Lastly, the emergence of virtual influencers and their impact on marketing is explored by [11], who examines switching intentions toward AI-generated personalities, indicating a shift in how consumers interact with brands in digital ecosystems.

In Colombia, for example, AI is redefining digital marketing, offering tools and capabilities that allow brands to better understand their audiences and optimize their strategies. This reflects the interest of brands in taking advantage of the digital environment and tools, based on campaign optimization, advanced segmentation, predictive analysis, among others. For its part, the Barranquilla Chamber of Commerce reaffirms its commitment to the business development of the region, focusing its portfolio of services on two key areas: AI and Marketing and Sales strategies. These initiatives will facilitate the integration of AI solutions in business processes, optimizing operations, improving decision-making and strengthening business efficiency.

The study of marketing trends measured by artificial intelligence not only represents a great advance for the improvement of organizations worldwide but also helps to strengthen the knowledge and understanding capacity of future marketers to make data-based decisions, improve the personalization of advertising campaigns and optimize digital strategies.

Artificial intelligence technology has revolutionized the way and processes in which companies manage their marketing strategies globally, from improving marketing plans to personalizing user experience and consumer behaviors. Process automation, highly personalized content creation, and real-time optimization thanks to artificial intelligence has caused technological advances in the accelerated development of machine learning algorithms, in turn, the increasing collection and availability of data provides a solid basis for AI to identify consumer patterns and behaviors. Intelligences advances bring with them a series of consequences such as the transformation of employment, where the automation of processes within organizations carried out by artificial intelligence is displacing certain traditional roles in marketing, in turn, ethical challenges regarding the use of artificial intelligence question data privacy and transparency in decision-making, which can lead in certain cases to consumer distrust. Considering the above, the following question arises what the trends in marketing mediated by artificial intelligence for the period are 2016–2025.

2 Methods

The present research is situated within the post-positivist paradigm, a revised interpretation of the classical positivist perspective. This paradigm is grounded in critical realism, acknowledging the existence of an objective reality while recognizing the inherent limitations in human understanding and interpretation of that reality [12]. Methodologically, the study adopts a quantitative approach, which allows for the systematic analysis of social phenomena through measurable variables and statistically supported interpretations [12], this investigation is descriptive in nature, aiming to characterize existing models of social innovation without manipulating variables or intervening in the phenomenon under study [13]. The research design is non-experimental and cross-sectional, as data collection occurs at a single point in time without any intentional influence on the variables being observed [12, 13], In terms of methodological tools, bibliometrics is employed as the primary analytical framework. Originally defined by [14], bibliometrics involves the application of statistical and mathematical techniques to assess the production and dissemination of scientific literature. As [15] explains, bibliometric analysis provides a macroscopic view of the evolution and current state of knowledge in each field by examining metadata from academic databases. Bibliometric networks, an extension of this methodology, aim to visualize and interpret research indicators, thereby offering both quantitative and qualitative insights into scientific output [15].

The bibliometric analysis conducted in this study follows the five-phase model proposed by [16]. The first phase, formulation, defined the objectives of the bibliometric review. The second phase, identification, involved establishing inclusion criteria based on a set of keywords social innovation, social innovation models, social transformation, social justice, sustainable development, collaborative networks, civic participation, social inclusion, social economy, and innovative solutions as well as delimiting the study to the last ten years.

For the implementation of the bibliometric analysis, the software VOS viewer was utilized. Developed by Nees Jan van Eck and Ludo Waltman at the Centre for Science and Technology Studies (CWTS), Leiden University (Netherlands), VOS viewer enables the creation and visualization of bibliometric networks based on citation, co-citation, and co-authorship analyses [17, 18].These networks illustrate the structure of scientific domains by linking journals, researchers, and individual publications, a total of 200 documents were retrieved, and the analysis was conducted based on the first 200 records with the highest relevance scores. The search equation is presented in detail in Table 1.

Table 1. Search Equation Parameters Used for the Bibliometric Analysis.

Search Equation	Subject Areas	Search Fields	Records Found
TITLE-ABS-KEY ("artificial intelligent OR intelligence AND marketing")	- (Computer Science) - (Business, Management and Accounting) - (Decision Sciences)	Title, Abstract, and Keywords	792
Language	**Source type**	**Open access**	**Documents**
English, Spanish	Journal, Conference proceeding	All open access, Gold	First 94 records sorted by relevance

3 Results

The bibliometric analysis reveals a strong and growing scholarly interest in the application of AI, within marketing and advertising domains. The most cited articles predominantly address the integration of AI into customer experience, personalization, and consumer behavior analysis. Particularly, the top-ranked publication focuses on generative AI within the hospitality sector, emphasizing its transformative role in enhancing customer engagement strategies. Table 2 reports the studies that comprise the top 10 within the analysis period of 2025.

Table 2. Top 10 Most Cited Articles.

Title	Year	Source Title	Cited by
Generative Artificial Intelligence in the Hospitality Sector	2025	Journal of Hospitality and Tourism Research	86
Perceived Anthropomorphism and Purchase Intentions	2025	Journal of Enterprise Information Management	42
Artificial Intelligence in Hospitality and Tourism	2025	Journal of Hospitality and Tourism Research	31
Digital Customer Engagement: A Systematic Literature Review	2025	Australian Journal of Management	13
The Use of Augmented Reality Technologies in Tourism	2025	European Journal of Innovation Management	11
The Dark Sides of AI Advertising	2025	Social Science Computer Review	9
Artificial Intelligence and Predictive Marketing	2025	Spanish Journal of Marketing - ESIC	7
Influence of Personalized Advertising Copy on Consumer Trust	2025	Electronic Commerce Research	6
Understanding the Switching Intention to Virtual Influencers	2025	Journal of Research in Interactive Marketing	6
Influence of Anthropomorphic Chatbots on Customer Loyalty	2025	Journal of Research in Interactive Marketing	5

Several studies underscore the relevance of anthropomorphic design in AI-driven advertising tools, suggesting a positive impact on purchase intentions and customer trust. The use of AI in personalized marketing is consistently associated with increased consumer loyalty and improved decision-making efficiency for businesses. Moreover, there is a clear emphasis on digital engagement and predictive marketing as critical components of competitive marketing strategies. Table 3 reports on the studies that comprise the top 10 on Marketing and Artificial Intelligence in 2025.

Table 3. Top 10 Marketing and Artificial Intelligence Publications of 2025.

Type	Title	Quartile	Impact Factor	H index	Documents
Book	Marketing 5.0: The Role of Human-Mimicking Technologies	N/D	N/D	N/D	9
Journal	Sustainability (Switzerland)	Q1	3.3	169	6
Book	Data Engineering for Data-Driven Marketing	N/D	N/D	N/D	6
Journal	Lecture Notes in Computer Science (LNCS)	Q3	0.32	446	5
Journal	Journal of Information Systems Engineering and Management	Q3	1.26	8	5
Journal	Journal of Business Research	Q1	7.55	189	4
Journal	Communications in Computer and Information Science (CCIS)	Q4	0.20	42	3
Journal	Social Science Computer Review	Q1	1.374	96	3
Journal	Journal of Marketing Research	Q1	6.96	212	2
Journal	Journal of the Academy of Marketing Science	Q1	6.89	221	2

The results reveal a strong presence of publications in high-impact journals within the fields of marketing and advertising, highlighting the academic and practical relevance of these disciplines in contemporary contexts. Sustainability (Switzerland), ranked in Q1 with an impact factor of 3.3, underscores the strategic positioning of sustainability as a core element in emerging marketing dynamics. The inclusion of the Journal of Business Research and the Journal of the Academy of Marketing Science, both with impact factors above 6 and classified in Q1, confirms the field's focus on applied research, consumer behavior, and data-driven business strategies.

Journals such as Lecture Notes in Computer Science and Communications in Computer and Information Science demonstrate the growing interest in interdisciplinary approaches that merge data engineering, information systems, and digital marketing essential components for understanding and anticipating consumer patterns in highly technologized environments. Publications in the Journal of Information Systems Engineering and Management further consolidate the focus on integrating intelligent systems in strategic decision-making for advertising and commercial communication. Collectively, these findings indicate a clear academic orientation toward innovation, advanced analytics, and sustainability as foundational pillars of modern marketing.

The findings correspond to a visualization of a keyword co-occurrence network, generated using VOS viewer, in which five color-coded thematic clusters are identified. This representation allows for the interpretation of the knowledge structure surrounding artificial intelligence applied to marketing from an academic and bibliometric perspective, see Fig. 1

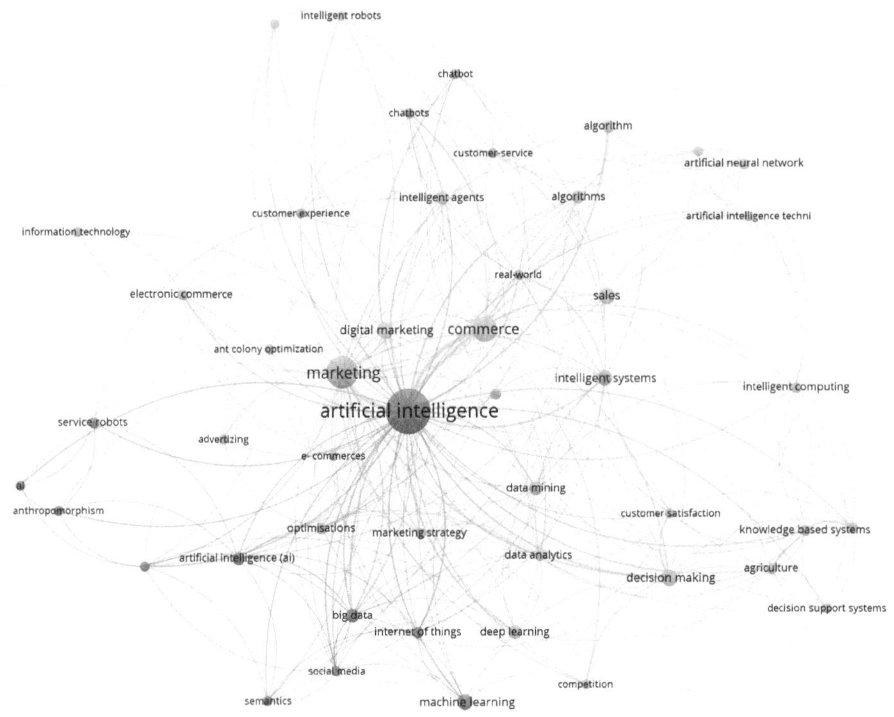

Fig. 1. Map of artificial intelligence applied to marketing.

The co-occurrence network visualization reveals a complex and interconnected thematic structure centered on AI, applied to marketing, organized into five main clusters. The red cluster includes terms such as "artificial intelligence," "chatbot," "automation," and "customer experience," indicating a predominant focus on process automation and personalized consumer engagement through emerging technologies. The blue cluster groups concepts like "marketing," "digital marketing," "strategy," and "advertising," highlighting AI's role as a strategic tool in multichannel environments and brand management. The green cluster emphasizes the technical and methodological dimension, showcasing the use of "machine learning," "data mining," and "prediction" to support data-driven decision-making. Meanwhile, the yellow cluster reflects a strong interest in user experience within e-commerce contexts, integrating terms such as "e-commerce," "recommendation systems," and "user experience," which underscores the centrality of the consumer in digital ecosystems. Lastly, the purple cluster addresses critical aspects related to "ethics," "privacy," and "trust," pointing to academic concerns about ethical challenges and governance in the use of AI in commercial settings. Collectively, the network demonstrates a convergence of technological innovation, consumer behavior, advanced analytics, and social responsibility, confirming AI's position as a transformative axis in contemporary marketing (Fig. 2).

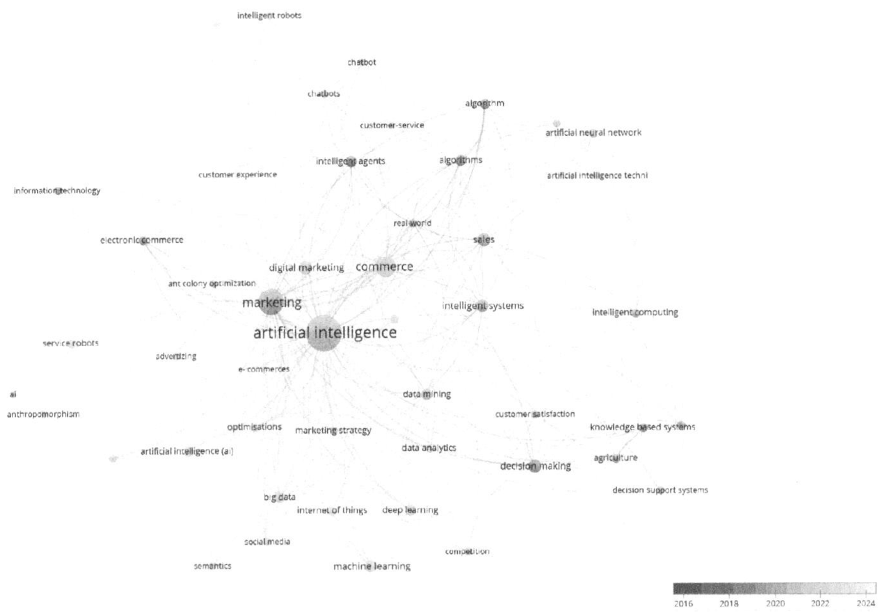

Fig. 2. Visualization map of trends over time.

Visualization map of trends over time illustrates a co-occurrence network of keywords related to artificial intelligence and marketing. The nodes represent concepts, with their size indicating frequency and relevance in scientific literature. The connections show associations between terms, highlighting thematic clusters such as artificial intelligence, marketing, machine learning, data analytics, customer experience, and intelligent systems.

The color scale reflects the temporal evolution of research (2016–2024). Yellow and green tones correspond to earlier studies, while blue shades indicate more recent trends. This progression reveals how initial concepts such as e-commerce and customer experience have evolved toward emerging notions like deep learning, decision support systems, and artificial neural networks.

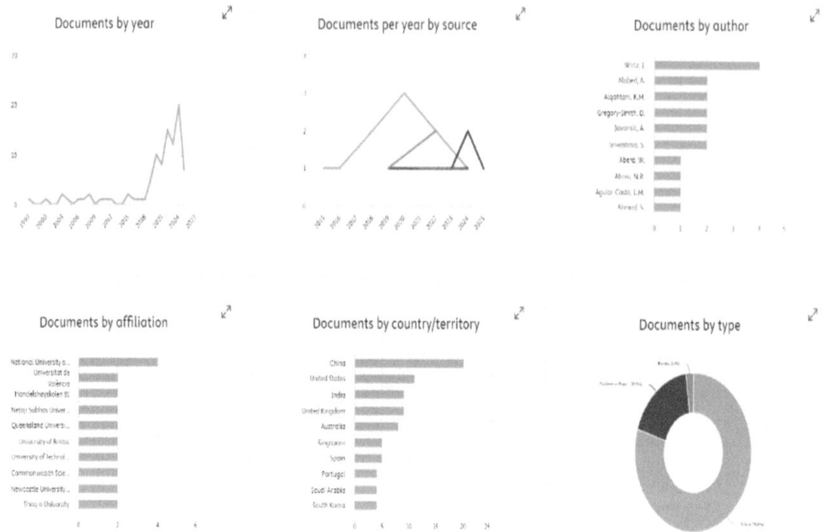

Fig. 3. Scopus bibliometric results dashboard

The graphs in Fig. 3 summarize key information. The 'Documents by Year' graph shows the number of publications, clearly indicating a significant increase starting in 2018, with notable peaks between 2021 and 2023. Meanwhile, the 'Documents per Year by Source' graph illustrates the distribution of contributions across various journals, emphasizing the multidisciplinary nature of this field. The Documents by author panel indicates the most active researchers, with Wang J. leading, followed by Ali R. and Alharthi A. The Documents by affiliation chart identifies institutions such as the National University of Singapore, Fondazione Bruno Kessler, and Queensland University of Technology among the most productive contributors. Geographically, the Documents by country/territory distribution shows China and the United States as the leading producers, followed by the United Kingdom, Australia, and several European and Asian countries, reflecting the global relevance of the subject. Finally, the Documents by type it evidences a predominance of journal articles over other formats such as conference papers or reviews, which reinforces the scientific consolidation of this research field.

4 Discussion

The dominance of articles focused on AI applications in hospitality and tourism marketing, such as Generative Artificial Intelligence in the Hospitality Sector and Artificial Intelligence in Hospitality and Tourism, highlights a sector-specific transformation. These studies align with the assertion that AI has moved from a futuristic trend to an operational imperative. Their high citation rates underscore their relevance in showcasing how AI personalizes experiences, automates service delivery, and enhances engagement core marketing objectives aimed at increasing organizational profitability. The anthropomorphizing of AI tools, as discussed in articles like Perceived Anthropomorphism and

Purchase Intentions and Influence of Anthropomorphic Chatbots on Customer Loyalty, reflects a growing academic interest in humanizing AI to foster emotional connections with consumers. This aligns with the theoretical claim that AI empowers brands to better understand and influence consumer behavior through mechanisms like predictive analytics and real-time personalization.

These findings affirm AI's role in optimizing customer journey touchpoints and increasing trust and loyalty. Topics such as The Dark Sides of AI Advertising reveal emerging ethical concerns within AI-mediated marketing. While the theory acknowledges the technological revolution AI has brought, it also warns of potential consequences, such as privacy violations and consumer mistrust. These studies contribute to the critical discourse around transparency and ethical data usage, reinforcing the need for marketers to adopt responsible AI practices to maintain brand credibility and long-term customer relationships.

AI, in marketing has emerged as a transformative catalyst, fundamentally reshaping the ways in which businesses engage with customers, analyzing data, and formulating strategic decisions. As noted by several scholars, AI is commonly understood as "the simulation of human intelligence that creates algorithms and computer systems capable of executing simple and complex tasks that people perform" [19]. This foundation supports the development of marketing technologies capable of automating, optimizing, and personalizing interactions across digital channels.

AI plays a critical role in enhancing operational efficiency across the marketing value chain. As previously analyzed by Bughin et al., companies that adopt AI technologies experience innovation in areas such as customer service, sales, and product development [20]. However, effective implementation requires more than just access to advanced tools; it depends on the availability of skilled professionals. As noted by Vergara, the involvement of experts and mentors in the field of AI and digital marketing is essential to maximizing its strategic potential [21].

One of AI's primary advantages in marketing lies in its ability to create highly personalized experiences. This personalization improves targeting accuracy and increases user engagement, which ultimately benefits business performance [22]. Achieving this level of precision requires a deep understanding of the data generated daily by customers. Thus, knowledge in AI-related domains such as machine learning, data processing, and learning models becomes indispensable [23].

Recent empirical research supports these observations. Figueroa et al. concluded that AI contributes significantly to digital marketing and content generation strategies for SMEs [24]. Nevertheless, a key obstacle to its successful adoption is the lack of digital skills and knowledge among marketing professionals. This barrier not only limits optimal use of AI tools but also reveals a broader issue of resistance or uncertainty in organizational environments.

This concern is echoed in the IAB Spain & Adevinta 2025 report, which identifies knowledge gaps as the primary barrier to AI implementation in marketing. Despite 69% of professionals actively using AI for personalization and data-based decision-making, 72% cite insufficient training as a limiting factor [25]. Complementary findings by PHD and WARC reinforce this perception, highlighting a disconnect between the theoretical potential of AI and its practical application in strategic marketing [26].

Similarly, a study by the IMMUNE Technology Institute indicates that 51% of companies consider lack of knowledge to be the main impediment to AI adoption, further reinforcing the necessity of investing in educational and training programs [27]. These findings converge on the conclusion that AI's strategic value is evident, but its impact remains constrained by human factors, particularly the need for upskilling in technological and analytical competencies.

The convergence of AI, and digital marketing has shaped an ecosystem driven by intelligent automation, hyper-personalization, and adaptive learning. A recent bibliometric analysis revealed that tools such as augmented reality, chatbots, and real-time adaptive algorithms are becoming strategic components in advertising campaigns, particularly for enhancing user experience and improving audience targeting [28]. Moreover, some of the most relevant patents in this field—developed by companies like Meta, Google, and Fuji Xerox—reflect a clear trend toward improving product recommendation and behavioral targeting using AI models trained to respond to cognitive, auditory, and emotional stimuli [29]. In parallel, case studies on customer segmentation with Big Data in the Colombian health sector confirm the strategic utility of the RFM model for identifying high-value clients, revealing its effectiveness in optimizing business decisions and enhancing service personalization [30, 31]. These trends suggest that AI not only acts as a technical driver of innovation but also as a structural axis for new customer-centric organizational dynamics.

5 Conclusions

Based on research conducted during the 2016–2025 period, it is evident that AI-mediated marketing is progressing toward a hybrid paradigm. This model integrates operational efficiency, emotional personalization, and digital governance, signifying a strategic shift from mere tactical implementation to comprehensive value creation. In sum, artificial intelligence emerges as a pivotal force in contemporary marketing, harmonizing technological innovation, consumer-centric strategies, and social responsibility to shape the discipline's future trajectory.

The comprehensive examination of influential publications alongside the thematic co-occurrence network compellingly reveals the multifaceted impact of artificial intelligence within modern marketing practices. AI is not merely a driver of innovation and strategic progress manifested through automation, personalized consumer engagement, and data-informed decision-making, but also a field deeply enmeshed with critical ethical considerations and sustainability concerns. The delineation of distinct thematic clusters highlights the complexity inherent in AI applications, encompassing technical methodologies, enhancements to consumer experience, strategic marketing integration, and governance-related challenges.

Furthermore, focused attention on hospitality and tourism marketing exemplifies AI's evolution from emergent technology to an indispensable operational instrument that customizes customer interactions and bolsters profitability. The anthropomorphizing of AI systems illustrates a sophisticated grasp of consumer-brand dynamics, where emotional resonance complements technological advancement.

However, this analysis thoroughly examines the ethical challenges associated with adoption of AI, particularly concerning privacy, transparency, and reliability. These issues underscore the necessity of adopting a balanced approach that fully leverages AI's transformative potential while steadfastly safeguarding consumer rights and advancing responsible marketing practices.

References

1. Toledo, A.: IA y el Nuevo Marketing en 2025: Tendencia de cambios inevitables que transformarán las estrategias de marcas y empresas. (2025). https://repositorio.utdt.edu/handle/20.500.13098/12832
2. Saleh, M.I.: Generative artificial intelligence in the hospitality and tourism industry: future capabilities, AI prompts and real-world applications. J. Hosp. Market. Manag. **34**(4), 1–32 (2025). https://doi.org/10.1080/19368623.2025.2458603
3. Uysal, M., Sirgy, M.J.: Artificial intelligence in hospitality and tourism: insights from industry practices, research literature, and expert opinions. J. Hospitality Tourism Res. **49**(1), 3–22 (2025). https://doi.org/10.1177/10963480241229235
4. Malhotra, G., Ramalingam, M.: Perceived anthropomorphism and purchase intention using artificial intelligence technology: examining the moderated effect of trust. J. Enterp. Inf. Manag. **38**(2), 1–15 (2023). https://doi.org/10.1108/JEIM-09-2022-0316
5. Chen, L., Zhang, Y.: Unveiling the influence of anthropomorphic chatbots on consumer behavioral intentions: evidence from China and Indonesia. J. Res. Interact. Mark. **19**(1), 67–89 (2025). https://doi.org/10.1108/JRIM-09-2023-0295
6. Srivastava, R., Gupta, P., Kumar, H., Tuli, N.: Digital customer engagement: a systematic literature review and research agenda. Aust. J. Manag. **50**(1), 220–245 (2025). https://doi.org/10.1177/03128962231177096
7. Guo, B., Jiang, Z.: Influence of personalised advertising copy on consumer engagement: a field experiment approach. Electron. Commer. Res. **25**(2), 1281–1310 (2025). https://doi.org/10.1007/s10660-023-09721-5
8. Çalışkan, G., Yıldız, S.: The use of augmented reality technologies in tourism businesses from the perspective of UTAUT2. Eur. J. Innov. Manag. **28**(1), 45–67 (2025). https://doi.org/10.1108/EJIM-04-2023-0271
9. Li, Y., Wang, X.: The dark sides of AI advertising: the integration of cognitive appraisal and information quality theories. Soc. Sci. Comput. Rev. **43**(2), 295–317 (2025). https://doi.org/10.1177/08944393241258760
10. Naz, H., Kashif, M.: Artificial intelligence and predictive marketing: an ethical framework from managers' perspective. Span. J. Market. - ESIC **29**(1), 22–45 (2025). https://doi.org/10.1108/SJME-06-2023-0154
11. Shao, Z.: Understanding the switching intention to virtual streamers in live streaming commerce: innovation resistances, shopping motivations, and personalities. J. Res. Interact. Mark. **19**(2), 123–145 (2024). https://doi.org/10.1108/JRIM-10-2023-0355
12. Hernández, R., Fernández, C., Baptista, P.: Metodología de la Investigación. McGraw-Hill Interamericana (2022)
13. Hernández-Sampieri, R., Mendoza, C.: Metodología de la investigación: Las rutas cuantitativa, cualitativa y mixta (1.ª ed.). McGraw-Hill Interamericana Editores S.A. de C.V (2019)
14. Pritchard, A.: Statistical bibliography or bibliometrics? J. Documentation **25**, 348–349 (1969)
15. Osareh, F.: Bibliometrics, citation analysis and co-citation analysis: a review of literature I. Libri **46**(3), 149–158 (1996). https://doi.org/10.1515/libr.1996.46.3.149
16. Ball, R.: Handbook Bibliometrics. De Gruyter, Berlin (2021)

17. Velt, H., Torkkeli, L., Laine, I.: Entrepreneurial ecosystem research: bibliometric mapping of the domain. J. Bus. Ecosyst. **1**(2), 1–31 (2020). https://doi.org/10.4018/JBE.20200701.oa1
18. Feijoo, G., Arias, A., Moreira, M.T.: Application of artificial intelligence in the preparation of review scientific articles: use of VOS viewer software with bibliometric networks. ResearchGate (2022). https://www.researchgate.net/publication/365593850
19. Londoño, P.: Artificial Intelligence: What It Is, How It Works, and Its Importance in 2023. HubSpot Blog (2023). https://blog.hubspot.com/marketing/how-does-ai-work
20. Bughin, J., Hazan, E., Ramaswamy, S.: Artificial Intelligence: The Next Digital Frontier? McKinsey Global Institute (2017). https://www.mckinsey.com/mgi2
21. Vergara Romero, A.: Educational Innovation and Skill Development in the 21st Century: Strategies, Training, and Digital Transformation in Education. Universidad ECOTEC (2023). https://libros.ecotec.edu.ec
22. Smart Panel. The Role of Artificial Intelligence in Marketing (2023). [No English source available]
23. Pimienta, S.X., Mosquera-Martínez, M.L.: Curricular, technological, and pedagogical considerations for the transition to a new AI-supported educational model in health sciences. Medicina **43**(4), 540–554 (2021). https://revistamedicina.net
24. Figueroa Mora, A.L., Meza Polo, G.M., Suárez Castro, M.F.: Analysis of artificial intelligence and its effect on SMEs' digital marketing strategies in Barranquilla. Universidad Simón Bolívar (2023). https://bonga.unisimon.edu.co
25. IAB Spain, Adevinta. Top Digital Trends Report 2025. IAB Spain (2025). https://iabspain.es/estudio/informe-top-tendencias-digitales-2025
26. PHD Worldwide, WARC. AI Knowledge Gaps and Conflicting Expectations Among Marketing Stakeholders. PHD & WARC (2024). https://www.prnewswire.com/news-releases/new-global-research-from-phd-and-warc-reveals-ai-knowledge-gaps-conflicting-expectations-among-marketing-stakeholders-302231708.html
27. IMMUNE Technology Institute. Study on Artificial Intelligence and Digital Skills in Companies. IMMUNE Institute (2024). https://immune.institute/en/programas/programa-avanzado-ia-data-science-for-business
28. Santamaría-Ruiz, M.J., Jiménez-Calderón, C.E., Osorio-Venecia, A.R., Álvarez-Santodomingo, A., Pardo-Forero, M.: Bibliometric behavior of artificial intelligence and digital marketing sustainability. Procedia Comput. Sci. **257**, 1047–1052 (2025). https://doi.org/10.1016/j.procs.2025.03.136
29. Santamaría-Ruiz, M.J., García-Samper, M.A., Pardo-Forero, M., Camero-Lara, P., Barragán-Morales, C., Sierra-Carpio, D.: Customer segmentation analysis with big data in health services companies in Colombia: case study. Procedia Comput. Sci. **257**, 1134–1139 (2025). https://doi.org/10.1016/j.procs.2025.03.150
30. Sukier, H.B., et al.: Análisis del marketing estratégico en pequeñas y medianas empresas: caso de la industria de la panadería en Colombia. Procedia Comput. Sci. **231**, 601–606 (2024). https://doi.org/10.1016/j.procs.2023.12.178
31. Molina, R.I.R., Ruiz, M.J.S., Castro, L.C.M., Raby, N.D.L., Hinojoza-Montañez, S., Samper, M.G.: Bibliometric behavior of big data and digital marketing as real-time multimedia. Procedia Comput. Sci. **241**, 526–532 (2024)

Classification of Emergency-Related Posts on Platform X Using Pretrained Generative Language Models

Marcelo Mendoza-Salazar[1](✉) and Gabriel Cotera-Ramírez[2]

[1] Maestría en Ciencia de Datos y Máquinas de Aprendizaje. Facultad de Posgrado, Universidad Técnica de Manabí, Avenida José María Urbina, 130105 Portoviejo, Ecuador
marcelomendoza1984@gmail.com

[2] Departamento de Sistemas Computacionales. Facultad de Ciencias Informáticas, Universidad Técnica de Manabí, Avenida José María Urbina, 130105 Portoviejo, Ecuador

Abstract. The generation of content on social media poses a significant challenge for data analysis and informed decision-making. This study explores the application of three generative artificial intelligence models for classifying posts related to emergency situations on Platform X (formerly Twitter). The corpus consisted of tweets labeled as Emergency or Non-emergency, which were normalized using natural language processing techniques. The CRISP-ML(Q) methodology was employed to ensure traceability and quality throughout each stage, from problem understanding to results evaluation. The evaluation metrics showed that, among the models evaluated, Gemini-2.0-Flash achieved the best overall performance with an F1-score of 0.7314; GPT-3.5-Turbo stood out for its Recall of 0.9155; whereas Mistral-small exhibited a lower Precision of 0.5350. The findings suggest that, through prompt engineering, it was possible to adapt pretrained generative models to classification tasks without additional training, providing a flexible, replicable, and adaptable solution for the automated detection of emergencies in risk management contexts.

Keywords: Emergencies · Generative Artificial Intelligence · Natural Language Processing · Social Media · Text Classification

1 Introduction

Social media platforms such as X (formerly known as Twitter) have become key channels for disseminating real-time information during critical events, such as natural disasters and social emergencies [1]. In this context, having proactive tools for incident detection represents a valuable communication resource for emergency response and public safety organizations [2].

In the existing literature, various approaches to the automated classification of social media posts during disaster situations have been explored. Early strategies focused on supervised machine learning techniques, as in [3], where a hybrid approach was implemented using algorithms such as Naive Bayes, Logistic Regression, J48, Random Forest,

T. Guarda et al. (Eds.): ARTIIS 2025, CCIS 2789, pp. 173–183, 2026.
https://doi.org/10.1007/978-3-032-16758-3_14

and Support Vector Machines (SVM), achieving up to 80% accuracy in the automatic identification of tweets related to both natural and man-made disasters. Subsequently, deep learning approaches emerged, such as the study by [4], which used tweet datasets available on the Kaggle platform and combined transformer architectures with deep neural networks, reaching F-score values of up to 80%. Continuing this line, [5] collected tweets related to traffic incidents through the Twitter Application Programming Interface (API) and proposed an optimized version of Bidirectional Encoder Representations from Transformers (BERT) enhanced with the AdamW optimizer, achieving a precision of 82%. More recently, studies like [6], have explored the application of generative models for zero-shot classification tasks, evaluating the performance of three Large Language Models (LLMs) applied to the open-access CrisisBench dataset.

While the reviewed studies show significant advances in the classification of social media posts, key limitations persist, such as the need for intensive training, high computational cost, and limited adaptability to new contexts; consequently, the adoption of generative models remains limited. These methodological constraints highlight the need to explore more efficient alternatives, such as those offered by Generative Artificial Intelligence (AI). Within this framework, the present study proposes a strategy based on pretrained models for classifying emergency-related posts on Platform X. This approach not only aims to reduce dependence on complex training processes but also offers a scalable, reproducible solution applicable to real-time monitoring systems, with potential value for institutions involved in risk management and public response.

Based on the above, this study addresses two fundamental questions: Can LLMs accurately classify emergency-related posts on Platform X without requiring additional training? Which generative model achieves the best Precision and Recall performance?

2 Methodology

To structure and guide the development of this project, the Cross Industry Standard Process for Machine Learning with Quality assurance (CRISP-ML(Q)) methodology was adopted—an approach widely recognized in the field of data science [7]. Figure 1 presents the overall process flow, which includes loading data from the Mendeley Data repository. The texts were processed using three pretrained generative language models: GPT-3.5-Turbo, Gemini-2.0-Flash, and Mistral-small. The corresponding outputs were generated in Comma-Separated Values (CSV) format, accompanied by their respective classification labels.

During the business understanding phase, the problem was contextualized. Subsequently, in the data understanding phase, an exploratory analysis was conducted to identify key insights. In the data preparation phase, Natural Language Processing (NLP) techniques were applied, including normalization, noise removal, and tokenization. During the modeling phase, pretrained generative language models were employed for the text classification task. Finally, performance metrics such as Accuracy, Precision, Recall, and F1-Score were used to evaluate the results. It is worth noting that, given the use of LLMs, the subsequent phases involving system deployment and monitoring were not addressed. The following subsections describe how each stage of the CRISP-ML(Q) methodology was carried out.

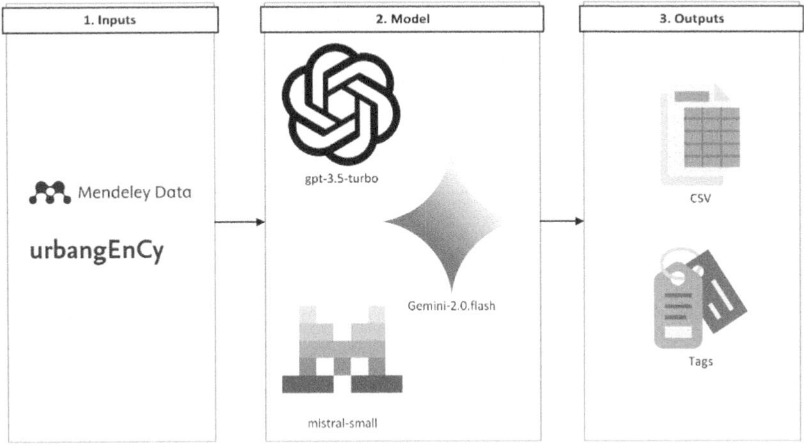

Fig. 1. Process Flow Diagram

2.1 Phase 1: Business Understanding

This phase aimed to understand the project requirements from a strategic perspective to define the objectives and stakeholders [8]. During this stage, the scope of the solution was outlined, setting as its main goal the recognition of critical information generated on social media, with application in operational contexts of risk management and emergency response. Identifying emergency-related posts on social media represents a significant challenge due to the unstructured nature, semantic noise, and linguistic diversity of user-generated content. These characteristics make processing particularly difficult when aiming for accurate classification of such information [9], In addition, there are limitations imposed by Platform X, including access restrictions and API-related costs, which constrain the large-scale collection of posts.

2.2 Phase 2: Data Understanding

The dataset used in this study was obtained from the urbangEnCy repository, developed by [10], It contains 25,000 posts related to emergency events, collected as part of a research initiative on citizen sensing in Ecuador. The dataset is structured into nine fields, including the textual content of the posts, temporal and geographic metadata, and the categories assigned to the reported event (Table 1).

During the initial exploratory analysis, the structure, completeness, and distribution of the dataset fields were evaluated. A significant imbalance was identified in the classification labels: approximately 6% of the posts corresponded to emergency situations, while 94% were classified as non-emergency. This distribution indicates a class imbalance scenario, which was taken into account in the subsequent phases of the CRISP-ML(Q) methodology.

Table 1. Dataset Fields.

Field	Description
ID	Unique identifier of the tweet
created_at	Date and time when the tweet was published
text	Textual content of the tweet
place_name	Name of the place associated with the post
center_name	Name of the center or institution related to the event
category1	The primary label assigned to the tweet is either Emergency or Non-Emergency
category2	Additional tags indicating specific categories
category3	This field contains supplementary labels assigned to the reported event
category4	Organization or authority that responded to the reported emergency

2.3 Phase 3: Data Preparation

In this stage, the relevant fields for the classification task were selected. The text attribute, which corresponds to the content of each post, was defined as the independent variable, while category1, which contains the classification label (Emergency or Non-Emergency), was established as the target or dependent variable, and was renamed tags for use in the subsequent phases of the process.

Based on this data structure, NLP techniques were applied for text cleaning, normalization, and transformation. The preprocessing included the removal of elements that do not contribute meaningful information to the text, such as URLs, emojis, HTML tags, numeric characters, and special symbols; conversion of text to lowercase; tokenization; and the removal of mentions, hashtags, and stopwords. Short phrases of fewer than three characters were also discarded, and the normalized texts were consolidated into coherent linguistic structures suitable for processing by LLMs.

As part of the exploratory analysis, a word cloud was generated to identify the most frequent terms in the corpus. Figure 2 shows that prominent words include death, robbery, accident, dead, victim, and fire, highlighting a strong presence of posts related to emergency situations.

Fig. 2. Word Cloud.

2.4 Phase 4: Modeling

This phase implemented an approach based on Large Language Models (LLMs) [11], with the objective of adapting the models to the classification task and enabling them to identify posts as either Emergency or Non-Emergency. Prompt engineering techniques were employed to optimize the formulation of instructions and effectively guide the response of the pretrained models [12]. This strategy enabled the configuration of model behavior without requiring additional training processes.

Although several relevant Generative AI models exist—such as LLaMA, Anthropic Claude, and DeepSeek, their integration into this study presented limitations in terms of infrastructure, performance, and language support. Therefore, priority was given to models that offered a balance between linguistic performance, accessibility, inference speed, and ease of integration.

Based on this premise, three LLMs were selected: the GPT-3.5 Turbo model, developed by OpenAI, was included due to its recognized versatility, stability, and linguistic quality in advanced text processing tasks [13]. The Mistral Small 3.1 model provided a lightweight and flexible alternative that enriched the comparative analysis [14]. Finally, Gemini-2.0-Flash, developed by Google DeepMind, was integrated for its suitability in multilingual classification tasks [15].

2.5 Phase 5: Evaluation

The performance of the generative models in the classification task was evaluated using metrics widely recognized in the field of supervised machine learning [16]. The following metrics were considered: Accuracy, which measures the overall proportion of correct predictions; Precision, which quantifies the proportion of true positives among all instances classified as positive; Recall, which assesses the model's ability to correctly identify actual positive instances; and F1-Score, which represents the harmonic mean of

Precision and Recall. The formulas used are as follows:

$$Accuracy = \frac{TP + TN}{TP + TN + FP + FN} \tag{1}$$

$$Precision = \frac{TP}{TP + FP} \tag{2}$$

$$Recall = \frac{TP}{TP + FN} \tag{3}$$

$$F1 - Score = 2 \times \frac{precision \times recall}{precision + recall} \tag{4}$$

where: TP (true positives) refers to cases correctly classified as Emergency; TN (true negatives) refers to cases correctly classified as Non-Emergency; FP (false positives) refers to posts incorrectly classified as Emergency; FN (false negatives) refers to posts incorrectly classified as Non-Emergency.

2.6 Configurations

For the manipulation and transformation of structured data, the Pandas library was used [17], while NLP tasks were performed using SpaCy [18], Text cleaning and normalization were complemented with regular expressions (regex) [19]. The integration of LLMs was implemented using LangChain [20], and error handling was managed through the Backoff library [21]. Multitasking processes were handled using the concurrent.futures module [22].

2.7 Testing

For the testing phase, a parallel processing scheme was implemented for the APIs, which significantly optimized classification times. The complete process on the test set was executed in approximately four hours. Table 2 illustrates the behavior of the models in specific cases.

Table 2. Sample of Post Classification

Post	Text	Tag	Gemini	Mistral	OpenAI
@ATMGuayaquil @ATM_Transito En esta calle que limita con el parque Samanes se acaba de salir una tapa de alcantarillado dejando un hueco y lo tapa en media calle Favor verificar antes que se produzca algún accidente https://t.co/2zx0Mugfcy	en esta calle que limita con el parque samanes se acaba de salir una tapa de alcantarillado dejando un hueco y lo tapa en media calle favor verificar antes que se produzca algún accidente	EMERGENCIA	EMERGENCIA	EMERGENCIA	EMERGENCIA

(*continued*)

Table 2. (*continued*)

Post	Text	Tag	Gemini	Mistral	OpenAI
@ecuainm_oficial @pichinchauniver Por favor solucion la empresa telefonica claro me esta robando la linea 0986466831pertenesco a movistar y desde 1 mes y medio otro señor la tiene e claro aclaro que me llegan llamadas de movistar y twenty y de claro a otro señor por favor atender reclamo	por favor solucion la empresa telefonica claro me esta robando la linea pertenesco a movistar y desde mes y medio otro señor la tiene e claro aclaro que me llegan llamadas de movistar y twenty y de claro a otro señor por favor atender reclamo	EMERGENCIA	NO EMERGENCIA	NO EMERGENCIA	EMERGENCIA
Sigue el Pais sumergido en el pantano de la corrupción… Sin temor a nada… ni nadie solo puedo decir que el dinero que roben es dinero de muerte desesperación y caos…! Son peor que cualquier virus…	sigue el pais sumergido en el pantano de la corrupción sin temor a nada ni nadie solo puedo decir que el dinero que roben es dinero de muerte desesperación y caos son peor que cualquier virus	NO EMERGENCIA	NO EMERGENCIA	NO EMERGENCIA	EMERGENCIA

The prompt explicitly requested that each post be categorized into one of two classes.

Given the bias present in the original dataset, with a notable imbalance toward the Non-Emergency class, an undersampling process was applied [23] to balance the class representation. As a result, a dataset of 6,377 posts was obtained, with an approximate distribution of 70–30 for the Non-Emergency and Emergency classes, respectively.

3 Results

In the classification process developed for identifying posts related to emergency situations on Platform X, the performance of three pretrained generative language models was evaluated (Fig. 3 and Table 3).

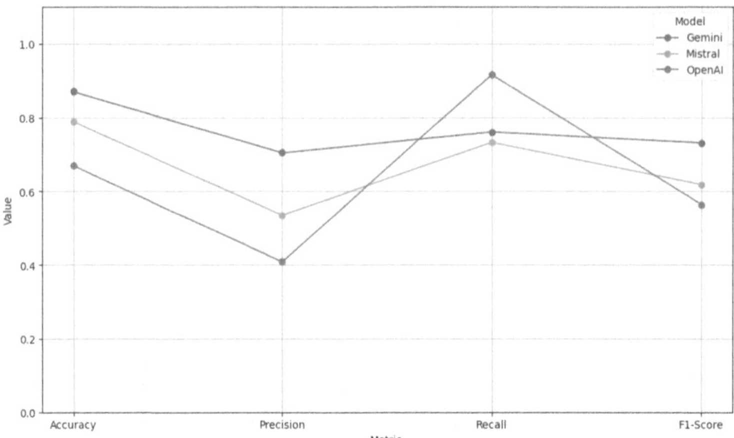

Fig. 3. Metrics by Model

Table 3. Performance Metrics

Model	Accuracy	Precision	Recall	F1-Score
Gemini (gemini-2.0-flash)	0.8694	0.7043	0.7606	0.7314
Mistral (mistral-small)	0.7886	0.5350	0.7324	0.6183
OpenAI (gpt-3.5-turbo)	0.6693	0.4077	0.9155	0.5642

Overall, the Gemini-2.0-Flash model demonstrated outstanding performance with an Accuracy of 0.8694, a Precision of 0.7043, and an F1-Score of 0.7314, indicating a favorable balance between Precision and Recall. Meanwhile, OpenAI's GPT-3.5-Turbo model achieved the highest Recall value at 0.9155, reflecting a high sensitivity in correctly identifying emergency cases. The Mistral-small model showed intermediate performance across most metrics, with a particularly notable Recall of 0.7324 (Fig. 4).

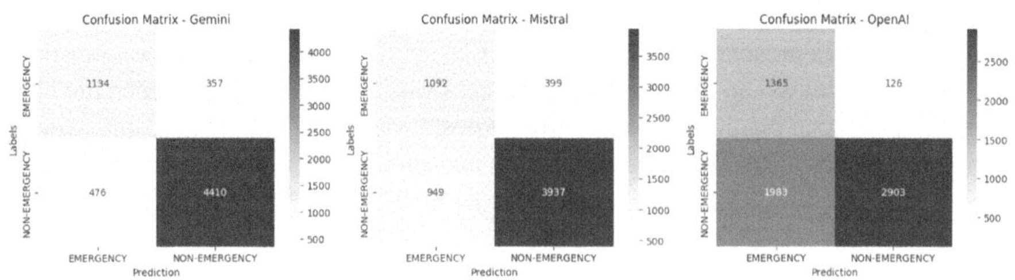

Fig. 4. Confusion Matrices

The Gemini-2.0-Flash model demonstrated balanced performance, correctly classifying a high proportion of posts in both the Emergency and Non-Emergency classes, while maintaining moderate levels of classification errors. In contrast, the Mistral-small model showed a slight decrease in its ability to detect emergencies, as evidenced by increased false negatives and false positives, suggesting lower precision in distinguishing between the two classes. OpenAI's GPT-3.5-Turbo model, on the other hand, exhibited high sensitivity, evidenced by a reduced number of false negatives. However, this was accompanied by a considerable increase in false positives.

4 Discussion

To address whether LLMs can accurately classify emergency-related posts on Platform X without requiring additional training—and which of these models delivers the best performance—the results showed that this task can be effectively carried out using prompt engineering techniques, without prior training or dataset segmentation. Gemini-2.0-Flash, developed by Google, achieved the best overall performance, while OpenAI's GPT-3.5-Turbo stood out for its high capacity to detect potential emergencies. Although the original dataset exhibited class imbalance, undersampling techniques were applied to mitigate potential bias without altering the original nature of the corpus.

When comparing these findings with previous studies, for instance, [5] employed an optimized version of BERT to classify tweets related to traffic-related disasters, reaching an F1-Score of 84%, although it required model training and fine-tuning. In a more closely related approach, [6] applied generative models to zero-shot classification tasks, obtaining a weighted F1-Score of 0.828 using GPT-4o, demonstrating the potential of LLMs for classification without task-specific training. Although the results obtained in the present study do not surpass these scores, it is worth noting that they were achieved without fine-tuning, with lower computational demand, and by focusing on lighter and more adaptable models.

It is important to highlight that the findings demonstrate that pretrained LLMs can serve as effective and reproducible tools for automatically classifying emergency-related posts. This capability positions them as a strategic alternative for developing real-time monitoring systems, particularly in contexts where scalability, rapid implementation, and operational efficiency are priorities. While factors such as prompt design, corpus quality, or inherent biases may affect accuracy, the distinctive contribution of this study lies in providing concrete evidence of the feasibility of integrating Generative AI into early warning systems based on social media—thus contributing to the advancement of knowledge in applications that combine NLP, risk management, and intelligent systems.

5 Conclusions and Future Work

In this study, LLMs were employed to classify emergency-related posts on Platform X using the urbangEnCy dataset. No additional training processes were required, as prompt engineering techniques were applied to adapt the models to a binary classification task. The results demonstrate that this strategy is effective and applicable in real-world crisis management scenarios.

Three generative AI models were evaluated, among which Gemini-2.0-Flash showed the best overall performance in terms of precision and recall balance. GPT-3.5-Turbo achieved the highest recall, making it suitable for scenarios where emergency detection is a priority. In contrast, Mistral-small exhibited a higher proportion of false positives, limiting its applicability in contexts that require high operational precision.

For future work, the integration of additional generative AI models is proposed, with the aim of analyzing their performance in similar classification tasks. Another line of research involves evaluating the proposed approach in different contexts, such as sentiment analysis and fake news detection, to assess the impact of prompt design on the quality of the results.

References

Garg, A., Mago, V.: Role of machine learning in medical research: a survey. Comput Sci Rev **40**, 100370 (2021). https://doi.org/10.1016/J.COSREV.2021.100370

Madichetty, S., Sridevi, M.: A stacked convolutional neural network for detecting the resource tweets during a disaster. Multimedia Tools Appl. **80**(3), 3927–3949 (2021). https://doi.org/10.1007/S11042-020-09873-8/TABLES/15

Algur, S.P., Venugopal, S.: Classification of disaster specific tweets - a hybrid approach. In: 2021 8th International Conference on Computing for Sustainable Global Development (INDIACom), pp. 774–777 (2021)

Balakrishnan, V., et al.: A comprehensive analysis of transformer-deep neural network models in twitter disaster detection. Mathematics **10**(24), 4664 (2022). https://doi.org/10.3390/MATH10244664

Prasad, R., Udeme, A.U., Misra, S., Bisallah, H.: Identification and classification of transportation disaster tweets using improved bidirectional encoder representations from transformers. Int. J. Inf. Manag. Data Insights **3**(1), 100154 (2023). https://doi.org/10.1016/J.JJIMEI.2023.100154

Mcdaniel, E.L., Scheele, S., Liu, J.: Zero-shot classification of crisis tweets using instruction-finetuned large language models (2024). https://arxiv.org/pdf/2410.00182. Accessed 26 May 2025

Studer, S., et al.: Towards CRISP-ML(Q): a machine learning process model with quality assurance methodology. Mach. Learn. Knowl. Extr. **3**(2), 392–413 (2020). https://doi.org/10.3390/make3020020

Plotnikova, V., Dumas, M., Milani, F.: Adaptations of data mining methodologies: a systematic literature review. PeerJ Comput. Sci. **6**, 1–43 (2020). https://doi.org/10.7717/PEERJ-CS.267/SUPP-2

Hanny, D., Schmidt, S., Resch, B.: Active learning for identifying disaster-related tweets: a comparison with keyword filtering and generic fine-tuning. In: Lecture Notes in Networks and Systems. LNNS, vol. 1066, pp. 126–142. Springer, Heidelberg (2024). https://doi.org/10.1007/978-3-031-66428-1_8

Parraga-Alava, J.: urbangEnCy, vol. 2 (2020). https://doi.org/10.17632/4X37ZZ82K8.2

Minaee, S., et al.: Large language models: a survey (2024). https://arxiv.org/pdf/2402.06196. Accessed 25 May 2025

Phoenix, J., Taylor, M.: Prompt Engineering for Generative AI (2024)

Ye, J., et al.: A comprehensive capability analysis of GPT-3 and GPT-3.5 series models (2023). https://arxiv.org/pdf/2303.10420. Accessed 23 May 2025

Ferrag, M.A., Tihanyi, N., Debbah, M.: Reasoning beyond limits: advances and open problems for LLMs (2025). https://arxiv.org/pdf/2503.22732. Accessed 23 May 2025

Ramachandran, A.: Unveiling Google's Gemini 2.0: A Comprehensive Study of its Multimodal AI Design, Advanced Architecture, and Real-World Applications (2024)

Alharthi, A., Alaryani, M., Kaddoura, S.: A comparative study of machine learning and deep learning models in binary and multiclass classification for intrusion detection systems. Array **26**, 100406 (2025). https://doi.org/10.1016/J.ARRAY.2025.100406

McKinney, W.: Python para análisis de datos. Manipulación de datos con pandas, Numpy y Jupyter, Actualización 2023. Anaya Multimedia, Madrid (2023)

Honnibal, M., Montani, I., Van Landeghem, S., Boyd, A.: spaCy: industrial-strength natural language processing in python (2020). https://doi.org/10.5281/zenodo.1212303

Friedl, J.E.F.: Mastering Regular Expressions (1997)

Chase, H.: LangChain (2022). https://github.com/langchain-ai/langchain

litl. backoff - Python library providing function decorators for configurable backoff and retry (2022). https://github.com/litl/backoff

Foundation, P.S.: concurrent.futures—Launching parallel tasks (2023). https://docs.python.org/3/library/concurrent.futures.html

Sadaiyandi, J., Arumugam, P., Sangaiah, A.K., Zhang, C.: Stratified sampling-based deep learning approach to increase prediction accuracy of unbalanced dataset. Electronics (Switzerland) **12**(21), 4423 (2023). https://doi.org/10.3390/ELECTRONICS12214423

Risk Perception and Risk Behavior. The Asian Disease Problem 40 years Later

Ingvar Tjostheim(✉) and Chris Wales

NLA Høgskolen, Linstows Gate 3, 0166 Oslo, Norway
ingvar.tjostheim@nla.no

Abstract. In most contexts, the word "risk" carries a negative connotation. However, in business and investment settings, it is not always perceived negatively. In this paper, we use the classic Asian disease problem and an investment scenario to examine the preferred choices of the general population versus specific groups: individuals with a high willingness to share personal data online, entrepreneurs, and the self-employed, compared to the average employee or citizen. The Asian Disease Problem involves a disease—an inherently negative event—but it can be framed either positively (as a gain) or negatively (as a loss). We recruited participants from a national population. Our analysis explores when the outcomes align with prospect theory and when they do not. We distinguish between the Asian Disease A (gain frame) and Asian Disease B (loss frame), as well as Investment Choice 1 (gain frame) and Investment Choice 2 (loss frame). Our findings indicate that the gain frame predicts the expected risk-seeking versus risk-averse behavior more frequently compared to the loss frame.

Keywords: Risk · risk perception · framing effect · prospect theory · national study

1 Introduction

In an open world, uncertainty and risk are inevitable. In many situations, we lack relevant information but must still make decisions. Prospect theory (Tversky & Kahneman, 1992) examines how people make decisions under uncertainty and risk, particularly when outcomes involve gains and losses. The Asian Disease Problem (AD) is a well-known example from behavioral economics and psychology that illustrates how framing effects influence decision-making. Introduced by Amos Tversky and Daniel Kahneman in 1981 (Tversky & Kahneman, 1981) as part of their research on cognitive biases, the scenario has been widely studied. Numerous experiments have been conducted, and the effect between conditions appears to range from negligible to small or medium (Kühberger, 1998).

The Asian Disease Problem (AD) is a hypothetical scenario, and it has been criticized for precisely that—being hypothetical. During the COVID-19 pandemic, the SARS-CoV-2 virus affected individuals personally, and although scientists do not universally agree on its origin, it was initially referred to, along with "China Virus" and "Wuhan

T. Guarda et al. (Eds.): ARTIIS 2025, CCIS 2789, pp. 184–193, 2026.
https://doi.org/10.1007/978-3-032-16758-3_15

Virus" as an "Asian virus", despite concerns of this being "inaccurate and xenophobic"(Vazquez, 2020). In the two studies presented in this paper, Norwegian citizens—both during and after the pandemic—responded to a survey that included the AD problem. The Norwegian government's strategy is to make the country the most digitized in the world by 2030, increasingly requiring citizens to use digital services and applications for most public services. A great number of citizens were therefore forced onto digital platforms by the onset of the COVID-19 pandemic, requiring greater digital literacy and competence within a brief time period. In the digital economy, risk is a crucial factor. Digital fraud is a growing problem, and with increased digital activity in the vast majority of the population has become a target and increasingly experiences being targeted. Citizens must repeatedly consider the question: When and how much should I share my personal data? Determining a safe choice is not necessarily straightforward.

In our two studies, we included a test measuring willingness to share personal data, which we named the Personal Data Disclosure Test. In the second study, some respondents answered questions about their employment and specifically whether they were self-employed or had started a business. Entrepreneurial activity inherently involves uncertainty, and we hypothesize that entrepreneurs are somewhat more willing to take risks compared to the average citizen. Additionally, we hypothesize that individuals willing to share personal data online exhibit risk characteristics similar to those of the risk-seeking group in the AD scenario.

The paper is structured as follows: Sect. 2 provides a brief description of the AD scenario, an investment scenario, and the Personal Data Disclosure Test. Section 3 presents the research questions and the results. In the final section, we conclude with a discussion of the results and their implications for future research.

2 The AD Scenario, the Investment Scenario and the Personal Data Disclosure Test

The AD scenario involves decision-making in the medical domain, focusing on a disease—specifically, a virus. In the gain frame, some individuals will be saved, while in the loss frame, some will die. To what extent can people understand and evaluate these alternatives? Before answering, do they relate to the situation and the disease itself? Nilson & Erikson (2020:17) write:

> *When looking at the asian disease used in the Asian Disease Problem, people might have a hard time understanding the effects of a fictional disease. They do not know how dangerous it is for the individual people nor the society, they do not know the symptoms or how they feel about the victims. When it comes to the coronavirus however, people know the symptoms, individual and societal risks. This is probably the main difference between the problem being fictional and real.*

During the pandemic in Norway, citizens were constantly presented with updates and statistics about the number of hospitalized patients with the coronavirus and the number of deaths either caused by or associated with the virus across mainstream- and social media platforms. Study 1 took place at a time when between 500 and 600 people had died with or from the virus—a number comparable to the figures used in the AD scenario by Tversky and Kahneman (1981), where in Scenario A, 600 would be saved, and in Scenario B, 600 would die. In our view, this enhances ecological validity, as there is reason to believe that respondents in the surveys could perceive these scenarios as real rather than purely hypothetical.

The investment scenario was inspired by monetary decision-making, particularly the win/loss dynamics in gambling, as discussed in Tversky & Kahneman (1981). The numbers used in the investment scenario were chosen to be relatable—for citizens who own shares in a company, an apartment, or other valuable assets, an amount comparable to $60,000 can be seen as realistic. Compared to a disease and potential death, choices in the monetary scenario have fewer social implications or emotional consequences, such as the loss experienced by a patient's family and close friends.

Market research panel members frequently participate in surveys. In our experiment on personal data disclosure, the participants had previously taken part in surveys. The market research company held their responses in a database, but did not however, share these with any other clients. Despite this, it is possible to link data and create detailed profiles based on past survey answers. In collaboration with the market research company, we inquired about accessing participants' past survey responses and their Facebook profiles to construct new, comprehensive profiles. We reiterate that at no time did the market research company, acting as the data processor, share past survey responses.

Similar to the AD scenario, respondents in our study had to make a choice: either give consent to share personal data with the client of the market research company or decline. We termed this assessment the Data Disclosure Test. This test has also been used in studies on digital vulnerability, phishing, identity theft, and sexting (Tjostheim & Waterworth, 2024, Tjostheim & Wales, 2024).

3 The ´Survey Data and the Research Questions

We commissioned two surveys in collaboration with the market research company Norstat AS, which recruited a representative sample of the population aged 16 to 69 years. The surveys included questions about online behavior related to the surveillance economy, the classic Asian Disease (AD) scenario, and the Personal Data Disclosure Test. In the second survey, we introduced an investment problem designed to mimic the AD scenario.

Human behavior varies across different domains, meaning financial risks do not necessarily align with health risks. Some individuals take risks in sports but avoid gambling, and vice versa. With this in mind, we reformulated the disease problem into the following investment scenarios:

- Investment Scenario 1: You have invested $60,000 in a company facing bankruptcy. You have two options: a) Sell and receive $20,000, or b) a 1/3 probability of recovering the full $60,000.
- Investment Scenario 2: You have two options: a) Lose $40,000, or b) a 2/3 probability of losing everything.

In the second survey, respondents received invitations to participate in a follow-up section containing questions about employment status and whether they had started a company. Based on their responses, we categorized them into two groups: Ordinary employees vs Self-employed individuals and entrepreneurs.

Similarly, we created two additional groups: Non-disclosure group (those unwilling to share personal data) vs. Willingness-to-share group (those open to sharing personal data).

To ensure demographic consistency, respondents were randomly assigned to AD groups so that subgroup profiles would closely match those of the general population.

Table 1. Descriptive statistics of the respondents, survey 1 and 2.

Survey 1 (N = 639)	Min	Max	Mean	SD	Skewness	Kurtosis
Gender	1	2	1.53	0.50	−0.10	−1.99
Age-groups	1	4	2.50	1.16	0.19	−1.46
Education	1	4	2.31	1.20	0.24	−1.49
Survey 2 (N = 1077)	Min	Max	Mean	SD	Skewness	Kurtosis
Gender	1	2	1.55	0.50	−0.19	−1.97
Age-groups	1	4	2.58	1.14	−0.03	−1.41
Education	1	4	2.63	1.01	0.38	−1.18

In a social science context, a kurtosis value greater than ±2.0, might indicate a tailedness problem. This was not the case for our variables – see Table 1. Similarly, a skewness between −1 and +1 is generally considered acceptable.

For this study, we have formulated the following research questions:

Research Question (RQ1): For the majority of respondents in the larger groups, the choices in the two AD scenarios will align with those presented in Tversky & Kahneman (1981). The majority refers to individuals who did not give consent in the Data Disclosure Test and those who are employees.

Research Question (RQ2): Respondents who gave consent in the Data Disclosure Test, as well as being self-employed individuals and entrepreneurs, tend to opt for riskier choices compared to other groups.

Research Question (RQ3): The direction of choices A or B will be consistent with the predictions of prospect theory in both the gain frame and the loss frame.

For further information on prospect theory, we refer to Kahneman & Tversky (1991) and the meta-analysis by Kühberger (1998).

4 Results and a Brief Discussion of Key Findings

Since the scenarios have only two alternatives, either A or B, we present our results in tables with the percentages as was presented in the Tversky & Kahneman 1981 article. In the gain frame, AD problem A, 72% chose the 200, referred to as the riskless alternative, a sure outcome. In the loss frame, 78% chose the riskier alternative, the probability choice. In the tables in the result section, we present our result in the same manner.

Table 2. Study 1 The choices in the two Asian disease scenarios (in parenthesis, the numbers from Tversky & Kahneman, 1981)

	The gain frame, the classic Asian disease problem, scenario A, N = 364	The loss frame, the classic Asian disease problem, scenario B N = 254
The riskless choice (risk averse)	67% (72%)	32% (22%)
The riskier choice (risk seeking)	33% (28%)	68% (78%)

Table 2 shows that the results for the two scenarios have the same pattern as in the original Tversky & Kahneman 1981 article. The finding is accordance with the prospect theory – decision making is affected by the framing, in this case in the health domain.

Study 1 included the personal data disclosure test. Although it is quite common to share personal data, it is safer not to share. The implication of the personal data disclosure test, the *I-give-consent* is that this reveals a lot about the respondent to the receiver of data. The *I-give-consent* answer is the riskier choice.

According to the numbers in Table 3, those with high willingness to share personal data measured by the data-disclosure test make choices similar to others in the gain frame. Notably, the riskless choice is 62% vs 70% in the AD scenario. In the loss frame, as many as 85% chose the riskier choice compared to 66% for the other. It can be interpreted as an indication of a high willingness take risk.

While study 1 only included the classic Asian disease problem, study 2 also included the investment scenario.

For the AD scenarios the choices are similar to the choices in study 1; 67% for riskless alternative in the gain frame, and 65% for the riskier alternative in the loss frame (see Table 4).

For the Investment scenario 1, nearly all our respondents, 96%, chose the riskless alternative, the sure gain. Interestingly, for the Investment scenario 2, it is closer to 50–50. The numbers are 56% for riskier choice and 44% for the riskless choice (see Table 4). According to prospect theory, people violate the invariance principle. It states that preferences should not change when the same choice is presented in different but logically equivalent ways. For the Investment scenario in the loss frame, the invariance principle is violated, but it is much closer to a 50–50 outcome compared to the other scenarios.

Table 3. Study 1. The choice of the two groups: not sharing vs sharing of personal data. Risk behaviour online measured with a personal data disclosure test.

	High willingness to share personal data online	**Not willing** to share personal data online		**Not willing** to share personal data online	**High willingness** to share personal data online	
	Gain frame The choice of the **Risk seeking behaviour group** in scenario A (N = 47)	Gain frame The choice of the **Risk averse behaviour** group in scenario A (N = 318)	The difference between the two groups	Loss frame The choice of the **Risk averse behaviour group** in scenario B (N = 227)	Loss frame The choice of the **Risk seeking behaviour group** in scenario A (N = 27)	The difference between the two groups
The fixed outcome. The **riskless** choice	70%	**62%**	–8%	34%	**15%**	–19%
The probability outcome. The **riskier** choice	30%	**37%**	+ 7%	66%	**85%**	+ 19%

Table 4. Study 2 The choice in the two Asian disease scenarios and the two Investment scenarios

	Gain frame. Asian disease scenario A (N = 327)	Loss frame. Asian disease scenario B (N = 243)	Gain frame. Investment scenario 1 (N = 270)	Loss frame. Investment scenario 2 (N = 237)
The fixed outcome. The riskless choice (risk averse)	**67%**	35%	**96%**	44%
The probability outcome. The riskier choice (risk seeking choice)	33%	**65%**	4%	**56%**

In the next table we present the results for the self-employed and entrepreneurs vs others. In the "other" group, many are employees, some are students, some are unemployed, and some are the oldest retirees. There are many reasons for being self-employed or for starting a company, but there is a risk involved.

Table 5. Study 2 the Asian scenario A and B and the investment scenario 1 and 2 for **self-employed and entrepreneurs vs other/employed**

	Asian disease scenario A, Gain frame	
	The **fixed outcome**. The riskless choice (risk averse),	The **probability outcome**. The riskier choice (risk seeking),
The choice of the group: self-employed or has started a company that has employees, N = 37	49%	51%
The choice of the group: the other (a broad group of people), N = 147	**70%**	30%
	Asian disease scenario B, Loss frame	
	The **fixed outcome**. The riskless choice (risk averse)	The **probability outcome**. The riskier choice
The choice of the group: self-employed or has started a company that has employees, N = 34	44%	56%
The choice of the group: the others (a broad group of people), N = 104	31%	**69%**
	Investment scenario, 1 Gain frame	
	The **fixed outcome**. The riskless choice (risk averse)	The **probability outcome**. The riskier choice
The choice of the group: self-employed or has started a company that has employees, N = 226	**93%**	7%
The choice of the group: the others (a broad group of people), N = 96	95%	5%
	Investment scenario 2, Loss frame	
	The **fixed outcome**. The riskless choice (risk averse)	The **probability outcome**. The riskier choice
The choice of the group: self-employed or has started a company that has employees, N = 18	**56%**	44%
The choice of the group: the others, (a broad group of people) N = 108	47%	**53%**

We refer to the other as the broad group of people that has not started a company or not being self-employed. Table 5 shows that broad group, for the Asian B, Asian B and in the Investment 1 gain frame make decisions as the prospect theory predicts. For the Investment 1 gain frame, nearly all, 93%, chose the riskless alternative.

For the self-employed, the entrepreneurs, it is only for the Investment 1 gain frame that the choice is the same as for the broad group – 95% chose the riskless alternative. For the three other scenarios, it is much closer to the 50–50. The percentages are 51, 56 and 56. We can speculate that they have made a calculation, and/or are less influenced by the framing.

Table 6. Study 2, the Asian scenario A and B and the investment scenario 1 and 2 for **high willingness to share personal data vs not willing to share personal data** (data disclosure t.)

	Asian disease scenario A, Gain frame	
	The **fixed outcome**. The riskless choice,	The **probability outcome**. The riskier choice,
The choice of the group: not giving consent to share personal data (cautions beh.), N = 230	**69%**	31%
The choice of the group, consent to share personal data (riskier beh.), N = 97	64%	36%
	Asian disease scenario B, Loss frame	
	The **fixed outcome**. The riskless choice (risk averse)	The **probability outcome**. The riskier choice
The choice of the group: not giving consent to share personal data (cautions beh.), N = 160	31%	**69%**
The choice of the group, consent to share personal data (riskier beh.), N = 70	45%	55%
	Investment scenario, A Gain frame	
	The **fixed outcome**. The riskless choice (risk averse)	The **probability outcome**. The riskier choice
The choice of the group: not giving consent to share personal data (cautions beh.), N = 194	**96%**	4%
The choice of the group, consent to share personal data (riskier beh.), N = 76	93%	7%
	Investment scenario B, Loss frame	
	The **fixed outcome**. The riskless choice (risk averse)	The **probability outcome**. The riskier choice
The choice of the group: not giving consent to share personal data (cautions behavior), N = 166	46%	54%
The choice of the group, consent to share personal data (riskier beh.), N = 64	36%	**64%**

Table 6 shows the same result as in Table 5 did for the broad group, the majority that answer no, *I do not give consent* in the personal data disclosure test. The members of this group show caution behavior. The interesting findings are with regard to the high willingness to share personal data group. In the gain frame, the Asian disease scenario, 64% chose the riskless alternative, as the majority group did. In the loss frame, the Asian disease scenario B, 55% chose the riskier alternative and closer to the 50–50.

For the investment scenario A, the gain frame, 93% chose the riskless alternative. But for the loss frame, Investment 2, that the riskier alternative is preferred by 64% compared to 54% for the majority group.

5 Concluding Remarks

In this paper we have used empirical data to discuss how prospect theory (Tversky & Kahneman, 1992) explains decision-making under risk, particularly through the Asian Disease (AD) Problem, a classic example of how framing (gain vs. loss) influences choices. The AD scenario, originally hypothetical, was revisited during the COVID-19 pandemic in Norway, where real-life parallels and experience increased its ecological validity.

Two studies were conducted in Norway—one during and one after the pandemic—using: The AD scenario (medical risk), An investment scenario (financial risk), and, a personal data disclosure test (digital risk).

The studies aimed to examine how people make decisions in different domains and whether risk preferences vary across contexts. Participants were also asked about their employment status (employee vs. entrepreneur) to explore if entrepreneurs are more risk-tolerant than other members of society, this considering that risk is inherent to such activity.

The studies replicated the Asian Disease (AD) problem and introduced investment and personal data disclosure scenarios to explore how people make decisions under risk, framed as either gains or losses. Our key findings align with prospect theory and mirror Tversky & Kahneman's original findings for the Asian disease scenarios. For the Investment scenario, the gain frame also aligns with prospect theory, but to a lesser degree for the loss frame.

The high willingness to share personal data and the self-employed, entrepreneur group show a somewhat higher aptitude for taking risk than respondents from the wider population. This suggests they may be less influenced by framing and more analytical in risk evaluation and a greater risk-taking tendency in the loss frames. This is especially clear in the Investment 2 scenario, the loss frame.

At a time when the world is faces greater uncertainty at both global and societal levels, while the media framework becomes more fragmented, and citizens are increasingly required, rather than encouraged, to communicate and transact digitally, understanding the nature of risk and factors related to it is becoming more and more important. While the results of our study align with a robust research programme from the 1980s, the intensity of change in current contexts requires further study.

References

Tversky, A., Kahneman, D.: Advances in prospect theory: cumulative representation of uncertainty. J. Risk Uncertain. **5**, 297–323 (1992)

Tversky, A., Kahneman, D.: The framing of decisions and the psychology of choice. Science **211**, 453–458 (1981)

Kuhberger, A.: The influence of framing on risky decisions: a meta-analysis. Organ. Behav. Hum. Decis. Process. **75**, 23–55 (1998)

Vasquez, M.: Called COVID-19 the "Wuhan Virus" or "China Virus" is inaccurate and xenophobic. Yale School of Medicine (2020). https://medicine.yale.edu/news-article/calling-covid-19-the-wuhan-virus-or-china-virus-is-inaccurate-and-xenophobic/

Nilsson, M., Eriksson, R.: Framing effect in time of a pandemic: A more realistic Asian disease problem (2020). https://lup.lub.lu.se/student-papers/search/publication/9016958

Kahneman, D., Tversky, A.: Prospect theory: an analysis of decision under risk. Econometrica **47**(2), 263–292 (1979)

Tjostheim, I., Waterworth, J.A.: Exploring susceptibility to phishing: the cognitive reflection test and other possible predictors. In: Proceedings of Annual Hawaii International Conference on System Scienced (HICSS), vol. 57, pp.4754–4763 (2024). https://doi.org/10.24251/HICSS.2024.570

Tjostheim, I., Wales, C.: Sexting, age and digital vulnerabilities. In: Proceeding 12th International Conference on Human Interaction and Emerging Technologies. AHFE Open Access (2024). https://doi.org/10.54941/ahfe1005513

Intelligent Parking Space Detection with ESP32 and SVM in Autonomous Vehicles at 1:10 Scale

Sebastián Burciaga-Sosa[1(✉)], José M. Celaya-Padilla[1], Rafael Reveles-Martínez[1], Héctor Burciaga-Sosa[2], Erika P. Sánchez-Femat[1], Javier Saldivar-Pérez[1], Carlos E. Galván-Tejada[1], Luis A. Flores-Chaires[1], Omar A. Guirette-Barbosa[3], and Juvenal Villanueva-Maldonado[1]

[1] Unidad Académica de Ingeniería Eléctrica. Universidad Autónoma de Zacatecas, Jardín Juárez 147, Centro, 98000 Zacatecas, Mexico
sburciagas1700@alumno.ipn.mx

[2] Independent Researcher, Zacatecas, Zacatecas, Mexico

[3] Department of Industrial Engineering, Universidad Politécnica de Zacatecas, Plan de Pardillo Sn, Parque Industrial, Fresnillo, 99059 Zacatecas, Mexico

Abstract. This paper presents the development of an intelligent system for the detection of parking spaces in 1:10 scale autonomous vehicles, using HC-SR04 ultrasonic sensors and machine learning techniques. Distance data were collected using an ESP32 microcontroller, allowing continuous transmission at a frequency of 250 Hz. This information was structured in windows of 60 samples and processed through metrics of central tendency, dispersion and distribution shape. Two supervised classification models were trained: multiple logistic regression and support vector machines (SVM) with an RBF kernel. Both models showed good predictive capacity, with the SVM model standing out for its slight superiority in precision and accuracy. The results validate the feasibility of using low-cost sensors and machine learning models in solving perception tasks for autonomous vehicles at scale. This proposal constitutes a solid basis for the development of real-time autonomous parking systems with low resource consumption, applicable in educational environments or functional prototypes.

Keywords: Autonomous driving · Vehicle control · Proximity sensing · Automatic learning

1 Introduction

Traffic accidents are one of the leading causes of death for people, with young people standing out among them [1]. This is because, in 2021, there were about 1.19 million deaths, which translates into 15 deaths per 100,000 inhabitants. Of those who died, about 69% were persons between 18 and 59 years of age, and 23% were persons over 60 years of age [2].

Traumatic injuries, besides being a major source of death and disability, represent a major economic impact on society, estimated at between 1% and 3% of the gross domestic product (GDP), a percentage that can reach 6% in some countries [3]. Therefore, they

T. Guarda et al. (Eds.): ARTIIS 2025, CCIS 2789, pp. 194–206, 2026.
https://doi.org/10.1007/978-3-032-16758-3_16

pose a great danger to the health and development sectors. In turn, it is predicted that, by 2030, motor vehicle accidents will become the seventh leading cause of death worldwide [4].

In Mexico, transportation accidents accounted for 42.9% of a total of 40,275 deaths in 2023, being one of the leading causes of death for young people aged 15 to 34 years [5]. Likewise, in 2021 it was recorded that, at the national level, 71.25% of the accidents occurred due to car users, meaning drivers. Circumstances that contributed to the accidents including: reckless driving, excessive speed, invasion of the oncoming lane, improper passing, failure to keep a safe distance, among others [6].

Autonomous driving seeks to replace human errors by developing algorithms that consider different situations, such as: maintaining a lane, performing passing maneuvers, considering the presence of pedestrians and traffic signals, as well as performing parking maneuvers. Unfortunately, there is currently no level of autonomy that would allow these tasks to be performed completely autonomously. The level of autonomy is classified in different degrees; Table 1 below summarizes these levels.

Table 1. Levels of autonomous vehicle assistance [7].

Level	Concept	Description
0	No Driving Automation	No vehicle automation
1	Driver Assistance	Automation in the control of the steering wheel or steering of the vehicle
2	Partial Driving Automation	Automation of the steering wheel and pedal system, under driver supervision
3	Conditional Driving Automation	Constant speed automation, driving assistance and autonomous parking
4	High Driving Automation	Almost complete automation, without contemplating climatological phenomena
5	Full Driving Automation	Full automation, where the driver is only a spectator

However, the development of this type of autonomous systems in full-scale automobiles is quite costly, since, due to the size of the vehicle, more sophisticated electronic components are required. This is evident in competitions that require full-scale automobile automation [8]. Therefore, the design of solutions for autonomous driving is usually done to scale, with 1:10 scale being the most common, and seeks to provide a solution to driving scenarios that arise in a driver's day-to-day life [9].

Internationally, there is an autonomous driving competition called Federation of International Robot-soccer Association (FIRA) RoboCup, which aims to develop 1:10 platforms. In this competition, two races must be completed in the Autonomous Cars category. The first consists of a race in which the vehicle must complete a circuit in the shortest possible time. The second is an urban circuit, in which the vehicle must follow the posted signs, and must make stops, changes of direction, among other maneuvers [10].

In Mexico there is a similar tournament, called Torneo Mexicano de Robótica, which includes the AutoModelCar category, which includes four tests: traffic sign recognition, autonomous navigation with obstacles, autonomous navigation with moving obstacles and autonomous parking.

The last test consists of vehicle parking in a designated area autonomously. To do this, the vehicle starts from a given distance and begins to move forward; once it detects an available parking space, it must use all the available space, as well as perform the necessary maneuvers to park successfully (Fig. 1) [11].

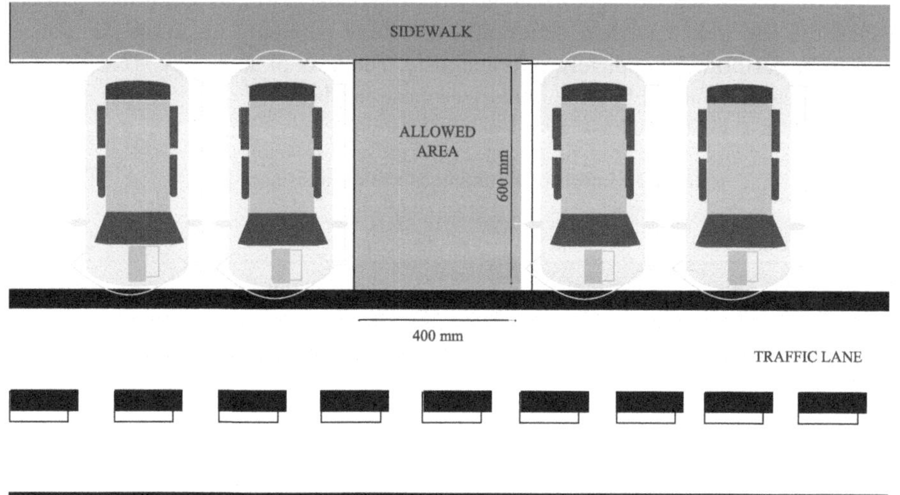

Fig. 1. Parking area TMR 2025.

Therefore, this study aims to present a methodology based on machine learning, allowing a scale model vehicle to identify available spaces for parking maneuvers in real time.

2 Related Work

Several studies have been carried out to solve this problem and allow a car to park in an empty space autonomously and successfully.

A study by Jhang, J.H. et al. [12] presented the design and implementation of an autonomous parking system, integrating Bidirectional Rapidly-Exploring Random Trees (Bi-RRT) algorithms in combination with model-based predictive control (MPC), which enabled the vehicle to perform efficient, accurate and collision-free parking maneuvers even in complex situations once it detected the space. This research focused on path planning, once it was assumed that the site was available.

In Rio de Janeiro, Brazil, an autonomous parking system based on light detection and localization (LIDAR) sensors as well as cameras was presented. As a LIDAR sensor, they used a Velodyne VLP-16 to detect obstacles and generate a map of the environment, and used a visual servoing technique with cameras, combined with localization, to guide the robot into the parking space. As results, they were able to detect available parking spaces, avoid obstacles, obtain real-time feedback and successfully park the vehicle, study conducted by Pérez-Morales, D. et al. [13].

On the other hand, Hongbo, G. et al. [14] presented an algorithm for autonomous parking control in intelligent vehicles. This algorithm employed optimization techniques with predictive control to plan and execute maneuvers to successfully and smoothly park the vehicle. They achieved a real-time search method that calculated the optimal trajectory to reach empty space, avoiding obstacles and focusing on precision.

A study conducted in Guyancourt, France, presented the design and implementation of a 1:1 scale parking system. For this purpose, an initial learning stage was included, in which the vehicle manually drove through the environment to map it, then allowing autonomous navigation through that space. Achieving by fusion of ultrasonic sensors and cameras vehicle localization, environment detection and safe navigation in previously learned spaces, study by Chirca, M. et al. [15].

Razinkova, A. et al. [16] proposed a scaled parallel parking assistance system, employing fuzzy logic, in which safe and efficient parking trajectories were generated. The system was generated by predefined rules for performing the movements, using sensors and actuators to validate the proposed fuzzy logic algorithm, demonstrating the feasibility of the system to perform parking maneuvers autonomously and without collisions with other objects.

In 2021, Heimberger, M. et al. [17] published a study in which, using computer vision techniques, an architecture for automated parking systems in full-scale cars was designed. With the help of four fisheye cameras, a 360-degree view was provided, avoiding blind spots in the vehicle, thus achieving the description of a system based on artificial vision to solve the problem of autonomous parking.

A study by Ma, S. et al. [18] presented an automatic parking system in which parking scenes, path planning, and tracking control were recognized, all using computer vision and pattern recognition techniques on vehicles in the parking area. An autonomous system implemented and tested in a full-scale vehicle was obtained, achieving vehicle parking and reducing the probability of accidents during maneuvers.

Wang, Y. et al. [19] addressed planning for autonomous parking in dynamic environments, where an approach that sequentially solved planning with static and moving obstacles was employed using a tree algorithm guided by bidirectional search and heuristics. The method was validated through several simulations, demonstrating its effectiveness in the planning of safe trajectories.

These approaches allow to understand that the development to autonomously park a car has been done previously. However, for the most part, they do not incorporate machine learning algorithms, the main focus of the present work.

3 Methods

Several In order to be able to robustly detect a parking space, the methodology was developed (Fig. 2), where in the first stage data collection is carried out using a low-cost device. Subsequently, the data is preprocessed so that it can be used in the learning process. Afterwards, the data are cleaned and standardized, followed by data balancing and analysis, culminating with the training of the learning model. The following sections describe each of the aforementioned stages.

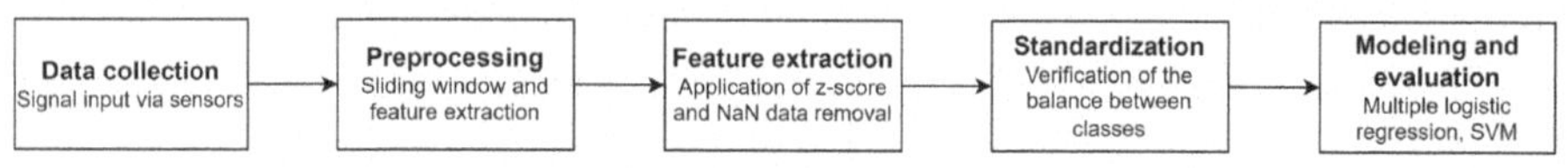

Fig. 2. Methodology.

Considering that we worked with HC-SR04 sensors, we designed a simple electrical circuit that included a button, a HC-SR04 ultrasonic sensor and an ESP32-WROOM-32D microcontroller. In this circuit, the echo and trigger pins of the ultrasonic sensor were connected to two digital pins of the ESP32, while the button was connected to another digital pin to send a logic value (1 or 0), depending on its state.

3.1 A Subsection Sample

The ESP32-WROOM-32D was programmed using the Arduino IDE software using two methods. In the first, the ultrasonic sensor transmitted via Bluetooth the distance data obtained (in millimeters), along with the time each reading was taken and the status of the button.

To indicate whether a parking space was available, two ranges were assigned: a value of 1 if the distance was between 400 mm and 600 mm (indicating free space), and a value of 0 if the distance was between 15 mm and 130 mm (indicating occupied space).

Using a Python script, the computer was linked to the ESP32 for real-time data reception, and a CSV document was written with three columns: time, distance, and button status. Once the code was executed, the circuit moved in a linear trajectory to verify whether or not an object was present (Fig. 3).

At the time the readings were taken, the distance (d) between objects occupying parking spaces was modified to have a different pattern of distance in each experiment performed, with the smallest distance being 400 mm and the largest being 900 mm.

Once the data was collected, a table with three columns and 60,077 sensor readings was obtained, where each reading was taken every 4 ms, resulting in a frequency of approximately 250 Hz.

As a second method, Micro-ROS was employed, a different modality of Robot Operating System, which aims to provide the capabilities of ROS in an embedded device with limited resources [20]. In this case, using the same ESP32 microcontroller, which was programmed to publish a node displaying the time of the reading, the distance recovered by the sensor and the status of the button. However, the data retrieved had a frequency of 32 Hz. Compared to the first method, the number of samples showed a large difference in the reading. Therefore, the 250 Hz database is the one that would be used for the machine learning algorithm.

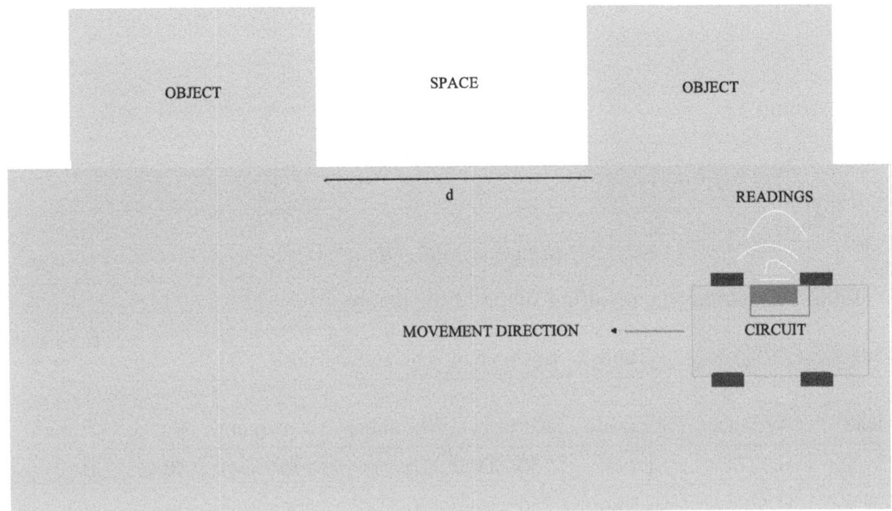

Fig. 3. Data collection scheme.

3.2 Data Preprocessing

To modify the database to be suitable for classification, an overlapping windowing process was used. This consisted in defining a sliding window of 60 samples, with a 50% overlap, in other words, each new window started 30 samples after the previous one, so as not to lose the continuity of information between each window created.

The selection of a window of 60 samples was purely empirical, because, with this number, we obtained a balance between a good number of windows for training (approximately 2000 windows), as well as having enough information for each individual window.

For each window, statistical measures such as mean, variance, skewness, kurtosis, minimum, maximum and range were calculated in order to extract more characteristics for the algorithm. Each of the statistics is shown below.

Mean:

$$\mu = \frac{1}{N}\sum\nolimits_{i=1}^{N} x_i \tag{1}$$

Variance:

$$\sigma^2 = \frac{1}{N}\sum\nolimits_{i=1}^{N} (x_i - \mu)^2 \tag{2}$$

Skewness:

$$skewness = \frac{1}{N}\sum\nolimits_{i=1}^{N} (x_i - \mu)^3 \tag{3}$$

Kurtosis:

$$kurtosis = \frac{1}{N}\sum\nolimits_{i=1}^{N}(x_i - \mu)^4 \tag{4}$$

Minimum:

$$\min(x_1, x_i, \ldots, x_n) \tag{5}$$

Maximum:

$$\max(x_1, x_i, \ldots, x_n) \tag{6}$$

Range:

$$Range = max - min \tag{7}$$

Table 2 illustrates the resulting shape of the database.

Table 2. Example of generated database.

Mean	Variance	Skewness	Kurtosis	Minimum	Maximum	Range	Button
129.996	0.327	-51.994	250.334	120	130	10	0
129.996	0.327	-51.994	250.334	120	130	10	0

The data were standardized using the z-score metric, which indicates the variance of a value from the mean, in units of standard deviation. As shown below.

$$z = \frac{x - \mu}{\sigma} \tag{8}$$

Moving on to the standardization of the data using z-score, which helps us to know how far away a value is from the mean in terms of standard deviation, as shown below.

When standardization was performed, data cleaning was required, since, on some occasions, they did not show any variation. For this purpose, the columns with missing data were filtered.

Verifying if the variable to be used as output (Button) was balanced, it was obtained that the values in "0" corresponded to 55.061% and the values in "1" to 44.939%, so it is concluded that the data are relatively balanced.

For the machine learning algorithms, two models were considered: multiple logistic regression and support vector machines (SVM).

3.3 Model Generation

It is proposed to perform a comparative analysis between two classification models: Multiple Logistic Regression and Support Vector Machine (SVM), to evaluate their performance in the task of line detection in autonomous vehicles at 1:10 scale. Both models will be trained and evaluated using a standard data set partitioning scheme, with 70% of the samples for training and the remaining 30% for testing. This approach will allow us to identify which of the two techniques is more efficient and robust to the computational constraints and the specific challenges of the small-scale context of the autonomous vehicle.

3.4 Multiple Logistic Regression

Logistic regression is a technique used to find the relationship between a dichotomous dependent variable (one that has only two possible values, such as 0 and 1) and one or more independent explanatory variables, whether quantitative or qualitative [21]. In this model, the dependent variable is calculated by combining the following independent variables. Each independent variable has a coefficient that shows how much it influences the result, which is obtained by summing these influences and applying a function known as sigmoid [22]. The formula is shown below.

$$y = \frac{1}{e^{-(b_0+b_1x_1+b_2x_2+\cdots+b_nx_n)}} \tag{9}$$

where y is the probability that the observation belongs to class 1, β_0 is the intercept and $\beta_1, \beta_2, \ldots, \beta_n$ are known as the coefficients associated with the variables $x_1, x_2, \ldots, x_n$.

The training of the model included 7 independent variables (Mean, Variance, Skewness, Kurtosis, Minimum, Maximum and Range) and a dichotomous dependent variable (Button).

3.5 Support Vector Machine (SVM)

Known as a pattern recognition technique that only works with two classes (works with binary data), it implements a principle called the Inductive Principle of Structural Risk Minimization [23]. This model divides the data into two groups, creating a line that performs this division. This line is not generated randomly, but is selected so that it is as far away as possible from the points closest to each class [24].

When the data cannot be linearly separated, a kernel such as Radial Basis Function (RBF) is used, which transforms the data into a higher dimensional space. For points that are very close to each other, the value will be high; otherwise, it will be practically 0 [25]. Its mathematical basis is as follows.

$$K(x, y) = \exp(-\gamma \|x - y\|^2) \tag{10}$$

where x, y are points in space, $\|x - y\|^2$ is the Euclidean distance between the points, and γ Controls how much each point influences. As in the Multiple Logistic Regression training, there were 7 independent variables and one dependent variable [26].

4 Results

4.1 Multiple Logistic Regression

Once the model was trained, the evaluation metrics were verified, obtaining Accuracy, which is the total percentage of correct predictions; Precision, which is the percentage of positive predictions that were actually positive; Re-call, which is the percentage of actual positive cases; and Specificity, which is the percentage of actual negative cases. The results corresponding to the testing part are shown below.

$$Accuracy = \frac{TP + TN}{TP + TN + FP + FN} = 0.953 = 95.3\% \tag{11}$$

$$Precision = \frac{TP}{TP + FP} = 0.959 = 95.9\% \tag{12}$$

$$\text{Recall} = \frac{TP}{TP + FN} = 0.937 = 93.7\% \tag{13}$$

$$\text{Specificity} = \frac{TN}{TN + FP} = 0.967 = 96.7\% \tag{14}$$

Likewise, in the logistic regression formula, where the values of the coefficients and the intercept are substituted, the variables $x_1, x_2, x_3, x_4, x_5, x_6, x_7$ correspond to the variables Mean, Variance, Skewness, Kurtosis, Minimum, Maximum and Range, respectively.

$$y = \frac{1}{e^{-(32.407+9.467x_1+0.051x_2-1.698x_3+0.015x_4+8.905x_5+9.355x_6+0.450x_7)}} \tag{15}$$

A graph was made to visualize the sigmoid curve (Fig. 4).

In order to analyze the performance of the logistic regression model, the value of the independent variable x on the abscissa axis is plotted against the estimated probability of the positive class on the ordinate axis. This graph allows us to visualize the model transforming the input values into probabilities by means of the sigmoid function.

In addition, it can be seen an increasing trend in the blue curve, while in red there is a dotted line representing the decision threshold at 0.5. This means that when the estimated probability exceeds this value, the model classifies the instance as belonging to the positive class; otherwise, as a negative class.

It is worth mentioning that variability peaks are perceived at the extremes of the curve, which is due to the few data in that range of values, generating predictions that are more sensitive to fluctuations, in other words, less reliable.

In general, the crossing of the curve by the threshold of 0.5 indicates that the model responds as expected: increasing the probability of belonging to the positive class as the value of the independent variable increases.

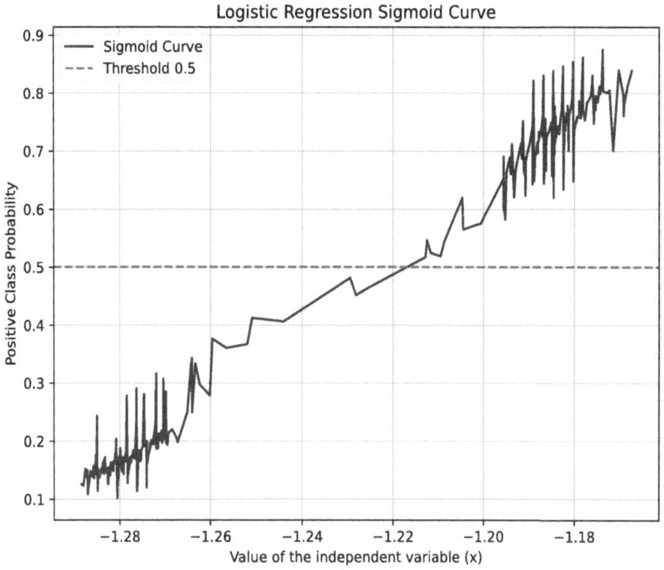

Fig. 4. Logistic Regression Sigmoid Curve.

4.2 Support Vector Machine

Reviewing the performance of the second model, the evaluation metrics Accuracy, Precision, Recall and Specificity are analyzed. The results corresponding to the testing part are shown below.

$$Accuracy = \frac{TP + TN}{TP + TN + FP + FN} = 0.959 = 95.9\% \tag{16}$$

$$Precision = \frac{TP}{TP + FP} = 0.963 = 96.3\% \tag{17}$$

$$\text{Recall} = \frac{TP}{TP + FN} = 0.946 = 94.6\% \tag{18}$$

$$\text{Specificity} = \frac{TN}{TN + FP} = 0.971 = 97.1\% \tag{19}$$

A graph is made to visualize the generated SVM model (Fig. 5).

Analyzing the performance, by means of the graph shown, two regions can be seen: the blue region represents class 0, while the red region represents class 1. The dots within the plot represent the training data, which have a color depending on their class. The black circles around some points indicate the support vectors, which are samples that are closer to the decision boundary.

In addition, it can be observed that the boundary separating the regions is not linear, which is a main feature of the RBF kernel used in this model. This kernel helps the classifier to adapt to nonlinear distributions, generating a complex decision boundary, but adjusted to the presented pattern.

Overall, the model indicates that the model is achieving good class separation, taking advantage of the flexibility of the selected kernel without overfitting.

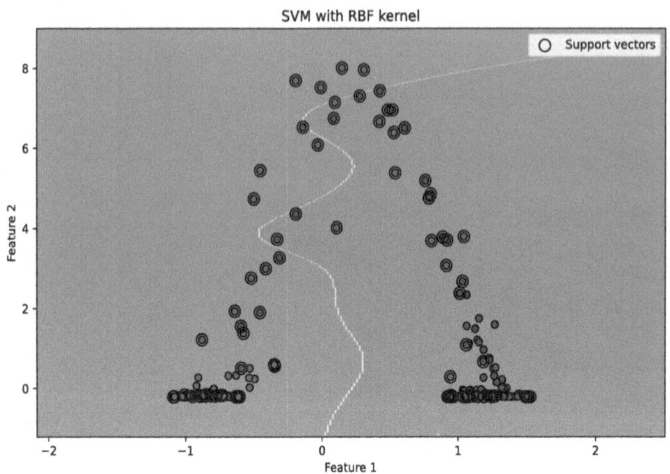

Fig. 5. Super Vector Machine with RBF kernel.

5 Conclusions

The lack of testing in real-world environments and a superficial analysis under adverse conditions are recognized as limitations of this work. However, the proposal represents a solid and practical foundation compared to other contributions in the field. Two models were implemented for classification: Multiple Logistic Regression and SVM, both trained on a database built from fenestration and statistical feature extraction techniques.

With favorable results when verifying the evaluation metrics. The Multiple Logistic regression reached an accuracy of 95.3%, precision of 95.9%, recall of 93.7% and specificity of 96.7%. On the other hand, the SVM model showed a slightly better performance, with an accuracy of 95.9%, precision of 96.9%, recall of 94.6% and specificity of 97.1%, being a better alternative for this type of binary classification.

This approach based on a combination of windowing of the collected data and standardization of the data proved to be an effective technique to generate a solid basis for classification, overcoming traditional methods based on fixed thresholds, as this approach allows us to adapt to different configurations when searching for available space.

Although this work does not include physical implementation, its performance can be approximated in a prototype. Since the data collection frequency is 250 Hz, it is possible to detect a gap every 4 ms, which is a fast response. Compared to other approaches, we present a low cost, simple and fast detection solution. Unlike other works that require the use of expensive hardware, our proposal only requires the use of an ultrasonic device costing less than 1 USD, as well as allowing all processing to be performed within the ESP32 unlike the post-processing required by techniques using artificial vision Heimberger, M. et al. [17].

However, one of the disadvantages of the ultrasonic sensor is the irregular surfaces or environmental conditions that generate noise in the readings, in addition to having a lower accuracy than more sophisticated hardware. Even so, the SVM approach shows promising, feasible and efficient results for autonomous parking systems at scale.

6 Future Work

The next objective is to implement the SVM algorithm on a 1:10 scale vehicle for competitive platforms, specifically FIRA (international) and TMR (national). Considering the frequency of the received data will allow for more efficient information synchronization. The implementation of a camera, in combination with the HC-SR04 sensors and algorithm, will facilitate real-time data processing, achieving low latency, which will help to make accurate decisions in a dynamic environment.

References

1. Shults, R.A.: Child passenger deaths involving drinking drivers – United States, 1997–2002. Morb. Mortal. Wkly Rep. **53**(4), 77–80 (2004)
2. World Health Organization (WHO): Global Status Report on Road Safety 2023. WHO, Geneva (2023). https://www.who.int/publications/i/item/9789240077614
3. Dalal, K., Lin, Z., Gifford, M., Svanström, L.: Economics of global burden of road traffic injuries and their relationship with health system variables. Int. J. Prev. Med. **4**, 1442–1450 (2013)
4. PIARC: Manual de Seguridad Vial – A guide for practitioners, pp. 1–27 (2021). https://roadsafety.piarc.org/es
5. INEGI: Estadísticas de defunciones registradas (Preliminar), pp. 29–31 (2023). _https://www.inegi.org.mx/contenidos/saladeprensa/boletines/2024/EDR/EDR2023_Dtivas.pdf
6. Instituto Mexicano del Transporte (IMT): Indicadores básicos de seguridad vial en México: propuesta metodológica para su construcción. Documento Técnico, no. 86 (2007). https://www.imt.mx/archivos/Publicaciones/DocumentoTecnico/dt86.pdf
7. SAE International: Taxonomy and Definitions for Terms Related to Driving Automation Systems for On-Road Motor Vehicles, Standard J3016_202104 (2022). https://saemobilus.sae.org/content/j3016_202104
8. Darms, M.S., Rybski, P.E., Baker, C., Urmson, C.: Obstacle detection and tracking for the urban challenge. IEEE Trans. Intell. Transp. Syst. **10**(3), 475–485 (2009)
9. Agnihotri, A., O'Kelly, M., Mangharam, R., Abbas, H.: Teaching autonomous systems at 1/10th-scale: design of the F1/10 Rracecar, simulators and curriculum. In: Proc. of the 52nd ACM Technical Symposium on Computer Science Education (SIGCSE), pp. 135–141 (2021)
10. FIRA World Cup: Autonomous Cars – FIRA Challenges. https://firaworldcup.org/leagues/fira-challenges/autonomous-cars/
11. FEMEX Robótica: Automodelcar – TMR 2025. https://femexrobotica.org/tmr2025/automodelcar/
12. Jhang, J.H., Lian, F.L.: An autonomous parking system of optimally integrating bidirectional rapidly-exploring random trees and parking-oriented model predictive control. IEEE Access **8**, 167848–167861 (2020). https://doi.org/10.1109/ACCESS.2020.3020859
13. Pérez-Morales, D., Domínguez-Quijada, S., Kermorgant, O., Martinet, P.: Autonomous parking using a sensor-based approach. In: HAL Id: hal-01396998v1, submitted on Nov. 15, (2016). https://inria.hal.science/hal-01396998v1

14. Hongbo, G., Guotao, X., Xinyu, Z., Bo, C.: Autonomous parking control for intelligent vehicles based on a novel algorithm. Sci. Direct **24**(4), 51–56 (2017). https://www.sciencedirect.com/science/journal/10058885
15. Chirca, M., Martin, G., Chapuis, R., Debain, C.: Autonomous valet parking system architecture, Renault – Dept. ADAS, Autonomous Vehicle and Electronic Technologies and Institut Pascal, Université Blaise Pascal, Guyancourt and Clermont-Ferrand, France
16. Razinkova, A., Cho, H.-C., Jeon, H.-T.: An intelligent auto parking system for vehicles. Int. J. Fuzzy Logic Intell. Syst. **12**(3), 226–231 (2012). https://doi.org/10.5391/IJFIS.2012.12.3.226
17. Heimberger, M., Horgan, J., Hughes, C., McDonald, J., Yogamani, S.: Computer vision in automated parking systems: design, implementation and challenges. arXiv preprint: arXiv:2104.12537
18. Ma, S., Jiang, H., Han, M., Xie, J., Li, C.: Research on automatic parking systems based on parking scene recognition. IEEE Access **5**, 21327–21335 (2017). https://doi.org/10.1109/ACCESS.2017.2760201
19. Wang, Y., Hansen, E., Ahn, H.: Hierarchical planning for autonomous parking in dynamic environments, Mitsubishi Electric Research Laboratories, TR2024–034 (2024). https://www.merl.com
20. MicroROS: MicroROS: ROS 2 for Embedded Systems. https://micro.ros.org/
21. Berea-Baltierra, R., Rivas-Ruiz, R., Pérez-Rodríguez, M., Palacios-Cruz, L., Moreno, J., Talavera, J.O.: Investigación clínica XX Del juicio clínico a la regresión logística múltiple. Rev. Méd. Inst. Mex. Seguro Soc. **52**(2), 192–197 (2014). ISSN: 0443-5117
22. Ochoa Sangrador, C., Molina Arias, M., Ortega Páez, E.: Fundamentos de medicina basada en la evidencia: Regresión logística múltiple. Pediatría Atención Primaria 2005(23), 27 (2023). ISSN: 1885-7388
23. Bustio Martínez, L., Mesa Rodríguez, A.: Estudio e Implementación de una Máquina de Soporte Vectorial. In: Reporte de Proyecto Final - Curso de Robótica, INAOE, México (n.d.). https://ccc.inaoep.mx/~emorales/Cursos/Robotica/Reporte%20Proyecto%20Fnal%20Aprendizaje.pdf. Accessed 14 Apr 2025
24. Cuevas Soto, V.M., Alvares Iriarte, S., Azcona Romero, M., Rodríguez Rogert, A.I.: Predictive power of the support vector machine: an application to financial planning. In: Revista Cubana de Ciencias Informáticas, vol. 13, no. 3, pp. 59–75. UCI, Havana (2019). http://rcci.uci.cu
25. Quesada Pérez, C.: Máquinas de Soporte Vectorial Cuánticas. Trabajo Fin de Grado, Facultad de Ciencias, Grado en Física, Universidad (2023)
26. Thurnhofer-Hemsi, K., López-Rubio, E., Molina-Cabello, M.A., Najarian, K.: Radial basis function kernel optimization for support vector machine classifiers (2020). https://arxiv.org/abs/2007.08233

Hybrid Project Management Methodologies in the Construction Industry

Bernardo Vilela[1], Anabela Tereso[2(✉)], and João Pedro Couto[3]

[1] Master's in Engineering Project Management, School of Engineering, University of Minho, 4800-058 Guimarães, Portugal
pg47354@alunos.uminho.pt

[2] ALGORITMI Research Centre, University of Minho, 4800-058 Guimarães, Portugal
anabelat@dps.uminho.pt

[3] Centre for Territory, Environment and Construction, Department of Civil Engineering, University of Minho, 4800-058 Guimarães, Portugal
jpc@civil.uminho.pt

Abstract. The aim of this study was to propose a project management strategy for a construction company specializing in the plasterboard niche market, integrated in a multinational company. The goal of this proposal was to improve the processes of monitoring and managing construction work by incorporating hybrid methodologies and agile tools, such as Kanban boards. To achieve this goal, a qualitative approach was adopted, based on participant observation, document analysis and consultations with experts, in order to guarantee an in-depth understanding of the organization's existing practices. The study reveals potential in the implementation of hybrid methodologies in the construction industry, evidencing both advantages and challenges, particularly in enhancing communication, optimizing workflows, and reducing rework and delays. However, the various limitations to the widespread application of these approaches cannot be ruled out, as a result of constraints such as rigid deadlines and the technical complexity of the work. Overall, the study highlights the need to customize hybrid methodologies in order to guarantee their effectiveness in the specific context of the construction industry. It therefore proposes the gradual adoption of visual tools, such as Kanban, as well as training initiatives capable of fostering a less rigid organizational culture that is more open to innovation. Therefore, despite having limitations related to the scope of the sample and resistance to change, this research represents a contribution to the advancement of project management in the construction industry, providing practical recommendations that can serve as a basis for future adaptations and research.

Keywords: Construction Industry · Hybrid Project Management Methodologies · Kanban

1 Introduction

The construction industry is one of the most important economic activities, both nationally and globally, contributing significantly to the Gross Domestic Product and absorbing a large amount of labor. It is an industry with a strategic impact on economic development,

T. Guarda et al. (Eds.): ARTIIS 2025, CCIS 2789, pp. 207–222, 2026.
https://doi.org/10.1007/978-3-032-16758-3_17

supported by a complex value chain that includes the production of materials, engineering services and emerging technologies. However, despite its importance, construction faces persistent structural challenges, such as inefficiencies in processes, wasted resources, low productivity and negative environmental impacts. These limitations are largely the result of resistance to innovation and the prevalence of traditional methodologies, which are poorly adapted to today's demands for sustainability and competitiveness. In response to these constraints, there has been growing investment in technological solutions, such as the digitization of processes and the introduction of tools like BIM and artificial intelligence, with the aim of modernizing the industry and aligning activity with the goals of energy efficiency, waste reduction and digital transition. In this regard, it is important to note that the construction industry, in spite of its strategic importance, has demonstrated significant resistance to the adoption of more modern project management practices. The introduction of more efficient and agile project management methodologies is, therefore, imperative in order to meet the industry's structural challenges. The ability to adapt, the elimination of waste and the promotion of more collaborative and autonomous teams are fundamental pillars to ensure the competitiveness and sustainability of the industry in a scenario of ever-growing demand.

This article is the result of research carried out within the context of a master's thesis in Engineering Project Management. The main objective of the study was to analyze and propose improvements to the project management methods currently used in a Portuguese company operating in the construction industry, through the integration of hybrid methodologies and agile tools, with a focus on process efficiency and transparency. The company under analysis was chosen on the basis of the fact that it is deeply rooted in the construction industry and is characterized by applying essentially traditional project management methodologies. The research was conducted within the organization's Production Department, allowing an in-depth and direct assessment of the current practices, as well as their limitations, in the specific context of drywall projects. This research arises from the need to develop a more effective approach to project management, not only in the company under study, but in the construction industry. The choice of topic is linked to the specific challenges faced by the company under study, which include communication difficulties, failures in resource management, cost control and meeting deadlines in highly complex projects. The proposal presented here aims to fill these gaps by integrating agile tools, namely Kanban boards, with the traditional project management methodologies. These visual management boards offer greater transparency and organization in monitoring tasks, promoting better coordination, greater predictability and continuous improvement. The overall aim of this study was to propose a systematic and innovative strategy capable of responding to the operational challenges identified and promoting management practices that are more in line with the contemporary imperatives of efficiency, innovation and sustainability. The methodological approach adopted is qualitative in nature, based on participant observation, document analysis and consultation with experts, ensuring an in-depth understanding of organizational dynamics. This research thus makes a double contribution: on the one hand, it responds to the practical needs of a real company; on the other hand, it provides the academic and professional community with a concrete reference for the application of hybrid methodologies in the construction industry.

2 Literature Review

2.1 Project Management in Construction

According to Pires and Varajão [1] project management consists of all the activities carried out by Project Managers, who are responsible for managing and leading the team implementing the project. The strategies required to carry out this activity, also known as Project Management, are generally defined as a set of methods, techniques, procedures, rules, models and good practices used throughout the life of the project. These are generally based on a specific approach that integrates a set of principles and guidelines that define how a project is managed [2]. The most frequently used method is the traditional one, based on a set of strategies and tools organized into a series of structured and sequential procedures, with a rigorous and predictable approach [3].

Project management in the construction industry faces numerous challenges that compromise the productivity and financial results of projects. Among the main barriers are low productivity, a shortage of manpower and rigid procedures. Despite recent efforts to automate processes, the construction industry is still far behind other industries (textile, mechanic, software, etc.) in terms of digitalization and industrialization. This delay makes management strategies less effective, especially in smaller-scale projects, where the degree of industrialization is even lower. Management teams tend to apply traditional methodologies, making it difficult to implement improvements. As a result, the growing complexity of construction processes and the specific nature of contract work emphasize the need to rethink current project management approaches [4].

2.2 Agile Project Management in Construction

Antlova [5] resorted to the dictionary, according to which agility means lively or active. According to the author, agility translates into the ability to change requirements during project execution, saving time and resources. This approach emerged in the 1990s as an alternative to traditional methodologies marked by bureaucracy. It involves short cycles with constant results, strong team organization and integration of the client in planning. Regarding the use of agile management tools, Barros-del Río et al. [6] introduced Kanban boards in an academic environment in order to ascertain the impact on collaborative work. The author concluded that these types of tools ensure free access, transparency and adaptability to different work contexts, whether in an academic or business environment. He also recommended that six lists be introduced into the framework, including "Diary", "Tasks to do", "Tasks in progress", "Tasks completed", "Critical reflection on progress and cooperation" and "Evaluation", making the adaptation process more accessible in both visual and practical terms. The author's concluded that the interactive nature of these tools promotes dialog, critical feedback and collaboration between participants, allowing changes to be made and improvements to be implemented at all stages of the project without compromising it. As referred by Mohammed and Karri [7], construction project management has evolved, seeking solutions to challenges such as delays and cost overruns, often caused by changes during the execution. Traditionally, the industry followed conservative methodologies, such as the waterfall method, where each stage is dependent on the previous one, making it difficult to incorporate changes.

However, given the dynamic nature of modern construction, this approach has proved inadequate. The application of agile methodologies, originally developed in computer science, emerged as a response to the need for more flexible and adaptive management. The agile methodology allows the plan to be adapted to the needs of the project, ensuring greater control over the impact of changes. Through iterative phases - initiation, planning and design, execution and monitoring, and closure - the project is organized into sprints, allowing changes to be incorporated continuously and efficiently. This approach minimizes risks, maximizes value, and contributes to delivering the project within the stipulated deadlines, quality and costs, promoting customer satisfaction. Figure 1 represents a management structure focused on change [7].

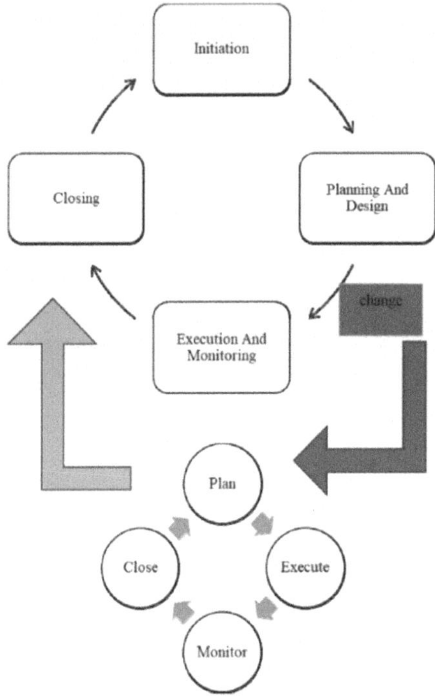

Fig. 1. Management structure focused on change (Retrieved from Mohammed and Karri [7]).

2.3 Hybrid Project Management in Construction

Hybrid management results from the combination of agile and traditional approaches [8]. A study conducted by Papadakis and Tsironis [9] revealed that companies are increasingly turning to agile methodologies, with around 71% of organizations reporting their use, while approximately one in five projects adopt a hybrid approach. This hybrid model, which integrates agile and traditional methods, allows for greater flexibility and versatility throughout the project lifecycle. According to the author, large-scale projects represent the best objects of study, since they present a series of difficulties and challenges, such as individual autonomy, team empowerment and the balancing of organizational responsibilities.

Lalmi *et al.* [10] argue that the hybrid approach to construction project management combines the advantages of agile, traditional and Lean methodologies, seeking to maximize the benefits of each and minimize their limitations. This methodology is flexible, allowing practices to be adapted to the specific needs of each project. The hybrid construction project management model presented by the authors (Fig. 2) integrates practices from the traditional, agile and Lean approaches, combining the structure and predictability of the traditional methods with the adaptability and waste reduction of the other approaches. It is divided into four main phases of a project's life cycle: initiation; planning and design; execution and controlling; and closing. Each phase incorporates proposed practices to optimize management and achieve better results. The model is flexible and can be adapted to the needs of each project and phase. For project management teams, this approach is interesting because it allows them to choose the most appropriate strategies, without being confined to a single methodology. The authors stated that validation of the model requires application in real situations, highlighting its strengths and weaknesses.

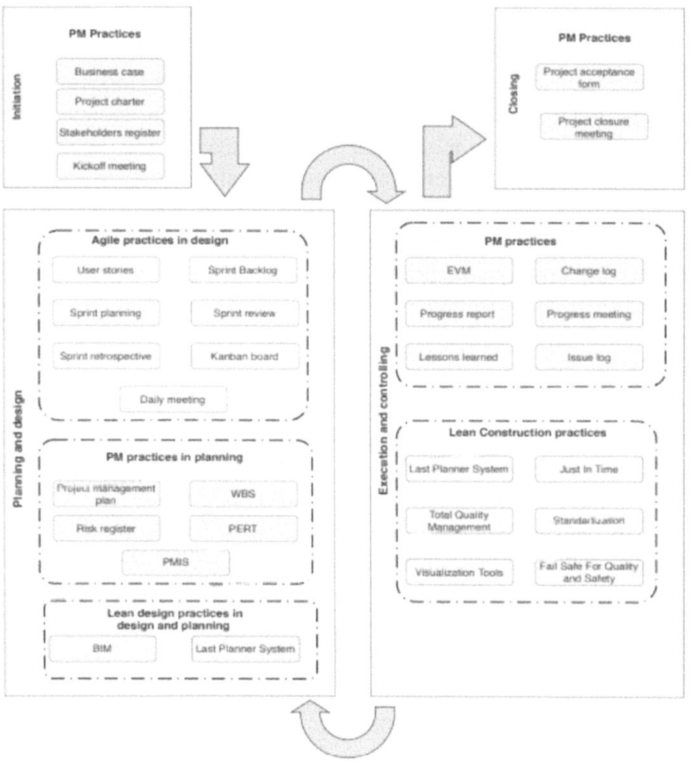

Fig. 2. Hybrid construction project management model. (Retrieved from Lalmi *et al.* [10]).

Despite the significant contribution of literature to the understanding of project management methodologies, there are still important gaps. Traditional approaches, while ensuring precision and predictability, prove to be inflexible in dynamic contexts. Agile methodologies, in turn, offer greater adaptability but face difficulties when applied to complex and highly dependent projects, such as construction. The hybrid model emerges as an attempt to reconcile these approaches, but, as recognized by the authors themselves, its validation remains limited to theoretical models, lacking practical application in real contexts.

In this sense, a relevant gap is identified: the scarcity of empirical studies that evaluate the application of these methodologies in the construction industry. Thus, this paper seeks to contribute to filling this gap by critically analyzing the potential and limitations of applying hybrid methodologies in real projects, promoting a closer relationship between theory and practice.

3 Methodology

3.1 Research Methodology

The research adopted a qualitative approach, considered appropriate due to its exploratory nature and ability to deepen understanding of project management practices in the construction sector. The study took place over 12 months in the company's production department, combining different data collection techniques to ensure triangulation and increase the validity of the analysis. Direct observation was the central method, allowing the researcher to monitor organizational dynamics in real time. Situations were recorded at weekly production meetings, planning meetings with clients, and site visits, making it possible to map workflows, decision-making processes, and communication patterns. To systematize this information, a field diary was kept, which served as the basis for categorizing the data into areas such as communication, construction monitoring, and task management. Documentary analysis complemented this process through the consultation of financial schedules, measurement reports, technical data sheets, and contracts, which are central planning and control tools. These elements provided an objective perspective on the organization, helping to identify gaps and inefficiencies in existing management methods. Informal interviews were also conducted with different stakeholders (production director, managers, sales and logistics technicians) in order to capture individual perceptions, identify practical difficulties, and gather suggestions for improvement. The data were analyzed systematically, cross-referencing evidence from different sources. This triangulation allowed us to generate a holistic and well-founded understanding, which served as the basis for the proposal to integrate hybrid and agile methodologies in the context studied, although we recognize limitations arising from the small sample size and the interpretive nature of the qualitative approach [11].

3.2 Data Analysis Methods

Data analysis was an essential step to transform the information gathered into structured knowledge relevant to the study's objectives. A qualitative content analysis approach was chosen, as it was suitable for identifying patterns, trends, and relationships in the project management practices observed. The process was conducted in three main phases: exploratory reading of the collected data (observations, internal documents, and meeting records), initial coding of the most significant elements, and finally, organization into categories and subcategories aligned with dimensions such as management methods and operational challenges. This procedure made it possible to map existing practices and highlight critical variables, such as dependencies in the procurement of materials or communication failures between departments. To reinforce validity, data triangulation was used, combining direct observations, document analysis, and informal interviews. Triangulation helped to reduce bias and ensure consistency of interpretations, offering a holistic view of organizational dynamics. During the process, systematic reviews of preliminary results were also carried out, allowing interpretations to be validated and emerging categories to be adjusted. This strategy reinforced the reliability of the conclusions and supported the proposal for improvements, namely the introduction of Kanban boards as a solution to increase the transparency and efficiency of processes. Despite its relevance, qualitative analysis faced limitations, particularly with regard to the generalization of results and the possibility of interpretive subjectivity. However, the rigorous application of content analysis, combined with triangulation and the comparison of perspectives among colleagues, ensured a robust and well-founded interpretation. Thus, the data analysis not only identified critical gaps in project management but also supported the formulation of practical solutions adapted to the context studied.

4 Presentation and Analysis of the Case Study

4.1 Case Study Description

The research focuses on analyzing the project management practices of a construction company specializing in the plasterboard niche, part of a multinational group. With several years of experience, the company stands out for its technical quality and the service it provides in different types of flooring and coverings. The organizational structure is divided into four main departments - Sales, Logistics, Finance and Production - under the supervision of the Business Unit Director. The Production Department, the focus of this research, is responsible for the execution and supervision of contracted work and is made up of a multidisciplinary team, comprising the Production Director, Project Designers, Project Managers and Foremen. The general structure of the company is shown in Fig. 3.

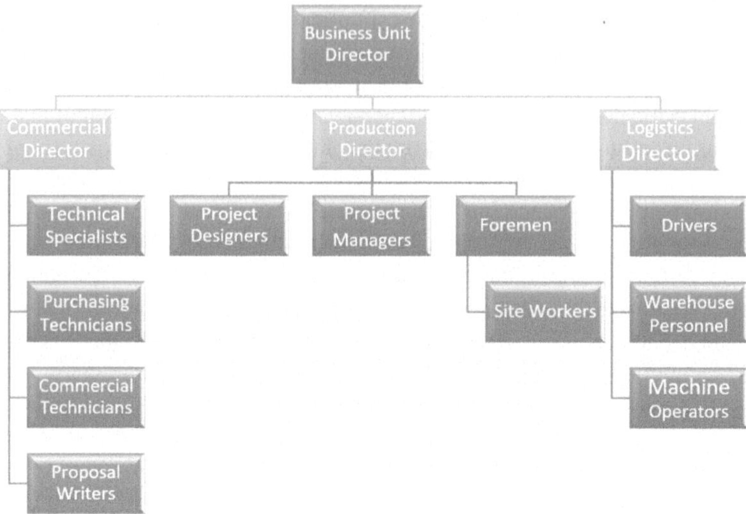

Fig. 3. Company's General Structure.

The Production Manager plays a strategic role, ensuring deadlines and budgets are met and aligning operational objectives with the company's commercial goals. Site preparers measure and quantify materials in the initial phase of projects, ensuring the correct planning of resources. On the other hand, Project Managers monitor all phases of projects, with technical and contractual responsibilities, namely in drawing up measurement records and managing additional work. In the field, Foremen ensure that tasks are carried out efficiently, monitoring labor and materials and reporting any needs to the Project Managers.

The company combines the resale of materials with the provision of specialized application services, which gives it an integrated offer. It works on large-scale projects of high technical complexity, standing out for its solutions such as decorative ceilings with special structures. Benefiting from well-defined processes and a strong international presence, it participates in industrial and residential projects, as well as providing services to other Portuguese construction companies. This combination of experience, innovation and interdepartmental collaboration allows the company to maintain high quality standards, adapting effectively to the demands of a dynamic and competitive industry.

4.2 Characterization of the Current Project Management

The organization's current project management is characterized by a structured and collaborative approach, starting with the preparation of a budget proposal by the Sales Department, technically validated by the Production Department. Once the subcontract has been awarded, a handover meeting takes place between the various departments, where crucial information such as profit margins, suppliers and schedules are discussed. However, difficulties have been identified in sharing information, which compromises strategic alignment and leads to operational failures. From this stage onwards, the Production Department takes over active management of the project. The Project Designer adapts the technical drawings and the Foreman carries out an assessment in the field, while the Project Manager focuses on contractual analysis, approval of materials and monitoring progress.

The execution phase is based on continuous coordination between the Foreman and the Project Manager, with regular meetings with the client to ensure technical and contractual compliance. The Foreman is responsible for supervising the work, recording time sheets and visually documenting progress, while the construction manager focuses on logistical and financial management, drawing up monthly billing proposals and communicating changes to the client. Despite the existence of formal mechanisms, there are still challenges related to internal communication, such as failures to communicate changes to the work and missed deadlines, which compromises the achievement of objectives and management efficiency. In the final phase, the Project Manager draws up the accounts closing statement to present to the client, but insufficient information provided by the Foreman can result in omissions that affect the profitability of the project. It is therefore clear that there is a need for stricter practices for recording and sharing information, as well as for greater alignment between the parties involved throughout all phases of the project.

A deeper analysis lead to the identification critical flaws described in Table 1. For the different areas, issues were identified together with the responsible party, cause of the issue and the mitigation proposal using Kanban.

Table 1. Critical Flaws

Area	Identified Issue	Responsible Party	Cause of the Issue	Mitigation Proposal using Kanban
Materials	Delay in material delivery due to uncommunicated long lead times	Sales Department	Poor communication between Sales and Production	Creation of 'Sales Approval' card with defined deadlines and due date alert
Materials	Lack of stock due to unawareness of material needs	Production/Logistics	Absence of needs registration by Production	'Project Needs' column updated weekly on the Kanban board
Materials	Lack of material on site due to untimely requisition	Site Foreman	Late communication of the need	Card with requisition deadline, checklist, and automatic alert

(continued)

Table 1. (*continued*)

Area	Identified Issue	Responsible Party	Cause of the Issue	Mitigation Proposal using Kanban
Materials	Loss of commercial discount due to lack of communication on expiry date	Sales Department	Omission in sharing contractual terms with other departments	'Commercial Discount' card with visible expiry date and validation checklist
Financial	Failure to communicate forecasted billing agreed with client	Production/Financial Department	Lack of formal alignment meetings	'Billing Forecast' card updated monthly on the shared board
Internal Production	Failure to communicate manpower reinforcement needs for a project	Site Foreman/Project Manager	No system for registering and sharing needs with Management	'Manpower Reinforcement' card requiring Production Director approval
Internal Production	Late or absent communication about additional tasks on site	Site Foreman	Lack of information sharing	'Additional Work' card created before the start of new tasks
Internal Production	Failure to communicate project delays	Site Foreman/Project Manager	Lack of systematic information flow to Production Director	'Delays/Alerts' column with weekly updates and technical comments
Internal Production	Failure to communicate the need to change workforce management strategy	Site Foreman/Project Manager	Isolated decision-making without hierarchical validation	'Strategic Review' task shared and scheduled, with joint validation on Kanban board

4.3 Critical Analysis

The case study's critical analysis reveals structural flaws in the company's communication and coordination, compromising the efficiency and effectiveness of project execution. Internal communication is fragmented, resulting in gaps in the sharing of information between departments, as evidenced by the gaps between the Purchasing Department and Production, and between the Foreman and the Project Manager. The absence of formal records and regular meetings contributes to incompatibilities in the execution of tasks, delays and rework. In addition, the lack of rigorous recording mechanisms makes it difficult to control the progress of activities and compromises the closing of accounts and the summary statement, crucial instruments for financial and operational evaluation.

The lack of an integrated decision-making structure between administrative and operational teams exacerbates the situation. Many decisions are made on the basis of incomplete data, without the involvement of the field teams, leading to deviations in schedules, inefficient allocation of resources and demotivation. This model, based on a rigid hierarchy, reduces organizational agility. The analysis also shows the direct impact of these failures in missed deadlines, increased costs and reduced quality, negatively affecting the company's reputation in the industry.

To address these challenges, measures such as restructuring the decision-making process, using digital tools and adopting Kanban boards are recommended. Kanban would allow for a clear visualization of tasks, greater transparency and integration between stakeholders. In addition, holding regular meetings in the Scrum format and training teams in effective communication would promote continuous alignment. These measures aim not only to mitigate the problems identified, but also to align project management with the organization's strategic objectives, strengthening its competitiveness and promoting more efficient and sustainable execution.

5 Improvement Proposal - Kanban

The implementation proposal for the Kanban method presented aims to optimize project management in the drywall production area, adjusting to the organizational specificities of the entity under study. This approach combines visual tools and agile practices, promoting greater operational efficiency, transparency in workflows and continuous improvement. The proposal responds directly to the gaps identified in the previous analysis, proposing a structured solution that combines the best practices of the method with the strategic needs of the organization. Kanban thus emerges as a tool capable of counteracting the negative trends observed, namely the lack of visibility, the inefficient management of multiple tasks and the absence of a system that promotes continuous improvement.

Implementation will follow four main phases: initial analysis and process mapping (around 3 weeks), definition of workflows and Kanban board configuration (3 to 4 weeks), testing and adjustments based on team feedback (6 weeks), and finally, full launch with ongoing monitoring. Success depends heavily on team preparation and training, ensuring their engagement and understanding of the system's operation. Workshops and practical sessions will be held, supported by instructional materials. The system will be configured using the Trello platform, adapting existing workflows into columns representing each work status phase, such as "Planned Tasks", "In Progress", "Approval" and "Completed". Each task will be represented by a card containing details like deadlines, responsible parties, and technical attachments, ensuring accurate and collaborative tracking. Figure 4 represents the proposed Kanban template board to be implemented in the company under study, with P.M. corresponding to the Project Manager, P.D. referring to the Project Designer and, finally, both Logistics and Sales refer to the respective departments.

The presented template resulted from a collaborative process with the Production Director, based on informal meetings and sketches drawn up during active participation in the department. The objective was to optimize project management by mitigating recurring communication failures between departments. As explained previously, various constraints were identified, such as delays in the delivery of materials, lack of stock, flaws in invoicing forecasts, and deficiencies in the management of labor and additional work. The structure of the Kanban board was designed to mitigate these shortcomings, promoting greater visibility, traceability and coordination between those involved. The model thus seeks to ensure more efficient management in line with the organization's strategic objectives. Continuous monitoring will rely on metrics such as lead time, throughput, and task completion rate. These indicators will help identify bottlenecks, assess team performance, and fine-tune Work in Progress (WIP) limits. Weekly team meetings will be held to assess the system's performance, supported by anonymous surveys and individual interviews to gather qualitative feedback. The creation of a group of trained "Kanban ambassadors" will also be essential to facilitate implementation, ensure team cohesion, and promote alignment with strategic goals.

The application of this proposal seeks to establish a resilient and adaptable project management model, transferable to other contexts, strengthening the company's competitiveness and fostering sustainable and efficient practices in the construction industry.

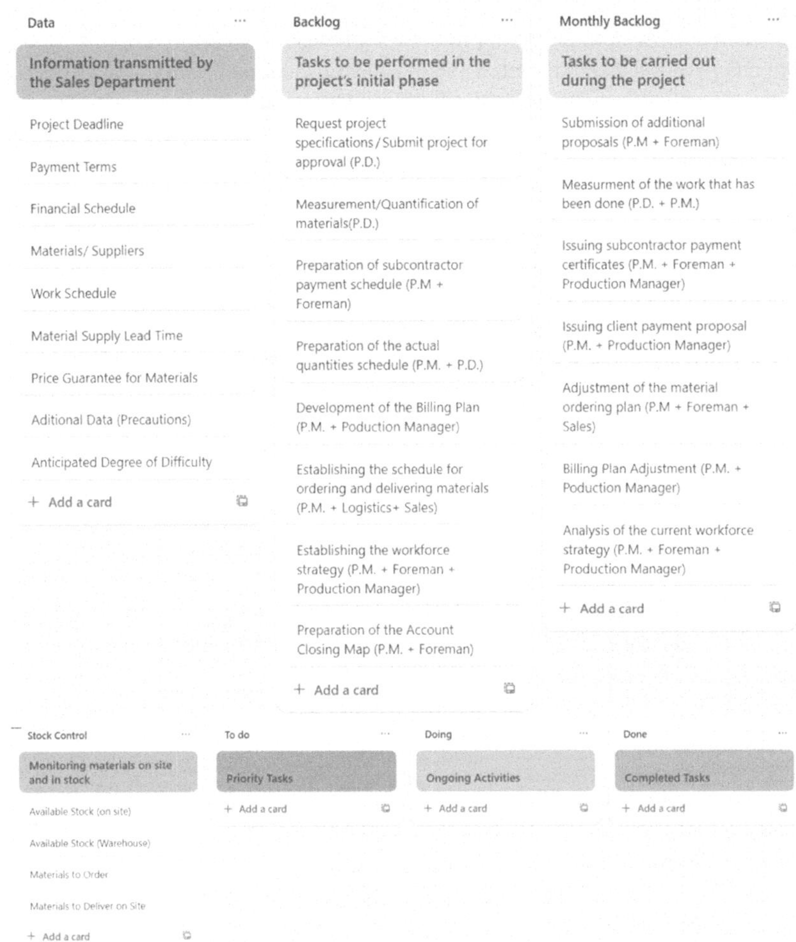

Fig. 4. Kanban Template Board.

6 Discussion

This chapter aims to provide a discussion of the results obtained, establishing connections with the defined objectives and the theoretical framework presented in the literature review. The application of the Kanban system arises as a strategic and adaptable approach, conceived to enhance operational efficiency and ensure consistency in workflow management in various organizational contexts [6]. Rooted in Lean principles, this method simplifies the organization and visualization of tasks, optimizing resource allocation and eliminating waste. In the context of the company under analysis, Kanban addresses specific challenges such as the limited task progress visibility and ineffective communication - both common problems that frequently jeopardize project deadlines and overall transparency. By supporting more dynamic resource management and enabling continuous monitoring, the system aligns with organizational needs and promotes increased sustainability in production processes.

From an operational standpoint, Kanban acts as a catalyst for efficiency by reducing waiting times and optimizing information flow. On construction sites, for instance, it allows for clearer scheduling of tasks, such as material procurement, preventing delays. Moreover, it enhances workforce tracking, financial analysis, and the overall coordination of project activities. Detailed visibility into task history, current status, and future projections supports more informed decision-making, risk mitigation, and agile adaptation to evolving project requirements.

In terms of communication and collaboration, Kanban has a transformative effect by providing a clear and accessible view of all tasks and their respective stages. It fosters transparency, enabling issues to be identified and resolved quickly and effectively, while encouraging a culture of individual and collective accountability, proactivity, and engagement. By reducing ambiguity and ensuring alignment between teams and project priorities, it strengthens trust and boosts team morale, contributing to a more collaborative and productive working environment.

Ultimately, integrating Kanban reinforces the principles of continuous improvement, promoting a systematic evolution of organizational operations. It encourages ongoing workflow analysis, the identification of inefficiencies, and the adoption of innovative practices. As such, Kanban positions itself as a strategic and indispensable solution for achieving organizational excellence and enabling continuous adaptation to the dynamic challenges of the construction industry.

7 Conclusion

This study synthesizes the key contributions of the research developed in the field of project management within the construction industry, with a particular focus on drywall subcontracting. With regard to the objectives initially proposed, the study came close to achieving them, highlighting the potential of applying hybrid project management approaches in the construction industry, particularly in the company under analysis. The findings confirmed the applicability of hybrid approaches that integrate traditional and agile methodologies, supported by tools such as Kanban. The proposed model has the potential to enable more efficient task tracking, greater transparency in workflow management, and significant improvements in team communication. These findings are consistent with previous studies that highlight the flexibility and operational efficiency provided by hybrid methodologies [9, 10]. Furthermore, the study stands out for proposing a practical model tailored to the specific characteristics of the construction industry, addressing gaps identified in the existing literature and contributing to the advancement of knowledge in this field.

Nevertheless, several methodological limitations were identified during the research that may affect the generalizability of the results. The sample used was limited in scope and diversity, focusing solely on drywall projects within a specific organizational context. Data collection relied predominantly on direct observation and document analysis, supplemented by qualitative insights gathered during informal interviews. Additionally, the proposed hybrid model was developed to be implemented only within the construction industry and did not consider external variables such as cultural factors or organizational changes, which could significantly influence outcomes in different environments. Furthermore, it should not be overlooked that cultural resistance to change and strict contractual deadlines may have hindered the adoption of innovative practices, thus narrowing the scope of application for the hybrid methodology. These contextual constraints should be taken into account in future studies, as they can significantly hinder the implementation and effectiveness of hybrid approaches in different organizational contexts.

It is also essential to acknowledge the constraints imposed by the specific context of the construction industry company and the region in which the study was conducted. The industry is characterized by unique dynamics, including the fragmentation of teams, the technical complexity of projects, and the influence of local regulations and market conditions on decision-making processes. These particularities may bias the results and limit their applicability to other companies with different organizational structures and practices. Moreover, the exclusive focus on drywall projects restricts the potential replication of the proposed model to other types of construction projects. Thus, it is crucial to consider these contextual specificities when interpreting the findings and to encourage future studies in diverse operational environments.

To expand and deepen the insights obtained, future research is recommended to explore the application of the developed hybrid model across industries with differing operational dynamics, including international settings or more volatile and complex environments. Such studies will help assess the model's versatility and resilience in the face of varying cultural, economic, and organizational factors. Integrating the model with other innovative approaches, such as artificial intelligence-based methodologies, could further enhance project management performance.

In conclusion, this study provides a valuable contribution to the construction industry, proposing a hybrid project management model adapted to the specificities of the sector and the organizational context of the company studied. The novelty of this research lies in the integration of agile and traditional approaches in one structured proposal designed for real-world application, filling a gap in the literature, where empirical studies on hybrid methodologies in construction remain scarce. Though the model hasn't been empirically validated yet, it offers a conceptual roadmap for future implementation and testing, contributing to the academic debate and laying the groundwork for the evolution of project management practices in response to the growing demands of a dynamic, sustainable, and competitive market.

Acknowledgements. This work has been supported by FCT—*Fundação para a Ciência e Tecnologia* within the R&D Unit Project Scope UID/00319/Centro ALGORITMI (ALGORITMI/UM) and within the R&D Unit Project of Centre for Territory, Environment and Construction.

References

1. Pires, L., Varajão, J.: Creativity as a topic in project management – a scoping review and directions for research. Think Skills Creat 101477 (2024). https://doi.org/10.1016/j.tsc.2024.101477

2. Špundak, M.: Mixed agile/traditional project management methodology – reality or illusion? Procedia Soc. Behav. Sci. **119**, 939–948 (2014). https://doi.org/10.1016/j.sbspro.2014.03.105
3. Miranda, C., Tereso, A., Manuela Gonçalves, A., Sousa, P., Engrácia, P.: Study on project management in Portugal within the scope of the Portuguese project management observatory. Procedia Comput. Sci. 1885–1892 (2023). https://doi.org/10.1016/j.procs.2023.01.487
4. Datta, S.D., Islam, M., Rahman Sobuz, M.H., Ahmed, S., Kar, M.: Artificial intelligence and machine learning applications in the project lifecycle of the construction industry: a comprehensive review. Heliyon **10**(5), e26888 (2024). https://doi.org/10.1016/j.heliyon.2024.e26888
5. Antlova, K.: Agile approach in the project management of the czech companies. Procedia Technol. **16**, 929–933 (2014). https://doi.org/10.1016/j.protcy.2014.10.045
6. Barros-del Río, M.A., López Nozal, C., Mediavilla-Martínez, B.: Practicum management and enhancement through an online tool in foreign language teacher education. Soc. Sci. Humanit. Open **6**(1) (2022). https://doi.org/10.1016/j.ssaho.2022.100273
7. Mohammed, K.N., Karri, S.C.: An analytical approach in usage of agile methodologies in construction industries - A case study. In: Materials Today: Proceedings, pp. 475–479. Elsevier Ltd. (2020). https://doi.org/10.1016/j.matpr.2020.05.045
8. Fernandes, G., et al.: Overcoming the 'use misfit' of project management practices in collaborative research, development and innovation. Project Leadersh. Soc. **5** (2024). https://doi.org/10.1016/j.plas.2024.100137
9. Papadakis, E., Tsironis, L.: Hybrid methods and practices associated with agile methods, method tailoring and delivery of projects in a non-software context. Procedia Comput. Sci. 739–746 (2018). https://doi.org/10.1016/j.procs.2018.10.097
10. Lalmi, A., Fernandes, G., Souad, S.B.: A conceptual hybrid project management model for construction projects. Procedia Comput. Sci. 921–930 (2021). https://doi.org/10.1016/j.procs.2021.01.248
11. Saunders, M.N.K., Lewis, P., Thornhill, A.: Research Methods for Business Students. Pearson Education (2023)

Comparative Analysis Between Bayesian Model and Maximum Likelihood Model for Predicting End-Effector Position from Robot Kinematics

Piero Vilcapoma[1], Robert Guaman-Rivera[2], Leonardo Guevara[3], Tito Arévalo-Ramirez[4], Oswaldo Menéndez[5], and Juan Pablo Vásconez[1](✉)

[1] Energy Transformation Center, Faculty of Engineering, Universidad Andres Bello, 7500971 Santiago, Chile
p.vilcapomacarhuamac@uandresbello.edu , juan.vasconez@unab.cl
[2] Institute of Engineering Science, Universidad de O'Higgins, Av. Libertador Bernardo O'Higgins, 2820000 Rancagua, Chile
robert.guaman@uoh.cl
[3] Lincoln Institute for Agri-Food Technology, University of Lincoln, Lincoln LN2 2LG, UK
lguevara@lincoln.ac.uk
[4] Department of Mechanical Engineering and Metallurgy, School of Engineering, Faculty of Engineering, Pontificia Universidad Católica de Chile, 7820436 Santiago, Chile
[5] Departamento de Ingeniería de Sistemas y Computación, Universidad Católica del Norte, 1249004 Antofagasta, Chile
oswaldo.menendez@ucn.cl

Abstract. Industrial manipulators require high precision and accuracy to perform repetitive tasks without affecting the robotic platform and the different agents interacting in the operating environment. Therefore, the end-effector position is important for accurate task execution. Machine learning and statistical methods using kinematic models to estimate the end-effector position have significant limitations in accuracy, robustness, and generating capacity in the face of dynamic or unmodeled conditions. In this context, a comparative analysis between a Bayesian regression model and a maximum likelihood-based model is proposed to estimate the end-effector position from kinematic information of the manipulator, considering a priori knowledge about the effector positions and joint angles. Error metrics such as the mean square error, coefficient of determination, and generalization capacity in untrained trajectories are used to evaluate the performance of the models. The results disclosed that the maximum likelihood model exhibits greater computational efficiency under ideal conditions. In contrast, Bayesian models demonstrate a superior capacity to represent the uncertainty inherent in the kinematic model.

Keywords: Bayesian regression · Maximum Likelihood · End-effector prediction

T. Guarda et al. (Eds.): ARTIIS 2025, CCIS 2789, pp. 223–236, 2026.
https://doi.org/10.1007/978-3-032-16758-3_18

1 Introduction

The Industry 5.0 paradigm aims to promote human-robot collaboration in industrial environments. Although the integration of robots can positively impact various businesses, such as agriculture, energy, construction or medicine, their adoption remains limited due to the perception threat or harm by workers [1].

Integrating robots in the industrial sector has allowed for optimizing time processes and reduced economic and energy costs. Automation, medicine, construction, and logistics have benefited from using robots for repetitive, physically demanding, or high-precision tasks [2]. In this context, the use of robotic manipulators in picking, package transfer, hazardous object handling, or assisted surgeries requires high positioning and orientation accuracy [3,4]. Therefore, accurate estimation of the end-effector's position and orientation ensures efficient performance that preserves the operator's integrity and the environment [4]. In addition, conventional robotic systems have limitations due to the uncertainties inherent in the environment and the robot model, which affect the accuracy of end-effector positioning.

Despite the advances and benefits provided by robotic systems, the precise position of the end-effector of manipulators represents a significant challenge, involving the detailed analysis of the workspace, degrees of freedom, and the implementation of high-precision estimation algorithms [5]. To address this problem, several methods have been developed, such as simulation software, manual testing, and field trials, which allow the identification of the robot's operational limitations and constraints. However, commonly used estimation techniques are based on geometric models, iterative methods, or analytical approaches, which, although they can provide accurate results, are often mathematically complex and computationally demanding [6].

1.1 State of the Art

The integration of cameras, LiDAR, optical and depth sensors, and kinematic modeling has made it possible to address the problem of end-effector position estimation in manipulator robots [7]. The study [8] reports the use of a virtual sensor in combination with a radial basis function (RBF) neural network for position estimation. In [9], a geometric triangulation-based strategy applied to a hydraulic excavator has been implemented. Finally, [10] presents a predictive control model oriented to manipulators mounted on unstable platforms, considering the base motion.

Artificial neural networks (ANN) also have several challenges predicting manipulator robots information, mainly due to the quality of the input data used for estimation. In [11], the K-means clustering algorithm was employed to enhance the accuracy of noisy joint angle measurements in a manipulator robot using a vision-based approach. A convolutional neural network (CNN) based on the YOLO (You Only Look Once) architecture was used to detect and estimate the joint positions. Subsequently, K-means clustering was applied to refine these estimations and provide more accurate joint angle measurements. The study

[12] develops a sensorimotor learning system that uses self-organizing neural networks (SOM) to track the end-effector's trajectory. In [13], the authors apply deep neural networks to estimate the force exerted by the end-effector based on measurements collected at the robot's base. Unlike [8–10], which relies on sensory data to estimate position, [12,13] focuses on processing large volumes of data and incorporates additional variables associated with the end-effector.

Accurate end-effector position estimation represents a determining factor for robot performance in efficient task execution. In this context, in this work we propose a comparative evaluation of the end-effector position estimation between a Bayesian model and the maximum likelihood estimation from the kinematics of a four-degree-of-freedom (6DOF) manipulator robot. Furthermore, our work proposes a different approach that relates the entries recorded in the joints and the positions recorded in a dataset. Based on this information, two statistical models will be used to compare their performances, and the necessary metrics will be calculated to determine efficiency and the relationship between the data and the results obtained.

1.2 Main Contributions

Considering the state of the art presented above, the contribution of this work can be summarized as follows:

- We applied descriptive statistics to analyze the dataset distribution that records different coordinates of the positioning of a 6DOF robot manipulator effector.
- We implemented Bayesian and Maximum Likelihood Estimation (MLE) models to predict the end effector position.
- We compared the results of the Bayesian and MLE models to evaluate their performance.

1.3 Outline

This work is organized as follows. Section 2 presents the proposed methodology workflow for the Bayesian and MLE for direct kinematics. In Sect. 3, we analyze the results obtained from the training processes. Finally, Sect. 4 presents the conclusions of this work, as well as a view of future work.

2 Methodology

This study uses a dataset containing records from a manipulator robot. From this dataset, two mathematical models are used to predict the position of the manipulator robot's end effector. The first stage of the methodology consists of collecting the dataset, followed by implementing the Bayesian model and the MLE model. Finally, in the results phase, the prediction values obtained are recorded, along with graphs representing the data distribution and the metrics used to compare both models. Figure 1 summarizes the phases of methodology.

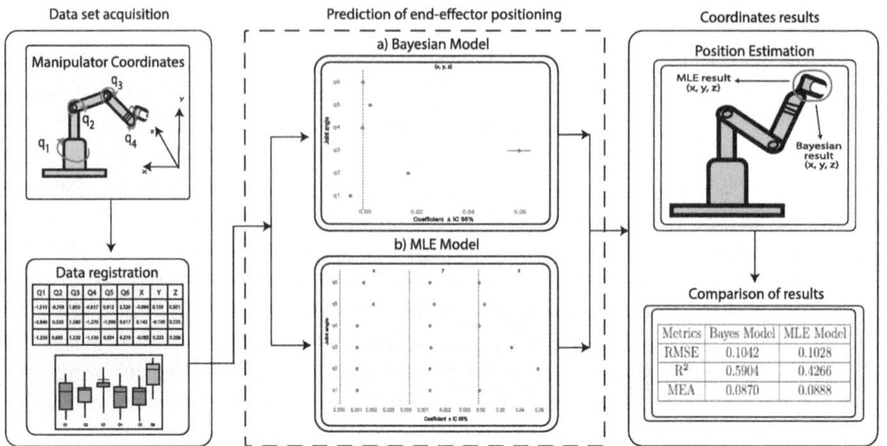

Fig. 1. Workflow for Predicting End-Effector Coordinates Based on Joint Data Using Bayesian and MLE Approaches.

2.1 Robot Kinematics Dataset Acquisition and Analysis

In this work, the publicly available Robot Kinematics Dataset from Kaggle was chosen because of its structured format and detailed recording of joint angles and end-effector positions, which enables controlled experimentation and benchmarking. Although this dataset has been previously analyzed, our study presents a new comparative perspective between Bayesian regression and MLE techniques, focusing on uncertainty representation and interpretability in position estimation. The dataset used for this work was obtained from the Kaggle webpage [14]. This dataset is made up of nine variables recorded from the kinematics of a manipulator robot. The first six variables correspond to the angles (in degrees) of the manipulator robot joints, while the other three variables correspond to the coordinates in the x, y, and z planes in which the robot's final effector will be positioned. This dataset has a total of 15,000 registered samples. In Table 1, the first five data samples comprising the dataset are presented.

Table 1. Structure and presentation of dataset records.

Q1	Q2	Q3	Q4	Q5	Q6	X	Y	Z
−1.510	−0.763	1.850	−0.817	0.912	2.320	−0.094	0.150	0.301
−2.840	0.520	1.58	−1.270	−1.390	0.617	0.142	−0.100	0.225
−1.230	0.695	1.22	−1.130	0.034	6.270	−0.083	0.223	0.206
−1.990	1.060	1.74	−1.760	−1.240	4.760	0.135	−0.031	0.370

The values of the recorded joints were randomly generated through the numpy.random.uniform module of Python, while the coordinates of the final effect were obtained through the kinematic model through the Denavit-Hartenberg operation. The initial variable will be the angles recorded, while the variables to be calculated with the models will be adjusted to the location of the final effector. To contrast the performance and effectiveness of the models, the arrangement of the articular and positional data of the robotic arm was examined. The dataset was randomly divided into 70% for training and 30% for testing in order to assess model generalization. To evaluate prediction accuracy on unknown configurations, performance metrics (RMSE, MAE, and R2) were calculated on the test set after both the Bayesian and MLE models were fitted to the training data.

It can be seen in Fig. 2 that the articular angles exhibit different degrees of dispersion. Specifically, the q3 variable presents a higher variability, while the q4 and q6 variables exhibit a greater concentration.

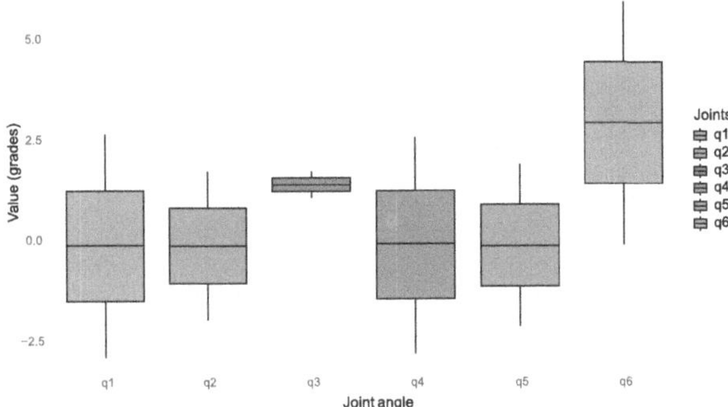

Fig. 2. Distribution of joint angles (q1 to q6) during the execution of movements.

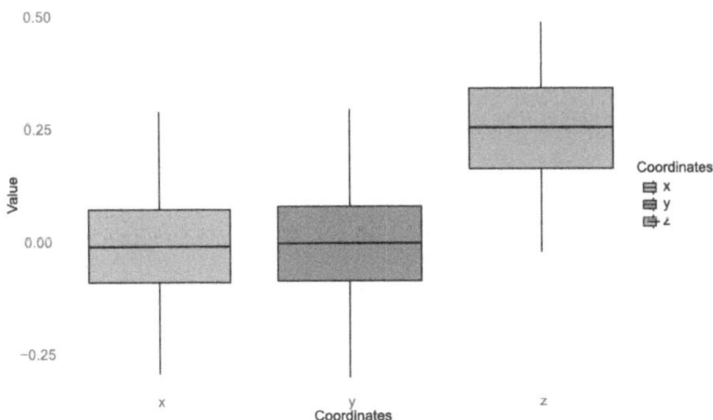

Fig. 3. Spatial distribution of the coordinates (x, y, z) of the end effector in the workspace.

Figure 3 shows the spatial variability of the final effector. It can be seen that the x and y coordinates have high variability (with values near ±0.5). However, the z coordinates have less dispersion, suggesting less movement on that axis. While the observed symmetry in the distribution could be interpreted as an indication of balanced behavior, the pronounced peaks could also indicate possible kinematic singularities or failures in the regulation system. The values obtained in the other coordinates can be attributed to the structural arrangement of the joints or the equipment's limitations. However, compared to the other axes, the lower dispersion recorded on the Z axis suggests greater stability in that direction, which could be interpreted as a fortunate exception or an inherent system characteristic.

Table 2. Statistical summary of kinematic variables: joints and spatial coordinates.

Variable	Average	Stan. dev.	Minimum	Maximum	Skewness	Kurtosis
Q1	0.00085	1.65504	−2.88000	2.88000	−0.00418	1.81189
Q2	−0.00916	1.11060	−1.92000	1.92000	0.00061	1.78958
Q3	1.57241	0.20166	1.22000	1.92000	−0.02040	1.79008
Q4	0.01861	1.61987	−2.79000	2.79000	−0.01884	1.79936
Q5	−0.00940	1.21111	−2.09000	2.09000	0.01250	1.79517
Q6	3.14329	1.81034	0.00044	6.28000	−0.00266	1.80609
X	−0.00519	0.10254	−0.29000	0.29200	0.05164	2.27360
Y	−0.00070	0.10562	−0.29800	0.29700	−0.01153	2.26495
Z	0.25729	0.11232	−0.02080	0.49000	0.08015	2.09202

Table 2 presents the descriptive statistics of nine variables. The mean of the variables q1 to q6 is observed to vary widely, with q6 exhibiting a remarkably high mean value (3.14), while the others are close to zero. With q6 and q2 showing the highest variability (SD = 1.1), the standard deviation reflects notable differences in data dispersion, pointing to greater heterogeneity in these particular observations. In terms of skewness, all variables exhibit values close to zero, suggesting that their distributions are approximately symmetric and free from significant asymmetry. Likewise, kurtosis values are around -1, indicating somewhat flatter (platykurtic) distributions than usual. The averages of the variables to be estimated are relatively near zero for x and y, while z has a larger mean (0.25) and a lower standard deviation (0.11), indicating a higher concentration of data around its mean.

Finally, a correlation calculation is performed to analyze the relation between the data, which is represented in Fig. 4. The correlation analysis shows that most of the variables have a low or no relationship with each other, which is favorable for the present study, since it allows a more controlled comparison of the maximum likelihood (MLE) and Bayesian approaches. These correlations allow for the independent evaluation of each procedure's performance free from collinear or redundant effects by demonstrating that the variables provide distinct, nonoverlapping information. Furthermore, weak correlations, such as that observed between q2 and z, allow us to analyze the extent to which the different methods can identify and model the underlying relationships present in the dataset.

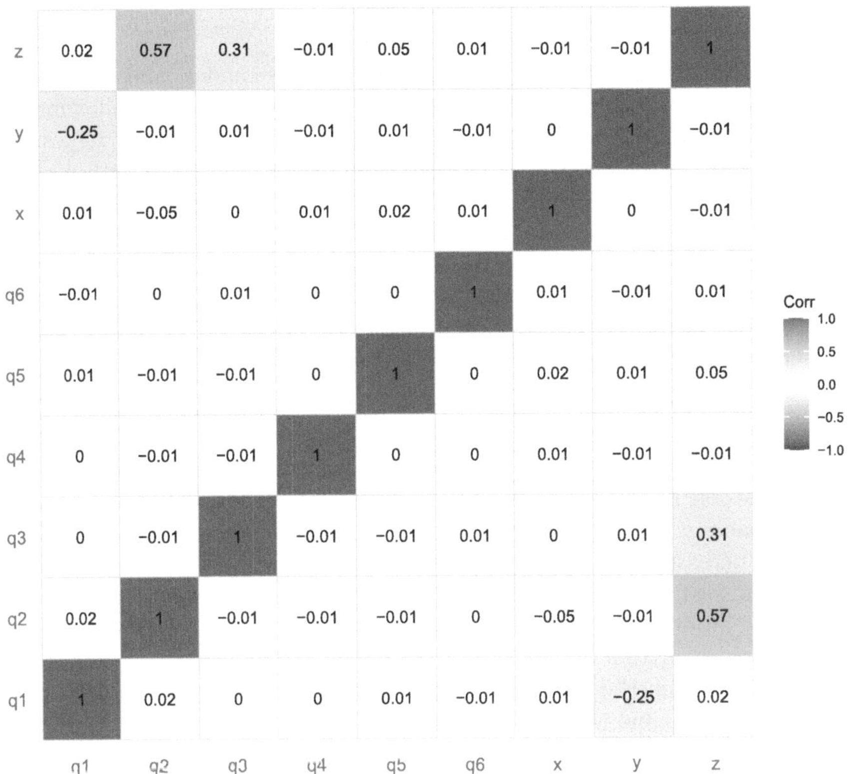

	q1	q2	q3	q4	q5	q6	x	y	z
z	0.02	0.57	0.31	−0.01	0.05	0.01	−0.01	−0.01	1
y	−0.25	−0.01	0.01	−0.01	0.01	−0.01	0	1	−0.01
x	0.01	−0.05	0	0.01	0.02	0.01	1	0	−0.01
q6	−0.01	0	0.01	0	0	1	0.01	−0.01	0.01
q5	0.01	−0.01	−0.01	0	1	0	0.02	0.01	0.05
q4	0	−0.01	−0.01	1	0	0	0.01	−0.01	−0.01
q3	0	−0.01	1	−0.01	−0.01	0.01	0	0.01	0.31
q2	0.02	1	−0.01	−0.01	−0.01	0	−0.05	−0.01	0.57
q1	1	0.02	0	0	0.01	−0.01	0.01	−0.25	0.02

Fig. 4. Correlation analysis between variables found in the Robot Kinematics Dataset. This dataset is the basis for the proposed comparison of Bayesian and maximum likelihood models.

2.2 Prediction of End-Effector Positioning

To analyze the relation between the articular variables (q1–q6) and the Cartesian coordinates (x, y, z) of the robot's final effector, assuming that the errors are random, two approaches are proposed: Bayesian regression and maximum likelihood estimation (MLE).

Bayesian Regression Model: To estimate the position of the end effector (x, y, z) from the joint angles ($q1$ to $q6$), a multilevel Bayesian regression model was implemented using the "brms" package in the RStudio software. The model considers both fixed and random effects to capture the relationship between articular variables and spatial coordinates, as well as the variability inherent in each axis [15]. The (1) equation specifies the model used.

$$value \sim q_1 + q_2 + q_3 + q_4 + q_5 + q_6 + (1|coordinate) \tag{1}$$

The angles are the introductory elements of the model, and the variable "(1|coordinate)" symbolizes a random intercept for the coordinates, allowing each axis to act differently even in the face of the same articulatory angles. The model was modified using Markov Chain Monte Carlo (MCMC) with 4 chains, 2000 iterations for each (1000 of heating), employing a Gaussian distribution for the response variable. Choosing a Bayesian approach allows for quantifying the uncertainty in the estimates by intervals, allowing the robot's kinematic model to be adapted for this type of application [15]. To validate the model, predictions were generated with new values of joint angles, obtaining the estimated position of the effector.

Maximum Likelihood Estimation (MLE) Model: To determine the location of the end effector (x, y, z), based on the joint angles ($q1$ to $q6$), a classical linear regression model estimated by maximum likelihood (MLE) was applied using the package "bbmle" in RStudio [16]. This perspective focuses on parameters that increase the possibility of examining data under the assumption of normality in waste, offering point estimators and standard errors for each coefficient. Three autonomous models were established, one for each Cartesian coordinate, considering that waste is distributed in a normal way. In contrast to the Bayesian model, the MLE model divides the estimation equations for each coordinate in the same way as they are illustrated in the Eqs. (2), (3), and (4).

$$x = \beta_0^x + \beta_1^x q1 + \beta_2^x q2 + \ldots + \beta_6^x q6 + \epsilon^x, \epsilon^x \sim N(0, \sigma_x^2) \tag{2}$$

$$y = \beta_0^y + \beta_1^y q1 + \beta_2^y q2 + \ldots + \beta_6^y q6 + \epsilon^y, \epsilon^y \sim N(0, \sigma_y^2) \tag{3}$$

$$z = \beta_0^z + \beta_1^z q1 + \beta_2^z q2 + \ldots + \beta_6^z q6 + \epsilon^z, \epsilon^z \sim N(0, \sigma_z^2) \tag{4}$$

Implementing the six joint angles as predictors and estimating the coefficients (B_i) in combination with the residual standard deviation, numerical optimization was used to minimize the negative log-likelihood function. To ensure convergence towards coherent estimators, the parameters were first set to zero and then changed using the Broyden-Fletcher-Goldfarb-Shanno (BFGS) method. The validation of the model included predictions for new joint values to represent the ability to estimate end-effector positions with minimal residual errors. Both models were implemented in R using different packages. The Bayesian regression model was trained with the brms package using 4 MCMC chains, 2000 iterations per chain, and a Gaussian family. It modeled the three spatial coordinates jointly via a multilevel structure with random intercepts for each axis. For the MLE model, the bbmle package was used to fit separate linear models for each coordinate, optimizing a custom negative log-likelihood function with the L-BFGS-B method. Input variables were normalized, and key metrics (RMSE, MAE, R^2) were extracted from predictions on the test set. Confidence intervals for coefficients were calculated in both approaches to assess uncertainty.

3 Results and Discussions

Bayesian and MLE models leverage the dataset's structure to address direct kinematics (coordinate prediction from angles). A comparison of the estimates of the proposed model is reported in Table 3, which comprises a total of six angles and the estimates obtained by entering those values in the proposed models. Both models used the same input values for joint angles ($q1$ to $q6$), allowing a direct comparison of their position estimates (x, y, z).

Table 3. Comparative Analysis of Test Values and Estimated Results: Bayesian Regression vs. MLE

Values						Position estimation (x, y, z)	
Q1	Q2	Q3	Q4	Q5	Q6	Bayes	MLE
0.000	0.000	0.00	0.000	0.000	0.000	(−0.100, −0.094, 0.162)	(−0.009, −0.080, −0.021)
1.000	−0.500	0.750	−0.250	0.300	−0.600	(−0.071, −0.061, 0.197)	(−0.004, −0.004, 0.084)
1.570	0.000	−1.570	0.000	0.000	0.000	(−0.203, −0.199, 0.059)	(−0.016, −0.016, −0.296)
0.300	0.700	−0.200	0.400	−0.100	0.500	(−0.101, −0.093, 0.160)	(−0.008, −0.008, −0.015)
−1.000	0.800	0.200	−0.600	0.400	−0.300	(−0.066, −0.065, 0.192)	(−0.008, −0.007, 0.061)

Data input values were selected considering that the first row represents the neutral position of the robot, the second row corresponds to a combination of values, the third row is designed to evaluate the limits of the joints, and the last two rows allow the analysis of both an intermediate configuration and an external combination of angles. Table 3 identifies a representative difference between the estimates obtained from the Bayesian and MLE models. The Bayesian model predicts the end-effector's position from the equation Eq. 1, whereas the equations Eq. 2, Eq. 3, and Eq. 4 were used for the MLE model.

To evaluate the influence of each angle of articulation ($q1$ to $q6$) on the prediction of the cartesian coordinates of the final effector (x, y, z), we analyzed the regression coefficients obtained from two different models: a Bayesian linear regression model (Fig. 5) and an MLE model (Fig. 6). Both figures present the estimated coefficients along with their 95% confidence intervals for each coordinate axis.

Figure 5 shows a Bayesian model that presents a more uniform and understandable distribution of coefficients in all joints. It is relevant to emphasize

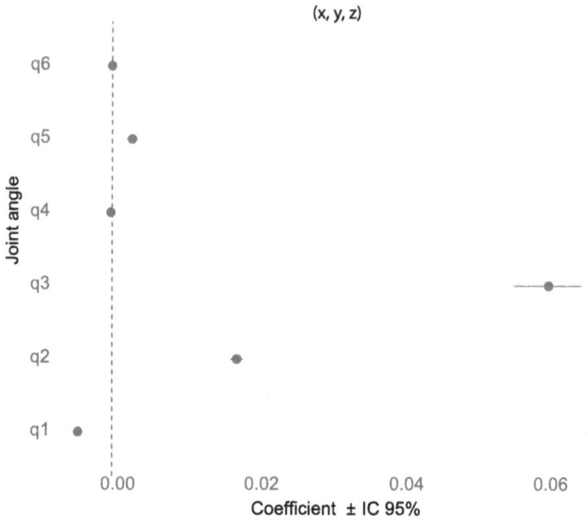

Fig. 5. Coefficients estimated by the Bayesian model for the prediction of the position of the final effector (x, y, z).

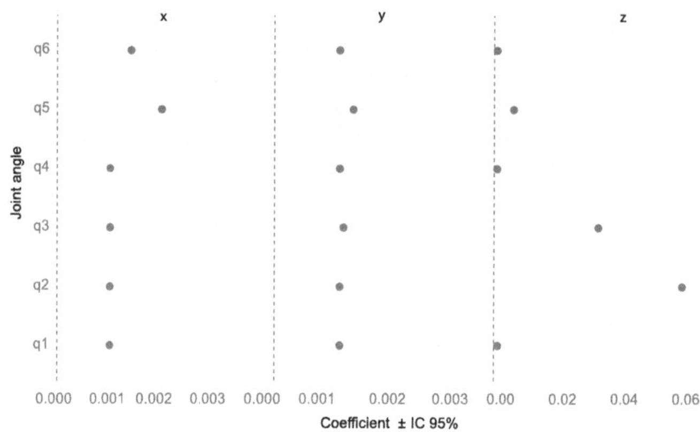

Fig. 6. Coefficients estimated by the Maximum Likelihood (MLE) model for predicting the position of the end effector (x, y, z).

that the articulatory angles $q2$ and $q4$ show relatively higher coefficients for the dimensions x and y, indicating a greater effect on vertical movement. However, the $q6$ joint appears more crucial in determining the z coordinate due to its high coefficient on that axis. Additionally, the Bayesian model's narrower and more consistent confidence intervals indicate less variability in the estimates and a more reliable fit, particularly in situations where the data is uncertain.

On the other hand, the MLE model shown in Fig. 6 exhibits significantly lower magnitude coefficients in all joint angles and output dimensions. Although the directionality of the impact is maintained to some extent (e.g., $q2$ and $q4$

Table 4. Statistical coefficients of the MLE model by coordinate (x, y, z).

Coordinate	Variable	Estimate	Standard Error	p-value
x	beta5	0.00197	0.00084	0.019
y	sigma	0.10597	0.00066	<0.001
z	beta2	0.06434	0.00069	<0.001

still contribute more significantly to x and y), the scale of the coefficients is markedly smaller, which could suggest a model with reduced sensitivity or over-regularization. In addition, the confidence ranges of the MLE model are not as uniform and, in certain situations, are more extensive, especially for the x and y coordinates, which indicates an increase in uncertainty in the estimation of the parameters. To better identify the contribution of each variable to the final estimate of the MLE model, the best results are structured for each coordinate, and Table 4 is constructed.

Table 5. Comparing performance metrics between the Bayesian model and the Maximum Likelihood (MLE) model.

Metrics	Bayes Model	MLE Model
RMSE	0.1042	0.1028
R^2	0.5904	0.4266
MEA	0.0870	0.0888

The results presented in Table 4 underline that the angle related to beta2 (Z coordinate) produces the most noticeable effect (Beta = 0.064, $p < 0.001$), while beta5 in X (Beta = 0.002, p = 0.019). This suggests that changes in these angles have a decisive influence on the location of the end effector, especially on the vertical axis. In contrast, low sigma values (Y: 0.106, Z: 0.085) corroborate the model's ability to identify variability in the data. This test supports the use of the model in applications that demand high accuracy, such as the handling of objects in structured environments. The final result of this research is the statistical comparison of the models, carried out through the use of Table 5.

Table 5 shows a numerical difference between the Bayesian regression model and the MLE model, using three standard metrics. Root Mean Square Error (RMSE), Normal of the Coefficient of Determination (R^2), and Mean Absolute Error (MEA). These evaluations provide information on the prediction accuracy and generalizability of each model by determining the location of the end effector based on articulatory angles. The RMSE results for both models are quite similar, with the MLE model reporting a slightly lower error (0.1028) relative to the Bayesian model (0.1042). This indicates that, relative to the mean deviation of the prediction, both models show similar performance. However, the RMSE does not, by itself, capture the model's ability to explain variability in the data. Regarding R^2, it shows a more significant difference. The Bayesian model arrives at an R^2 value of 0.5904, considerably higher than the 0.4266 achieved by the MLE model. This indicates that the Bayesian method provides an increase in the overall adaptation to the data, achieving an increase in the variability of the results.

Finally, the MEA values are again very similar between the two models, with the Bayesian model standing out a little more than the MLE model (0.0870 vs. 0.0888). Although the change is minimal, this consistency, coupled with the high R^2 value, supports the conclusion that the Bayesian model provides more reliable and robust performance, particularly in situations where capturing the underlying data structure is crucial. In general, although the MLE model achieves slightly lower error values in RMSE and MEA, the Bayesian model demonstrates superior explanatory capacity, which is critical for applications that require interpretability and confidence in the model's predictions.

4 Conclusions

In this work, we present a comparative study between a Bayesian regression model and an MLE-based model to predict the location of the end effector of a robotic manipulator using the joint angles information. Through a statistical method that links the joint structures ($q1$ to $q6$) with the spatial coordinates (x, y, z), we were able to determine the location of the end effector and assess the performance of each model through error metrics such as RMSE, R^2, and MEA. The Bayesian model obtained a higher mean R^2 value (0.5904) compared to the MLE model (0.4266), indicating a more efficient fit to the information and a greater ability to explain the variability in the position estimation. This demonstrates that it is possible to accurately perform forecasting of the position of the end effector of a manipulator robot (direct kinematics) despite the significant challenges related to uncertainty and nonlinear dynamics of robotic manipulator joints. We demonstrate that the Bayesian method is more appropriate for handling these uncertainties since it offers more stable coefficient calculations and more accurate confidence intervals, despite the MLE model having slightly lower error metrics in certain situations. However, this study presents certain limitations. First, the dataset used was synthetically generated using a kinematic model, which may not fully reflect real-world sensor noise and environmental uncertainties. Additionally, the models were evaluated only under ideal simulated conditions, without testing on real hardware or datasets collected from physical robots. These factors may limit the generalizability of the results to real-world applications. In future works, we will analyze sequential relations between joint angles and the end effector position by incorporating time series methods, which may further enhance the accuracy of the estimation.

Acknowledgments. This work has been supported by ANID under grant Fondecyt Iniciación 11240105 and 11241171. It was also funded by FONDECYT Postdoctorado 3240116.

A Annexes

The dataset was extracted from the Kaggle page, which can be found under the name Robot Kinematics Dataset in [14].

References

1. Guamán-Rivera, R., et al.: Assessment of convolutional neural networks for asset detection in dynamic automation construction environments. In: 2023 IEEE CHILEAN Conference on Electrical, Electronics Engineering, Information and Communication Technologies (CHILECON), pp. 1–6 (2023)
2. Hjorth, S., Chrysostomou, D.: Human-robot collaboration in industrial environments: a literature review on non-destructive disassembly. Robot. Comput.-Integr. Manuf. **73**, 102208 (2022)
3. Chiaverini, S., Siciliano, B., Egeland, O.: Review of the damped least-squares inverse kinematics with experiments on an industrial robot manipulator. IEEE Trans. Control Syst. Technol. **2**(2), 123–134 (1994)
4. da Veiga, T., et al.: Challenges of continuum robots in clinical context: a review. Progr. Biomed. Eng. **2**(3), 032003 (2020)
5. Alebooyeh, M., Jill Urbanic, R.: Neural network model for identifying workspace, forward and inverse kinematics of the 7-DoF Yumi 14000 abb collaborative robot. IFAC-PapersOnLine **52**(10), 176–181 (2019). 13th IFAC Workshop on Intelligent Manufacturing Systems IMS 2019
6. Guamán Rivera, R., García Alvarado, R., Martínez-Rocamora, A., Cheein, F.A.: Workspace analysis of a mobile manipulator with obstacle avoidance in 3D printing tasks. Appl. Sci. **11**(17) (2021)
7. Velásquez, E.I.C., Del Río Caldumbide, J.A., Romo, Á.J.P., Granizo, O.A.M.: Visual-aid positioning using point cloud compression and RGB-D cameras for robotic manipulators (2023)
8. Adel, M., Ahmed, S.M., Fanni, M.: End-effector position estimation and control of a flexible interconnected industrial manipulator using machine learning. IEEE Access **10**, 30465–30483 (2022)
9. Yamamoto, Y., Kikuuwe, R.: End-effector position estimation and control of hydraulic excavators with total stations. In: 2024 IEEE/SICE International Symposium on System Integration (SII), pp. 345–350. IEEE (2024)
10. Lertpiriyasuwat, V., Berg, M.C.: Adaptive real-time estimation of end-effector position and orientation using precise measurements of end-effector position. IEEE/ASME Trans. Mechatron. **11**(3), 304–319 (2006)
11. Vásconez, J.P., et al.: Joint angle estimation for an industrial manipulator robot via convolutional object detection and k-means clustering. In: International Conference on Advanced Research in Technologies, Information, Innovation and Sustainability, pp. 290–305. Springer (2024)
12. Lin, J., Ye, C., Yang, J., Zhao, H., Ding, H., Luo, M.: Contour error-based optimization of the end-effector pose of a 6 degree-of-freedom serial robot in milling operation. Robot. Comput.-Integr. Manuf. **73**, 102257 (2022)
13. Liu, X., Zuo, G., Zhang, J., Wang, J.: Sensorless force estimation of end-effect upper limb rehabilitation robot system with friction compensation. Int. J. Adv. Rob. Syst. **16**(4), 1729881419856132 (2019)
14. Essiegota, S.: Robot kinematics dataset. https://l1nq.com/dWltb

15. Bürkner, P.-C.: brms: an R package for Bayesian multilevel models using stan. J. Stat. Softw. **80**(1), 1–28 (2017)
16. Bolker, B., Development Core Team: bbmle: tools for general maximum likelihood estimation. R package version 1.0.25 (2025)

A Retrieval Augmented Generation Approach for Planning on General Purpose Service Robots

Eden Attenborough[1], Hariharan Arunachalam[3], Juan Pablo Vásconez[4], Francesco Del Duchetto[2], Riccardo Polvara[2], and Leonardo Guevara[2(✉)]

[1] School of Computer Science, University of East Anglia, Norwich, UK
e.attenborough@uea.ac.uk

[2] Lincoln Centre for Autonomous Systems, University of Lincoln, Lincoln, UK
{fdelduchetto,rpolvara,lguevara}@lincoln.ac.uk

[3] LAAS-CNRS, Universite de Toulouse, Toulouse, France
harunachal@laas.fr

[4] Energy Transformation Center, Faculty of Engineering, Universidad Andres Bello, Santiago, Chile
juan.vasconez@unab.cl

Abstract. The introduction of Large Language Models (LLMs) in the past few years has disrupted the fields of natural language understanding and embodied artificial intelligence. LLMs have previously been used to generate plans from human instructions, enabling a physical agent (robot) to complete abstract long-form tasks without direct programming, when provided with a list of capabilities. On the other hand, Retrieval Augmented Generation (RAG) extends the capabilities of LLMs by querying an easily-updated knowledge base 'on the fly', outside of its own parameters, to generate a response. This work is one of the pioneers in exploring the usability of a RAG-based approach to generate robot plans, with RAG used to inform about the capabilities of the robot, and the context in which it is operating, instead of being stored them in the LLM itself. The usability of this approach was evaluated in the context of general purpose service robots (GPSR). Experimental results revealed that the proposed approach outperforms by 15% state-of-the-art LLM-based techniques for robot planning in terms of generating valid plans from 'implicit' queries where a GPSR is expected to understand and perform an action based on environmental context, without being explicitly instructed on every detail. Our approach runs locally on with low computational requirements enabling real-time robot operations.

Keywords: RAG · LLM · NLU · GPSR · Service Robots · Embodied AI · Robot Planning

T. Guarda et al. (Eds.): ARTIIS 2025, CCIS 2789, pp. 237–250, 2026.
https://doi.org/10.1007/978-3-032-16758-3_19

1 Introduction

Traditionally, robots have been programmed to complete successfully a single task or a limited set of tasks. This limits their wider adoption and overall usefulness in the real world. If robotic systems are to become more ubiquitous in the real world, they will have to complete tasks that they were not specifically programmed to do. In this context, this work focuses on what is called a General Purpose Service Robot (GPSR), which is capable of understanding a generic human command/task such as 'I'm hungry, please give me a gluten-free food item please', and then generate a list of discrete atomic actions to be executed in sequence, such that: '1. Go to the kitchen; 2. Identify a food item that doesn't contain gluten; 3. Grasp the food item; 4. Go back to the requester; 5. Offer gripper; 6. Done'.

The advent of Large Language Models (LLMs), most famously ChatGPT [14], revolutionised the fields of Natural Language Understanding (NLU), Artificial Intelligence (AI), and robotics. Their ability to accurately represent human syntax and encode common sense knowledge makes them highly appropriate to be used for GPSR high level planning from natural language instructions.

Using LLMs for robot task decomposition from a generic instruction is not a new idea, several works have been proposed in this field including [2,6,12]. While the outputs of LLMs are semantically correct when using them for robot planning, the generated task plans may not accurately map to acceptable/feasible actions the robot can perform and might encompass various linguistic ambiguities [13]. These approaches may require high computational capabilities [10] or access to cloud models [12]. Moreover, the so-called LLMs hallucinations pose another challenge for robot task planning, which results in content that is nonsensical or inconsistent with real-world facts [4].

In this context, this work explores the use of Retrieval-Augmented Generation (RAG) techniques to improve LLM high-level robot planning accuracy by reducing hallucinations. RAG is a method by which LLMs query a knowledge base of external information (up to the relevant knowledge cut-off date), before producing a result; rather like an 'open-book' test. This means that, unlike traditional LLMs, RAG-augmented models don't have to rely solely on pre-trained datasets, which are quickly outdated. Utilising RAG has also the advantage of lower computational requirements, as it allow to use smaller models due to the fact that the knowledge base is kept externally rather than needing to be stored into the model weights via training. This is why RAG is commonly used in businesses to query documentation or databases specific to that business [19], but has not been used widely for robotic applications.

Previous works on the robotics domain have used retrieval augmentation for generating manipulation control policies from a database of examples of the ongoing task [21] or, more similar to our work, for continually generating high-level plans to explore the environment and satisfy requirements provided in natural language [18]. Differently from these previous works, we propose utilising RAG to store the *context* in which the robot is operating, namely its surroundings and capabilities, more specifically the action primitives the robot can perform. Additionally, we propose pre and post-validation stages that check the feasibility of requested commands and executability of generated plans, which further reduces the chances of hallucinations.

The main contributions of our work are:

- a RAG approach to task decomposition from natural language instructions that effectively integrates information about environmental context and robot's capabilities;
- a pre-prompter and rule-based plan validation approach to ensure the generation of valid plans;
- an LLM planning method that can run offline on the robot hardware and with low computational requirements (approximately 6 GB of VRAM);
- extensive evaluation on a GPSR robotics competition benchmark against state-of-the-art approaches.

2 Related Work

2.1 General Purpose Service Robots

Service robots, as defined by the International Organization for Standardization(ISO), are machines that perform helpful tasks for humans or equipment [5]. However, not all such robots qualify as "general purpose"; to merit this description, a robot must be able to handle a wide variety of tasks in its environment. A prominent showcase of this versatility is the RoboCup[1] competition, particularly the *RoboCup@Home* league, which evaluates robots' ability to solve randomly assigned tasks without a predetermined script or order, through its GPSR and Extended GPSR tests. Given RoboCup's popularity, numerous research teams have published robot planning approaches, with recent efforts including rule-based validation systems to ensure logical sequencing of actions (for example, requiring navigation before grasping an object) [11,17].

A preliminary iteration of the planning methodology discussed here was employed by the LCASTOR team [7] in RoboCup@Home 2024, and has since undergone further refinements described in Sect. 3.

2.2 Large Language Models for Robot Planning

A large language model is a large-scale deep learning architecture, pre-trained on substantial datasets to generate text from human-language prompts. In robot planning, LLMs effectively translate natural-language instructions into executable actions. An early example, *PaLM-SayCan* [2], decomposes complex tasks via Google's proprietary PaLM model but remains closed-source, limiting reproducibility. Another approach, *TGenBot* [6], produces behaviour trees through an LLM trained on hundreds of examples, risking domain shifts on robots with differing capabilities or environments. By contrast, *ROS-LLM* [9]

[1] https://www.robocup.org/.

is fully open-source and integrates with the Robot Operating System (ROS), though its reliance on OpenAI-hosted LLMs complicates offline or local deployment. *LLM-Planner* [12] splits planning between high-level and low-level LLMs. This structure isolates low-level failures, preventing an entire plan from collapsing if a step falters. Additionally, it employs multimodal models for contextual grounding, enabling the robot to recognise when a prompt's object reference corresponds to a specific item in its environment. Similarly, Hi Robot [10] proposes a hierarchical multimodal framework for robot planning from natural instructions enabling to perform complex tasks and accepting users' interjections during execution. This approach however requires a large-scale data collection for the task domain in which it is applied and two GeForce RTX 4090 gpus for real-time inference. In contrast, our approach leverages pre-trained large models (no training required), acquires domain knowledge from external knowledge-bases through RAG (limited data collection required) and can run locally in real-time on 6 GB of virtual memory.

2.3 Retrieval Augmented Generation for Robot Planning

Previous research has shown that LLMs can effectively break down robot tasks into subtasks, yet a key challenge lies in grounding these subtasks within the robot's capabilities and its environment [13]. Many approaches rely on existing machine learning models to handle environment grounding [9,11,12], while some leverage multimodal LLMs [2] to associate prompt-referenced objects with those in the scene. However, even multimodal grounding is susceptible to hallucinations, in which the LLM outputs a function or capability the robot does not possess [11]; for instance, generating subtasks requiring the robot to detect or grasp objects it cannot identify or handle (due to weight, size, or fragility).

Hallucinations arise because LLMs rely on static training data that may be outdated, inaccurate, or overly general. A practical remedy, short of retraining these models, is Retrieval-Augmented Generation (RAG) [8], which retrieves domain-specific or current information from internal sources, merges it with the user's query, and then prompts the LLM with this combined input. In robot planning, RAG thus reduces hallucinations by grounding the LLM's responses in an up-to-date knowledge base, including robot capabilities and environmental constraints. Such a knowledge base is inherently relational: for example, it might encode that an `apple`, as a type of fruit, is graspable, typically located on a `kitchen table`, which itself belongs in the `kitchen`.

Although some works propose knowledge graphs to minimise hallucinations [1,3], we are unaware of any direct use of RAG for robot planning in precisely this manner. Instead, Yamao *et al.* [16] suggests using RAG to "save and accumulate experiences" from a robot's prior tasks, and two existing RAG-based methods for robot planning [15,20] indeed store previous states and instructions to inform longer task sequences. However, these approaches focus on incorporating temporal data rather than using knowledge graphs to provide environment-level grounding.

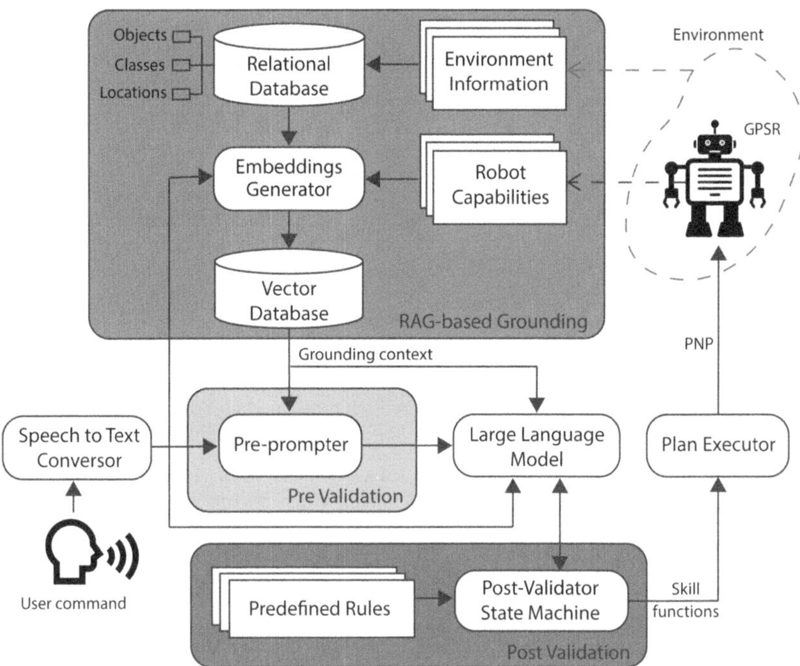

Fig. 1. A block diagram showing the workflow of the proposed planning approach.

3 Methodology

This section presents the proposed approach for planning on GPSR[2]. The workflow of the proposal is illustrated in Fig. 1. Important steps and components are described in the subsections below.

3.1 RAG-Based Grounding

Embeddings Generator. In RAG, embeddings are used to retrieve relevant information from a large corpus based on the user's query. In our case, the query is the transcript (generated by a speech-to-text conversor) with a command for the robot to do and the corpus consists of prior knowledge about the environment and robot capabilities. The query and corpus are both processed, generating embeddings that map the text into a high-dimensional vector space. The system then compares the query embedding with all the corpus embeddings in the vector database. It calculates similarity scores and retrieves the most relevant information that is then used as grounding context to generate a response from the LLM. The embedding model used was `BGE` (BAAI general embedding), specifically `BAAI/bge-base-en-v1.5`[3], an English only model.

[2] https://github.com/LCAS/rag_gpsr.git.

[3] https://huggingface.co/BAAI/bge-base-en-v1.5.

Table 1. Examples of skill functions including their required arguments and description.

Function	Argument(s)	Description
goto_location	location_name	Go to a named location, such as 'side tables', 'bedroom' or 'cabinet' or 'bedside table'.
grasp_object	object_location object_name	Grasps a given object, for example 'fruit' or 'bowl' at a given location, e.g. 'kitchen table'.
offer_object_to_me	–	Give the previously grasped object to me. 'grasp_object()' must previously have been called.
offer_object_to_person	person_location person_name	Offer a previously grasped object to a specific named person at a named location. You must be grasping an object, so 'grasp_object()' must have previously been called.
identify_people	people_location what_to_identify	Identifies and counts the number of people in a given room doing a given action. For example what_to_identify could be 'standing persons' or 'pointing to the right'.
identify_objects	object_location what_to_identify	Given something to look for, for example, the biggest food item or the smallest toy, or the number of plates, do perception to identify this.

Adding Robot Capabilities. To ensure the generated plans include tasks that are feasible for the robot, all known robot capabilities are added to the RAG knowledge base from a single file that contains the definition of all the admissible skill functions the specific GPSR is capable of doing. Some examples of robot skill functions are shown in Table 1. The robot capabilities were added using LlamaHub's `llama-index-readers-docstring-walker` which uses the `ast` library to analyse Python abstract syntax trees.

Adding Environment Information. In addition to the skill functions as capabilities, the RAG knowledge base needs to store information about the environment in which the robot is operating, such as the rooms in the scene, the names of the people in the scene, all of the graspable objects, and their locations. This information is stored in *markdown* format (as the files provided by the `RoboCup@Home` GitHub[4]) and is added to the knowledge base with the use of `llama-index-readers-file`.

Unlike the robot capability information that goes directly to the embedding generator, the environmental information such as object names, classes, and their locations needs to first be stored in a relational database and then can be vectorized. For instance, for the query 'Where would I find an apple?' it has to chain the information:

1. The user is looking for an apple, which is an object
2. The object 'apple' is in the class 'fruit' (and not 'snacks' or 'food')
3. 'Fruit' objects are stored on the 'coffee table'

[4] https://github.com/RoboCupAtHome/Eindhoven2024/.

```
SELECT objects.object_name AS object, object_classes.class_name AS class,
↪  locations.location_name AS locations
FROM objects
INNER JOIN object_classes ON objects.class_id = object_classes.class_id
INNER JOIN locations ON locations.class_id = objects.class_id;
```

Listing 1: Query used to select the objects, classes and locations in the scene, as shown in Table 2, which are then made into vector embeddings.

Table 2. Examples of objects, classes and locations as made into vector embeddings with database encoder.

Object	Class	Location
soap	cleaning supplies	shelf
milk	drinks	kitchen cabinet
cornflakes	food	kitchen counter
candle	decorations	desk
apple	fruits	coffee table
candy	snacks	dinner table
cup	dishes	dishwasher

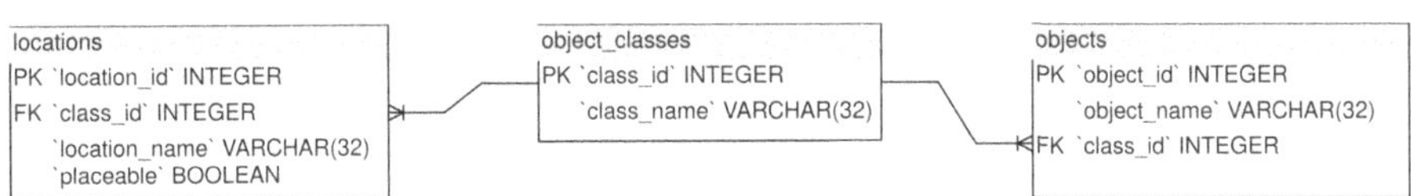

Fig. 2. Database entity relationships diagram.

Table 3. Examples of explicit and implicit tasks used to evaluate the GPSR planning solution.

Task Type	Examples
Explicit	give me a glass of water from the kitchen cabinet
	guide the person in the kitchen from the dinner table to the hallway
	bring me a clean cup from the dishwasher
Implicit	bring me a pear
	fetch a drink and deliver it to me
	take a plate to the dinner table

This was achieved by parsing the markdown as HTML with the `markdown` Python library, and then parsing that HTML with the `lxml` library. The HTML tree is read, and the information is appended to an *SQLite* database with the use of the `sqlite3` library. An entity relationship diagram showing the structure of the relational database is shown in Fig. 2. The SQL query to retrieve the information for vectorization is shown in Listing 1, with an example output being shown in Table 2.

3.2 Pre-validator for Unfeasible Tasks

Table 3 shows examples of commands that GPSRs are expected to understand and complete. When it comes to the so-called implicit tasks such as 'bring me a pear', where the location of the object of interest is not specified, the GPSR should be able to chain the knowledge that objects 'pear' is in the class 'fruit', and objects in the 'fruit' class are stored at the location 'coffee table'.

To accomplish this, a *pre-prompter* was implemented to assist with chaining knowledge, spreading out the knowledge chaining over multiple queries. The pre-prompter assists with getting the location of objects if they weren't specified in the prompt and then appends the result to the main query. Taking the example task 'bring me a pear' again, the pre-prompter would append the text 'pears are located on the coffee table' to the main LLM query, assisting it. Moreover, since LLMs can struggle with chaining knowledge from different sources, the pre-prompter was also introduced as a task pre-validation stage to determine if the required command is unfeasible. For example, in the task 'fetch me a cola from the desk', the LLM must evaluate that 'cola' is in the category 'drinks' and 'drinks' are in the location 'kitchen cabinet' and not the location 'desk'. In this case, the prompt contradicted the knowledge base and thus the LLM responded by saying that the task was not possible. In the end, the implementation of the pre-prompter aims to complement the benefits of RAG to reduce hallucinations on LLM planning outputs.

3.3 Post-validator for Generated Plans

The following is a subset of the rules that were identified as useful to validate a generated plan from the LLM. These rules are recursive and are used to define the parameters of the robot skill functions.

1. The robot can only grasp an object if it has moved to a specific location first.
2. The robot can only perceive objects if it has moved to a specific location first.
3. The robot can only answer a quiz if it has asked for a human first.
4. The robot can only ask a human to follow it if it has asked for a human first.
5. A robot can only offer an object to a human if it has *both*:
   (a) At some point previously grasped an object.
   (b) Lastly has asked for a human *or* is at the instruction point.
6. The robot can only report information if it has *both*:
   (a) At some point previously perceived an object *or* perceived a human.
   (b) Lastly has asked for a human *or* is at the instruction point.

With a set of rules defined, a post-processing validator was implemented to check the produced function adheres to these rules. Whilst we have also implemented a system that handles and replans if a task decomposition fails, having another validator before this enables us to replan without having to attempt an invalid plan first. The post-validator ensures that the produced decomposition adheres to the user's predefined rules with the use of a state machine. Moreover, it also checks that the produced code only contains function calls, with no sequence or selection (if statements or iteration), and that the function signature is correct.

4 Experimental Validation

The proposed planning solution was evaluated on a dataset of 80 GPSR commands, half of which were generated by the RoboCup@Home 2024 `Command Generator`[5], that we are going to refer as `explicit` tasks since they provide detailed information to the GPSR about where to go. The other half of the commands, which we are going to refer to as `implicit` tasks, were manually generated to make them more difficult to complete since they don't provide information on where to find specific objects of interest (expecting the GPSR to infer where those objects are within the known environment). Table 3 shows some examples of explicit and implicit tasks that were used as commands for the GPSR to generate a plan.

To systematically evaluate the contribution of every component of our proposal, we performed an ablation study that compared the performance of a full implementation including RAG, Plan Post-validator, and Task Pre-validator against three variations: a) RAG only b) RAG and Task Pre-validator c) RAG and Plan Post-validator. For all of them, the LLM model used was llama3.1 8b 4-bit quantised[6]. Moreover, to validate the capabilities of our proposal for reducing hallucinations, we compared its performance against a state-of-the art alternative called LLM-Planner [12] which used GPT-3[7] as LLM model.

The planning performance evaluation consisted of passing the 80 commands in our dataset through the systems mentioned above, and then manually labelling the produced task decomposition, classifying it into one of the following categories[8]:

1. **Correct (score = 0)**: For decompositions that perfectly decomposed the requested task (see Listing 2).
2. **Correct, but not concise (score = 1)**: For decompositions that completed the requested task, but performed some redundant subtasks (see Listing 3).
3. **Partially correct (score= 2)**: For runs that generated *some* of the required subtasks, but not enough to complete the overall goal (see Listing 4).
4. **Incorrect (score = 3)**: When the decomposition did not attempt any valid subtasks for the main task, or when the LLM generated a solution that would crash the planner, such as generating a function hallucination, that would make the whole attempt fail (see Listing 5).

[5] https://github.com/RoboCupAtHome/gpsr_command_generator.
[6] https://ai.meta.com/blog/meta-llama-3-1/.
[7] https://platform.openai.com/docs/models.
[8] The complete command dataset including the labeled task decompositions, environmental information, and robot capabilities considered for the experiments can be found in https://github.com/LCAS/rag_gpsr.git.

```
def do_func(p):
    grasp_object(p, object_location='dishwasher', object_name='fruit')
    offer_object_to_person(p, person_location='hallway', person_name='the
    ↪ person pointing to the right')
```

Listing 2: Example of 'Correct' task decomposition, from the command `fetch a fruit from the dishwasher and give it to the person pointing to the right in the hallway`. Here the task decomposition is perfect and there are no superfluous subtasks.

```
def do_func(p):
    goto_location(p, location_name="TV table")
    grasp_object(p, object_location="TV table", object_name="Pringles")
    offer_object_to_me(p)
```

Listing 3: Example of 'Correct, but not concise' task decomposition, from the command `give me a pringles from the TV table`. It is classified as 'Correct, but not concise' because the `goto_location()` function call is superfluous, the `grasp_object()` task already moves the robot to the correct location according to the `object_location` parameter.

```
def do_func(p):
    engine_say(p, "I'd be happy to help you with that!")
    identify_people(p, people_location="office",
    ↪ what_to_identify="raising their right arm")
    greet_person(p, person_location="office", person_name="the person
    ↪ raising their right arm")
    ask_for_person(p, person_location="office", person_name="the person
    ↪ raising their right arm")
    engine_say(p, "The current day of the week is...")
    get_date(p)
    engine_say(p, "Ah, and now I'll tell you that!")
```

Listing 4: Example of 'partially correct' task decomposition, from the command `tell the day of the week to the person raising their right arm in the office`. It is classified as 'partially correct' because the `get_date()` function needs to be embedded inside the `engine_say()` function call for it so say the date out loud correctly. It also calls `identify_people()` and `greet_person()`, which despite being superfluous, do not affect how well the task decomposition ultimately reaches its goal.

Figure 3 shows the results of running every system evaluated in the dataset of 80 commands, splitting it into explicit (see plots (a)–(e)) and implicit tasks (see plots (f)–(j)). Every plot shows the distribution of resultant plans according to the four categories defined above.

```
def do_func(p):
    goto_location(p, location_name="hallway")
    follow_person(p, person_name="the sitting person",
    ↪  from_location="hallway", to_location=None)
    ask_for_person(p, person_location="hallway", person_name="the sitting
    ↪  person")
    answer_quiz(p)
```

Listing 5: Example of 'incorrect' task decomposition, from the command `go to the hallway then find the sitting person and answer a quiz`, here the LLM generates the function `follow_person()` incorrectly, but more importantly sets its `to_location` parameter to `None`, which break the task decomposition action completely.

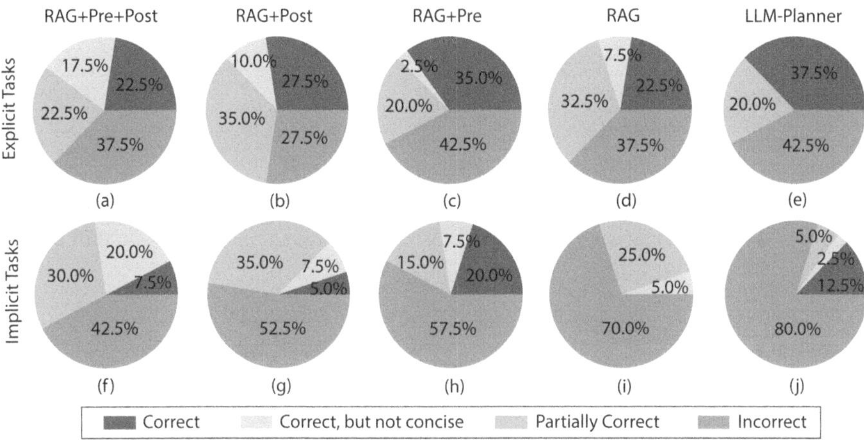

Fig. 3. Results of each system by testing it on explicit and implicit tasks. The plots show the distribution of generated responses according to the four possible categories

Then, to quantify the performance of the task decomposition in percentage 0–100%, we used the formula $(1 - (score/3)) * 100$, where the $score$ value is replaced by the numerical score corresponding to the given label (0,1,2 or 3).

5 Results and Discussion

Table 4 summarizes the task decomposition performance results from each of the approaches evaluated. If we focus on the ablation study, the implementation of RAG without any validation stage was the least effective approach among all of them while the implementation of RAG with Task Pre-validation demonstrated to be the best alternative overall. If we consider their performance for specific task types, then the RAG with Plan Post-validation obtained the higher performance for explicit tasks while the full implementation was the best option for

Table 4. Task decomposition evaluation results generated after testing the 80 commands in the dataset.

Task Type	Average Task Decomposition Performance (%)				
	RAG+Pre+Post	RAG+Post	RAG+Pre	RAG	LLM-Planner
Explicit	41.67	**45.84**	43.34	38.34	44.17
Implicit	**30.84**	21.67	30	11.67	15.84
All Tasks	36.25	33.75	**36.67**	25	30

Table 5. Percentage of improvement with respect to LLM-Planner. Positive values represent improvements, and negative values represent a decrease in performance.

Task Type	Change Calculation	Improvement with respect to LLM-Planner (%)			
		RAG+Pre+Post	RAG+Post	RAG+Pre	RAG
Explicit	Relative	–5.66	**3.77**	–1.88	–13.20
	Absolute	–2.5	**1.66**	–0.83	–5.83
Implicit	Relative	**94.74**	**36.84**	**89.47**	–26.31
	Absolute	**15**	**5.83**	**14.16**	–4.16
All	Relative	**20.83**	**12.5**	**22.22**	–16.66
	Absolute	**6.25**	**3.75**	**6.66**	–5

implicit tasks. The overall results suggest that the Task Pre-validation step is a more critical component of the system than the Plan Post-validation step.

When comparing the performance of RAG and its variations (that used a small size LLM model with 8B parameters) against LLM-Planner (that used a larger size LLM model with 175B parameters), it is interesting to see that our RAG-based solution with pre and post-validation stages outperforms the LLM-Planner for the decomposition of implicit tasks. The percentages of improvement with respect to LLM-Planner are summarized in Table 5, showing that the implementation of RAG with Plan Post-validation is the only variation that does not have negative values (i.e. only improvements). However, the overall improvement is not as significant as the other variations that include Task Pre-validation. In fact, the full implementation achieved a relative improvement of almost 95% for implicit tasks which on an absolute scale represents a 15% improvement. These results clearly demonstrate that our RAG-based approach together with Pre and Post validation steps is able to reduce hallucinations typical of GPSR commands that do not provide detailed information.

6 Conclusions

This work reported the results of implementing a first-in-its-kind RAG-based approach for planning on GPSR. The results showed that the RAG implementation by itself was not as effective as when pairing it with pre and post-validation stages which allowed the system to handle better unfeasible plans and reduce the hallucinations typical of other state-of-the-art LLM-based approaches. Moreover, the proposed planning solution demonstrated that by using RAG, it is not necessary to use a large LLM and cloud services, making this approach suitable for applications where GPSR requires to operate off-line or when onboard computational resources are limited. These results encourage further exploration of the use of RAG for planning and integrating prompt engineering to obtain the best possible output from LLMs. While RAG has a practical advantage over fine-tuning/retraining models to keep the LLMs updated, in this work, we have assumed that objects within the known environment are always located in specific places. This assumption won't work in every environment, and there will be occasions where an item was misplaced by my mistake or on purpose in a different location, thus, the GPSR should be able to continuously update the knowledge base to be able to locate the misplaced objects. This challenge will be addressed in future work by exploring the integration of multimodal LLMs with RAG, allowing the knowledge base of the environment to be updated in real-time.

Acknowledgments. This work was supported by the Engineering and Physical Sciences Research Council and AgriFoRwArdS CDT [EP/S023917/1], and ANID under grant Fondecyt Iniciación 11240105.

References

1. Agrawal, G., Kumarage, T., Alghami, Z., Liu, H.: Can knowledge graphs reduce hallucinations in LLMs?: A survey (2023). https://doi.org/10.48550/arXiv.2311.07914
2. Ahn, M., et al.: Do As I Can, Not As I Say: Grounding Language in Robotic Affordances (2022). https://arxiv.org/abs/2204.01691
3. Fatehkia, M., Lucas, J.K., Chawla, S.: T-RAG: lessons from the LLM trenches (2024). https://doi.org/10.48550/arXiv.2402.07483
4. Huang, L., et al.: A survey on hallucination in large language models: principles, taxonomy, challenges, and open questions. ACM Trans. Inf. Syst. (2024). https://doi.org/10.1145/3703155
5. ISO: Robotics—vocabulary (2021). https://www.iso.org/standard/75539.html
6. Izzo, R.A., Bardaro, G., Matteucci, M.: BTGenBot: Behavior Tree Generation for Robotic Tasks with Lightweight LLMs (2024). https://arxiv.org/abs/2403.12761
7. LCASTOR: Lcastor 2024 team description paper (2024). https://repository.lincoln.ac.uk/articles/report/LCASTOR_2024_Team_Description_Paper/25853875?file=46405942
8. Li, J., Yuan, Y., Zhang, Z.: Enhancing LLM factual accuracy with rag to counter hallucinations: a case study on domain-specific queries in private knowledge-bases (2024). https://doi.org/10.48550/arXiv.2403.10446
9. Mower, C.E., et al.: ROS-LLM: A ROS framework for embodied AI with task feedback and structured reasoning (2024). https://arxiv.org/abs/2406.19741v1

10. Shi, L.X., et al.: Hi robot: open-ended instruction following with hierarchical vision-language-action models. arXiv preprint arXiv:2502.19417 (2025)
11. Shirasaka, M., et al.: Self-recovery prompting: promptable general purpose service robot system with foundation models and self-recovery. In: 2024 IEEE International Conference on Robotics and Automation (ICRA), pp. 17395–17402. IEEE (2024). https://doi.org/10.1109/ICRA57147.2024.10611640
12. Song, C.H., Wu, J., Washington, C., Sadler, B.M., Chao, W.L., Su, Y.: LLM-planner: few-shot grounded planning for embodied agents with large language models. In: Proceedings of the IEEE/CVF International Conference on Computer Vision, pp. 2998–3009 (2023) https://doi.org/10.48550/arXiv.2212.04088
13. Wang, R., Yang, Z., Zhao, Z., Tong, X., Hong, Z., Qian, K.: LLM-based robot task planning with exceptional handling for general purpose service robots (2024). https://doi.org/10.48550/arXiv.2405.15646
14. Wu, T., et al.: A brief overview of ChatGPT: the history, status quo and potential future development. IEEE/CAA J. Automatica Sinica **10**(5), 1122–1136 (2023). https://doi.org/10.1109/JAS.2023.123618
15. Xu, W., Wang, M., Zhou, W., Li, H.: P-RAG: progressive retrieval augmented generation for planning on embodied everyday task. In: Proceedings of the 32nd ACM International Conference on Multimedia, MM '24, pp. 6969–6978. Association for Computing Machinery, New York (2024). https://doi.org/10.1145/3664647.3680661
16. Yamanaka, J., Kido, T.: Evaluating large language models with RAG capability: a perspective from robot behavior planning and execution. In: Proceedings of the AAAI Symposium Series, vol. 3, pp. 452–456 (2024). https://doi.org/10.1609/aaaiss.v3i1.31254
17. Yamao, K., Kanaoka, D., Isomoto, K., Mizutani, A., Tanaka, Y., Tamukoh, H.: Development of a SayCan-based task planning system capable of handling abstract nouns. In: Proceedings of International Conference on Artificial Life & Robotics (ICAROB2024), pp. OS15-4. ALife Robotics (2024). https://doi.org/10.5954/ICAROB.2024.OS15-4
18. Yoo, M., Jang, J., Park, W.J., Woo, H.: Exploratory retrieval-augmented planning for continual embodied instruction following. In: The Thirty-eighth Annual Conference on Neural Information Processing Systems (2024). https://openreview.net/forum?id=LpXV29Ggl3
19. Yu, C., Yang, G., Chen, X., Liu, K., Zhou, Y.: Bashexplainer: retrieval-augmented bash code comment generation based on fine-tuned codebert. In: 2022 IEEE International Conference on Software Maintenance and Evolution (ICSME), pp. 82–93. IEEE (2022). https://doi.org/10.1109/ICSME55016.2022.00016
20. Zare, A., Niu, Y., Ayyubi, H., Chang, S.f.: RAP: Retrieval-Augmented Planner for Adaptive Procedure Planning in Instructional Videos (2024). https://doi.org/10.48550/arXiv.2403.18600
21. Zhu, Y., Ou, Z., Mou, X., Tang, J.: Retrieval-Augmented Embodied Agents. In: Proceedings of the IEEE/CVF Conference on Computer Vision and Pattern Recognition. pp. 17985–17995 (2024) https://doi.org/10.1109/CVPR52733.2024.01703

Sentiment Analysis of Climate Change Tweets: Tool Comparison and Evaluation of Impact Based on Post Reach

María Guadalupe Celaya-Padilla(✉), Roberto Solís-Robles, Luis C. Reveles-Gómez, Carlos H. Espino-Salinas, Vanessa Alcalá-Rmz, and José María Celaya-Padilla

Universidad Autónoma de Zacatecas, Zacatecas, Mexico
{34152203,rsolis,luiscarlosreveles,carlos.espino,vdrar.06,
jose.celaya}@uaz.edu.mx

Abstract. This study evaluates the performance of three predefined sentiment analysis tools in Python—TextBlob, VADER, and transformer-based models—on a dataset of 396 climate change-related tweets. Each tool was combined with classification algorithms (SVM, Naive Bayes, KNN, and Random Forest) to assess emotional responses based on post reach (followers, likes, retweets, and account verification). A subset of tweets was manually annotated to serve as ground truth. Results show that transformer models paired with Naive Bayes achieved the highest F1-Score, while VADER with SVM performed best in terms of ROC AUC. To formally assess tool reliability, Cohen's Kappa coefficient was used to measure agreement with human labels, revealing limited alignment across tools. These findings highlight the challenge of interpreting sentiment in social media contexts and the need for models attuned to nuance, sarcasm, and emotional ambiguity in environmental discourse.

Keywords: Sentiment analysis · Climate change · Twitter · Classification · Machine Learning

1 Introduction

Climate change is one of the most pressing global issues of our time, directly affecting ecosystems, public health, and the global economy [1]. In recent years, social media has played a central role in shaping public discourse about climate-related topics. Platforms like Twitter have become essential arenas for users to share opinions, spread information, and express emotions about environmental issues [2,3]. However, these platforms also facilitate the rapid spread of misinformation, increasing the need for accurate tools to assess public sentiment.

Sentiment analysis—an area of Natural Language Processing (NLP)—offers valuable techniques to detect and classify the emotional tone of text. Through it,

T. Guarda et al. (Eds.): ARTIIS 2025, CCIS 2789, pp. 251–265, 2026.
https://doi.org/10.1007/978-3-032-16758-3_20

we can explore how the public responds to climate events, environmental policies, and awareness campaigns in real time. The effectiveness of such analyses largely depends on the tools and models used, which include lexicon-based tools and machine learning algorithms.

Among the most used lexicon-based tools are TextBlob [4] and VADER (Valence Aware Dictionary and Sentiment Reasoner) [5], known for their efficiency in handling informal and social media language. Additionally, transformer-based models like BERT (Bidirectional Encoder Representations from Transformers) [6] have shown strong performance in contextual understanding of language.

On the machine learning side, classifiers such as Support Vector Machines (SVM) [7], Naive Bayes (NB) [8], Random Forest (RF) [9], and k-Nearest Neighbors (k-NN) [10] are commonly applied for text classification. These models allow for the prediction of sentiment categories (e.g., positive, neutral, negative) based on features extracted from the text or its metadata.

This paper presents a comparative evaluation of three sentiment analysis tools—TextBlob, VADER, and BERT-based models—and their performance when combined with machine learning classifiers. Moreover, we investigate the relationship between tweet reach (e.g., follower count, likes, retweets) and the emotional impact perceived in climate-related posts. By comparing automated sentiment classifications against human annotations, we aim to determine which approaches are most robust and contextually reliable.

2 Literature Review

The undergraduate thesis *Sentiment Analysis on Social Networks* by Rafael Reyes Podadera explores how verbal communication through natural language has evolved alongside the rise of social media platforms. The work focuses on using Artificial Intelligence (AI) techniques to process text and analyze public sentiment on platforms like Twitter. This analysis is approached from a business perspective, employing models such as Naive Bayes and Support Vector Machines, along with tools like TextBlob and VADER [11].

Climate change communication on social media has become a prominent research topic for understanding public awareness and reactions to environmental challenges. Several studies demonstrate that emotions expressed in social media posts can significantly influence the diffusion of climate-related information. For instance, Segado-Boj et al. highlight how habits, attitudes, and expectations shape university students' interactions with climate news on social media [12]. Their results underscore the importance of emotional content for designing effective awareness campaigns.

In the Spanish-language context, Rosenbrock, Trossero, and Pascal [13] examine sentiment analysis across various domains, emphasizing its potential to capture tone, polarization, and public discourse. This line of work can be extended to climate discourse, where capturing nuanced emotions is crucial.

Beyond environmental topics, Colón-Ruiz et al. analyze emotional reactions to pharmaceuticals on social media to inform content regulation [14]. Their findings suggest that emotional cues in digital communication are valuable not only for monitoring but also for guiding public messaging—an idea relevant to climate communication strategies.

Llopis [15] presents a data mining-based analysis of decentralized platforms like Mastodon to explore climate change debates. His work reveals a wide range of opinions and emotional tones, indicating that decentralized media are also viable channels for studying environmental discourse. Although the study addresses climate-related conversations, it was not included in our comparative evaluation of sentiment analysis tools since its focus lies on data mining techniques rather than textual sentiment classification.

From an educational perspective, Villafuerte [16] demonstrates the role of social media in preparing young audiences for climate-related risks, reinforcing the potential of emotionally resonant content to foster awareness and resilience.

Rodrigo-Cano and Fernández Rial [17] analyze how social platforms encourage reflection and adaptation to climate change, while González shows how social media can bridge the consensus gap across South American countries. These findings point to the platform's importance in shaping perceptions and promoting action.

Despite the diversity of methodologies in the literature, most studies rely on a single sentiment analysis technique—either lexicon-based or machine learning-based—without cross-method comparison. This gap limits the identification of the most robust and generalizable tools. To address this, our study proposes a systematic comparison of several sentiment analysis techniques on the same dataset under uniform conditions, contributing a more comprehensive perspective to the field.

3 Methodology

The sentiment analysis in this study was conducted using an integrated approach that combined multiple sources and techniques to enable result comparison. First, a dataset specifically collected for analyzing emotions in climate change-related texts was used. Data processing included three main categorization approaches: automated analysis using Python tools (VADER, TextBlob, and Transformers), human categorization, and keyword-based classification. Each method generated labeled texts that were evaluated and compared with one another.

Subsequently, five supervised learning models—SVM, NB, KNN, and RF—were applied to predict emotional classification based on post reach. These models were trained and evaluated using the labels obtained from the aforementioned categorization methods.

Cohen's Kappa coefficient was then calculated to measure the agreement between the results of each Python-based tool and the human assessments, with the latter serving as the ground truth [18].

The outcomes were analyzed to assess the relative performance of different categorization approaches and classification models, helping to identify the most suitable method for predicting emotions based on the emotional impact of climate change-related posts.

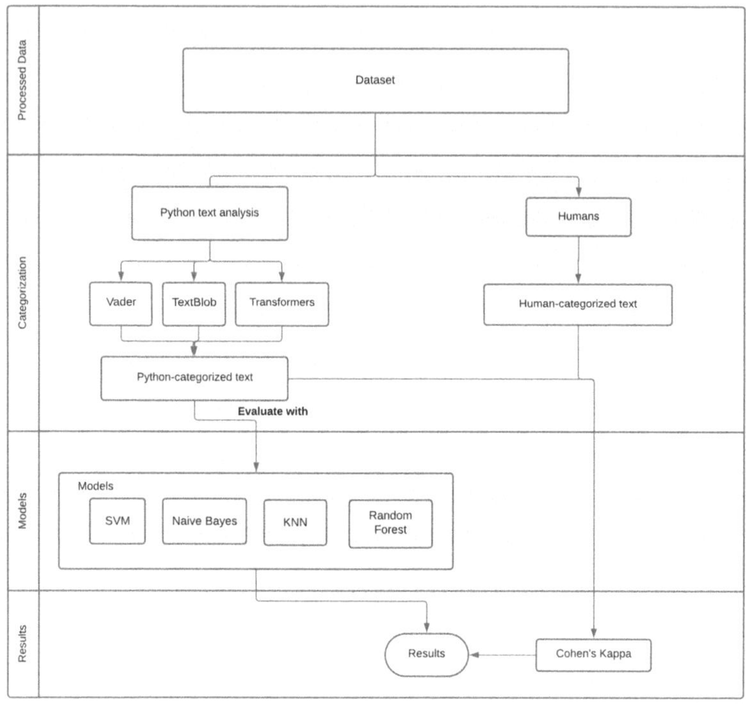

Fig. 1. Methodological process diagram for model development and workflow.

Figure 1 illustrates the overall workflow of this study, which ranges from text analysis (automated and human) to classification model evaluation and agreement measurement using Cohen's Kappa coefficient.

3.1 Data Collection

The data for this research was obtained from José Guzmán's *Climate Sentiment in Twitter* dataset [19], collected using tools such as the Twitter API and filtering for posts that included climate change-related terms (e.g., *"climate change"*, *"global warming"*). The dataset comprised 396 tweets published between January 1, 2020, and December 24, 2020 [20].

A new version of the dataset was created by processing the post content using GPT-4 to clean and enhance message interpretation while preserving the original semantic content.

To support the automated sentiment analysis, a group of four people helped classify 396 tweets as positive, neutral, or negative. All annotators were adults (18 years or older) and were chosen because they could understand the informal language used on social media. They were not experts, but this type of human annotation is common in studies where emotional meaning is subjective. Having several people label the tweets helps reduce individual bias and improves the reliability of the results.

3.2 Data Preprocessing

The following transformations were applied to the text data:

- Removal of irrelevant characters (e.g., mentions, URLs, hashtags).
- Conversion of text to lowercase for uniformity.
- Replacement of numbers using regular expressions (e.g., with the word `"num"`).
- Segmentation of text into smaller units for individual processing.
- Removal of punctuation marks after segmentation.

To ensure the original message remained semantically intact, cosine similarity was calculated between original and processed text. This metric evaluates similarity based on the angle between two text vectors in a multidimensional space. The cosine similarity between two vectors $\boldsymbol{A}$ and $\boldsymbol{B}$ is defined as:

$$\text{cosine\_similarity}(\boldsymbol{A}, \boldsymbol{B}) = \frac{\boldsymbol{A} \cdot \boldsymbol{B}}{\|\boldsymbol{A}\| \cdot \|\boldsymbol{B}\|} \tag{1}$$

where $\boldsymbol{A} \cdot \boldsymbol{B}$ is the dot product and $\|\boldsymbol{A}\|$ is the Euclidean norm of vector $\boldsymbol{A}$.

After preprocessing, the dataset retained all 396 tweets. The average similarity score between the original and cleaned versions was 0.892, indicating a high level of semantic preservation.

3.3 Sentiment Analysis

The study applied five complementary approaches for sentiment analysis, combining lexicon-based methods, machine learning techniques, and human evaluation.

- **TextBlob:** A Python library for processing textual data that provides two main metrics:
  - *Polarity* (-1 to 1): Indicates sentiment strength, where -1 is extremely negative, 0 is neutral, and $+1$ is extremely positive. It is calculated as:

$$\text{Polarity} = \frac{\sum_{i=1}^{n} \text{sentiment}(word_i)}{n} \tag{2}$$

    where n is the number of sentiment-bearing words [4].

  - *Subjectivity* (0 to 1): Measures how opinionated the text is, with 0 being fully objective and 1 fully subjective.

  Although it uses a predefined lexicon, it can be extended with domain-specific terms. Its simplicity makes it computationally efficient, though it may lack accuracy in specialized contexts [4,21].

- **VADER (Valence Aware Dictionary and Sentiment Reasoner):** A rule-based model designed for social media text. It:
  - Uses a sentiment lexicon with intensity scores (e.g., "happy" = +1, "sad" = −1)
  - Accounts for capitalization emphasis and degree modifiers (e.g., "very good" = +1.5 vs. "good" = +1)
  - Interprets emojis and slang (e.g., ":)" = +0.6)
  - Recognizes contrastive conjunctions (e.g., "but" shifts sentiment emphasis)

  The compound score, normalized to the range $[-1, 1]$, is computed as:

$$\text{Compound} = \frac{\sum_i s_i}{\sqrt{(\sum_i s_i)^2 + \alpha}} \tag{3}$$

  where s_i are the individual sentiment scores and α is a normalization constant (default = 15) [5,22].

- **Transformer Models:** Advanced neural architectures that:
  - Use self-attention to weigh the relevance of each word in context:

$$\text{Attention}(Q, K, V) = \text{softmax}\left(\frac{QK^T}{\sqrt{d_k}}\right)V \tag{4}$$

    where Q (queries), K (keys), and V (values) are learned matrices.
  - Leverage pretraining on large corpora and fine-tuning for domain-specific tasks.
  - Were implemented via Hugging Face's pipeline using a pretrained BERT model fine-tuned for sentiment classification.

- **Human Evaluation:** Conducted through structured surveys:
  - Four annotators independently labeled 200 randomly selected tweets.
  - A codebook with sentiment examples was used for consistency.
  - Inter-annotator agreement reached $\kappa = 0.72$ (substantial agreement). Although Cohen's Kappa is traditionally used for two raters, in this study we computed pairwise Cohen's Kappa scores between all annotator combinations and reported the average. We acknowledge that Fleiss' Kappa may be more appropriate for multi-rater agreement and will include it in future work.
  - Discrepancies were resolved through consensus meetings. The final label for each tweet was determined through majority voting among the four annotators. When no majority was reached, discrepancies were resolved through discussion and consensus.

  This method provides high-quality ground truth data but is time-consuming (approx. 45 s per annotation).

- **ChatGPT-4o:** The multimodal Large Language Model (LLM) was prompted as follows:

  ```
  "Classify this tweet's sentiment about climate change as
  POSITIVE, NEUTRAL, or NEGATIVE. Consider both content
  and context. Respond only with the label."
  ```

  Advantages of this method include:
  - Context-aware world knowledge
  - Improved ability to detect sarcasm and irony
  - Multilingual capabilities

  However, the model may exhibit positional bias and inconsistencies across runs [23]. Quadratic Weighted Kappa was not used because our sentiment labels (positive, neutral, negative) are considered nominal categories without a strict ordinal relationship. For this reason, unweighted Cohen's Kappa was applied (Fig. 2).

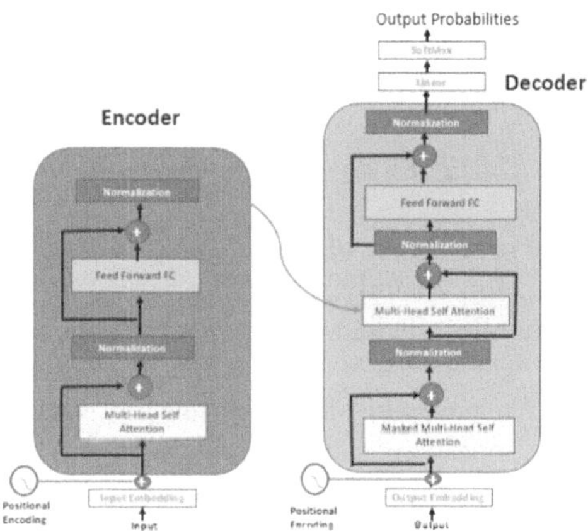

Fig. 2. Transformer architecture: Input embeddings pass through multiple encoder layers. Self-attention heads (right) compute contextual relationships. The clasiffication token aggregates sentence-level features for classification tasks.

3.4 Classification Models

Before conducting the experiments, a comparison was made between the AI-interpreted dataset (processed with ChatGPT) and the original dataset to verify semantic similarity. Cosine similarity was used, leveraging vector embeddings (e.g., Word2Vec or Sentence Transformers), yielding an average score of 0.8920.

This indicates that, despite the cleaning and reinterpretation steps, the semantic content of the messages remained largely unchanged.

For model implementation, the following features were selected as predictors: follower count and account verification status. Sentiment classification results obtained from VADER, Transformers, and TextBlob were used as target variables. To assess classification performance, four algorithms were applied:

- **Support Vector Machines (SVM):** A supervised learning algorithm used for classification and regression tasks. SVM constructs an optimal hyperplane that separates classes by maximizing the margin between them. For non-linear problems, it employs kernel functions to project data into higher-dimensional spaces where separation becomes feasible [7].
  In this study, the Radial Basis Function (RBF) kernel was selected, as it is suitable for handling non-linearly separable data. This kernel maps input features to a higher-dimensional space, facilitating more flexible decision boundaries. Since predictor variables such as follower count and likes may exhibit non-linear relationships with sentiment labels, the RBF kernel enhances the model's ability to capture these patterns [24].
- **Naive Bayes:** A probabilistic classifier based on Bayes' theorem, commonly used in text classification. It estimates the posterior probability that an instance belongs to a given class, assuming conditional independence among features. The classification rule is defined as:

$$P(C|X) = \frac{P(X|C)P(C)}{P(X)} \tag{5}$$

  where $P(C|X)$ is the probability of class C given feature set X. Although the independence assumption is rarely true in practice, Naive Bayes remains effective and computationally efficient, especially for high-dimensional datasets [8].
- **Random Forest:** An ensemble learning method that constructs multiple decision trees using bootstrap samples and randomly selected feature subsets. It aggregates individual tree predictions via majority voting (for classification) or averaging (for regression). Random Forest is robust to overfitting and performs well with noisy or unbalanced data [9].
- **k-Nearest Neighbors (k-NN):** A non-parametric algorithm that classifies new instances based on the majority label among their k closest neighbors in the feature space. Distance metrics such as Euclidean distance are commonly used to compute proximity. Although intuitive and easy to implement, k-NN can be sensitive to irrelevant features and to data scaling [10].

$$d(\mathbf{x}, \mathbf{y}) = \sqrt{\sum_{i=1}^{n} (x_i - y_i)^2} \tag{6}$$

4 Results and Discussion

The performance of the classification models applied to the sentiment outputs was evaluated using a train-test split of 70% and 30% respectively. The evaluation metrics included *Accuracy*, *Area Under the Curve (AUC)*, *Precision*, *Recall*, and *F1-Score* (Tables 1 and 2).

Table 1. Classifier results with TextBlob, VADER, and Transformers on test data

Model	Accuracy	AUC	Precision	Recall	F1-Score
TextBlob - RF	0.4202	0.5885	0.42	0.42	0.42
TextBlob - SVM	0.4202	0.6080	0.18	0.42	0.25
TextBlob - KNN	0.4454	0.6214	0.45	0.45	0.45
TextBlob - NB	0.3866	0.4673	0.17	0.39	0.24
VADER - RF	0.5546	0.8012	0.53	0.55	0.54
VADER - SVM	0.6303	0.8205	0.40	0.63	0.49
VADER - KNN	0.6218	0.8290	0.60	0.62	0.61
VADER - NB	0.6134	0.8124	0.48	0.61	0.49
Transformers - RF	0.5882	0.4500	0.54	0.59	0.56
Transformers - SVM	0.6807	0.4780	0.46	0.68	0.55
Transformers - KNN	0.5882	0.4449	0.49	0.59	0.52
Transformers - NB	0.6807	0.5404	0.63	0.68	0.59

Table 2. Best results obtained from classification models

Model	Accuracy	AUC	Precision	Recall	F1-Score
VADER - SVM	0.6303	0.8205	0.40	0.63	0.49
Transformers - Naive Bayes	0.6807	0.5404	0.63	0.68	0.59
TextBlob - KNN	0.4454	0.6214	0.45	0.45	0.45

The *Positive* class consistently achieved higher precision and recall values, whereas the *Neutral* and *Negative* classes showed weaker performance across most models. This disparity may be attributed to the inherent ambiguity and subjectivity of language in social media contexts. Although some models performed reasonably well according to standard metrics, their agreement with human annotators remained limited. To formally evaluate this, we applied Cohen's Kappa coefficient, as presented in the following section.

Cohen's Kappa Coefficient. To quantify the agreement between automated classification and human-labeled data, Cohen's Kappa coefficient (κ) was calculated for each tool (Figs. 3, 4, 5 and 6):

- **VADER:** $\kappa = 0.1437$
- **Transformers:** $\kappa = 0.1842$
- **TextBlob:** $\kappa = 0.1353$

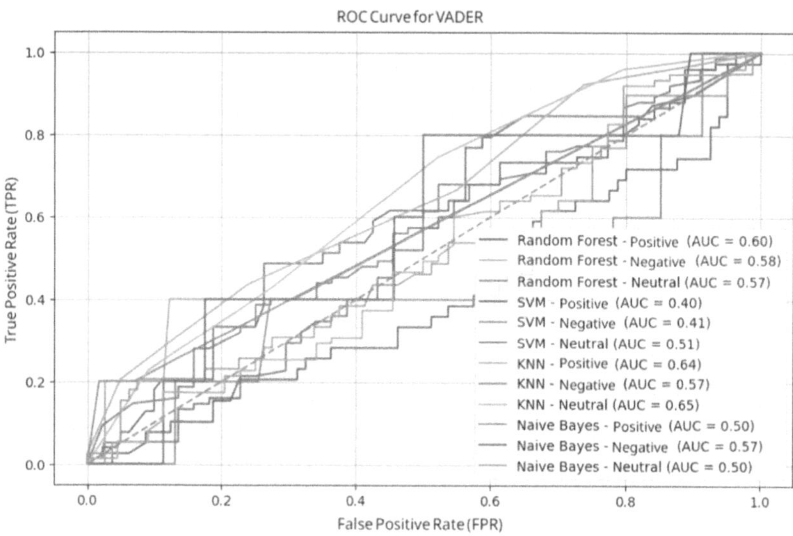

Fig. 3. ROC curves for different classifiers using VADER (positive, negative, and neutral).

The κ values indicate a low level of agreement between the automated tools and human annotations. This confirms the challenge of accurately capturing nuanced emotional content through predefined models. Moreover, several sections of the ROC curves fall below the diagonal, revealing cases where models performed worse than random guessing.

This behavior may be explained by the ambiguity and subjectivity in user-generated content. For instance, comments such as *"How wonderful to destroy the planet faster!"* or *"Amazing how we keep polluting, bravo humanity"* contain superficially positive words but convey a clearly negative sentiment—posing difficulties for lexicon-based systems.

Additionally, domain-specific context and cultural nuances often go unrecognized by traditional algorithms. These limitations highlight the need for models better attuned to the subtleties of emotional expression in climate change discourse.

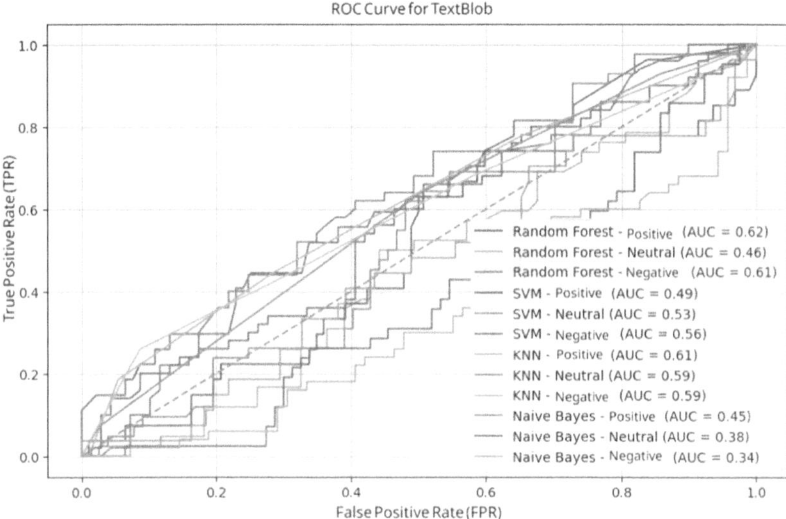

Fig. 4. ROC curves for different classifiers using TextBlob (positive, negative, and neutral).

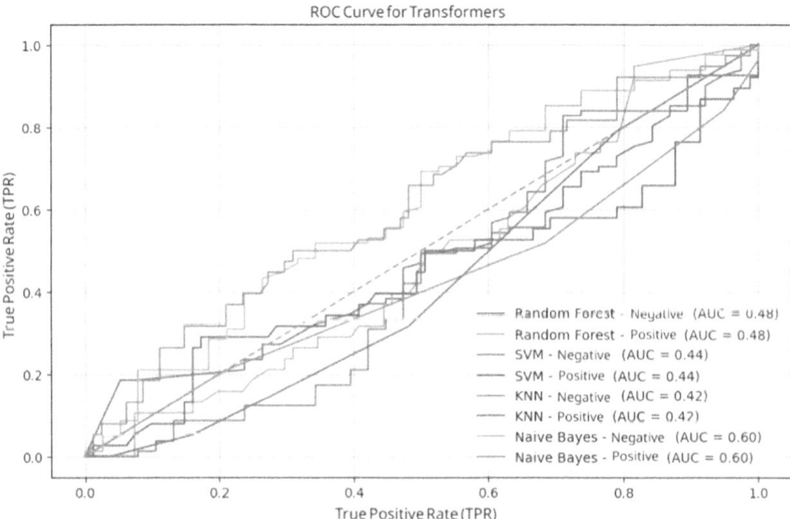

Fig. 5. ROC curves for different classifiers using Transformers (positive, negative, and neutral).

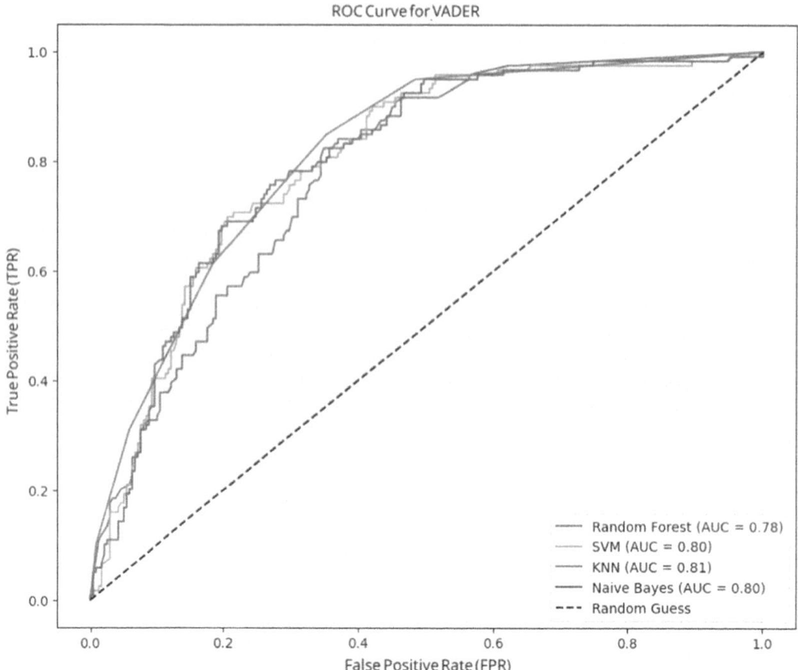

Fig. 6. Micro-average ROC curves for different classifiers using VADER. While the Positive classification may perform well, the model struggles to distinguish between Negative and Neutral categories.

5 Conclusions

This study examined the relationship between tweet reach (e.g., likes, retweets, follower count) and the emotional responses they generate, evaluating whether higher reach correlates with increased emotional impact. The findings suggest that post reach has minimal and statistically insignificant influence on sentiment classification outcomes.

Several factors may explain this result, including the nature of the post, the audience's prior attitudes, or the sociopolitical context in which the tweet circulates. For instance, even content with seemingly high impact—such as "Significant temperature increase forecasted for 2025"—may not trigger strong emotional reactions in all users.

A major limitation in the current approach is the presence of irony or sarcasm, which presents a challenge for automated sentiment analysis. Phrases like *"Great, more wildfires this year. Just what we needed!"* contain positive lexical cues but convey negative sentiment—often misclassified by rule-based or shallow models. This reinforces the complexity of interpreting emotional language in climate-related discourse.

Although features such as account verification or follower count showed some association with emotional patterns, they were not sufficient for reliably predicting sentiment. Among the models evaluated, VADER in combination with SVM performed best in terms of ROC AUC, while Transformers with Naive Bayes achieved the highest F1-Score.

Notably, Cohen's Kappa coefficient was incorporated as an additional metric to assess the agreement between machine and human labels. Its use in sentiment classification contexts is uncommon, and our findings suggest it may be a valuable tool for evaluating reliability in emotionally ambiguous domains. This opens the door for further methodological refinement in future studies.

Finally, a comparative summary with previous studies is presented in Table 3, highlighting key differences in methodology and coverage.

Table 3. Comparison with related sentiment analysis studies

Study	Tools	Domain	Focus
Reyes Podadera (2023)	VADER, TextBlob	Brand opinion	Business use
Rosenbrock et al. (2021)	Lexicon + ML	Spanish text	No transformers
Llopis (2024)*	Data mining	Mastodon (climate)	Decentralized platform
This study	VADER, Transformers	Twitter (climate)	Tool comparison, Kappa

* *Note: Although Llopis (2024) addresses climate change debates, it focuses on data mining in decentralized networks rather than text-based sentiment analysis, and was thus excluded from our comparative evaluation.*

Although ROC curves provide a general overview of classifier performance, future work will include confusion matrices to better visualize misclassifications between sentiment classes, especially the confusion between neutral and negative cases observed in climate-related discourse.

Overall, the study highlights the limitations of current tools and the importance of incorporating more context-aware, culturally sensitive, and sarcasm-aware models for analyzing sentiment in climate change communication.

6 Future Work

Future research will focus on enhancing sentiment analysis techniques through multilingual approaches and model integration. One key direction is the development of a sentiment analysis framework capable of processing both Spanish and English texts, allowing better adaptability to bilingual social media environments.

In addition, efforts will be made to create a new Spanish-language dataset specifically curated for climate change-related discussions. This dataset will be manually annotated by human evaluators to ensure the capture of nuanced emotional expressions, which are often overlooked by automated methods.

Another promising line of work involves the implementation of ensemble systems that combine multiple classifiers. These systems would integrate predictions from different models using majority voting (for classification) or averaging (for regression), with the goal of improving both accuracy and robustness. The ensemble approach seeks to capitalize on the strengths of lexicon-based, machine learning, and transformer-based methods.

Lastly, the use of Cohen's Kappa coefficient as a tool for assessing reliability in automated sentiment classification could be further explored. Given that it is rarely applied in this domain, its inclusion may represent a valuable methodological contribution for future studies aimed at aligning machine predictions with human perception, especially in emotionally ambiguous contexts.

References

1. IPCC. Climate change 2021: The physical science basis (2021). https://www.ipcc.ch/report/ar6/wg1/. Intergovernmental Panel on Climate Change
2. Kirilenko, A.P., Stepchenkova, S.O.: Climate change and geography: twitter as a tool for mapping public sentiment. Appl. Geogr. **60**, 190–197 (2015)
3. Jang, S.M., Hart, P.S.: Climate change and social media: a computational text analysis of twitter content. J. Environ. Commun. **15**(2), 131–146 (2021)
4. Loria, S.: Textblob: Simplified text processing (2018). Accessed 13 May 2025. https://textblob.readthedocs.io/en/dev/quickstart.html
5. Hutto, C., Gilbert, E.: Vader sentiment analysis. Official GitHub repository (2014). https://github.com/cjhutto/vaderSentiment
6. Devlin, J., Chang, M.-W., Lee, K., Toutanova, K.: Bert: pre-training of deep bidirectional transformers for language understanding. In: Proceedings of NAACL-HLT, pp. 4171–4186 (2019)
7. Cortes, C., Vapnik, V.: Support-vector networks. Mach. Learn. **20**(3), 273–297 (1995)
8. IBM. Naive bayes: Introduction and applications. IBM's official website (2024). https://www.ibm.com/mx-es/topics/naive-bayes
9. IBM. Random forest: Introduction and applications. IBM's official website (2024). https://www.ibm.com/mx-es/topics/random-forest
10. IBM. K-nearest neighbors (knn): Introduction and applications. IBM's official website (2024). https://www.ibm.com/mx-es/topics/knn
11. Podadera, R.R.: Sentiment analysis in social networks (2023). https://riuma.uma.es/xmlui/handle/10630/35235. Accessed 2 Dec 2024
12. Segado-Boj, F., Díaz-Campo, J., Navarro-Sierra, N.: Emotions and the spread of climate change news on social media. Influence of habits, previous attitudes and uses and gratifications among university students. Revista Latina de Comunicación Social (2020). https://hal.science/hal-03213358/
13. Rosenbrock, G., Trossero, S., Pascal, A.: Sentiment analysis techniques applied to opinion evaluation in Spanish language. In: Memorias del Congreso Argentino en Ciencias de la Computación - CACIC 2021, pp. 291–300 (2021). https://sedici.unlp.edu.ar/handle/10915/130344
14. Colón-Ruiz, I. S.-B.C., Martínez, P.: Sentiment analysis in the health domain: analyzing drug comments. Procesamiento del Lenguaje Natural **63**, 15–22 (2019). http://journal.sepln.org/sepln/ojs/ojs/index.php/pln/article/view/6090

15. Llopis, V.R.: Analysis of climate change on mastodon using data mining and social network techniques (2024). https://titula.universidadeuropea.com/handle/20.500.12880/8876
16. González, M., Rodríguez, L.: Social networks as a tool for resilience to climate change. Revista Cubana de Meteorología **25**(3), 443–456 (2019). http://scielo.sld.cu/scielo.php?script=sci_arttext&pid=S1727-81202019000300443
17. Rodrigo-Cano, D., Chávez, R.M., Rial, R.F.: Climate change communication, a tool for the great challenge. Dykinson (2021). https://www.torrossa.com/en/resources/an/5093569
18. Andalusian Society of Intensive, Emergency and Coronary Medicine (SAMIUC), Cohen's kappa (2018). https://www.samiuc.es/estadisticas-variables-binarias/medidas-de-concordancia/kappa-de-cohen/. Accessed 13 May 2025
19. Guzmán, J.: Climate sentiment in twitter. Dataset available on Kaggle (2023). https://www.kaggle.com/datasets/joseguzman/climate-sentiment-in-twitter
20. Leskovec, A.R.J., Ullman, J.D.: Mining of Massive Datasets. Cambridge University Press, Cambridge (2014)
21. del Val, R.: Sentiment analysis techniques with python (part 1) (2021). https://raqueldelval.medium.com/t%C3%A9cnicas-de-an%C3%A1lisis-de-sentimientos-1fde113dc189. Accessed 13 May 2025
22. G. for Geeks. Sentiment analysis using vader in python (2021). https://www.geeksforgeeks.org/python-sentiment-analysis-using-vader/. Accessed 13 May 2025
23. OpenAI. Introducing gpt-4o (2024). https://openai.com/index/introducing-gpt-4o. Accessed 13 May 2025
24. Schölkopf, B., Smola, A.J.: Learning with kernels: support vector machines, regularization, optimization, and beyond. In: Adaptive Computation and Machine Learning. MIT Press, Cambridge (2002)

A Two Stage Approach to Supporting Human Judgment in Literature Review Using Latent Dirichlet Allocation

Lucia González[1(✉)], Lorena Espinoza Pérez[1,2,3], Andrea Espinoza Pérez[1,2], and Óscar C. Vásquez[1,2]

[1] Faculty of Engineering, Department of Industrial Engineering, University of Santiago of Chile (USACH), Santiago, Chile
lucia.gonzalez.v@usach.cl

[2] Faculty of Engineering, Program for the Development of Sustainable Production Systems (PDSPS), University of Santiago of Chile (USACH), Santiago, Chile

[3] Université de Lorraine, ERPI, 54000 Nancy, France

Abstract. This paper proposes a two-stage method that uses Latent Dirichlet Allocation (LDA) to help organize and review academic articles. The goal is to support researchers when exploring large amounts of literature. In the first stage, LDA is trained on a small set of articles that were selected by reading their titles and abstracts. This allows the model to find common topics and related keywords. In the second stage, the topics are used to classify the full dataset, and the results are checked for consistency. A case study on sustainable supply chain design is used, based on 541 articles from the Web of Science. Three different subsets are tested to see how the selection method affects the model's performance. The results show that when one person selects the articles, the topics are more consistent and easier to interpret. In contrast, when several people choose the articles, the results vary more and are harder to group. Statistical tests support this difference, confirming that human selection can strongly influence automated topic models. And highlight the usefulness of combining machine learning and human judgment to help with literature reviews.

Keywords: Latent Dirichlet Allocation · Literature Review · Topic Modeling

1 Introduction

Literature review plays a fundamental role in developing scientific research, as it helps identify advances, gaps, and emerging trends in a given field [5]. However, the continuous growth in academic production has made it difficult to manually analyze large volumes of information, especially during the initial exploratory phases. In this context, automated text mining techniques have emerged as an alternative to support this process. Recent research by Hairani et al. (2024)

T. Guarda et al. (Eds.): ARTIIS 2025, CCIS 2789, pp. 266–276, 2026.
https://doi.org/10.1007/978-3-032-16758-3_21

illustrated that the application of Latent Dirichlet Allocation (LDA) to thesis titles and abstracts effectively identified predominant research domains and enhanced topic classification precision when integrated with supervised learning techniques, underscoring its utility for structuring extensive academic datasets [7].

Among the most commonly used approaches is the Latent Dirichlet Allocation (LDA) model, which allows the discovery of latent thematic structures within text collections [6]. LDA is a probabilistic generative model that represents documents as combinations of hidden topics, with each topic represented as a distribution of words. Its application has been documented in tasks such as document classification, content analysis, and pattern visualization [2]. Considering its popularity, LDA's dependence on the Dirichlet prior may constrain its capacity to represent relationships among topics, and conventional inference techniques may encounter difficulties with large-scale datasets. Innovations like the Latent Generalized Dirichlet Allocation (LGDA) and cross-collection extensions tackle these challenges by facilitating more sophisticated topic correlation analysis and scalable processing across various document collections [8].

The potential of LDA to improve literature reviews has been highlighted from various points of view. Kometani and Nagaoka [1] developed a support system for university students that enables the exploration of articles and the organization of thematic reviews through visualization of similarities and topic-based structures. Kongthon et al. [2] proposed an author-topic model that identifies thematic profiles from bibliographic data, helping to detect academic communities and emerging research lines. Asmussen and Moller [3] introduced a replicable methodological framework for exploratory literature reviews, structured in three phases: preprocessing, topic modeling, and postprocessing, with an emphasis on transparency and reproducibility.

In practice, many literature reviews begin with a filtering stage based on reading titles and abstracts, which may involve hundreds or thousands of articles. This process often relies on the researcher's judgment, which may not be clearly defined at the early stages of the study. In this regard, incorporating machine learning tools such as LDA can help structure and support the initial filtering process by combining automated analysis with human validation. Empirical evidence demonstrates that LDA can serve as a first-pass filter to group extensive collections into coherent topics, which can subsequently be further refined through human judgment, thereby demonstrating the efficacy of such an approach [7]. This hybrid approach ensures both efficiency and interpretability and is in line with recent methodological developments that extend topic modeling to comparative and large-scale settings [8].

Although LDA has primarily been used for topic detection and thematic segmentation, this study proposes its use as a preliminary step in literature reviews. Specifically, it suggests using topics generated from the analysis of titles and abstracts to classify and organize large volumes of information, aiming to bridge automated analysis with human judgment.

2 Methods and Methodology

The methodology is divided into two main stages: (i) training the LDA model on subsets of the dataset, and (ii) cross-validating the generated topics using the complete dataset. Diagram 1 presents a graphical overview of the methodology.

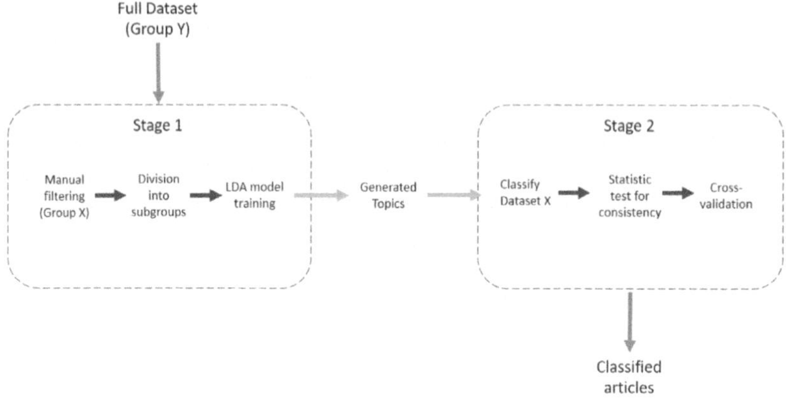

Fig. 1. Flow chart of the Methodology.

2.1 Stage 1

From the initial dataset Y, composed of titles and abstracts extracted from a search engine using a search equation, a subset X is derived, containing only those articles classified as relevant based on human reading of titles and abstracts. From this set X, a group of n subsets is defined and used to explore the topics generated under different input configurations. Each subset X_n is processed individually using a script with the following structure:

As a first step, the relevant fields (title and abstract) are combined into a single text body. Then, non-alphabetic characters are removed, all text is converted to lowercase, and a lemmatization process is applied. These steps help normalize the content and reduce the lexical variability, making the text more consistent for further analysis.

In the second step, a bag-of-words numerical representation of the text is built using the Gensim library. Terms with extremely low or high frequencies are removed to reduce noise and improve the quality of the topic model.

The LDA model is then trained using the LdaMulticore function, exploring different numbers of topics. To determine the optimal configuration, each model is evaluated based on its coherence score, which estimates the semantic consistency of the topics.

Each model run generates two main outputs: (i) a list of keywords associated with each topic, along with their weights, and (ii) a topic distribution matrix for each document, including the dominant topic and its estimated probability.

2.2 Stage 2

Once the model has been trained on each subset n, cross-validation is performed using the entire set X. The topics generated from each corresponding subset n are used as a reference to classify documents in the complete set, verifying whether the articles from the training subset are consistently selected.

Based on the keywords and weights associated with each topic, a script is used to calculate the topic membership distribution for each document. The proportion of correctly classified documents is then analyzed based on predefined criteria.

This analysis is complemented by visualizations that illustrate how topics behave and how keywords relate to each topic. Additionally, Cohen's Kappa coefficient and McNemar's test are used to quantify the level of agreement between topic assignments and to detect significant differences between model executions. These indicators provide empirical evidence of the model's stability and thematic coherence.

3 Case Study

To implement the proposed methodology, a case study is conducted based on a literature review developed in 2023 [4]. This review collects articles published in the Web of Science (WoS) database until December 2020, using the following keyword combination: ((“Green Supply Chain” OR “Sustainable Supply Chain”) AND (Design OR Conception)) OR ((“Supply Chain Design”) AND (Sustainable OR Sustainability)). This search yielded a total of 1,147 articles, which constitute the dataset Y. Subsequently, a team of six students and researchers manually reviewed titles and abstracts to select 541 relevant articles. This subset, labeled X, was stored in Excel spreadsheets, preserving titles and abstracts for later analysis.

From the dataset X, three subsets were defined:

- X_1: the first 100 articles in the spreadsheet, selected by a team member.
- X_2: the last 100 articles in the spreadsheet, selected by a different team member.
- X_3: 100 randomly selected articles. A random number was assigned to each article using Excel's `RAND()` function, and the first 100 sorted by this value were chosen. Multiple team members selected those articles.

Each subset was processed independently in Python using Jupyter Notebook. The code used was adapted to automate the export of results for comparative analysis.

During development, it was confirmed that parameter choices influence the results. Therefore, stable configurations were defined for future applications on larger datasets:

- `BATCH_SIZE = 40`: number of texts processed per iteration.

- `NUM_CHUNKS = 20`: division of the dataset into segments to optimize memory usage.
- `START_TOPICS = 2`, `LIMIT_TOPICS = 7`, `STEP_TOPICS = 2`: range defined for evaluating the number of topics, based on six thematic dimensions identified in the initial literature review.

The model was executed on a computer with an `Intel(R) Core(TM) i5-9300H 2.40 GHz` processor, 8 GB RAM, and 64-bit Windows OS. Python libraries used include:

- `pandas`: data manipulation and analysis in tabular form.
- `numpy`: efficient numerical operations and multidimensional arrays.
- `matplotlib` and `seaborn`: data visualization and plotting.
- `gensim`: topic modeling and NLP, especially for LDA.
- `spaCy`: advanced linguistic processing, including lemmatization.
- `scikit-learn`: preprocessing, evaluation metrics, and cross-validation.
- `nltk`: complementary NLP tasks like tokenization and filtering.

4 Results

For each subset, three executions of Stage 1 were performed using the same parameter settings. In all cases, the results showed high consistency, with variations in the relative weights of the keywords at the second decimal place. The dominant words remained constant across the runs, and the associated probabilities varied only at the second decimal place. The supplementary material shows this in detail.

The GEPHI platform was used to visualize the relationships between keywords associated with each topic and their estimated probability, as shown in Fig. 2. It allows for the graphical representation of the semantic network generated from the LDA model results.

The strength of topic-word connections can be analyzed using built-in features in GEPHI, particularly the modularity calculation, which helps identify thematic communities within the graph and distinguish tightly grouped words and topics.

The generated graph shows 5 distinct communities, represented with different colors, yielding a modularity score of 0.396, suggesting a moderately strong community structure, indicating the presence of well-defined thematic clusters across the topic model. Each community is visually centered around a dominant topic label, P for X_1 data, U for X_2, and R for X_3, with keywords grouped according to thematic affinity. This figure reveals three main thematic axes within the network: (1) sustainability and performance evaluation, with terms like sustainability, performance, impact, and efficiency occupying central positions; (2) optimization and decision-making under uncertainty, centered around keywords such as optimization, uncertainty, solve, and stochastic; and (3) supply chain and production systems, characterized by the clustering of terms like logistics, distribution, supplier, and production.

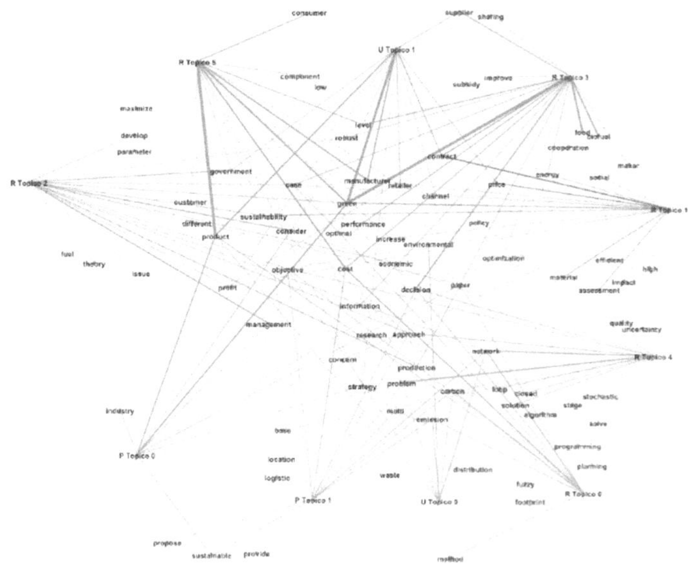

Fig. 2. Topic distribution generated in GEPHI.

Then, Fig. 3 displays the topic probability distribution of dataset X_1 after applying Stage 1 and Stage 2, respectively. In Stage 1, where the model was trained directly on the subset, the resulting topic probabilities are generally higher, indicating greater confidence in topic assignment. In contrast, Stage 2–where topics were predefined and the model was applied solely for classification–yields lower probability values, suggesting a more uncertain or balanced distribution under those constraints. A similar pattern can be observed in Fig. 4, which exhibits comparable distributions across groupsets.

In the case of Fig. 5, the behavior is similar to that observed in the other subsets. However, Fig. 5a shows a wider data distribution with a higher probability range. In contrast, Fig. 5b presents more compressed values concentrated in lower probability levels, which can suggest that the model is not confident in the classification in stage 2.

In terms of thematic substance, the topic groups generated from the subsets X_1, X_3, X_2, and *Non selected articles* were compared. The thematic profiles of each group were unique, yet partially overlapping. The first 100 articles reviewed by a single reviewer made up the X_1 group, which was characterized mainly by themes related to emission regulation, network-oriented decision-making, and industrial sustainability. A heavy emphasis on the environment was reflected by often used terminology like "green", "emission", and "network", which emphasized industrial modeling with organized decision-making within production processes and sustainable product design.

With 100 randomly chosen articles, the X_3 group showed a wider range of themes. It included subjects such as green contracting, bioenergy, and public

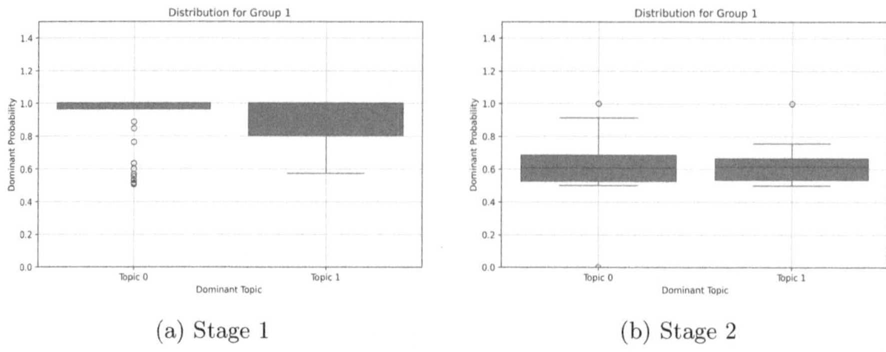

(a) Stage 1 (b) Stage 2

Fig. 3. Topic probability distribution for X_1 under two modeling stages.

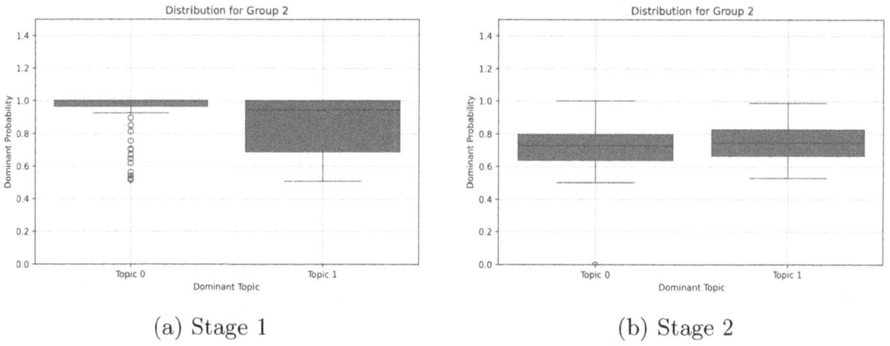

(a) Stage 1 (b) Stage 2

Fig. 4. Topic probability distribution for X_2 under two modeling stages.

policy in addition to environmental concerns (such as carbon, contracts, and decision-making). This thematic diversity, which was reinforced by phrases like biofuel, food, and loop, demonstrated how technical discourse was integrated with institutional and policy viewpoints.

Drawn from the end of the dataset, the X_2 group showed thematic similarities to both X_1 and X_3. It frequently utilizes words like green, product, network, and carbon to highlight the environmental effects of logistics networks and sustainable contracts. This group prioritized implementation above conceptual modeling and tended toward real-world applications of sustainability in supply chains and retail settings.

Lastly, a clear thematic structure emerged from the *Non selected articles* group, which included items that were not included in the first manual evaluation. Energy optimization, environmental decision-making, sustainable supply chains, and organizational management were among its primary subjects. In addition to introducing new themes like internal practices and managerial methods that were less prevalent in the other groups, it preserved analytical patterns found in previous subgroups, such as economic–environmental trade-offs.

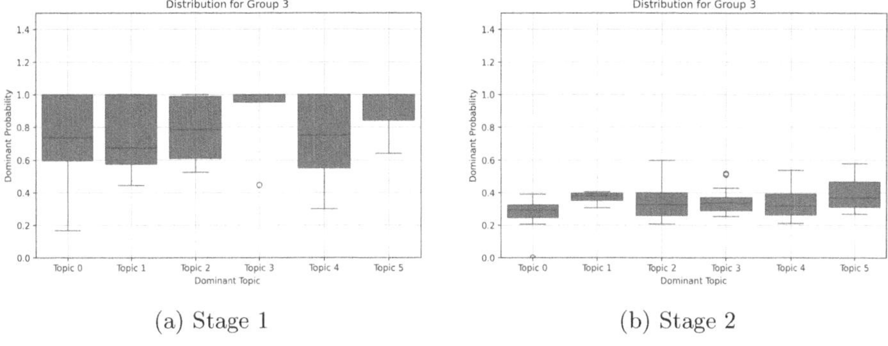

(a) Stage 1

(b) Stage 2

Fig. 5. Topic probability distribution for X_3 under two modeling stages.

Finally, Table 1 summarizes the Cohen's Kappa coefficient and McNemar's test results, which were used to evaluate the level of agreement between classification stages and to detect significant differences in topic assignment.

Table 1. Statistical test results for each subset

Subset	Cohen's Kappa	McNemar *p-value*
X_1 (First 100)	0.698 (substantial agreement)	0.3018 (no significant difference)
X_2 (Last 100)	0.781 (substantial agreement)	0.0117 (significant difference)
X_3 (Random)	0.423 (moderate agreement)	Not applicable (non-binary matrix)

In this case, the subsets X_1 and X_2 show substantial agreement, indicating that when fewer topics are defined, the classification tends to be more consistent. However, only X_2 shows a statistically significant difference according to McNemar's test, suggesting that the classification behavior changed between stages for that subset.

Table 2 shows the distribution of documents by dominant topic across the three subsets and both stages. In stage 1, the code generated only two topics for the subsets X_1 and X_2, which explains their exclusive distribution between Topics 0 and 1. This limited topic granularity results in a more concentrated and interpretable classification structure, where most documents are consistently assigned to one of the two categories. In contrast, X_3 was modeled with six topics in Stage 1, resulting in a broader distribution that reflects greater thematic diversity within the subset.

In stage 2, X was used to classify the documents using each subset n, but the number of topics used in the classification matched those from Stage 1: two topics for X_1 and X_2, and six topics for X_3. As a result, the documents in X_1 and X_2 remained heavily concentrated in Topics 0 and 1, confirming consistent behavior between stages. In contrast, X_3 exhibited a broader distribution across

Table 2. Number of articles per dominant topic in Stage 1 and Stage 2 across subsets

Topic	X_1	X_2	X_3
0	48	48	24
1	51	51	15
2	–	–	13
3	–	–	5
4	–	–	31
5	–	–	12

Stage 1

Topic	X_1	X_2	X_3
0	266	266	126
1	275	275	10
2	–	–	68
3	–	–	123
4	–	–	94
5	–	–	120

Stage 2

all six topics, consistent with the greater topic granularity used in its Stage 1 configuration.

These results suggest that subsets X_1 and X_2 contain more thematically homogeneous content, which is effectively captured even with simpler models. In contrast, the random subset X_3 displays greater thematic diversity, which may require a more granular topic structure to be adequately represented or may indicate inconsistencies in classification.

5 Discussion and Conclusion

The results obtained from the different subsets allowed for analyzing the topic model's behavior under varying input and validation conditions. In general, using the LDA model as a support tool in literature reviews proved effective for organizing large volumes of information with a reasonable level of thematic coherence. This was particularly evident in subsets X_1 and X_2, where the article selection was conducted by a single person, resulting in greater consistency in topic classification.

In contrast, subset X_3, which was randomly selected and reviewed by multiple individuals, showed less internal consistency. This was reflected in a lower Kappa value (0.423) and greater dispersion in the dominant topic probabilities. Additionally, the McNemar test could not be applied due to the non-binary nature of the confusion matrix, further suggesting reduced stability in topic assignments for this group.

A possible explanation for this heterogeneity is the involvement of different people in the article selection process, introducing variability in the inclusion criteria. This indicates that when human judgment is not standardized, the resulting dataset may lack thematic consistency, affecting both model training and topic assignment.

Based on this observation, future model iterations are planned for subset X_3, incorporating adjustments in topic definition and preprocessing. The aim is to evaluate how the thematic content changes and whether consistent results can still be obtained under more heterogeneous human criteria. This will help assess the model's sensitivity to different configurations and reflect on the role of manual selection in the early stages of literature review.

The suggested two-stage LDA method provides a scalable and methodical strategy to organizing extensive document collections, in contrast to a wholly manual literature review, while maintaining the interpretive benefits of human expertise. A completely manual process necessitates the individual reading and categorization of each article, which can be unnecessarily time-consuming for datasets surpassing several hundred articles. In contrast, our methodology utilizes topic modeling to create semantically coherent clusters, exemplified by the X_1 and X_2 groups, enabling reviewers to focus their reading on the most thematically pertinent subsets. This targeted reading approach diminishes cognitive burden and enhances efficiency while maintaining thematic richness, as evidenced by the correspondence between automated topic clusters and specialized themes (e.g., industrial sustainability, emission regulation, and logistics network optimization). Thus, the hybrid methodology enhances both the efficiency of the initial filtering phase and the uniformity of topic coverage relative to unstructured manual assessment. This study's findings affirm that the LDA model is an effective instrument for organizing and categorizing scientific literature, especially during the exploratory research phase. It can be particularly advantageous for early-career academics, helping them recognize essential themes and acquire a comprehensive understanding of available literature. Nonetheless, the quality of the outcomes is significantly contingent upon the initial keyword selection and article screening choices; if they are inconsistent or ambiguous, thematic coherence may diminish. In this context, computational analysis ought to be regarded not as a substitute for human judgment, but as an adjunct that enhances and fortifies it.

Disclosure of Interests. The authors have no competing interests to declare that are relevant to the content of this article.

References

1. Kometani, Y., Nagaoka, K.: Construction of a literature review support system using latent Dirichlet allocation. In: Yamamoto, S. (ed.) HIMI 2016. LNCS, vol. 9735, pp. 159–167. Springer, Cham (2016). https://doi.org/10.1007/978-3-319-40397-7_16
2. Kongthon, A., Haruechaiyasak, C., Thaiprayoon, S.: Enhancing the literature review using author-topic profiling. In: Buchanan, G., Masoodian, M., Cunningham, S.J. (eds.) ICADL 2008. LNCS, vol. 5362, pp. 335–338. Springer, Heidelberg (2008). https://doi.org/10.1007/978-3-540-89533-6_38
3. Asmussen, C.B., Møller, C.: Smart literature review: a practical topic modelling approach to exploratory literature review. J. Big Data **6**(1), 1–18 (2019). https://doi.org/10.1186/s40537-019-0255-7
4. Espinoza Pérez, A.T., Vásquez, Ó.C.: How to measure sustainability in the supply chain design: an integrated proposal from an extensive and systematic literature review. Sustainability **15**(9), 7138 (2023)

5. Snyder, H.: Literature review as a research methodology: an overview and guidelines. J. Bus. Res. **104**, 333–339 (2019)
6. Thakur, K., Kumar, V.: Application of text mining techniques on scholarly research articles: methods and tools. New Rev. Acad. Librariansh. **28**(3), 279–302 (2022)
7. Hairani, H., Janhasmadja, M., Tholib, A., Ximenes Guterres, J., Ariyanto, Y.: Thesis topic modeling study: latent Dirichlet allocation (LDA) and machine learning approach. Int. J. Eng. Comput. Sci. Appl. **3**(2), 51–60 (2024). https://doi.org/10.30812/ijecsa.v3i2.4375
8. Luo, Z., Amayri, M., Fan, W., Ihou, K.E., Bouguila, N.: Parallel inference for cross-collection latent generalized Dirichlet allocation model and applications. Expert Syst. Appl. **238**, 121720 (2024). https://doi.org/10.1016/j.eswa.2023.121720

Exploring Road Crash Injury Risk Factors with Random Forest

Maria P. G. Martins[1(✉)], Isabel M. Lopes[1,2,3,4], and Paulo D. F. Gouveia[1]

[1] Instituto Politécnico de Bragança, Campus de Santa Apolónia, 5300-253 Bragança, Portugal
{prud,isalopes,pgouveia}@ipb.pt
[2] UNIAG, Instituto Politécnico de Bragança, Campus de Santa Apolónia, 5300-253 Bragança, Portugal
[3] Algoritmi, Universidade do Minho, Largo do Paço, 4704-553 Braga, Portugal
[4] CEDRI, Instituto Politécnico de Bragança, Campus de Santa Apolónia, 5300-253 Bragança, Portugal

Abstract. A Random Forest model was trained on a large real-world road-crash dataset (328,407 cases) to predict the occurrence of physical injury. A total of 19 explanatory variables were considered, covering driver, vehicle, environmental, and contextual characteristics. To address the significant class imbalance, eight resampling techniques were tested, including SMOTE, undersampling, and Tomek Links. The model was optimized through an exhaustive grid search combined with 10-fold cross-validation, using F1-score as the optimization criterion. The best model achieved an F1-score of 58.4, an AUC of 85.1, and a G-Mean of 75.4 on the hold-out test set. The feature importance analysis confirmed several well-established findings in road safety research, notably the strong influence of vehicle category (with motorcycles standing out), accident type, and the greater vulnerability of teenage drivers. At the same time, the model revealed less intuitive patterns: run-off-road crashes were identified as the most likely to result in injuries, whereas collisions with obstacles within the roadway were associated with the lowest injury rates. These results demonstrate the potential of Random Forest for identifying relevant risk factors, combining predictive performance with interpretability, and supporting more effective injury prevention strategies. Furthermore, the model validated known risk factors while uncovering less intuitive patterns, reinforcing its value for evidence-based road safety analysis.

Keywords: machine learning · random forest · traffic accident injury · risk factor identification · data resampling

1 Introduction

Road traffic accidents remain one of the most critical global safety challenges, ranking among the leading causes of mortality, serious injuries, and permanent disabilities. Understanding the factors that contribute to the occurrence

T. Guarda et al. (Eds.): ARTIIS 2025, CCIS 2789, pp. 277–290, 2026.
https://doi.org/10.1007/978-3-032-16758-3_22

of physical injuries in road crashes is therefore essential for developing effective preventive strategies, planning infrastructure, improving driver education, and enhancing emergency response systems.

The complexity of road accidents makes this task particularly demanding. Human factors – such as driver behavior – interact with environmental conditions, road infrastructure, vehicle characteristics, and even surrounding traffic, making it difficult to assess all these determinants in an integrated manner.

In this context, machine learning methods – particularly Random Forest – have gained increasing relevance. These algorithms offer significant advantages in modeling complex relationships, extracting patterns from large datasets, and estimating the relative importance of predictive variables. Random Forests are especially notable for their high accuracy, robustness to overfitting, tolerance to noise and computational efficiency, even when applied to large-scale data. They are therefore a valuable tool both for predicting crash outcomes and for understanding their underlying causes.

Random Forest (RF), introduced by Breiman [2], are an ensemble learning method that builds multiple decision trees during training and combines their predictions to improve overall performance. Based on the principle that a set of weak learners can produce a strong classifier, RF introduces randomness in data and feature selection, increasing tree diversity and reducing variance without increasing bias.

In this study, we apply RF to investigate the key risk factors associated with injuries resulting from road crashes. To this end, we use a large-scale, high-dimensional real-world dataset that includes variables related to the driver, the vehicle, the infrastructure, and the surrounding context. With this research, we aim to generate actionable knowledge that can support the development of public road safety policies and more effective prevention measures.

2 Literature Review

Traffic accident severity prediction has increasingly relied on machine learning, with RF emerging as a popular choice due to its ability to handle high-dimensional nonlinear data, its built-in interpretability, and its high computational efficiency when compared to other commonly used techniques such as Support Vector Machines (SVM) and Artificial Neural Networks (ANN). RF ensembles of decision trees yield strong predictive performance while providing feature–importance scores to elucidate influential variables.

A review conducted by Santos et al. [5], based on 56 peer-reviewed articles obtained from major scientific databases and citation analysis, showed that RF was the algorithm with the best overall performance, achieving superior results in 70% of the cases in which it was applied, outperforming models such as SVM and ANN.

Numerous empirical studies across different countries have confirmed the utility and adaptability of RF in crash severity prediction. In Bangladesh, Bhuiyan et al. [1] compiled crash data from newspapers and applied RF with feature selection, finding RF outperformed Decision Tree and Naïve Bayes. The RF model highlighted nine of 14 variables as significant including driver gender, license type, seatbelt use, vehicle type, road surface, road class, crash day/time, and injury location. These results underscore how RF-based analysis can reveal a diverse mix of driver, vehicle, roadway and temporal factors contributing to severe crashes in a developing-country context. In a separate study, also from Bangladesh, Sakib et al. [4] proposed an ensemble-based approach to investigate the factors influencing the occurrence of fatalities in road traffic accidents, using an imbalanced dataset containing 20,381 records. The study evaluated eight machine learning algorithms, including RF, and applied eight resampling techniques combined with bagging strategies. The best performance was achieved with the combination of Gradient Boosting Machine, Random Under-Sampling and bagging optimized via Bayesian Optimization, reaching a G-mean score of 65.23 and an Macro F1 score of 60.06. Among the most relevant factors identified for fatal outcomes were collision type, vehicle type, road classification, vehicle movement, and the presence of traffic control.

In Thailand, Mohamad et al. [3] trained eight algorithms on 112,837 crash records. RF achieved the best binary classification performance (AUC = 0.768, accuracy = 0.777, precision = 0.752, recall = 0.777), outperforming SVM, ANN, etc. The top predictors were road type (highway), speeding, time of day (daylight), absence of lighting at night, and driver gender. The RF model, however, had low recall for fatal crashes (0.198), reflecting the rarity and complexity of fatality prediction.

In China, Wang et al. [7] combined RF with SHAP (Shapley Additive Explanations) to identify critical risk factors, analyzing crash data from Shenyang city (20182020) using 19 variables related to road, temporal, environmental, and at-fault driver characteristics. The dataset was divided into two categories based on the at-fault party: vulnerable road users and motor vehicle drivers. The RFSHAP analysis revealed that travel mode, season, and road speed limit were the most influential risk factors in accidents where motor vehicle drivers were at fault. Additionally, the Apriori algorithm was used to explore multi-factor interaction patterns in fatal crashes.

In the United States, Wang et al. [8] developed a metaheuristic-optimized RF model to analyze 2020 interstate crash data. The model, tuned using the Crown Porcupine Optimizer, achieved over 90% accuracy, recall, F1-score, and precision – high results that are rarely observed in real-world applications. GIS-based analysis of feature importance revealed that temperature and weather conditions were among the most influential factors in crash severity. The authors used the RF-derived importance scores to propose safety recommendations, such as improved roadway lighting and fatigue alert systems at night.

All these studies illustrate important methodological insights, with RF's intrinsic feature-importance scores standing out as a widely used tool to highlight critical risk factors. To finalize, in comparative evaluations, RF typically matches or exceeds the performance of techniques like SVM, ANN and Naïve Bayes. For example, in the Thailand case, Mohamad et al. [3] found RF superior to SVM,

K-Nearest Neighbors, ANN, Decision Tree, Naïve Bayes, Logistic Regression, and Gradient Boosting. However, some contexts, such as in the study by Sakib et al. [4], favor other methods. Arifeen et al. [6] also noted that a Bayesian neural network[1] outperformed RF on Hong Kong pedestrian crash data – although RF still provided interpretability advantages in a study focused on identifying key risk factors. Overall, RF and other tree ensembles (e.g. Gradient Boosting and its variants) often achieve state-of-the-art accuracy in crash severity tasks, but RF's strength lies in its balanced predictive performance and transparent risk–factor analysis.

3 Dataset Description

The original dataset contained records of road traffic accidents that took place across Portuguese roads during the period from 2022 to 2024. These data, properly anonymized, were organized into two distinct tables: one containing accident-related information, with 34 columns and over 250,000 entries; and another comprising data on the vehicles involved, with 27 columns and over 430,000 records.

3.1 Preprocessing

Given that the objective of this study is to identify the main factors associated with the occurrence of physical injuries in vehicles involved in traffic accidents, the vehicle table was used as the primary source for constructing the training dataset. Selected features from the accident table were subsequently integrated. This was achieved through a left join operation between the two tables, using the accident identifier as the key. Prior to merging, a feature selection step was performed, excluding from both tables all columns lacking explanatory value or containing a significant amount of missing data.

Due to the large size of the dataset, missing, invalid, or anomalous values were handled by removing the corresponding rows, thereby ensuring data consistency and reliability.

Non-motorized vehicles, such as bicycles and animal-drawn vehicles, were excluded. Additionally, highly specific or non-standard motorized vehicles, such as electric personal mobility devices, scooters, tractors, and other agricultural machinery, were also removed.

To exclude buses and similar passenger transport vehicles, all entries involving more than ten occupants were eliminated. Likewise, vehicles involved in pedestrian collisions were excluded, as the focus of the study is on injuries sustained by the occupants of the vehicles.

All types of motorcycles were uniformly recoded under a single category: motorcycle. To reduce computational complexity and eliminate low-informative

[1] A sophisticated machine learning technique which combines the benefits of ANN and Bayesian theory.

data, rare categories in nominal categorical variables were aggregated into a new 'other' category.

The time of the accident was categorized into four time periods – dawn, morning, afternoon, and night – and the accident date, together with the vehicle registration date, was used to compute the vehicle's age.

Nominal categorical features were encoded using one-hot encoding, whereas ordinal categorical variables were transformed using ordinal encoding to preserve their inherent order.

Outlier removal was approached conservatively. Instead of applying generic filtering techniques, specific and controlled exclusions were performed. For example, vehicles driven by individuals younger than 15 or older than 90 years were removed, as well as vehicles older than 50 years.

Injury data, originally provided as separate quantitative counts for fatal, serious, and minor injuries recorded independently for drivers and passengers, were first consolidated into a single ordinal variable, severity, with the following ordered categories: fatal injuries, serious injuries, minor injuries, and no injuries. Subsequently, considering the ordinal nature of injury severity and in order to avoid multiclass classification, a hierarchical formulation was adopted using cumulative boolean targets: (i) fatal_injury; (ii) serious_injury, which includes both serious and fatal cases; and (iii) injury, which encompasses all injury cases, including serious and fatal ones.

As a result of the preprocessing steps, the final dataset comprised 19 features, 328,407 instances, and three alternative target variables. The feature names, along with their types, representative values, and distributions, are summarized in Table 1.

4 Methodology

All data processing and modeling tasks were performed in a Python environment, using a set of widely adopted machine learning libraries, including pandas, numpy, imblearn, matplotlib, seaborn, and most notably, scikit-learn.

The dataset was initially split into training and testing subsets using an 80–20 stratified random sampling strategy, resulting in 262,725 instances for training and 65,682 for testing. Successive RF models were trained and fine-tuned on the training data and subsequently evaluated on the reserved test set to assess their final performance.

Given the significant class imbalance in the dataset – clearly observable in the distribution of the three boolean target variables shown in Table 1 – we attempted to mitigate this issue through eight different resampling techniques, as proposed in [4]: SMOTE, Random Under-Sampling (RUS), Random Over-Sampling (ROS), ADASYN, Tomek Links, Near Miss, SMOTETomek, and SMOTEENN.

Despite these efforts, it became apparent that meaningful performance could not be achieved for severely imbalanced subsets, such as those used for predicting serious and fatal injuries, which contained only 1.4% and 0.3% positive cases,

Table 1. Overview of the preprocessed dataset: 19 features, 3 target variables, and 328,407 cases.

Name	Category	Type	Values	cases	Rate
vehicle class	vehicle	nominal	light	292847	89.2%
			heavy	15670	4.8%
			motorcycle	19890	6.1%
plate country	vehicle	binary	portugal	317888	96.8%
			other	10519	3.2%
vehicle status	vehicle	binary	moving	325279	99.0%
			parked	3128	1.0%
num occupants	vehicle	discrete	1..10	–	–
vehicle age	vehicle	discrete	0..50	–	–
accident type	accident	nominal	frontal	27226	8.3%
			side with moving vehicle	101725	31.0%
			rear with moving vehicle	73389	22.3%
			single vehicle runoff	33352	10.2%
			in lane vehicle collision	23816	7.3%
			in lane obstacle collision	15318	4.7%
			off lane collision	15281	4.7%
			separator crossing	1129	0.3%
			with rollover	7480	2.3%
			chain collision	9691	3.0%
			other	20000	6.1%
probable cause	accident	nominal	distraction	174696	53.2%
			excessive speed	13007	4.0%
			drunk driving	6108	1.9%
			other	134596	41.0%
rollover	accident	boolean	–	10162	3.1%
num vehicles involved	accident	discrete	1..17	–	–
num heavy vehicles	accident	discrete	1..4	–	–
driver gender	driver	binary	female	102039	31.1%
			male	226368	68.9%
driver age	driver	discrete	15..90	–	–
driver bac	driver	continuous	0..4.6	–	–
road	road	nominal	highway	33559	10.2%
			main itinerary	2217	0.7%
			complementary itinerary	7763	2.4%
			national road	74965	22.8%
			street	172339	52.5%
			other	37564	11.4%
urban area	road	boolean	–	241901	73.7%
weather	atmospheric	nominal	clear	269201	82.0%
			rain	56628	17.2%
			fog	1974	0.6%
			snow	604	0.2%
time of day	time	nominal	dawn	13145	4.0%
			morning	99146	30.2%
			afternoon	136515	41.6%
			night	79601	24.2%
weekend	time	boolean	–	90793	27.6%
holiday	time	boolean	–	7822	2.4%
fatal injury (target)	accident	boolean	–	822	0.3%
serious injury (target)	accident	boolean	–	4457	1.4%
injury (target)	accident	boolean	–	54424	16.6%

respectively. Consequently, our study focused solely on the detection of all injury cases – light, serious, or fatal – which together represented 16.6% of the total dataset. Even so, the resulting dataset remained highly imbalanced.

Hyperparameter tuning was conducted using GridSearchCV() from scikit-learn, a common method for exhaustive search over specified parameter grids. This process employed 10-fold cross-validation and used the F1-score as the primary evaluation metric to identify the best-performing model.

Once the best model was trained and optimized, it was evaluated on the test set, which had been kept isolated throughout the process. Although seven different evaluation metrics were considered in this final assessment, the comparison of model variants and the interpretation of results were always grounded in the F1-score. This metric was selected for its conservative nature and its ability to reflect real-world performance in highly imbalanced scenarios. Since the F1-score is highly sensitive to low values of either precision or recall (as it is their harmonic mean), a high F1-score necessarily indicates strong model performance, as it ensures that neither metric is excessively low. As will be shown in the results, F1-score consistently proves to be more conservative than its counterparts, including macro-F1, AUC, G-Mean, and accuracy.

Finally, the core objective of this study – identifying and analyzing the most relevant explanatory variables – was addressed. For this purpose, we leveraged a key feature of the RF algorithm: its ability to compute the importance of predictive variables based on their contribution to decision-making across the ensemble. In the context of this work, this functionality enabled us to rank all features according to their relevance in predicting injury occurrence (see Fig. 2). Once the most influential risk factors were identified, a more detailed analysis was conducted to examine the nature and direction of their impact on the probability of injury.

5 Results and Discussion

As described in the methodology, the goal was to induce a RF model capable of predicting the occurrence of physical injuries in vehicles involved in crashes. The preprocessed dataset was initially split into training and testing subsets. Eight resampling techniques were applied to the training data in order to address class imbalance.

For each resampled training subset, a separate RF model was trained and fine-tuned. Table 2 presents the performance of each of these models, evaluated across seven different metrics. For comparison, the table also includes a baseline model trained on the original, imbalanced training set. Additionally, a model using the class_weight = 'balanced' parameter of the RF algorithm was tested – referred to in the table as the "balanced RF" model – which automatically adjusts class weights inversely proportional to class frequencies in the target variable.

Interestingly, the F1-score, which combines precision and recall, consistently yielded lower values than all other metrics. This empirical evidence supports the

Table 2. Comparison of different resampling techniques – including the inherent balancing performed by RF – using various classification metrics (the highest value in each column is underlined).

Method	F1	Macro-F1	Precision	Recall	AUC	G-Mean	Accuracy
Imbalanced data	54.3	73.7	<u>74.2</u>	42.8	85.7	64.4	<u>88.0</u>
balanced RF	<u>58.4</u>	74.6	53.7	63.8	85.1	75.4	84.9
SMOTE	58.3	<u>75.2</u>	61.6	55.3	85.0	71.8	<u>86.9</u>
SMOTETomek	58.2	<u>75.2</u>	61.7	55.2	85.0	71.7	<u>86.9</u>
ROS	57.8	73.9	51.0	66.7	85.4	76.3	83.9
ADASYN	57.7	74.8	59.0	56.4	<u>89.8</u>	72.1	86.3
SMOTEENN	56.4	72.7	47.7	69.1	85.1	76.6	82.3
RUS	56.1	72.1	45.9	<u>71.9</u>	85.6	<u>77.3</u>	81.3
TomekLinks	55.9	74.5	72.5	45.5	85.7	66.3	88.1
NearMiss	43.7	62.2	32.4	67.1	78.2	69.6	71.3

notion that F1-score is the most robust and reliable metric for evaluating models trained on imbalanced datasets. Based on this metric, none of the resampling techniques outperformed the inherent capacity of the RF algorithm to manage class imbalance. The “balanced RF” model achieved the highest F1-score (58.4), along with a Macro-F1 of 74.6, G-Mean of 75.4, AUC of 85.1, accuracy of 84.9 (less meaningful in imbalanced settings), precision of 53.7, and recall of 63.8. A precision above 50% in a dataset with significant class imbalance is considered encouraging, particularly when accompanied by a similarly positive recall, as is the case here.

It is also worth noting that the results reported in [4] are of the same order of magnitude as those obtained here. However, they refer to a different context: on one hand, they are more challenging as they focus on predicting fatal injuries (a more imbalanced problem); on the other hand, their evaluation relies on Macro-F1, a metric that tends to be higher but less conservative, as it gives equal weight to performance on both positive (minority) and negative (majority) classes.

Given these results, the remainder of this study focused on the “balanced RF” model, whose ROC curve is shown in Fig. 1. This model was fine-tuned with the following hyperparameters: max_depth = 20, criterion = ‘entropy’, and max_features = ‘sqrt’ – controlling tree depth, split quality metric, and feature sampling, respectively. Additionally, class_weight = ‘balanced’, as previously mentioned, was used to address class imbalance, and the number of trees was set to n_estimators = 201, as higher values were not expected to yield significant performance gains relative to the increased computational cost. All other hyperparameters were left at their default values.

Using the relative feature importances provided by the RF algorithm, we constructed the plot in Fig. 2, which highlights the most relevant explanatory variables for predicting physical injuries in (the occupants of) crashed vehicles.

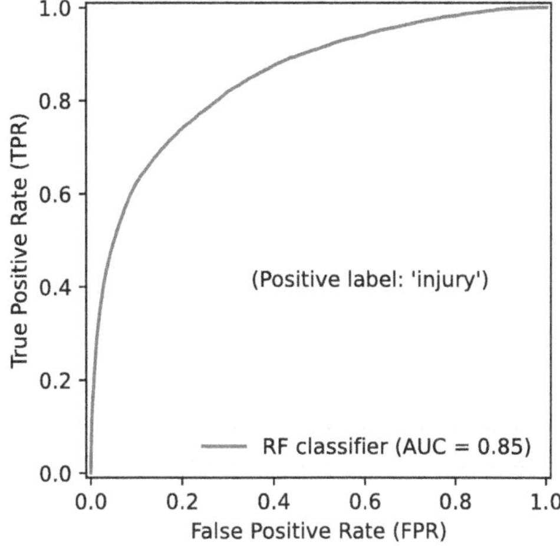

Fig. 1. ROC curve of the RF binary classifier for injury prediction.

The top five factors, in descending order of importance, were: vehicle class, accident type, vehicle age, number of vehicles involved, and driver age.

Two of these, vehicle age and driver age, were somewhat unexpected. To better understand the role of these and the other three most important factors, we conducted a more detailed analysis of how each influences injury occurrence.

1. **Vehicle class** – Figure 3 shows the relative importance of each vehicle class. As expected, motorcycles have a strong positive influence on the likelihood of injury, while heavy vehicles show lower influence. However, the next chart (Fig. 4), which compares injury rates for presence and absence of each category, reveals the direction of these effects more clearly. Motorcycles increase injury risk, while other classes tend to reduce it.
2. **Accident type** – Figure 5 presents the importance of each accident type. The four types with greatest influence on injury probability are: single run-off-road, collision with a roadside object, head on collision, and rollover. Interestingly, as shown in Fig. 6, collisions with roadside objects are associated with a lower likelihood of injury.
3. **Vehicle age** – Figure 7 illustrates normalized injury rates by vehicle age. Injuries are least frequent in vehicles around 7 years old and become more common after about 32–33 years.
4. **Number of vehicles involved** – Figure 8 shows that the probability of injury among the occupants of a crashed vehicle decreases as the number of other vehicles involved in the accident increases. However, this reflects a logical probabilistic relationship rather than a meaningful explanatory factor, as a greater number of vehicles increases the likelihood that the vehicle under analysis was not among those most directly involved in the crash.
5. **Driver age** – Figure 9 shows normalized injury rates by driver age. The lowest rates occur between ages 40 and 45, with a gradual increase beyond

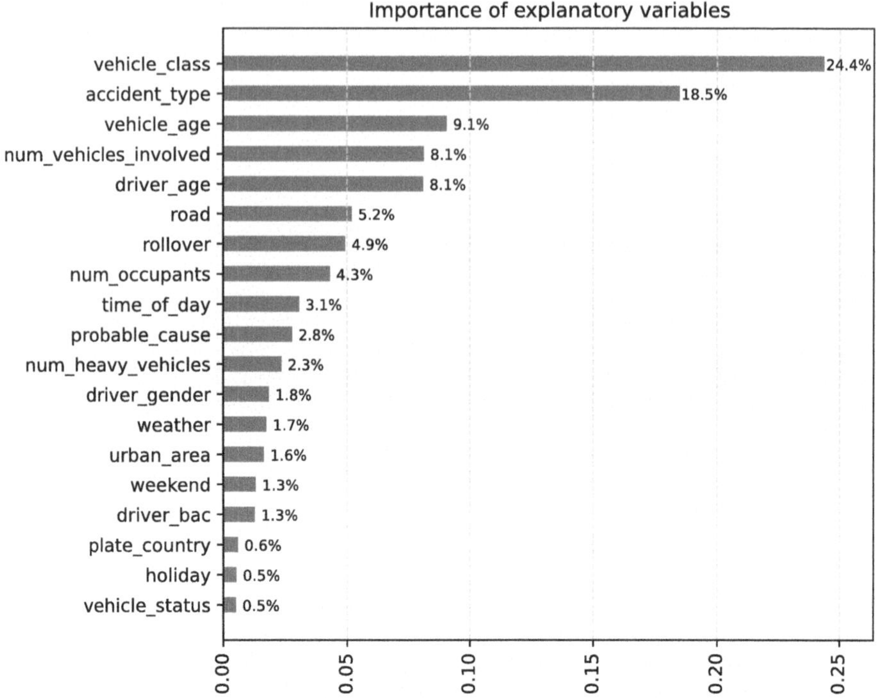

Fig. 2. Relative importance of features in injury occurrence.

that. But the most striking evidence is the sharp increase in the likelihood of injury as driver age drops below 19, with the proportion of injury cases approaching 80%. This may reflect both the popularity of motorcycles among younger drivers and their relative inexperience and riskier behavior.

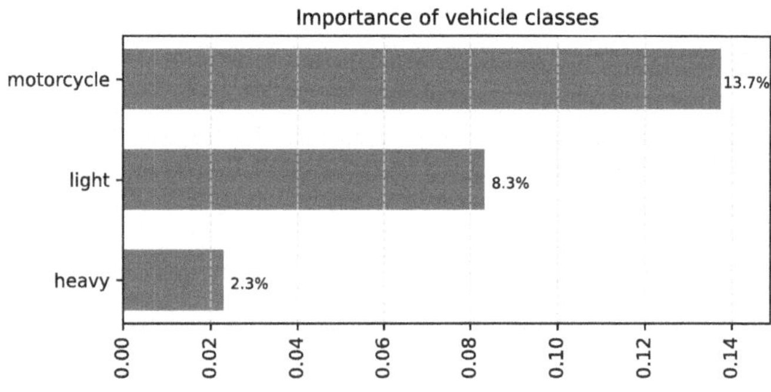

Fig. 3. Importance of vehicle classes in injury prediction.

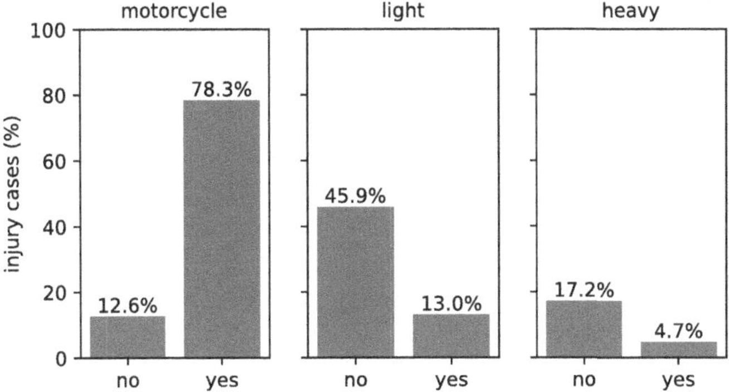

Fig. 4. Nature of the effect of vehicle classes on injury occurrence.

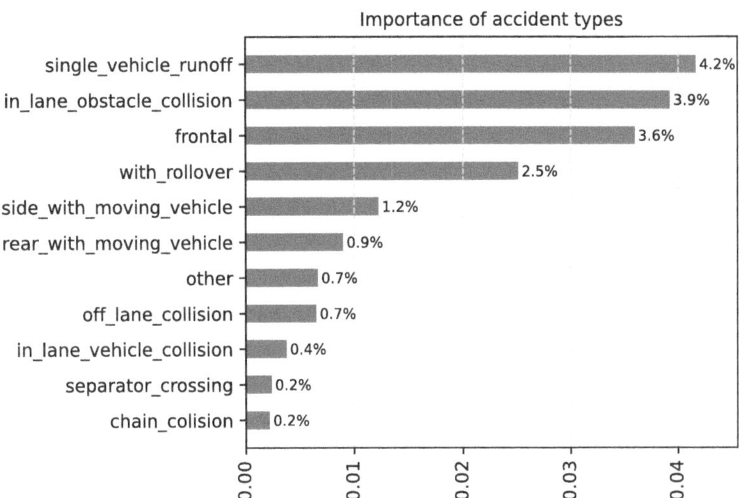

Fig. 5. Importance of accident types in injury prediction.

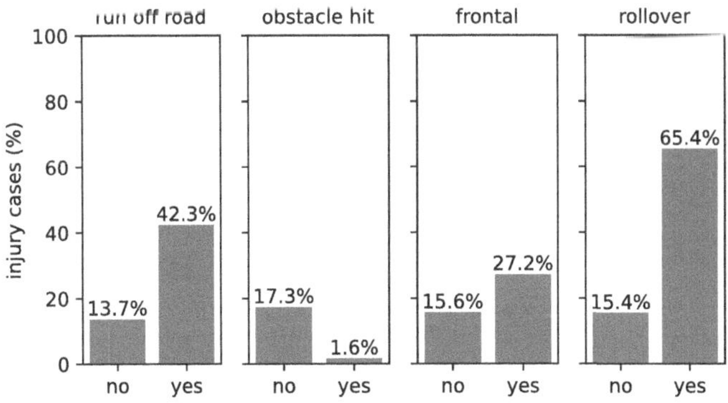

Fig. 6. Nature of the effect of accident types on injury occurrence.

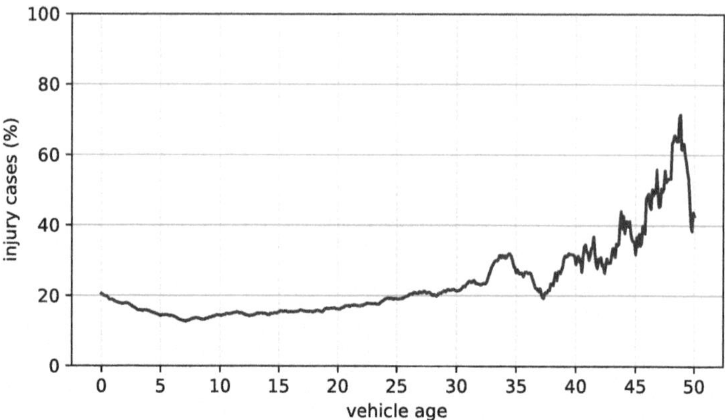

Fig. 7. Proportion of injury cases by vehicle age.

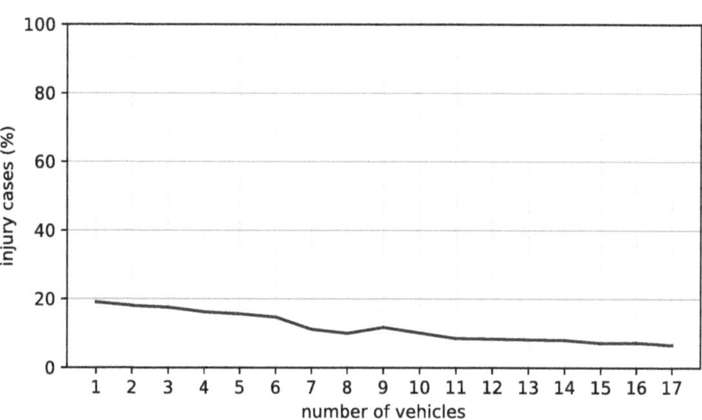

Fig. 8. Proportion of Injury Cases by number of vehicles involved in the accident.

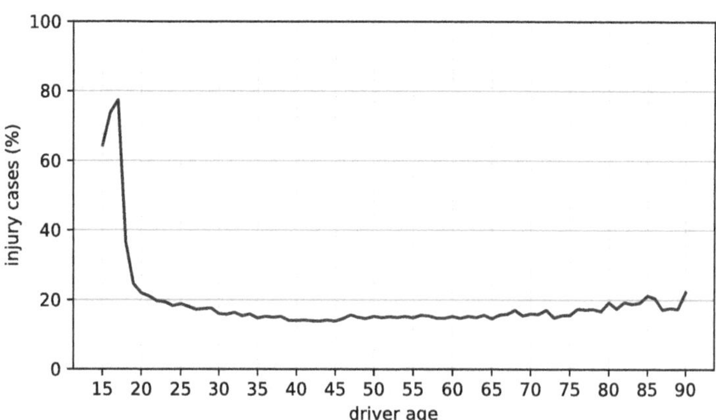

Fig. 9. Proportion of injury cases by driver age.

6 Conclusions

This study aimed to identify the key risk factors that contribute to the occurrence of physical injuries among occupants of vehicles involved in road crashes, using one of the most prominent machine learning algorithms – the Random Forest.

The top five most influential factors identified, in descending order of importance, were: vehicle class, accident type, vehicle age, number of vehicles involved, and driver age.

The results, on the one hand, reinforce well-established knowledge – such as the critical role of vehicle category and accident type; the elevated injury risk associated with motorcycles and older vehicles; and the increased vulnerability of teenage drivers. On the other hand, the study also uncovered less intuitive findings, such as the fact that single-vehicle crashes (roff-road accidents) are the most likely to result in injuries, while collisions with roadside obstacles are the least likely.

These insights may support the development of more targeted and effective traffic safety interventions.

It is important to note, however, that several well-known factors associated with injury – such as collision speed[2], the presence or absence of passive safety systems (e.g. seat belts, airbags), and even falling asleep at the wheel – were not included in the analysis due to the unavailability of such data in the recorded crash reports. Nonetheless, we have no doubt that incorporating these variables – particularly collision speed – would significantly enhance the predictive performance of the models.

This limitation, along with the use of a particularly conservative evaluation metric (the F1-score), likely explains why the performance of our models did not always reach the levels reported in some of the referenced studies. Despite these limitations, the study relied on a large-scale, high-dimensional real-world dataset, which enhances the robustness and practical relevance of the findings. The principal contribution of this work lies in the application of the proposed methodology to Portuguese road traffic data, thereby demonstrating its effectiveness in this specific context.

From a more technical perspective, this study also highlighted the ability of Random Forest to effectively handle imbalanced datasets, thereby partially alleviating the need for additional balancing techniques. Furthermore, the F1 score was shown to be an appropriate metric for evaluating models induced from such datasets, due to its ability to correctly balance precision and recall in scenarios with unequal class distributions.

Future research could benefit from incorporating additional contextual and behavioral factors, and in-vehicle safety technologies, to further refine predictive models and deepen the understanding of injury risk dynamics in road traffic accidents. Moreover, future work may also explore alternative machine learning

[2] Although excessive speed is one of the classes of the categorical variable probable cause, it is believed that it was not recorded with sufficient accuracy (only 4% of the cases, as shown in Table 1).

techniques or even deep learning approaches to enhance model performance and uncover more complex patterns.

Disclosure of Interests. The authors have no competing interests to declare that are relevant to the content of this article.

References

1. Bhuiyan, H., et al.: Crash severity analysis and risk factors identification based on an alternate data source: a case study of developing country. Sci. Rep. **12**(1), 21243 (2022). https://doi.org/10.1038/s41598-022-25361-5
2. Breiman, L.: Random forests. Mach. Learn. **45**, 5–32 (2001)
3. Mohamad, I., JomnonKwao, S., Ratanavaraha, V.: Machine learning predictive performance in road accident severity: a case study from Thailand. Results Eng. **26**, 104833 (2025)
4. Sakib, N., Paul, T., Anwari, N., Hadiuzzaman, M.: Ensemble-based model to investigate factors influencing road crash fatality for imbalanced data. Transp. Eng. **18**, 100284 (2024)
5. Santos, K., Dias, J.P., Amado, C.: A literature review of machine learning algorithms for crash injury severity prediction. J. Saf. Res. **80**, 254–269 (2022). https://doi.org/10.1016/j.jsr.2021.12.007
6. Ul Arifeen, S., Ali, M., Macioszek, E.: Analysis of vehicle pedestrian crash severity using advanced machine learning techniques. Arch. Transp. **68** (2023)
7. Wang, J., Ma, S., Jiao, P., Ji, L., Sun, X., Lu, H.: Analyzing the risk factors of traffic accident severity using a combination of random forest and association rules. Appl. Sci. **13**(14), 8559 (2023). https://doi.org/10.3390/app13148559
8. Wang, X., Su, Y., Zheng, Z., Xu, L.: Prediction and interpretive of motor vehicle traffic crash severity based on random forest optimized by meta-heuristic algorithm. Heliyon **10**(16), e35595 (2024). https://doi.org/10.1016/j.heliyon.2024.e35595

Benchmarking YOLO and RT-DETR Models for Streaks Detection

Diogo Ramalho Fernandes and Olivier Parisot(✉)

Luxembourg Institute of Science and Technology (LIST), 5 Avenue des Hauts-Fourneaux, 4362 Esch-sur-Alzette, Luxembourg
{diogo.ramalho-fernandes,olivier.parisot}@list.lu

Abstract. Artificial satellites and space debris increasingly contaminate astronomical sky images with linear streaks caused by reflected sunlight. These artifacts compromise the quality of long-exposure observations and pose challenges for automated image analysis. These streaks, usually coming from satellites and debris, can also come from near-Earth asteroids (NEAs) that can produce similar patterns when illuminated by the Sun during long exposures. This work explores object detection using Deep Learning to automatically identify these streaks. We train declinations of YOLO and RT-DETR architectures on StreaksYoloDataset, a dataset of 2,388 annotated raw astronomical images captured between 2022 and 2023. The models are evaluated under different background conditions and illumination levels. Our results show that both YOLO models achieve high mean average precision (mAP), demonstrating their effectiveness in detecting streaks even in noisy or low-contrast conditions. This study lays the foundation for automated streak removal or restoration into astronomical image analysis pipelines and opens the door to future integration of generative restoration techniques and intelligent monitoring systems of real-time detection.

Keywords: Streaks · Object detection · Deep Learning

1 Introduction

Modern astronomy is entering an era of unprecedented data acquisition, with large telescopes capturing deep-sky images at increasing volume and frequency [26], requiring AI-driven approaches for efficient processing. However, the increasing number of artificial satellites and space debris now poses a major challenge: linear streaks appearing due to solar reflections, contaminating long-exposure images and degrading data quality. This incident is becoming worse due to the large number of artificial objects in orbit. According to the United Nations Office for Outer Space Affairs (UNOOSA), in 2024, more than 2,800 objects were launched [22], and the total number of objects recorded since 1957 exceeds 20,000 [23].

T. Guarda et al. (Eds.): ARTIIS 2025, CCIS 2789, pp. 291–300, 2026.
https://doi.org/10.1007/978-3-032-16758-3_23

The streaks, often caused by satellites and debris, can also be the effect from the fast movement of natural objects like near-Earth asteroids (NEAs), creating similar linear patterns when illuminated by the Sun during long exposures [7].

In traditional approaches, streaks were manually processed by masking filters or by image processing using techniques such as Hough [14] or Radon transforms [19] within temporal co-addition pipelines. While effective for small datasets or controlled conditions, these methods are not very well adapted for large observatory projects such as the Vera C. Rubin Observatory and its Legacy Survey of Space and Time (LSST), where thousands of images must be processed each night.

More recently, Deep Learning techniques have been introduced to improve automated streak detection. A U-Netbased segmentation model was proposed and shown to outperform traditional methods in both accuracy and processing time [9], confirming the potential of neural networks in astronomical imaging tasks. To overcome these limitations, we propose a data-driven approach using Deep Learning. Specifically, we explore variants of the YOLO (You Only Look Once), a Convolutional Neural Network (CNN) as an object detection model for real-time streak identification. This study includes a dataset of annotated astronomical images taken in recent years fully annotated with satellite and debris streaks, as well as a comparison of two YOLO models, YOLOv8 and YOLOv11, and a recent transformer for detection task called RT-DETR (Real-Time Detection Transformer), to detect streaks. Our goal is to develop a robust and accurate streak detection model that can be integrated into automated astronomical image processing pipelines, and to lay the groundwork for future enhancements such as generative restoration and intelligent interpretation to achieve fully automated astronomical image analysis.

2 Related Work

As satellite constellations are deployed more frequently, the emergence of linear streaks in astronomical images has become a significant issue [5]. Traditional approaches to address this problem consist of image stacking, temporal background elimination, and feature identification methods like the Hough or Radon transformations. For example, a method to detect streaks using image filtering and spatial correlation to monitor debris in optical images [24], or an enhanced Radon transform for better sensitivity and speed [14] have been presented. While these methods worked well on controlled or small datasets, they may no longer be effective with today's rapid and large-scale collection of astronomical data.

To tackle these issues, recent research has investigated Machine Learning and Deep Learning methods. A use case refers to a supervised pipeline utilizing U-Net segmentation trained on artificial sky images [9], which outperformed traditional techniques such as Pyradon and ASTRiDE in terms of accuracy and processing speed [16]. While U-Net excels at identifying pixel-level details, it may be excessively slow and resource-intensive for real-time applications.

Alternative U-Net-based approaches like ASTA (Automated Satellite Tracking for Astronomy) combine segmentation with probabilistic Hough transforms to enhance the detection of satellite trails [19]. Nonetheless, these techniques still require significant time to execute and demand considerable memory. In a similar way, SatStreaks [2] is a model that includes additional layers to enhance the detection of faint streaks but demands significant computing resources, which complicates scalability.

Compared to segmentation models, object detection models like YOLO offer a faster and lighter solution for streak detection. YOLO detects the desired features using bounding boxes, enabling faster inference without requiring large computational resources. Outside of astronomy, YOLO has been successfully applied to detect linear patterns such as pavement cracks [6] and rail defects [12], same features as satellite streaks. These studies show that YOLO can identify unwanted lines by extracting their fine and long structure and, in addition, with the presence of noise. Therefore, it becomes an excellent choice for real-time detection in astronomical images to detect streaks.

Besides detection, generative models are also gaining attention for their use in preprocessing. One approach used an improved Pix2Pix network with residual and self-attention layers, showing better recovery of faint signals in noisy astronomical images [25]. These techniques could help make streaks more visible before detection, making them a promising option for future research.

3 Methodology

3.1 Data

The present study is based on StreaksYoloDataset [15], a collection of 2,388 sky photos labelled as astronomical images captured with a fixed exposure time of 10 s using smart telescopes and fully annotated with the positions of actual satellite streaks present in the images. Data was initially collected between March 2022 and February 2023 in the Luxembourg Greater Region using a Stellina smart telescope. This automated instrument features a f/5 ED doublet and is equipped with an IMX178 CMOS sensor (6.4 million pixels).

After acquisition, each image was manually reviewed to discard those affected by excessive motion blur, cloud cover or sensor noise artifacts. After filtering, each remaining image was annotated with bounding boxes to indicate visible linear streaks caused by satellites or orbital debris. To improve training robustness, we included a subset of backgrounds, images without visible streaks, allowing the models to better distinguish between signal and noise during training.

The images were resized to 640×640 and converted to grayscale. Annotations were made in YOLO format with a single class label named: *streak*. The dataset was randomly divided into 1,722 training images (72%), 333 validation images (14%), and 333 test images (14%).

A sample from StreaksYoloDataset is displayed in Fig. 2, manually annotated to illustrate the type of streaks the models should identify.

3.2 Model Training

We trained two versions of YOLO using the Ultralytics framework [10,11]. Each model, YOLOv8 and YOLOv11, was used with pretrained weights and fine-tuned for a single class detection. We selected YOLOv8 and YOLOv11 for comparison as they represent two of the most recent and widely adopted versions with major architectural improvements relevant to real-time linear feature detection, while YOLOv10 is primarily experimental and lacks stable benchmarks for astronomical applications. As in a recent work for weed detection [18], we already trained RT-DETR (Real-Time Detection Transformer) models to compare to the YOLO models. RT-DETR is an object detection model based on transformers, designed to achieve fast and accurate real-time detection by combining the efficiency of one-stage methods with the power of transformer architectures [27].

Training was set up to 800 epochs, with early stopping (patience as default for 100 epochs) based on validation loss to avoid overfitting. All training and validation metric curves for the YOLOv11n model, including loss, precision, recall and mPA, are shown in Fig. 1.

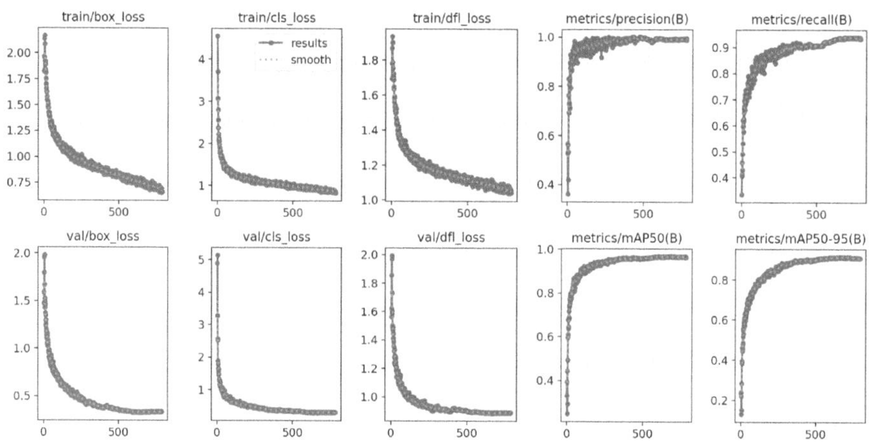

Fig. 1. Training curves of the YOLO11n model on StreaksYoloDataset, showing the evolution of training and validation loss, precision, recall and mAP metrics over epochs.

Our models were trained on a server equipped with an NVIDIA Tesla V100 GPU (32 GB VRAM), CUDA 11.4, and NVIDIA driver version 470.256.02.

The training hyperparameters for all models are listed below:

- epochs: 800
- patience: 100
- batch size: 4
- Optimizer: SGD with momentum (0.937)
- Learning rate: 0.01
- Weight decay: 0.0005
- Image size: 640 × 640
- Loss weights: box = 7.5, cls = 0.5, dfl = 1.5

These values were chosen for both performance and compatibility with the training hardware. The batch size of 4 was determined from prior experiments as the optimal setting for the available GPU memory on our system. Momentum, learning rate, weight decay, and loss weights are set as default values from Ultralytics recommendations, which have proven effective across various object detection tasks. An image size of 640 × 640 was selected to balance detection accuracy with reduced training and inference time. The high number of epochs (800) allows the models to reach a performance plateau, while early stopping with a patience of 100 epochs prevents overfitting. Various data augmentations were used, including random flips, scaling, translations, and backgrounds to increase robustness under different sky conditions. Performance was evaluated using the standard object detection metrics: precision, recall, mAP@50 and mAP@50–95.

Fig. 2. Example from the StreaksYoloDataset showing an astronomical image with manual annotation indicating satellite or debris streak. The bounding box illustrate the expected detection target for the evaluated models.

3.3 Evaluation Metrics

To evaluate model performance, we use standard object detection metrics:

- **Precision** $= \frac{TP}{TP+FP}$: Measures the proportion of predicted streaks that are correct.
- **Recall** $= \frac{TP}{TP+FN}$: Measures how many actual streaks were correctly detected.
- **mAP@50** (mean Average Precision at IoU threshold 0.50): Captures detection performance with a relaxed overlap requirement.
- **mAP@5095**: mAP over multiple IoU thresholds (from 0.50 to 0.95, step of 0.05), reflecting both localization and classification accuracy.

4 Results

Training results were collected and introduced in Table 1 summarizing the performance of all evaluated models: YOLOv8 and YOLOv11, in three different sizes: nano (n), medium (m) and extra-large (x). Metrics are presented for the training, validation, and testing splits for precision, recall, mAP@50 and mAP@50–95. The highest mAP@50–95 score for the test set, which represents the future inferences, was YOLOv11m with 0.934. But the lightweight model YOLOv11n follows very close with a score of 0.933 and outperforming its larger structure YOLOv11x, which performed slightly worse despite having a higher number of parameters. This suggests that large models might not benefit from the default training settings and may require more precise hyperparameter tuning to avoid overfitting or instability. Version 8, YOLOv8x achieved the best mAP@50 (0.979), while YOLOv8n achieved very similar results considering its very small structure. These results highlight the surprising power of smaller architectures for this type of detection task. Something surprising is that the nano models finished with extremely high precision scores when they have a few parameters compared to large models (2.6–3.0M vs. 56-68M). This efficiency makes them an excellent choice for real-time applications on resource-constrained systems. In general, YOLOv11n appears to offer the best compromise between model complexity and performance, making it the best option for robust detection while remaining lightweight enough to be deployed in low-resource and real-time monitoring systems. An inference made by this nano model can be seen in Fig. 3 with different streak patterns: (i) a background image, where the model correctly doesn't detect any streaks; (ii) a small, faint streak correctly detected; (iii) a medium-length streak also well detected; and (iv) a long and high-contrast streak also recognized by the model. These results give a demonstration of the model's ability to distinguish signal from noise based on the intensity and size of the streaks.

And lastly, the RT-DETR-L model ended up with the highest mAP@50–95 score on the test split. Despite using an architecture based on transformers, its performance remains very close to YOLO models. This highlights that both CNN-based and transformer-based models are competitive for this task.

Table 1. Performance comparison of all models on streak detection. Results are reported for each dataset split (training, validation, and test), along with the number of parameters for each model size, the best epoch (corresponding to the highest performance), Precision (P), Recall (R), and mAP at IoU thresholds of 0.50 and 0.500.95.

Model	Size	Best ep.	Set	P.	R.	@50	@50–95
RT-DETR-L	32 M	386	train	0.992	0.966	0.989	0.948
			val	0.985	0.946	0.971	0.908
			test	0.995	0.978	0.985	0.942
YOLOv8n	3 M	579	train	0.995	0.919	0.962	0.904
			val	0.995	0.918	0.962	0.903
			test	0.993	0.929	0.968	0.925
YOLOv8m	26 M	235	train	0.975	0.873	0.939	0.866
			val	0.964	0.884	0.939	0.866
			test	0.981	0.920	0.965	0.895
YOLOv8x	68 M	266	train	0.972	0.935	0.966	0.910
			val	0.972	0.934	0.967	0.910
			test	0.991	0.942	0.979	0.923
YOLOv11n	3 M	687	train	0.990	0.938	0.966	0.912
			val	0.990	0.938	0.966	0.911
			test	0.994	0.951	0.971	0.933
YOLOv11m	20 M	608	train	0.981	0.914	0.979	0.929
			val	0.981	0.915	0.979	0.927
			test	0.983	0.929	0.982	0.934
YOLOv11x	57 M	298	train	0.899	0.917	0.947	0.889
			val	0.899	0.917	0.947	0.888
			test	0.924	0.916	0.966	0.918

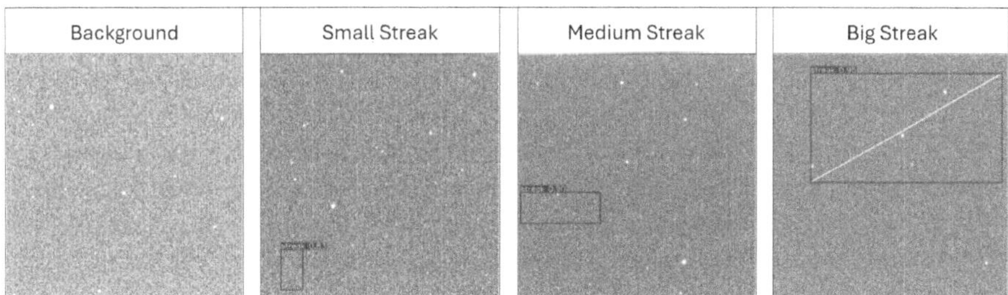

Fig. 3. Example YOLOv11n detections: (i) background image with no false positives; (ii) detection of a small, faint streak; (iii) detection of a medium streak; (iv) detection of a large, high-contrast streak. Blue squares indicate the prediction boxes. (Color figure online)

5 Discussion

Detecting faint streaks remains a major challenge due to their low SNR and variable brightness along the images, making the identification of such streaks challenging [4]. Conventional thresholding and detection pipelines often fail when streaks are indistinguishable from background noise. While basic preprocessing techniques, such as grayscale normalization, improve contrast consistency, they are often insufficient to improve weaker signals. On the other hand, generative restoration methods such as GANs have shown their effectiveness in denoising astronomical images while preserving critical features [17]. Additionally, deep generative approaches (e.g., variational autoencoders and GANs) have demonstrated effectiveness in detecting certain anomalies in astronomical datasets, suggesting their potential utility in identifying faint streaks [13,21].

Our results confirm that YOLO models maintain extremely high precision detecting streaks accurately while avoiding false positives due to the noise of the background. Thanks to their lightweight architectures, both versions better meet the requirements of low resource restrictions such as smartphones, embedded systems or for tracking, without compromising speed by optimization frameworks like YOLObile [1]. Additionally, lightweight models have been successfully implemented in IoT environments, demonstrating robust performance in real-time detection tasks on embedded devices [3].

These developments highlight the versatility of YOLO models in various applications, ranging from mobile object detection to real-time surveillance systems, highlighting their potential for universal adoption in scenarios requiring both speed and accuracy.

While this work focuses on detection, a fully automated process would integrate advanced restoration and interpretation tools. GANs could improve image quality through intelligent denoising, while large language models (LLMs) could add contextual features (semantic labeling, anomaly classification, and natural language explanations) [20], transforming outputs into scientific information.

6 Conclusion and Future Work

In this work, we explored the use of YOLO in the object detection model to automatically identify satellite and debris streaks in astronomical images. We trained and evaluated two versions, YOLOv8 and YOLOv11, on a dataset of long-exposure sky images annotated with streaks. The models performed excellently across all standard detection metrics, with YOLOv11m delivering the best overall performance in terms of precision, recall, and mAP@5095, while maintaining a reasonable model size suitable for deployment.

Beyond the global high accuracy, the results demonstrate the potential of lightweight models, such as YOLOv11n, for resource-constrained real-time applications. Their ability to generalize to diverse environments and lighting conditions makes them particularly suitable for operational use in automated pipelines at astronomical observatories.

As sky surveys expand, particularly with observatories like the Vera C. Rubin Observatory and LSST [8], the demand for automated and scalable image analysis is more critical than ever. Our work contributes to this need by enabling fast and accurate streak filtering, ensuring data quality in high-performance astronomical imaging systems.

In the future, we plan to integrate Generative Adversarial Networks (GANs) for denoising and signal enhancement, and Large Language Models (LLMs) for semantic interpretation and labeling. These developments could support a broader automation framework for sky monitoring, enabling enhanced filtering, classification, and reporting of anomalies directly from image data.

Acknowledgements. This research was funded by the Luxembourg Institute of Science and Technology (LIST), during the NEOD project (https://www.list.lu/en/informatics/project/neod/).

Data Availability. StreaksYoloDataset can be retrieved from this page: https://doi.org/10.5281/zenodo.14047944. Additional materials used to support the results of this paper are available from the corresponding author upon request.

References

1. Cai, Y., et al.: YOLObile: real-time object detection on mobile devices via compression-compilation co-design. In: Proceedings of the AAAI Conference on Artificial Intelligence, vol. 35, pp. 955–963 (2021)
2. Chatterjee, S., Kudeshia, P., Kollo, N., Agowun, M.A., Peethambaran, J., Akiyama, Y.: SatStreaks: towards supervised learning for delineating satellite streaks from astronomical images. In: Proceedings of the Conference on Robots and Vision. PubPub (2024)
3. Chen, R., et al.: An optimized lightweight real-time detection network model for IoT embedded devices. Sci. Rep. **15**(1), 3839 (2025)
4. Cvrcek, V., Sára, R.: Detection and certification of faint streaks in astronomical images. In: VISIGRAPP (5: VISAPP), pp. 498–509 (2019)
5. Hainaut, O.R., Williams, A.P.: Impact of satellite constellations on astronomical observations with ESO telescopes in the visible and infrared domains. Astron. Astrophys. **636**, A121 (2020)
6. Hu, G.X., Hu, B.L., Yang, Z., Huang, L., Li, P.: Pavement crack detection method based on deep learning models. Wirel. Commun. Mob. Comput. **2021**(1), 5573590 (2021)
7. Irureta-Goyena, B.Y., et al.: Deep learning to improve the discovery of near-earth asteroids in the Zwicky transient facility. Publ. Astron. Soc. Pac. **137**(5), 054503 (2025)
8. Ivezić, Ž, et al.: LSST: from science drivers to reference design and anticipated data products. Astrophys. J. **873**(2), 111 (2019)
9. Jeffries, C., Acuña, R.: Detection of streaks in astronomical images using machine learning. J. Artif. Intell. Technol. **4**(1), 1–8 (2024)
10. Jocher, G., Chaurasia, A., Qiu, J.: Ultralytics YOLOv8 (2023). https://github.com/ultralytics/ultralytics

11. Jocher, G., Qiu, J.: Ultralytics YOLO11 (2024). https://github.com/ultralytics/ultralytics
12. Luo, H., Cai, L., Li, C.: Rail surface defect detection based on an improved YOLOv5s. Appl. Sci. **13**(12), 7330 (2023)
13. Margalef-Bentabol, B., et al.: Detecting outliers in astronomical images with deep generative networks. Mon. Not. R. Astron. Soc. **496**(2), 2346–2361 (2020)
14. Nir, G., Zackay, B., Ofek, E.O.: Optimal and efficient streak detection in astronomical images. Astron. J. **156**(5), 229 (2018)
15. Parisot, O.: StreaksYoloDataset: labeled raw astronomical images for streaks detection (2024). https://doi.org/10.5281/zenodo.14047944
16. Parisot, O., Jaziri, M.: Impact of satellites streaks for observational astronomy: a study on data captured during one year from Luxembourg greater region. In: Proceedings of the 13th International Conference on Data Science, Technology and Applications - Volume 1: DATA, pp. 417–424. INSTICC, SciTePress (2024). https://doi.org/10.5220/0012787800003756
17. Rahman, M.M., Warren, H.P.: Application of a conditional generative adversarial network to denoising solar observations. Front. Astron. Space Sci. **12**, 1541901 (2025)
18. Saltık, A.O., Allmendinger, A., Stein, A.: Comparative analysis of YOLOv9, YOLOv10 and RT-DETR for real-time weed detection. In: European Conference on Computer Vision, pp. 177–193. Springer (2025)
19. Stoppa, F., et al.: Automated detection of satellite trails in ground-based observations using U-net and hough transform. Astron. Astrophys. **692**, A199 (2024)
20. Stoppa, F., et al.: Large language models enable textual interpretation of image-based astronomical transient classifications (2025)
21. Storey-Fisher, K., et al.: Anomaly detection in astronomical images with generative adversarial networks. arXiv preprint arXiv:2012.08082 (2020)
22. United Nations Office for Outer Space Affairs: Annual number of objects launched into space – UNOOSA. Dataset via Our World in Data. https://ourworldindata.org/grapher/yearly-number-of-objects-launched-into-outer-space. Accessed 16 June 2025
23. United Nations Office for Outer Space Affairs: Cumulative number of objects launched into space – UNOOSA. Dataset via Our World in Data. https://ourworldindata.org/grapher/cumulative-number-of-objects-launched-into-outer-space. Accessed 16 June 2025
24. Vananti, A., Schild, K., Schildknecht, T.: Streak detection algorithm for space debris detection on optical images. In: Proceedings of AMOS Conference (2015)
25. Xu, M.: Denoising astronomical images using an enhanced pix2pix model. Appl. Comput. Eng. **88**, 259–266 (2024). https://doi.org/10.54254/2755-2721/88/20241760
26. Yuan, P.: Big data in the astronomical field. Open Access J. Astron. **2**, 1–4 (2024). https://doi.org/10.23880/oaja-16000116
27. Zhao, Y., et al.: DETRs beat YOLOs on real-time object detection. In: 2024 IEEE/CVF Conference on Computer Vision and Pattern Recognition (CVPR), pp. 16965–16974. IEEE (2024)

Humanoid Robot Classification via Xception Deep Neural Network

Juan Pablo Vásconez[1,4,5(✉)], Vicente Águila[1,4,5], Alvaro Javier Prado[2,4,5], Viviana Moya[3,4,5], Miguel Torres-Torriti[3,4,5], and Patricio J. Cruz[3,4,5]

[1] Energy Transformation Center, Faculty of Engineering, Universidad Andres Bello, 7500971 Santiago, Chile

[2] Departamento de Ingeniería de Sistemas y Computación, Universidad Católica del Norte, 1249004 Antofagasta, Chile
alvaro.prado@ucn.cl

[3] Facultad de Ciencias Técnicas, Universidad Internacional Del Ecuador UIDE, Quito 170411, Ecuador
vimoyago@uide.edu.ec, mtorreto@uc.cl

[4] Department of Electrical Engineering, School of Engineering, Faculty of Engineering, Pontificia Universidad Católica de Chile, 7820436 Santiago, Chile
juan.vasconez@unab.cl

[5] Departamento de Automatización y Control Industrial (DACI), Escuela Politécnica Nacional, Ladrón de Guevara, Quito 170517, Ecuador
patricio.cruz@epn.edu.ec

Abstract. Humanoid robots have emerged as a key research field in recent years, driven by their potential in diverse applications, including industry, entertainment, assistance, logistics, and others. In this work, we propose a convolutional neural network architecture for the classification of state-of-the-art humanoid robots using the Xception Convolutional Neural Network (CNN). A comprehensive dataset comprising 5,399 RGB images across 31 different humanoid robot classes was curated from online sources, including official websites and public multimedia resources. To enhance model performance, data augmentation techniques were applied, including random rotations, reflections, translations, scaling, and shearing, with all images resized to a uniform 299 × 299 pixel resolution. The dataset was divided into 70% training, 15% validation, and 15% test subsets for model evaluation of overfitting and underfitting. The Xception model achieved high performance on the test set, with average metrics across classes of 99.72% specificity, 79.00% precision, 71.46% recall, 75.34% F1-score, 0.759 MCC, and 0.608 Jaccard index. These results highlight the model's high accuracy and robustness in real-time humanoid robot classification, demonstrating its potential for applications in dynamic, real-world environments, such as in multi-humanoid collaborative environments.

Keywords: Robotics · Humanoid Robots · Xception · Image Classification · Convolutional Neural Networks

T. Guarda et al. (Eds.): ARTIIS 2025, CCIS 2789, pp. 301–315, 2026.
https://doi.org/10.1007/978-3-032-16758-3_24

1 Introduction

Humanoid robots have gained significant interest in recent years, particularly in fields such as collaborative robotics, human-robot interaction, autonomous navigation, and service applications [4,6,24,29,30]. Their anthropomorphic design enables seamless integration into human-centric environments, supporting a diverse range of platforms, from research-oriented robots like NAO [14] and Pepper to advanced robots capable of performing tasks in industry, such as Tesla Optimus and Atlas. As the adoption of humanoid robots grows, robust and real-time systems for recognizing and classifying these platforms are increasingly critical for applications such as behavior analysis, fleet management, and mixed-environment collaboration [3,8,19,25,26].

Detection and classification of humanoid robots is a relevant problem, among other reasons, because tracking humanoid robots across environments enables better data for urban planning, workplace optimization, and usage trends. In social robotics, accurate classification is critical in applications like elder care, education, or therapy, where appearance and behavior must be matched appropriately to task and context. There are also safety, surveillance, and situational awareness needs, in which detection of human or robots in work or urban environments is necessary for the safe operation of other autonomous machines or access control to restricted areas [3,8,19,25,26].

Advancements in Computer Vision (CV), Machine Learning (ML), Deep Learning (DL), or artificial intelligence (AI) in general have significantly enhanced the capabilities of humanoid robots, enabling them to perform complex tasks with human-like proficiency. For instance, NVIDIA's GR00T N1 model employs a dual-system architecture inspired by human cognition, integrating vision-language processing with real-time motor action generation [16]. Specialized hardware accelerators, such as Graphics Processing Units (GPUs) and Tensor Processing Units (TPUs), have further improved the computational efficiency of AI models, enabling large-scale training and real-time deployment of sophisticated neural networks [2]. These developments have made vision-based AI systems indispensable for humanoid robots, which rely on image classification, object detection, and semantic segmentation to interpret their environments and interact with other robots or humans [27,28].

In this context, vision-based classification systems are essential because they allow humanoid robots to recognize objects, detect obstacles, and identify other robots during collaborative tasks. By doing so, these systems improve operational efficiency. For example, they support accurate fleet coordination in industrial environments and enable smooth human-robot interaction in assistive applications [26]. Then, the large variety of humanoid robot designs creates a strong demand for comprehensive datasets and models that are specifically developed for this purpose.

1.1 State-of-the-Art

To the best of our knowledge, no prior work has been found that directly addresses the classification of humanoid robot images using CV or AI. Taking this into account, this section examines three interconnected threads in the state of the art related to humanoids, AI, and vision: general developments in humanoid and bipedal robotics [1], deep learning models for detecting and understanding human shapes and postures [12], and the application of architectures for visual classification.

Regarding the development of humanoid robots, a comprehensive technological review by [23] presents a historical and functional overview of this type of robot, emphasizing their mechanical and sensory evolution. These works outline challenges such as energy efficiency, dynamic balancing, and real-time perception, underscoring the need for intelligent visual recognition systems integrated into humanoid platforms. Several research works (e.g., [15] and [14] contribute to this context by showcasing teleoperation architectures for humanoid robots, including systems capable of intercontinental control and delayed bilateral feedback. Such studies, although focused on control, illustrate deployment environments where autonomous detection and classification of robot types would be valuable.

Furthermore, research on human body form and pose detection is a key precedent for humanoid classification. Methods based on silhouettes, skeletons, and semantic body parts offer a basis for shape-based recognition. The work of [12] applied neural-fuzzy networks on shape projections to classify human postures. Later, [7] and [10] showed the effectiveness of silhouettes in conjunction with multi-class SVMs and CNNs for posture classification and fall detection. Building on research into the classification of humanoid shape and characteristics, advanced detection and segmentation strategies are also explored in works such as [13], which proposes a hierarchical part-template tree for fine-grained detection and segmentation of human forms. Additionally, [11] extends the work by incorporating volumetric 3D shape tracking via the Skinned Multi-Person Linear (SMPL) model fitting, thus bridging surface-to-volume analysis. Similarly, the work in [21] used silhouette-based inverse estimation pipelines to recover 3D pose and shape with indirect learning. These studies collectively establish the importance of body shape and silhouette modeling as core components of vision-based recognition.

Lastly, recent studies, such as those found in [17] and [10], underscore the superiority of DL models over classical ML in classifying postures from low-dimensional silhouettes. Mask R-CNN is increasingly adopted to extract high-quality silhouettes from RGB input as a precursor to CNN-based classification. On the other hand, regarding the development of robust and efficient models for generic image classification, as technology allowed for more complex architectures, one prominent development is the Xception model, built upon depthwise separable convolutions, which is an efficient and robust architecture for image classification. Its applications in person re-identification and fine-grained recognition were explored by [18], who used a dual-branch Xception-based model for parsing body parts and classifying identity. Furthermore, the work of [22] used a modified Xception for clothing image classification, achieving a top-1 accuracy of 92.19%, which outperforms Inception-ResNet-v2 and the baseline Xception. These results demonstrate the architecture's capacity for detailed visual discrimination, making it ideal for classifying humanoid robot images with subtle morphological differences.

Based on the analyzed literature, no prior studies have been identified that specifically focus on the classification of humanoid robot images using AI and computer vision, highlighting a significant research gap. Therefore, this work addresses this need by proposing a methodology based on the Xception CNN model for the classification of humanoid robot images. This approach is particularly valuable in multi-humanoid collaborative scenarios, where precise identification and differentiation of humanoid robots are critical for effective coordination and task allocation.

1.2 Contributions

This work presents the following main contributions:

- A comprehensive dataset of 5,399 images across 31 humanoid robot classes (approximately 180 images per class) was developed to address the challenge of visual diversity and classification scale.
- The Xception convolutional neural network was trained and calibrated to fit the distribution of the humanoid dataset for the proposed classification task.
- Model evaluation used a wide range of performance metrics, including specificity, precision, recall, F1-score, Matthews Correlation Coefficient (MCC), and Jaccard index, alongside analytical techniques such as receiver operating characteristic (ROC) curves.

2 Materials and Methods

In this work, it is proposed an architecture to train, validate, and test the Xception deep learning classification model for humanoid robot image classification, which is presented in Fig. 1. To this end, it was created a dataset containing state-of-the-art humanoid robots such as ASIMO, Atlas, iCub, G1, Optimus (Tesla), JAXON, among others. Next, we use the Xception convolutional neural network for image classification. Finally, we perform a multi-metric approach to evaluate our models using different metrics such as specificity, precision, recall (sensitivity), F1 score, Matthews correlation coefficient, and Jaccard similarity coefficient. We explain each stage of the proposed architecture in detail below.

2.1 Dataset Structure

In this work, it was created a dataset composed of 5,399 RGB (red-green-blue) images with 31 state-of-the-art humanoid robots, which are detailed in Table 1.

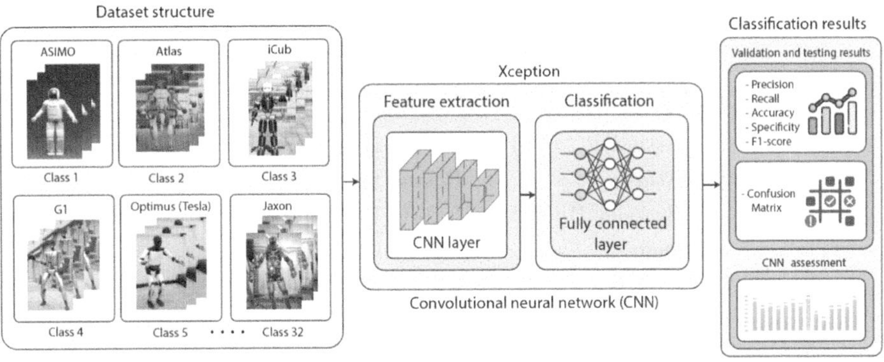

Fig. 1. Proposed architecture for humanoid robot image classification using the Xception convolutional neural network.

Approximately 180 images per humanoid class were collected from the internet, including official websites, publicly accessible multimedia resources, and published videos. The dataset was then divided into training (70%), validation (15%), and test (15%) subsets, resulting in 3,779 training images, 810 validation images, and 810 test images. To improve the classification model performance, we applied data augmentation with the following parameters: random rotation between −20 and 20°, random X-axis reflection, random translations of -10 to 10 pixels in both X and Y directions, random scaling of 0.9 to 1.1 for X and Y axes, and random shearing of −5 to 5° for both X and Y axes. During training, the augmented image datastore randomly augments the training data each epoch, ensuring varied data without changing the number of images or storing transformed versions. Additionally, all images were resized to a uniform resolution of 299×299 pixels to match the input layer size of the Xception network. The dataset was divided into training (70%), validation (15%), and test (15%) subsets for model development and evaluation. The training set was used to train the Xception model, the validation set was employed to fine-tune its weights, and the test set was used for the final evaluation of the model's performance, which includes underfitting and overfitting evaluation. It is worth mentioning that the 31 classes of humanoid robots represent a diverse range of manufacturers, sizes, functionalities, etc. For instance, the ASIMO and NAO robots are well known for their role in research and education, while others, such as the Atlas robots, Tesla's Optimus, or Digit, are more focused on environments such as industry or field assistance tasks.

2.2 Xception Convolutional Neural Network

The Xception Convolutional Neural Network (CNN) is a deep learning model optimized for image classification that uses depthwise separable convolutions to achieve high computational efficiency [20]. Its 71-layer architecture includes convolutional layers, batch normalization, ReLU activations, and residual con-

Table 1. Dataset details of Humanoid Robots and Their Manufacturers

N	Name	Maker
1	Apollo	Apptronik
2	Atlas DRC (V3)	Boston Dynamics
3	Atlas V4	Boston Dynamics
4	Berkeley Humanoid	Hybrid Robotics
5	Digit	Agility Robotics
6	Draco3	Apptronik
7	ergoCub	IIT
8	G1	UNITREE Robotics
9	H1	UNITREE Robotics
10	iCub	IIT
11	JAXON	JSK
12	NAO	SoftBank Robotics
13	Robonaut 2	NASA JSC Robotics
14	Romeo	Aldebaran Robotics
15	Sigmaban	Rhoban
16	TALOS	PAL Robotics
17	Valkyrie	NASA JSC Robotics
18	WALK-MAN	IIT
19	ASIMO	Honda
20	HRP Series	AIST/Kawada
21	Kengoro & Kenshiro	JSK, Universidad de Tokio
22	TORO	DLR
23	iCub 3	IIT
24	EveR Series	KIST
25	Atlas (Actual)	Boston Dynamics
26	Tesla Optimus	Tesla
27	UBTech Walker X	UBTech
28	Aeolus Robot	Aeolus Robotics
29	Pepper	SoftBank Robotics
30	Roboy	Universidad de Múnich
31	Sophia	Hanson Robotics

nections to enhance gradient flow during training. With 22.9 million parameters and an input size of 299 × 299 pixels for RGB images, Xception offers a good balance of performance and efficiency. We fine-tuned a pre-trained Xception model, originally trained on ImageNet (1000 categories), to classify 31 distinct humanoid robot categories. Compared to architectures like VGG or ResNet,

Xception's reduced parameter count and efficient feature extraction make it ideal for datasets with high visual variability, such as humanoid robot images.

A key feature of Xception is its modular structure, comprising entry, middle (repeated eight times), and exit flows, with residual connections mitigating gradient vanishing in deep networks [5,9]. For training, we optimized the model using categorical cross-entropy loss, a standard choice for multi-class classification, defined as:

$$L = -\sum_{i=1}^{N}\sum_{c=1}^{C} y_{i,c}\log(\hat{y}_{i,c}), \tag{1}$$

where N is the number of samples, C is the number of classes (31 in this case), $y_{i,c}$ is the true label (1 if class c is correct, 0 otherwise), and $\hat{y}_{i,c}$ is the predicted probability for class c [9]. This loss function ensured stable convergence, effectively handling the diverse visual features of humanoid robots. The Xception model's robust feature extraction and transfer learning capabilities make it well-suited for the humanoid image classification task for the dataset that we describe in Sect. 2.1.

2.3 Performance Metrics

To evaluate the Xception model's performance in classifying images across 31 humanoid robot categories, we used six key metrics: Accuracy, Precision, Recall, F1-Score, Matthews Correlation Coefficient (MCC), and Jaccard Index [9]. These metrics were used to evaluate the validation and test sets, providing a complete assessment of the model's ability to classify the diverse humanoid robot images. Accuracy measures overall correctness, Precision and Recall assess class-specific reliability and completeness, F1-Score balances Precision and Recall, MCC ensures robustness against class imbalance, and the Jaccard Index quantifies prediction overlap, all critical for robust classification in this multi-class task [9].

3 Results

In this section, we present the assessment results of the Xception model for the humanoid robot classification problem.

3.1 Validation Results

The validation results of the proposed Xception model are presented in Table 2, with the validation confusion matrix shown in Fig. 2a and the ROC curves for each humanoid class in Fig. 3a. It can be observed that the Xception model obtains high performance results on several humanoid robot classes, such as G1 (100.0%), H1 (100.0%), Bostondinamycs (95.2%), and iCub (95.7%), achieving high Precision, Recall, F1-score, and MCC values–indicating accurate and consistent classification. However, notable performance issues arise for classes like

Table 2. Classification results for the validation test.

Class	Specificity	Precision	Recall	F1-Score	MCC	Jaccard
ASIMO	99.8%	88.9%	80.0%	84.2%	0.840	0.727
Aeolusrobot	99.6%	87.5%	70.0%	77.8%	0.775	0.636
Bostondinamycs	99.8%	95.2%	100.0%	97.6%	0.975	0.952
EveRSeries(KIST)	99.2%	33.3%	20.0%	25.0%	0.247	0.143
G1	100.0%	100.0%	100.0%	100.0%	1.000	1.000
H1	100.0%	100.0%	100.0%	100.0%	1.000	1.000
HRP-SERIES	100.0%	100.0%	95.0%	97.4%	0.974	0.950
ICub3(IIT)	99.8%	83.3%	50.0%	62.5%	0.640	0.455
JAXON	99.8%	80.0%	80.0%	80.0%	0.798	0.667
KengoroyKenshiro	100.0%	100.0%	90.0%	94.7%	0.947	0.900
NAO	99.6%	80.0%	40.0%	53.3%	0.554	0.364
Robotnaut	100.0%	100.0%	20.0%	33.3%	0.444	0.200
Roboy	99.4%	76.9%	100.0%	87.0%	0.874	0.769
Romeo	100.0%	100.0%	40.0%	57.1%	0.625	0.400
SigmanBan	100.0%	100.0%	100.0%	100.0%	1.000	1.000
SoftbanksRobotics	93.5%	39.6%	100.0%	56.8%	0.609	0.396
Sophia	96.6%	54.1%	100.0%	70.2%	0.722	0.541
TALOS	99.6%	75.0%	60.0%	66.7%	0.665	0.500
TORO(DLR)	100.0%	100.0%	90.0%	94.7%	0.947	0.900
TeslaOptimus	99.4%	86.4%	95.0%	90.5%	0.902	0.826
UbtechWalkerX	98.0%	37.5%	60.0%	46.2%	0.461	0.300
Valkyrie	100.0%	100.0%	10.0%	18.2%	0.313	0.100
WALK-MAN	99.8%	50.0%	14.3%	22.2%	0.262	0.125
WalkerXUbtech	99.2%	50.0%	40.0%	44.4%	0.437	0.286
apollo	100.0%	100.0%	100.0%	100.0%	1.000	1.000
atlas drc	99.4%	88.5%	88.5%	88.5%	0.878	0.793
atlas v4	100.0%	100.0%	100.0%	100.0%	1.000	1.000
berkeley	99.6%	92.9%	100.0%	96.3%	0.962	0.929
digit	98.0%	71.4%	100.0%	83.3%	0.836	0.714
draco3	100.0%	100.0%	100.0%	100.0%	1.000	1.000
ergoCub	100.0%	100.0%	33.3%	50.0%	0.573	0.333
iCub	99.8%	95.7%	100.0%	97.8%	0.977	0.957

EveRSeries(KIST) (33.3%), SoftbanksRobotics (39.6%), Valkyrie (54.1%), and WALK-MAN (50.0%), which exhibit low Precision or Recall. The low performance might be because of visual similarity with other robots, complexity of the images, or even limited training data variability.

Table 3. Classification results for the test set.

Class	Specificity	Precision	Recall	F1-Score	MCC	Jaccard
ASIMO	99.8%	85.7%	60.0%	70.6%	0.713	0.545
Aeolusrobot	99.4%	76.9%	52.6%	62.5%	0.625	0.455
Bostondinamycs	100.0%	100.0%	80.0%	88.9%	0.891	0.800
EveRSeries(KIST)	98.4%	46.7%	77.8%	58.3%	0.594	0.412
G1	100.0%	100.0%	90.9%	95.2%	0.952	0.909
H1	100.0%	100.0%	100.0%	100.0%	1.000	1.000
HRP-SERIES	100.0%	100.0%	50.0%	66.7%	0.700	0.500
ICub3(IIT)	99.8%	85.7%	60.0%	70.6%	0.713	0.545
JAXON	100.0%	100.0%	40.0%	57.1%	0.631	0.400
KengoroyKenshiro	99.8%	94.7%	94.7%	94.7%	0.945	0.900
NAO	99.0%	61.5%	40.0%	48.5%	0.480	0.320
Robotnaut	100.0%	100.0%	50.0%	66.7%	0.704	0.500
Roboy	99.2%	63.6%	77.8%	70.0%	0.698	0.538
Romeo	100.0%	100.0%	65.0%	78.8%	0.800	0.650
SigmanBan	100.0%	100.0%	100.0%	100.0%	1.000	1.000
SoftbanksRobotics	95.7%	50.0%	100.0%	66.7%	0.692	0.500
Sophia	98.4%	71.4%	100.0%	83.3%	0.838	0.714
TALOS	99.6%	75.0%	66.7%	70.6%	0.702	0.545
TORO(DLR)	99.8%	95.2%	100.0%	97.6%	0.975	0.952
TeslaOptimus	99.6%	90.5%	95.0%	92.7%	0.924	0.864
UbtechWalkerX	96.0%	25.9%	70.0%	37.8%	0.408	0.233
Valkyrie	99.4%	50.0%	30.0%	37.5%	0.378	0.231
WALK-MAN	99.8%	85.7%	85.7%	85.7%	0.855	0.750
WalkerXUbtech	99.2%	0.0%	0.0%	0.0%	-0.012	0.000
apollo	99.8%	92.9%	76.5%	83.9%	0.838	0.722
atlas drc	98.8%	76.0%	76.0%	76.0%	0.748	0.613
atlas v4	99.6%	89.5%	100.0%	94.4%	0.944	0.895
berkeley	99.6%	92.9%	100.0%	96.3%	0.962	0.929
digit	98.8%	80.6%	100.0%	89.3%	0.892	0.806
draco3	100.0%	100.0%	100.0%	100.0%	1.000	1.000
ergoCub	100.0%	100.0%	54.5%	70.6%	0.735	0.545
iCub	99.8%	95.5%	100.0%	97.7%	0.976	0.955

3.2 Test Results

The test results of the proposed Xception model are presented in Table 3, with the test confusion matrix shown in Fig. 2b and the corresponding ROC curves for each humanoid class in Fig. 3b. Similar to the validation performance, the

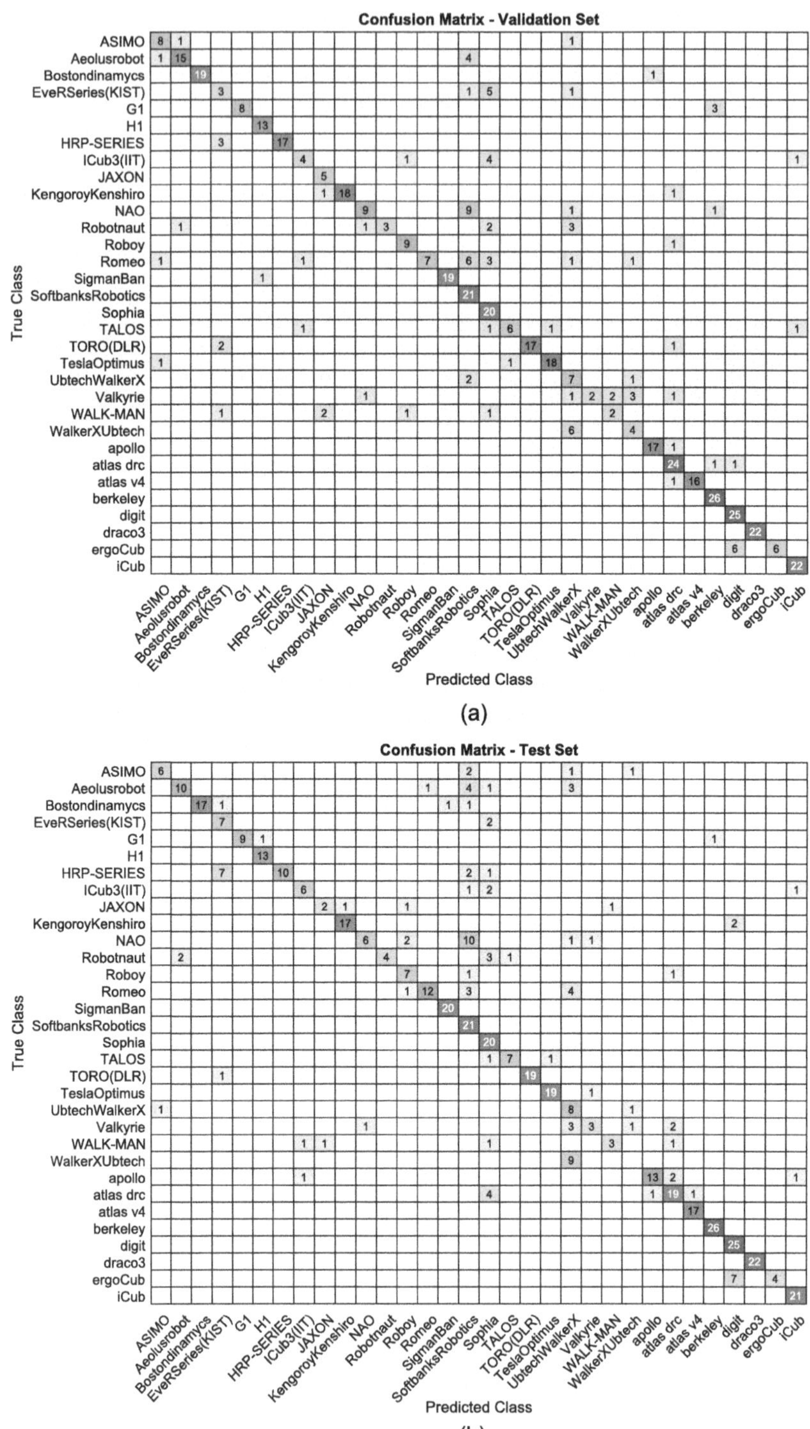

Fig. 2. Confusion matrices of the Xception model. (a) Test set. (b) Validation set.

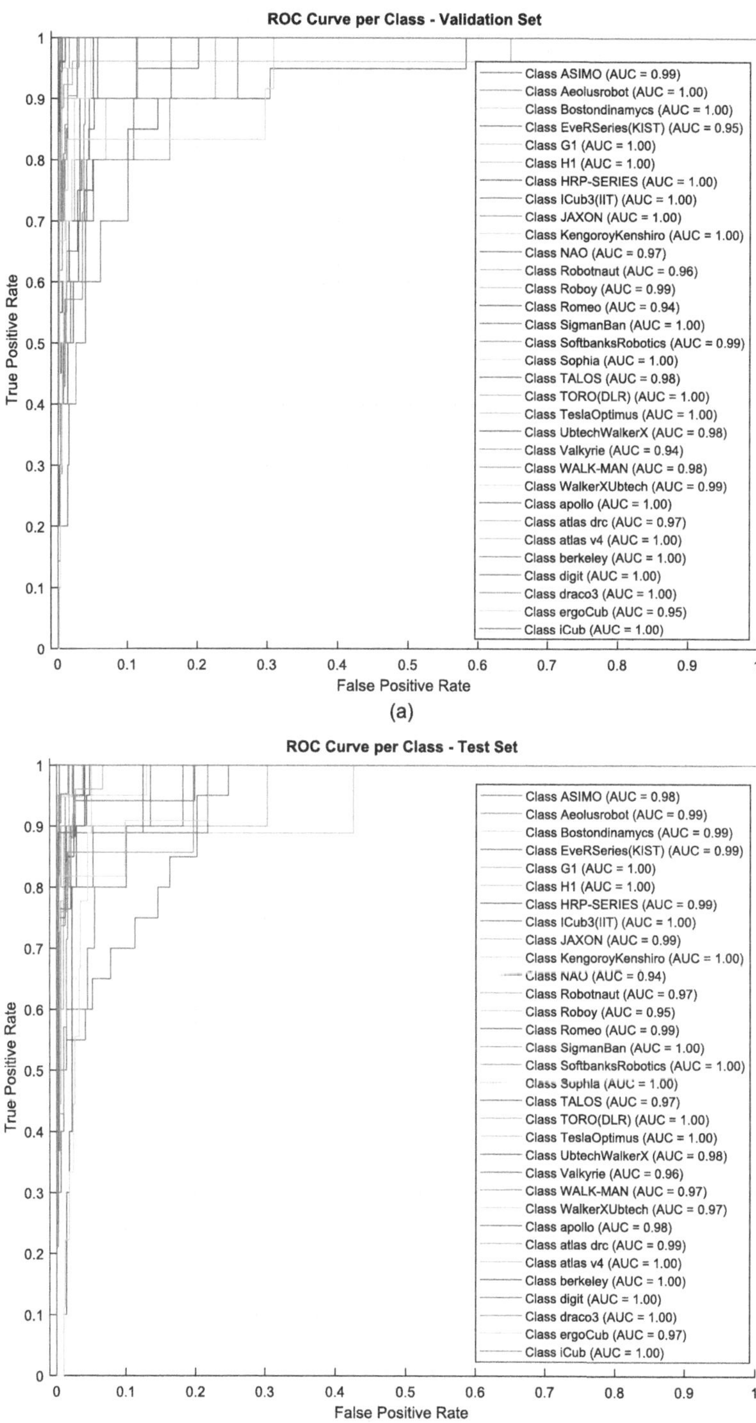

Fig. 3. ROC curves by humanoid class obtained with the Xception model. (a) Validation set. (b) Test set.

Table 4. Average validation and test results of the proposed Xception model for humanoid image classification.

Metric	Validation Set	Test Set
Specificity	99.37% ± 1.30	99.35% ± 1.03
Precision	83.32% ± 21.21	80.81% ± 24.28
Recall	74.25% ± 31.14	74.79% ± 25.63
F1-Score	74.24% ± 26.19	75.27% ± 22.59
MCC	0.757 ± 0.241	0.759 ± 0.222
Jaccard	0.652 ± 0.309	0.648 ± 0.260

Xception model achieves high performance results for several classes, such as H1 (100.0%), SigmanBan (100.0%), draco3 (100.0%), and iCub (95.5%) in Precision, showing high accuracy and generalization capability. However, a drop in performance is still observed for other classes like UbtechWalkerX (25.9%) and Valkyrie (30.0%) in Recall, indicating potential limitations in feature discrimination or insufficient representation in the training data. The class WalkerX-Ubtech obtained 0.0% in Precision and F1-score, suggesting a strong bias or lack of learning for this particular robot. These variations may point to overfitting for classes with high validation but lower test scores, or underfitting in cases where both validation and test metrics are low. These results highlight the effects of possible class imbalance and intra-class variability. Nevertheless, our Xception model obtained outstanding classification results for most of the humanoid robot classes.

3.3 Summary of Evaluation Metrics

The average performance metrics across the validation and test sets are summarized in Table 4. Overall, the model exhibits strong generalization capability. Specificity remains consistently high in both sets, indicating a stable true negative rate and reliable identification of non-target classes. Precision shows a slight decrease in the test set, suggesting a marginal decline in the model's accuracy when predicting positive instances, which may be attributed to class imbalance or unseen variations in the test data. Recall remains relatively stable, reflecting the model's consistent ability to detect relevant instances. The F1-Score shows minimal variation between validation and test sets, indicating a balanced trade-off between precision and recall. Similarly, the Matthews Correlation Coefficient (MCC) and Jaccard Index values reflect strong agreement between predicted and actual labels, with low generalization loss. Importantly, the close alignment of validation and test metrics suggests that the model does not suffer from significant overfitting (where validation performance greatly exceeds test performance) nor underfitting (where both are consistently low). These results confirm the robustness and reliability of the Xception-based architecture for the classification of 31 humanoid robot classes.

4 Conclusions

In this study, we proposed a deep learning architecture for classifying 31 state-of-the-art humanoid robots using the Xception CNN model. Our dataset, consisting of 5,399 curated and augmented RGB images, was used to train and evaluate the model. The results demonstrate robust performance, with an average F1-Score of $74.24\% \pm 26.19$ on the validation set and $75.27\% \pm 22.59$ on the test set, as well as a Matthews Correlation Coefficient (MCC) of 0.757 ± 0.241 and 0.759 ± 0.222, respectively. Despite the strong overall performance, the relatively large standard deviation indicates variability in classification accuracy across different robot classes. We also observed a significant performance gap between high-accuracy classes (e.g., *G1*, *H1*) and low-performing ones (e.g., *EveRSeries*, *WalkerXUbtech*), suggesting underfitting for certain humanoid robots. Conversely, a drop in test performance for some classes (e.g., *WalkerXUbtech* with 0% test Precision) despite moderate validation results suggests localized overfitting. To mitigate these issues, we applied data augmentation and used separate validation and testing sets to ensure fair evaluation. Overall, the Xception model demonstrates strong potential for state-of-the-art humanoid robot classification, achieving a test F1-Score of up to 75.27% across 31 humanoid robot classes. For future work, we plan to explore additional classification algorithms and novel object detection and segmentation methods based on artificial intelligence and computer vision.

Acknowledgments. This work has been supported by ANID (National Research and Development Agency of Chile) under Fondecyt Iniciación 2024 Grant 11240105 and Fondecyt Iniciación 2023 Grant 11230962.

References

1. Modeling, stability and control of biped robots–a general framework. Automatica **40**(10), 1647–1664 (2004). https://doi.org/10.1016/j.automatica.2004.01.031
2. Evolutionary deep learning: a survey. Neurocomputing **483**, 42–58 (2022). https://doi.org/10.1016/j.neucom.2022.01.099
3. Aro, K., Guevara, L., Torres-Torriti, M., Torres, F., Prado, A.: Robust nonlinear model predictive control for the trajectory tracking of skid-steer mobile manipulators with wheel–ground interactions. Robotics **13**(12) (2024). https://doi.org/10.3390/robotics13120171. https://www.mdpi.com/2218-6581/13/12/171
4. Chico, A., et al.: Hand gesture recognition and tracking control for a virtual UR5 robot manipulator. In: 2021 IEEE Fifth Ecuador Technical Chapters Meeting (ETCM), pp. 1–6. IEEE (2021)
5. Chollet, F.: Xception: deep learning with depthwise separable convolutions. In: Proceedings of the IEEE Conference on Computer Vision and Pattern Recognition (CVPR), pp. 1251–1258 (2017). https://doi.org/10.1109/CVPR.2017.195
6. Cruz, P.J., et al.: A deep q-network based hand gesture recognition system for control of robotic platforms. Sci. Rep. **13**(1), 7956 (2023)

7. Foroughi, H., Rezvanian, A., Paziraee, A.: Robust fall detection using human shape and multi-class support vector machine. In: 2008 Sixth Indian Conference on Computer Vision, Graphics & Image Processing, pp. 413–420 (2008). https://doi.org/10.1109/ICVGIP.2008.49
8. García, I., et al.: Human-robot interaction based on hand gesture detection using yolo algorithm. In: International Conference on Advanced Research in Technologies, Information, Innovation and Sustainability, pp. 351–365. Springer, Cham (2024)
9. Goodfellow, I.: Deep learning (2016)
10. Hasib, R., Khan, K.N., Yu, M., Khan, M.S.: Vision-based human posture classification and fall detection using convolutional neural network. In: 2021 International Conference on Artificial Intelligence (ICAI), pp. 74–79 (2021). https://doi.org/10.1109/ICAI52203.2021.9445263
11. Huang, C.H.P., et al.: Tracking-by-detection of 3D human shapes: from surfaces to volumes. IEEE Trans. Pattern Anal. Mach. Intell. **40**(8), 1994–2008 (2018). https://doi.org/10.1109/TPAMI.2017.2740308
12. Juang, C.F., Chang, C.M.: Human body posture classification by a neural fuzzy network and home care system application. IEEE Trans. Syst. Man Cybern. Part A Syst. Hum. **37**(6), 984–994 (2007). https://doi.org/10.1109/TSMCA.2007.897609
13. Lin, Z., Davis, L.S.: Shape-based human detection and segmentation via hierarchical part-template matching. IEEE Trans. Pattern Anal. Mach. Intell. **32**(4), 604–618 (2010). https://doi.org/10.1109/TPAMI.2009.204
14. Moya, V., Slawiñski, E., Mut, V.: Delayed bilateral teleoperation of the speed and turn angle of a bipedal robot. Robotica **39**(4), 633–651 (2021). https://doi.org/10.1017/S0263574720000636
15. Moya, V., Slawiñski, E., Mut, V., Wagner, B.: Intercontinental bilateral-by-phases teleoperation of a humanoid robot. IEEE Lat. Am. Trans. **20**(1), 64–72 (2022). https://doi.org/10.1109/TLA.2022.9662174
16. NVIDIA: Bjorck, J., et al.: Gr00t n1: an open foundation model for generalist humanoid robots (2025). https://arxiv.org/abs/2503.14734
17. Ogundokun, R.O., Maskeliūnas, R., Misra, S., Damasevicius, R.: A novel deep transfer learning approach based on depth-wise separable CNN for human posture detection. Information **13**(11) (2022). https://doi.org/10.3390/info13110520
18. Qiao, S., et al.: Human body multiple parts parsing for person reidentification based on xception. Int. J. Comput. Intell. Syst. **14**, 482–490 (2020). https://doi.org/10.2991/ijcis.d.201222.001
19. Romero, R., et al.: Hand gesture and arm movement recognition for multimodal control of a 3-DOF helicopter. In: Kim, J., et al. (eds.) RiTA 2021. LNNS, vol. 429, pp. 363–377. Springer, Cham (2022). https://doi.org/10.1007/978-3-030-97672-9_32
20. Shaheed, K., et al.: DS-CNN: a pre-trained xception model based on depth-wise separable convolutional neural network for finger vein recognition. Expert Syst. Appl. **191**, 116288 (2022)
21. Tan, J., Budvytis, I., Cipolla, R.: Indirect deep structured learning for 3D human body shape and pose prediction (2017). https://doi.org/10.17863/CAM.21421
22. Tan, Z., Hu, Y., Luo, D., Hu, M., Liu, K.: The clothing image classification algorithm based on the improved xception model. Int. J. Comput. Sci. Eng. **23**(3), 214–223 (2020). https://doi.org/10.1504/IJCSE.2020.111426
23. Tong, Y., Liu, H., Zhang, Z.: Advancements in humanoid robots: a comprehensive review and future prospects. IEEE/CAA J. Automatica Sinica **11**(2), 301–328 (2024). https://doi.org/10.1109/JAS.2023.124140

24. Vásconez, J.P., Cheein, F.A.A.: Workload and production assessment in the avocado harvesting process using human-robot collaborative strategies. Biosys. Eng. **223**, 56–77 (2022)
25. Vasconez, J.P., Kantor, G.A., Cheein, F.A.A.: Human-robot interaction in agriculture: a survey and current challenges. Biosys. Eng. **179**, 35–48 (2019)
26. Vasconez, J.P., Admoni, H., Cheein, F.A.: A methodology for semantic action recognition based on pose and human-object interaction in avocado harvesting processes. Comput. Electron. Agric. **184**, 106057 (2021)
27. Vasconez, J.P., Carvajal, D., Cheein, F.A.: On the design of a human-robot interaction strategy for commercial vehicle driving based on human cognitive parameters. Adv. Mech. Eng. **11**(7), 1687814019862715 (2019)
28. Vasconez, J.P., Cheein, F.A.: Finding a proper approach to obtain cognitive parameters from human faces under illumination variations. In: 2018 5th International Conference on Control, Decision and Information Technologies (CoDIT), pp. 946–951. IEEE (2018)
29. Vasconez, J.P., Guevara, L., Cheein, F.A.: Social robot navigation based on HRI non-verbal communication: a case study on avocado harvesting. In: Proceedings of the 34th ACM/SIGAPP Symposium on Applied Computing, pp. 957–960 (2019)
30. Vasconez, J.P., Viscaino, M., Guevara, L., Cheein, F.A.: A fuzzy-based driver assistance system using human cognitive parameters and driving style information. Cogn. Syst. Res. **64**, 174–190 (2020)

Identifying Key Drivers of Academic Performance in Colombian Engineering Students: A Machine Learning Approach

Nathalia Orozco Morales[1(✉)], Leonardo Valderrama Garcia[1], Luis Rabelo[2], and Cristian Rincón-Guio[1]

[1] Corporación Universitaria Minuto de Dios, Bogotá 110110, Colombia
nathalia.orozco@uniminuto.edu

[2] University of Central Florida, Orlando, FL 32816, USA

Abstract. This study proposes a machine learning-based model, specifically using the Random Forest algorithm, to analyze the factors influencing the performance of engineering students in the Saber Pro test, administered by the Colombian Institute for Educational Evaluation (ICFES). The model is designed to integrate academic records, socioeconomic variables, and institutional data in order to identify and prioritize the key factors associated with student achievement. The proposed methodology includes data collection, preprocessing, feature selection, and hyperparameter optimization using GridSearchCV. Techniques such as categorical variable encoding, normalization, and cross-validation will be applied to ensure methodological rigour and model robustness. Rather than presenting experimental results, this proposal outlines the conceptual and technical foundation for developing a predictive tool that can inform evidence-based educational strategies. The ultimate aim is to support institutional efforts to enhance academic outcomes, reduce dropout rates, and provide a scalable analytical framework applicable to other higher education contexts.

Keywords: Random Forest · Educational Data Mining · Feature Importance · Dropout Prediction · Artificial Intelligence

1 Introduction

The Colombian Institute for Educational Evaluation (ICFES) administers the Saber Pro tests as psychometric tools to assess undergraduate students who have completed at least 75% of their studies. These tests measure key skills for professional life, using a scoring scale from 0 to 300, and include a socio-economic questionnaire that gathers information about students' family environment, home conditions, internet access, and entertainment habits [1].

General competencies in higher education include intellectual and social skills essential for learning and teamwork, along with academic abilities like communication and argumentation [2]. However, standardized tests such as Saber Pro face issues like grading subjectivity, limited feedback, and lack of adaptability. Studies show that performance is influenced by social, cultural, and academic factors, which affect dropout

T. Guarda et al. (Eds.): ARTIIS 2025, CCIS 2789, pp. 316–327, 2026.
https://doi.org/10.1007/978-3-032-16758-3_25

rates and learning quality [3, 4]. Technology integration can address diverse learning needs and improve engagement [5], while identifying key competencies helps strengthen educational strategies [6].

This study applies to a Random Forest model to identify variables that best explain engineering students' performance on Saber Pro. Its ability to handle large data, detect complex patterns, and reduce overfitting makes it suitable for this task. The analysis focuses on students from private universities (2021-2 to 2023-1) to support improvements in professional training and align skills development with industry needs [2].

The next section reviews literature on ML techniques for predicting academic performance. Section 3 presents the proposed model, and validation approach. Then, Sect. 4 examines its implications for Colombian universities, focusing on Uniminuto as a private university. Finally, Sect. 5 concludes with suggestions for future research, particularly regarding defining and developing specific engineering competencies.

2 Literature Review

2.1 Machine Learning in Education

ML has emerged as a transformative tool in education, enabling the analysis of complex datasets to uncover patterns and predict outcomes [1]. Ensemble algorithms have proven to be an effective strategy for improving the accuracy of predictive models in various contexts, including academic performance [4]. These algorithms combine multiple supervised models to reduce errors and optimise performance. They can identify the most relevant variables when paired with feature selection methods, enhancing the model's effectiveness [1, 3]. Hyperparameter optimization further refines these models, ensuring robust performance across diverse datasets [7].

AI in education has revolutionized teaching and learning processes. For instance, AI has transformed legal education and practice in the legal sector by optimizing tasks and enabling advanced conceptual analysis [7, 8]. In education, AI facilitates personalized learning through intelligent tutoring systems and online platforms, although it also raises challenges and concerns in higher education [9, 10]. Combining AI and Big Data has led to new approaches in virtual learning environments and the study of 21st-century skills [6, 11]. ML models, such as artificial neural networks and decision trees, have been instrumental in evaluating the impact of social programs on educational outcomes. These models enable student performance and dropout risk predictions, providing actionable insights for policymakers and educators [3].

2.2 Random Forest: Fundamentals and Applications in the Academic Field

Random Forest is an ensemble method based on the combination of multiple decision trees using the bagging technique [12]. This approach trains different trees with random subsets of data, allowing each to contribute a vote to the final decision. As a result, model accuracy improves, and the risk of overfitting a common issue in individual decision tree models is reduced. Additionally, Random Forest includes a mechanism to estimate feature importance, providing key insights into the factors influencing the prediction of a given phenomenon [13].

Various algorithms that address classification and regression problems have driven advancements in ML. In this context, decision trees have been widely used, as they generate rules based on continuous and categorical input variables to predict different types of outcomes [9, 14]. Specifically, classification trees predict categorical outcomes, while regression trees handle continuous values. Their flexibility has made these models fundamental tools in ML.

In the academic field, Random Forest has been used to classify students based on their risk of low performance and to predict outcomes in specific assessments [4]. Its popularity is due to its ability to handle large volumes of heterogeneous data and its robustness against outliers and missing data. Furthermore, its application in educational settings has enhanced personalized learning through intelligent tutoring systems and online education platforms [15]. Additionally, integrating Random Forest with Big Data analysis techniques has expanded its use in evaluating 21st-century skills and improving virtual learning environments [16]. From a broader perspective, Random Forest has been shown to assess the impact of social programs on educational support. Models based on artificial neural networks and decision trees have achieved prediction accuracy of up to 71%, allowing for identifying students at risk of repeating courses and developing strategies to prevent academic failure and dropout [11].

2.3 Socioeconomic and Academic Variables Affecting Performance

Various studies indicate that academic performance depends not solely on cognitive abilities but also on socioeconomic, cultural, and contextual factors [11, 17]. The key factors influencing student performance include [18]: 1) Economic and family conditions: Family income, socioeconomic status, parental education level, internet access. 2) Access to education: Geographical location, availability of technological resources, study hours. 3) Academic trajectory: Cumulative grade point average, history of course repetition, critical subjects, class attendance, and participation.

ML techniques have enabled more accurate predictions of academic performance. [18] conducted a study examining variables using feature selection methods to identify the most influential ones. They then applied supervised models such as KNN, SVC, Naïve Bayes, and decision trees, optimized with Python, demonstrating the effectiveness of these models in predicting university performance.

Similarly, [19] used ML models such as linear regression, decision trees (Random Forest), Lasso regression, and Ridge regression to address regression problems. Their study focused on forecasting the number of students enrolled under Colombia's "over-age" condition. Model evaluation was conducted using metrics such as the coefficient of determination (R^2), root mean square error (RMSE), and mean absolute percentage error (MAPE), achieving an accuracy of 73%. This AI-based approach aids educational policy planning by forecasting student enrollment across diverse groups. The findings support strategies to boost academic achievement and retention.

2.4 Research Gap and Expected Contributions

Despite the growing use of ML in education, research on its application to Saber Pro data, particularly in Colombian engineering programs, remains limited. This gap presents an opportunity to propose a model that predicts academic performance and identifies the key factors influencing it. By focusing on Random Forest, this study provides a clear methodological framework for future research, emphasizing both predictive accuracy and interpretability.

The expected contributions of this study include: 1) A validated ML model to predict academic performance in engineering students using Saber Pro data. 2) Identification of the most influential socioeconomic and academic variables affecting performance. 3) Actionable insights for institutional policies and pedagogical strategies to reduce dropout rates and improve learning outcomes. 4) A scalable framework that can be adapted by other institutions in similar contexts, particularly in Latin America.

3 Proposed Model

Random Forest was chosen for this study due to its ability to perform feature selection during model training, allowing evaluation of each variable's importance. Its high predictive power, achieved by combining multiple decision trees through bagging, enhances accuracy, reduces overfitting, and improves prediction quality, making it well-suited for educational data analysis [20].

3.1 Data

The Saber Pro test is an external assessment that measures the quality of higher education in Colombia. It evaluates students in five general modules: Critical Reading, Written Communication, Quantitative Reasoning, Citizenship Competencies, and English. Additionally, it offers 40 specific modules, assigned according to the core knowledge area and the academic program's level of training, as classified by the National Higher Education Information System of the Ministry of National Education [19]. For this study, five differentiated databases will be used: SaberPro_2021.txt (246,498 records), SaberPro_Específicas_2021_2.txt (198,167 records), SaberPro_2022–1.TXT (42,734 records), DATA_ICFES_SABERPROPROFESIONAL_2022–2.TXT (127,342 records), and DATA_ICFES_SABERPRO_PROFESIONAL_20231.TXT (139,288 records).

The dataset includes generic and specific competencies by study area. A filtering process will focus on engineering students from a private university (UNIMINUTO), specifically in Agroecological, Civil, Systems, Industrial, and Logistics Engineering. Independent variables (X) include sociodemographic factors such as nationality, location, internet access, gender, and parents' education. Dependent variables (Y) include performance scores in Critical Reading, Written Communication, Quantitative Reasoning, Citizenship Competencies, English, Global Score, and Global Percentile.

3.2 Data Preprocessing and Modelling

The proposed model integrates preprocessing, feature engineering, and data modeling to optimize prediction. Techniques like Random Forest and cross-validation will be used to enhance accuracy and generalization. In line with Raschka's recommendations [21], the approach also considers challenges related to data quality and availability.

1. Data Integration and Consolidation:
   - Data Loading: Four national Saber Pro databases (from 2021-2 to 2023-1) were imported into a unified workspace.
   - Structure Unification: Verify that all datasets have a homogeneous structure regarding column names and data types.
   - Dataset Merging: The five cohorts were consolidated into a single DataFrame containing 452,020 student records and 83 variables.
2. Data Cleaning and Correction of Inconsistencies:
   - Duplicate Removal: Identify and remove duplicate records.
   - Handling Missing Values: If there are missing values in categorical variables (access to internet, household assets), they can be filled with the mode. For numerical variables, it can be completed with the median or mean, depending on the distribution.

Or if a variable has a high percentage of missing values (>50%), consider removing it. In addition, verify typographical errors, date formats, out-of-range values, and atypical records. After the cleaning process, the dataset was reduced from 83 to 71 variables, preserving only those relevant and consistent for modelling and analysis.

3. Feature Engineering.
   - Target Variable Construction: The response variable corresponds to the global score, which ranges from 0 to 300. To mitigate class imbalance, it will be discretized into three categories: Low: scores $\leq$ 135.5, Medium: scores between 135.6 and 157.5
   - High: scores > 157.5, this transformation will allow the modelling task to be addressed as a multiclass classification problem.
   - Predictor Variables: The modelling process will consider a wide set of predictor variables, including sociodemographic, academic, and familial characteristics:
   - Student-related variables and Family and household variables.
   - Relevant Feature Selection: Apply feature selection techniques, such as correlation analysis or feature importance-based selection using Random Forest.
   - Categorical Variable Encoding: One-Hot Encoding for nominal variables (academic programmes, universities), or label encoding for ordinal variables (socioeconomic level).
   - Numerical Data Transformation: Normalization (MinMaxScaler) for disparate scales, or Standardization (StandardScaler).
   - Creation of New Variables: Average performance scores in general competencies, exam participation indexes, and variables derived from socioeconomic characteristics.
4. Exploratory Data Analysis (EDA).
   - Distribution Visualisation: histograms, boxplots, and scatter plots to identify patterns.
   - Outlier Detection: Use Interquartile Range or DBSCAN to detect score anomalies.

- Correlation Analysis: Use a correlation matrix to identify relationships between variables and prevent multicollinearity.

5. Data Splitting.

   Split the data into training and testing sets using an 80/20 ratio, where 80% of the data is allocated for training the model and 20% for testing its performance. This division allows the model to learn from a substantial portion of the data while assessing its ability to generalize to unseen examples. Although the 80/20 ratio is widely used, it can be adjusted depending on the dataset size and the specific objectives of the task [22, 23].
6. Cross-validation strategy.

   Use Stratified K-Fold Cross-Validation to assess the model's robustness. This method divides the dataset into K equal parts, preserving the original class distribution in each fold. The model is trained on K-1 folds and tested on the remaining fold, repeating the process K times. The final performance is obtained by averaging the results across all iterations, ensuring a robust evaluation [24, 25].

3.3 Model Implementation

Random Forest is applied for feature selection and performance prediction, improving model efficiency Fig. 1. This figure presents a basic model of a Random Forest based on [24]. Subsequently, hyperparameter optimization uses GridSearchCV or RandomizedSearch to prune trees and adjust parameters, preventing overfitting. GridSearchCV combines grid search and cross-validation to evaluate all possible parameter combinations within a defined range. Its objective is to minimize the Mean Squared Forecasting Error (MSFE), calculated as [24, 25]:

$$MSFE = \frac{1}{n}\sum\nolimits_{i=1}^{n} \left(yi - \hat{y}_i\right)^2 \tag{1}$$

where y_i represents actual values and $\hat{y}_i$ are the model's predictions. In k-fold cross-validation, the MSFE is averaged across k partitions:

$$MSFE_f = \frac{1}{k}\sum\nolimits_{i=1}^{n} MSFE_j \tag{2}$$

GridSearchCV systematically evaluates all parameter combinations and selects the one that minimizes the final MSFE, ensuring optimal model configuration.

3.4 Metrics

Evaluating model performance involves analysing the factors influencing test results and comparing evaluation metrics across different models, such as (MSE), coefficient determination, sensitivity, precision, and specificity [26]. Additionally, interpreting the results and analysing the importance of predictive features provides valuable insights into the model's effectiveness and ability to generalise to new data.

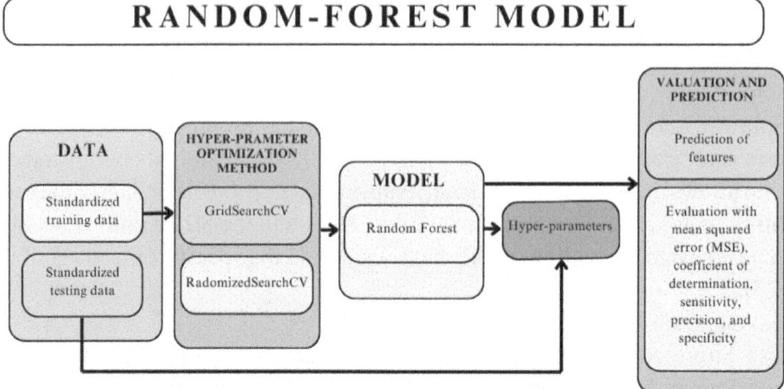

Fig. 1. Model Implementation, Random Forest

3.5 Current Limitations

This study presents several limitations that may affect the accuracy and development of the analysis. One of the main challenges is the time required for ICFES to provide the databases, which can delay the research process. Data quality poses a challenge, as the information may often contain inconsistencies, missing values, or erroneous records, requiring extensive cleaning and preprocessing. Furthermore, handling sensitive data demands strict security and confidentiality measures to ensure its protection and prevent unauthorized access.

4 Implications

4.1 Model Relevance

The Random Forest algorithm is machine learning tool for identifying critical variables significantly influencing academic performance due to its robust feature selection capabilities and interpretability [27]. This model leverages an ensemble of decision trees trained on diverse subsets of data, thereby effectively capturing complex, nonlinear relationships between predictors and academic outcomes while mitigating the risks associated with overfitting [28].

The inherent ability of Random Forest to rank variables based on their importance enables educational researchers and institutions to pinpoint precise socio-economic, academic, and institutional factors that have the most substantial impact on student performance [29]. Consequently, this facilitates an informed and systematic analysis of each variable's contribution and significance, guiding educational institutions in formulating targeted, evidence-based intervention strategies and personalized action plans. Beyond predicting academic performance at the student level, the insights derived from the Random Forest model provide actionable guidance at broader institutional and policymaking levels [30]. Educational leaders and policymakers can leverage these analytical insights to address systemic issues, such as socioeconomic disparities and unequal access to educational resources, thus promoting equitable education policies aligned with broader educational goals and national priorities [31].

Furthermore, integrating data-driven methodologies within engineering education supports optimizing pedagogical approaches [32]. It allows educators to identify precise learning patterns, trends, and performance gaps, contributing significantly to refining teaching methods, curriculum design, and student support systems to enhance educational quality and reduce dropout rates [33, 34]. Additionally, this research aligns with global educational standards and initiatives, such as the United Nations Sustainable Development Goals (SDGs), particularly SDG 4 (Quality Education). It demonstrates how advanced data-driven techniques like Random Forest can promote equitable and inclusive education, thus facilitating improved educational outcomes, resource optimization, and long-term socio-economic benefits at regional and national scales.

4.2 Impact on Decision-Making

The proposed Random Forest model enhances academic management by enabling data-driven decision-making in higher education. It supports student affairs teams in delivering targeted interventions such as mentoring, counselling, psychosocial support, and academic reinforcement. Predictive analytics allow early detection of issues like absenteeism, course failure, and dropout risk, improving retention and student success [35]. By identifying performance patterns, institutions can allocate resources effectively and personalize support, boosting engagement, achievement, and well-being while reducing dropout rates [3, 36].

The proposed approach creates avenues for future research, particularly in examining the alignment between specific academic competencies and labour market demands within engineering disciplines [37]. By linking predictive insights with industry requirements, institutions can better prepare students to meet evolving workforce challenges, fostering long-term professional success and institutional excellence [38]. This data-driven framework enhances immediate decision-making capabilities and supports the broader objective of aligning educational practices with industry standards and market demands, ultimately driving continual improvement and innovation in engineering education [39].

4.3 Future Research Lines

Considering the impact of ML in education, this study opens the door to exploring new research directions. Specifically, it suggests applying various analytical models, such as Clustering, KNN, and Artificial Neural Networks, to gain deeper insights into the socioeconomic and cultural factors influencing students' performance in the Saber Pro exams. Additionally, future research could delve into the relationship between academic competencies and the skills required in the job market. These methodologies will help identify hidden patterns in the data and develop more precise strategies to improve academic performance and align educational programs with industry needs.

4.4 Limitations

His study is presented as a methodological proposal and does not yet include complete experimental results. While Random Forest provides robust predictive capabilities, its performance is dependent on data quality, feature selection, and class balance. Limitations include delays in accessing updated Saber Pro datasets, potential noise in self-reported socioeconomic variables, and the computational cost of training models on large-scale data. These aspects should be addressed in future stages to strengthen the empirical contribution and ensure broader applicability.

5 Conclusions

The proposed Random Forest model offers a scalable and adaptable framework for higher education institutions, particularly in Latin America, by supporting the transition from traditional approaches to personalized, data-driven strategies. Its ability to optimize resources and enhance pedagogical and student welfare initiatives demonstrates practical value across academic settings. Future research should validate the model using updated and diverse data, expand its application beyond engineering disciplines, and explore the integration of deep learning techniques to improve predictive accuracy and interpretability. Longitudinal studies could further reveal the long-term impact of targeted educational interventions.

Applying ML techniques in higher education to private institutions such as Uniminuto presents a significant opportunity to enhance academic quality and optimize resource allocation. Integrating predictive models into educational management enables data driven decision-making, personalized teaching strategies, and early intervention plans for at-risk students.

This work provides a methodological foundation for applying Random Forest in large-scale educational assessment, specifically the Saber Pro exams. Although empirical results are still under development, the proposed framework highlights the potential of machine learning to transform academic management in Latin America. Future research will validate the model with updated data, compare it with advanced algorithms such as XGBoost and neural networks, and extend its application across disciplines. By aligning predictive analytics with institutional goals and global initiatives like SDG 4 (Quality Education), this approach can contribute to reducing inequalities and fostering innovation in higher education.

References

1. Zhao, Y., Chen, X., Xue, H., Weiss, G.M.: A machine learning approach to graduate admissions and the role of letters of recommendation. PLoS ONE **18**(10), e0291107 (2023). https://doi.org/10.1371/journal.pone.0291107
2. Wang, K., Cui, W., Yuan, X.: Artificial intelligence in higher education: the impact of need satisfaction on artificial intelligence literacy mediated by self-regulated learning strategies. Behav. Sci. (Basel) **15**(2) (2025). https://doi.org/10.3390/bs15020165

3. Goran, R., et al.: Identifying and understanding student dropouts using metaheuristic optimized classifiers and explainable artificial intelligence techniques. IEEE Access **12**, 122377–122400 (2024). https://doi.org/10.1109/access.2024.3446653
4. Beaulac, C., Rosenthal, J.S.: Predicting university students' academic success and major using random forests. Res. High. Educ. **60**(7), 1048–1064 (2019). https://doi.org/10.1007/s11162-019-09546-y
5. Yuetqi, L., Lin, G.S.S., Mamat, R.B., Noorani, T.Y.: Student's perception of hybrid team-based and case-based learning in undergraduate endodontics education. BMC Oral Health **25**(1), 43 (2025)
6. Vargas, A.M.C., Espinoza Mina, M.A., López Catálan, L., López Catalán, B.: Computational intelligence, educational robotics, and artificial intelligence in the educational field. A bibliometric study and thematic modelling. Int. J. Educ. Res. Innov. **22**, 1–19 (2024). https://doi.org/10.46661/ijeri.10369
7. Gao, Y., Bu, S.: Genetically optimized neural network for college English teaching evaluation method. Educ. Inf. Technol. **29**(17), 22371–22405 (2024). https://doi.org/10.1007/s10639-024-12736-6
8. Contreras, L.E., Bermúdez, G.M., Cardona, A.P.: Machine learning aplicado al rendimiento académico en educación superior: factores, variables y herramientas. Editorial Universidad Distrital Francisco José de Caldas (2023)
9. Plant, E.A., Ericsson, K.A., Hill, L., Asberg, K.: Why study time does not predict grade point average across college students: implications of deliberate practice for academic performance. Contemp. Educ. Psychol. **30**(1), 96–116 (2005)
10. Vanegas-Ayala, S.C., Leal-Lara, D.D., Barón-Velandia, J.: Prediction of student performance saber protest in pandemic together with socio-economic characteristics. Tecnol. Investig. Acad. TIA **9**(2), 5–16 (2021)
11. Mary, M.C., Jennath, H.S., Asharaf, S.: Explainable optimal random forest model with conversational interface. Eng. Appl. Artif. Intell. **145**(110134), 110134 (2025)
12. Jain, K.K., Raghuram, J.N.V.: Gen-AI integration in higher education: predicting intentions using SEM-ANN approach. Educ. Inf. Technol. (2024). https://doi.org/10.1007/s10639-024-12506-4
13. Kavitha, K., Joshith, V.P.: Pedagogical incorporation of artificial intelligence in K-12 science education: a decadal bibliometric mapping and systematic literature review (2013–2023). J. Pedagog. Res. (2024). https://doi.org/10.33902/jpr.202429218
14. Syed Mustapha, S.M.F.D.: Predictive analysis of students' learning performance using data mining techniques: a comparative study of feature selection methods. Appl. Syst. Innov. **6**(5) (2023)
15. Shoaib, M., Sayed, N., Singh, J., Shafi, J., Khan, S., Ali, F.: AI student success predictor: enhancing personalized learning in campus management systems. Comput. Human Behav. **158**(108301), 108301 (2024). https://doi.org/10.1016/j.chb.2024.108301
16. Ang, K.L.-M., Ge, F.L., Seng, K.P.: Big educational data & analytics: survey, architecture and challenges. IEEE Access **8**, 116392–116414 (2020). https://doi.org/10.1109/access.2020.2994561
17. Korous, K.M., Causadias, J.M., Bradley, R.H., Luthar, S.S., Levy, R.: A systematic overview of meta-analyses on socioeconomic status, cognitive ability, and achievement: the need to focus on specific pathways. Psychol. Rep. **125**(1), 55–97 (2022). https://doi.org/10.1177/0033294120984127
18. Karim-Abdallah, B., Ayitey Junior, M., Appiahene, P., Harris, E., Binful, D.K.: Application of machine learning algorithms in predicting academic performance of students in higher education institutes (HEIs): a systematic review and bibliographic analysis. Afr. J. Appl. Res. **11**(1), 536–559 (2025). https://doi.org/10.26437/ajar.v11i1.869

19. Ordoñez, H., Ordoñez, C., Buchelis, V.: Identificación de las tendencias del estado actual de la extraedad en el acceso a la educación básica en Colombia aplicando inteligencia artificial. Investig. Innov. Ing. **10**(2), 106–118 (2022)
20. Breiman, L.: Random forests. Mach. Learn. **45**(1), 5–32 (2001). https://doi.org/10.1023/a:1010933404324
21. Raschka, S.: Python machine learning: machine learning and deep learning with python, scikit-learn, and TensorFlow. Sebastian Raschka y Vahid Mirjalili (2017)
22. Gedeck, P., Bruce, P., Bruce, A.: Estadística Práctica Para Ciencia De Datos Con R Y Python Más de 50 conceptos esenciales. Marcombo (2022)
23. Zhao, Y., Zhang, W., Liu, X.: Grid search with a weighted error function: hyper-parameter optimization for financial time series forecasting. Appl. Soft Comput. **154**(111362), 111362 (2024)
24. Xu, J., Liu, X., Gu, Z., Xiao, G.: A rapid cross-validation computing for three-way decisions in imbalanced data. Inf. Sci. (Ny) **707**(122016), 122016 (2025)
25. Vuralli, D., Polat, S., Isık, E.I., Öksüzler, M., Özel, A.S., Göker, P.: Crista Galli morphometry and morphology: an anatomical, radiological, and machine learning application study. Int. J. Morphol. **41**(3), 749–757 (2023)
26. Liu, C., Balasubramanian, P., An, J., Li, F.: Machine learning prediction of ammonia nitrogen adsorption on biochar with model evaluation and optimization. NPJ Clean Water **8**(1) (2025)
27. García-González, J.R., Sánchez-Sánchez, P.A., Orozco, M., Obredor, S.: Extracción de conocimiento para la predicción y análisis de los resultados de la prueba de calidad de la educación superior en Colombia. Form. Univ **12**(4), 55–62 (2019)
28. Almalawi, A., Soh, B., Li, A., Samra, H.: Predictive models for educational purposes: a systematic review. Big Data Cogn. Comput. **8**(12) (2024)
29. Nnadi, L.C., Watanobe, Y., Rahman, M.M., John-Otumu, A.M.: Prediction of students' adaptability using explainable AI in educational machine learning models. Appl. Sci. (Basel) **14**(12), 5141 (2024). https://doi.org/10.3390/app14125141
30. Barnes, E., Hutson, J., Perry, K.: Optimizing adult learner success: applying random forest classifier in higher education predictive analytics. Int. J. Multidiscip. Curr. Educ. Res. **6**(3) (2024)
31. Yingsoon, G.Y., Yiming, C., Suyan, Z., Haiyan, Z., Xiaoyao, T.: Elevating equity in education: programmatic strategies for supporting disadvantaged learners. In: Mitigating Learner Disadvantages in Teaching and Learning, pp. 29–58. IGI Global Scientific Publishing (2025)
32. Rahmani, S., Aghalar, H., Jebreili, S., Goli, A.: Optimization and computing using intelligent data-driven approaches for decision-making. In: Optimization and Computing Using Intelligent Data-Driven Approaches for Decision-Making. CRC Press (2024)
33. Ahmad, K., et al.: Data-driven artificial intelligence in education: a comprehensive review. EdArXiv (2020). https://doi.org/10.35542/osf.io/zvu2n
34. Kurilovas, E.: On data-driven decision-making for quality education. Comput. Hum. Behav. **107**(105774), 105774 (2020). https://doi.org/10.1016/j.chb.2018.11.003
35. Salloum, S.A., Alomari, K.M., Alfaisal, A.M., Aljanada, R.A., Basiouni, A.: Emotion recognition for enhanced learning: using AI to detect students' emotions and adjust teaching methods. Smart Learn. Environ. **12**(1) (2025). https://doi.org/10.1186/s40561-025-00374-5
36. Vetrivel, S.C., Vidhyapriya, P., Arun, V.P.: data science for learning analytics: understanding and improving learning processes. In: Driving Quality Education Through AI and Data Science. IGI Global Scientific Publishing (2025)
37. OrozcoMorales, N., OsorioGarcía, P.A.: Aplicación de modelos de inteligencia artificial en pruebas estandarizadas para la optimización del rendimiento académico en educación superior. Eur. Public Soc. Innov. Rev. **9**, 1–21 (2024). https://doi.org/10.31637/epsir-2024-1605

38. Silva, M., Ferreira, A., Alves, K., Valenca, G., Brito, K.: A new perspective for longitudinal measurement and analysis of public education in Brazil based on open data and machine learning. In: Proceedings of the 17th International Conference on Theory and Practice of Electronic Governance, pp. 130–138. ACM, New York (2024)
39. AbRahman, N.F., Wang, S.L., Ng, T.F., Ghoneim, A.S.: Artificial intelligence in education: a systematic review of machine learning for predicting student performance. J. Adv. Res. Appl. Sci. Eng. Tech. **54**(1), 198–221 (2024). https://doi.org/10.37934/araset.54.1.198221

Comparative Study of Closed Vision-Language Models for Ki-67 Index Prediction in Breast Cancer Histopathology Images

Harold Brayan Arteaga-Arteaga[1,2,3(✉)], Juan Andrés Giraldo-Arias[2], Esteban Mercado-Ruiz[1], Miguel Angel Londoño-Salgado[1], Cristina Juárez Landín[4], Mario Alejandro Bravo-Ortiz[1,2], Pablo Guillen-Rondon[5,6], and Reinel Tabares-Soto[1,2,7]

[1] Departamento de Electrónica y Automatización, Universidad Autónoma de Manizales, Manizales 170001, Caldas, Colombia
harold.arteagaa@autonoma.edu.co

[2] Departamento de Sistemas e Informática, Universidad de Caldas, Manizales 170002, Caldas, Colombia

[3] CDI Interactive, Ariadna Communications Group, Manizales 170001, Caldas, Colombia

[4] Centro Universitario UAEM Valle de Chalco, Universidad Autónoma del Estado de México, Valle de Chalco Solidaridad 56615, Estado de México, Mexico

[5] Department of Computer Science, University of Houston Downtown, Houston, TX 77002, USA

[6] Biomedical and Energy Solutions LLC, Houston, TX 77001, USA

[7] Faculty of Engineering and Sciences, Universidad Adolfo Ibáñez, Diagonal Las Torres 2640, 7941169 Santiago de chile, Chile

Abstract. This study delivers the first multi-vendor comparison of closed source Vision-Language Models (VLMs) for automated Ki-67 index estimation in breast cancer histopathology. This study applies a single guideline-based prompt to seven proprietary VLMs to identify Ki-67 positive and negative nuclei, compute the proliferation index, and show the calculation steps. On the expert-annotated BCData test set (402 images), performance varies substantially: GPT-4.5 achieves the highest concordance with pathologists ($R^2 = 0.86$, RMSE = 7.97), while Gemini 1.5 Pro and Grok-2 Vision score lower ($R^2 = 0.62$ and 0.28, respectively). Inference time per image ranged from 1.5 to 6 s, reflecting different speed-cost trade-offs. This study shows that closed VLMs can estimate Ki-67 without retraining at a level that may be clinically useful; however, accuracy and cost vary by provider.

Keywords: Vision-Language Models · Breast Cancer · Histopathology · Ki-67 Index · Deep Learning · Comparative Study

T. Guarda et al. (Eds.): ARTIIS 2025, CCIS 2789, pp. 328–342, 2026.
https://doi.org/10.1007/978-3-032-16758-3_26

1 Introduction

Breast cancer is the most common cancer in women and a leading cause of death worldwide. It accounts for about 25% of female cancers and 15.4% of related deaths [6]. Clinical management relies heavily on reliable biomarkers to guide treatment decisions and personalize care [8,17]. Among these, the Ki-67 proliferation index quantifies the fraction of Ki-67-expressing tumor cells, offering key prognostic and predictive insights [4]. Yet, manual scoring of Ki-67 is laborious and subject to significant inter-observer variability, limiting reproducibility in routine practice [7,26,31,34].

The advent of artificial intelligence (AI), particularly deep learning (DL), has revolutionized digital pathology by automating biomarker evaluation and improving throughput and consistency [3,25,29,30]. A variety of deep learning (DL) architectures, ranging from segmentation networks to specialized classifiers (e.g., piNET, PathoNet, Lite-UNet), have demonstrated accurate Ki-67 scoring [12,13,20,32]. However, these systems need many labeled images, significant computing power, and periodic retraining, which hinders broad clinical adoption [9,11].

Figure 1 illustrates the transition from manual counting, following the guidelines of the International Ki-67 Working Group, to DL-based automation. In the manual approach, pathologists identify and tally Ki-67-positive and Ki-67-negative cells, a process prone to subjective bias and inter-reader differences [26,31].

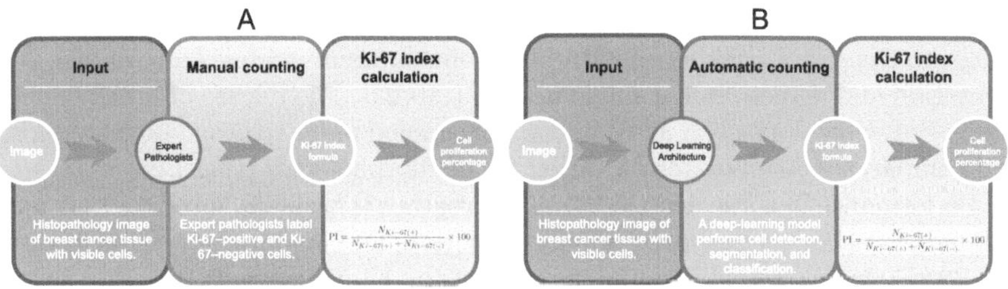

Fig. 1. Ki-67 index assessment in breast cancer histopathology: (A) manual counting and (B) deep learning-assisted automation.

Automated DL methods substantially improve consistency and speed by standardizing cell detection and classification, reducing the variability inherent to manual review [24].

Vision-Language Models (VLMs) combine image analysis with natural language. With a prompt, they can interpret images without retraining. With structured prompts, VLMs can extract quantitative biomarkers such as the Ki-67 index. This approach reduces the need for custom training and makes advanced analysis more accessible where deep-learning infrastructure is limited.

This work presents the first multi-provider evaluation of closed-source VLMs for Ki-67 prediction. The same guideline-based prompt was run on seven models, and outputs were compared with BCData labels using standard regression metrics (R^2, MAE, MSE, RMSE).

This paper contributes: (i) a zero-shot, prompt-based method to estimate the Ki-67 index; (ii) a cross-vendor benchmark that reports accuracy, cost, and latency; and (iii) practical recommendations for selecting and integrating these models in pathology workflows.

The remainder of the paper is organized as follows: Sect. 2 reviews related work in DL-based Ki-67 prediction; Sect. 3 describes the materials and methods; Sect. 4 presents the experimental results; Sect. 5 discusses the findings and their implications; and Sect. 6 concludes.

2 Related Work

Early efforts in automating Ki-67 scoring relied on classical machine learning and image processing techniques for nucleus detection and classification. While these methods demonstrated feasibility, their robustness and scalability were constrained when faced with diverse, large-scale histopathology datasets [4].

The introduction of convolutional neural networks (CNNs) marked a major advance, enabling end-to-end frameworks for cell segmentation, detection, and classification in digital pathology [5,29]. Pioneering studies by Saha et al. showed that deep architectures could reliably score Ki-67, spurring subsequent work on U-Net variants, MobileUNet, and custom networks like PathoNet [25,30].

Further developments include hybrid and multi-branch architectures that integrate DenseNet backbones with fully convolutional modules or combine segmentation and detection in a single model [1,10,23]. The release of large, expert-annotated collections such as BCData has enabled more rigorous benchmarking and comparative studies across varied tissue morphologies [16,20,25].

Performance in these deep learning approaches is typically measured via metrics such as mean average precision for detection, Dice and IoU for segmentation, and MAE, MSE, or RMSE for regression of the Ki-67 index [9,19,32].

Moreover, conventional deep learning pipelines require extensive labeled data, substantial computing resources, and periodic retraining to maintain performance across new clinical domains. These requirements hinder rapid deployment and adaptation in routine pathology settings.

Automated Ki-67 scoring has relied on DL pipelines that achieve high accuracy but demand large annotated datasets, significant computational resources, and frequent retraining to generalize across different settings [1,2,10,12,13,15, 18–23,25,27,32].

Recently, Vision-Language Models have emerged, offering zero-shot image understanding coupled with natural language reasoning. To date, no study has systematically compared closed-source VLMs from multiple commercial providers for the quantitative prediction of biomarkers. This work fills that gap by benchmarking OpenAI, Google, and xAI models on Ki-67 index estimation.

3 Materials and Methods

3.1 Dataset

BCData, a public dataset with expert cell-level annotations, was used as the evaluation benchmark [16]. The test split contains 402 images spanning diverse tissue patterns and expression levels (see Table 1).

Table 1. Composition of the BCData dataset (adapted from [16]).

Set	Number Positive Cell	Number Negative Cell	Number Total Cell	Number Images
Train	33,058	60,780	93,838	803
Validation	7,701	14,103	21,804	133
Test	21,864	43,568	65,432	402
Total	**62,623**	**118,451**	**181,074**	**1,338**

3.2 Ki-67 Index Calculation

The *Ki-67 index* (proliferation index, PI) is the percentage of Ki-67-positive cells among all tumor cells (positive and negative) as shown in Eq. 1. It is an objective indicator of proliferation and tumor aggressiveness [4].

$$PI = \frac{N_{\text{Ki-67}(+)}}{N_{\text{Ki-67}(+)} + N_{\text{Ki-67}(-)}} \times 100\% \tag{1}$$

where $N_{\text{Ki-67}(+)}$ is the number of Ki-67-positive (immunopositive) cells and $N_{\text{Ki-67}(-)}$ is the number of Ki-67-negative (immunonegative) cells within the analyzed region.

Figure 2 illustrates three histopathological examples with distinct PIs: (A) 6.31%, (B) 61.60%, and (C) 87.27% [25]. These variations highlight the heterogeneity of tumor proliferation and underscore the need for accurate quantification.

3.3 Prompting Strategy and VLM Configuration

Seven closed-source VLMs (OpenAI, Google, and xAI) were evaluated via their APIs. A single guideline-aligned prompt instructed each model to (i) distinguish positive and negative nuclei, (ii) count both, (iii) compute the PI, and (iv) report counts, calculation, and final percentage in a structured output. All analyses relied only on the models' built-in vision-language reasoning [26].

The prompt was designed to mirror a pathologist's workflow: find nuclei, count positives and negatives, then compute PI using Eq. 1. The prompt was checked on images with low, medium, and high Ki-67. Minor rephrasing produced similar results, but removing the stepwise instructions or the formula reduced consistency; therefore, one guideline-aligned prompt was used for all experiments.

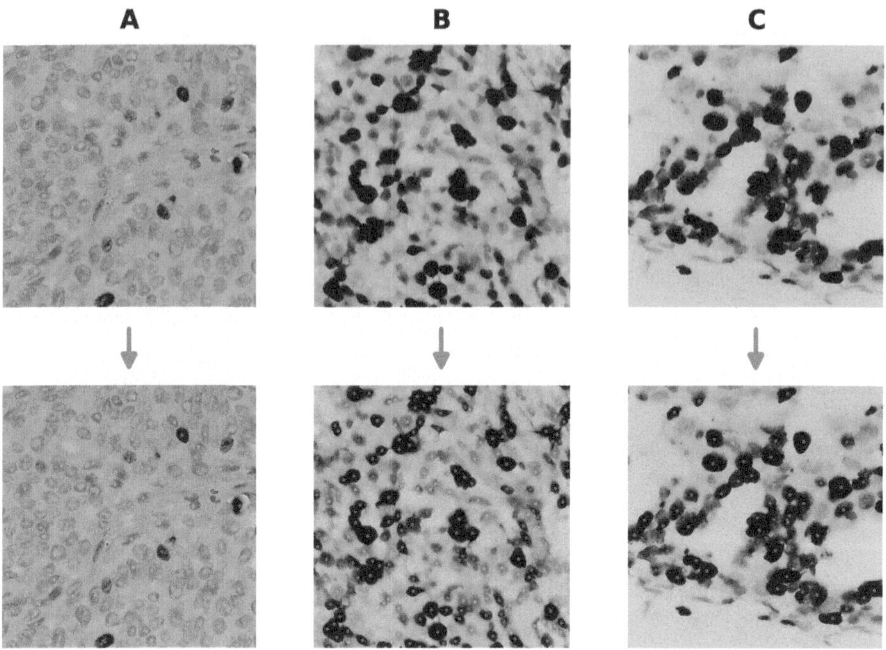

Fig. 2. Examples of Ki-67 index variation: (A) 6.31%, (B) 61.60%, and (C) 87.27%. Adapted from [25].

3.4 Automated Inference Pipeline

An automated Python pipeline was implemented to streamline batch inference. For each image, the pipeline sent the prompt and image to the API and saved the response. Positive and negative counts, calculation steps, and the final PI were logged for evaluation. Images for which the VLM declined or failed to provide valid counts were omitted from the quantitative assessment.

3.5 Reference Standard

Ground truth Ki-67 values for every test image were sourced from expert-annotated dataset labels, which were reviewed and confirmed by board-certified pathologists. These annotations serve as the definitive benchmark against which model outputs are compared.

3.6 Regression Metrics

Predictive performance was evaluated by comparing each predicted Ki-67 index $\hat{y}_i$ to its true counterpart y_i over n samples using established regression measures (see Eqs. 2, 3, 4):

- Mean Absolute Error (MAE):

$$\text{MAE} = \frac{1}{n}\sum_{i=1}^{n}\left|y_i - \hat{y}_i\right| \tag{2}$$

- Mean Squared Error (MSE):

$$\text{MSE} = \frac{1}{n}\sum_{i=1}^{n}\left(y_i - \hat{y}_i\right)^2 \tag{3}$$

- Root Mean Squared Error (RMSE):

$$\text{RMSE} = \sqrt{\text{MSE}} = \sqrt{\frac{1}{n}\sum_{i=1}^{n}\left(y_i - \hat{y}_i\right)^2} \tag{4}$$

where y_i is the true Ki-67 index for sample i, $\hat{y}_i$ is the predicted value, and n is the number of samples.

Additionally, the coefficient of determination (R^2) quantifies the fraction of variance in y that is explained by $\hat{y}$, and scatter plots are used to visualize the agreement between the prediction and the reference.

3.7 Ethical Considerations

All images originate from an anonymized, publicly accessible dataset. This research is intended for academic purposes and must not replace clinical judgment or decision-making by qualified professionals.

3.8 Resources

The code and resources are available at GitHub: https://github.com/BioAITeam/ki67-vlm-comparative-study-artiis-conf-2025. Alternatively, resources can be requested by contacting the authors. The GitHub repository includes: (i) end-to-end batch-inference code, (ii) the standardized prompt template, (iii) provider API configs (OpenAI, Google, xAI), (iv) evaluation and plotting scripts to reproduce Tables and Figures, (v) latency and cost logging utilities, and (vi) a quick-start README with environment file and usage examples.

4 Results

This section reports the quantitative evaluation of seven closed-source VLMs—GPT-4.5, GPT-4.1 mini, GPT-4.1, GPT-4o (OpenAI), Gemini 1.5 Pro, Gemini 1.5 Flash (Google), and Grok-2 Vision (xAI)—for zero-shot Ki-67 index estimation on the BCData test set. All indices were computed as per Eq. 1.

Table 2. Predictive performance of closed-source VLMs on the BCData test set

Provider	Model	R^2	MAE	MSE	RMSE
OpenAI	**GPT-4.5**	**0.8570**	**6.1507**	**63.5334**	**7.9708**
	GPT-4.1 mini	0.7523	8.3774	110.0709	10.4915
	GPT-4.1	0.6369	9.9281	161.3309	12.7016
	GPT-4o	0.3352	14.0849	295.3649	17.1862
Google	Gemini 1.5 Pro	0.6210	9.7350	168.3996	12.9769
	Gemini 1.5 Flash	0.5634	10.8133	183.2869	13.5383
xAI	Grok-2 Vision	0.2821	14.5148	318.9832	17.8601

4.1 Performance on BCData

Table 2 presents the coefficient of determination (R^2), MAE, MSE, and RMSE for each model, quantifying the agreement with expert pathologist annotations.

Figure 3 shows that most predictions lie near the diagonal (high concordance), with greater spread at higher Ki-67 values.

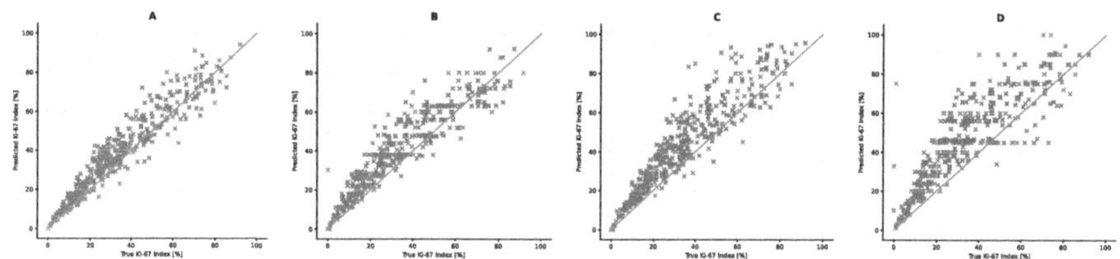

Fig. 3. Observed vs. predicted Ki-67 index for OpenAI VLMs: (A) GPT-4.5, (B) GPT-4.1 mini, (C) GPT-4.1, (D) GPT-4o. The diagonal denotes perfect agreement.

Figure 4 displays the same comparison for Google and xAI models. Predictions spread farther from the diagonal—especially at high Ki-67—indicating lower consistency.

The plots show greater variability between providers, especially at high Ki-67. This indicates differences in agreement and robustness across commercial models.

4.2 Summary and Interpretation

GPT-4.5 leads with an R^2 of 0.857 and RMSE of 7.97, demonstrating high fidelity to pathologist scores. Google's Gemini models perform moderately (R^2 0.6210 and 0.5634), while Grok-2 Vision trails ($R^2 = 0.2821$). Error metrics (MAE, RMSE) align with these trends, illustrating a trade-off between model size and capacity, as well as predictive accuracy.

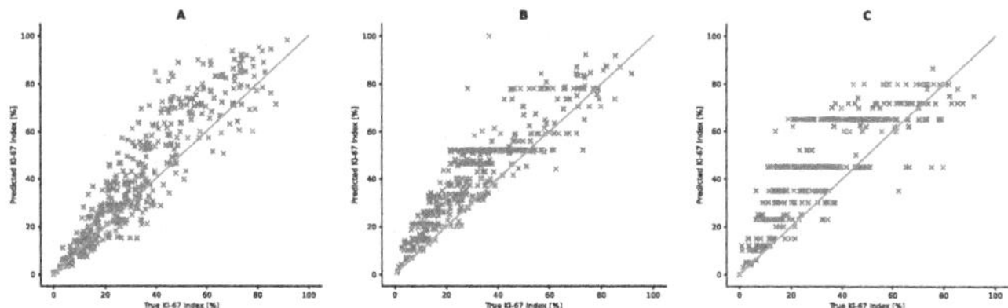

Fig. 4. Scatter plots of predicted versus true Ki-67 index on the BCData test set for Google and xAI models: (A) Gemini 1.5 Pro, (B) Gemini 1.5 Flash, and (C) Grok-2 Vision. Each point represents a test image, and the diagonal line indicates perfect prediction ($y = x$).

Visual analysis of the scatter plots supports quantitative findings, with most cases exhibiting close alignment between predictions and reference values. However, a few outliers exist, primarily in cases with high Ki-67 indices. These discrepancies may be related to challenges in image quality, staining variability, or cellular density.

Each VLM is proprietary, with its own internal design and training/inference setup; results therefore vary across providers. Consistent with capacity trends, larger or better-performing models (e.g., GPT-4.5) are typically more robust on Ki-67 index prediction.

4.3 Inference Time and Cost Analysis

Inference times per image varied according to the algorithm, ranging from approximately 1.5 to 6 s. Table 3 lists the estimated per-image costs from each provider at the time of the study. Overall costs were low enough to consider VLMs as an initial tool, including in resource-limited labs.

Table 3. Inference time and cost per image

Provider	Model	Avg Time [sec]	Cost [USD]
OpenAI	GPT-4.5	5.44	$0.12514
	GPT-4.1 mini	2.07	$0.00081
	GPT-4.1	2.84	$0.00353
	GPT-4o	3.17	$0.00408
Google	Gemini 1.5 Pro	2.43	$0.00420
	Gemini 1.5 Flash	1.59	$0.00084
xAI	Grok-2 Vision	5.21	$0.00673

These results affirm that closed VLMs can deliver clinically relevant Ki-67 quantification without retraining, though accuracy, latency, and cost profiles differ substantially across vendors.

5 Discussion

This work delivers the first comparative assessment of closed-source VLMs from multiple commercial providers—OpenAI, Google, and xAI—for the automated prediction of the Ki-67 index in breast cancer histopathology. Using a unified, clinically guided prompt and a curated dataset, this study shows that VLMs can reach accuracy comparable to traditional deep learning methods; performance still depends on the provider and model.

5.1 Comparison with Prior Work

Traditional automated Ki-67 scoring methods, mainly based on deep learning, require extensive annotated datasets, specialized model training, and continuous retraining to adapt to new data distributions or clinical settings [1,2,10,12,13,15,18–23,25,27,32]. These requirements can limit scalability and slow clinical translation. Our findings show that VLMs, especially larger models such as GPT-4.5, can achieve strong agreement with expert annotations ($R^2 > 0.85$ for GPT-4.5 from OpenAI), rivaling conventional deep learning pipelines, without requiring any retraining or domain-specific adaptation. This zero-shot, prompt-based paradigm has the potential to accelerate adoption and lower the barriers to implementing AI in digital pathology.

5.2 Performance, Interpretability, and Deployment Trade-Offs

Among the evaluated models, GPT-4.5 from OpenAI achieves the highest predictive performance, both in terms of explained variance and low error margins. Google's Gemini models and xAI's Grok-2 Vision, while capable of processing images and following prompts, exhibit lower accuracy and greater variability in predictions, particularly for high Ki-67 values. This highlights substantial vendor-dependent differences that must be considered for real-world integration.

A key advantage of prompt-based VLMs is their "explainability by construction." Unlike black-box deep learning models, VLMs can output explicit cell counts and provide detailed reasoning for each prediction, thereby increasing transparency and supporting clinical acceptance.

Inference time and cost analyses further highlight trade-offs. While larger models yield superior performance, they require more computational resources and have higher per-image costs. However, the ability to process hundreds of cases within minutes and at a low price makes this technology feasible for routine pathology, even in resource-limited environments.

To minimize costs, this study recommends validating per hospital (local scanners and stains) to pick the best cost-accuracy model. Reduce input tokens by shortening the prompt and by downscaling images, selecting the smallest resolution that maintains accuracy.

This tool is decision-support only. This work recommends implementing a human-in-the-loop protocol and reporting with full audit trails.

5.3 Limitations and Sources of Error

Despite promising results, several limitations exist. The accuracy of VLM predictions depends strongly on the quality and clarity of the prompt, and there is currently no consensus on the optimal prompt engineering for pathology tasks. Additionally, all results are based on a single, public dataset (BCData); performance on other staining protocols, tissue types, or in prospective clinical workflows remains to be validated. These findings are limited to BCData and may not transfer to other sites. A local pilot—with pathologist review of outputs—is recommended to validate the pipeline under each institution's scanners, resolutions, staining, and workflow.

Some models exhibited systematic errors—particularly at higher Ki-67 indices—potentially due to challenges in distinguishing densely packed or weakly stained nuclei. The outlier analysis reveals that while GPT-4.5 maintains robust performance, smaller and less capable models, or those from other providers, may struggle in such challenging scenarios.

5.4 Analysis of Outliers at High Ki-67 Indices

To highlight prediction discrepancies at elevated Ki-67 index values, Fig. 2 (C) shows a representative case with a true index of 87.27% (corresponding to 48 positive and seven negative cells). Model outputs for this image varied notably:

- *GPT-4.5*: 42 positive cells, 6 negative cells (87.50%).
- *GPT-4.1 mini*: 48 positive cells, 4 negative cells (92.31%).
- *GPT-4.1*: 38 positive cells, 2 negative cells (95.0%).
- *GPT-4o*: 45 positive cells, 5 negative cells (90.0%).
- *Gemini 1.5 Pro*: 70 positive cells, 28 negative cells (71.42%).
- *Gemini 1.5 Flash*: 87 positive cells, 13 negative cells (87.0%).
- *Grok-2 Vision*: 72 positive cells, 28 negative cells (72.0%).

These results indicate that higher-capacity models such as GPT-4.5 provide more accurate estimates for challenging, high-proliferation images, while other VLMs may fail to quantify Ki-67 in these contexts. This highlights the importance of selecting robust models for accurate biomarker assessment.

5.5 Hard Cases and Reference Benchmark

Lower robustness occurs in images with very high Ki-67 and marked nuclear crowding—cases that are difficult even for experts. Zero-shot VLMs show the same limitations. This paper and its results serve as the reference benchmark for such cases, encouraging the community to build on it with improved preprocessing and prompt strategies to strengthen robustness.

5.6 Practical and Clinical Implications

The ability to obtain reproducible, quantitative Ki-67 scores rapidly and at scale has direct implications for breast cancer prognosis and treatment planning. VLMs could help reduce inter-observer variability, improve workflow efficiency, and provide explainable outputs to support pathologists' trust. Furthermore, prompt-driven multimodal AI delivers a practical approach to deploying robust algorithms in settings where large-scale model retraining is impractical.

Clinical implications and risk mitigation. The models are intended strictly as decision-support and always require pathologist review and sign-off. A threshold-aware policy is recommended, using our predefined cut-offs (Low: Ki-67 $< 16\%$ (less proliferative), Medium: $16\% \leq$ Ki-67 $< 30\%$ (intermediate proliferation), High: Ki-67 $\geq 30\%$ (highly proliferative)), with manual recount for boundary cases or when AI and human assessments disagree. Models are decision-support only with mandatory pathologist review and sign-off [14,28,33]

5.7 Scientific Contribution and Future Directions

This study introduces a robust benchmark and open evaluation suite to advance research in multimodal AI for digital pathology. The findings indicate that closed-source VLMs offer considerable potential. Yet, their performance remains highly dependent on the provider, is sensitive to prompt design, and may not generalize well across domains, highlighting key areas for future research.

This research compares proprietary VLMs because most state-of-the-art, production-ready systems are closed and dominate current adoption; this study quantifies their accuracy, latency, and cost. Code, unified prompt, and inference scripts are publicly available; see the GitHub repository referenced in *Resources*.

Going forward, it will be essential to conduct systematic benchmarking of both closed and open-source VLMs from a wider variety of vendors and to evaluate their use in other histopathological scenarios. Efforts to develop standardized prompting protocols and to validate model performance in clinical practice will be essential for ensuring the safe and effective integration of these technologies. Ultimately, developing and training open-source VLMs will be key to establishing best practices for implementing multimodal AI in pathology, fostering broader accessibility, and enhancing the reliability of diagnostic tools.

6 Conclusion

This work presents the first comparative analysis of closed-source vision-language models from multiple vendors for automated estimation of the Ki-67 index in breast cancer histopathology images. By employing a unified, clinically relevant prompting protocol on the BCData database, this study demonstrates that VLMs—particularly high-capacity models such as GPT-4.5—can achieve strong agreement with pathologist annotations, matching or surpassing the performance of traditional deep learning methods, while requiring no training.

However, the findings also show marked variability across providers and model variants, underscoring the need for careful model selection and standardized prompting for robust clinical use. While these results are promising, further validation in diverse real-world settings is crucial, as is systematic evaluation of both proprietary and open-source VLMs to ensure reliability and generalizability across different pathology domains.

Vision-Language Models are poised to make quantitative digital pathology more accessible, reproducible, and interpretable. Their rapid deployment, ability to follow explicit clinical instructions, and explainable outputs offer a practical pathway to AI integration in diagnostic workflows. Continued benchmarking and open evaluation will be key to advancing best practices and maximizing the clinical impact of multimodal AI in cancer care.

Acknowledgements. Harold Brayan Arteaga-Arteaga is supported by a Ph.D. grant Convocatoria 22 OCAD for Science, Technology, and Innovation of the Sistema General de Regalías de Colombia and the Ministerio de Ciencia, Tecnología e Innovación de Colombia. Harold Brayan Arteaga-Arteaga thanks the Universidad Autónoma de Manizales and Universidad Autónoma de Bucaramanga for their support in completing this publication, which is an integral part of his M.Eng. and Ph.D. in Engineering studies. We would like to thank Universidad Autónoma de Manizales for making this publication possible as part of the projects "Development of a novel ViT-based Deep Learning architecture to predict the Ki-67 index in histopathological images of Breast Cancer", "Development of a pipeline based on Vision-Language Models for Ki-67 Index prediction in Breast Cancer histopathological images", *"Clasificación de los estadios del Alzheimer utilizando Imágenes de Resonancia Magnética Nuclear y datos clínicos a partir de técnicas de Deep Learning"* with code 873-139, *"Diagnóstico del Cáncer Cérvico-Uterino a través de Modelos de Inteligencia Artificial (IA), como aporte a la Salud Integral de las Mujeres" with code 922-151"*, and *"Aplicación de Vision Transformer para clasificar estadios del Alzheimer utilizando imágenes de resonancia magnética nuclear y datos clínicos"* with code 847-2023 TD. The Universidad de Caldas also supported the development of the publication with *"Sistema para la detección y prevención de Ciberataques No Convencionales a partir de aprendizaje profundo para Servicios de Ciberdefensa"* with code PRY-80; *"Diagnóstico del cáncer Cérvico-Uterino a través de modelos de Inteligencia Artificial, como aporte a la Salud Integral de las mujeres"* with code PRY-276, *"Desarrollo de modelos de Ciencia de Datos para apoyo diagnóstico en el S.E.S. Hospital Universitario De Caldas"* with code PRY-178; *"Plataforma Tecnológica para la clasificación de los estadios de la enfermedad de Alzheimer utilizando imágenes de Resonancia Magnética Nuclear, datos clínicos y técnicas de Deep Learning"* with code PRY-89; *"Generar un modelo de ML que sea capaz de predecir las condiciones idóneas que contribuya a la administración de los recursos de hidrocarburos gaseosos en la cuenca del Valle Inferior del Magdalena"* with code PRY-345; and *"Familia, Diversidad y Territorio: dinámicas familiares en el Eje Cafetero"* with code PRY-389. This publication was also supported by Agency for Research and Development (ANID), Applied Research Subdirection (SIA), through the instrument IDeA I+D 2023, code ID23I10357; ANID+SUBDIRECCIÓN DE INVESTIGACIÓN APLICADA/IT25I0161; ANID FONDECYT 1230315, ANID-MILENIO-NCN2024_103, ANID-MILENIO-NCN2024_047, ANID PIA/BASAL AFB240003, and

Centro de Modelamiento Matemático (CMM) FB210005, BASAL funds for centers of excellence from ANID-Chile.

Disclosure of Interests. Harold Brayan Arteaga-Arteaga is employed by Ariadna Communications Group. Pablo Guillen-Rondon is employed by Biomedical & Energy Solutions LLC.

References

1. Anglada-Rotger, D., Sala, J., Marques, F., Salembier, P., Pardàs, M.: Enhancing Ki-67 cell segmentation with dual U-Net models: a step towards uncertainty-informed active learning. In: 2024 IEEE/CVF Conference on Computer Vision and Pattern Recognition Workshops (CVPRW), pp. 5026–5035. IEEE (2024). https://doi.org/10.1109/CVPRW63382.2024.00509, https://ieeexplore.ieee.org/document/10678018/
2. Aniq, E., Chakraoui, M., Mouhni, N.: Artificial intelligence in pathological anatomy: digitization of the calculation of the proliferation index (Ki-67) in breast carcinoma. Artif. Life Robot. (2024). https://doi.org/10.1007/s10015-023-00923-6
3. Arteaga-Arteaga, H.B., Candamil-Cortés, M.S., Breaux, B., Guillen-Rondon, P., Orozco-Arias, S., Tabares-Soto, R.: Machine learning applications on intratumoral heterogeneity in glioblastoma using single-cell RNA sequencing data. Briefings Funct. Genomics (2023). https://doi.org/10.1093/bfgp/elad002
4. Barricelli, B.R., et al.: ki67 nuclei detection and ki67-index estimation: a novel automatic approach based on human vision modeling. BMC Bioinform. **20**(1), 733 (2019). https://doi.org/10.1186/s12859-019-3285-4
5. Bravo-Ortiz, M.A., et al.: CVTStego-Net: a convolutional vision transformer architecture for spatial image steganalysis. J. Inf. Secur. Appl. **81** (2024). https://doi.org/10.1016/j.jisa.2023.103695
6. International Agency for Research on Cancer, W.: Data visualization tools for exploring the global cancer burden in 2022 (2022). https://gco.iarc.fr/today/en, https://gco.iarc.who.int/media/globocan/factsheets/cancers/20-breast-fact-sheet.pdf
7. Catteau, X., Zindy, E., Bouri, S., Noël, J.C., Salmon, I., Decaestecker, C.: Comparison between manual and automated assessment of Ki-67 in breast carcinoma: test of a simple method in daily practice. Technol. Cancer Res. Treat. **22** (2023). https://doi.org/10.1177/15330338231169603
8. Choi, S.B., et al.: Ki-67 and breast cancer prognosis: does it matter if Ki-67 level is examined using preoperative biopsy or postoperative specimen? Breast Cancer Res. Treat. **192**(2), 343–352 (2022). https://doi.org/10.1007/s10549-022-06519-1
9. Dawe, M., et al.: Reliability and variability of Ki-67 digital image analysis methods for clinical diagnostics in breast cancer. Lab. Invest. **104**(5) (2024). https://doi.org/10.1016/j.labinv.2024.100341
10. Feng, M., et al.: An advanced automated image analysis model for scoring of ER, PR, HER-2 and Ki-67 in breast carcinoma. IEEE Access **9**, 108441–108451 (2020). https://doi.org/10.1109/ACCESS.2020.3011294
11. Fernando, G.P., Brayan, A.A.H., Florina, A.M., Liliana, C.B., Héctor-Gabriel, A.M., Reinel, T.S.: Enhancing intrusion detection in IoT communications through ML model generalization with a new dataset (IDSAI). IEEE Access **11**, 70542–70559 (2023). https://doi.org/10.1109/ACCESS.2023.3292267

12. Fulawka, L., Blaszczyk, J., Tabakov, M., Halon, A.: Assessment of Ki-67 proliferation index with deep learning in DCIS (ductal carcinoma in situ). Sci. Rep. **12**(1), 3166 (2022). https://doi.org/10.1038/s41598-022-06555-3
13. Geread, R.S., et al.: piNET–an automated proliferation index calculator framework for Ki67 breast cancer images. Cancers **13**(1), 11 (2020). https://doi.org/10.3390/cancers13010011, https://www.mdpi.com/2072-6694/13/1/11
14. Haltaufderheide, J., Ranisch, R.: The ethics of ChatGPT in medicine and healthcare: a systematic review on Large Language Models (LLMs) (2024). https://doi.org/10.1038/s41746-024-01157-x
15. Huang, J., Hu, Y., Xue, Y., Yao, Y., Wang, H., He, J.: A deep learning model for assessing Ki-67 and tumor-infiltrating lymphocytes using multiscale attention and pixel channel fusion. IEEE Access **12**, 167856–167865 (2024)
16. Huang, Z., et al.: BCData: a large-scale dataset and benchmark for cell detection and counting. In: Martel, A.L., et al. (eds.) MICCAI 2020. LNCS, vol. 12265, pp. 289–298. Springer, Cham (2020). https://doi.org/10.1007/978-3-030-59722-1_28
17. Kamal, A.M., Sakorikar, T., Pal, U.M., Pandya, H.J.: Engineering approaches for breast cancer diagnosis: a review. IEEE Rev. Biomed. Eng. **16**, 687–705 (2023). https://doi.org/10.1109/RBME.2022.3181700
18. Lakshmi, S., Ritwik, K.V.S., Vijayasenan, D., S., S.D., Sreeram, S., Suresh, P.K.: Deep learning model based Ki-67 index estimation with automatically labelled data. In: 2020 42nd Annual International Conference of the IEEE Engineering in Medicine & Biology Society (EMBC), pp. 1412–1415. IEEE (2020). https://doi.org/10.1109/EMBC44109.2020.9175752, https://ieeexplore.ieee.org/document/9175752/
19. Lakshmi, S., Vijayasenan, D., Sumam, D.S., Sreeram, S., Suresh, P.K.: An integrated deep learning approach towards automatic evaluation of Ki-67 labeling index. In: IEEE Region 10 Annual International Conference, Proceedings/TENCON, vol. 2019-Octob, pp. 2310–2314 (2019). https://doi.org/10.1109/TENCON.2019.8929640
20. Li, B., Zhang, Y., Ren, Y., Zhang, C., Yin, B.: Lite-UNet: a lightweight and efficient network for cell localization. Eng. Appl. Artif. Intell. **129**, 107634 (2024). https://doi.org/10.1016/j.engappai.2023.107634, https://linkinghub.elsevier.com/retrieve/pii/S0952197623018183
21. Liu, Y., et al.: A domain adaptive and label-efficient deep learning method for Ki-67 scoring in infiltrative breast ductal carcinoma cells. In: 2022 3rd International Conference on Control, Robotics and Intelligent System, pp. 211–218. ACM, New York (2022). https://doi.org/10.1145/3562007.3562048
22. Lu, W., et al.: AI-based intra-tumor heterogeneity score of Ki67 expression as a prognostic marker for early-stage ER+/HER2- breast cancer. J. Pathol. Clin. Res. (2023). https://doi.org/10.1002/cjp2.346
23. Mirjahanmardi, S.H., et al.: Preserving dense features for Ki67 nuclei detection, vol. 12039, pp. 220–227 (2022). https://doi.org/10.1117/12.2611212
24. Mora-Rubio, A., et al.: Multi-subject identification of hand movements using machine learning. In: Corchado, J.M., Trabelsi, S. (eds.) SSCTIC 2021. LNNS, vol. 253, pp. 117–128. Springer, Cham (2022). https://doi.org/10.1007/978-3-030-78901-5_11
25. Negahbani, F., et al.: PathoNet introduced as a deep neural network backend for evaluation of Ki-67 and tumor-infiltrating lymphocytes in breast cancer. Sci. Rep. **11**(1), 1–13 (2021). https://doi.org/10.1038/s41598-021-86912-w

26. Nielsen, T.O., et al.: Assessment of Ki67 in breast cancer: updated recommendations from the international Ki67 in breast cancer working group. J. Natl Cancer Inst. **113**(7), 808–819 (2021). https://doi.org/10.1093/jnci/djaa201
27. Phan, T.C., Phan, A.C., Le, T.M.T., Trieu, T.N.: Deep learning for detection and classification of nuclear protein in breast cancer tissue. In: Communications in Computer and Information Science, vol. 1950, pp. 15–28. Springer Science and Business Media Deutschland GmbH (2024). https://link.springer.com/10.1007/978-981-99-7666-9_2
28. Ranisch, R., Haltaufderheide, J.: Foundation models in medicine are a social experiment: time for an ethical framework. npj Digit. Med. **8**(1), 525 (2025). https://doi.org/10.1038/s41746-025-01924-4, https://www.nature.com/articles/s41746-025-01924-4
29. Reinel, T.S., et al.: GBRAS-Net: a convolutional neural network architecture for spatial image steganalysis. IEEE Access **9**, 14340–14350 (2021). https://doi.org/10.1109/ACCESS.2021.3052494
30. Saha, M., Chakraborty, C., Arun, I., Ahmed, R., Chatterjee, S.: An advanced deep learning approach for Ki-67 stained hotspot detection and proliferation rate scoring for prognostic evaluation of breast cancer. Sci. Rep. **7**(1), 1–14 (2017). https://doi.org/10.1038/s41598-017-03405-5
31. Shim, V.C., et al.: Evaluation of the international Ki67 working group cut point recommendations for early breast cancer: comparison with 21-gene assay results in a large integrated health care system. Breast Cancer Res. Treat. **1**(0123456789) (2023). https://doi.org/10.1007/s10549-023-07118-4
32. Wang, W., et al.: Quantitative immunohistochemistry analysis of breast Ki67 based on artificial intelligence. Open Life Sci. **19**(1), 20221013 (3 2024). https://doi.org/10.1515/biol-2022-1013, https://www.degruyter.com/document/doi/10.1515/biol-2022-1013/html
33. WHO: Ethics and Governance of Artificial Intelligence for Health. World Health Organization (2024). https://www.who.int/publications/i/item/9789240084759
34. Zehra, T., Shams, M., Ahmad, Z., Chundriger, Q., Ahmed, A., Jaffar, N.: Ki-67 quantification in breast cancer by digital imaging AI software and its concordance with manual method. J. Coll. Phys. Surg. Pak. **33**(5), 544–547 (2023). https://doi.org/10.29271/jcpsp.2023.05.544

3D Design and CNC Machining with YOLOv8-Based Shape Detection

Joel Molina[1], Joel Rubio[1], Mathew Lara[1], Angélica Quito[1(✉)], Andrea Pilco[1], and Viviana Moya[2]

[1] Faculty of Technical Sciences, International University of Ecuador UIDE, Quito 170411, Ecuador
anquitoca@uide.edu.ec

[2] Departamento de Automatización y Control Industrial, Escuela Politécnica Nacional, Quito 170517, Ecuador

Abstract. CNC machining of 3D files has an automatization issue, which is still time-consuming with significant use of manual work and CAD experience. This paper addresses the issue of minimizing human intervention in the production of 3D models for use in CNC milling operations. The models are traditionally created manually in a CAD environment, which is time-consuming and needs special skills. As a reaction, the proposed project includes the design and development of an automated CNC milling machine with an artificial intelligence feature, which can recognize geometric figures and create IPT files directly based on 2D images. The offered system incorporates a homemade CNC milling machine with a 3-axis GRBL board and NEMA-23 motors, as well as a segmentation model based on YOLOv8, trained on a set of 338 labeled photos. The precision of this model was 95.21% in identifying and isolating simple geometric objects, including rectangles, circles, and triangles. The resulting segmented outputs are fed into the dimension parameters, which produce automation of 3D models in Autodesk Inventor. Real-world images were used to confirm the experimental results, which showed that the system could handle quality fluctuations in the input images, saving a tremendous amount of time in the modeling process without compromising accuracy in dimensions. The results hold promise for a promising way ahead, although some challenges remain, including sensitivity to image noise and shape overlap. The given strategy helps to develop intelligent manufacturing, as it provides scalable use in industrial automation and instruction in engineering education regarding Industry 4.0.

Keywords: Computer Numeric Control (CNC) · Artificial Intelligence · YOLOv8 · Implemented Machine

1 Introduction

The use of computer numeric control (CNC) milling machines has aided in modernizing the manufacturing sector, as they provide accurate and flexible cutting and shaping of various materials. Many experts investigate the significant

T. Guarda et al. (Eds.): ARTIIS 2025, CCIS 2789, pp. 343–358, 2026.
https://doi.org/10.1007/978-3-032-16758-3_27

peculiarities of these machines, from design to more sophisticated applications. The kinds of materials used have a substantial impact on the buildings. Due to its strength and stiffness, aluminum is widely used in the construction of aerospace vehicles. Nevertheless, wood and polymers are frequently applied as they are more cost-effective [1,4,6]. The application of Artificial Intelligence (AI) in manufacturing has redefined CNC milling and 3D scanning. The input (a square-shaped nylon piece) is transformed into a 3D model, and G-code using AI can enhance precision and production speed in the process of automated production.

Currently, the field of computer vision and photogrammetry relies heavily on deep learning, improving image recognition algorithms, and creating 3D models from pictures. Combining these approaches has allowed image-based 3D reconstruction to be adopted in video game design, working with maps, inspecting land through drones, and similar activities. Image recognition means we can group and identify objects [2,11], fruits [12], vegetables [9], people or various features in a photo. These days, Convolutional Neural Network (CNNs) are commonly used as they can accurately identify complex patterns in photos. Recently, some advanced networks, including ResNets and GANs, are used to enhance the accuracy of classification and segmentation of objects in challenging images by considering the context. Recent research has explored the application of YOLO (You Only Look Once) algorithms for shape recognition across various domains [10].

1.1 State of Art

Since Industry 4.0 started, merging AI and deep learning with CNC machining is playing a key role in improving how well work is done, how efficiently things run, and how well issues are detected in advance. Using a variety of physical sensors for monitoring may be too expensive and disruptive for very precise work. Recent studies have used technology based on data and vision systems to help improve intelligent tracking. As an illustration, [18] decided to apply three approaches from deep learning, including CNN and DBN, together with SAE, to estimate the energy used by CNC turning. [15] also created a model that predicts tool wear on DBNs by using readings from CNC sensors reached through OPC UA, achieving nearly perfect results without the need for new devices. The research team of [7] used a BiLSTM neural network and an algorithm that selects key temperatures to model the displacement caused by heat on the spindle in CNC machines and the RMSE of their results was 0.6 μm or less. With a Raspberry Pi and multi-angle cameras, [8] developed a CNN system to detect surface faults in CNC-machined pieces without any additional operator assistance.

The study by [3] uses CNNs and shows that with 99.34% accuracy, one can recognize statuses of CNC machine HMI panels. At the same time, their system design involves cloud support, making adding new data and adjusting the learning parameters simple. According to [5], to generate CAD data for CNC (computer numerical control) machines using deep learning, first use CNNs and edge detection to change a bitmap image into a vector format for reverse engineering, then perform object recognition and draw the outline from real-world photos. A research team studied 5-axis ultra-precision CNC machines using 1D-CNN models with multiple outputs and trained them on energy consumption data to help determine the machine's status and predict its feed rate with a standard deviation of 21.9 [19]. To add to this, an RGB-D cameraCNNbased cyber-physical system was made to ensure NC code execution in real space without directly linking to the CNC controller. By displaying the virtual job in augmented reality, users can safely practice with real-time movements of their cutting tools [16]. These papers suggest that using computer vision, machine learning, and automated data collection is leading to better accuracy, lower prices, and faster monitoring in CNC manufacturing equipment. The mixing of CNN, DBN, BiLSTM, and AR allows the smart factory to be well-organized and flexible, supporting fault detection, forecasts, energy efficiency, and reading from interfaces.

Despite the rapid advances in smart manufacturing and the integration of artificial intelligence in industrial processes, there is still a significant gap in the direct transformation of 2D image data into actionable 3D models suitable for CNC machining. Most current solutions require extensive manual intervention between image interpretation and model fabrication, leading to increased design time, higher costs, and susceptibility to human error. Moreover, few implementations integrate real-time object detection algorithms with in-house built CNC machines, particularly within low-resource or academic environments, where accessibility and affordability are crucial.

To develop and validate an end-to-end, low-cost pipeline that converts top-view 2D images into manufacturing-ready 3D models and G-code by combining real-time YOLOv8 object detection with a custom-built CNC milling machine, minimizing manual intervention and accelerating prototyping. Therefore, the main contributions of this research are:

1. A fully automated workflow that converts top-view 2D images into manufacturing - ready 3D models and G-code by coupling real-time YOLOv8 detection with parametric extrusion/subtraction - eliminating manual CAD steps and accelerating prototyping.
2. A custom, affordable CNC milling platform interfaced with open-source motion control and a modular software stack, enabling reproducible deployment in low-resource and academic environments.
3. Experimental results on representative shapes/materials demonstrating high detection performance (accuracy and overall precision) and a substantial reduction in design-to-fabrication time compared to a manual CAD reconstruction baseline.

1.2 Outline

This document is divided into several sections to detail the development and findings of the project. Section 2 describes in detail the system's operation process, from image uploading to the generation of 3D models and their preparation for the CNC milling machine. Additionally, in Sect. 3 presents the results obtained, including examples of generated models and their validation in terms of efficiency, accuracy, and applicability. Finally, Sect. 4 summarizes the conclusions of the project, the benefits achieved, and potential extensions or future improvements that could be explored.

2 Materials and Methods

The CNC machine system integrates an artificial intelligence module based on image recognition. The system includes a custom-built CNC milling machine developed as part of this work. It is capable of identifying three geometric shapes—triangle, rectangle, and circle—through the implementation of a YOLOv8 large model (Yolov8l).

The process begins by taking a photo of the geometric shape to be drilling. Using the pre-trained model, it recognizes the shape, obtains its bounding box, and class label. This information is sent to the inventor via the API. The measurements of the identified shapes are customized. From this information, the system generates two different 3D representations: one where the detected shapes are extruded and another where the cut is applied (eliminating the identified regions to create cavities or holes). The computer contains a preloaded G-code template, which is manually updated with the G-code corresponding to the newly generated part from Inventor. Once the updated G-code is transmitted to the CNC system, the machining process begins. The entire process is illustrated in Fig. 1.

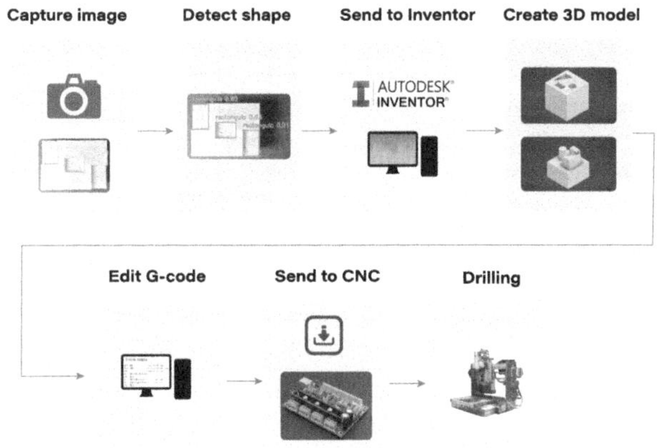

Fig. 1. Flow Diagram of CNC Milling Machine Integrated with AI Model.

2.1 CNC Milling Machine

The CNC milling machine was built using aluminum and stainless steel profiles. Aluminum was used for the side supports and the Z-axis frame, while stainless steel made up the main arms and bases. The machine dimensions are 402 mm in width, 435 mm in height, and 458 mm in length. Both the X and Y axes are made entirely of stainless steel, providing durability and precision.

The milling machine used ball screws and linear guides on the X, Y, and Z axes, controlled by NEMA-23 motors, all of which are driven by NEMA-23 stepper motors. The system was equipped with a 300W, 12,000 RPM R-11 spindle motor, capable of cutting materials such as aluminum, nylon, and wood. A 3-axis GRBL CNC controller board manages the NEMA-23 motors and the spindle motor. The machine is powered by a 110V power supply and includes safety features such as emergency stop buttons, limit switches, and monitoring systems that automatically interrupt operations in the event of anomalies. Fig. 2 illustrates all the key components of the CNC milling machine.

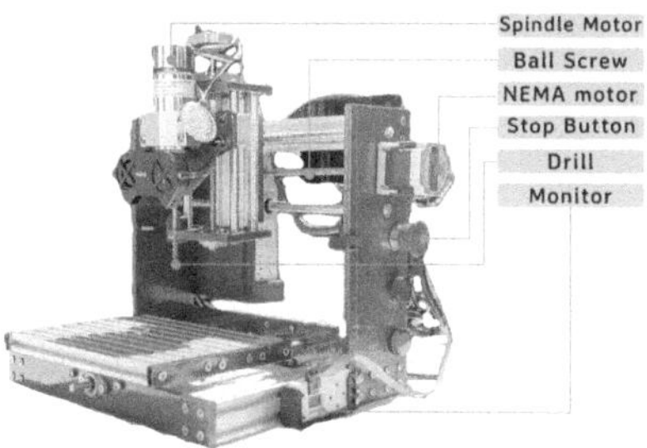

Fig. 2. CNC Milling Machine.

2.2 Geometric Shape Segmentation

YOLOv8l was used to segment geometric shapes such as rectangles, triangles, and circles. Unlike previous versions, which simply identified and delimited objects with boxes, YOLOv8l accurately segments each object at the pixel level, effectively delineating its shape and isolating it from the background. This model not only identifies the geometric but also determines its position and contour within the image. This research adopted the CRISP-DM (Cross Industry Standard Process for Data Mining) methodology, which is used for guiding machine learning projects. CRISP-DM consists of six phases: business understanding, data understanding, data preparation, modeling, evaluation, and deployment [13]. The first four phases are described in this section, while the evaluation and deployment phases are addressed in Sect. 3. The process used to create the segmentation model is illustrated in Fig. 3 and was performed following a series of steps, as detailed below.

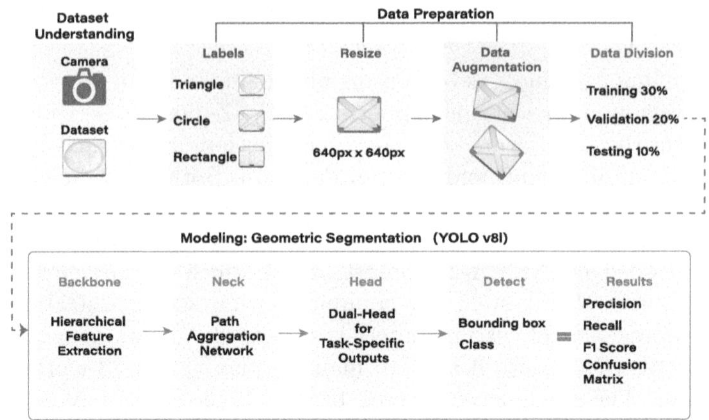

Fig. 3. Pipeline for Geometric Shape Segmentation Using YOLOv8l.

Business Understanding: The main objective was to reduce manual intervention in CAD modeling for CNC machining by developing an automated end-to-end pipeline that converts 2D images of geometric shapes into 3D models and machining code.

Data Understanding: To create the dataset, 50×50×50 mm cubes were 3D printed. One of the cube's faces had the shapes to be detected: circle, triangle, or rectangle. Fig. 4 shows the captured images. Figure 4(a) displays rectangles, Fig. 4(b) includes rectangle, triangle and a circle, and Fig. 4(c) contains a triangle. A total of 167 images were collected. The images were captured using a camera whose specifications are detailed in Table 1.

Data Preparation: The preparation stage included dataset building, image resizing, data augmentation, and data splitting. Each of these steps is described in detail below.

Table 1. Camera Specifications.

Parameter	Specification
Resolution	4032 × 3024 pixels
Focal Length	24 mm
ISO	149

– **Data Labeling:** The dataset was manually labeled in Roboflow, with labels created in Spanish: triángulo (triangle), círculo (circle), and rectángulo

(a) 3D Printing of a Rectangle.

(b) 3D Printing of a Rectangle, Circle and Triangle.

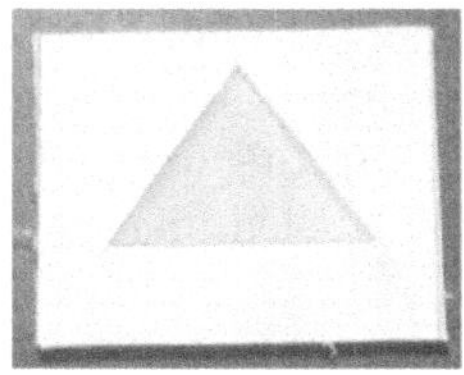

(c) 3D Printing of a Triangle.

Fig. 4. Overview of Dataset Creation.

(rectangle)—each corresponding to a different geometric shape. Furthermore, all images were resized to 640×640 pixels.

- **Data Augmentation:** A data augmentation process was applied to increase variability and robustness, resulting in a final dataset of 399 images.
- **Data Division:** The data was also divided into training, testing and validation, leaving 70% for training, 20% for validation and 10% for testing. Data distribution is showed in Table 2.

Table 2. Dataset information.

Category	Details
Training (70%)	279
Validation (20%)	80 images
Testing (10%)	40 images
Labels	Meaning
Triángulo	Triangle
Circulo	Circle
Rectángulo	Rectangle

Modeling: To segment the geometries, the YOLOv8l model was employed. YOLOv8 is an open-source architecture capable of performing both object detection and instance segmentation in a unified manner [20]. The YOLOv8l variant corresponds to the large-sized version within the YOLOv8 family. This variant provides an optimal trade-off between computational efficiency and accuracy, making it particularly suitable for real-time applications on resource-limited devices. The architecture of YOLOv8 is composed of three main components: a backbone network for hierarchical feature extraction, a neck module based on a Path Aggregation Network (PAN) to enhance multi-scale feature fusion, and a dual-head design for task-specific outputs [14]. The detection head handles object classification and bounding box regression, while the segmentation head produces high-resolution binary masks corresponding to each detected object [17]. In this work, the YOLOv8l model was trained using a dataset consisting of 399 labeled images.

Training: A training environment was set up in a Google Colab. The characteristics of the environment used are presented in Table 3. The specific training parameters used in this setup are detailed in Table 4.

Table 3. Training Environments

Environment	Component	Capacity
Google Colab Pro	RAM	12.7 GB 2-3
	GPU	T4 GPU (15 GB VRAM)

Table 4. Training Parameters

Parameter	Value
Model Size	YOLOv8l
Number of epochs	200
Batch size	16
Image size	640 pixels
Number of Classes	3
Optimizer	Automatic
Learning Rate	Automatically adjusted by model

2.3 3D Model and CNC Code Generation

Once the model has been trained, it returns the bounding box and the class of each detected shape. Based on this information, the system automatically generates two variations of a 3D model: one in which the recognized shapes are extruded (raised in 3D space), and another where slicing is applied (removing the identified regions to create cavities or holes). The implementation uses Python in combination with the Autodesk Inventor API to programmatically generate files in the `.ipt` format, which corresponds to part files compatible with Inventor's 3D CAD environment. The detected geometries are thus transformed into 3D components within this format. Finally, G-code is generated and sent to the GRBL CNC controller, which performs the milling operation to fabricate the physical part.

3 Results and Validation

3.1 Experimental Process

The main objective of integrating artificial intelligence into the CNC milling system is to automate the creation of three-dimensional models (IPT) from a single image, using a shape classification and segmentation approach. This process is divided into three main stages: **shape identification**, **relative position determination**, and **3D model creation**. These stages work sequentially to analyze the figures in the base image, determine their geometric characteristics, and position them in a final three-dimensional model, which is generated and stored in multiple formats.

The detection and 3D modeling process relies on high-resolution images in PNG or JPG format that clearly display a rectangular base figure containing other shapes (circles, triangles, or smaller rectangles). Images must be taken perpendicularly to the shape plane to avoid distortions. A YOLO-based segmentation model identifies the geometric shapes and creates masks for each. Then, the system calculates the relative position of each shape within the base rectangle using centered coordinates. Using this data, a 3D model is generated in Autodesk Inventor, extruding each shape and exporting the model in IPT, STL, and image formats for design and manufacturing purposes.

3.2 Model Training

The images obtained from the objects designated for detection were employed for data augmentation in training the large YOLOv8 model. The training process utilized the Ultralytics framework version 8.3.145 on a GPU (Tesla T4 with 15 GB of VRAM). The model underwent training for a total of 200 epochs, with an image size set at 640 pixels and a batch size of 16. The metrics derived from this training are presented in Fig. 5.

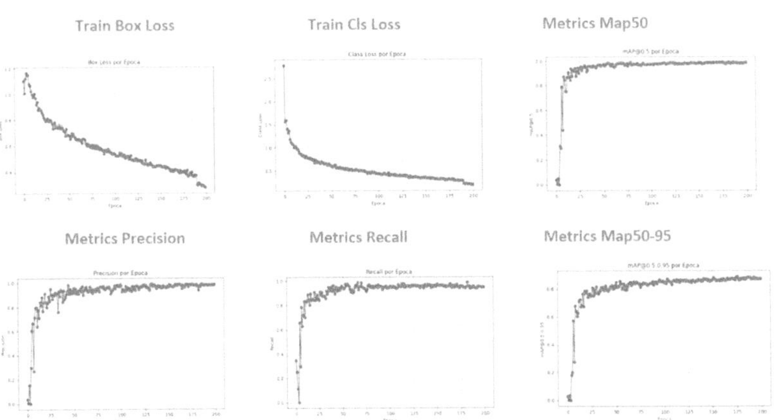

Fig. 5. Training Results.

On the other hand, training itself was carried out on the original images and the augmentation technique was not applied. The strategy resulted to unique performances in the observed behaviour measures. The comparisons underscore the importance of data augmentation to model efficacy in that different input representations can greatly affect the performance. The result is supported by the figure presented together with the article where the value of data augmentation is quite noticeable in improving the performance of models. These insights will help in perfecting the methodologies in image processing and machine learning leading to more reliable and valid predictive models in our field (Fig. 6).

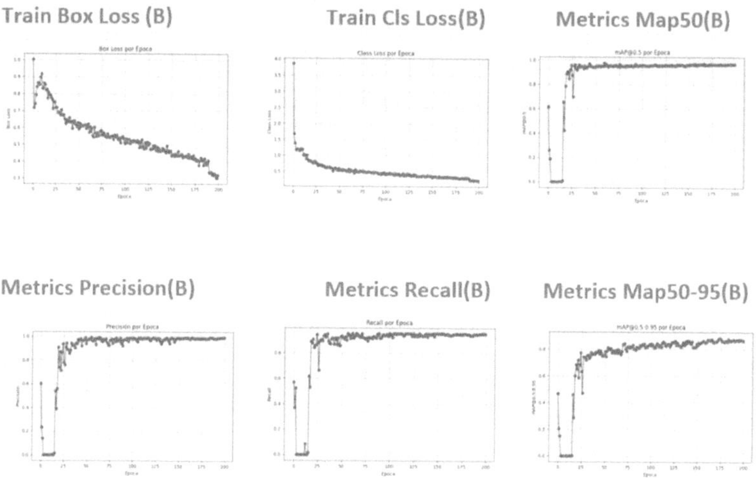

Fig. 6. Training Results without data augmentation.

3.3 Models Simulations

This section presents a summary of the metrics derived from the employed model. Additionally, it includes the computation of a metric that correlates precision with recall, specifically the F1 score. The results of this analysis are satisfactory, indicating a high percentage of effectiveness within the model, as illustrated in Table 5, which summarizes the performance metrics, including precision, recall, and F1 score, as well as their adaptability to the project's workflow. Additionally, visual results from the models applied to test images are included, allowing for an evaluation of which model is most suitable for accurately generating contours and the necessary data for 3D modeling in Autodesk Inventor.

$$F1 = 2 \cdot \frac{\text{Precision} \cdot \text{Recall}}{\text{Precision} + \text{Recall}} = 2 \cdot \frac{0.9826 \cdot 0.9462}{0.9826 + 0.9462} \approx 0.9640 \tag{1}$$

After the training has been carried out and the Precision and Recall metrics have been calculated, the F1 score value can be obtained through Equation (1) [12], which indicates the balance between precision and recall, indicating how balanced the trained model is.

Table 5. Results of Trained YOLOv8 Model

YOLOv8 Model	
Feature	Detection
Yolov8l model	Object detection 200 epochs
Precision (%)	98.26
Recall (%)	94.62
F1 Score (%)	96.00

The validation results for the various classes of geometric figures indicate the following levels of accuracy: circles exhibited a high precision of 98.43%, rectangles achieved a precision of 97.64%, and triangles recorded a precision of 89.56%. These figures underscore the effectiveness of the validation process employed. A detailed summary of the metrics associated with each analyzed geometric object will be found in Table 6, providing a comprehensive overview of the findings.

Table 6. Performance by Class

Class	Precision	Recall	mAP@0.5	mAP@0.5:0.95
Circle	0.9843	0.9552	0.9837	0.8867
Rectangle	0.9764	0.9552	0.9841	0.8867
Triangle	0.8956	0.9697	0.9309	0.8337

These results highlight the differential performance of each geometric class, thereby contributing to the overall understanding of the validation methodology and its implications for future research.

In the case of training without data augmentation, the results shown in the Table 7 have been witnessed.

Table 7. Performance by Class- Training 2

Class	Precision	Recall	mAP@0.5	mAP@0.5:0.95
Circle	0.967	1	0.995	0.847
Rectangle	1	0.992	0.995	0.972
Triangle	0.984	0.857	0.91	0.83

After performing the analysis of both training sessions, it has been observed that through the use of data augmentation techniques, it has been possible to obtain better overall results, including the number of true positives, giving the training used initially as a more reliable model, which is described in the methodology of this research.

3.4 Model Tasting Results

The confusion matrix reveals strong performance across all shape categories. The circle class achieved excellent results, with nine instances correctly classified and only one misclassified as background. Rectangles were correctly identified 66 times, though five were incorrectly labeled as background, indicating a slight detection weakness. Similarly, triangles had 29 accurate predictions, and four were misclassified as background. In all cases, no shape was misclassified as a different geometric figure, which suggests the model distinguishes well between classes. However, the model struggled to detect the background class itself, as no background instances were correctly classified, and several shapes were mistakenly labeled as such—specifically, one circle, five rectangles, and four triangles—resulting in a total of 10 false negatives. These errors may be due to the lack of clearly labeled negative samples in the dataset. Overall, the model exhibits high intra-class accuracy, with most classification errors resulting from background confusion rather than shape confusion, indicating robust object recognition behavior, as can be seen in Fig. 7.

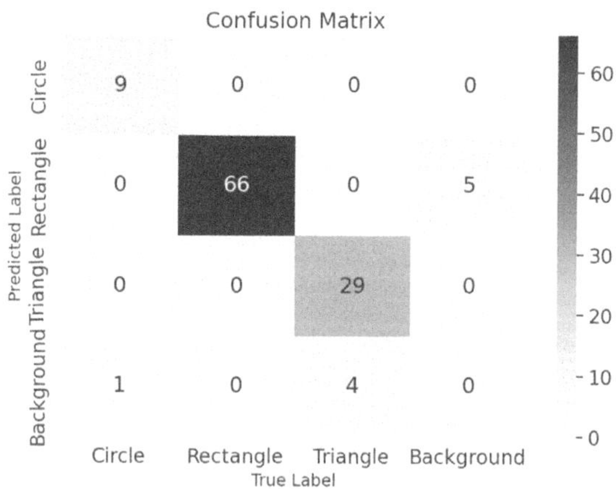

Fig. 7. Confusion Matrix Initial Training.

The model demonstrates a high level of precision for each class and minimal confusion between distinct classes, indicating effective learning of the visual characteristics unique to each shape. Most false negatives are concentrated in instances where objects were misclassified as background, which may be attributed to inconsistent labeling of background regions, low contrast between objects and their surroundings, or the model's internal tolerance threshold for low-confidence detections.

3.5 User Interface

This project automates the creation of IPT files using Python, YOLOv8, and the Autodesk Inventor API. The process begins with uploading a top-view image containing various shapes. The YOLOv8 model detects and locates these shapes within the image. Based on the detection, two 3D model versions are generated: one with extrusions to raise shapes into reliefs and another with cuts to form cavities. The data is converted into IPT files through the Inventor API, creating solid models with the specified features. This automated workflow enhances design speed, improves precision, and minimizes human error in 3D modeling tasks.

3.6 Tabulation of Data Obtained

The Table 8 presents a detailed summary of the model's performance on a wide range of test images. It demonstrates how the system recognized different shapes, indicating both the type it identified and the level of confidence it had in each decision. By reviewing these results, we can gain a better understanding of how accurately the model performs and whether it tends to miss or misclassify specific shapes. The information helps highlight patterns, strengths, and areas where the system may struggle—such as with images that are unclear or less defined. This overview is essential to evaluate how well the model might work in real-world scenarios that involve identifying basic figures.

The table confirms that the model performs well in visual classification, with outstanding accuracy in rectangles, robust results in triangles, and a modest improvement in circle detection.

3.7 Validation in Real Images

To verify the trained model, a verification process has been carried out using machined printed figures, which can include circles, rectangles, and triangles within the same block. In this way, the model's accuracy can be verified, and the percentage of detection accuracy for each figure is displayed within the bounding boxes (Fig. 8). The model accurately detects multiple geometric shapes with consistently high confidence scores, highlighting its strong performance and reliability. This demonstrates its robustness when applied to real-world conditions, where variations in lighting, material texture, and surface reflections often pose significant challenges. The results confirm that the model can generalize well beyond synthetic training data, making it suitable for practical applications involving physical components and diverse environmental factors.

Table 8. Detected Class and Confidence by Image

Image	Detected Class	Average confidence per class
1	rectangle	0.9496
2	circle	0.8391
3	circle	0.6646
4	triangle	0.9570
5	triangle	0.9547
6	rectangle	0.9436
7	triangle	0.9151
8	rectangle	0.9498
9	triangle	0.9363
...		
53	triangle	0.9514
54	rectangle	0.9481
55	triangle	0.9290
56	rectangle	0.9521
57	rectangle	0.9338
58	rectangle	0.9238
59	rectangle	0.9234
60	rectangle	0.9648
61	rectangle	0.9647
62	rectangle	0.9523

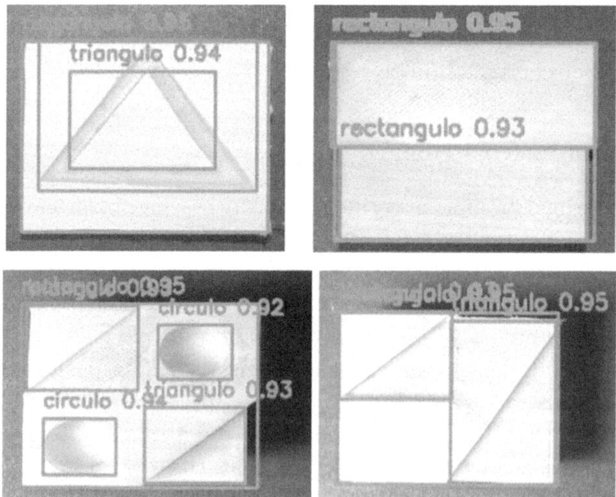

Fig. 8. Validation results with real 3D-printed geometric figures.

4 Conclusions

This work presents an essential contribution to the automation of digital manufacturing by integrating artificial intelligence with computer-aided design and CNC. Developing a low-cost, custom-built milling machine, combined with a YOLOv8-based segmentation model, enabled the automatic generation of 3D IPT models from top-view images of basic geometric shapes. The segmentation model achieved an overall precision of 0.9521, showing solid performance across all classes. Precision reached 0.9843 for circles, 0.9764 for rectangles, and 0.8956 for triangles. Recall was highest for triangles at 0.9697, with circles and rectangles both at 0.9552.

Despite these results, the project encountered challenges, particularly related to variations in image quality, the model's limited ability to handle overlapping shapes, and reduced accuracy when detecting triangles, likely due to dataset imbalance. These limitations highlight areas for further refinement. Future work will focus on incorporating depth sensors to enhance 3D spatial perception, expanding the dataset with more diverse conditions to improve generalization, and optimizing the model for deployment on resource-constrained hardware. Additionally, integrating the system with more advanced CNC platforms and enabling remote operation could extend its industrial applicability. Overall, this work represents a solid step toward intelligent and cost-effective manufacturing systems aligned with the objectives of Industry 4.0.

References

1. Ali, S., Mohsin, H.: Design and fabrication of 3-axes mini cnc milling machine. In: IOP Conference Series: Materials Science and Engineering, vol. 1094 (2021). https://doi.org/10.1088/1757-899X/1094/1/012005
2. García, I., et al.: Human-robot interaction based on hand gesture detection using yolo algorithm. In: Guarda, T., Portela, F., Gatica, G. (eds.) Advanced Research in Technologies, Information, Innovation and Sustainability, pp. 351–365. Springer, Cham (2025). https://doi.org/10.1007/978-3-031-83210-9_26
3. Guo, B., Lee, F.S., Lin, C.I., Lin, Y.J.: An optimization strategy for HMI panel recognition of CNC machines using a CNN deep-learning network. Concurr. Eng. **29**(1), 35–48 (2021). https://doi.org/10.1177/1063293X21998083
4. Hu, S.: A method of chatter-free milling parameters optimization for processing with high energy efficiency. In: IOP Conference Series: Materials Science and Engineering, vol. 382, p. 042038. IOP Publishing (2018). https://doi.org/10.1088/1757-899X/382/4/042038
5. Kaur, A.: Cad design for CNC equipments and industrial manufacturing using cnn. In: 2023 International Conference on Data Science and Network Security (ICDSNS), pp. 1–7 (2023). https://doi.org/10.1109/ICDSNS58469.2023.10245143
6. Kim, B., Ro, S., Park, J.K.: Development of a 3-axis desktop milling machine and a CNC system using advanced modern control algorithms. Int. J. Precis. Eng. Manuf. **11**, 39–47 (2010). https://doi.org/10.1007/S12541-010-0005-4
7. Liu, Y.C., Li, K.Y., Tsai, Y.C.: Spindle thermal error prediction based on LSTM deep learning for a CNC machine tool. Appl. Sci. **11**(12) (2021). https://doi.org/10.3390/app11125444. https://www.mdpi.com/2076-3417/11/12/5444

8. Medojevic, M., Ilic, V.: A CNN network-driven autonomous work-piece surface anomalies detection in CNC manufacturing (2023)
9. Moya, V., Quito, A., Pilco, A., Vásconez, J.P., Vargas, C.: Crop detection and maturity classification using a yolov5-based image analysis. Emerg. Sci. J. **8**(2), 496–512 (2024)
10. Peña, S., Moreano, D., Buele, F., Moya, V., Pilco, A., Quito, A.: Color classification using a 3-dof robotic arm based on the yolov5 model. In: 2024 IEEE Eighth Ecuador Technical Chapters Meeting (ETCM), pp. 1–6 (2024). https://doi.org/10.1109/ETCM63562.2024.10746227
11. Peña, S., Pilco, A., Moya, V., Chamorro, W., Vásconez, J.P., Zuniga, J.A.: Color sorting system using yolov5 for robotic mobile applications. In: 2024 6th International Conference on Robotics and Computer Vision (ICRCV), pp. 1–5 (2024). https://doi.org/10.1109/ICRCV62709.2024.10758571
12. Pilco, A., Moya, V., Quito, A., Vásconez, J.P., Limaico, M.: Image processing-based system for apple sorting. J. Image Graph. **12**(4), 362–371 (2024)
13. Schröer, C., Kruse, F., Gómez, J.M.: A systematic literature review on applying crisp-dm process model. Procedia Comput. Sci. **181**, 526–534 (2021)
14. Terven, J., Córdova-Esparza, D.M., Romero-González, J.A.: A comprehensive review of yolo architectures in computer vision: from yolov1 to yolov8 and yolo-nas. Mach. Learn. Knowl. Extract. **5**(4), 1680–1716 (2023)
15. Wang, M., Li, J., Zhou, X.: Real-time optimization in CNC milling using artificial intelligence. Int. J. Manuf. Eng. **58**(4), 567–580 (2021). https://doi.org/10.1080/ijme.2021.0223
16. Wang, P., Yang, W.A., You, Y.: A cyber-physical prototype system in augmented reality using RGB-d camera for CNC machining simulation. J. Intell. Manuf. **34**, 3637–3658 (2023)
17. Wu, W., He, Z., Li, J., et al.: Instance segmentation of tea garden roads based on an improved yolov8n-seg model. Agriculture **14**(7), 1163 (2024)
18. Xiao, Q., Li, C., Tang, Y., Du, Y., Kou, Y.: Deep learning based modeling for cutting energy consumed in cnc turning process. In: 2018 IEEE International Conference on Systems, Man, and Cybernetics (SMC), pp. 1398–1403 (2018). https://doi.org/10.1109/SMC.2018.00244
19. Xu, Z., Selvaraj, V., Min, S.H.: State identification of a 5-axis ultra-precision CNC machine tool using energy consumption data assisted by multi-output densely connected 1d-cnn model. J. Intell. Manuf. **35**, 147–160 (2024)
20. Yang, T., Zhou, S., Xu, A., Ye, J., Yin, J.: Yolo-segnet: a method for individual street tree segmentation based on the improved yolov8 and the segformer network. Agriculture **14**(9) (2024). https://doi.org/10.3390/agriculture14091620. https://www.mdpi.com/2077-0472/14/9/1620

Visuals as a Context for NLP Systems When Dealing with Linguistic Polysemy

Yasena Chantova(✉)

University of Library Studies and Information Technologies, Blvd "Tsarigradsko Shose" 119, 1784 Sofia, Bulgaria
y.chantova@unibit.bg

Abstract. Polysemy, the capacity of a single linguistic unit to possess multiple related meanings, is a fundamental phenomenon in natural languages, deeply intertwined with the socio-historical and emotional experiences of language speakers. This study explores the characteristics of polysemous units, the challenges they present to linguistic analysis and computational processing, and recent advancements in addressing these challenges. It examines contemporary research trends from 2020 to 2024 that focus on distinguishing, categorizing, and disambiguating polysemous meanings, highlighting both theoretical insights and technological innovations, particularly in Natural Language Processing (NLP). The article emphasizes the importance of context recognition and word sense disambiguation, outlining the evolution from knowledge-based systems to contextual embeddings and multimodal models such as GPT-4V and CLIP. An illustrative case study of the word *apple* demonstrates how polysemy is influenced by contextual categories such as characters, space, time, and social values, revealing the dynamic and culturally embedded nature of the construction of meaning. Ultimately, the study argues for an open-ended and flexible categorization framework capable of accommodating new manifestations of polysemy, as language continues to evolve. By integrating linguistic theory, cognitive science and artificial intelligence, this research contributes to a deeper understanding of polysemy and the development of more context-sensitive language technologies.

Keywords: Visual · Polysemy · NLP systems

1 Introduction

Polysemy, the phenomenon wherein a single linguistic unit has multiple related meanings, is a fundamental characteristic of natural languages. Its pervasive presence across linguistic systems reflects the dynamic interaction between language and the evolving cognitive, social, and historical experiences of the speakers. The study of polysemy not only sheds light on the processes of semantic change and language evolution, but also reveals important aspects of human categorization and conceptualization.

In recent years, polysemy has emerged as a major focus of interdisciplinary research at the intersection of linguistics, cognitive science, and Natural Language Processing

T. Guarda et al. (Eds.): ARTIIS 2025, CCIS 2789, pp. 359–372, 2026.
https://doi.org/10.1007/978-3-032-16758-3_28

(NLP). Scholars have sought to address several critical challenges posed by polysemy, namely: the identification and differentiation of distinct meanings, the mapping of relationships among these meanings, and the resolution of semantic ambiguities in discourse. These challenges are particularly salient in the development of artificial intelligence systems that aim to process human language effectively.

The study examines the phenomenon of polysemy from both theoretical and applied perspectives. It explores the socio-historical and emotional dependencies of polysemous units; it discusses current research trends in the field, and analyses the difficulties polysemy presents for computational language models. Special attention is devoted to modern strategies for context recognition and word sense disambiguation, including the role of multimodal systems integrating visual and linguistic information.

Furthermore, the article offers an illustrative case study on the polysemous lexical unit *apple*, using cultural and historical contexts to exemplify how different meanings arise and are anchored in specific frames of reference. This analysis provides a categorization of contextual features – characters, space, time, and social values – that contribute to the dynamic shaping of polysemous meanings. It also highlights the need for flexible, open-ended frameworks capable of accommodating the emergence of new manifestations of polysemy in evolving linguistic and technological environments.

2 Dealing with Polysemy

2.1 Some Characteristics of Polysemy

Polysemy is a linguistic phenomenon which is common to natural languages and which refers to the capacity of one linguistic unit to have multiple meanings. The meanings of linguistic units develop throughout the evolution of languages and are closely related to uses of linguistic units by language speakers [1]. Language speakers and their activities are thus the main factor for the creation of polysemous linguistic units, whose features are determined by the speakers. Therefore, speakers of a certain language and their circumstances play a crucial role in defining the polysemy of linguistic units. In the first place, polysemous linguistic units are closely related to the socio-historical context of their appearance. This context can enlarge or restrict the meaning of a word. The word of French origin 'gain', for example, used to mean only the agricultural production and profit obtained, while today it refers to all kinds of acquisition as a result of the multiplication of human work-related activities (gain popularity; financial gain). On the other hand, the diversification of social and professional human activities can lead to the specialization of words and their meanings. In French, the meaning of "operation" has acquired different uses when referring to professional areas like medicine (surgical activity), the armed forces (military operation) or finance (financial operation). Secondly, polysemous linguistic units are related to the emotional experiences and attitudes of the language speakers. Pejorative and euphemistic meanings and uses of linguistic units are due to such attitudes. In this way, some features of the polysemous linguistic units appear and all of them are conditioned by the speakers' circumstances. Multiple meanings are heavily dependent on context and this contextual dependency is of two kinds: the socio-historical one and the emotional one.

The phenomenon of polysemy with its two kinds of contextual dependency is so commonly spread within natural languages that it raises at least three closely related issues [2]: distinguishing between the different meanings, both discovering and defining them; pointing out relationships between these meanings; and resolving ambiguities at the level of the discourse.

2.2 Actual Research Challenges on Polysemy

These three issues have become the main focus of research interest in recent (2020–2024) years. On the topic of distinguishing between the different meanings, recent studies have emphasised the importance of identifying and clearly defining the various meanings that polysemous words can carry.

Crucially, polysemy can be classified into two principal types, regular and irregular polysemy [3, 4]. Regular polysemy refers to predictable, systematic shifts in meaning that follow identifiable patterns. Examples include systematic extensions like institution/building ("school" as institution vs. "school" as physical structure) or content/container ("bottle" as object vs. "bottle" as contents). Irregular polysemy, by contrast, denotes idiosyncratic or context-bound meaning extensions that resist pattern generalization. These are less predictable and often culturally embedded, such as the polysemy of *apple* in different mythological or technological contexts. These classifications are further shaped by socio-historical evolution and affective connotation. For instance, metaphorical or euphemistic senses often emerge from culturally shared emotional frameworks. Multiple methodologies have been applied to uncover these meanings, including corpus-based behavioral profiling [5, 6], semantic clustering [7, 8], and vector-based word representations [9, 10]. Cognitive experiments [11] have shown that speakers mentally store and possess literal, metaphorical and metonymic meanings differently. In addition to that, in-depth analyses of lexical conversion and domain-specific terminology (such as legal or medical language) [12, 13] reveal that meaning differentiation is influenced by both linguistic form and conceptual categorization. These approaches help clarify how meanings are represented in the mind and how they evolve in usage.

Pointing out relationships between these meanings involves understanding the internal structure of polysemous words. Studies have explored how meanings are interconnected through mechanisms such as metaphor, metonymy, colexification, synonymy, and hyponymy [14, 15]. Copredication – where a single word simultaneously supports multiple predicates – illustrates [16, 17] how distinct meanings can co-occur in discourse. Cognitive and conceptual models [18–20] map these relations using image schemas, radial structures, and even circular diagrams of conceptual categories. Hierarchical models derived from dictionary data or user perception also show how meanings cluster and overlap [21, 22]. By mapping these relations, researchers provide insights into how language users navigate among related senses and how polysemy reflects broader cognitive processes.

One of the most practical challenges of polysemy lies in resolving ambiguities in actual communication and automated processing. In discourse, context is key for disambiguating meanings, a task that humans perform intuitively but machines struggle with. Computational approaches have introduced neural networks [23], attention-based models [24], and topic modelling techniques [9] that dynamically adapt meaning representations based on usage. These models aim to interpret meanings in real time [25] and resolve ambiguity using context-aware mechanisms [26, 27]. In parallel, mathematical [28] and semiotic models [29] attempt to formalise how multiple meanings can coexist or compete in discourse.

Such interdisciplinary efforts – combining linguistics, cognitive science, and artificial intelligence – seek to enable accurate interpretation and effective language use across various platforms, from natural conversations to machine translation and semantic search systems.

2.3 Focused Research Question: Integrating Vision in Polysemy Disambiguation

This study narrows its scope to the following question: how can multimodal (vision-language) models enhance the disambiguation of polysemous terms by leveraging contextual visual cues?

This question arises from observed limitations in text-only systems, particularly in handling irregular polysemy. By analyzing multimodal architectures, this paper investigates whether grounding word meanings in visual contexts improves interpretability, especially for metaphorical or culturally loaded senses.

3 NLP Systems Dealing with Polysemy

3.1 Some Challenges

The complexity of polysemous linguistic units presents the most persistent challenge in the development of artificial intelligence systems that process natural languages. While language speakers intuitively disambiguate multiple meanings using context, computational models must rely on formal representations and on probabilistic inference to resolve polysemous ambiguity. Thus, the main difficulties come from context recognition and word sense disambiguation.

Context Recognition and Word Sense Disambiguation

A core challenge for NLP systems lies in correctly identifying the intended meaning of a polysemous linguistic unit within a given context. Context recognition lies at the heart of resolving polysemy in artificial intelligence systems that process natural languages. Since polysemous words carry multiple related meanings, the ability to determine their correct sense in a given use is essential for achieving accurate understanding, translation, and interaction. In NLP, this challenge is addressed through a process known as Word Sense Disambiguation (WSD) – the task of identifying the intended meaning of a word based on context [30, 31]. This process is essential for accurate understanding of language since NLP systems often have to distinguish between metaphorical meaning and literal meaning, or between denotated and connotated meanings. In the following cases of the word *apple*:

- *She reached into the basket and took out a small red apple.*
- *The apple of my eye has always been my youngest daughter.*

NLP systems must distinguish between the literal meaning, which refers to the edible fruit by taking into account the nutrition context, and the metaphorical meaning, which is idiomatically used to point out deep affection.

For artificial intelligence systems that process natural languages, determining the correct meaning requires interpreting surrounding lexical cues, syntactic structure, and even pragmatic cues. Without this, systems might produce irrelevant or nonsensical outputs. In contrast to language speakers who resolve the ambiguity of words effortlessly by relying on background knowledge and linguistic experience, NLP systems must algorithmically infer meaning from data.

3.2 Some Possible Solutions

Early Approaches to Context Recognition

Initial approaches to WSD relied on knowledge-based systems such as WordNet [32], where definitions (glosses) and semantic relationships between word senses were used to identify meaning. Algorithms are also used for disambiguated words [33] by comparing overlaps between dictionary definitions and surrounding context.

While these methods offered foundational insights, they were limited by the static nature of lexical resources and their inability to generalise across domains.

Statistical and Machine Learning Methods

With the advent of large text corpora, statistical and supervised learning (labelled datasets) approaches became dominant. These methods trained classifiers on annotated datasets, where each instance of a word was labelled with the correct sense (e.g. from corpora like SemCor corpus). While effective in constrained settings, they required large amounts of manually labelled data, which is costly and domain-specific.

Unsupervised learning methods (clustering contexts) later emerged aiming to cluster instances of words based on distributional similarity – i.e. words used in similar contexts likely to share meaning [34]. These methods, however, often struggled to map clusters to interpretable senses.

Contextual Embeddings and Neural Language Models

A major breakthrough in context recognition came with the development of contextual word embeddings in models like Embeddings from Language Models (ELMo) [35], Bidirectional Encoder Representations from Transformers (BERT) [36], and later Generative Pretrained Transformer (GPT) variants. These models no longer represent words as fixed vectors. Instead, each token's representation is dynamically computed based on its sentence-level context using deep neural networks and self-attention mechanisms.

Modern transformer-based models like BERT generate contextualised word embeddings, and unlike earlier models that produced static vector representations for words, these models output different embeddings for the same word depending on its surrounding context. This allows the same polysemous word to have distinct vector identities depending on usage. Thus, the same word *apple*, for example, receives different vector representations depending on its usage. In BERT, the word *apple* would have significantly different embeddings in the above-mentioned contexts, allowing downstream tasks (e.g. question answering or sentiment analysis) to process them accordingly. This allows models to implicitly distinguish between senses without explicit annotation.

Contextual models like ELMo and BERT mitigate the problem of context recognition and of polysemous linguistic units by learning to attend to different parts of the sentence using self-attention mechanisms to dynamically adjust the focus of the model. These models, however, still depend on the distribution and frequency of senses in the training data. Less common senses may be poorly represented or entirely absent leading to biased disambiguation.

Remaining Challenges

Despite the progress of contextual models, challenges remain. Rare senses or those that are underrepresented in training data may still be misunderstood or collapsed into more dominant interpretations. Furthermore, multi-sense or discourse-level context, which is often needed for full disambiguation, is still imperfectly modelled by most current systems [37].

In addition, metaphorical language, sarcasm, or domain-specific usage can further obscure sense resolution demanding richer representations and integration of external knowledge sources (e.g. knowledge graphs, ontologies).

Multilingual transformer models, such as mBERT and XLM-R, attempt to reduce such errors by jointly modelling polysemy across languages [38]. Yet even these systems can fail when cultural or domain-specific knowledge is required for accurate interpretation.

Another possible solution for artificial intelligence systems that process natural languages to deal with polysemy is multimodal models [39]. Recent advances in multimodal artificial intelligence have led to the development of models that integrate vision and language understanding, notably OpenAI's GPT-4 with Vision (GPT-4V) and Contrastive Language-Image Pretraining (CLIP). These models represent complementary approaches to visual-linguistic reasoning enabling new capabilities in image interpretation, grounding, and visual semantics.

GPT-4 with Vision

GPT-4V is a multimodal extension of the GPT-4 architecture that enables the model to process and respond to visual inputs alongside text. While the core transformer architecture remains text-based, GPT-4V incorporates a vision encoder to project images into a latent space compatible with textual representations. This allows the model to perform a range of tasks, such as image captioning, visual question answering, and diagram interpretation.

Importantly, GPT-4V demonstrates emergent multimodal reasoning. It can combine visual information with textual context to solve complex tasks that no modality alone would suffice for. For example, it can describe the content of a meme while interpreting the humour, or analyse a scientific plot by referring to its caption and axes. These abilities suggest a form of cross-modal grounding where the semantics of one modality are anchored through the other [40].

However, GPT-4V's capabilities are not without limitations. it is susceptible to produce plausible but incorrect interpretations and struggles with occluded or abstract images. Additionally, the precise architectural details and training data remain proprietary, leaving open questions about how it internalises visual features.

CLIP: Contrastive Vision-Language Pretraining

CLIP, also developed by OpenAI, takes a different approach. it consists of two encoders, one for text and one for images, trained jointly using a contrastive learning objective: to bring representations of matching image-text pairs closer together in a shared embedding space, and push apart non-matching pairs [41]. This enables CLIP to perform zero-shot classification and image-text retrieval without task-specific fine-tuning.

The power of CLIP lies in its flexibility. Given a text prompt, it can retrieve the most relevant images from a dataset, or vice-versa. Its training on a massive, noisy corpus of image-caption pairs scraped from the web allows it to generalize to a wide range of concepts. Importantly, CLIP is capable of compositional reasoning (e.g. identifying "a red cube on top of a blue sphere"), and can distinguish between fine-grained textual variations. CLIP has also proven influential as a component in generative systems like DALL·E and Stable Diffusion, where it serves as a semantic controller, guiding image generation towards text-based goals.

GPT-4 with Vision and CLIP: Some Critical Limitations

Despite recent progress, some critical limitations persist.

Concerning domain generalization, most models struggle to transfer learned representations to new domains without fine-tuning. For example, the sense of *apple* in a biblical text diverges markedly from its technological or mythological uses. Pre-trained models like BERT, trained on general corpora, often fail to generalize across such divergent contexts.

Some limitations also persist concerning data bias. Predominant senses dominate training data (e.g., *apple* as the brand), leading to skewed outputs. GPT-4V, although multimodal, inherits these biases if its image-caption pairs have overrepresented popular culture or tech-oriented meanings.

Multimodality as a Possible Solution

Though developed separately, GPT-4V and CLIP can be seen as complementary systems. While CLIP excels at aligning modalities in vector space and matching or retrieving content, GPT-4V builds on this alignment to support generative, contextual, and inferential reasoning across modalities.

These systems echo longstanding cognitive theories that emphasise the integration of perceptual input with symbolic reasoning. Empirical studies indicate [42] performance gains in multimodal Word Sense Disambiguation. In zero-shot classification tasks, CLIP achieves over 75% top-1 accuracy on datasets like ImageNet-R and Flickr30k. Just as human cognition is grounded in sensory experience, GPT-4V and CLIP reflect a move towards multimodal grounding in artificial systems, which is an essential step for capturing phenomena like polysemy, where meaning is often shaped by both linguistic and perceptual contexts.

Such multimodal systems, especially CLIP [43], are aimed to deal with visual concepts relying on a wide variety of natural language supervision. For image-text retrieval, CLIP scores an average Recall@1 of 59.2% on MS-COCO, outperforming unimodal baselines. As a result, CLIP can be instructed in natural language to perform a variety of visual classification. However, NLP systems also need to be trained on visuals to learn linguistic concepts, especially polysemous ones. For more successful training of systems on visuals, it would be useful to point out some context-related visual features of polysemous units.

These findings suggest that visual input can sharpen semantic distinctions, particularly for irregular polysemy. However, model performance still hinges on training diversity and cross-modal alignment quality.

4 The Polysemy of *Apple*: A Multimodal Case Study

Collected from Facebook, the image "…who ordered the *apple*?" [44] illustrates in a clever way the polysemous lexical unit *apple* by bringing together around the table some iconic characters, who come from mythology, religion, literature, history, and pop culture and who are associated in some way with an *apple* (Fig. 1).

4.1 Methodological Framework and Visual Selection Criteria

This study adopts a curated multimodal stimulus centered on the visual meme "Who ordered the *apple*?", which juxtaposes characters embodying culturally diverse interpretations of the word *apple*. The selection of visual elements was guided by four primary criteria. First, semantic anchoring ensures that each image corresponds to a culturally recognizable sense of *apple*, thereby providing a stable referential point for analysis. Second, semantic domain diversity is maintained by incorporating representations from a wide array of cultural framework, including mythological, religious, scientific, technological, literary, and historical contexts. Third, the selected visuals span a broad temporal range, encompassing references from biblical times to contemporary digital culture, thus allowing for a diachronic perspective on semantic evolution. Finally, visual distinctiveness was a determining factor, with each character chosen for its symbolic salience and clear visual differentiation. This multimodal configuration enables the investigation of how visually embedded cultural cues support or shape sense disambiguation in both computational and cognitive processing frameworks.

4.2 Some Visual Contexts of Polysemous *Apple*

The above Facebook image provides mythological, religious, scientific, technological, literary, and historical visual contexts to the polysemous lexical unit *apple*.

Each figure represented in the visual meme serves as a semantic anchor that activates a specific conceptual interpretation of the word *apple*, drawing on socio-culturally and historically embedded associations.

As biblical characters, the serpent, Adam and Eve refer to the *Book of Genesis* and thus, the *apple* symbolizes the forbidden fruit from the Tree of Knowledge and the moment of the Fall of Man. This visual context evokes the *apple of temptation*, foregrounding themes of religious morality and original sin. Isaac Newton's depiction refers to the *apple of scientific discovery*, symbolizing scientific inspiration and the birth of modern physics. The juxtaposition of Snow White and the Evil Queen introduces the *apple of poison*, encapsulating the dichotomy between innocence and deception in fairy-tale logic. In today's culture, Steve Jobs and the half-bitten *Apple* logo represent

Fig. 1. Visual representation of the polysemous lexical unit *apple*

more than just a brand: the *apple of brand identity* indexes themes of digital technological innovation, trade mark, and consumer culture. The classical figures of the Trojan warrior Paris and the Greek goddess Aphrodite allude to the *apple of discord*, invoking mythological narratives of rivalry, destruction, and conflict. Finally, William Tell with his iconic shot at the target *apple* on the head of his son evokes the *apple of precision*, which connotes courage, precision, but also trust, resistance, fight for freedom.

These characters function not merely as illustrative references but as narrative and cognitive anchors that activate distinct conceptual frames. Crucially, their visual co-presence within a single meme foregrounds how multimodal cues can facilitate the disambiguation of polysemous terms by situating them within culturally saturated, visually distinct interpretive contexts.

Table 1. Categorization of visual contexts of polysemy

Characters	Space	Time	Social values	Meaning of *apple*
the serpent, Adam and Eve	Book of Genesis	biblical	the forbidden knowledge, the Fall of Man, (original) sin	*apple of temptation*
Isaac Newton	both Britain and fictional	both 17–18 centuries and fictional	scientific inspiration and discovery	*apple of scientific discovery*
Snow White and the Evil Queen	fairy tale	fairy tale	innocence, deception	*apple of poison*
Steve Jobs with his MacBook	*Apple* Inc	High Tech 20 century	digital technological innovation, trade mark, consumer culture	*apple of brand identity*
Paris and Aphrodite	mythological Greece	mythological	rivalry, destruction, conflict	*apple of discord*
William Tell and his son	both Switzerland and Swiss legend	both 14–15 centuries and legendary	courage, trust, resistance, fight for freedom	*apple of precision*

4.3 Categorization of Visual Contextual Features in Polysemy

Various identified features emerge from the visual context in which the polysemous unit apple appears and are thus instrumental in determining the specific meanings that apple may assume. Table 1 illustrates the meanings of apple mediated by these visual contextual features. These visual contextual features of polysemy can be classified into four principal categories: characters, space, time and social values. Each of these categories is further subdivided into more specific subcategories.

With regard to the polysemy of the word *apple*, the category of characters includes references to real historical figures, mythological characters, fairy tale protagonists, and legendary figures.

The space category encompasses various settings, ranging from historically attested locations to fictional realms, corporate entities, and biblical landscapes.

Time likewise plays a critical role in the interpretation of meaning, as the accepted or typical image of *apple* evolves according to the historical period and cultural milieu. Meanings attributed to *apple* often reflect the temporal context in which the term was employed. Temporal reference varies from biblical, medieval, modern, and timeless one.

Furthermore, the category of social values profoundly influences the connotations associated with the word. Over time, these values have imbued *apple* with meanings ranging from highly negative (the forbidden knowledge, the Fall of Man, the original sin) and negative (deception, destruction, conflict) to neutral (rivalry, innocence, trade mark, consumer culture), positive (courage, trust, resistance, fight for freedom), and highly positive (digital technological innovation, scientific inspiration and discovery).

Ultimately, the interplay among these contextual categories shapes the multifaceted meanings of *apple*, according to its various symbolic representations – from a symbol of temptation and sin, to scientific discovery, a poisonous fruit, from a corporate brand to a metaphor of discord and an emblem of precision.

The proposed categorization is not intended to be exhaustive and remains an open and dynamic framework, capable of incorporating additional categories as further examples of polysemy emerge through ongoing linguistic analysis. This categorization enables systematic mapping between context and sense, offering a structured input for vision-language modelling.

4.4 Toward an Integrated Framework: Visual Contextualization for NLP

We propose the creation of a specialized dataset and tagging schema for the systematic annotation of polysemous units across four contextual axes: (1) character types, (2) temporal frame, (3) spatial grounding, and (4) social value. This multidimensional encoding framework is intended to support the fine-tuning of multimodal transformers on contextually rich, visually anchored instances of polysemy, thereby enhancing both semantic disambiguation accuracy and model interpretability in word sense disambiguation benchmarks. Furthermore, such a resource would enable cross-cultural evaluation of semantic generalization, addressing the transferability of contextually grounded meanings across domains and traditions. An illustrative pilot corpus might integrate annotated visual materials – including memes, historical imagery, and educational illustrations – paired with curated sense inventories to serve as a testbed for multimodal semantic analysis.

5 Conclusion

This study has demonstrated that polysemy presents persistent challenges to NLP systems, especially when irregular meanings are heavily context-dependent. The study has highlighted the complexities inherent in distinguishing, categorizing, and disambiguating the multiple meanings of polysemous linguistic units.

Despite significant progress in both theoretical and applied approaches to polysemy, several challenges remain unresolved, particularly in computational processing. Rare senses, discourse-level ambiguities, and culturally embedded meanings continue to pose difficulties for NLP systems.

The analysis of the polysemous lexical unit *apple* has provided an illustrative case study, revealing how cultural, historical, and social contexts contribute to the layering and diversification of meaning. By proposing a structured framework for representing contextual dimensions (characters, time, space, values), this study enhances polysemy modelling. Importantly, this framework remains open-ended, reflecting the dynamic and evolving nature of language itself. Future research should therefore develop annotated multimodal datasets and evaluate multimodal systems on polysemy-focused benchmarks to validate cross-modal disambiguation. Future research should also continue to explore integrative approaches that combine linguistic theory, cognitive modelling, and multimodal processing in order to achieve a deeper and more nuanced understanding of polysemy.

By combining theoretical linguistic insights with AI architectures, this interdisciplinary work contributes to more robust, context-sensitive semantic modelling.

Acknowledgments. This research would not be possible without the financial support of the following project: "Libraries – Learning – Artificial Intelligence: Symbiosis Possibilities", funded by Bulgarian National Science Fund of the Ministry of Education and Science of the Republic of Bulgaria with Contract №KP–06–N85/9 from 05.12.2024, led by Senior Assist. Prof. Elisaveta Tsvetkova, PhD.

References

1. Bréal, M.: Essai de sémantique: science des significations, pp. 155–172. Hachette, Paris (1897)
2. Martin, R.: Esquisse d'une analyse formelle de la polysémie. Trav. Ling. Litt. Strasbourg **10**(1), 125–136 (1972)
3. Carston, R.: Polysemy: pragmatics and sense conventions. Mind Lang. **36**(1), 108–133 (2021). https://doi.org/10.1111/mila.12329. Accessed 14 Feb 2025
4. Lombard, A., Huyghe, R., Barque, L., Gras. D.: Regular polysemy and novel word-sense identification. Mental Lexicon **18**(1), 94–119 (2023). https://doi.org/10.1075/ml.21002.lom. Accessed 14 Feb 2025
5. Wu, S., Ou, Y.: A Quantitative study of the polysemy of mandarin Chinese perception Verb Kàn 'Look/See.'. Aust. J. Linguist. **43**(3), 191–218 (2023). https://doi.org/10.1080/07268602.2023.2289194. Accessed 14 Feb 2025
6. Wang, H., Kanamaru, T., Li., K.: The polysemy of the Japanese temperature adjective atsui: a behavioral profile analysis. Rev. Cogn. Linguist. (2023). https://doi.org/10.1075/rcl.00156.wan. Accessed 14 Feb 2025
7. Proos, M.: Feeling your neighbour: an experimental approach to the polysemy of tundma "to feel" in Estonian. Lang. Cogn. **12**(2), 282–309 (2020). https://doi.org/10.1017/langcog.2019.44. Accessed 14 Feb 2025
8. Veismann, A., Proos, M., Taremaa, P.: Are jam and bus still standing? Polysemy of seisma 'to stand' in Estonian and the physical experience of standing [Kas moos ja buss seisavad endiselt? seisma-verbi polüseemia ja seismise kehaline kogemus]. Eesti ja Soome-Ugri Keeleteaduse Ajakiri **14**(2), 321–347 (2023). https://doi.org/10.12697/jeful.2023.14.2.13. Accessed 14 Feb 2025
9. Corbett, J., Li, L.: Polysemy, synonymy, and metaphor: the use of the historical thesaurus of English in translation studies. Digit. Scholarsh. Humanit. **36**(4), 827–839 (2021). https://doi.org/10.1093/llc/fqab008. Accessed 14 Feb 2025

10. Yoshida, T., Hisano, R., Ohnishi, T.: Gaussian hierarchical latent Dirichlet allocation: bringing polysemy back. PLoS ONE **18**(7), 1–18 (2023). https://doi.org/10.1371/journal.pone.0288274. Accessed 14 Feb 2025
11. Apresjan, V., Lopukhina, A., Zarifyan, M.: Representation of different types of adjectival polysemy in the mental lexicon. Front. Psychol. **12**, art. N 742064 (2021). https://doi.org/10.3389/fpsyg.2021.742064. Accessed 14 Feb 2025
12. Valera, S., Ruz, A.E.: Conversion in English: homonymy, polysemy and paronymy. Engl. Lang. Linguist. **25**(1), 181–204 (2021). https://doi.org/10.1017/S1360674319000546. Accessed 14 Feb 2025
13. Pannain, R., di Pace, L.: Metonymy and the polysemy of Covid-19 in Italian. Rev. Cogn. Linguist. **20**(1), 231–257 (2022). https://doi.org/10.1075/rcl.00109.pan. Accessed 14 Feb 2025
14. Ursini, F.-A., Long, H., Zhang, S.Y.: Polysemy and semantic relations in Italian spatial prepositions. Rev. signos **55**(108), 173–198 (2022). https://doi.org/10.4067/S0718-09342022000100173. Accessed 14 Feb 2025
15. Ursini, F.-A., Long, H.: Polysemy and semantic relations in Aquilan prepositions. Onomázein **54**, 203–223 (2021). https://doi.org/10.7764/onomazein.54.06. Accessed 14 Feb 2025
16. Michel, C., Löhr. G.: A cognitive psychological model of linguistic intuitions: polysemy and predicate order effects in copredication sentences. Lingua **301**(April) (2024). https://doi.org/10.1016/j.lingua.2024.103694. Accessed 14 Feb 2025
17. Viebahn, E.: Copredication, polysemy and context-sensitivity. Inquiry **65**(8), 1066–1082 (2022). https://doi.org/10.1080/0020174X.2020.1822911. Accessed 14 Feb 2025
18. Liu, M.: Mental Imagery and polysemy processing. J. Conscious. Stud. **29**(5–6), 176–189 (2022). https://doi.org/10.53765/20512201.29.5.176. Accessed 14 Feb 2025
19. Li, J., Joanisse, M.F.: Word senses as clusters of meaning modulations: a computational model of polysemy. Cogn. Sci. **45**(4), 1–30 (2021). https://doi.org/10.1111/cogs.12955. Accessed 14 Feb 2025
20. Fortescue, M.: Polysemy, Diachrony and the Circle of Cognition. Introduction. Brill, Boston (2021)
21. Bond, F., Maziarz, M., Piotrowski, T., Rudnicka, E.: Models of polysemy in two English dictionaries. Int. J. Lexicogr. **37**(2), 196–225 (2024). https://doi.org/10.1093/ijl/ecad033. Accessed 14 Feb 2025
22. Richard-Bollans, A., Álvarez, L. G., Cohn. A. G.: Identifying and modelling polysemous senses of spatial prepositions in referring expressions. Cogn. Syst. Res. **77**, 45–61 (2023). https://doi.org/10.1016/j.cogsys.2022.09.004. Accessed 14 Feb 2025
23. Ma, R., Jin, L., Liu, Q., Chen, L., Yu, K.: Addressing the polysemy problem in language modeling with attentional multi-sense embeddings. In: ICASSP, IEEE International Conference on Acoustics, Speech and Signal Processing - Proceedings, 2020-May, art. no. 9053503, pp. 8129–8133 (2020). https://doi.org/10.1109/ICASSP40776.2020.9053503. Accessed 14 Feb 2025
24. Zhong, X., Ding, C., Qu, X., Tao, D.: Polysemy deciphering network for robust human-object interaction detection. Int. J. Comput. Vision **129**(6), 1910–1929 (2021). https://doi.org/10.1007/s11263-021-01458-8. Accessed 14 Feb 2025
25. Lai, H.-L., Hsu, H.-L., Liu, J.-S., Lin, C.-H., Chen, Y.: Supervised word sense disambiguation on taiwan hakka polysemy with neural network models: a case study of BUN, TUNG and LAU. In: Proceedings of the 35th Pacific Asia Conference on Language, Information and Computation 2021, pp. 731–741 (2021)
26. Iftikhar, S., Jabeen, F., Nasir, H., Fida, S.: WordNet and wiki based approach for finding polysemy tags in a tag set. In: International Conference on Intelligent Systems and Computer Vision, ISCV 2020, art. no. 9204288 (2020). https://doi.org/10.1109/ISCV49265.2020.9204288. Accessed 14 Feb 2025

27. Zhao, Q., Gao, T., Guo, N.: A novel Chinese relation extraction method using polysemy rethinking mechanism. Appl. Intell. **53**(7), 7665–7676 (2023). https://doi.org/10.1007/s10489-022-03817-5. Accessed 14 Feb 2025
28. Priss, U.: A semiotic perspective on polysemy. Ann. Math. Artif. Intell. **90**(11/12), 1125–1138 (2022). https://doi.org/10.1007/s10472-022-09795-1. Accessed 14 Feb 2025
29. Haber, J., Poesio, M.: Polysemy - evidence from linguistics, behavioural science, and contextualized language models. Comput. Linguist. **50**(1), 351–417 (2024). https://doi.org/10.1162/coli_a_00500. Accessed 14 Feb 2025
30. Navigli, R.: Word Sense Disambiguation: a Survey. ACM Comput. Surv. **41**(2), 1–69 (2009). https://doi.org/10.1145/1459352.1459355. Accessed 14 Feb 2025
31. Mitkov, R. (ed.): The Oxford Handbook of Computational Linguistics, pp. 249–265. Oxford University Press (2009)
32. Miller, G.A.: WordNet: a lexical database for English. Commun. ACM **38**(11), 39–41 (1995). https://doi.org/10.1145/219717.21974. Accessed 14 Feb 2025
33. Lesk, M.: Automatic sense disambiguation using machine readable dictionaries: how to tell a pine cone from an ice cream cone. In: Proceedings of the 1986 SIGDOC Conference, Toronto, Canada, pp. 24–26 (1986)
34. Schütze, H.: Automatic word sense discrimination. Comput. Linguist. **24**(1), 97–123 (1998)
35. Peters, M.E., et al.: Deep contextualized word representations. In: Proceedings of the 2018 Conference of the North American Chapter of the Association for Computational Linguistics: Human Language Technologies, 1, Long Papers, pp. 2227–2237 (2018)
36. Devlin, J., Chang, M.-W., Lee, K., Toutanova, K.: BERT: pre-training of Deep Bidirectional Transformers for Language Understanding. In: Proceedings of the 2019 Conference of the North American Chapter of the Association for Computational Linguistics: Human Language Technologies, vol. 1, pp. 4171–4186 (2019)
37. Wiedemann, G., Remus, S., Chawla, A., Biemann, C.: Does BERT make any sense? Interpretable word sense disambiguation with contextualized embeddings. In: Proceedings of the 15th Conference on Natural Language Processing (KONVENS 2019), Long Papers, 161–170 (2019)
38. Pires, T., Schlinger, E., Garrette, D.: How multilingual is multilingual BERT? In: Proceedings of the 57th Annual Meeting of the Association for Computational Linguistics, pp. 4996–5001 (2019)
39. Mitkov, R. (ed.): The Oxford Handbook of Computational Linguistics, pp. 650–669. Oxford University Press (2009)
40. Bisk, Y., et al.: Experience grounds language. In: Proceedings of the 2020 Conference on Empirical Methods in Natural Language Processing (EMNLP), pp. 8718–8735 (2020). https://doi.org/10.18653/v1/2020.emnlp-main.703. Accessed 14 Feb 2025
41. Radford, A., et al.: Learning transferable visual models from natural language supervision. In: Proceedings of the 38th International Conference on Machine Learning (ICML), pp. 8748–8763 (2021). http://proceedings.mlr.press/v139/radford21a/radford21a.pdf. Accessed 14 Feb 2025
42. Barsalou, L.W.: Perceptual symbol systems. Behav. Brain Sci. **22**(4), 577–660 (1999). https://doi.org/10.1017/s0140525x99002149. Accessed 14 Feb 2025
43. Open AI CLIP: Connecting text and images. https://openai.com/index/clip. Accessed 03 Apr 2025
44. … who ordered the *apple*?. https://www.facebook.com/photo/?fbid=322909453864969&set=a.102334505922466. Accessed 03 Apr 2025

Braille Character Recognition Using Machine Vision Algorithm

Sánchez-Luévano Abril Natalia[1], García-Cruz Azalia Guadalupe[1], Chávez-Almaraz Marlon[1], Domínguez-Sánchez Sergio[1](✉), Hernández-González Umanel Azazael[1], Mirelez-Delgado Flabio[1], and De-La-Rosa-Priego Willehado Armando[2]

[1] Unidad Profesional Interdisciplinaria de Ingeniería Campus Zacatecas, Instituto Politécnico Nacional, Calle Circuito Cerro del Gato No. 202, 98160 Zacatecas, Zac., Mexico
sdominguez@ipn.mx

[2] Centro de Estudios Científicos y Tecnológicos No. 18 "Zacatecas", Instituto Politécnico Nacional, Calle Circuito Cerro del Gato No. 202, 98160 Zacatecas, Zac., Mexico
https://www.zacatecas.ipn.mx/, https://www.cecyt18.ipn.mx

Abstract. This system seeks to provide a support tool for the visually impaired community, allowing them to preserve, share, and consult braille in a more accessible way. It also represents a valuable resource for educators, students, and people interested in learning the braille system, by facilitating the interpretation and automated translation of physical documents into digital formats. It presents the development of a computational algorithm of traditional computer vision for the identification of characters according to the standard established by the Spanish National Organization of the Blind (ONCE, by its acronym in Spanish) of distance between points and composition of the cells of the tactile reading-writing system. The system was implemented on an embedded hardware platform based on a Raspberry Pi 4 Model B, in charge of processing the image captured by an OV5647-based wide-angle camera. To facilitate the detection of the point, dark field illumination was used. Image processing was carried out using the OpenCV library in Python, with tasks such as contrast enhancement, noise elimination, morphological analysis, segmentation of lines and cells, identification of dots by region in the cell clustering techniques and finally, translation into grade 1 braille, i.e., with no contraction, generating as output the transcription of the text in alphanumeric characters.

Keywords: Braille · Visual impairment · Computer Vision · Character recognition · Image processing · Segmentation

1 Introduction

Access to information is one of the most important aspects of education at all levels; for this reason, people with or without visual impairment should be

T. Guarda et al. (Eds.): ARTIIS 2025, CCIS 2789, pp. 373–385, 2026.
https://doi.org/10.1007/978-3-032-16758-3_29

aware of the importance of the braille system in facilitating access to written texts, mathematics, music, and literature [9]. Dr. Eduardo Chávez Mondragón, president of the Mexican Society of Ophthalmology, stated that in Mexico, there are an estimated 2,237,000 people with visual impairment and more than 415,800 with blindness [1]. However, there are disadvantages due to the difficulty in accessing information in braille. Reading is an essential skill both in the school environment and for accessing the wealth of human cultural information [8].

In the capital city of Zacatecas, "Roberto Cabral del Hoyo" library has a collection of 560 books in braille, which have been preserved since their printing in 1961. For about 25 years there has been a braille reading and writing education project led by Ricardo Vela Vicencio, a Bachelor in Special Education focused in blindness and visual impairment, who in an interview on September 20th, 2023 expressed the difficulty in obtaining material that has not been damaged by use and the passage of time, since this material is brought from other states and the machinery to generate braille texts is very expensive.

According to the description given by Professor Vela Vicencio, braille is a "communication system for people with or without visual impairment, which is based on reading by touch"; this system of reading and writing was conceived by Louis Braille in 1825 [3].

In the braille system, each character is composed of six embossed dots, which can be used to make up to sixty-four different combinations. The characters are distinguished from each other due to the presence and arrangement of the dots. Figure 1 shows the braille version of each of the letters of the alphabet, according to ONCE.

Each cell must have a specific distance between its points and between them, and each point a specific height. The horizontal center-to-center spacing of points in the same cell can be from 2.4 to 2.7 mm. The distance between points' centers of the same cell vertically has the same range as the distance between horizontal centers, while the horizontal distance between the centers of the initial points from one cell to the other is from 6 to 6.9 mm. The vertical separation between the centers of the initial points from one cell to the other can be 10 to 11.26 mm; the diameter of the points is 1.2 to 1.9 mm; and the recommended height for the dots can be defined between 0.2 to 0.5 mm [5], as shown in Fig. 2.

In this context, computer vision is a combination of image processing and pattern recognition, and it offers an effective alternative for capturing, interpreting, and translating information contained in braille texts. The result of the computer vision process is the understanding of images; the development of this field is realized by adapting the human vision capability to obtain information [10].

Optical Character Recognition (OCR) technology encompasses a set of techniques based on statistics, character shapes, transformations, and comparisons, which, complementing each other, are used to automatically distinguish between different existing characters [7]. Table 1 identifies the characteristic stages in any OCR system.

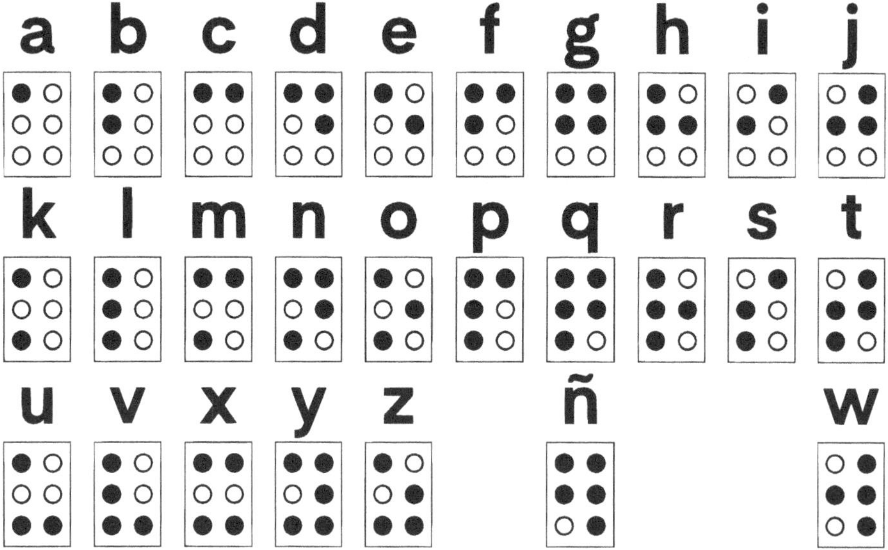

Fig. 1. The braille alphabet.

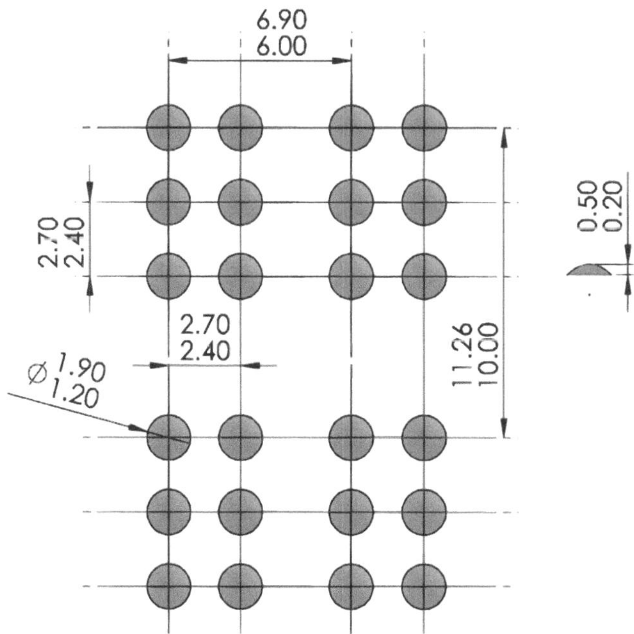

Fig. 2. Distance between points (lengths in millimeters).

Table 1. Stages of an OCR system.

Stage	Concept	Description
1	Preprocess	Image adequacy
2	Segmentation	Selection of the area of interest
3	Feature extraction	Digital representation of the image
4	Recognition	Distinction of the characters contained in the image

The aim is to develop this braille character recognition system not only to facilitate access to information for the visually impaired but also to promote education and professional inclusion for anyone interested in learning braille, achieving a more equitable society in which economic barriers are not an obstacle to personal and academic development.

To achieve this, diverse alternatives for braille recognition were explored, as outlined in Sect. 2. The methodology for the chosen solution is explored in Sect. 3, and its results are discussed in Sect. 4.

2 Related Work

There is a wide variety of methods for implementing computer vision to process images computationally to identify characters, geometric shapes, patterns, object recognition, etc.

Many modern methods are based on object recognition using neural networks. For example, in Cusco, Peru, Fernandez C. Y. et al. [4] developed a mobile application for Android for text recognition and speech conversion, using extreme programming and neural networks. These methods offer an accuracy close to 100%, however they require extensive computational power.

Another way to recognize braille characters is to use a combination of sensors. Park B. S. et al. [6] compared the effectiveness of computer vision methods with the use of a tactile sensor based on a capacitive array. The use of sensors complements computer vision methods, but it requires specialized and difficult-to-manufacture hardware.

A low-level approach was taken by Badaya Y. [2], who used a combination of traditional computer vision techniques such as edge detection and the Hough transform to create horizontal and vertical segments of the original image, dividing it into individual braille cells. There remain significant challenges related to accuracy with this method.

Building on the limitations identified in previous approaches, this work aims to generate a low-cost, embedded solution that can be later integrated into a braille copying system, which is why a traditional computer vision approach was also adopted, incorporating additional preprocessing techniques, image processing methods and a controlled lighting environment.

3 Methods

This section describes the methodology used for the machine vision algorithm to go from image capturing to image processing, segmentation, point and braille translation to obtain a digital file with the corresponding alphanumeric characters.

3.1 Experimental Setup and Image Capture

The image processing starts from the capture of the image. For the development of this system, a camera based on the OV5647 sensor of 12 MP and 130° of aperture with ± 10° of tolerance, coupled with a Raspberry Pi 4 Model B processing card, due to the compatibility of connection between them. The distance between the camera and the document to be scanned is 20 cm.

A diffuse light was used in a dark field illumination arrangement, which consists of thin strips of LED lights on the sides of the sheet at the same height, to highlight the braille dots on the sheet, as shown in Fig. 3. With a controlled environment, constant image captures can be obtained, and processing can begin to scan one braille page at a time.

Fig. 3. Image Captured.

3.2 Image Preprocessing

As a first step, the fisheye effect of the camera is eliminated using the defisheye library. Subsequently, the perspective of the area to be analyzed is adjusted, the image is passed through a high-pass filter to homogenize the background of the image, converted to grayscale, binarized, and the morphological kernel operation is applied to clearly see the braille dots of the document.

3.3 Segmentation of Rows and Cells

With OpenCV operations, the braille dots are horizontally dilated so that each line can be identified as white rectangles. With the Canny tool, the edges of the rectangles are identified and with the Hough transform, the start and end coordinates of each line are obtained, saving the position of each line.

The Hough transform is used to detect straight lines by the number of intersections between curves. With polar coordinates, the equation of a family of lines passing through a point is given below.

$$r_\theta = x_\theta \cos(\theta) + y_\theta \sin(\theta) \tag{1}$$

Therefore, each pair $(r_\theta,\ \theta)$ corresponds to a line passing through a point $(x_\theta,\ y_\theta)$. This process is repeated, but now with a vertical dilation of the braille dots, to identify the separation between cells. In this way, the separation of each cell is stored in each line, taking the whole document as a reference.

As a next step, each line is extracted and scrolled through with its respective separation of cells, it is analyzed if it has white dots (braille) or if it has a minimum height, so that it is saved for later analysis of its content or as a paragraph break.

For cells, a similar condition is taken into account, in which each cell is extracted from the line, checked for white dots or minimum width, and saved to view its contents or as a space between words.

3.4 Identification of Braille Dots

To identify the points of a braille cell, the contours of these points are searched by clustering techniques and by the condition that if they have a minimum of five pixels, then their centroid is calculated, and their coordinates are stored. To find the centroid of a shape in an image, first its moments must be calculated according to the addition of the intensities of the pixels in the matrix, as shown from (2) to (4).

$$M_{00} = \sum_x \sum_y I(x, y) \tag{2}$$

$$M_{10} = \sum_x \sum_y xI(x, y) \tag{3}$$

$$M_{01} = \sum_x \sum_y yI(x, y) \tag{4}$$

Each of the moments is divided to obtain the x and the y coordinates of the centroid of the analyzed shape as shown in (5).

$$x = \frac{M_{10}}{M_{00}}, \quad y = \frac{M_{01}}{M_{00}} \tag{5}$$

The technique of identifying centroids prevents errors in which a braille dot, because of the generated shadow, appears to belong to more than one region in the cell. Thus, only the region to which it belongs the most is counted.

Subsequently, the cell is divided into six regions (Fig. 4); two columns and three rows, to identify to which sector of the cell the braille dots belong, a '0' is coded for the absence of a braille dot and a '1' for the presence of the dot in the region, so that every braille cell will be coded by a six digit binary number.

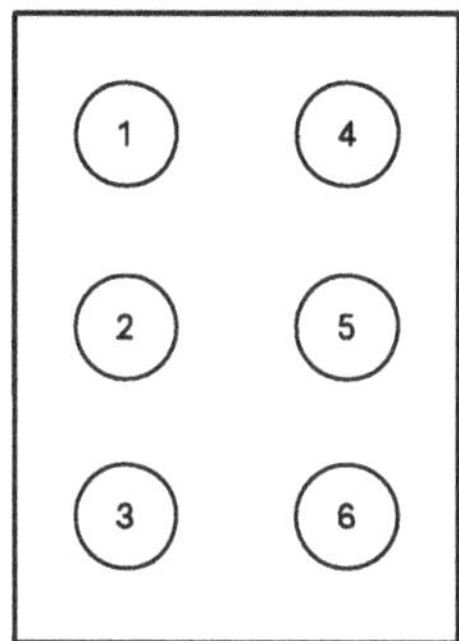

Fig. 4. Regions of the braille cell.

3.5 Conversion to Alphanumeric Characters

Dictionaries with the equivalent of each braille character are stored in four variables.

1. For indicators that the next cell is a number or a capital letter.
2. For the alphabet.
3. For numbers.
4. For signs.

It opens a text file to write the results of each cell, first, it checks if the line has content or if it is empty. In the latter case, it writes a paragraph break. If it has content, then it continues to compare the binary digit of the analyzed cell with the corresponding dictionary to write the correct character in the text file. Once it finishes analyzing the cells in the line, it makes a line break. This process is repeated until it finishes going through all the lines of the document and obtains a complete translation.

4 Results

Table 2 shows the input text for test one, in alphanumeric characters in spanish and in braille.

Table 2. Input text for test1

Alphanumeric characters	Braille
Benjamín pidió una bebida de kiwi y fresa. Noé, sin vergüenza, la más exquisita champaña del menú.	[illegible] [illegible] [illegible] [illegible]

Figure 5 shows the result of the defisheye operations and perspective shift, which produces an orthogonal view of the image.

(a) Rotated image, without effect. (b) Perspective adjustment.

Fig. 5. Defisheye operations on image.

Figure 6 shows the main preprocessing operations: the application of a high-pass filter, grayscale conversion, Kernel morphological analysis, and binarization.

With the preprocessing done, the dilation of points horizontally (Fig. 7) and vertically (Fig. 8) it was possible to detect each line and each braille cell in them, fulfilling the objective of referencing the information from the whole document to be precise in the division of cells.

By superimposing these results on the preprocessing image, the segmentation obtained is clearer (Fig. 9). The extraction of the main image is done from the start and end coordinates of the line, as shown in Fig. 10.

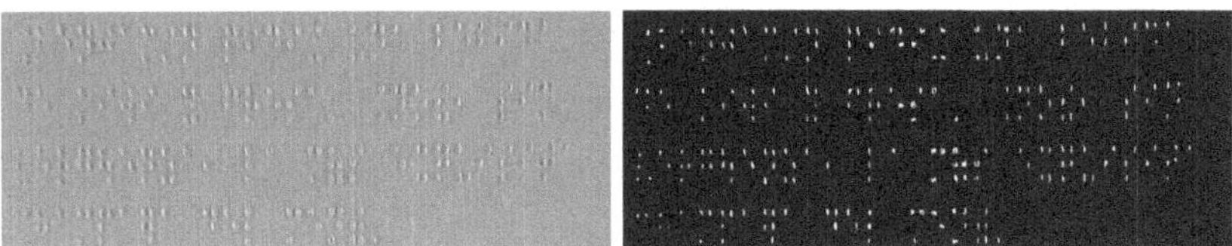

(a) Image after application of the high-pass filter. (b) Preprocessing result.

Fig. 6. Main preprocessing operations.

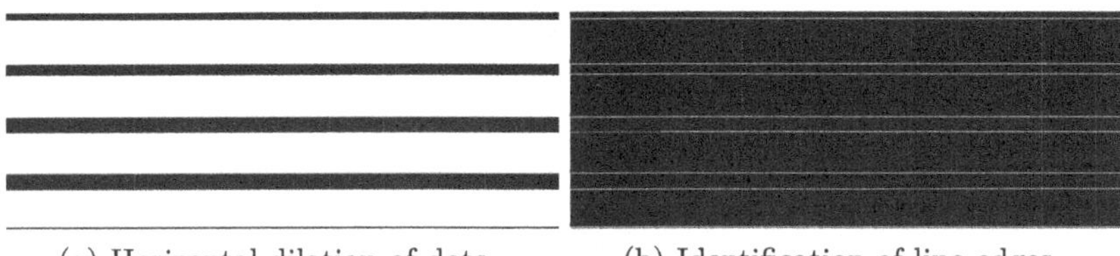

(a) Horizontal dilation of dots. (b) Identification of line edges.

Fig. 7. Dilation of points horizontally.

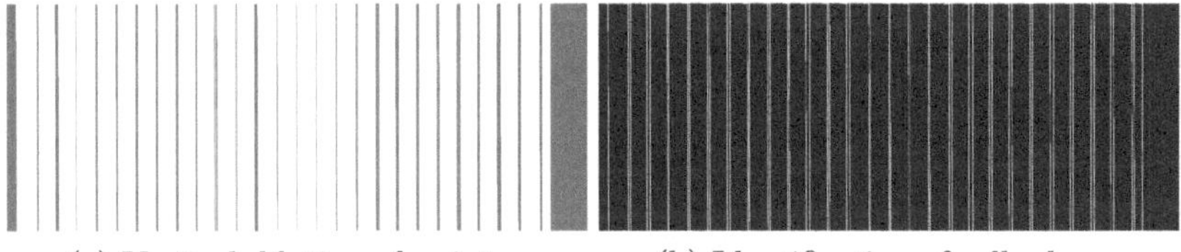

(a) Vertical dilation of points. (b) Identification of cell edges.

Fig. 8. Dilation of points vertically.

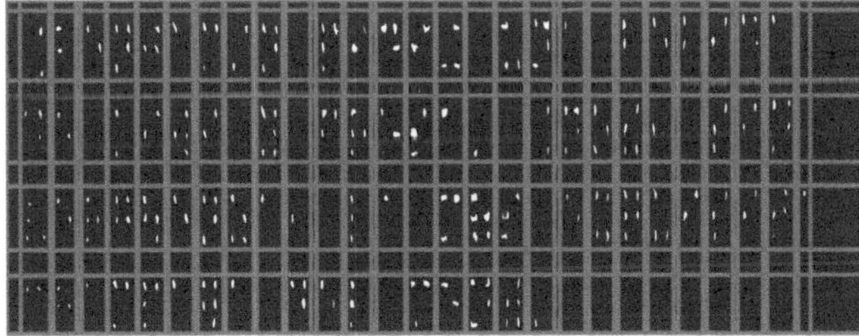

Fig. 9. Segmentation of rows and cells.

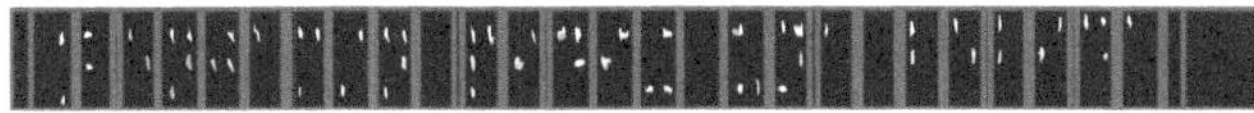

Fig. 10. Braille line extraction and analysis.

Subsequently, each braille cell is extracted from the line under analysis, for example, in Fig. 11, the first character of the first line is analyzed, the divisions of the regions of the cell are shown in red, the braille dots in white and the centroids located in each dot in green. As a result, this cell has dots in regions four and six, so it is saved as '000101'.

Fig. 11. Braille character identification.

After completing the image processing, the result is a text file with the translation of the scanned braille document, Table 3 shows the scanned text and its Braille equivalent:

Table 3. Output text for test 1.

Alphanumeric characters	**Braille**
Benjamín pidió una bebida	⠨⠃⠑⠝⠚⠁⠍⠌⠝ ⠏⠊⠙⠊⠬ ⠥⠝⠁ ⠃⠑⠃⠊⠙⠁
de kiwi y fresa. Noé, sin	⠨⠙⠑ ⠅⠊⠺⠊ ⠽ ⠋⠗⠑⠎⠁⠄ ⠨⠝⠕⠮⠂ ⠎⠊⠝
vergüenza, la más exquisit	⠨⠧⠑⠗⠛⠳⠑⠝⠵⠁⠂ ⠇⠁ ⠍⠷⠎ ⠑⠭⠟⠥⠊⠎⠊⠞
champaña del menú.	⠨⠉⠓⠁⠍⠏⠁⠻⠁ ⠙⠑⠇ ⠍⠑⠝⠾⠄

To evaluate the performance of the system, the accuracy of the detections was calculated as shown in (6).

$$\text{Accuracy} = \frac{\text{Correctly detected characters}}{\text{Total characters}} \tag{6}$$

The processing time is around 1.55 s. With one misidentified character out of a total of ninety-six, the accuracy for this test if of 98.9%.

Further scanning tests were carried out with other braille documents, varying in length and position on the page. In each case, it was verified that the processing steps were followed; evaluating if the segmentation of lines and cells were correct in order to identify the equivalent braille characters. A line-by-line comparison was made between the text on the page and the digital file obtained.

In a writing covering most of the page, the result in the text file was:

```
El triste, José Joss

Qué triste fue decirnos
adiós
Cando nos adorábamos más
hasta la golondrina emigr
Sresagiando el final
Qé triste luce todo sin
los mares de las playas s

se tiñen los colores de
ris
hoy todo es so;edac

t! sé si vuelva a verje
cessués
No sé si vuelva a verte
después
No sé qué de mi vida serz
Sin el lucero azu; de tu
ser
Qué no me alumbra más
```

Table 4 shows a comparison between the braille in the document and the braille equivalent of the scanned text.

With 333 characters correctly identified out of a total of 354, i.e., 94.07% error rate, in a processing time of 2.54 s.

On the other hand, in a document that is only a line and a half long, the digital file obtained the following text:

```
ko esencaasesinuis
aos ojos"
```

Table 5 shows a comparison between the braille in the document and the braille equivalent of the scanned text for this test.

Twenty-three out of thirty-seven characters were correctly identified with a processing time of 1.67 s, i.e., 62.16% accuracy.

Table 4. Comparison of input and output braille for test 2.

Braille document	Braille of scanned text
[illegible]	[illegible]
[illegible]	[illegible]
[illegible]	[illegible]
[illegible]	[illegible]
[illegible]	[illegible]
[illegible]	[illegible]
[illegible]	[illegible]
[illegible]	[illegible]
[illegible]	[illegible]
[illegible]	[illegible]
[illegible]	[illegible]
[illegible]	[illegible]
[illegible]	[illegible]
[illegible]	[illegible]
[illegible]	[illegible]
[illegible]	[illegible]
[illegible]	[illegible]
[illegible]	[illegible]
[illegible]	[illegible]

Table 5. Comparison of input and output braille 3.

Alphanumeric characters	Braille
[illegible]	[illegible]
[illegible]	[illegible]

5 Conclusions

In the development of this work, a computer system for the identification and translation of braille characters to a digital file was developed, providing an accessible solution to the interpretation of grade 1 braille documents, through the use of low-cost hardware, combining image processing techniques in Python, achieving a high percentage of accuracy.

Unlike other works on the same subject, the technique of identifying the clusters' centroids by regions of the braille cell represents an advance, since if only the presence of pixels were identified, the accuracy in detecting the braille dots would be considerably reduced.

The proposal not only addresses a technical problem of braille pattern interpretation but also provides a social value by facilitating the preservation, access, and learning of documents in this reading and writing system.

Demonstrating the potential of artificial vision technologies applied to the field of accessibility, laying the groundwork for the development of more inclusive tools that contribute to the elimination of barriers for visually impaired people.

6 Future Work

The future goal is to expand the processing system for the identification and translation of grade 2 braille, which uses abbreviations to represent words and common groups of letters, allowing a more efficient reading than grade 1. This challenge involves not only the correct recognition of dot patterns but also the contextual interpretation of character and word combinations. Also, the improvement of segmentation and recognition algorithms is planned.

References

1. Agencia Internacional para la Prevención de la Ceguera: IAPB Vision Atlas, Global Vision Database Maps (2025). http://atlas.iapb.org/gvd-maps/#AllAges, archived at https://web.archive.org/web/20200919131030/http://atlas.iapb..org/gvd-maps/#AllAges
2. Badaya, Y.: MUSoC 2017 - Braille OCR (2017). https://medium.com/musoc-2017-braille-ocr/week-i-preprocessing-of-the-braille-scan-14475d8beaee
3. Cobos-Granada, V.: Construcción de una impresora Braille de bajo costo. B.S. Thesis, Universidad Técnica del Norte, Ecuador (2023)
4. Fernandez-Guevara, C., Vargas-Pantoja, J.: Aplicación para el reconocimiento de textos y transformación de voz, y desarrollo de un prototipo de impresora braille orientado a personas con discapacidad visual. B.S. Thesis, Universidad Nacional De San Antonio Abad Del Cusco, Perú (2018)
5. Organización Nacional de Ciegos Españoles: Documento técnico b1: Parámetros dimensionales del braille. Tech. rep., ONCE, Madrid (2014)
6. Park, B.S., et al.: Visual and tactile perception techniques for braille recognition. Micro Nano Syst. Lett. **11**(1), 23 (2023). https://doi.org/10.1186/s40486-023-00191-w
7. Sanchez-Fernandez, C., Sandonis-Consuegra, V.: Reconocimiento Óptico de Caracteres. B.S. Thesis, Universidad Carlos III, Madrid (2009)
8. Sarango-Espinoza, J., Chamba-Zzaragocín, W., Espinoza-León, M.: Aprendizaje del sistema de lectura y escritura braille basado en las tic. CEDEMAZ **12**(1), 77–84 (2022)
9. Serpa-Valdes, M., Rondon-Rojas, I., González-Cabrera, Y.: Consideraciones históricas sobre el sistema braille. Revista Cubana de Oftalmología **35**(3) (2022)
10. Wiley, V., Lucas, T.: Computer vision and image processing: a paper review. Int. J. Artif. Intell. Res. **2**(1), 22 (2018)

Predicting Customer Churn in Certification Services Using Supervised Learning

Oscar Javier Novoa-Nuñez and Ixent Galpin(✉)

Facultad de Ciencias Naturales e Ingeniería, Universidad de Bogotá - Jorge Tadeo Lozano, Bogotá, Colombia
{oscarj.novoan,ixent}@utadeo.edu.co

Abstract. Customer retention is a critical challenge for companies in an ever-changing environment. This project focuses on a leading certification services organization in Colombia with an extensive portfolio and an average of 25,000 customers. The organization faces the challenge of anticipating customer needs and behaviors, with certificate renewal being a key indicator of satisfaction and continuity in the business relationship.The main objective of this study is to develop a predictive model to identify customers with a high probability of not renewing their certificates. Using the Cross Industry Standard Process for Data Mining (CRISP-DM) methodology, historical customer data is analyzed, relevant features are selected, and several classification models are compared to predict the probability of renewal. The evaluation of the models includes the optimization of classifiers and the evaluation of their performance using the confusion matrix, a tool that allows measuring the accuracy of the predictions. The classification model with the best performance to identify customers with a potential risk of leakage is decision trees, with an accuracy of 98%.

The predictive model provides the organization with an effective tool to anticipate certificate renewals, allowing the implementation of customized proactive retention strategies. These actions may include loyalty campaigns and adjustments to service protocols, tailored to the specific needs of each client.

Keywords: Customer Retention · Predictive Modeling · Machine Learning · Certification Renewal · Decision Trees · CRISP-DM · Churn Prediction

1 Introduction

Customer churn is one of the most critical issues faced by many companies today [16]. As such, it is crucial for organizations to act proactively in understanding customer needs and behaviors in order to ensure the success of a business. Furthermore, customer retention is also considered a critical factor for

T. Guarda et al. (Eds.): ARTIIS 2025, CCIS 2789, pp. 386–400, 2026.
https://doi.org/10.1007/978-3-032-16758-3_30

companies seeking to build a sustained and strong relationship with their target audience. In the certification services sector, large competitors anticipate with actions that provide a competitive advantage. Failing to do so, companies leave highly valuable opportunities in favor of their peers. This proposal uses a classification model to identify customers with a high probability of not renewing their certificates, thereby enabling actions that can prevent churn. Such actions may involve personalized retention campaigns or a more tailored customer protocol.

Currently, the organization, one of the leaders in providing certification services in Colombia, recognizes the importance of understanding and forecasting customer churn. This renewal not only represents a commercial transaction but also a crucial indicator of customer satisfaction and their willingness to maintain a continuous relationship with the company.

To address this need, the project develops a classification model that can be used to predict which customers are more likely to renew or not renew their certificate with the organization. Using the *Cross Industry Standard Process for Data Mining* (CRISP-DM) methodology [17], a detailed analysis of historical customer data, the main selected feature sets, and the optimization and scoring of several classifiers are performed. As a result, the organization obtains a predictive tool that accelerates the renewal anticipation process, with a strategic decision based on evidence, data understanding, data preparation, modeling, evaluation, and deployment. Moreover, the process of implementing the optimized model in a production environment is described, enabling real-time execution of all predictions related to the renewal of certified professionals. This ensures not only the effectiveness of the predictions but also the sustainability of the model over time, allowing the company to make proactive and informed decisions in managing customer retention. The contributions of this paper are:

- The development of a high-accuracy predictive model to identify clients at risk of not renewing certifications, enabling proactive retention strategies.
- The application of the CRISP-DM methodology to systematically address data imbalance and optimize model performance, comparing techniques like SMOTE, undersampling, and ADASYN across multiple algorithms (e.g., XGBoost, logistic regression).
- The practical deployment of the model as a REST API using Flask, facilitating real-time integration into business workflows for dynamic customer retention interventions.

The paper is structured as follows: Sect. 2 presents related work. Section 3 discusses the business understanding phase, where the importance of customer retention is addressed. Section 4 covers data understanding. Section 5 describes the data preparation process and the selection of relevant features. Section 6 presents the machine learning models employed. Section 7 compares the models and the results obtained. Section 8 discusses the deployment of the application in a production environment. Section 9 reflects on the performance of the models. Finally, Sect. 10 concludes communicating suggestions for exploring new approaches or improving models to achieve better results in the business context.

2 Related Work

Huang *et al.* [7] presents an approach to predict customer churn using seven different models, including logistic regression, linear classification, Naive Bayes, decision trees, neural networks, support vector machines (SVM), and an evolutionary data mining algorithm [7]. Rinika *et al.* [12] discusses student churn in its different forms within the educational system [12].

Xie *et al.* [18] observes that banks in China consider customer loss a priority, attempting to retain their customers despite resource constraints. This paper introduces a novel learning approach, called improved balanced random forests, to address the problem of class imbalance in data distribution [18]. Lu *et al.* examines the prediction of customer churn in digital customer relationship management (CRM) systems. They recommend using boosting techniques to identify and isolate high-risk consumers from others. Additionally, they implement models such as logistic regression and develop prediction models for each cluster, comparing them with an initial model [10].

Seyed *et al.* highlights that this is a major challenge for companies offering subscription-based services, as customer retention is critical for sustainable growth. This study analyzes prediction in three highly imbalanced public datasets from different sectors, including telecommunications, e-commerce, and banking [5]. Anurag *et al.* proposes K-Nearest Neighbors (KNN) as a better option for predicting customer loss, as logistic regression proved to be less effective in this case with labeled data [3].

Renato *et al.* [9] finds that the random forest technique outperforms decision trees, nearest neighbors, elastic net, logistic regression, and support vector machines across multiple metrics [9]. Youngjung *et al.* [15] focuses on analyzing the behavior of customers from a water purifier rental company, where churn is very frequent. Lazarov *et al.* [8] discusses the need to put more effort into predicting and preventing supplier churn. Burez et al. [4] investigates models for customer loss across six different companies.

The aforementioned projects provide different approaches to understand the challenges surrounding customer churn and retention. The goal is, through a comprehensive data analysis related to an algorithmic model, to better predict which customers are likely to stay with the organization and which might be considering leaving. This approach not only aims to recognize customer behavior patterns, but also attempts to anticipate their requirements and expectations. Having a more solid understanding of the relationship between the reasons that lead a customer to specifically leave the organization could allow us to identify requirements that help improve the customer experience and foster loyalty towards the organization.

3 Business Understanding

This project is conducted in the city of Bogotá within an organization that promotes, develops, and guides the application of technical standards. The organization has an extensive portfolio and an average of 25,000 clients. However, it has become increasingly challenging and competitive to anticipate the needs and behaviors of each customer, which has become essential for the success of organizations. In this context, customer retention and loyalty are strategic priorities for companies that wish to build strong and lasting relationships with their clients.

This project focuses on one of the leading entities in providing certification services, recognizing that the re-certification pattern of its clients should never be an overlooked area. This renewal process is not just a commercial transaction; it is a fundamental parameter that measures the potential continuation of the relationship between a company and its client, as well as the client's level of satisfaction with that relationship.

To address this need, the project develops a classification model to predict which clients are most likely to renew or not renew their certificates with the organization. Using the CRISP-DM methodology, an analysis of historical customer data is conducted, selecting relevant features and evaluating and comparing different classification models. Additionally, a reference to the confusion matrix is made, which helps visualize the performance of the classification model and better understand how it predicts certificate renewals. This matrix compares the model's predictions with the actual labels (i.e., whether the customer renewed or not). It consists of four elements:

- *True Positives* (TP): Customers predicted to renew who indeed renewed.
- *False Positives* (FP): Customers predicted to renew, but did not.
- *True Negatives* (TN): Customers predicted not to renew who indeed did not renew.
- *False Negatives* (FN): Customers predicted not to renew, but did.

The most critical metric in this context is the False Positive (FP) rate, which represents customers who were expected to renew but did not. Incorrectly predicting these cases can have a significant impact on the organization's retention strategy.

In this context, a data source from SQL Server 2012 is used, as described in Sect. 4. A stored procedure is generated to efficiently extract the customer history along with other relevant variables for analysis. Once the data is gathered, it is processed in Python for training the supervised model, exploring different classification algorithms. This equips the organization with a predictive tool that facilitates the anticipation of renewal processes and the making of evidence-based strategic decisions.

The document covers the phases of business understanding, data analysis, data preparation, modeling, evaluation, and deployment. Additionally, it details the process of implementing the optimized model in a production environment, allowing for real-time predictions regarding customer certificate renewals [19].

Finally, this project aims not only to improve customer retention but also to provide a deeper understanding of the factors that influence the decisions of customer churn. This enables proactive management of customer relationships and more effective decision-making, identifying opportunities for improvement in the organization's current processes. Thus, reverse engineering of each process does not only ensure customer retention but also lead to a better understanding of customer behavior and market needs.

4 Data Understanding

This project explores a data source that contains information stored in a SQL Server 2012 database schema. It includes historical data about customers who have or have not renewed their certificates with the company. During the exploration, several relevant variables are identified, as there is a stored procedure that returns 17 variables considered the most significant for analysis. Using these columns, a total of 21,704 records were processed. These records are then exported to a flat file to be loaded into a DataFrame in Python, enabling the necessary analysis processes to make more accurate predictions for each of the customers.

Table 1. Churn statistics for company clients

Category	Quantity	Percentage
Did not renew	17,893	82.44
Renewed	3,811	17.56

Table 1 summarizes the number of clients who have renewed and those who have not renewed throughout the company's history. These figures show an extremely high proportion of customer churn within the organization, with the majority of customers not renewing with the company. This highlights the imperative need for improvement in the processes and a stronger relationship with customers in order to enhance the service provided to each of them. Therefore, a balancing technique must be employed, as there is an imbalance in the data. This allows the machine learning model to apply balancing techniques to improve either the majority or minority classes depending on the results provided by each.

The variables in the dataset are the following:

- `Business Name`: The name of the company or entity registered in the system.
- `Tax Identification Number (NIT)`: A unique fiscal identifier assigned to each company or legal entity in Colombia.
- `Address`: The physical address or main office of the company, where its commercial activity is located.
- `Phone`: The contact phone number of the company.
- `City`: The city where the company is located. This helps identify its location within the country or region.
- `Department`: The department or province where the company is located. In some cases, like in Colombia, it refers to a territorial subdivision within the country.

- `Country`: The country where the company is located. This could be Colombia, Chile, Ecuador, Nicaragua, the Dominican Republic, and other international countries.
- `Region`: An internal or external regional classification of the company. In many cases, this column seems to indicate the geographical area or administrative division within the country that the company belongs to (e.g., "Antioquia Chocó and Eje Cafetero" or "Centro and Sur Oriente").
- `Account Executive`: The name of the executive or person responsible within the company who manages the certificates or clients related to the company.
- `Certificate Number`: The unique identifier assigned to the quality certificate or management system granted to the company. This number is used to track the certificate.
- `Management System`: Indicates the type of management system or ISO standard (e.g., ISO 9001, ISO 14001, ISO 45001, etc.) under which the company is certified. This system refers to the policies and procedures the company implements to ensure quality, safety, environment, etc.
- `Version`: Indicates the version of the ISO management system or other standard the company is using. The versions of standards may change over time, and each version has specific requirements. For example, "ISO 9001:2008" or "ISO 9001:2015."
- `Grant Date`: The date the quality certificate or management system was granted to the company. This marks the start of the certificate's validity period.
- `Renewal Date`: The date when the certificate should be renewed, i.e., the day a new evaluation or inspection is expected to confirm that the company continues to meet the standard requirements.
- `Expiration Date`: The date when the certificate will no longer be valid if not renewed. Once this date is reached, the company loses its certification until it is renewed.
- `Client Renewal`: This field indicates whether the company has renewed its certification on the corresponding date. If the answer is "YES," the renewal has been made; if "NO," the renewal has not been completed.
- `Customer Tenure`: This field indicates how many years the company has been a client (or how long the company has been using the management system). This helps understand the length of the relationship the company has maintained with the management systems, which can also indicate its stability or experience in the matter.

Figure 1 presents a summary of clients who have and have not renewed by region. This information allows for a detailed analysis of clients distributed across the country's different regions, highlighting whether they have renewed their certificates with the organization throughout their history. This approach not only helps understand the historical behavior of our clients but also allows us to identify specific regions that have great potential to enhance reliability in the services we offer. Through the implementation of strategic actions, we can improve the customer experience in these areas.

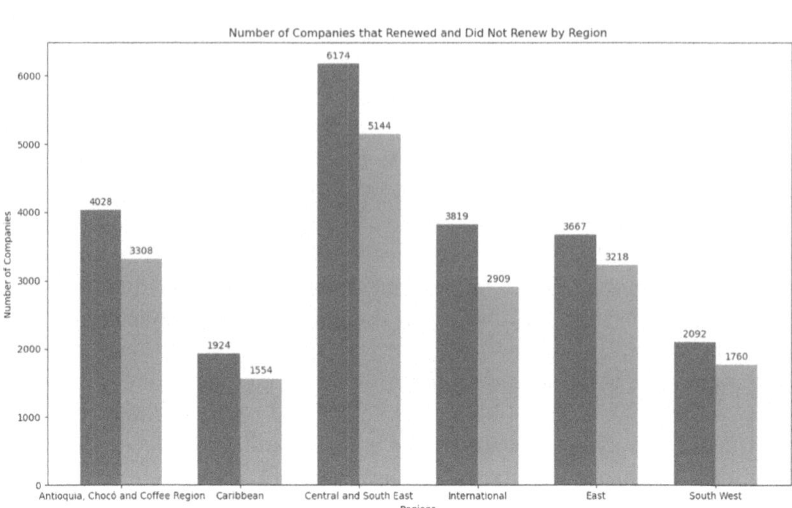

Fig. 1. Analysis of customer churn by region

Particularly in the central region, where the majority of the client base is concentrated, a deeper analysis is essential. The objective is to identify the characteristics of this population and assess whether competitors are offering better opportunities, products, or added value that could attract our current clients. This includes a thorough examination of activities that the company is not engaging in, in order to identify areas for improvement. By doing so, concrete actions may be taken to optimize business processes and ultimately strengthen the company market position.

Additionally, this analysis allows marketing and sales strategies to be adjusted, focusing on the specific needs and preferences of clients in each region. By better understanding the competitive environment and consumer expectations, more effective value propositions can be developed, and stronger relationships built with clients, ensuring their long-term loyalty. To achieve this, a confusion matrix is employed, which is an output generated by the model to identify the critical business factors, such as false positives or false negatives. These are evaluation metrics, including F1-score and recall, which are key to understanding how a model performs, especially in problems where classes are imbalanced or where it is more important to capture the positive class in order to determine better predictions in customer evaluations.

5 Data Preparation

This study, conducted on September 25, 2024, identified a database with approximately 84 tables, which are structured to store various aspects of customer information and their transactions. These tables include data on:

- **Clients**: Contact information.
- **Certificates**: Details about the issued certificates, including issue and expiration dates.
- **Demographics or Location**: Location data by region, department, and country where the client is certified.
- **Client Tenure**: Information about how long the client has been with the organization.
- **Account Executive**: Data about the person who manages the client at the first level.
- **Dates**: Various dates associated with each certificate, to identify the issuance and expiration dates.

Therefore, we can validate that the proportion of clients in the central region is much higher. This indicates that the majority of clients are located in this region, reflecting 23%, suggesting that efforts to strengthen ties with these clients should continue. There are also regions that need improvement, with a 1.53% increase required to generate growth and client renewal. This relational schema allows for efficient data management, facilitating integration and analysis from various perspectives. It highlights a dataset that provides an integrated view of client behavior in relation to certificate renewal, which is crucial for developing a predictive model.

Figure 2 shows that the organization has a high client tenure, reflecting a considerable level of trust in the company. However, the goal of this project is to enhance customer loyalty by implementing various strategies across different areas of the organization. This has a positive effect on our processes and, consequently, on the overall customer experience.

As such, it is essential to implement a machine learning model that efficiently identifies potential customer churn. This approach is envisioned to not only help detect those who may not renew their certificates, but also provide the opportunity to take proactive measures to retain them. By anticipating their needs and concerns, we can offer them the confidence and security they need to view our organization as a key partner in the service they require.

To carry out this process, we use the Python programming language, which is widely recognized for its versatility and efficiency in data analysis. Libraries such as Pandas are used to manage and manipulate data effectively by creating a DataFrame. This allows for the organization, cleaning, and analysis of the necessary information for the model.

Additionally, it is important to address the class imbalance problem, as this can affect the model's accuracy. To do so, we implement under-sampling,

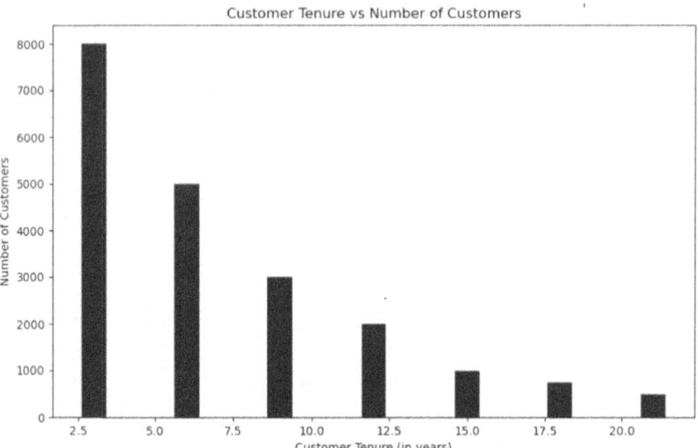

Fig. 2. Client Tenure

SMOTE (Synthetic Minority Over-sampling Technique) and ADASYN (Adaptive Synthetic Sampling), a data balancing technique used to improve the performance of machine learning models in imbalanced classification problems. Undersampling allows us to reduce the size of the majority class, while SMOTE generates synthetic examples for the minority class. These combined techniques help balance the dataset, which is crucial for improving the performance of our machine learning models.

Once the data is prepared and balanced, we proceed to develop and evaluate various machine learning models. We use methods such as logistic regression, decision trees, and more advanced algorithms like Random Forest, Regression, and XGBoost. Through rigorous analysis, we compare the performance of these models using metrics such as accuracy, recall, and F1-score. This helps determine which model best meets specific needs and offers the best performance in identifying customer churn.

By implementing this approach, we not only help retain current clients but also improve relationships with them. By better understanding their behavior and needs, we ensure that they feel valued and supported by the organization. This contributes to increasing their long-term loyalty and ultimately strengthens the company position in the market.

6 Modeling

Machine learning models are algorithms and techniques that enable computers to learn from data and make predictions or decisions based on that data, without the need to be explicitly programmed to perform those tasks [21]. They are based on the idea that, by exposing a model to a set of data, it can identify patterns and relationships that allow it to generalize to new situations. These are powerful tools that enable organizations to extract value from data and make more informed decisions. The choice of the appropriate model depends on the type of available data and the specific problem to be solved.

6.1 Naive Bayes

Naive Bayes is a set of classification algorithms based on Bayes' theorem, widely used in statistics and machine learning. It is called "naive" because it assumes that the input features are independent of each other, which is rarely true in practice, but simplifies the model significantly [1]. The model calculates the probability that a given data point belongs to a specific class, based on the features of the data. There are several types of Naive Bayes, such as Gaussian Naive Bayes, which is used for continuous data, and Multinomial Naive Bayes, which is commonly used for text classification.

6.2 Logistic Regression

This type of classification analysis is used to predict the outcome of a categorical variable based on independent variables, meaning an outcome with two possible categories (such as "yes" or "no", "1" or "0") [13]. Logistic regression is a fundamental tool in data analysis, especially in contexts where it is necessary to classify observations into two or more categories. Its ability to model probabilistic relationships in an interpretable and efficient manner makes it a popular choice across various disciplines.

6.3 XGBoost

XGBoost is a highly efficient and flexible machine learning algorithm, mainly used for supervised learning problems, where a training dataset is used to predict a target variable. It is known for its outstanding performance in data science competitions and its ability to handle large volumes of data [20]. Its ability to handle complex data, its flexibility in applications, and its superior performance make it a popular choice for many data analysts and data scientists.

6.4 Decision Trees

Decision trees are a machine learning method used for classification and regression, representing decisions and their possible outcomes in the form of a tree-like graph structure. They are intuitive and easy to interpret, making them a popular tool in data analysis. A decision tree consists of nodes (where decisions are made) and leaves (final outcomes). Each node represents a feature (variable), and each branch represents a decision outcome. The leaves indicate the class or the final predicted value [11].

These models illustrate the rich diversity of techniques available in machine learning, each with its own advantages and disadvantages. The choice of the appropriate model depends not only on the type of data and the problem to be solved but also on the specific context and interpretability requirements. As tools and techniques continue to evolve, understanding and properly selecting these models becomes crucial to maximize the value extracted from data across a wide range of applications and domains.

7 Evaluation

In this section, we present the evaluation of each of the models previously described, using data balancing techniques such as SMOTE, undersampling, and ADASYN [6]. A five-fold cross-validation was performed, which involves dividing the dataset into five equal parts. In each iteration of the validation process, one of these folds is used as the test set, while the other four folds are used to train the model. This process is repeated five times, each time with a different fold as the test set, and the results are averaged to obtain a more robust evaluation of the model. Table 2 shows the performance of the models using the precision, accuracy, recall, and F1-score metrics. This evaluation allows us to identify which model performs most effectively in the classification tasks.

Table 2. Results of Implemented Models

Model	Technique	Precision	Recall	F1-score	Accuracy
Naive Bayes	Smote	0.30	0.60	0.48	0.77
Logistic Regression	Smote	0.35	0.77	0.46	0.72
Ridge Regression	Smote	0.44	1.00	0.61	0.78
XGBoost	Under-sampling	0.75	0.93	0.86	0.94
Naive Bayes	Under-sampling	0.39	0.60	0.47	0.77
Logistic Regression	Under-sampling	0.35	0.66	0.46	0.72
Ridge Regression	Under-sampling	0.76	1.00	0.61	0.78
XGBoost	Under and Smote	0.44	1.00	0.86	0.94
XGBoost	ADASYN	0.75	1.00	0.86	0.94
Decision Trees	Under-sampling	0.92	0.98	0.95	0.98
Decision Trees	Smote	0.92	0.96	0.96	0.98

In the performance analysis of these models, we observe that precision and accuracy are crucial metrics that allow us to evaluate how well a model is performing. The decision tree models achieve 0.99 of accuracy for both the *Yes* and *No* classes. The model that reaches 0.98 of accuracy in both classes is not only more effective in the correct classification of instances, but it also provides a reliable framework for decision-making. This makes it a superior option compared to other models with lower performance, where the risks associated with classification errors could be significantly higher.

8 Deployment

The deployment of the application is carried out using a model that has been previously stored, containing all the logic and Python code needed to implement the model. After training the model, it is saved in a serialized format such as `trained-model.pkl`, which allows its reuse in future deployments or analyses, ensuring that the model's functionality and performance remain consistent. To facilitate access to the model and enable smooth interaction with other applications, the Flask library[1] is used. This microframework is widely recognized in the Python development community for its simplicity and flexibility. Through Flask, key functions such as `jsonify` and `request` are implemented, which allow handling requests and responses in JSON format. This format is especially useful for developing services that follow the RESTful API paradigm, as it allows clear and structured communication between the client and server [2]. The main goal of this architectural approach is for the application to be published and consumed via queries to a REST API. As described in the work of Richardson and Ruby [14], this architecture not only facilitates the integration of different clients, such as mobile applications or web frontends, but also promotes better separation of concerns, which in turn improves the system's maintainability and scalability. In addition, implementing a REST API allows tools such as Postman to connect and make queries to the service efficiently and easily. This is crucial for developers, who can perform quick tests and get immediate responses, thus facilitating iteration in development and debugging. Through different endpoints defined in the application, users can interact with the model to perform specific tasks, such as obtaining predictions, sending data for processing, or querying the system's status (Fig. 3).

We can verify through a web service consumption client like Postman that by running APIs, we can send data to the model, and it predicts whether a customer is likely to renew their services with the company.

This approach also favors integration with other services and platforms, allowing the creation of more complex ecosystems where multiple applications can be interconnected. Furthermore, the ability to scale the service horizontally (by adding more instances) or vertically (by improving infrastructure) becomes much more feasible, ensuring that the application can handle an increase in workload without compromising performance.

9 Discussion

The superior performance of decision trees in this study can be attributed to several key factors. First, decision trees inherently handle non-linear relationships and interactions among features without requiring complex transformations, making them well-suited for the dataset's structure, which includes categorical variables like region, management system, and client tenure. Second, their interpretability allows for clear identification of critical renewal predictors (e.g.,

[1] https://flask.palletsprojects.com/.

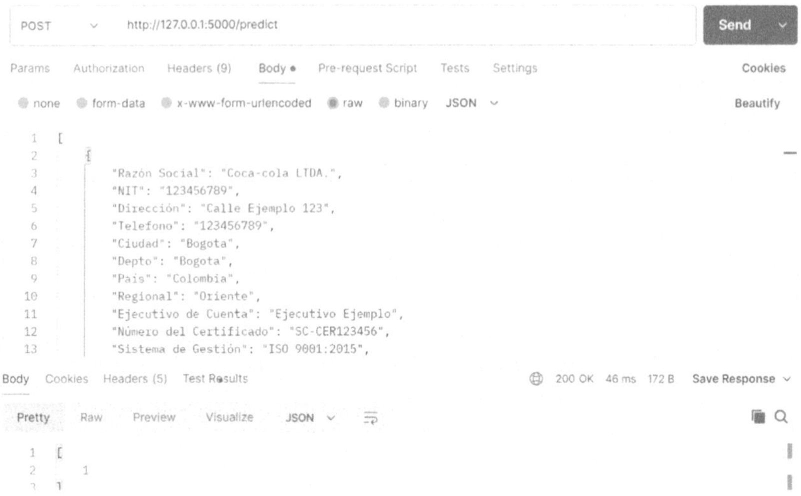

Fig. 3. Program Execution

expiration dates or regional trends), aligning with the business need for actionable insights. While XGBoost and logistic regression struggled with class imbalance (82% non-renewals), decision trees, especially when combined with SMOTE or undersampling, effectively minimized false positives (misclassified renewals), a critical metric for retention strategies. Additionally, decision trees' robustness to outliers and missing values likely reduced noise in the historical certification data, whereas logistic regression's linear assumptions and XGBoost's sensitivity to hyperparameter tuning may have limited their adaptability. The results suggest that, for this specific problem of imbalanced, feature-rich customer data, the simplicity and flexibility of decision trees outweighed the ensemble advantages of XGBoost or the probabilistic rigor of logistic regression.

The high performance of the decision tree model (98% accuracy) is unlikely to be a result of overfitting due to several methodological safeguards. First, the study employed 5-fold cross-validation, ensuring that the model's performance was consistently evaluated across multiple subsets of the data, reducing the risk of overfitting to any single partition. Second, the use of data balancing techniques (SMOTE, undersampling, and ADASYN) mitigated bias toward the majority class, preventing the model from artificially inflating accuracy by simply predicting the dominant outcome. Additionally, the model's strong performance metrics, including precision, recall, and F1-score, were validated across both balanced and imbalanced datasets, demonstrating robustness. Finally, the practical deployment of the model in a real-world setting (via a Flask API) provided further validation of its generalizability beyond the training data. These measures collectively suggest that the results reflect genuine predictive power rather than overfitting.

10 Conclusions and Future Work

This study successfully developed a high-accuracy predictive model for customer churn in certification services, achieving a 98% accuracy rate using decision trees. The model enables the organization to proactively identify clients at risk of not renewing their certificates, allowing for targeted retention strategies such as personalized campaigns and service adjustments. By leveraging the CRISP-DM methodology, the project systematically addressed data imbalance and optimized model performance, ensuring actionable insights for business decision-making.

The deployment of the model as a REST API using Flask facilitates real-time integration into business workflows, enhancing the organization's ability to respond dynamically to customer needs. This not only improves retention rates but also strengthens customer relationships by anticipating their requirements and fostering long-term loyalty. The results underscore the value of machine learning in transforming raw data into strategic tools for competitive advantage.

To further enhance the model's effectiveness and expand its applications, the following future directions are proposed: (i) Incorporating additional variables, such as customer interaction logs, service feedback, and external market trends, to refine predictions and capture nuanced behavioral patterns; (ii) Enhancing the model by integrating real-time data streams, enabling continuous learning and adaptation to evolving customer behaviors; (iii) Developing tools to improve model interpretability, ensuring stakeholders understand the factors driving churn predictions and can trust the model's recommendations; and (iv) Testing model generalizability by applying it to other sectors within the organization or similar industries, so as to identify universal and context-specific churn drivers. By pursuing these initiatives, the organization can further solidify its leadership in customer retention and set new benchmarks for data-driven decision-making in certification services.

References

1. Ahmad, Z., Shahid Khan, A., Wai Shiang, C., Abdullah, J., Ahmad, F.: Network intrusion detection system: a systematic study of machine learning and deep learning approaches. Trans. Emerg. Telecommun. Technol. **32**(1), e4150 (2021)
2. Bassett, L.: Introduction to JavaScript Object Notation: A To-the-Point Guide to JSON. O'Reilly Media, Inc., Sebastopol (2015)
3. Bhatnagar, A., Srivastava, S.: A robust model for churn prediction using supervised machine learning. In: 2019 IEEE 9th International Conference on Advanced Computing (IACC), pp. 45–49. IEEE (2019)
4. Burez, J., Van den Poel, D.: Handling class imbalance in customer churn prediction. Expert Syst. Appl. **36**(3), 4626–4636 (2009)
5. Haddadi, S.J., Farshidvard, A., dos Santos Silva, F., dos Reis, J.C., da Silva Reis, M.: Customer churn prediction in imbalanced datasets with resampling methods: a comparative study. Expert Syst. Appl. **246**, 123086 (2024)
6. He, H., Bai, Y., Garcia, E.A., Li, S.: Adasyn: adaptive synthetic sampling approach for imbalanced learning. In: 2008 IEEE International Joint Conference on Neural Networks (IEEE World Congress on Computational Intelligence), pp. 1322–1328. IEEE (2008)

7. Huang, B., Kechadi, M.T., Buckley, B.: Customer churn prediction in telecommunications. Expert Syst. Appl. **39**(1), 1414–1425 (2012)
8. Lazarov, V., Capota, M.: Churn prediction. Bus. Anal. Course. TUM Comput. Sci **33**, 34 (2007)
9. de Lima Lemos, R.A., Silva, T.C., Tabak, B.M.: Propension to customer churn in a financial institution: a machine learning approach. Neural Comput. Appl. **34**(14), 11751–11768 (2022)
10. Lu, N., Lin, H., Lu, J., Zhang, G.: A customer churn prediction model in telecom industry using boosting. IEEE Trans. Ind. Inf. **10**(2), 1659–1665 (2012)
11. Pal, M.: Random forest classifier for remote sensing classification. Int. J. Remote Sens. **26**(1), 217–222 (2005)
12. Paul, R., Rashmi, M.: Student satisfaction and churn predicting using machine learning algorithms for edtech course. In: 2022 10th International Conference on Reliability, Infocom Technologies and Optimization (Trends and Future Directions)(ICRITO), pp. 1–6. IEEE (2022)
13. Peláez, I.M.: Modelos de regresión: lineal simple y regresión logística. Revista Seden **14**, 195–214 (2016)
14. Richardson, L., Amundsen, M., Ruby, S.: RESTful Web APIs: Services for a Changing World. O'Reilly Media, Inc., Sevastopol (2013)
15. Suh, Y.: Machine learning based customer churn prediction in home appliance rental business. J. Big Data **10**(1), 41 (2023)
16. Tu, Y.T., Chang, H.C.: Corporate brand image and customer satisfaction on loyalty: an empirical study of Starbucks coffee in Taiwan. J. Soc. Dev. Sci. **3**(1), 24–32 (2012)
17. Wirth, R., Hipp, J.: CRISP-DM: towards a standard process model for data mining. In: Proceedings of the 4th International Conference on the Practical Applications of Knowledge Discovery and Data Mining, vol. 1, pp. 29–39. Manchester (2000)
18. Xie, Y., Li, X., Ngai, E., Ying, W.: Customer churn prediction using improved balanced random forests. Expert Syst. Appl. **36**(3), 5445–5449 (2009)
19. Xie, Y., Li, X., Ngai, E., Ying, W.: Customer churn prediction using improved balanced random forests. Expert Syst. Appl. **36**(3), 5445–5449 (2009)
20. Zhang, J., et al.: Insights into geospatial heterogeneity of landslide susceptibility based on the shap-xgboost model. J. Environ. Manag. **332**, 117357 (2023)
21. Zhou, Z.H.: Machine Learning. Springer, Singapore (2021). https://doi.org/10.1007/978-981-15-1967-3

Evaluating Prompt Strategies for Generative AI-Based Readability Improvement of Pillar 3 Disclosures

Ľubomír Benko(✉) and Lucia Benkova

Department of Informatics, Faculty of Natural Sciences and Informatics, Constantine the Philosopher University in Nitra, Tr. A. Hlinku 1, 949 01 Nitra, Slovakia
{lbenko,lbenkova}@ukf.sk

Abstract. Pillar 3 disclosures are critical regulatory documents intended to inform the public and promote transparency. However, their technical complexity often renders them inaccessible to non-expert audiences. This study evaluates the use of Generative Artificial Intelligence (GenAI) models to improve the readability of these financial documents without omitting key information. Two state-of-the-art GenAI models, GPT-4o and GPTo3, were tested with six prompt strategies, including standardized, enriched, roleplay, and Chain-of-Thought approaches. Readability was measured using the Gunning Fog Index and LIX metrics, and results were further examined using residual analysis and human review for financial accuracy and tone. All prompts significantly reduced text complexity, with the Chain-of-Thought prompt achieving the most substantial improvement, particularly for GPTo3. However, GPT-4o occasionally failed to complete outputs and showed higher variability in quality. Human evaluation confirmed that while GenAI models preserved most key financial information, some prompts led to oversimplification or informal wording. The results show that Chain-of-Thought prompt improved the readability by an average 12.30 for Gunning Fog Index and 37.99 for LIX, with statistically significant improvements across all prompts and models. These findings highlight the potential of GenAI to assist in simplifying financial disclosures, provided human oversight and further prompt design optimization are maintained.

Keywords: Finance Documents · Text Readability · Generative Artificial Intelligence · Prompt Engineering

1 Introduction

Pillar 3 disclosures, mandated under the Basel Framework [1], are intended to promote transparency and market discipline in the banking sector by requiring institutions to publish detailed information about their risk profile. The complexity of these documents often makes them inaccessible to non-expert stakeholders. Although formal and technical language is necessary to meet legal and regulatory requirements, it leads to low readability scores [2]. Improving the readability of these documents without compromising

T. Guarda et al. (Eds.): ARTIIS 2025, CCIS 2789, pp. 401–413, 2026.
https://doi.org/10.1007/978-3-032-16758-3_31

their legal integrity is a non-trivial challenge. Traditional approaches to simplification, such as manual language rewriting or editorial support, require expert knowledge and are time-consuming tasks. The introduction of Large Language Models (LLMs), such as OpenAI GPT models [3], offers a novel approach to summarization and simplification of various types of documents. These models, when prompted appropriately, are capable of paraphrasing, summarizing, or rewriting complex text into more readable forms. Dong et al. [4] explored the use of LLMs in the finance domain with a focus also on summarization of banking documents. However, summarization or simplification that omits critical information or shifts the tone inappropriately could introduce legal or reputational risk. In financial and regulatory settings, simplification must preserve both accuracy and compliance.

This study is aimed at evaluating the use of Generative Artificial Intelligence (GenAI) to improve the readability of financial documents. The research builds upon the previous study, which examined the influence of Pillar 3 disclosure documents readability and complexity on stakeholder behavior on the web portals of banking institutions [2]. The aims of this study can be divided into the following parts:

- To analyze the readability of GenAI-generated versions of financial disclosures using established readability metrics, such as the Gunning Fog Index and LIX. Two state-of-the-art GenAI models have been compared and their outputs evaluated to identify relative strengths and weaknesses.
- To assess the differences of various prompting strategies on GenAI model output, in order to improve document readability without requiring model training or fine-tuning.

This study evaluates two GenAI models accessed through API interface, GPT-4o and GPTo3, across six prompt strategies, where readability is measured using Gunning Fog Index and LIX metrics. The outputs are assessed using residual analysis and human validation with dataset compromising segmented Pillar 3 disclosures from a banking institution.

The structure of the paper is divided into sections as follows. The second section introduces related work in the domain of financial documents summarization and simplification. The third section contains the methodology of our experiment with documents preprocessing. The results are presented in the fourth section where the readability of generated documents was evaluated using automatic metrics. The Discussion and Conclusion sections summarize the obtained findings and argue the limitations of the study.

2 Related Work

Automatic summarization of financial documents has been addressed by several studies [5]. Financial texts, such as annual or financial reports, are usually long and linguistically complex. The authors in [2] highlight the importance of presenting financial information in a manner that improved readability to better engage stakeholders. The analysis showed that stakeholders preferred texts with lower complexity and accessible language and were less likely to access documents that were linguistically demanding, such as Pillar 3 disclosures. Simplification methods have evolved from basic statistical and rule-based approaches to the use of GenAI and Large Language Models (LLMs) [6]. Traditional approaches included techniques like Term Frequency-Inverse Document Frequency [6], statistical features with heuristic approaches [7], and classification algorithms [8]. For example, Abdaljalil and Bouamor [7] used a sentence embedding model based on BERT to encode documents and generate summarizations. The authors compared sentence-based with section-based models. Higher ROUGE scores were achieved for section-based models when creating extractive summarization of texts. LLMs are focused on transformer architecture with self-attention mechanisms and can process large documents and generate readable outputs without labeled training data [9]. Guidroz et al. [10] employed a GenAI model (Gemini 1.5 Flash) for simplification of domain-specific texts, followed by a randomized comprehension study to validate effectiveness. The study showed that participants achieved significantly higher comprehension when reading the simplified versions, which were derived from PubMed domain texts. These results indicate the practical benefits of GenAI based simplification in specialized domains. Another study conducted in the financial domain used four GenAI models (Llama, Pegasus, FastChat, and Alpaca) to simplify Spanish financial texts [11]. The performance of these models was evaluated using BLEU and other metrics. The results showed that FastChat achieved the best performance and was recommended for further fine-tuning process. On the other hand, Pegasus performed poorly in BLEU scores but showed better results in lexical simplification. The achieved results suggest that LLMs could be integrated into simplification of non-English financial texts. Farajidizaji et al. [12] introduced a readability-controlled text modification approach. The outputs' readability was assessed using Flesch reading ease. The authors used ChatGPT and Llama-2 using zero-shot approach to generate texts. The results showed that the models struggled to map the readability of texts to the target readability ranges with accuracy below 0.25. The authors concluded that higher change between source and target texts indicates lower semantic similarity and higher lexical divergence between the texts. Kim et al. [13] investigated bloated parts of financial documents, as the documents length is increasing in the years. They used LLMs to summarize corporate disclosures and conclude that these summaries are beneficial for stakeholders. The authors propose a novel metric (disclosure bloat) that measures the extent of less relevant information in the documents.

While these studies present the value of GenAI for summarization and simplification tasks in general and domain-specific contexts, there is limited research focused on the structured simplification of regulatory documents. These documents require a balance between readability, terminology precision, and preservation of key information. This study builds on previous work [2] by focusing specifically on Pillar 3 disclosures. These documents require not only syntactic simplification but also preservation of terminology, risk classifications, and structural consistency.

3 Methodology

The methodology (Fig. 1) was inspired by previous research [2, 14] and extends it to test GenAI performance on real-world financial disclosures represented by financial reports documents. The aim was to assess whether GenAI can improve readability of such texts using various prompting strategies, without training or fine-tuning on domain-specific data. The methodology was designed into the following steps:

1. Data acquisition – public financial reports documents were extracted from a banking institution website, using a log file of accesses to these documents by stakeholders.
2. Data preparation – nine documents were selected from the financial reports category, and each document was separated into three logical parts. This was done because each document contained more than 12,000 words and would pose a big volume of tokens for the GenAI model to work with. As the documents are structured and consist of similar sections, the division was done based on this logic and each created part consisted of the same sections.
3. GenAI models application – using various prompt strategies, GenAI models were prompted using OpenAI API to improve the readability of the examined documents.
4. Calculation of readability scores – using Python Spacy library TextDescriptives were calculated the Gunning Fog Index and LIX scores for each separated document.
5. Comparison of GenAI models outputs – using statistical analysis the GenAI outputs and prompts influence on readability was examined.
6. Interpretation and evaluation of results.

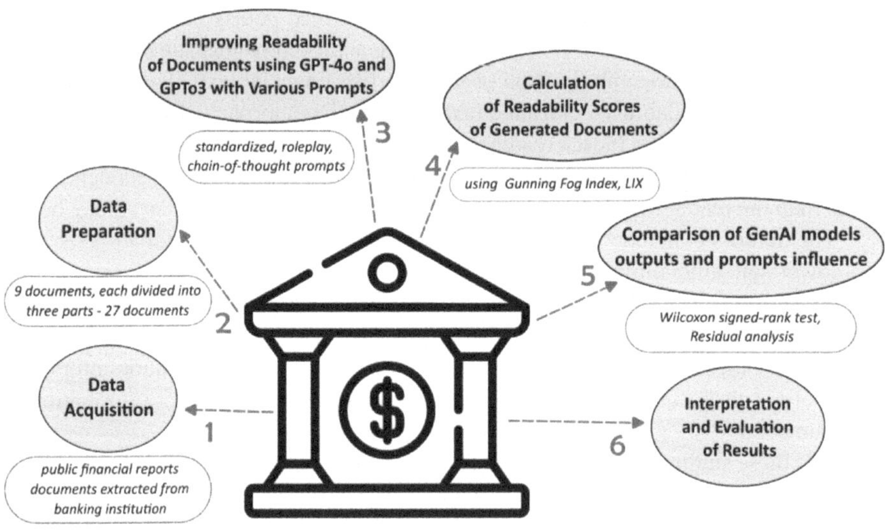

Fig. 1. Experiment methodology workflow.

A homogenous sample of financial reports from a banking institution's web portal was selected. Each document is long (approximately 12,000 words on average) divided into three distinct parts based on logical content segmentation and document length. Each part contained approximately 3,800 words on average. The document structure is as follows:

- Executive summary and performance report (business development, financial highlights, segment performance, client initiatives).

- Risk management and corporate governance (risk exposure, internal control systems, board structure, general assembly actions).
- Statutory disclosures and board committees (shareholder structure, general meeting procedures, committee responsibilities).

The created document parts consisted of 105 sentences on average, which were mostly longer and contained 25 words on average. The most frequent words used in the examined documents are depicted on Fig. 2.

During the monitored period, the Asset and Liability Management Committee met 14 times.

The Credit Risk Committee

Discusses the documentation regarding Organizational Risk Management and the system of principles and procedures in credit risk management and approves changes in them, sets and reviews the risk level of individual portfolios as well as their return and income, exposure limits according to the portfolios of sections, products, maturities and currencies , reviews rules of engagement vis-à-vis industries, business sectors, geographic regions, individual borrowers and economically connected groups, negotiates and decides on new loan product proposals and rating matters. It also reviews and approves the level of provisioning for credit losses on the portfolio of client assets.

Fig. 2. Sample of the content of financial reports documents and a word cloud of most frequent words in the examined documents.

Each document was preprocessed to remove style, figures and tables. Only the raw textual content was used as input for the GenAI models. Two GenAI models from OpenAI were selected based on the performance and API interface availability [3]:

- GPT-4o (gpt-4o-2024-08-06): A model optimized for complex tasks, such as summarization, and general-purpose Natural Language Processing tasks.
- GPTo3 (o3-2025-04-16): A model optimized for structured reasoning and complex content transformation.

Model parameters were aligned where possible. Temperature was set to 0.2 for GPT-4o to encourage consistent and deterministic outputs. GPTo3 as a reasoning model does not allow temperature adjustment, so its default value (1.0) was retained. Other parameters were fixed for both models (Table 1).

Table 1. GenAI models parameter configuration.

Parameter	GPT-4o	GPTo3
Temperature	0.2	1.0
Top_p	1.0	1.0
Frequency_penalty	0.0	0.0
Presence_penalty	0.0	0.0

To assess how prompt variation affects GenAI outputs, six distinct prompting strategies were implemented. These were inspired by recent work on prompt engineering [15, 16]. Six prompts (Table 2) were created based on [15, 16], from which three were standardized with the aim of examining the models' capabilities to generate similar quality output based on readability measures. The fourth prompt was deviated from the standardized prompt and enriched with the Gunning Fog Index average score for the examined documents. This way it was possible to specify for GenAI the aim of improving readability of the documents. Inspired by Hedlin et al. [15], a roleplay prompt was designed, where the model took the role of financial editor. Lastly, the sixth prompt was created as a Chain-of-Thought, where the model obtained a specific example of how to improve the readability.

Table 2. Prompt design for the readability improvement of financial texts.

Prompt Approach	Prompt Design
Prompt1 Standard - Instruction	You are going to rewrite a text that is difficult to read into a text that is easier to read. The information from the original text should be preserved as far as possible in the rewritten, easy-to-read text. Do not shorten the text and do not use bullet points. You do not have to answer anything, just rewrite the text
Prompt2 Standard - Plain English	Rewrite the following Pillar 3 disclosure in plain English suitable for a general audience, without removing key financial concepts. Do not shorten the text and do not use bullet points. You do not have to answer anything, just rewrite the text
Prompt3 Standard - Clarity Focused	Rewrite the following text to improve clarity and reduce sentence length, while preserving the technical terminology and regulatory integrity. Do not shorten the text and do not use bullet points. You do not have to answer anything, just rewrite the text
Prompt4 Standard - Readability Targeted	Rewrite the following Pillar 3 disclosure in plain English suitable for a general audience, without removing key financial concepts. [This is defined according to readability index, Gunning Fog Index. It considers the number of sentences, number of words, and the number of complex words consisting of three or more syllables in the text. The lower the index score, the easier it is for readers to understand what they are reading. On average the index for this text is around 22, I want it less than 14]. Do not shorten the text and do not use bullet points. You do not have to answer anything, just rewrite the text

(*continued*)

Table 2. *(continued)*

Prompt Approach	Prompt Design
Prompt5 Roleplay	You are a professional financial editor working for a regulatory compliance team at a major bank. Your job is to improve the readability and clarity of internal Pillar 3 disclosure reports before they are submitted to external stakeholders, such as regulators and non-expert financial analysts. Your objective is to rewrite the following text to make it clearer and more accessible, while retaining all content and financial detail. Do not summarize, do not omit information, and do not shorten unless necessary for clarity. The structure, terminology, and meaning must remain accurate and complete. Your output should be approximately the same length as the original, but significantly more readable. Do not shorten the text and do not use bullet points. You do not have to answer anything, just rewrite the text
Prompt6 Chain-of-Thought	Rewrite the following Pillar 3 disclosure in plain English suitable for a general audience, without removing key financial concepts. Do not shorten the text and do not use bullet points. You do not have to answer anything, just rewrite the text. To do this, we replace long words, words over 6 letters long with shorter synonyms and possibly replace a long word with several short ones. We also try to break up long sentences into several short ones. Example: "For 2009, the bank set itself the goal of maintaining a leading position in the banking sector and continuing the trend of increasing efficiency, which it managed to achieve". We see the sentence is complex, so we paraphrase it and replace long words with shorter synonyms, this lowers the complexity and improves readability. We can write: "In 2009, the bank aimed to stay a leader in the banking sector and keep improving its efficiency a goal it successfully met". This is the way

The Gunning Fog Index (GFI) [17], widely used in financial readability research [2], was one of the two primary metrics. It estimates years of formal education required to understand a text (1), where *complex words* consist of three or more syllables.

$$GFI = 0.4 * \left[\left(\frac{n\_words}{n\_sentences} \right) + 100 * \left(\frac{complex\ words}{n\_words} \right) \right] \tag{1}$$

A GFI score above 18 indicates a highly technical document suited for graduates. Our sample averaged at score 22. The target was a reduction to 13–14, aligning with college-level readability. The second metric was LIX [18], which is language independent, where a score higher than 55 represents graduates' level of readability. The score uses standard text characteristics for its calculation (2), where *n_words* is the number of words, *n_periods* number of punctuation marks and *long words* are defined as words consisting of more than six characters.

$$LIX = \frac{n\_words}{n\_periods} + \frac{long\ words * 100}{n\_words} \tag{2}$$

The examined document sample averaged with a LIX score of 68. The aim of the experiment was to decrease the complexity of the texts but keeping the important information contained in the original documents. The target was a LIX score around 56–57, that would represent the lower threshold for college level readability.

In addition to computing readability metrics GFI and LIX scores, a residual analysis was conducted to examine the difference between the original and GenAI-generated texts. Where negative residuals indicate a reduction in complexity and improvement in readability. Documents with residuals beyond $\pm 2\sigma$ were examined to identify extreme cases. The output text from the OpenAI API was not further modified and analyzed as it was generated.

4 Results

The comparison of the GPT models and prompt strategies was conducted across multiple levels. GFI and LIX were calculated for each original and GenAI-generated document. The original documents averaged $GFI = 21.85$ and $LIX = 67.98$, confirming high complexity across the dataset. Across all examined prompts and models, readability scores were significantly reduced (Table 3). However, GPT-4o failed to generate valid outputs for five documents under prompts 3, 4, and 5. Repeated attempts to re-generate these outputs produced the same failure: the model either returned a refusal or truncated content. On average, GPT-4o outputs were 915 tokens long, while GPTo3 outputs averaged 2,268 tokens closed to the original document length of 3,937 tokens. All other documents were generated without functional errors and results of the human validation are presented in the discussion section.

Table 3. Average GFI and LIX Scores by Prompt and Model.

Prompt	GPT-4o		GPTo3	
	GFI	LIX	GFI	LIX
Prompt 1	16.67	57.80	16.91	57.05
Prompt 2	15.75	56.21	17.41	58.96
Prompt 3	16.38*	57.78*	17.57	60.16
Prompt 4	14.15*	51.67*	14.16	49.70
Prompt 5	15.92*	56.23*	17.98	60.78
Prompt 6	14.42	52.27	9.56	30.00

Note: Asterisks indicate averages excluding failed generations from GPT-4o

First were tested significant differences in readability scores across prompt types using the Friedman test. Since the same documents were used across all prompt conditions and the assumption of normality was violated for several score distributions ($p < 0.05$), this non-parametric test was appropriate. The results indicated statistically significant differences ($p < 0.001$) across prompts for both GFI and LIX. Subsequently, pairwise Wilcoxon signed-rank tests were applied to compare readability scores of the generated documents with their original, across all 12 prompt-model combinations. All combinations showed statistically significant differences ($p < 0.001$) in both GFI and LIX, confirming that all prompts improved readability. Further comparisons across prompts showed statistically significant differences in performance. For prompt 6 (Chain-of-Thought), statistically significant differences ($p < 0.001$) were identified between all prompts for GPTo3 and between prompts 1, 2 for GPT-4o. Standard prompts (1–3) produced similar quality of readability with no statistically significant differences ($p > 0.05$) across either model, suggesting minimal influence of wording differences within standard instruction formats. Prompt 4, which incorporated explicit readability guidance using the GFI, led to statistically significant differences between all prompts for GPTo3 ($p < 0.001$). For GPT-4o, difference was only significant when compared with prompt 2 ($p < 0.001$). This shows that adding readability context helps the reasoning model (GPTo3) to better understand the task and produce significantly different results in comparison to other prompting strategies. The roleplay strategy did not yield statistically significant differences between the prompts in the case of GPT-4o ($p > 0.05$). In the case of GPTo3, statistically significant differences between prompt 5 and prompts 4, 6 were identified ($p < 0.001$). This indicates that both models do not consider the role of the financial expert and produce similar outputs as with standardized prompts.

To analyze prompt-model interactions further, residual analysis was conducted following the methodology from the previous research [19, 20], to identify document parts with extreme values of readability scores (GFI and LIX) between GPT-4o and GPTo3. Residuals were computed using the $\pm 2\sigma$ rule, where values outside this range were considered extreme. In all cases (Fig. 3 and 4), residuals were negative, which indicates reductions in complexity of texts. GPT-4o showed a more extreme residual reductions than GPTo3, but some were influenced by incomplete outputs. Specifically, documents 11, 14, 20, and 23 showed residuals skewed by GPT-4o's inability to produce full text. On the other hand, GPTo3 provided complete outputs in all cases and showed more stable reductions across document parts. When analyzing document parts, outputs related to "Executive summary and performance report" showed smaller residuals, which indicates readability scores closer to the original documents (document IDs: 0, 3, 6, 9, 12, 15, 18, 21, 24). The other two document parts showed stronger reductions in both GFI and LIX across both GenAI models.

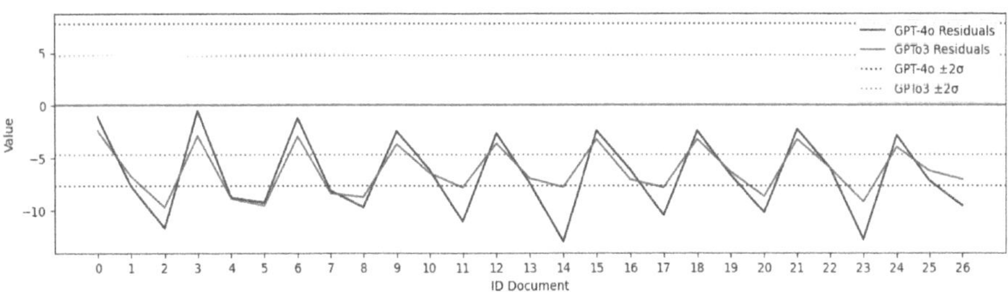

Fig. 3. Visualization of GPT-4o and GPTo3 residuals for Gunning Fog Index.

To quantify readability improvements, mean residuals were calculated for each prompt. Prompt 6 (Chain-of-Thought) was the most effective in the case of GPTo3, where the largest average score reduction was identified in both GFI (−12.30) and LIX (−37.99) scores. These reductions were statistically greater than all other prompts

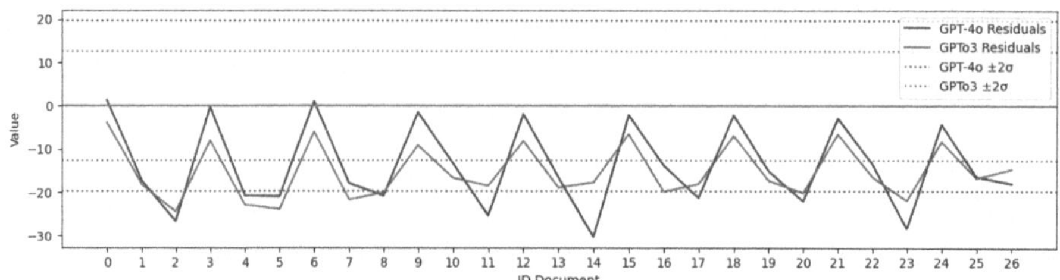

Fig. 4. Visualization of GPT-4o and GPTo3 residuals for LIX.

(Wilcoxon test, $p < 0.001$). GPT-4o also showed substantial reductions using prompt 6 (*GFI*: −7.43; *LIX*: −15.72). Prompt 4, that was standardized with information about GFI, was the most effective prompt for GPT-4o (*GFI*: −8.48; *LIX*: −18.66) and second most effective for GPTo3 (*GFI*: −7.70; *LIX*: −18.28). These findings suggest that integrating readability guidance (e.g., GFI targets) or using structured rewriting examples (one-shot) significantly improves GenAI performance for financial document simplification.

5 Discussion

While the results of the analysis showed that all prompts significantly improved readability scores according to both Gunning Fog Index and LIX metrics, human evaluation revealed important limitations and qualitative differences across models and prompts. Manual examination of all generated documents was conducted, with a focus on whether key financial information was preserved and whether the language remained appropriate for formal regulatory reporting. In general, both GPT-4o and GPTo3 kept most of the critical content across most document parts. However, GPT-4o failed to produce valid outputs for five documents, returning the error message "I'm sorry, but I can't assist with that request." These failures occurred exclusively in the document part "Statutory disclosures and board committees" and were likely related to the presence of named entities, such as board members. These failures were consistent even after multiple re-generations and limited to specific prompts (3–5). Outside these cases, the models generated 162 documents per model (27 documents x 6 prompts), all of which were processed successfully and contained no functional errors. In terms of linguistic quality, GPT-4o kept the text style professional and structured, while GPTo3 (especially with prompt 6) produced more informal and generalized outputs. For example, in one document, GPTo3 substituted the phrase "clients" with "folks", which is stylistically inappropriate in the context of financial regulation. This aligns with the observation that while GPTo3 generated longer and more readable documents, it occasionally compromised on domain-specific terminology.

The readability analysis further supports this interpretation. For instance, in the "Statutory disclosures and board committees" document part, readability scores with prompt 6 were significantly lower for both models in comparison to the original text (GPT-4o *GFI* = 18.00; GPTo3 *GFI* = 10.98; Original *GFI* = 27.42). GPT-4o retained more structure and formalism, although its average output length (1,096 tokens) was much shorter than that of GPTo3 (2,268 tokens), and considerably shorter than the original documents (3,937 tokens). GPTo3 used plain language with lower terminology usage with prompt 6. The financial information is accurate in both versions, but the simplification of words in the case of GPTo3 made the text less technical. This could indicate that the Chain-of-Thought strategy in GPTo3 case oversimplified the text and decreased the expected level of financial terminology.

The document part "Executive summary and performance report" showed the lowest reduction in readability scores compared to the original among all three document parts. One of the documents showed very similar readability scores between the models using prompt 4, and not significantly lower scores compared to the original (GPT-4o $GFI = 13.86$; GPTo3 $GFI = 12.31$; Original $GFI = 16.68$). GPT-4o omitted capital actions and dividend details from the original in this document and used more general terms and simplified terminology. Overall, the text was more informal but very clear. GPTo3 included all the important information from the original and maintained a more formal phrasing, even with a lower readability score than GPT-4o. GPTo3 in this case preserved most key disclosures while improving the readability of the original text.

In the document part "Risk management and corporate governance", both models showed strong performance with prompt 4 (standardized prompt with Gunning Fog Index information). Both GenAI models covered the core areas crucial for Pillar 3 and market discipline. A sample document from this category achieved a lower GFI score in favor of GPT-4o (GPT-4o $GFI = 12.52$; GPTo3 $GFI = 15.03$; Original $GFI = 23.47$) with prompt 4. A detailed examination of the generated documents showed that both models produced simplified terminology, where GPT-4o used general wording and GPTo3 used less legally precise language. The models occasionally lost specificity in technical areas like risk measurement and were weak in terminology precision. Overall, both GPT-4o and GPTo3 produced useful summaries but should not replace the original in formal or legal contexts.

These results highlight a key limitation of prompt engineering, where prompts optimized for linguistic simplification may lead to oversimplification, loss of terminology, or outputs that are not suitable for regulatory or professional stakeholders. Another limitation of this study was its relatively small sample of texts. Although 27 documents across 6 prompts and 2 models (324 outputs in total) were analyzed, the dataset was confined to financial reports, and all evaluations were conducted manually without a structured, multi-question protocol. While the insights gained could prove beneficial, more robust annotation schemes are needed to formally assess financial accuracy, terminology use, and suitability of tone. Ideally, these annotations should be performed by domain experts. Lastly, GenAI models available through API interface are financially costly, which could be a significant limitation in deploying these models for large-scale applications. Using self-hosted or fine-tuned LLMs could be a viable alternative but requires significant investment in computing infrastructure.

6 Conclusion

The experiment showed the potential of GenAI models to improve the readability of financial reports without the need to train models on new sets of documents. Two different models from OpenAI GPT-4o and GPTo3 were examined. Prompting strategies were used to generate simplified versions of original documents with varying levels of accuracy. Overall, both models and all prompts yielded improved readability, as measured by lower scores in the Gunning Fog Index and LIX metrics. The residual analysis further clarified model behavior across document sections. Residuals were consistently negative, indicating that all GenAI outputs reduced complexity relative to the original text. However, in document parts such as the "Executive summary and performance report", residuals were less extreme, suggesting the original text in these sections was already closer to natural language and required less intervention. Both models still managed to simplify the texts but GPT-4o did so at the cost of terminology inaccuracy. On the other hand, parts such as "Risk management and corporate governance" showed more distinct reductions in complexity, particularly under GPTo3 with prompt 6. Nevertheless, the residual analysis showed that GPT-4o produced more outlier documents with excessively reduced Gunning Fog Index scores, indicating a risk of overshooting simplification in certain contexts. From a practical perspective, these findings suggest that while GenAI can be used to assist in making financial disclosures more accessible, especially for non-expert stakeholders, it cannot yet replace human editorial oversight. The models are capable of significant improvements in syntactic simplicity and surface-level clarity but struggle with domain-specific nuance, formal tone, and preservation of regulatory detail. Moreover, model outputs are sensitive to prompt design, with large differences observed between standard, enriched, and Chain-of-Thought prompting styles. This has implications for deployment, where any implementation of GenAI-based rewriting in financial contexts would require strong quality control measures, human validation loops, and likely a hybrid human-AI editorial workflow. The current study was limited by the size of the dataset (27 documents) and lack of multi-rater annotation for human evaluation. Future research should aim to expand the sample to include a broader range of document types, introduce structured expert annotation protocols, and include or develop quantitative metrics for semantic reliability and hallucination risk already mentioned by Nie et al. [5]. Future work should include comparison and integration of other GenAI, not only OpenAI models. Overall, this study presents a practical view of what current GenAI systems can and cannot do in regulatory documents.

Acknowledgements. This work was supported by the Scientific Grant Agency of the Ministry of Education of the Slovak Republic (ME SR) and Slovak Academy of Sciences (SAS) under the contract No. VEGA-1/0734/24 and Slovak Research and Development Agency under contract No. APVV-23-0554.

References

1. BIS Connect: Pillar 3 framework - Executive Summary (2019)
2. Benko, Ľ, Pilkova, A., Munk, M., Eley, S.: Pillar 3: the impact of language complexity on the preferences of commercial bank website users. Expert Syst. Appl. **259**, 125326 (2025). https://doi.org/10.1016/j.eswa.2024.125326
3. Achiam, J., et al.: GPT-4 Technical Report, pp. 1–100 (2024)
4. Dong, M.M., Stratopoulos, T.C., Wang, V.X.: A scoping review of ChatGPT research in accounting and finance. Int. J. Account. Inf. Syst. **55**, 100715 (2024). https://doi.org/10.1016/j.accinf.2024.100715

5. Nie, Y., et al.: A survey of large language models for financial applications: progress, prospects and challenges, pp. 1–39 (2024)
6. Xia, B., Rawte, V.D., Zaki, M.J., Gupta, A.: FETILDA: an effective framework for fin-tuned embeddings for long financial text documents, pp. 1–20 (2022)
7. Abdaljalil, S., Bouamor, H.: An exploration of automatic text summarization of financial reports. In: Proceedings of the Third Workshop on Financial Technology and Natural Language Processing, pp. 1–7. Association for Computational Linguistics, Financial Technology and Natural Language Processing (FinNLP) (2021)
8. Giannakopoulos, G., Pittaras, N.: The summary evaluation task in the MultiLing - RANLP 2019 workshop. In: Proceedings of the Workshop MultiLing 2019: Summarization Across Languages, Genres and Sources associated with RANLP 2019, pp. 11–16. Incoma Ltd., Shoumen (2019). https://doi.org/10.26615/978-954-452-058-8_003
9. Trott, S., Rivière, P.: Measuring and modifying the readability of English texts with GPT-4. In: Proceedings of the Third Workshop on Text Simplification, Accessibility and Readability (TSAR 2024), pp. 126–134. Association for Computational Linguistics, Stroudsburg (2024). https://doi.org/10.18653/v1/2024.tsar-1.13
10. Guidroz, T., et al.: LLM-based text simplification and its effect on user comprehension and cognitive load, pp. 1–32 (2025). https://doi.org/10.48550/arXiv.2505.01980
11. Brenes-Brenes, B.C., Calderón-Ramírez, S.: Exploration and selection of LLM models for financial text simplification. Rev. Tecnol. Marcha (2024). https://doi.org/10.18845/tm.v37i7.7297
12. Farajidizaji, A., Raina, V., Gales, M.: Is it possible to modify text to a target readability level? An initial investigation using zero-shot large language models. In: Proceedings of the 2024 Joint International Conference on Computational Linguistics, Language Resources and Evaluation (LREC-COLING 2024), pp. 9325–9339. ELRA and ICCL, Torino (2024)
13. Kim, A.G., Muhn, M., Nikolaev, V.V.: Bloated disclosures: can ChatGPT help investors process information? SSRN Electron. J. (2023). https://doi.org/10.2139/ssrn.4425527
14. Munkova, D., Stranovska, E., Munk, M.: Communication models in a foreign language in relation to cognitive style category width and power distance. Front. Psychol. **14** (2024). https://doi.org/10.3389/fpsyg.2023.1272370
15. Hedlin, E., Estling, L., Wong, J., Demmans Epp, C., Viberg, O.: Got it! Prompting readability using ChatGPT to enhance academic texts for diverse learning needs. In: Proceedings of the 15th International Learning Analytics and Knowledge Conference, pp. 115–125. ACM, New York (2025). https://doi.org/10.1145/3706468.3706483
16. Pecuchova, J., Drlik, M.: The role of generative artificial intelligence in the assessment of open-ended questions. In: International Conference on Interactive Collaborative Learning, pp. 394–405. Springer, Tallinn (2025). https://doi.org/10.1007/978-3-031-85652-5_40
17. Spiers, H., Amin, N., Lakhani, R., Martin, A.J., Patel, P.M.: Assessing readability and reliability of online patient information regarding vestibular Schwannoma. Otol. Neurotol. **38**, e470–e475 (2017). https://doi.org/10.1097/MAO.0000000000001565
18. Björnsson, C.H.: Lasbarhet. Bokforlaget Liber, Stockholm (1968)
19. Benko, Ľ., Munkova, D., Munk, M., Benkova, L., Hajek, P.: The use of residual analysis to improve the error rate accuracy of machine translation. Sci. Rep. **14**, 9293 (2024). https://doi.org/10.1038/s41598-024-59524-3
20. Kapusta, J., Munk, M., Drlík, M.: Analysis of differences between expected and observed probability of accesses to web pages. In: Computational Collective Intelligence. Technologies and Applications. ICCCI 2014. Lecture Notes in Computer Science (including subseries Lecture Notes in Artificial Intelligence and Lecture Notes in Bioinformatics), pp. 673–683 (2014). https://doi.org/10.1007/978-3-319-11289-3_68

A Scalable Python Framework for Static Malware Classification Using Feature Optimization and Ensemble Learning

Iliyan Barzev and Daniela Borissova(✉)

Institute of Information and Communication Technologies, Bulgarian Academy of Sciences, 1113 Sofia, Bulgaria
{iliyan.barzev,daniela.borissova}@iict.bas.bg

Abstract. The article describes a framework for automated malware classification based on Python that incorporates ML algorithms to learn from files (Portable Executable) from the EMBER 2018 dataset. A complete pipeline with 616 extracted features, model training, optimization, and evaluation is coded in Python 3.8 and implemented LIEF 0.16.5 library to account for older malware, with multiple file implementations through the code practice. Four ML algorithms – Random Forest, XGBoost, LighGBM, and CatBoost, are trained on multiple training set sizes and optimized using Optuna hyperparameter tuning. Feature selection is explored using SelectKBest metric with multiple dimensions. A scanner in a command line interface is created, which gives even more offline malware detection. A variety of metrics, graphics, and deployment considerations are described. The proposed solution allows malware detection with different use cases in constrained conditions or legacy systems that must be highly interpretable and scalable. The conducted investigations demonstrate very promising results regarding the ability to automate malware classification.

Keywords: Python-Based Framework · Malware Classification · Static Analysis · Machine Learning · Ensemble Models · Optuna Optimization · CLI Scanner

1 Introduction

Artificial intelligence in cybersecurity systems can be recognized in the use of intelligent algorithms and machine learning techniques to improve the detection, prevention, and response to cyber threats. By incorporating these approaches, cybersecurity systems become capable of analyzing vast amounts of data, identifying patterns, and helping to make informed decisions that go beyond human capabilities. The authors show that artificial intelligence has a significant effect on cybersecurity and vice versa, for subsamples driven by increased automation, the sophistication of cyberattacks that outpace defensive capabilities [1]. Therefore, various new and hybrid algorithms are being developed to improve protection against malware [2].

T. Guarda et al. (Eds.): ARTIIS 2025, CCIS 2789, pp. 414–429, 2026.
https://doi.org/10.1007/978-3-032-16758-3_32

Cybersecurity and malware are closely related topics focusing on protecting computer systems, applications, devices, data, financial assets and people from malicious software and cyberattacks. Malware attacks continue to grow, and experts predict that their frequency will only increase in the coming years. Among the variety of ways to detect malware, the most common is to scan the computer for malicious files or programs. There is no universal way to remove malware, because it depends on the specific malware installed. However, some common methods for removing malware are the use of an antivirus program or a malware removal program. That is why many researchers' efforts are focused on developing different approaches to cope with malware problems [3]. Some of them implement different deep learning algorithms for malware classification [4, 5]. Other researchers aim to detect invisible malware attacks via a framework for Windows based on API and deep learning techniques [6]. A new framework for detecting malicious actions is also proposed as a mechanism for recognizing and preventing attacks [7], as well as a malware detection framework for Android devices [8].

To develop a software system capable of detecting and identifying malware, it is necessary to analyze the behavior of the malware. There are two main categories of malware analysis: static analysis and dynamic analysis [9]. Static malware analysis has several key advantages – early detection, it is signature-based, and can use various techniques to understand the nature of the threat. Static analysis evaluates the properties of malware, such as metadata, strings, and structure. This process can be automated by using disassemblers, decompiles, and debuggers to quickly analyze large numbers of malware samples. Static analysis relies on reverse engineering, code inspection, and digital signature-based approaches for malware detection [10].

With all these considerations in mind, this article describes a malware detection and analysis framework that aims to protect data as cybersecurity remains critical not only for individuals but also for businesses of all sizes. An ML-based architecture for malware detection and classification based on Python libraries is proposed. This framework combines several ML algorithms such as Random Forest, XGBoost, LightGBM, and CatBoost [11, 12]. The presented results show that the proposed framework effectively extracts distinctive features for each malware type. The proposed framework relies on a modular architecture and can easily add additional modules with different ML algorithms.

The rest of the article is organized as follows: Sect. 2 describes methodology of proposed framework development; Section 3 presents experimental results; Section 4 refers to the practical use of CLI scanner; Section 5 contains results and discussion; while the conclusion and future research directions are drawn in Sect. 6.

2 A Methodology of Python-Based Framework for Static Malware Classification Using Feature Optimization and Ensemble Learning

The proposed methodology of the developed Python-based framework for automatic classification of malware is illustrated in Fig. 1.

The proposed framework is based on using the following Python libraries and modules for the specific purpose:

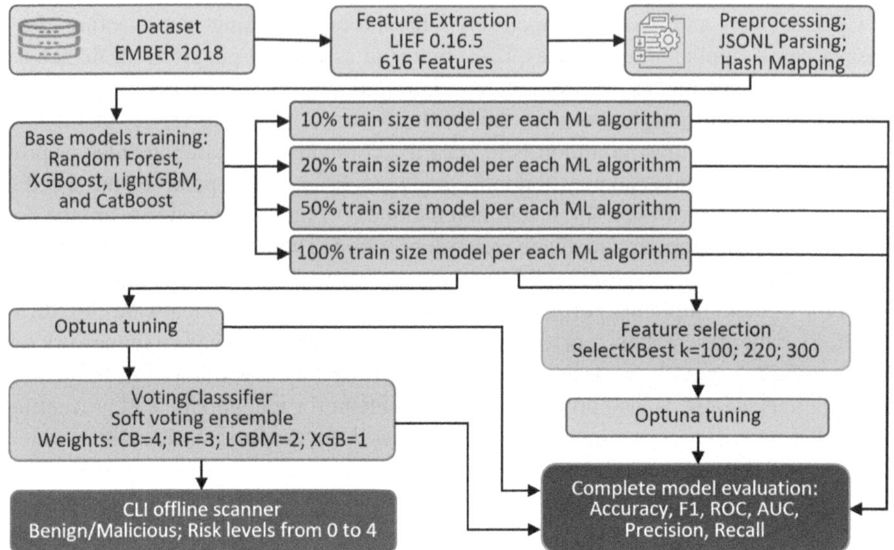

Fig. 1. Methodology of the developed Python-based framework for static malware classification.

- Dataset: A publicly available, well-structured dataset – EMBER 2018 [13], containing 616 pre-extracted features from PE files. Data is split 80% to 20% training to testing. We performed a set of new experiments on the 10%, 20%, 50%, and 100% training dataset completion to assess the impact of training data size on model performance.
- Data processing: pandas, numpy – to handle data structuring, transforming and numerical analysis; json – for.jsonl feature representation files.
- File and path handling: os, pathlib, re, hashlib, sys – for file handling, regex, hashing and directories.
- Machine Learning and Models: (a) scikit-learn – for base models, feature selection, and evaluation (VotingClassifier, RandomForestClassifier, SelectKBest, mutual_info_classif, permutation_importance, FeatureHasher, accuracy_score, precision_score, recall_score, f1_score, roc_auc_score, confusion_matrix, roc_curve); (b) xgboost (XGBClassifier), lightgbm (LGBMClassifier), catboost (CatBoostClassifier) – for gradient-boosting models [14]; (c) optuna – for hyperparameter optimization.
- Visualization: matplotlib.pyplot, seaborn, plotly.graph_objects – for graphical representation of results.
- PE Analysis and Feature Extraction: lief – to extract statistical and structural features from PE files.
- Utilities to support connections between models such as: joblib, tqdm, logging, argparse, concurrent.futures, time – serialisation, logging, progress bars, command line argument for features, parallel processing.

3 Experimental Results

The feature extraction is performed by modifying the existing python code for features from the EMBER Project to work with lief 0.16.5 and Python 3.8. The entropy value, the section names, the imports/exports items, and reported statistics for metadata, strings, etc. were the extracted features. Each PE file is represented as a vector of 616 variables.

The environment lief 0.16.5 and Python 3.8 are selected after major refinement to fix compatibility issues, to try and duplicate an environment closely related to the EMBER 2018 timeframe. Any version newer than this of LIEF or Python did either not extract or were no longer compatible with some binary objects that were commonly used for malware at that time. When coding, we had to alter our code when traversing sections, handling imports, and coding contingency plans for dealing with edge cases from samples of the older malware.

The following steps in data preparation are included: (1) Read in all train_features_*.jsonl and test_features.jsonl files; (2) Map sha256 hash to associated label; (3) Delete sha256 field; (4) Create arrays X_train, y_train, X_test, y_test. This preparation lays the foundation for all further experimentation as we try different models, data sizes, and trying nuances of optimization.

3.1 Model Training and Initial Results

For each experiment for each algorithm (one for each training set), four models are trained, resulting in 16 baseline models. All models were saved as.pkl files for reproducibility and comparison. Four ML algorithms are tested: Random Forest, XGBoost, LightGBM, and CatBoost are trained on 4 different proportions of training data, 100%, 50%, 20%, and 10%. One of the primary questions that we wanted to answer is whether the model performance is impacted by the amount of training data, as well as what metrics would be used to quantify this question. The evaluation metrics of these 45 trained models is shown in Table 1.

CatBoost had the best values by a considerable margin model using the whole dataset. Random Forest model is able to convert to code consistently with the least training time. The training time for 100% training data set is around 15–30 min for all models (depending on the model). For the smaller training sizes, substantially less training time is used. Increasing the amount of data trained on from 10% to 100% improved performance in terms of accuracy for every model. XGBoost and CatBoost provided the most improvement. LightGBM, the fastest to train, while its accuracy in default mode is slightly lower than the others.

Table 1. Results with different training set.

#	Model Name	K	Accuracy	F1-Score	ROC AUC	Precision	Recall	Optuna	Train Size
1	RandomForest	616	0.9391	0.9392	0.9796	0.9353	0.9433	Yes	100%
2	RandomForest	616	0.9245	0.9241	0.9542	0.9285	0.9198	No	

(continued)

Table 1. (*continued*)

#	Model Name	K	Accuracy	F1-Score	ROC AUC	Precision	Recall	Optuna	Train Size
3	RandomForest	300	0.9117	0.9116	0.9426	0.9129	0.9093	No	
4	RandomForest	300	0.9362	0.9369	0.9777	0.9332	0.9387	Yes	
5	RandomForest	200	0.9371	0.9371	0.962	0.9344	0.9394	Yes	
6	RandomForest	200	0.9188	0.9184	0.9435	0.9193	0.9175	No	
7	RandomForest	100	0.9357	0.9356	0.9506	0.9328	0.9382	Yes	
8	RandomForest	100	0.9154	0.9154	0.9454	0.9161	0.9145	No	
9	XGBoost	616	0.9173	0.9184	0.9728	0.9063	0.9308	Yes	
10	XGBoost	616	0.9082	0.9171	0.9482	0.8926	0.9281	No	
11	XGBoost	300	0.9283	0.9287	0.9586	0.9207	0.9368	Yes	
12	XGBoost	300	0.7762	0.8027	0.9124	0.7176	0.9106	No	
13	XGBoost	200	0.9268	0.9269	0.9735	0.9201	0.9336	Yes	
14	XGBoost	200	0.7604	0.7781	0.9007	0.7246	0.8412	No	
14	XGBoost	100	0.9255	0.9258	0.9407	0.9191	0.9324	Yes	
15	XGBoost	100	0.8294	0.8215	0.8394	0.8616	0.7852	No	
16	LightGBM	616	0.9389	0.9391	0.9691	0.9351	0.9432	Yes	
17	LightGBM	300	0.9441	0.9438	0.9853	0.9445	0.9437	Yes	
18	LightGBM	200	0.9424	0.9425	0.9841	0.9399	0.9451	Yes	
19	LightGBM	100	0.9427	0.9425	0.9576	0.9432	0.9418	Yes	
20	LightGBM	200	0.9011	0.9036	0.9283	0.8815	0.9268	No	
21	LightGBM	616	0.8970	0.8993	0.9645	0.8795	0.9201	No	
22	LightGBM	300	0.8257	0.8408	0.9232	0.7739	0.9203	No	
23	CatBoost	616	0.9405	0.9406	0.9706	0.9388	0.9424	Yes	
24	CatBoost	616	0.9292	0.9298	0.9597	0.9215	0.9382	No	
25	CatBoost	300	0.9341	0.9342	0.9757	0.9299	0.9385	Yes	
26	CatBoost	300	0.8447	0.8503	0.8795	0.8206	0.8823	No	
27	CatBoost	200	0.9355	0.9359	0.9608	0.9307	0.9411	Yes	
28	CatBoost	200	0.9237	0.9236	0.9689	0.9246	0.9226	No	
29	CatBoost	100	0.9315	0.9313	0.9464	0.9275	0.9351	Yes	
30	CatBoost	100	0.8507	0.8517	0.8665	0.8457	0.8578	No	
31	VotingClassifier (XGB, LGBM, CB, All Features)	616	0.9461	0.9461	0.9864	0.9468	0.9454	No	
32	RandomForest	616	0.8652	0.8533	0.9253	0.9338	0.7856	No	50%

(*continued*)

Table 1. *(continued)*

#	Model Name	K	Accuracy	F1-Score	ROC AUC	Precision	Recall	Optuna	Train Size
33	XGBoost	616	0.8668	0.8621	0.9216	0.8934	0.8329	No	
34	LightGBM	616	0.8659	0.8605	0.9352	0.8967	0.8272	No	
35	LightGBM	100	0.8827	0.8841	0.8989	0.8735	0.8951	No	
36	CatBoost	616	0.8891	0.8846	0.9543	0.9223	0.8498	No	
37	RandomForest	616	0.7855	0.7375	0.9247	0.9497	0.6028	No	20%
38	XGBoost	616	0.8381	0.8244	0.9256	0.9003	0.7603	No	
39	LigghtGBM	616	0.8349	0.8141	0.9244	0.9314	0.7234	No	
40	CatBoost	616	0.8625	0.8487	0.9408	0.9433	0.7713	No	
41	RandomForest	616	0.5972	0.3336	0.7517	0.9663	0.2016	No	10%
42	XGBoost	616	0.6626	0.5165	0.8121	0.9112	0.3604	No	
43	LigghtGBM	616	0.7463	0.6683	0.9034	0.9658	0.5112	No	
44	CatBoost	616	0.6458	0.4664	0.7613	0.9458	0.3096	No	

3.2 Feature Selection and Hyperparameter Optimization

All models and optimizations in this section used the feature set produced with the adapted features.py script and compatible with lief version 0.16.5 and Python version 3.8 to establish a controlled and consistent environment with EMBER 2018.Two important methods are applied to optimize and systematize performance: dimensionality reduction via SelectKBest and hyperparameter optimization using Optuna.

In total, 45 models are trained and evaluated with the following combinations: 4 ML algorithms (Random Forest, XGBoost, LightGBM, CatBoost), 4 different training set sizes (10%, 20%, 50%, 100%), Optuna on and off, and different SelectKBest values, $k = 100; 200; 300;$; each model is evaluated from an independent test set on 5 core metrics (see Table 1).

The SelectKBest feature selection algorithm using mutual_info_classif is employed to identify which features are most informative. In comparing the number of features and performance the parameter k is tested using 100, 200, and 300 features respectively. There is a small loss of accuracy trading off fewer features selected, however, both $k = 200$ and $k = 300$ did not differ much from the entire features set, meaning fewer features can be useful in situations where compute resources are a factor. Optimizing different models fully with Optuna takes significant amount of compute and time resources: each of the 4 algorithms (CatBoost, XGBoost, LightGBM, Random Forest) ran 50 trials plus various feature dimensions and model depths, which took approximately 100 to 140 h of pure compute time. The work involved long validation loops, logging, reviewing the results, and saving the top performing models. The time put in reflects the rigor and commitment to creating a reliable high-performing ML architecture.

3.3 Optimized Hyperparameters from the Best-Performing Configurations

Since hyperparameter tuning is essential for optimizing the performance of machine learning algorithms [15], the best hyperparameters achieved for each of the applied algorithms are described here. Each parameter is selected based upon Optuna's selection of a total of 50 trials for each parameter so they can yield good performance, generalizability, and shorten training times. Short descriptions for each of the relevant parameter characteristics are included in parentheses.

- The hyperparameters are genuinely optimized based upon the 50 trial Optuna process performed on each of the models. They are the best configurations based upon F1-score on the validation set and the final model comparisons used these values. The hyperparameters described are well-balanced measures of performance/speed and they are validated using the full feature set (616 features) with SelectKBest transformations ($k = 100; 200; 300$).
- LightGBM: max_depth = 6 (maximum tree depth to remove risk of overfitting), *learning_rate* = 0.07 (models speed of adaptation to the data), *n_estimators* = 420 (number of iterations are sufficient for a medium learning rate)
- CatBoost: *depth* = 8 (maximum depth of the tree, enough to capture indirect relationships), l *earning_rate* = 0.05 (mean learning rate, is slower but converged steadily), *iterations* = 500 (number of iterations needed for a low learning rate)
- XGBoost: *n_estimators* = 468 (number of boosting rounds), *max_depth* = 10 (deep trees to model complex dependencies), *learning_rate* = 0.0942 (standard value for stable learning), *subsample* = 0.7039 (overfitting controlled by using a single sample from all sample data), c *olsample_bytree* = 0.8392 (the number of features used per tree)
- Random Forest: *n_estimators* = 132 (number of trees in the forest for stable predictions), *max_depth* = 28 (can make relatively deep trees while vowing to only allow reasonable overfitting), *min_samples_split* = 5 (branches excessive), *min_samples_leaf* = 2 (has too sensitive branches), *max_features* = *ʼlog2ʼ* (the number of features when the decision trees build the splits are all dimensions, so samples grow diversity of the trees)

It is worth noting that the time to execute this training – the Optuna optimization with full configuration of all training data (100%)/SelectKBest ($k = 300$) – is extremely time consuming. A single trial for either CatBoost or XGBoost in its full extent in trial time can take anywhere from 20 to 90 min based on model depth, number of iterations and input data. Therefore, for ideally up to 50 runs for a single model takes up to approximately 20 to 50 h of pure computation time.

Optuna provided clear improvements over the baseline configurations and expectedly improved the performance for CatBoost and Random Forest. The largest improvement on accuracy is for LightGBM which improved from 0.8970 to 0.9389. With different values of $k = 100; 200; 300$, SelectKBest gave some models with less data dimensionality performance rivaling or exceeding performance in using all features. For example, XGBoost with $k = 300$ and Optuna is able to achieve an accuracy of 0.9283 and F1-score equal to 0.9287 which is better than the same model using 616 total features (Accuracy = 0.9173, F1 = 0.9184). So also, LightGBM at with $k = 300$ did show with some marginal accuracy (Accuracy = 0.9392) better than its full version (0.9389). Finally, CatBoost with $k = 300$ showed it could perform highly also (Accuracy = 0.9341, F1 = 0.9342) while approaching its version with full-input results (0.9405). Thus, SelectKBest could be effective as a strategy in resource limited or time constrained situations. However, for the final ensemble model (see the next section), the full data set of 616 features is used, so a single benchmark number is achieved to provide balanced input for all models in the ensemble.

3.4 Ensemble Model with Voting Classifier

The ensemble method that combines optimized models with unique architectures produced the most beneficial outcome in the analysis. The VotingClassifier model which applied Soft Voting with defined weights made predictions stronger than the individual models, including the CatBoost which had the best performance. This is evidence of leveraging the power forth by unique models with unique beneficial algorithms.

Once the individual experiments are performed and the hyper tuning is completed on each model, the ensemble configuration is formed using the VotingClassifier. The goal of the ensemble is to be able to combine all the strengths of all the algorithm potential and minimize the individual models risks using Soft Voting as support.

Voting Classifier Composition is as follows: CatBoost (Optuna, 616 features); LightGBM (Optuna, 616 features); Random Forest (Optuna, 616 features); and XGBoost (Optuna, 616 features). Soft Voting is used to pool model probabilistic outputs. Soft Voting is chosen over Hard Voting, because Soft Voting allows merging predictions in a far more informative manner as the predicted probabilities can be pooled together and considered, rather than only pooled and hard decided on classifications. In addition, using Soft voting allows models to express their confidence, which is particularly important with models that differ in their false positive/negatives mixed with sensitivity and specificity.

All models are trained on the entire 100% training set. Each model used the full 616 feature vector to ensure the input structure is similar. Weighted classifications for VotingClassifier (based on performance) is as follows: CatBoost: 4; Random Forest: 3; LightGBM: 2; and XGBoost: 1. These weights represent the relative strength of each model after Optuna tuning, with the objective to allow the power of the best possible predictors to deliver the best outcome. Lastly, direct Optuna did not apply to the VotingClassifier since it is an ensemble of base models already optimized, and applying an ensemble level of tuning would have significant compute costs with very little expected gains from performance to justify. Expert defined weights and Soft Voting are both fine tuning and helped make the voting a little more computable. Results from the VotingClassifier are shown in Table 1.

VotingClassifier achieved the highest values for all core evaluation metrics. It surpassed all non-voting models; even the overall best CatBoost model (0.9405). An ensemble modeled with pre-tuned base models also allowed for diminished individual model weaknesses. Practical advantages are that the model has high stability and reliability when put into real-world use. The application of the model would be well-suited for incorporation in an actual CLI (Command Line Interface) scanner (detailed in the next section) with a strong balance between accuracy and interpretability.

Not only did the weighted Soft Voting ensemble exceed all of the non-voting models for measures, but it also had strong stability and adaptability in realistic environments. The voting ensemble setup used exceptionally well-optimized base models and controlled voting to deliver the highest classification accuracy among the study (Accuracy: 94.61%).

4 CLI Scanner: Practical Use Case

The CLI scanner is purposely created to be used in the same environment (Python 3.8 and lief 0.16.5) to guarantee full compatibility with the EMBER 2018 feature extraction and in order to prevent issues with newer PE file structures. The CLI scanner provides a command-line environment that utilizes an input argument provided by the user (the path to the PE file) to extract features (using an embedded mechanism), load the final VotingClassifier model, and yield a risk level. The developed CLI scanner is completely offline, so it can work in isolated networks and environments (i.e., virtual). It is created in Python environment and is also a packaged.exe application using PyInstaller. Features are extracted using lief and are exactly 616. The CLI scanner is capable to generate and maintains a log file showing detailed status of the scan and probability scores.

The performance of the CLI scanner is as follows: Average single PE file scan time is ~ 1.0 s. Every console output is both recorded and logged, which includes all details as you would see in the console output: date and time, path of the file, predicted probability, risk score, and final class. The scanner can process a single file or multiple files at once (with paths their paths given), but directory scanning will be developed in the future. An example command of the CLI scanner is:

```
python scanner.py --file suspicious.exe
```

An example output of the CLI scanner is:

```
[INFO] Scan result: suspicious.exe: Malicious | Ciritcal Risk | Probability: 95%
```

Actual console output from a CLI scanner in which an example of a scan is shown for 2 PE files, a benign PE file (python-3.8.10-amd64.exe) and a malicious PE file (malicious_file_sample.exe). Risk category, probability score, and a log entry are provided in the output. All output is written to scan_log.txt, as shown in Fig. 2.

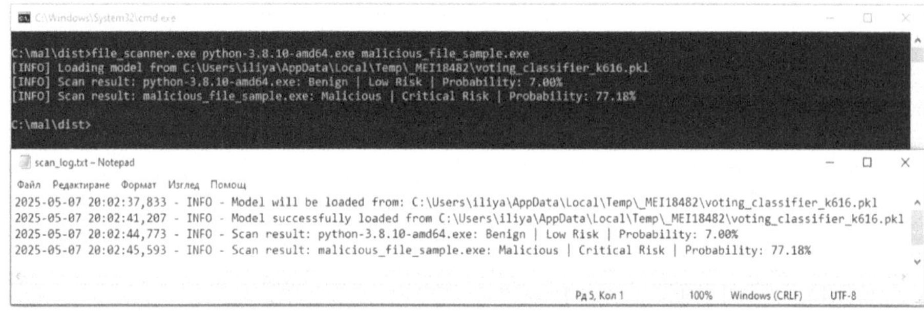

Fig. 2. Actual console output from a CLI scanner.

CLI scanner identified 5 levels of risk: 0: Benign; 1: Low Risk; 2: Medium Risk; 3: High Risk; and 4: Critical Risk. The proposed CLI scanner can be used by IT administrators on government or corporate systems that do not have internet access. The CLI scanner is compatible with obsolete hardware with legacy operating systems. This scanner can be used as part of script automation or internal defensive systems.

4.1 Visualizations and Metrics

This section presents a collection of visualizations that facilitate interpretation and analysis of model behavior, completely from the test set (20% from EMBER 2018) that is not included in training or optimization in any way. These figures serve as complements to the numerical results discussed in the previous section and allow for visual comparative analysis across architectures, optimization levels, and amounts of training data. In terms of visualizations, the top 20 models to visualize are determined based on accuracy with F1-score serving as a secondary option to break any resulting ties. The visualizations to be presented include model rankings, heatmaps, comparisons by key metric, false positive/false negative model evaluations, feature importance classifications, and ROC curves. Each figure will include a brief descriptor and interpretation.

The heatmap of the top 20 models is shown in Fig. 3.

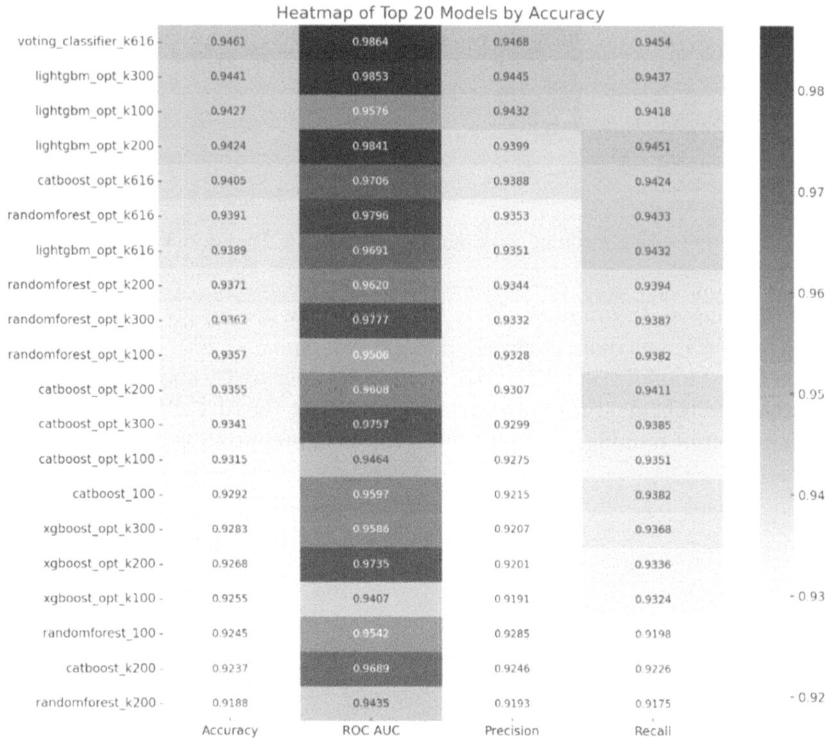

Fig. 3. Heatmap of accuracy, F1, precision, recall, and ROC AUC for top 20 models.

It contains all of the core metrics for the top 20 models which have values for (accuracy, F1-score, precision, recall, Roc AUC) for 5 selected metrics. The color gradient is especially useful to see how models stack up with strong values over models in each of the 5 selected measures. From this heatmap, it is evident that VotingClassifier is better than the other models in nearly all situations, so we can confirm using this metric, that the model is robust.

Figure 4 shows grouped bar chart illustrated three different representative models, from three different classes of strength – strong (VotingClassifier), medium (Random Forest with $k = 200$), and weak (Random Forest with 10% training set) – with respect to five evaluation metrics.

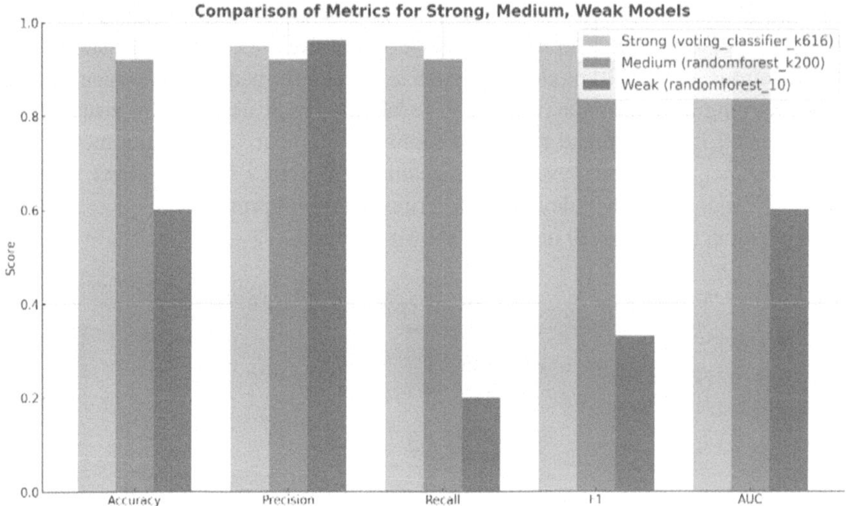

Fig. 4. Comparing strong-medium-weak models on Accuracy, Precision, Recall, F1 and AUC.

The ROC curve, shown in Fig. 5, is realized to view the results of a strong model (VotingClassifier), a medium model (Random Forest with $k = 200$), and a weak model (Random Forest training size, 10%). The VotingClassifier AUC is highest (0.9424); the weak model barely better than random guessing (0.5972). The AUC difference, in general shows the point of training size is less powerful than optimization upon classification ability.

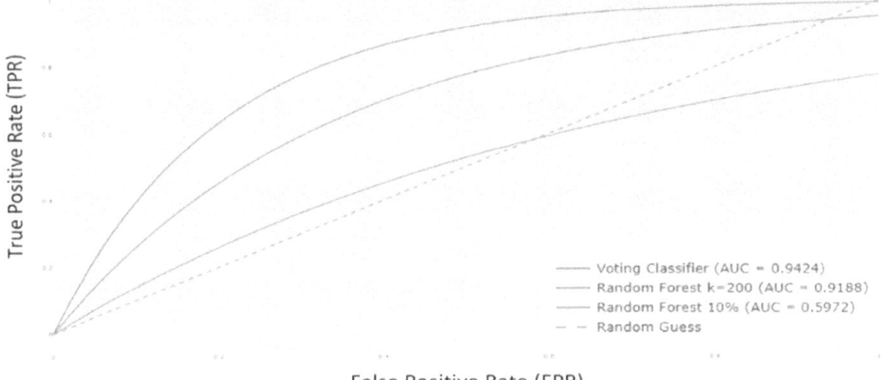

Fig. 5. Comparative ROC curves.

The confusion matrix (see Fig. 6) illustrates the true and false positives, and true and false negatives from the VotingClassifier in total executed on the test set. The overall performance in prediction started to show a balanced, fewer errors, and that confusion matrices are helpful in understanding real-world behavior of one system.

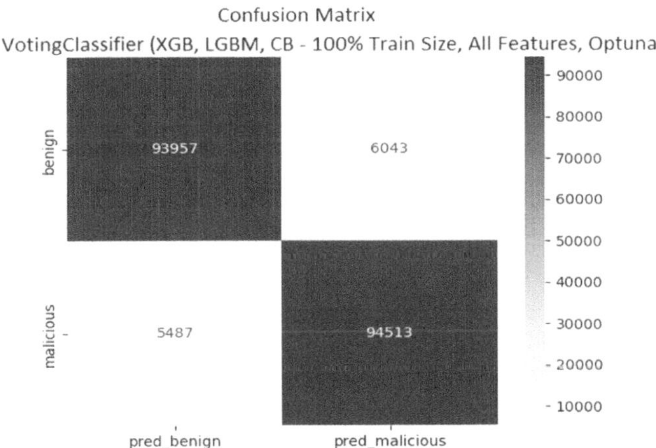

Fig. 6. VotingClassifier confusion matrix.

Figure 7 illustrates most influential 20 features based on VotingClassifier.

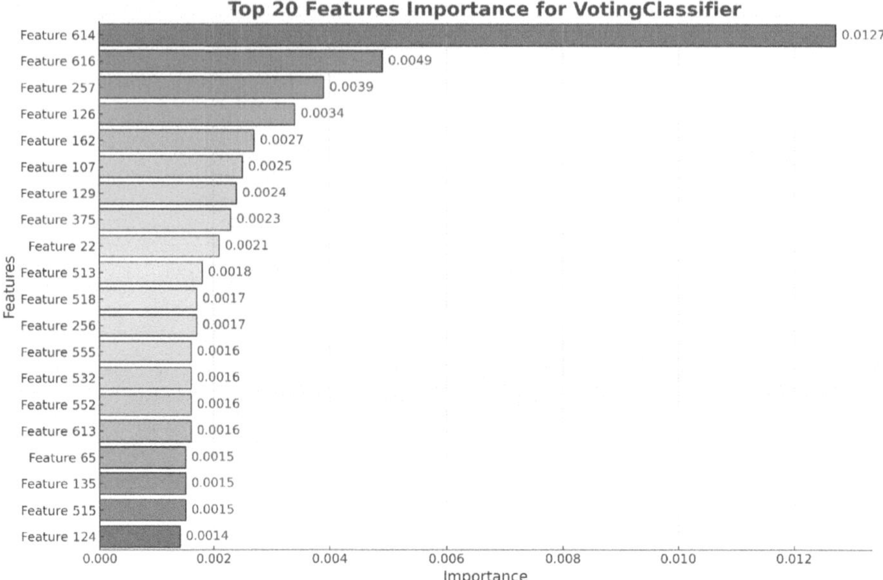

Fig. 7. 20 most influential features based on VotingClassifier.

The features are ordered from largest to smallest influence as Feature ID (based on descending values), where Feature 614 is the most influential. The chart is for model explainability and shows which features are responsible for the most impact on decisions. Due to the nature of the EMBER 2018 dataset, feature names are only presented as numeric (Feature 614 etc.) as semantic labels for the features are not publicly available. However, the empirical importance value gives important understanding about how the model works.

5 Discussion and Results

With our experiments with smaller training sets (10% and 20%) we saw much more variability, and also the model overfitting in cases of basing in particular on CatBoost and XGBoost. This also illustrates the need for regularization or, at least, more complete subset in order to receive acceptable prediction states. SelectKBest testing ($k = 100/200/300$) showed that some models are particularly sensitive to reductions in features; XGBoost is especially harmed by excessive reduction.

Optuna optimization demonstrated that smaller training sizes often resulted in hyperparameters that are aggressively base-trained well, but poorly generalizing to the test set, overfitting has been shown. It is important to note that the VotingClassifier's performance is evaluated only using the pre-split test set (20% from EMBER) data that is not used for training, and therefore not seen before. This ensures of measurement is unbiased. The results starkly show the benefits of using the VotingClassifier over the single models. All metrics (Accuracy, F1, AUC, Precision, Recall) achieved consistently high performance, where VotingClassifier achieved an accuracy of 94.61%.

CatBoost and Random Forest independently achieved good performance without feature selection, and improved further after using Optuna for optimization. LightGBM, being the quickest model to train, holds a unique advantage in situations where compute is limited. Models can be speed by feature reduction with SelectKBest, without restricting accuracy – especially $k = 200/300$. VotingClassifier, combining models of separate feature dimensions, is impractical. As such, an ensemble with a unified input of 616 features is used. Only one dataset (EMBER 2018) is evaluated, which restricts the ability to generalize these results. The scanner only performs static-analysis; dynamic behavior is not considered. Multi-class classification (e.g. Trojan, Worm) is not yet implemented.

FP/FN analysis of false positives for the ensemble is significantly lower than the individual models. Visualization of the feature importance indicates relative few features have a significant part in making an accurate prediction. While EMBER 2018 provides a reliable benchmark, its age may introduce dataset bias. The use of newer datasets in future experiments will help evaluate the generalizability of the proposed system.

6 Conclusion and Future Research

The proposed system for automated classification of PE files is considered highly effective, especially owing to the ensemble (VotingClassifier), which is combining four optimized ML algorithms. Overall, the experimental results confirm that high accuracy and robustness in any malware detection task can be achieved through combining human expertise in static analysis with objectively tuned machine learning classifiers.

A key find in this study is the use of historical data - specifically, the dataset EMBER 2018. Although this dataset serves as a good, standard foundation dataset, the structures and techniques it incorporates may no longer be a true representation of current malware. This leads to the concept of feature drift, which suggests that the statistical properties and characteristics of the malware, may shift over time. This also means that the performance of any model will likely deteriorate, particularly in production situations where there is a continuously emerging emergence of new malware families and evasion techniques. So to preserve detection effectiveness consistently over time – mechanisms to identify, and alleviate the drift, need to be included in this study. Possible solutions may include tracking feature distribution, updating the training set periodically, or drift aware retraining pipelines.

The most significant contribution of the entirety of the system is practical – an offline, CLI-based scanner, which be implemented in isolated and legacy environments, and provides a faster, interpretable result than analyzing an offline PE using a whole trained ensemble model. Every component is optimized for reproducibility, modularity, and extensibility.

This work offers several opportunities for future work. Some of those opportunities include the following: Expanding from binary to multiclass classification – e.g. producing labels such as Trojan, Worm, Ransomware, etc. Factoring in more options for dynamic analysis and behavioral indicators to enable detection. Performing temporal validation, to determine how much impact feature drift has, and then updating our model overtime with recent datasets or live feeds of malware. Detecting drift feature over-time based on distributions of features, and performing retraining as needed. Adding more contemporary, diverse malicious samples to our datasets (e.g. VirusShare, honeypot samples from inside company). Adding a graphical user interface (GUI) or web-based front end if we want less technical users to use this tool. Improving explainability with visualization insights, making it easier for analysts to understand why a relevant file is determined to be malicious. This project has engineering value, scientific rigor and real-world applications – great foundations for auras of publishable academic articles, as well as possibilities for practical implementations.

References

1. Khan, K., Khurshid, A., Cifuentes-Faura, J.: Is artificial intelligence a new battleground for cybersecurity? Internet Things **28**, 101428 (2024). https://doi.org/10.1016/j.iot.2024.101428
2. Barzev, I., Borissova, D.: An improved static analysis approach for malware detection by optimizing feature extraction combining different ML algorithms. In: Communications in Computer and Information Science, vol. 2304, pp. 102–115 (2025). https://doi.org/10.1007/978-3-031-82153-0_8
3. Baghirov, E.: A comprehensive investigation into robust malware detection with explainable AI. Cyber Secur. Appl. **3**, 100072 (2025). https://doi.org/10.1016/j.csa.2024.100072
4. Aslan, Ö., Yilmaz, A.A.: A new malware classification framework based on deep learning algorithms. IEEE Access **9**, 87936–87951 (2021). https://doi.org/10.1109/ACCESS.2021.3089586
5. Brown, A., Gupta, M., Abdelsalam, M.: Automated machine learning for deep learning based malware detection. Comput. Secur. **137**, 103582 (2024). https://doi.org/10.1016/j.cose.2023.103582
6. Maniriho, P., Mahmood, A.N., Chowdhury, M.J.M.: API-MalDetect: automated malware detection framework for windows based on API calls and deep learning techniques. J. Netw. Comput. Appl. **218**, 103704 (2023). https://doi.org/10.1016/j.jnca.2023.103704
7. Parmar, A., Brahmbhatt, K.: An optimized intelligent malware detection framework for securing digital data. Wireless Pers. Commun. **133**, 351–371 (2023). https://doi.org/10.1007/s11277-023-10771-z
8. Smmarwar, S.K., Gupta, G.P., Kumar, S., Kumar, P.: An optimized and efficient android malware detection framework for future sustainable computing. Sustain. Energy Technol. Assess. **54**, 102852 (2022). https://doi.org/10.1016/j.seta.2022.102852
9. Arora, P., Gupta, R., Malik, N., Kumar, A.: Malware analysis types & techniques: a survey. In Proceedings of 5th International Conference on Information Management & Machine Intelligence (ICIMMI 2023), vol. 135, pp. 1–6. Association for Computing Machinery, New York (2024), https://doi.org/10.1145/3647444.3652439
10. Omar, M., Gouveia, L.B., Al-Karaki, J., Mohammed, D.: Reverse-engineering malware. In: Dawson, M., Tabona, O., Maupong, T. (eds.), Cybersecurity Capabilities in Developing Nations and Its Impact on Global Security, pp. 194–217 (2022). https://doi.org/10.4018/978-1-7998-8693-8.ch010
11. Thai, H.-T.: Machine learning for structural engineering: a state-of-the-art review. Structures **38**, 448–491 (2022). https://doi.org/10.1016/j.istruc.2022.02.003
12. Hancock, J.T., Khoshgoftaar, T.M.: CatBoost for big data: an interdisciplinary review. J. Big Data **7**, 94 (2020). https://doi.org/10.1186/s40537-020-00369-8
13. Anderson, H.S., Roth, P.: EMBER: An open dataset for training static PE malware machine learning models (2018). https://doi.org/10.48550/arXiv.1804.04637
14. Rizkallah, L.W.: Enhancing the performance of gradient boosting trees on regression problems. J. Big Data **12**, 35 (2025). https://doi.org/10.1186/s40537-025-01071-3

15. Lujan-Moreno, G.A., Howard, P.R., Rojas, O.G., Montgomery, D.C.: Design of experiments and response surface methodology to tune machine learning hyperparameters, with a random forest case-study. Expert Syst. Appl. **109**, 195–205 (2018). https://doi.org/10.1016/j.eswa.2018.05.024

Factors Influencing Graduation Delays Among Master's Students: An AI Analysis in a Faculty of Engineering

Alejandro Caroca[1], David Ruete[1], Danilo Leal[1], and Jean Paul Maidana[1,2(✉)]

[1] Universidad Andres Bello, Viña del Mar, Chile
[2] Instituto de Tecnología para la Innovación en Salud y Bienestar, Universidad Andrés Bello, Quillota 980, Viña del Mar, Chile
jean.maidana@unab.cl

Abstract. The delay in completing graduate studies in programs is crucial for higher education institutions. Global research has focused on the relevance of timely graduation, which is essential to academic accreditation processes. Institutions are interested in implementing tactics to reduce this delay, considering an approach based on analyzing the risk factors that impact student progress. This study presents a descriptive analysis that explores the interrelationship between student characteristics, such as gender and age, and program aspects, such as duration and modality. The analysis takes a sample of engineering students (1257/1496 records) from the last five years and documents the risk elements that play an essential role in explaining the reasons behind graduation delays. Findings reveal that students who do not pass their first thesis project face a significant extension in their graduation time. Among the factors influencing this delay are individual peculiarities, such as gender (with a minor impact), students' educational background (previous education, pass rate, with substantial implications), and institutional context (program type, location, with a moderate impact). The results highlight the need to support students in improving their academic performance, avoiding unnecessary delays in obtaining the degree, and for institutions to seek strategies that promote efficient progression toward graduation.

Keywords: dropout rate · higher education · graduation delay · master's degree

1 Introduction

Late graduation poses a significant challenge in master's programs, regardless of discipline or institution. This phenomenon becomes most apparent when examining student behavior. Ideally, universities would use data from statistical analyses on late graduations to address and prevent this issue. However, research into the motivations or perceptions driving master's students to drop out remains limited.

T. Guarda et al. (Eds.): ARTIIS 2025, CCIS 2789, pp. 430–444, 2026.
https://doi.org/10.1007/978-3-032-16758-3_33

Every year, millions of individuals work, save, and strive to enroll in master's programs with the goal of improving their circumstances, securing better jobs, higher incomes, and an enhanced lifestyle. Academic and social experiences shape students' perceptions of the value of a master's degree [1,2]. Despite such investments, nearly half of those who begin a master's program leave before completion [3,4], delaying their path to graduation.

Dropping out of programs, and consequently graduating late, presents a global challenge in higher education [5,6]. Students' experiences, including their expectations, professional development opportunities, performance standards, and unexpected academic transitions, often hinder their progress and lead to attrition [1].

Leaders of master's programs must gather and analyze this data from day one to ensure students graduate successfully and on time. They should implement monitoring and support mechanisms to reduce dropout rates. Academic administrators must consider a complex web of evolving factors related to students: their availability of time, health, past and present experiences, future goals, personal or work circumstances, and success expectations [7]. Many causes of dropout, such as unforeseen personal situations, health crises, or financial setbacks, fall outside students' control [8]. However, these do not explain every case. Some causes are personal, while others stem from institutional factors [9]. Therefore, targeted research is necessary to identify what influences on-time graduation rates.

A literature review shows few studies analyzing late graduation in master's programs. The systematic review also observes that no studies use technology to assist in the analysis of results.

This research provides a study focused on the early stage of the graduation process through descriptive and statistical analysis (modeling the student's profile and study program) using data from the Learning Management System (LMS). The study demonstrates how quantitative variables of the academic experience can be a projection of student dropout intentions that affect graduation.

It is crucial to reflect on the broader implications of this issue. Graduation delays entail significant socioeconomic consequences, as graduates who postpone degree completion face a salary penalty of 8% to 15% in later earnings, affecting individuals, the educational system, and human capital development [10]. Timely completion is also linked to higher student achievement and institutional efficiency, highlighting the importance of strengthening academic process management [11]. In graduate programs, where progress depends on milestones such as examinations, proposals, and thesis defenses, monitoring mechanisms are needed to anticipate delays and enable timely interventions [12]. Thus, this study, centered on the early identification of risks related to delayed graduation, contributes to improving outcomes, institutional effectiveness, and the social value of postgraduate education.

The research focuses on master's students in a Faculty of Engineering who completed coursework and entered the thesis stage over the last five academic years (1,257 records). Modeling uses variables from institutional systems

(LMS/SIS), prioritizing real-time operationalization for early alerts. As a result, individual causes of attrition (e.g., financial, health, work–study balance), extensively reported in the literature [13–17], are not directly observed. We prioritized scalability and real-time deployment, acknowledging reduced explanatory detail while recognizing these broader causal factors as directions for future data enrichment.

2 Related Works

This section presents a review of the literature on predictive models applied to undergraduate student dropout and its impact on graduation time. Although no studies specifically address the prediction of late graduation in master's programs, the review highlights the variables and techniques employed, the results obtained, and the evaluation metrics used in these models.

Higher-education institutions that offer postgraduate studies, including master's programs, are being urged to optimize their educational processes by integrating information and communication technologies (ICTs). These tools enable the analysis of large volumes of data and variables using intelligent systems, data mining, and machine learning, among other resources, transforming educational data into relevant and practical information [18].The integration of ICTs is critical as it supports the development of predictive models that can effectively analyze and interpret vast datasets, providing insights crucial for improving educational outcomes and reducing dropout rates.

Various variables have been employed to feed predictive models for dropout and delayed graduation, including student performance indicators like cumulative average, tests, exams, and attendance and demographic factors such as age, gender, and family history [19]. These variables provide a comprehensive view of the factors influencing student retention and timely graduation. Algorithms such as Decision Trees, Neural Networks, and Support Vector Machines have been utilized to develop predictive models, with Neural Networks and Decision Trees showing high accuracy rates. The Decision Tree algorithm is the most widely used predictive model for identifying student dropout in higher education institutions [20].

Studies have employed a range of methodologies, including multi-layer morphological neural networks, support vector machines, and probabilistic analysis techniques, to predict dropout and late graduation. These methodologies leverage different mathematical and computational approaches to model and analyze student data. Models based on fuzzy-ARTMAP neural networks and Hidden Mark"ov Models have also been explored, demonstrating promising accuracy levels [21]. Additionally, logistic regression algorithms have been employed to create predictive models aimed at student retention and timely graduation policies. Results from these models have shown reductions in dropout rates [22]. Logistic regression is particularly notable for its ability to handle binary outcomes, such as dropout or continuation, and its flexibility in incorporating various predictor variables.

While existing studies have focused on student dropout at various stages, there is a gap in research addressing late graduation risks, particularly in master's degree programs. This study aims to address this gap by leveraging machine learning algorithms fed with cognitive data from Learning Management Systems to provide early warnings on late graduation risks due to dropout at the final degree project preparation stage. By utilizing real-time data collection, this approach seeks to enhance the effectiveness of predictive models in identifying and mitigating late graduation risks [23].

The review highlights the importance of integrating advanced data analysis techniques and machine learning algorithms in predicting student dropout and graduation timelines. The insights gained from these predictive models can inform institutional policies and practices to improve student retention and timely graduation. Future research should focus on expanding the application of these models to graduate programs and exploring additional variables that may influence late graduation risks.

University dropout is a multifaceted concept that demands a precise definition to eliminate ambiguity. Larsen et al. [13] examined various dimensions of the term and chose to define it negatively, as the "non-completion" of a university program. It is crucial to specify where dropout occurs: a student might switch majors but remain enrolled in higher education, transfer to another university for different reasons, or exit the university system entirely [14].

In Fernández-Mellizo's [15] report on undergraduate dropout at on-campus universities in Spain, abandonment refers to discontinuing any undergraduate program—excluding major changes. Researchers calculated the rate based on a cohort of new students who did not re-enroll for two consecutive years. Specifically, first-year dropout describes those who enrolled initially but did not register in the following two years. They calculated the dropout rate by dividing this number by the total number of new entrants. The report indicates that the first year carries the highest dropout risk; after that period, attrition rates decline.

To reduce dropout rates, we must pinpoint both the triggers and the profiles of students who leave university. A prior study [16] identified several key predictors: enrollment status (part-time versus full-time), admission score, and field of study. That study used multilevel logistic regression and decision tree analysis to describe how these factors relate to dropout.

This research aims to detect at-risk students as early and accurately as possible. Data-mining methods let us combine multiple factors—personal, academic, and non-academic—into unified models that predict dropout, program changes, or continued enrollment [24]. For a comprehensive review of educational data mining, consult Romero and Ventura [25].

According to Frawley, Piatetsky-Shapiro, and Matheus [26], data mining involves extracting meaningful, hidden, and potentially useful information from large datasets using machine learning algorithms to detect patterns or relationships—an essential component of predictive modeling. In this study, we apply multiple techniques, such as Decision Tree, KNN, SVM, ANN, and Logistic Regression, to compare outcomes, identify significant overlaps, and assess each method's unique contributions.

Academic success in higher education is fundamental for accessing employment opportunities, advancing social justice, and driving economic growth. Student dropout remains the key challenge institutions must address to improve educational outcomes. There is no single definition of "dropout," and reported rates vary depending on how it is defined, the data source, and calculation methods [14]. Many researchers categorize dropout based on timing (early vs. late) [27], but inconsistent reporting standards complicate comparisons across institutions [28]. Here, we adopt a micro-level definition: any change of field or institution counts as dropout, regardless of timing. This yields substantially higher dropout rates than macro-level definitions, which include only those who entirely exit the higher education system.

An independent report from the European Commission notes that too many students fail to complete their higher education programs [17]. Even in the top-performing country (Denmark), only about 80% graduate, while in Italy that figure drops to around 46%. The report attributes dropout primarily to socioeconomic factors.

Namoun and Alshanqiti [29] conducted a comprehensive review of 62 peer-reviewed articles published between 2010 and 2020 that presented intelligent models for predicting student performance. Furthermore, growing interest in early prediction of academic outcomes has emerged in recent years [30–34]

. However, despite this growing research focus and the volume of data universities generate, there remains a need for more comprehensive administrative datasets—especially regarding reasons for dropout or transfer [27].

The study of school dropout is relevant across all educational levels. Reducing student dropout is a significant challenge for both secondary and higher education. The loss of students at the beginning of secondary or undergraduate studies is a global concern [35–38]. Research has identified various contributing factors, including adverse sociodemographic conditions, insufficient academic support, limited economic resources, and deficiencies in academic or social skills. Numerous quantitative studies analyze these causes and potential solutions to dropout [35,37,39].

Investigating student dropout is complex because multiple variables can act simultaneously. Academic failure may stem from teaching content that lacks practical relevance or from low motivation resulting in sporadic attendance. Additionally, some students exhibit behavioral problems due to weak family support structures. Unrealistic expectations set by families that lack sufficient support, as well as the absence of engaged parents or academic role models at home, are also critical factors. First-generation students, in particular, often require a stronger school environment to compensate for the lack of academic structure at home. To address this issue, the Institute of Education Sciences (USA) issued six key evidence-based recommendations to prevent high school dropouts [40], including early-warning systems and personalized supports:

- Implement data systems to detect at-risk students early.
- Offer individual tutoring for these students.
- Provide academic support (additional office hours, Y assignments, etc.).
- Include social skills development programs and specialized experiences that enrich the classroom.
- Ensure personalized academic instruction is available.
- Emphasize lifelong competencies alongside rigorous and relevant teaching.

Analysis of the multiple factors affecting dropout rates in secondary and higher education has led institutions to conduct statistical studies that identify the relative importance of these factors and implement timely interventions to identify at-risk students [38]. In this context, the integration of learning analytics—which combines social and academic performance data—has uncovered the most influential factors and improved predictive model accuracy in recent years [41,42]. Modern data analysis techniques applied to large datasets facilitate a deeper understanding of the relationships among the many involved variables.

3 Methodology

This article presents a descriptive analysis of how student attributes (gender, age, academic background) and program characteristics (duration, campus, major, schedule) influence delayed graduation. The study examines a dataset comprising 1,257 master's-level engineering students from the past five years, all of whom have completed coursework and are currently working on their thesis. Through descriptive methods, it identifies risk factors associated with prolonged time to degree. The dataset includes demographic information (age, gender) and academic performance metrics (course completion rate, faculty affiliation, dropout rate, and time to degree), all sourced from university information systems. The institutional LMS/SIS extract used in this study did not include individual-level socioeconomic indicators (e.g., household income, financial-aid/scholarship status, parental education, or employment while studying). To avoid bias from ad-hoc imputation or unstable proxies, we restricted modeling to system-native variables available in real time.

Certain demographic variables—such as address, funding type, time commitment, family background, and other personal details—were deliberately excluded since they rely on survey data and are not available in real time. Instead, our prototype integrates directly with the university's Learning Management System (LMS) to generate live alerts. However, its implementation lies outside the scope of this study.

We categorized variables into two types: input and output. Input factors were further divided into student-level and program-level variables. Student inputs include gender, years of delay, prior dropout history, and number of courses passed. Program inputs cover metrics such as program duration (in semesters and years), program type and major, campus location, and schedule. The only output variable is the time it takes each student to complete the degree.

Finally, we carried out combined descriptive and predictive analyses on the input-output dataset. The results will assess these variables, highlight key findings, offer interpretations, and draw conclusions based on the observed trends.

3.1 Descriptive Analytic

We provide a descriptive analysis derived from the primary findings regarding the relationship between input and output variables in the database. The results will be used to evaluate these variables, forming the final dataset for the predictive analysis.

3.2 Predictive Analytics

Six experiments have been prepared and programmed using the R language for the predictive analysis. Based on the database from the previous section, we designed six experiments aimed at detecting timely student graduation. Early detection of this issue within any academic cycle allows for intervention through remediation and mitigation processes, ensuring timely graduation.

The experiments will employ six supervised machine learning algorithms to generate predictive models: Logistic Regression, Support Vector Machine, Naive Bayes, Decision Tree, Random Forest, and K-Nearest Neighbors. The different models will be compared to identify the best-performing one.

3.3 Training and Testing

The database was divided into a training set and a test set. The training set, comprising 80% of the database, is used to train the model. The remaining 20% constitutes the test set, which will be used to evaluate the performance of the prediction model.

The database includes eleven input variables and one output variable (timely graduation). The output variable is categorized into two classes: Yes timely graduation (YES TG) or No timely graduation (NO TG). To assess the performance of the prediction models, confusion matrices will be employed.

3.4 K Fold Cross-Validation

To avoid overlap between training and test sets, we use k-fold cross-validation. In this method, the dataset is shuffled and split into k roughly equal folds. In each iteration, k-1 folds are used for training and the remaining fold for validation, rotating through all folds. After completing all k rounds, we compute accuracy and error for each model, then average these metrics to assess overall performance.

Once we obtain the average accuracy for a particular model, the same cross-validation process is applied to the other classification models. We then select the model exhibiting the highest average accuracy and lowest mean error.

In our study, we set k=5, meaning each experiment uses four folds for training and one for validation. Consequently, each algorithm undergoes five validation runs. With six algorithms under evaluation, this leads to a total of 30 experiments. This setup enhances generalization and reduces the risk of overfitting.

4 Results and Discussion

4.1 Descriptive Analytic

The rate of untimely graduation, considering all postgraduate programs at the university, including master's, doctoral, and medical specialties, reaches a value of 34.65%, equivalent to 5164 students. As seen in Fig. 1, this problem is exacerbated in doctoral programs with a rate of 64.29%, followed by master's programs with a rate of 34.32%, and finally medical specialties with a rate of 32.12

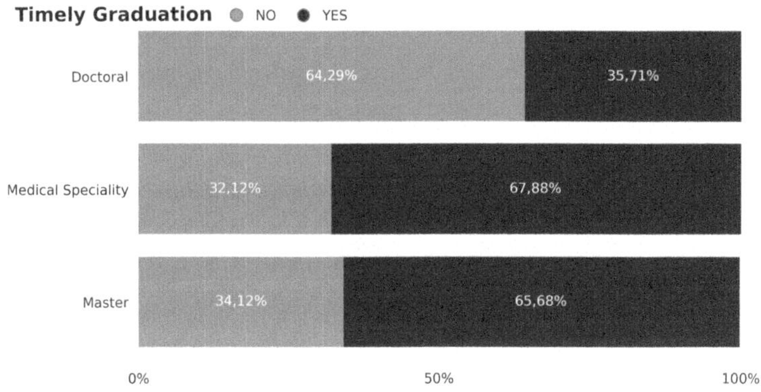

Fig. 1. Untimely Postgraduate Graduation University.

This 30/70 pattern is repeated in the analysis by campus, with Viña del Mar at 27.95%, Concepción at 28.64%, and Santiago at 36.63%. For the analysis of the schedule, a rate of 25.97% is observed for daytime programs, 29.63% for evening programs, and 44.5% for online programs. Regarding gender, a rate of 33.25v% is observed for men and 35.74% for women for untimely graduation.

As a preliminary conclusion, it is observed that special attention should be given to doctoral programs, programs at the Santiago campus, and online programs. Untimely graduation by gender is similar between women and men.

The Faculty of Engineering, as shown in Fig. 2, has an untimely graduation rate of 26.89%, 7.76 points below the university average. It also shows better performance compared to other faculties. Figure 3) focuses on the analysis of master's programs, where the untimely graduation rate is 26.89%, 7.43 points below the university's master's graduation average.

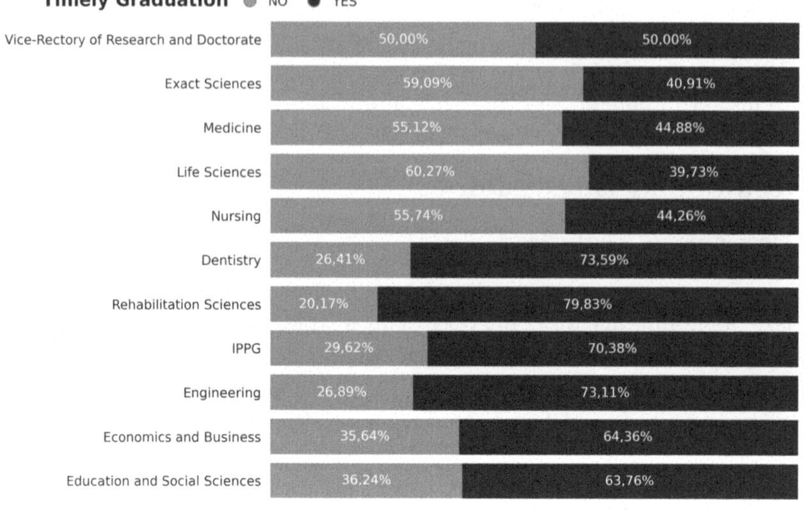

Fig. 2. Untimely Postgraduate Graduation by Faculty.

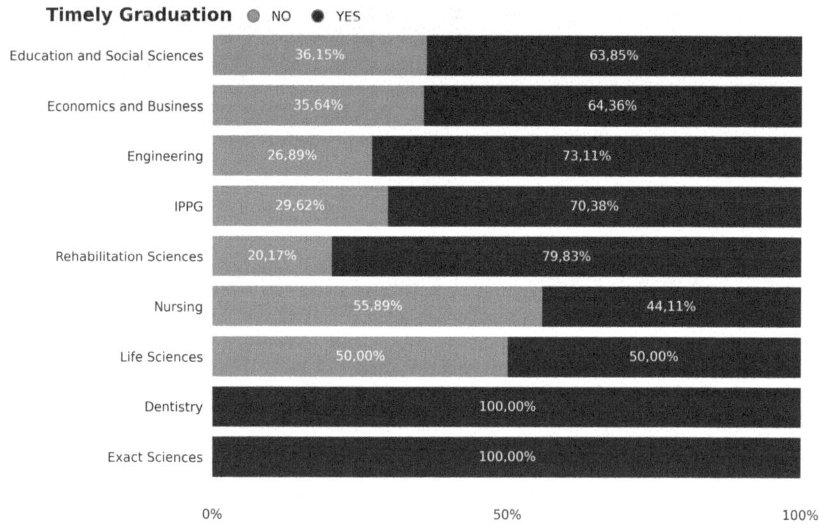

Fig. 3. Untimely Master's Graduation by Faculty.

The Faculty of Engineering does not administer doctoral programs but does offer academic and professional master's programs. The untimely graduation rate in the Faculty of Engineering by campus is Viña del Mar at 27.33%, Concepción at 11.61%, and Santiago at 28.54%. For the analysis of the schedule, a rate of 15.38% is observed for daytime programs, 25.78% for evening programs, and

29.03% for online programs. Regarding gender, a rate of 27.26% is observed for men and 24.56% for women. The low value observed in Concepción is due to the closure of master's programs' admissions. A low rate is also observed in the daytime schedule, explained by the fact that daytime programs require 100% dedication, while evening and online programs are for professionals who have jobs. In terms of gender, parity in results is observed again, but it is also noted that in this case, women have a lower rate compared to men, unlike the same analysis at the university level.

Delving into the problem, it is observed that professional master's programs need to be intervened to decrease untimely graduation rates.

4.2 Model Performance Comparison

Table 1 summarizes the evaluation results obtained through 5-fold cross-validation on the graduate student dataset. Reported metrics include the Area Under the ROC Curve (AUC), Accuracy, and Cohen's Kappa, which together provide a balanced assessment of classification performance.

Table 1. Cross-validation results of machine learning models for predicting timely graduation, using AUC, Accuracy, and Kappa.

Model	AUC	Accuracy	Kappa
Decision Tree	0.887 ± 0.011	0.922 ± 0.007	0.817 ± 0.018
GLM	0.977 ± 0.004	0.914 ± 0.009	0.803 ± 0.022
KNN	0.948 ± 0.032	0.935 ± 0.009	0.855 ± 0.021
Naïve Bayes	0.976 ± 0.004	0.891 ± 0.004	0.768 ± 0.008
Random Forest	0.987 ± 0.003	0.946 ± 0.006	0.880 ± 0.015
SVM	0.986 ± 0.003	0.938 ± 0.009	0.862 ± 0.019

The Random Forest (RF) model achieved the best overall performance, with the highest AUC (0.987 ± 0.003), accuracy (94.6% + 0.6%), and Kappa (0.880 ± 0.015). These results indicate not only strong discriminative capacity but also high reliability beyond chance, highlighting the robustness of this approach across folds. The Support Vector Machine (SVM) closely followed, confirming its role as a strong alternative, while KNN also performed competitively. In contrast, GLM and Naive Bayes obtained high AUC values but comparatively lower Kappa scores, suggesting reduced agreement. The Decision Tree achieved acceptable accuracy but lagged behind in stability, reflecting its greater susceptibility to overfitting.

Beyond numerical performance, the models shed light on key factors influencing graduation outcomes. Academic background variables—such as program length, adherence to expected timelines, and course completion rates—emerged as the strongest predictors. Institutional factors, including campus location and delivery modality, showed a moderate but consistent impact. Individual-level variables, such as gender, displayed smaller yet statistically significant effects.

The predictive analysis also revealed that students failing their first master's thesis course faced substantially delayed graduation, while those enrolled in full-time day programs showed lower rates of late completion (15.38%). Conversely, students in evening or part-time programs exhibited higher risks of non-completion, underscoring the importance of designing tailored academic support mechanisms. Finally, the positive association between engagement in thesis research and timely graduation reinforces the central role of program structure in shaping outcomes.

Taken together, these results not only confirm the superiority of ensemble-based models such as Random Forest for predicting timely graduation but also provide actionable insights into how institutional and academic factors can be leveraged to improve student success.

4.3 Limitations and Threats to Validity

First, the study does not explicitly model self-reported reasons for attrition; the features are system-native (LMS/SIS) proxies and therefore may omit relevant personal, financial, or health circumstances discussed in prior research [13–17]. Second, the sample comprises students who reached the thesis stage, which may introduce selection effects relative to earlier-leaver populations. Third, the analysis is single-institution and single-faculty, so institutional and program heterogeneity could limit external validity. While we mitigated overfitting with 5-fold cross-validation, true external validation across cohorts and campuses remains future work. Finally, measurement error may exist in LMS-derived indicators, as noted in the broader educational data mining literature [25].

4.4 Implications and Transferability to Other Contexts

Despite these limitations, the pipeline is designed to be portable. The feature schema (academic progress, course completion, program modality, and milestone attainment) can be mapped to other graduate programs and faculties with minimal engineering effort; only calibration (thresholds and class balance) and program-specific covariates would need tuning. Milestone-based monitoring is general across graduate education (e.g., proposal submission, preliminary examinations, thesis defense) [12], and on-time completion aligns with both individual and institutional benefits [10,11]. We outline a stepwise replication plan: (i) variable mapping to local LMS/SIS fields, (ii) re-training with stratified cross-validation by campus/program, (iii) prospective evaluation via early-alert workflows, and (iv) governance and bias monitoring (e.g., by gender and modality) to ensure equitable interventions.

5 Conclusions and Final Considerations

Late graduation is a concerning factor at the master's level. Understanding the risk factors faced by these students becomes increasingly relevant as it threatens their educational continuity. This study has presented a descriptive analysis addressing and explaining the delays in graduation observed in the master's degree student graduation process.

There are two major findings in this study that, when detected early, enable institutions to implement remedial measures such as targeted academic tutoring. First, students who fail the initial course associated with their master's thesis tend to experience significant graduation delays. Second, dedicating sufficient time to the thesis is positively correlated with on-time degree completion. These effects are most pronounced among students enrolled in evening programs, placing them at heightened risk of delayed graduation.

The key insight of this study is that the risk of failing to graduate on schedule can be identified early using variables obtained from the Learning Management System (LMS) and artificial intelligence–based prediction tools. Early detection enables institutions to intervene before students enter thesis courses, thereby improving on-time graduation rates and strengthening accreditation-relevant indicators.

Moreover, by leveraging predictive analytics and machine learning models, institutions can continuously monitor students' progress and provide timely interventions tailored to individual needs. Such proactive measures can be integrated into the academic support framework to ensure a more personalized approach to student retention and success.

In light of these findings, we recommend further research into the role of "student support," as it may be vital for enhancing student outcomes. We also suggest expanding the dataset to include demographic information, assessments of active learning methodologies, tutoring interactions, and other personal variables to enrich and robustly enhance the predictive model. Furthermore, understanding the socio-economic background and personal commitments of students can provide deeper insights into the challenges they face and help in formulating more effective support strategies.

Higher education institutions should use the study results to develop proactive initiatives that help reduce students' graduation time. This could include the establishment of comprehensive support systems encompassing academic advising, mental health services, and peer mentoring programs. By fostering an environment that addresses both academic and personal challenges, institutions can significantly enhance student outcomes and contribute to the overall improvement of educational quality and institutional reputation.

Addressing late graduation at the master's level requires a multifaceted approach that integrates early detection, personalized interventions, and continuous support. By implementing these strategies, educational institutions can not only improve graduation rates but also ensure that students have a more fulfilling and less stressful educational experience, ultimately leading to better preparedness for their professional careers.

Acknowledgments. The presentation of this article was funded by the Faculty of Engineering of Andrés Bello University.

References

1. Rizzolo, S., DeForest, A., DeCino, D., Strear, M., Landram, S.: Graduate student perceptions and experiences of professional development activities. J. Career Dev. **43**(3), 195–210 (2016)
2. Spaulding, L., Rockinson-Szapkiw, A.: Hearing their voices: factors doctoral candidates attribute to their persistence. Int. J. Dr. Stud. **7**, 99–219 (2012)
3. Council of Graduate Schools. Ph.D. completion and attrition: Analysis of baseline program data from the Ph.D. completion project. Washington, DC (2008)
4. Nettles, M., Millett, C.: Three magic letters-Getting to PhD. The Johns Hopkins University Press, Baltimore, MD (2006)
5. Carlhed, C.: Resistances to scientific knowledge production of comparative measurements of dropout and completion in European higher education. European Educ. Res. J. **16**(4), 386–406 (2017)
6. Soares, T., Fernandes, N., Nóbrega, M., Nicolella, A.: Factors associated with dropout rates in public secondary education in Minas Gerais. Educ. Pesqui. **4**(3), 757–772 (2015)
7. Friedenberg, J., Silverman, G.: Cognitive science: an introduction to the study of mind, 3rd edn. Sage, Los Angeles (2015)
8. DeClou, L.: Who stays and for how long: examining attrition in Canadian graduate programs. J. Higher Educ. **46**(4), 174–198 (2016)
9. Sullivan, W., Rosin, M.: New agenda for higher education: Shaping a life of the mind for practice. San Francisco: Jossey Bass.Normas APA 7Âł edición (2008)
10. Witteveen, D., Attewell, P.: Delayed time-to-degree and post-college earnings. Res. High. Educ. **62**, 230–257 (2021)
11. Moraga-Pumarino, A., Salvo-Garrido, S., Polanco-Levicán, K.: Profiles of university students who graduate on time: a cohort study from the chilean context. Behav. Sci. **13**(7), 582 (2023)
12. Young, M.E., Miller, M., Urban, C.: Tracking student progress through graduate programs. Discover Educ. **3**, 43 (2024)
13. Larsen, M.S. , Kornbeck, K.P., Kristensen, R., Larsen, M.R., Sommersel, H.B.: Dropout phenomena at universities: what is dropout? why does dropout occur? What can be done by the universities to prevent or reduce it?. Danish Clearinghouse for Educational Research (2013)
14. Behr, A., Giese, M., Teguim Kamdjou, H.D., Theune, K.: Dropping out of university: a literature review. Rev. Educ. **8**(3), 614–652 (2020)
15. Fernández-Mellizo, M.: Análisis del abandono de los estudiantes de grado en las universidades presenciales en España. Ministerio de Universidades (2022)
16. Constante-Amores, A., Fernández-Mellizo, M., Florenciano Martínez, E., Navarro Asencio, E.: Factores asociados al abandono universitario. Educación XX1, **24**(1), 17–44 (2021)
17. Quinn, J.: Dropout and completion in higher education in Europe among students from under-represented groups. An independent report authored for the NESET network of experts. Brussels, Belgium, European Commission (2013)
18. Publishing, E., E. Group, Limited, Reserved, P., Url, A., Uri, E.: Catalysing change in higher education for sustainable development: a review of professional development initiatives for university educators. Int. J. Sustainabil. Higher Educ. **18**(5), 798 (2017)
19. Shahiri, A., Husain, W., Rashid, N.: A review on predicting student's performance using data mining techniques. Procedia Comput. Sci. **72**, 414–422 (2015)

20. Alban, M., Mauricio, D., Mauricio, D.: National University of San Marcos, and Artificial Intelligence
21. Lykourentzou, I., Giannoukos, I., Nikolopoulos, V., Mpardis, G., Loumos, V.: Dropout prediction in e-learning courses through the combination of machine learning techniques. Comput. Educ. **53**, 950–965 (2009)
22. Burgos, C., Campanario, M., de la Peña, D., Lara, J., Lizcano, D., Martínez, M.: Data mining for modeling students' performance: a tutoring action plan to prevent academic dropout. Comput. Electric. Eng. **66**, 541–556 (2018)
23. Asif, R., Merceron, A., Ali, S., Haider, N.: Analyzing undergraduate students' performance using educational data mining. Comput. Educ. **113**, 177–194 (2017)
24. Rodriguez-Muniz, L.J., Bernardo, A.B., Esteban, M., Diaz, I.: Dropout and transfer paths: what are the risky profiles when analyzing university persistence with machine learning techniques?". PLoS ONE, **14**, (8), e0218796 (2019)
25. Romero, C., Ventura, S.: Educational data mining: a review of the state of the art. IEEE Trans. Syst. Man Cybern. Part C (Appl. Rev.) **40**(6), 601–618 (2010)
26. Frawley, W.J., Piatetsky-Shapiro, G., Matheus, C.J.: Knowledge discovery in databases: an overview. AI Mag. **13**(3), 57–70 (1992)
27. Kehm, B.M., Larsen, M.R., Sommersel, H.B.: Student dropout from universities in Europe: a review of empirical literature. Hungarian Educ. Res. J. **9**(2), 147–164 (2020)
28. Atchley, W., Wingenbach, G., Akers, C.: Comparison of course completion and student performance through online and traditional courses. Int. Rev. Res. Open Distributed Learn. **14**(4), 104–116 (2013)
29. Namoun, A., Alshanqiti, A.: Predicting student performance using data mining and learning analytics techniques: a systematic literature review. Appl. Sci., **11**(237) (2020)
30. Saa, A.A., Al-Emran, M., Shaalan, K.: Mining student information system records to predict students' academic performance. Adv. Intell. Syst. Comput. **921**, 229–239 (2020)
31. Akçapınar, G., Altun, A., Aşkar, P.: Using learning analytics to develop early-warning system for at-risk students. Int. J. Educ. Technol. Higher Educ., **16**(40) (2019)
32. Daud, A., Lytras, M.D., Aljohani, N.R., Abbas, F., Abbasi, R.A., Alowibdi, J.S.: Predicting student performance using advanced learning analytics. In: Proceedings of the 26th International World Wide Web Conference 2017, WWW 2017 Companion, pp. 415–421 (2017)
33. Martins, M.V., Tolledo, D., Machado, J., Baptista, L.M.T., Realinho, V.: Early prediction of student's performance in higher education: a case study. Adv. Intell. Syst. Comput. **1365**, 166–175 (2021)
34. Amare, M.Y., Simonova, S.: Global challenges of students' dropout: a prediction model development using machine learning algorithms on higher education datasets. In: Proceeding of the 21st International Scientific Conference Globalization and its Socio-Economic Consequences. SHS Web of Conferences, vol. 129, no. 09001 (2021)
35. Aulck, L., Velagapudi, N., Blumenstock, J., West, J.: Predicting student dropout in higher education. arXiv [Preprint], arXiv:1606.06364 (2016)
36. Heublein, U.: Student drop-out from German higher education institutions. Eur. J. Educ. **49**, 497–513 (2014)
37. Hsu, C.W., Yeh, C.C.: Mining the student dropout in higher education. J. Test. Eval. **48**, 4563–4575 (2019)

38. Olaya, D., Vásquez, J., Maldonado, S., Miranda, J., Verbeke, W.: Uplift modeling for preventing student dropout in higher education. Decision Support Syst., **134**(113320) (2020)
39. Garg, A., Lilhore, U., Ghosh, P., et al.: Machine learning-based model for prediction of student's performance in higher education. In: Proceedings of the 8th International Conference on Signal Processing and Integrated Networks, SPIN, Noida, pp. 162–168 (2021)
40. Dynarski, M., Clarke, L., Cobb, B., Finn, J., Rumberger, R., Smink, J.: Dropout prevention: a practice guide (NCEE 2008–4025). National Center for Education Evaluation and Regional Assistance (2008)
41. Saravanan, T., Nagadeepa, N., Mukunthan, B.: The effective learning approach to ICT-TPACK and prediction of the academic performance of students based on machine learning techniques. In: Sharma, H., Shrivastava, V., Kumari Bharti, K., Wang, L. (eds) Communication and Intelligent Systems. Lecture Notes in Networks and Systems, vol. 461. Singapore: Springer (2022)
42. Amare, M.Y., Simonova, S.: Global challenges of students' dropout: a prediction model development using machine learning algorithms on higher education datasets. In: Proceeding of the 21st International Scientific Conference Globalization and its Socio-Economic Consequences. SHS Web of Conferences, vol. 129, no. 09001 (2021)

Identifying Key Radiomic Features in Breast Cancer Images

Erika Sánchez-Femat[1], Carlos-Eric Galván-Tejada[1], Rafael Reveles-Martínez[1,2], Manuel-Alejandro Soto-Murillo[1], Jorge-Issac Galván-Tejada[1], Hamurabi Gamboa-Rosales[1], and José-María Celaya-Padilla[1(✉)]

[1] Unidad De Ingeniería Eléctrica, Universidad Autónoma De Zacatecas, Zacatecas, Zacatecas, Mexico
jose.celaya@uaz.edu.mx

[2] Unidad Profesional Interdisciplinaria De Ingeniería Campus Zacatecas, Instituto Politécnico Nacional, Zacatecas, Mexico

Abstract. This paper presents a comprehensive study on the identification of key radiomic features for breast cancer classification using mammographic images from the CBIS-DDSM dataset. Four independent experiments were conducted, corresponding to two lesion types—masses and calcifications—across two standard mammographic views: craniocaudal (CC) and mediolateral oblique (MLO). Radiomic features were extracted from segmented regions of interest and evaluated through a diverse feature selection pipeline, including Variance Thresholding, Correlation Filtering, SelectKBest, Recursive Feature Elimination (RFE), Lasso regularization, Boruta, and Permutation Feature Importance. The objective was to identify features consistently selected across methods, under the hypothesis that such consensus features may serve as robust radiomic biomarkers. The selected features were used to train Random Forest classifiers and evaluated through cross-validation using metrics such as accuracy, AUC, and F1-score. Among all configurations, the calcification-CC subgroup demonstrated the most robust and consistent predictive performance across all metrics, achieving an AUC of 0.90, F1-score of 0.81, and accuracy of 0.86. These findings highlight the utility of consensus-driven feature selection and support its role in future multimodal breast cancer diagnostic frameworks.

Keywords: Feature selection · Mammographic images · Radiomic biomarkers

1 Introduction

Breast cancer remains one of the leading causes of mortality among women worldwide, highlighting the importance of early detection and accurate diagnosis. Radiomics—the high-throughput extraction of quantitative features from medical images—has emerged as a promising approach to support clinical decision-making in oncology. By capturing subtle imaging characteristics that may elude

T. Guarda et al. (Eds.): ARTIIS 2025, CCIS 2789, pp. 445–460, 2026.
https://doi.org/10.1007/978-3-032-16758-3_34

the human eye, radiomic features offer an opportunity to enhance diagnostic accuracy, risk stratification, and treatment planning in breast imaging.

Despite its promise, the reproducibility and generalizability of radiomics-based studies are often limited by inconsistencies in data sources, segmentation quality, and feature selection methods. Many computer-aided detection (CADe) and diagnosis (CADx) systems have relied on private or unspecified subsets of public datasets, making their findings difficult to replicate or compare. The Curated Breast Imaging Subset of the Digital Database for Screening Mammography (CBIS-DDSM) addresses this limitation by providing a standardized and well-annotated public dataset that includes improved mass segmentations, pathology-confirmed labels, and curated metadata [7].

In this study, it was conducted a systematic evaluation of radiomic feature selection methods across four key configurations derived from CBIS-DDSM: masses and calcifications, each viewed in craniocaudal (CC) and mediolateral oblique (MLO) orientations. Radiomic features were extracted from lesion-specific ROIs using `PyRadiomics` and filtered through eight feature selection techniques, including filter-based, wrapper, and embedded methods. it was hypothesize that consensus-selected features—those chosen by multiple selection algorithms—represent stable and discriminative radiomic biomarkers.

Unlike previous works that focused on a single view or lesion type, this methodology enables a cross-comparative analysis of radiomic feature robustness and model performance across all standard mammographic views and lesion types. Classifiers trained with the selected features were evaluated using multiple metrics, including accuracy, AUC, F1-score, precision, and recall. Notably, the Calcification-CC subgroup exhibited the strongest performance across all metrics, with an AUC of 0.90 and an F1-score of 0.81.

These results demonstrate the value of ensemble feature selection for radiomic biomarker discovery and support the development of interpretable and reproducible pipelines for AI-assisted breast cancer diagnosis.

2 Related Work

Feature selection plays a pivotal role in the development of robust machine learning models for medical diagnosis, particularly in radiomics-based cancer detection tasks where high-dimensional data is common. Numerous studies have proposed and compared different approaches for selecting informative and non-redundant features to enhance predictive accuracy and model interpretability.

Comprehensive reviews by Saeys et al. [1] and Remeseiro et al. [2] highlight the classification of feature selection methods into three main categories: filter, wrapper, and embedded approaches. Filter methods rely on statistical measures to independently evaluate feature relevance, such as mutual information and correlation metrics, offering scalability and speed. However, they often overlook feature interactions and model dependencies. Wrapper methods evaluate subsets of features based on model performance, providing better accuracy at the cost of higher computational overhead. Embedded methods, such as those involving

Lasso regularization or tree-based models like Random Forests, integrate feature selection within the model training process, balancing efficiency and predictive power.

The importance of combining multiple feature selection techniques has been emphasized in biomedical studies [3,4]. For instance, Pudjihartono et al. [4] demonstrated how consensus-based selection from diverse methods can address the "curse of dimensionality" and enhance generalizability in disease risk prediction. This notion aligns with our approach, where we evaluated features repeatedly selected by multiple techniques—such as RFE, Lasso, Boruta, SelectKBest, and Permutation Importance—under the hypothesis that such overlap signals feature robustness and biological relevance.

In the context of radiomics, Alongi et al. [5] applied Pyradiomics for Alzheimer's disease prediction using PET/CT data, employing statistical parametric mapping and ML-based feature reduction. Their findings reinforce the predictive power of second-order texture features (e.g., GLCM and GLRLM), which are likewise found to be significant in breast cancer classification, as confirmed in our mass-CC experiments.

Several benchmark studies [1,6] have discussed the limitations of relying on single-method selection pipelines, noting that ensemble strategies help mitigate overfitting and enhance model reproducibility. This is particularly important in biomedical applications where interpretability and statistical stability are critical.

This study utilizes the CBIS-DDSM dataset [7], a curated version of the original DDSM that includes standardized train-test splits, accurate mass segmentation, and detailed metadata, allowing reproducible experimentation. The dataset's size and scope (891 mass cases and 753 calcification cases) make it one of the most comprehensive public resources for breast imaging research. Its structure supports experiments on craniocaudal (CC) and mediolateral oblique (MLO) views separately, which we leverage to evaluate the consistency of selected features across different anatomical perspectives.

In summary, the methodology builds upon prior work by integrating a diverse set of feature selection algorithms, employing robust statistical validation (e.g., ANOVA, t-test), and using a widely accepted, preprocessed mammographic dataset. This positions our study within the growing body of research advocating for ensemble feature selection and reproducibility in radiomics-based cancer diagnostics.

3 Methodology

3.1 Dataset Description

The Curated Breast Imaging Subset of the Digital Database for Screening Mammography (CBIS-DDSM) is a standardized and enhanced version of the original DDSM, developed to facilitate reproducible research in computer-aided detection (CADe) and diagnosis (CADx) of breast cancer. It includes decompressed mammography images with updated, more accurate lesion segmentations and detailed metadata curated by trained mammographers. The dataset comprises 753 cases of calcifications and 891 cases of masses, totaling approximately 3,288 mammogram images when considering the two standard views per case (craniocaudal and mediolateral oblique). These include 970 mass abnormalities and 1,045 calcification abnormalities, each labeled with pathology-confirmed diagnoses, BI-RADS descriptors, and other semantic features such as shape, margin, and density. To improve usability, images are provided in DICOM format, and binary masks are included for lesion analysis. By offering a well-annotated, publicly accessible dataset, CBIS-DDSM addresses the challenges of inconsistent evaluation protocols in breast imaging and provides a benchmark resource for developing and testing machine learning models in mammographic cancer detection [7]. A sample of mammogram images from the dataset is shown in Fig. 1.

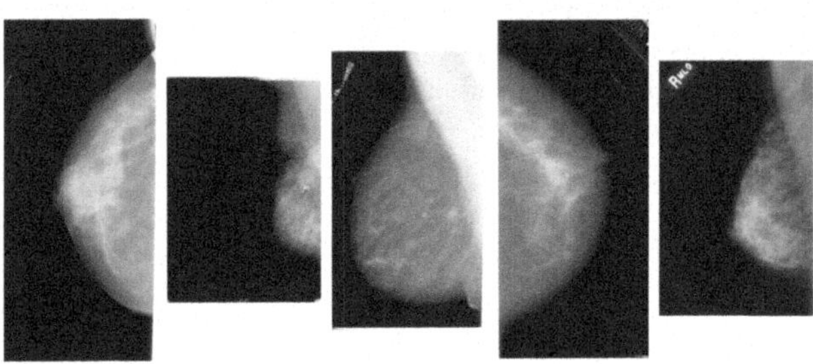

Fig. 1. Mammogram sample from the CBIS-DDSM dataset showing the CC and MLO views.

3.2 Image Preprocessing

To ensure the reliability and reproducibility of radiomic feature extraction, all mammography images underwent a rigorous preprocessing pipeline, designed to standardize image intensities, enforce spatial consistency, and isolate lesion-specific regions.

Image Loading and ROI Alignment. Images in DICOM format were parsed using the `pydicom` library and transformed into NumPy arrays. Each mammogram was associated with a corresponding binary mask that delineated the Region of Interest (ROI), extracted from the CBIS-DDSM annotations. ROI masks were validated for spatial alignment and dimension consistency with their respective images.

Intensity Normalization via Linear Contrast Stretching. To correct for inter-image intensity disparities caused by scanner variation and acquisition parameters, linear contrast stretching was applied. This process enhances contrast by remapping the pixel intensities $I(x, y)$ to a fixed range $[0, 255]$, based on specified percentiles:

$$I_{\text{norm}}(x, y) = 255 \times \frac{I(x, y) - I_{\min}}{I_{\max} - I_{\min}} \tag{1}$$

where $I_{\min}$ and $I_{\max}$ represent the 1st and 99th percentile values of the intensity histogram, respectively. Pixel values below $I_{\min}$ were clipped to 0, and values above $I_{\max}$ were clipped to 255.

Gaussian Smoothing. Gaussian filtering was evaluated as a denoising strategy. It smooths the image by convolving with a 2D Gaussian kernel $G(x, y)$:

$$G(x, y) = \frac{1}{2\pi\sigma^2} \exp\left(-\frac{x^2 + y^2}{2\sigma^2}\right) \tag{2}$$

The filtered image I_G is obtained via convolution:

$$I_G = I * G \tag{3}$$

This operation reduces high-frequency noise but was excluded from the radiomic pipeline to avoid altering texture features.

CLAHE. Contrast Limited Adaptive Histogram Equalization (CLAHE) was considered for local contrast enhancement. Unlike standard histogram equalization, CLAHE operates on image tiles and applies contrast enhancement limited by a clip threshold T to prevent noise overamplification. The enhanced intensity is computed as:

$$I_{\text{clahe}} = \text{CDF}_{\text{clipped}}(I(x, y)) \cdot (L - 1) \tag{4}$$

where $\text{CDF}_{\text{clipped}}$ is the cumulative distribution function of the clipped local histogram and L is the number of gray levels.

ROI Masking. Lesion-specific radiomic features were extracted exclusively from the annotated ROIs. Given an image I and its binary mask M, the masked image I_{ROI} is defined as:

$$I_{\text{ROI}}(x, y) = \begin{cases} I(x, y), & \text{if } M(x, y) = 1 \\ 0, & \text{otherwise} \end{cases} \tag{5}$$

This masking ensures that only lesion pixels contribute to the computed feature vectors.

Quality Control and Data Stratification. Only cases with complete image-mask pairs, valid metadata, and dimensionally consistent annotations were retained. Samples failing these criteria were excluded. The remaining data were stratified into four subsets: masses (CC), masses (MLO), calcifications (CC), and calcifications (MLO), enabling view- and lesion-specific modeling.

3.3 Feature Extraction

Radiomic feature extraction was performed using the `PyRadiomics` library, a robust and standardized tool for quantitative imaging analysis [8]. The extraction process begins with the preprocessing of the images, where each image is resampled to a uniform voxel spacing (typically 1×1 mm for 2D mammograms) to ensure spatial consistency. Intensity normalization is applied to reduce variability due to differences in acquisition settings. `PyRadiomics` then takes as input the medical image and its corresponding binary mask, which delineates the region of interest (ROI), and computes a comprehensive set of handcrafted features that quantitatively describe the image texture, intensity, and shape characteristics within that ROI.

By default, `PyRadiomics` extracts a total of **107 radiomic features**, which are grouped into **seven feature classes**. These classes capture different aspects of the image:

- **First Order Statistics** (18 features): summarize the distribution of intensity values within the ROI, including metrics such as mean, median, entropy, skewness, and energy.
- **Shape-based (2D)** (14 features): describe the geometric properties of the ROI, such as area, perimeter, elongation, and compactness.
- **Gray Level Co-occurrence Matrix (GLCM)** (24 features): evaluate how often pairs of pixels with specific values and in a specified spatial relationship occur in an image, providing measures such as contrast, correlation, homogeneity, and dissimilarity.
- **Gray Level Run Length Matrix (GLRLM)** (16 features): measure the length of consecutive runs of pixels with the same gray level value in a given direction.
- **Gray Level Size Zone Matrix (GLSZM)** (16 features): quantify the size of homogeneous zones (groups of connected pixels that share the same gray level) and the distribution of zone sizes and gray levels.
- **Gray Level Dependence Matrix (GLDM)** (14 features): measure the number of connected voxels within a distance that are dependent on the center voxel.
- **Neighboring Gray Tone Difference Matrix (NGTDM)** (5 features): describe the difference between a gray value and the average gray tone of its neighbors, capturing local texture variations.

The following table summarizes the categories and the number of features in each (Table 1):

Table 1. Radiomic feature categories and number of features extracted by `PyRadiomics`

Feature Class	Count	Description
First Order Statistics	18	Intensity distribution metrics (mean, entropy, kurtosis, etc.)
Shape-based (2D)	14	Geometric properties (area, perimeter, elongation, compactness, etc.)
GLCM	24	Gray level spatial relationships (contrast, correlation, homogeneity, etc.)
GLRLM	16	Length of homogeneous pixel runs in given directions
GLSZM	16	Size and intensity of homogeneous zones
GLDM	14	Dependence of gray levels in a local neighborhood
NGTDM	5	Difference between a pixel and average gray tone of its neighbors
Total	**107**	

3.4 Feature Selection Methods

To identify the most relevant radiomic features for breast cancer classification, we employed eight well-established feature selection techniques. Each method provides unique insights into feature importance by leveraging different statistical or model-based criteria. The feature selection process was conducted independently for each view (CC and MLO) and abnormality type (mass and calcification).

Recursive Feature Elimination (RFE). RFE iteratively removes the least important features based on the weights assigned by an estimator (Random Forest in our case). It fits the model multiple times and ranks features by their impact on model accuracy [9].

$$\text{Rank}(x_i) = \arg\min_{x_i \in X} \mathbb{E}[L(f(X_{-i}), y)] \tag{6}$$

where X_{-i} is the dataset without feature x_i, and L is the loss function.

Recursive Feature Elimination with Cross-Validation (RFECV). RFECV extends RFE by integrating cross validation to automatically select the optimal number of features. It avoids overfitting by identifying the point where adding more features does not improve model performance.

$$\text{Optimal number of features} = \arg\min_{k} \frac{1}{K} \sum_{j=1}^{K} L(f_k^{(j)}, X^{(j)}, y^{(j)}) \tag{7}$$

where $f_k^{(j)}$ is the model with k features trained on fold j, and K is the number of folds.

SelectKBest (with ANOVA F-Value). SelectKBest selects the top k features with the highest scores based on univariate statistical tests. We used the ANOVA F-test for this analysis [10].

$$F = \frac{\sum_{i=1}^{m} n_i(\bar{x}_i - \bar{x})^2/(m-1)}{\sum_{i=1}^{m}\sum_{j=1}^{n_i}(x_{ij} - \bar{x}_i)^2/(N-m)} \tag{8}$$

where m is the number of classes, n_i is the sample size of class i, and N is the total number of samples.

Permutation Feature Importance. This method measures the increase in prediction error when a feature's values are randomly shuffled. Features that significantly affect the model's predictions will yield a greater drop in accuracy [11].

$$I_{\text{perm}}(x_i) = \mathbb{E}_\pi\left[L(f(X), y) - L(f(X^{\pi(i)}), y)\right] \tag{9}$$

where $\pi(i)$ denotes a random permutation of feature x_i.

Variance Threshold. This filter method removes features with low variance across samples, assuming that low-variance features are less informative.

$$\text{Var}(x_i) = \frac{1}{n}\sum_{j=1}^{n}(x_{ij} - \bar{x}_i)^2 \tag{10}$$

Features with $\text{Var}(x_i) < \theta$ are discarded.

Correlation-Based Feature Selection. This method removes features that are highly correlated with others to reduce redundancy. The Pearson correlation coefficient is used for pairwise comparison.

$$\rho_{x_i,x_j} = \frac{\text{Cov}(x_i, x_j)}{\sigma_{x_i}\sigma_{x_j}} = \frac{\sum_{k=1}^{n}(x_{ik} - \bar{x}_i)(x_{jk} - \bar{x}_j)}{(n-1)\sigma_{x_i}\sigma_{x_j}} \tag{11}$$

Features with $|\rho| > \tau$ are filtered out.

Lasso (L1-Regularization). Lasso performs both feature selection and regularization. Features with zero coefficients are removed, promoting sparsity in the model [12].

$$\hat{\beta} = \arg\min_{\beta}\left\{\sum_{i=1}^{n}(y_i - \beta_0 - \sum_{j=1}^{p}\beta_j x_{ij})^2 + \lambda\sum_{j=1}^{p}|\beta_j|\right\} \tag{12}$$

Boruta. Boruta is a wrapper method built around Random Forest. It compares the importance of real features with that of random,"shadow" features to assess significance [13].

$$\text{If } Z_{x_i} > \max(Z_{\text{shadow}}) \Rightarrow x_i \text{ is important} \tag{13}$$

where Z_{x_i} is the importance score of the original feature and Z_{shadow} are scores from permuted features.

3.5 Classification

The classification stage was designed to evaluate the predictive capacity of the most relevant radiomic features selected by multiple feature selection strategies. We conducted independent classification experiments for each of the four configurations: masses in craniocaudal (CC) view, masses in mediolateral oblique (MLO) view, calcifications in CC view, and calcifications in MLO view.

Combinatorial Feature Consensus. Instead of relying on individual feature selection methods, we explored a consensus-based approach to construct multiple feature subsets. Specifically, we generated feature sets based on the number of methods that agreed on the importance of a given feature. That is, a feature was included in the final subset if it was selected by at least n methods, where n ranged from 1 to 8. This approach aimed to identify stable and robust features that consistently appear across diverse selection strategies.

Classification Workflow. For each of the eight cumulative feature sets, we trained a separate Random Forest classifier. This process was repeated for each of the four lesion/view configurations, resulting in a total of 32 classification models.

The classification pipeline consisted of the following steps:

1. **Data Standardization**: Features were standardized using z-score normalization based on the training set.
2. **Train/Test Split**: The official CBIS-DDSM partitions were preserved to ensure external validity.
3. **Cross-Validation**: A stratified 5-fold cross-validation was applied to the training set to optimize the Random Forest hyperparameters, including the number of estimators, tree depth, and minimum samples per leaf.
4. **Model Training**: Each model was trained using the full training set and the corresponding feature subset.
5. **Evaluation**: Performance was measured on the test set using five metrics: accuracy, sensitivity, specificity, F1-score, and AUC.

Selection of Top Models. To prioritize the most effective models, we ranked the 8 classifiers per configuration by their test accuracy and retained the top 10 classifiers globally (across all configurations) for detailed analysis and interpretation. This strategy allowed us to compare the predictive performance of feature subsets with varying levels of selection consensus, and to investigate whether highly stable features (i.e., selected by many methods) yield better classification performance.

4 Experimental Validation and Results

4.1 Distribution of Radiomic Features by Class

To investigate the discriminative potential of radiomic features extracted from mammographic images, we visualized the distribution of 12 features from the `firstorder` class across all four experimental configurations: masses and calcifications, each in craniocaudal (CC) and mediolateral oblique (MLO) views. These features were plotted separately for patients diagnosed with breast cancer and those without, using kernel density estimation (KDE) and overlaid histograms. In each chart, red curves represent cancer cases and blue curves represent non-cancer cases.

Figure 2 displays the feature distributions for each dataset. Several features exhibited distinct distributional patterns between cancer and non-cancer classes:

- **First-order features such as** `MeanAbsoluteDeviation`, `Energy`, `Kurtosis`, and `InterquartileRange` showed notable divergence between the two classes in most datasets-particularly Calcification-CC-suggesting strong potential for use in classification.
- **Mass datasets** (CC and MLO) showed overlapping but slightly shifted distributions, indicating moderate discriminative potential that may require combination with texture-based features for better separation.
- **Calcification-CC** displayed the most pronounced separation between cancer and non-cancer groups, reinforcing its top-performing status in our classification experiments.
- **Some features like** `Mean` and `Median` demonstrated overlapping distributions across all views, indicating limited standalone utility.

These findings validate the presence of statistically meaningful differences in feature distributions between benign and malignant lesions. They support the need for feature selection techniques and multivariate modeling to harness complementary information from multiple features and improve classification performance.

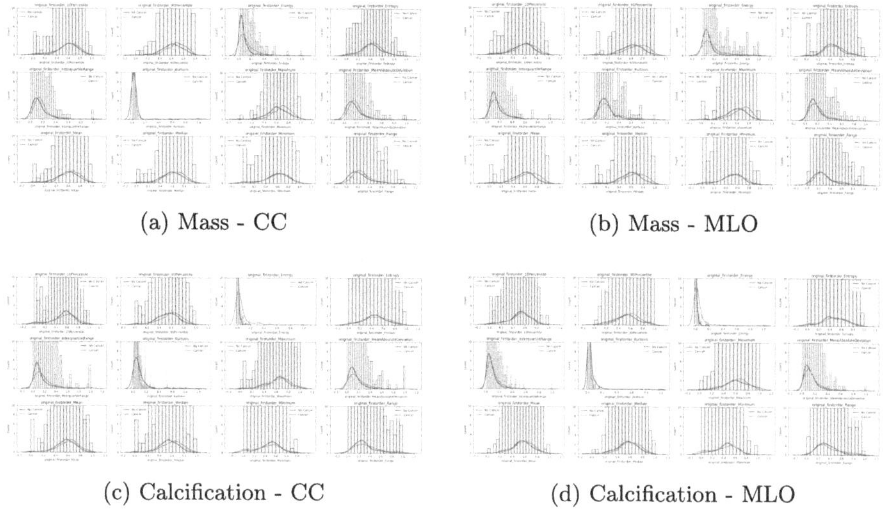

Fig. 2. Distribution of selected first-order radiomic features across the four lesion/view configurations.

4.2 Feature Importance by Method Agreement

To assess the robustness and relevance of selected radiomic features, we examined the agreement across eight different feature selection techniques. Figure 3 presents binary heatmaps for each of the four lesion/view configurations: masses and calcifications, each in CC and MLO views. In each heatmap, rows correspond to selection methods and columns to individual radiomic features. A black square indicates that the method selected the corresponding feature.

This visualization highlights both consensus and divergence among selection strategies:

- **Calcification-CC** exhibits the strongest agreement across methods, particularly in texture-related features such as `GLCM_ClusterProminence` and `GLSZM_ZoneEntropy`, reinforcing the superior classification performance observed for this dataset.
- **Mass-CC** shows moderate consensus, especially among first-order and GLRLM features, suggesting a stable but slightly less discriminative feature space.
- **Mass-MLO** and **Calcification-MLO** display more scattered patterns of agreement, with fewer features consistently selected by multiple methods, indicating potential sensitivity to imaging view and increased feature variability.

Boruta, RFECV, and Correlation Filtering tended to select broader sets of features, while Lasso and Permutation Importance were more conservative. The convergence of different selection methods on certain features-especially when spanning filter, wrapper, and embedded approaches-suggests that these features are more likely to generalize well and avoid overfitting. Conversely, features selected by only one method may be less reliable and should be interpreted cautiously in downstream modeling.

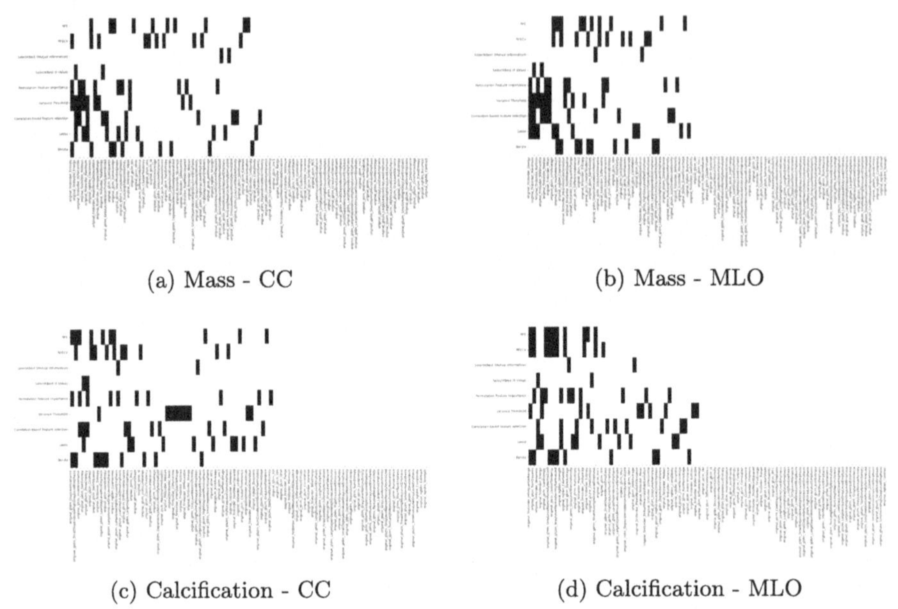

(a) Mass - CC

(b) Mass - MLO

(c) Calcification - CC

(d) Calcification - MLO

Fig. 3. Binary heatmaps of feature selection agreement across methods for each configuration. Black squares indicate that the feature was selected by the corresponding method.

4.3 Top Performing Classification Models

To validate the discriminative power of the selected radiomic features, we trained Random Forest classifiers using the top-ranked feature subsets for each of the four experimental configurations: Mass-CC, Mass-MLO, Calcification-CC, and Calcification-MLO. Each model used the most effective combination of feature selection methods based on cross-validation performance.

Figure 4 shows the ROC curves and confusion matrices for the best-performing model in each configuration. These visualizations allow a direct comparison of classifier behavior across lesion types and mammographic views.

- **Calcification - CC:** This configuration achieved the highest overall performance, with an AUC of 0.90, F1-score of 0.81, accuracy of 0.86, and balanced sensitivity (recall = 0.75) and precision (0.87). Features were selected using `SelectKBest (Mutual Information + F-Value)`, `Variance Threshold`, `Lasso`, and `Boruta`.

- **Calcification - MLO:** The second-best result came from this configuration, achieving an AUC of 0.86 and accuracy of 0.74 using features selected by `SelectKBest (Mutual Information)`, `Permutation Importance`, `Variance Threshold`, and `Correlation-based feature selection`. The model showed moderate recall (0.62) and precision (0.62).
- **Mass - CC:** This model performed moderately well, with an AUC of 0.73 and F1-score of 0.69. The best features came from `Variance Threshold`, capturing mostly first-order and texture metrics.
- **Mass - MLO:** This configuration yielded an AUC of 0.80 and F1-score of 0.74 using features selected by `SelectKBest (F-Value)`. The model achieved the highest recall among mass cases (0.76), making it sensitive to malignant detections.

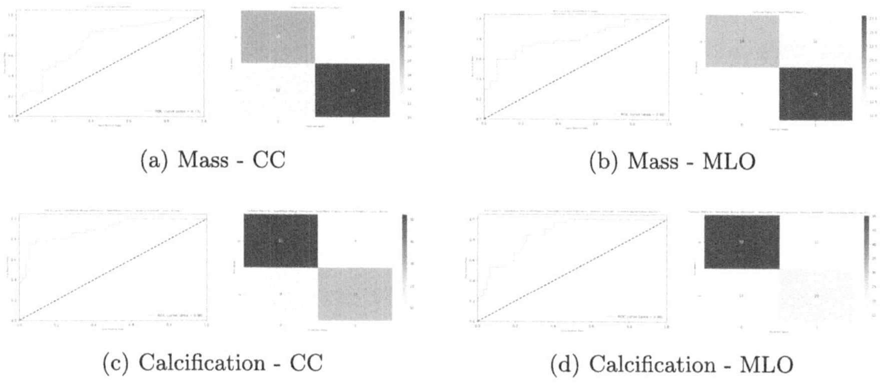

(a) Mass - CC (b) Mass - MLO

(c) Calcification - CC (d) Calcification - MLO

Fig. 4. ROC curves and confusion matrices for the best-performing model in each lesion/view configuration.

Table 2. Performance metrics for the best model in each lesion/view configuration.

Configuration	Accuracy	F1 Score	Precision	Recall	AUC
Calcification - CC	0.86	0.81	0.87	0.75	0.90
Calcification - MLO	0.74	0.62	0.62	0.62	0.86
Mass - CC	0.66	0.69	0.71	0.68	0.73
Mass - MLO	0.70	0.74	0.72	0.76	0.80

Table 2 summarizes the classification performance of the top model for each dataset. Notably, the Calcification-CC model outperformed the rest, with an

AUC of 0.90 and a balanced combination of precision (0.87) and recall (0.75), confirming its robustness and clinical potential.

Although the Calcification-MLO model achieved a similar AUC (0.86), its F1 score and recall were lower, indicating a less favorable trade-off between sensitivity and precision. Among mass datasets, Mass-MLO slightly outperformed Mass-CC in AUC and F1, yet both models lagged behind the calcification-based configurations in all key metrics.

These results reinforce that view and lesion type significantly impact radiomic feature stability and classifier performance, supporting the use of per-configuration optimization in diagnostic model design.

4.4 Cross-Validation and Statistical Comparison of Top Models

To ensure the generalizability of the best-performing classifiers, we conducted stratified 10-fold cross-validation for the top models of each of the four lesion/view configurations. Table 3 summarizes the average cross-validation metrics for these models.

Table 3. Cross-validation performance metrics for the top model in each configuration.

Configuration	Accuracy	F1 Score	Precision	Recall	AUC
Calcification - CC	0.741	0.599	0.682	0.555	0.812
Calcification - MLO	0.728	0.601	0.647	0.568	0.814
Mass - CC	0.642	0.659	0.637	0.685	0.686
Mass - MLO	0.509	0.527	0.534	0.531	0.556

The results confirm that both calcification configurations outperform the mass-based models during cross-validation. Specifically, the **Calcification-CC** and **Calcification-MLO** models achieved AUCs above 0.81, while maintaining balanced precision and recall. The **Mass-MLO** configuration yielded the weakest results, with an average accuracy of 0.509 and AUC of 0.556, highlighting its lower generalization capability.

To determine whether the performance differences were statistically significant, we conducted pairwise post-hoc t-tests comparing the accuracy and AUC scores of the top model in each configuration against all other evaluated models (n=10) per dataset.

Across all configurations, none of the post-hoc tests for AUC or accuracy reached statistical significance at the $p < 0.05$ threshold. While some comparisons approached marginal significance (e.g., Calcification-CC vs. Model 10, $p = 0.100$; Mass-CC vs. Model 10, $p = 0.091$), the results overall suggest that performance differences among feature subsets, though numerically distinct, may be partly influenced by sample variance.

These findings reinforce the importance of rigorous cross-validation and statistical testing in radiomic model evaluation. Although models like Calcification-CC showed superior metrics, formal significance testing helps clarify that no single feature subset was universally dominant under all metrics. The convergence of good performance and inter-method feature agreement remains a strong indicator of robustness.

5 Discussion

The results demonstrate that radiomic features from the CBIS-DDSM dataset provide discriminative information for classifying breast lesions. Among the four lesion/view configurations, Calcification-CC achieved the highest performance across all metrics and exhibited the strongest agreement among feature selection methods, suggesting robust biomarker potential.

In contrast, Mass-MLO showed the weakest performance, indicating lower feature stability or reduced lesion visibility in that view. Simpler feature selection strategies, particularly combinations of `SelectKBest (Mutual Information)` and `F-Value`, consistently outperformed more complex, multi-method pipelines. Statistical tests confirmed that additional selection complexity did not significantly improve performance.

Texture-based features, especially from GLCM and first-order classes, were frequently selected and contributed most to model accuracy. These findings underscore the relevance of tailoring feature selection to specific lesion types and imaging views.

Importantly, the use of interpretable and lightweight radiomic models makes this approach suitable for integration into clinical decision support systems. The methodology is computationally efficient and based on public data and open-source tools, promoting reproducibility and sustainability - two key aspects for translational impact in real-world diagnostic workflows.

6 Conclusion

This study demonstrates that consensus-driven radiomic feature selection with Random Forest classifiers can achieve performance competitive while addressing critical limitations that make deep learning unsuitable for clinical breast cancer diagnosis.

The decision to focus on machine learning approaches rather than deep learning was driven by fundamental clinical requirements that deep learning cannot satisfy:

1. Clinical Interpretability Imperative: Medical diagnosis requires explainable decisions where experts can understand and validate the reasoning. Deep learning's "black box" nature fundamentally conflicts with clinical practice standards and regulatory requirements for medical AI systems.

2. Clinical Impact: These findings support the development of interpretable, view-specific radiomic models that can be readily integrated into clinical decision support systems. The approach's reliance on lightweight computation and mathematically interpretable features addresses the key barriers that have prevented widespread clinical adoption of AI in medical imaging.

References

1. Saeys, Y., Inza, I., Larrañaga, P.: A review of feature selection techniques in bioinformatics. Bioinformatics **23**(19), 2507–2517 (2007)
2. Remeseiro, B., Bolón-Canedo, V.: A review of feature selection methods in medical applications. Comput. Struct. Biotechnol. J. **17**, 1437–1451 (2019)
3. Drotár, P., Gazda, J., Smékal, Z.: An experimental comparison of feature selection methods on two-class biomedical datasets. Comput. Biol. Med. **66**, 1–10 (2015)
4. Pudjihartono, N., Fadason, T., Kempa-Liehr, A.W., O'Sullivan, J.M.: A review of feature selection methods for machine learning-based disease risk prediction. Front. Bioinform. **2**, 927312 (2022). https://doi.org/10.3389/fbinf.2022.927312
5. Alongi, P., et al.: Radiomics analysis of brain [^{18}F]FDG PET/CT to predict Alzheimer's disease in patients with amyloid positivity. Diagnostics **12**(3), 738 (2022)
6. Chandrashekar, G., Sahin, F.: A survey on feature selection methods. Comput. & Elect. Eng. **40**(1), 16–28 (2014)
7. Lee, R.S., Gimenez, F., Hoogi, A., Miyake, K.K., Gorovoy, M., Rubin, D.L.: A curated mammography data set for use in computer-aided detection and diagnosis research. Scientific Data **4**, 170177 (2017). https://doi.org/10.1038/sdata.2017.177
8. van Griethuysen, J.J.M., Fedorov, A., Parmar, C., et al.: Computational radiomics system to decode the radiographic phenotype. Can. Res. **77**(21), e104–e107 (2017). https://doi.org/10.1158/0008-5472.CAN-17-0339
9. Guyon, I., Weston, J., Barnhill, S., Vapnik, V.: Gene selection for cancer classification using support vector machines. Mach. Learn. **46**, 389–422 (2002)
10. De, A., Bhattacharya, R., Das, S., Chattopadhyay, S.: Feature selection techniques for classification and clustering. In: International Conference on Computational Intelligence and Networks (2014)
11. Breiman, L.: Random forests. Mach. Learn. **45**(1), 5–32 (2001)
12. Tibshirani, R.: Regression shrinkage and selection via the lasso. J. Royal Statis. Soc.: Ser. B **58**(1), 267–288 (1996)
13. Kursa, M.B., Rudnicki, W.R.: Feature selection with the Boruta package. J. Statis. Softw. **36**(11), 1–13 (2010)

Data Mining Patterns in Virtual Classrooms in Online Higher Education

Kevin Pacheco-Mera[1(✉)], Leticia Vaca-Cárdenas[2], and Ricardo Ordoñez-Ávila[2]

[1] Maestría en Ciencia de Datos y Máquinas de Aprendizaje, Facultad de Posgrado, Universidad Técnica de Manabí, Portoviejo, Manabí, Ecuador
kpacheco7075@utm.edu.ec

[2] Departamento de Sistemas Computacionales, Facultad de Ciencias Informáticas, Universidad Técnica de Manabí, Portoviejo, Manabí, Ecuador

Abstract. Virtual classrooms have become essential in higher education due to their flexibility and accessibility, but they also present challenges in monitoring student engagement and predicting academic success. This study proposes a hybrid data mining framework to analyze student behavior by integrating clustering, association rule mining, and classification techniques. We analyzed over four million interaction records from the Moodle platform of the online Psychology program at the Technical University of Manabí. After data cleaning and transformation, clustering revealed four distinct behavioral profiles, from highly engaged and high-performing students to those with low interaction and academic risk. Association rules identified key activities linked to better performance, such as forum participation and timely assignment submissions. Classification models, particularly Random Forest and Support Vector Machines (SVM), achieved up to 91% accuracy in predicting student performance. The proposed framework allows early detection of at-risk students and offers valuable insights into behavioral patterns in virtual learning environments. These results contribute to the development of effective, data-driven strategies aimed at improving student retention and academic outcomes in online education.

Keywords: Educational Data Mining · Virtual Classrooms · Predictive Models · Clustering · Association Rules

1 Introduction

Online education in higher education has brought with it significant challenges in understanding and improving student engagement in the classroom. Unlike face-to-face environments, virtual environments make it difficult to detect early signs of disinterest or academic difficulties due to the absence of immediate physical interactions [1, 2].To address this limitation, the use of Learning Management Systems (LMS) has intensified, allowing for the collection of large volumes of data on student behavior, such as the number of visits, session duration, interaction with resources, and assignment submission [3, 4].

T. Guarda et al. (Eds.): ARTIIS 2025, CCIS 2789, pp. 461–474, 2026.
https://doi.org/10.1007/978-3-032-16758-3_35

These records, if properly analyzed, offer a valuable opportunity to identify patterns of behavior and make informed decisions that improve educational processes. In this context, Educational Data Mining (EDM) emerges as a discipline that applies computational, statistical, and machine learning techniques to analyze data generated in digital learning environments [1, 5]. Its objective is to discover hidden patterns that improve pedagogical decision-making and academic management [6].

Among the most widely used techniques in EDM are clustering, association rules, and classification models. Clustering, such as the k-means algorithm, has been used to identify student profiles, such as those who are highly active, moderately active, or inactive [7, 32, 33]. Association rules allow frequent relationships between events or behaviors to be discovered, for example, the correlation between the number of resources consulted and academic performance [8, 9]. On the other hand, classification models—such as decision trees, logistic regression, support vector machines (SVM), KNN, and random forest—have been used to predict outcomes such as academic success or failure [10–12].

In recent years, more sophisticated approaches have been developed that integrate techniques such as deep learning for knowledge tracking [16], hybrid models for real-time monitoring [18], and recommendation systems that adjust the student's trajectory according to their progress [17]. A/B testing and causal inference strategies assisted by auxiliary data have also been proposed to improve experimental interpretation in digital learning platforms [19]. In addition, innovative contexts such as the metaverse are being explored to design immersive and personalized experiences in virtual education [13, 14].

Most of these advances have been implemented in institutions in regions of the global north—such as North America, Europe, and East Asia—where there are greater technical, economic, and organizational capacities to adopt complex educational analytics systems. However, in the Latin American context, particularly in countries such as Ecuador, the implementation of these technologies still faces significant barriers, such as infrastructure limitations, limited access to actionable data, and a weak culture of evidence-based decision-making [4, 15].

In addition, many studies apply these techniques in isolation, without integrating them to obtain a more complete view of student behavior. This lack of methodological coordination limits the potential of EDM to significantly improve teaching and learning processes [20, 21].

To address these limitations, the present study proposes a hybrid educational data mining framework that integrates clustering, association rules, and classification models to achieve three specific goals: (1) to identify behavioral profiles among students based on their activity patterns; (2) to discover frequent behavior patterns linked to academic performance; and (3) to build predictive models capable of anticipating academic success. The research was conducted at the Technical University of Manabí (Ecuador), with an emphasis on generating insights that are both interpretable and applicable to teaching staff and academic decision-makers, thereby promoting adaptive and evidence-based pedagogical practices.

2 Methodology

This study implements a structured data mining approach to analyze student participation in virtual environments. The proposed framework combines supervised and unsupervised learning techniques to extract behavior patterns, identify risk profiles, and generate accurate predictions of academic performance. The methodological phases include: data collection and preprocessing, clustering segmentation, association rule extraction, and predictive modeling using classification algorithms.

2.1 Data Collection and Preprocessing

A real dataset extracted from the Moodle LMS system corresponding to the online Psychology degree program at the Universidad Técnica de Manabí was used. The dataset comprises approximately 4,100,000 records generated by 1,939 students during one academic semester.

The interactions collected are shown in Table 1:

Table 1. Interactions extracted from the online activity log

Type of interaction	Description
Login	Number of times the student accesses the platform
Access to resources	Viewing of materials such as PDFs, videos, or external links
Participation in forums	Includes posts, replies, and views of discussion threads
Assignment submission	Recorded submissions of assigned activities
Quiz attempts	Number of attempts to complete online assessments
Final grades	Student's final grade in each subject

The Preprocessing Steps Included:

- Treatment of missing values by imputation using median values for categorical variables [22].
- Normalization of continuous variables (e.g., session duration, number of accesses) using min-max scaling.
- Generation of aggregate variables (count of activities per student).
- Sequential pattern mining (SPM) to capture temporal interaction dynamics and study strategies [23].
- Binary coding of performance: 1 = academic success (grade ≥ 70), 0 = risk of failure.

A moderate imbalance was identified in the target classes: 63% of students passed and 37% were at risk. This imbalance was subsequently addressed using techniques such as SMOTE and class weight adjustment in the classification models.

2.2 Clustering Segmentation

The K-Means algorithm was applied to the key interaction variables, using Euclidean distance as a similarity metric. The optimal value of k was determined using the elbow and silhouette index methods, both of which suggested four distinct groups. This segmentation allows for the identification of behavioral profiles that guide adaptive pedagogical decisions. A detailed interpretation of these clusters is presented in the results section [24, 25].

2.3 Association Rules Extraction

The Apriori algorithm was used to discover frequent patterns between student activities and academic success. Previously, the interaction variables were binarized using a simple threshold (value 1 if the activity was present, 0 otherwise), generating a transactional representation in which each student corresponds to a transaction composed of activities performed. On this transformed basis, the support, confidence, and lift metrics were calculated, which allowed us to identify combinations of behaviors with a strong correlation with academic performance. These rules provide interpretable knowledge for teachers about effective practices to promote [9, 22].

2.4 Predictive Modeling Using Classification Algorithms

Five classification models were trained to predict students' academic performance, defined as a binary variable: "academic success" if the final grade exceeds 70 points, and "at risk" otherwise. The algorithms used were: Logistic Regression, Decision Trees, Random Forest, K-Nearest Neighbors (KNN), and Support Vector Machines (SVM). The choice of these models is based on studies that highlight their performance in educational contexts and their balance between accuracy and interpretability [11, 17, 26, 27].

The models were validated using 10-fold stratified cross-validation and evaluated using standard metrics: accuracy, precision, recall, F1-score, and ROC-AUC. The formulas applied are described below:

1. Accuracy:

$$\frac{(TP + TN)}{(TP + TN + FP + FN)}$$

2. Precision:

$$\frac{TP}{(TP + FP)}$$

3. Recall:

$$\frac{\mathrm{TP}}{(TP + FN)}$$

4. F1-score:

$$2\frac{(Precision)(Recall)}{(Precision + Recall)}$$

5. ROC-AUC:

   Represents the area under the ROC curve. Evaluates the model's ability to discriminate between positive and negative classes at different decision thresholds.

To mitigate the imbalance of classes in the target variable, oversampling techniques with SMOTE and class weight adjustment were applied.

2.5 Development Environment and Tools

The processing was implemented in Python 3.11 using libraries such as Pandas 2.2.3, NumPy 2.2.5, Scikit-learn 1.6.1, and imbalanced-learn 0.13.0, supported by custom scripts to handle large volumes of records.

2.6 Integration and Justification of the Framework

The proposed pipeline is structured on three complementary levels:

- Clustering allows us to understand the aggregate behavior of students.
- Association rules reveal latent patterns between activities and performance.
- Classification enables early predictions of academic risk (Fig. 1).

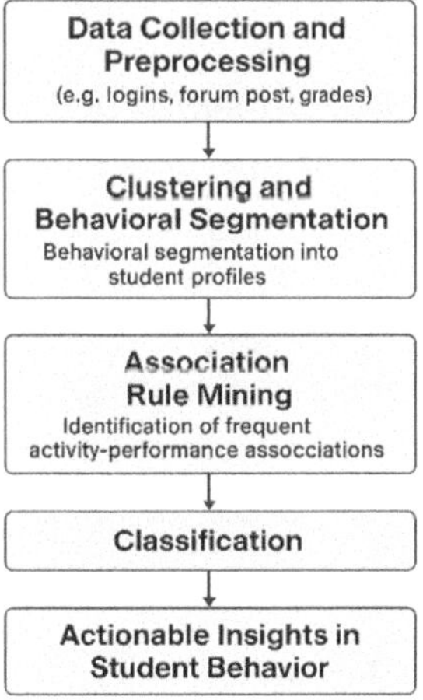

Fig. 1. Data mining pipeline

This integrated approach responds to recent calls in the literature for educational analytics systems that are interpretable, actionable, and contextualized [13, 18, 28].

2.7 Ethical and Privacy Considerations

All student data used in this study were fully anonymized prior to analysis, ensuring that no personally identifiable information (PII) was retained or processed. Data collection and usage complied with institutional policies and ethical standards for educational research. The analysis was conducted solely for academic purposes and posed no risk to participants' privacy or academic standing.

3 Results and Discussion

3.1 Profile Segmentation Through Clustering

Segmentation was performed to discover student behavior profiles based on variables such as visits to resources, assignment submissions, forum participation, and questionnaire interactions using the K-Means algorithm. The optimal number of clusters was selected using the silhouette method, which showed a significant inflection at $k = 4$.

Characterization of the Groups

The segmentation revealed four groups of student behavior, identified after normalizing the data using StandardScaler to ensure all features contributed equally to the analysis. Dimensionality reduction was then performed using PCA, which retained 88.86% of the variance, to visualize the clusters effectively (Fig. 2). The average characteristics per group are summarized in Table 2.

Table 2. Mean Values of Student Activity and Performance by Cluster

Cluster	Visits to resources	Task submissions	Forum participation	Questionnaire interactions	Final grade
0	5.61	24.61	0.81	3.01	24.05
1	15.47	79.30	1.17	9.92	83.30
2	32.32	154.55	1.61	11.30	87.01
3	19.28	83.72	3.15	11.10	86.10

Description of Profiles

- **Cluster 0 – low engagement, low performance:** This group has the lowest levels in all activity metrics, which is reflected in significantly lower academic performance. It represents the classic profile of a student at risk.
- **Cluster 1 – Moderate participation, high performance:** Although their activity is not the highest, especially in forum participation, these students achieve remarkable academic performance, which may indicate effective time management or more autonomous learning.

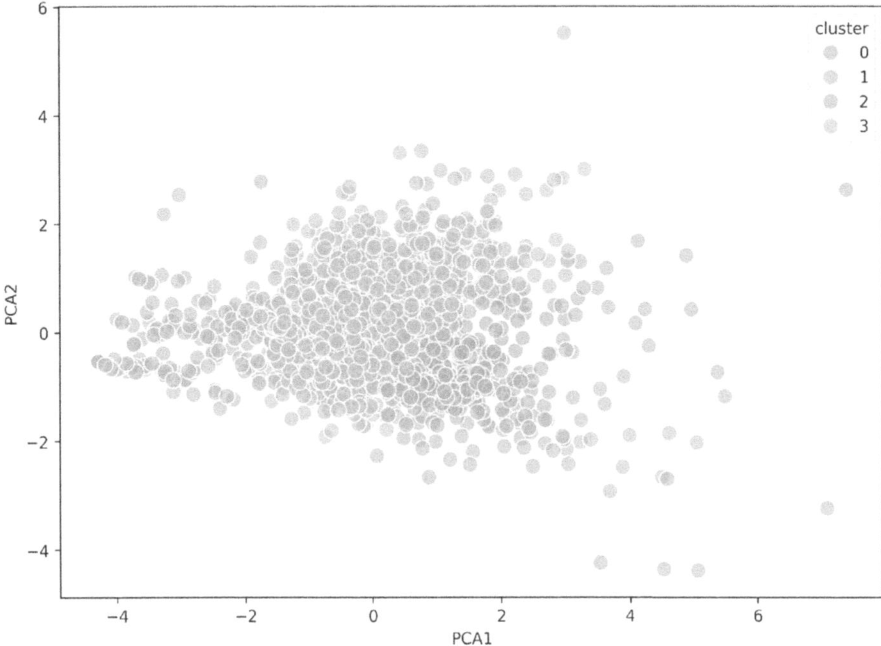

Fig. 2. K-means PCA Visualization

- **Cluster 2 – Highly engaged, excellent performance:** This group shows the highest level of interaction with the platform. Their academic performance is the highest of the group, suggesting a strong correlation between digital engagement and academic success.
- **Cluster 3 – Active participation in fórums, high performance:** Despite having a lower volume of visits and tasks than cluster 2, this group compensates with greater participation in forums, which seems to correlate with equally high performance.

These profiles allow for the design of differentiated intervention strategies, in line with previous work on segmentation in EDM [24, 29].

3.2 Pattern Extraction Through Association Rules

The Apriori algorithm was applied to discover patterns between student activities and academic performance (considered "good" if the grade was ≥ 70). With appropriate support and confidence thresholds, 13 relevant rules were obtained (Table 3).

Among the most relevant rules with a single antecedent is forum_participation → good_performance, which had a confidence of 0.92 and a lift of 1.06. This suggests that students who actively participate in forums have a 92% chance of achieving good performance—6% more than expected by chance. Notably, this group also had a high average final grade of 84.2, one of the best across all rules.

Another strong single-antecedent rule is quiz_interactions → good_performance, with a confidence of 0.89 and a lift of 1.02. Although its lift is lower, it still shows

Table 3. Association Rules Between Student Activities and Performance

Antecedent	Consequent(s)	Support	Confidence	Lift	Average Final Grade
quiz_interactions, resources_visits	good_performance	0.4215	0.9313	1.066	84.81
quiz_interactions, forum_participation	good_performance	0.4264	0.9303	1.065	84.76
assignment_submissions, forum_participation, resources_visits	good_performance	0.4215	0.9270	1.061	84.46
forum_participation, resouces_visits	good_performance	0.4215	0.9267	1.061	84.44
assignment_submissions, forum_participation	good_performance	0.4264	0.9246	1.058	84.30
forum_participation	good_performance	0.4264	0.9238	1.058	84.23
assignment_submissions, quiz_interactions, rcsource_visists	good_performance	0.8570	0.8906	1.020	82.56
quiz_interactions,resource_visits	good_performance	0.8570	0.8904	1.019	82.54
assignment_submissions, quiz interactions	good_performance	0.8593	0.8893	1.018	82.47
quiz_interactions	good_performance	0.8693	0.8888	1.017	82.42
assignment_submissions, resource_visits	good_performance	0.8606	0.8819	1.009	81.86
resource_visits	good_performance	0.8606	0.8814	1.009	81.81
assignment_submissions	good_performance	0.8736	0.8760	1.003	81.38

that quiz activity is positively associated with academic success, and students with this behavior had an average grade of 82.4.

Among the rules with combined antecedents, quiz_interactions + forum_participation + resource_access → good_performance stands out with the highest confidence (0.93) and highest lift (1.07). This indicates a robust association between broad engagement and good performance. Students matching this pattern had an average grade of 84.8, the highest in the set.

Additionally, rules such as forum_participation + resource_access → good_performance and assignments + forum_participation → good_performance also show high confidence (92% +) and lift (≈1.06), reinforcing the role of forum engagement as a consistent indicator of strong academic outcomes.

These results are in line with previous findings [34–36], which show that the combination of task engagement and interaction with resources strongly predicts positive outcomes.

3.3 Evaluation of Predictive Models to Classify Academic Performance

The objective was to predict students' final academic performance, with grades equal to or higher than 70 considered "academic success" and those below 70 considered "academic risk".

Given that the original distribution of the target variable was significantly unbalanced—with a majority of students in the success category—the SMOTE technique was implemented to generate a balanced training set. This improved the sensitivity of the models to the minority class and reduced learning bias.

Five classification models were trained: Decision Tree, K-Nearest Neighbors (KNN), Logistic Regression, Random Forest, and Support Vector Machines (SVM). Each model was evaluated using repeated cross-validation and then tested on an independent test set with the original class distribution. The average metrics obtained in both stages are detailed in Table 4:

Table 4. Average performance metrics of classification models for predicting student success

model	acc_cv	prec_cv	rec_cv	auc_cv	acc_test	prec_test	rec_test	auc_test
Decision Tree	0.898	0.903	0.892	0.898	0.865	0.948	0.893	0.791
KNN	0.909	0.950	0.864	0.966	0.847	0.952	0.867	0.846
Logistic Regresion	0.824	0.805	0.857	0.905	0.854	0.960	0.866	0.892
Random Forest	0–933	0.926	0.943	0.982	0.912	0.945	0.945	0.890
SVM	0.850	0.811	0.913	0919	0.895	0.919	0.919	0.884

During cross-validation, the Random Forest model performed best overall, achieving an accuracy of 92.6%, a sensitivity of 94.2%, and an AUC of 0.982. It was followed by the KNN model with an accuracy of 95.0% and an AUC of 0.966, although its sensitivity was lower (86.4%). In contrast, Logistic Regression showed a more moderate performance, with a sensitivity of 85.7% and an AUC of 0.905.

In the final test, the Random Forest model remained the most effective, achieving an accuracy of 91.2%, a precision of 95.3%, and a sensitivity of 94.5%. The SVM and Logistic Regression models also performed well on the test set, with precisions above 95% and sensitivities above 86%, although with slightly lower AUC values. On the other hand, the Decision Tree and KNN models showed a greater difference between validation and test performance, which could indicate greater sensitivity to overfitting or lower generalization capacity.

These metrics suggest that the Random Forest model not only offers high accuracy in classifying students with satisfactory academic performance (final grade ≥ 70), but also maintains a good ability to correctly identify those at academic risk.

Figure 3 shows the ROC curves corresponding to each of the models evaluated on the test set. The Random Forest model curve stands out, with the highest AUC, confirming its discriminative ability between classes.

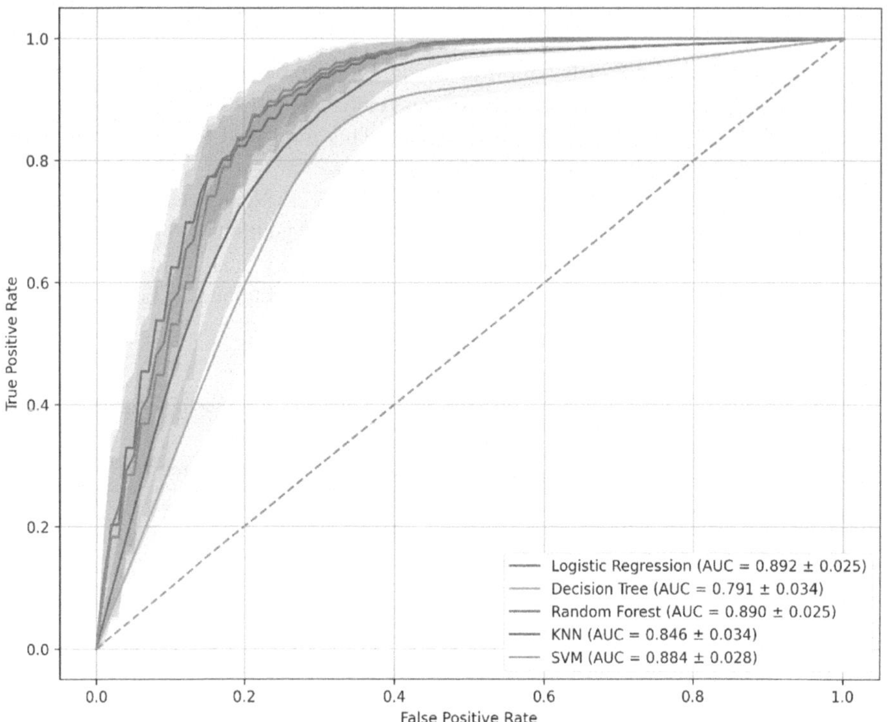

Fig. 3. ROC Curve comparison in test set

Statistical Analysis

To determine whether there were statistically significant differences between the models evaluated, the nonparametric Friedman test was applied, using the average accuracy in cross-validation (acc_cv) as the main metric. The result was statistically significant (statistic = 120.0, $p < 0.001$), indicating that at least one model performed significantly differently compared to the others.

Subsequently, Nemenyi's post-hoc test was performed to identify which pairs of models showed significant differences. The results indicated that Random Forest and Logistic Regression significantly outperformed Decision Tree ($p = 0.000$). KNN and SVM also performed better than Logistic Regression ($p = 0.000$). No significant differences were found between Random Forest and KNN ($p = 0.102$), nor between SVM and Decision Tree ($p = 0.102$), suggesting similar performance in these pairs.

Figure 4 graphically summarizes the p-values of the Nemenyi test, where darker colors indicate greater statistical significance:

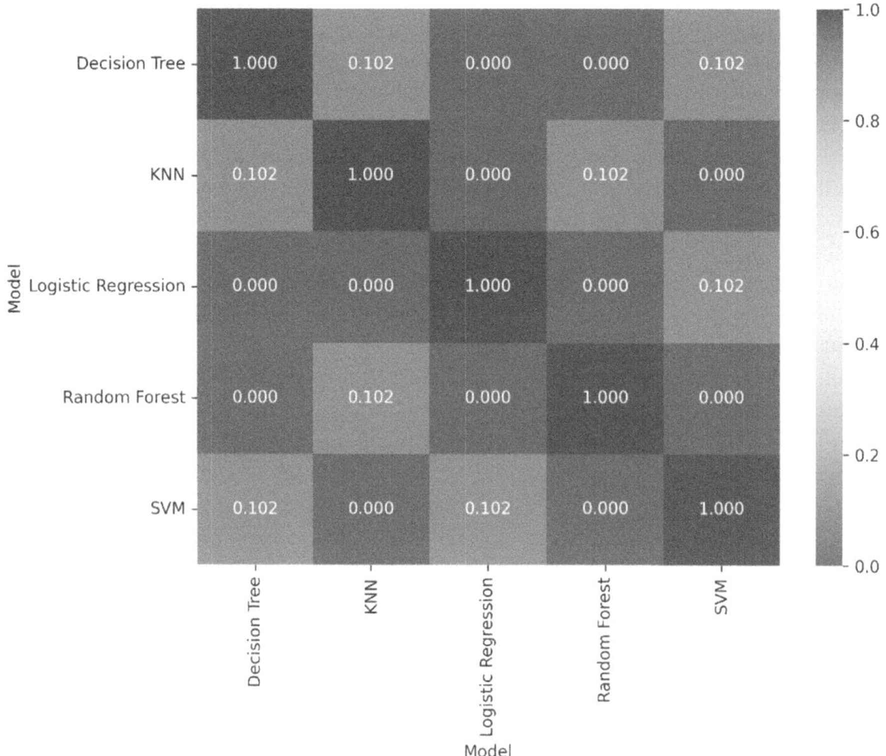

Fig. 4. Nemenyi Post-hoc Test (accuracy_cv)

These findings support the effectiveness of ensemble models, such as Random Forest, whose results are consistent with those reported in previous studies. This suggests that this type of model performs well when applied in virtual environments, where data often reflect complex and varied behaviors. Likewise, other approaches such as SVM also present results aligned with those found in the literature, which reinforces the validity of the approach adopted in this study [3, 30, 31].

4 Conclusion

This study proposed a hybrid data mining framework for analyzing student behavior in virtual higher education environments, integrating clustering, association rule mining, and classification techniques. Applied to a real dataset from the Technical University of Manabí, the approach identified four distinct profiles of student participation, characterized by their interaction patterns and performance levels.

The results demonstrate that the combination of activities—such as participation in forums, assignment submission, and interaction with resources—is highly correlated with academic success. Likewise, classification models based on Random Forest and SVM showed remarkable performance in predicting performance.

Beyond descriptive analysis, the framework presented offers practical value by facilitating the early detection of at-risk students and supporting data-driven pedagogical decisions. Its interpretive capacity makes it suitable for incorporation into LMS systems as tools for monitoring and personalizing learning.

This study is limited to behavioral data from a single academic program, which may affect the generalizability of the findings. In addition, affective and contextual factors were not included, and the real-time implementation of the proposed framework remains unexplored.

Future research could focus on deploying the framework as a real-time monitoring tool integrated into platforms like Moodle, enabling timely identification of at-risk students and immediate pedagogical intervention.

Future research could also focus on expanding the analysis to other disciplines and institutions to validate the model across diverse academic settings. Another promising direction involves incorporating affective, motivational, and self-efficacy variables to enhance predictive capacity and better reflect the complexity of student learning.

This work responds to the need for contextualized analytical solutions for virtual education in Latin America, providing empirical evidence and a replicable framework to move toward more inclusive, adaptive, and data-driven learning ecosystems.

References

1. Romero, C., Ventura, S.: Educational data mining and learning analytics: an updated survey. Wiley Interdiscip. Rev. Data Min. Knowl. Discov. **10**, e1355 (2020). https://doi.org/10.1002/WIDM.1355
2. Celik, I., Gedrimiene, E., Silvola, A., Muukkonen, H.: Response of learning analytics to the online education challenges during pandemic: Opportunities and key examples in higher education. Policy Futures Educ. **21**, 387–404 (2023). https://doi.org/10.1177/14782103221078401
3. Yağcı, M.: Educational data mining: prediction of students' academic performance using machine learning algorithms. Smart Learn. Environ. **9**, 1–19 (2022). https://doi.org/10.1186/S40561-022-00192-Z
4. Hilliger, I., et al.: Towards learning analytics adoption: a mixed methods study of data-related practices and policies in Latin American universities. Br. J. Edu. Technol. **51**, 915–937 (2020). https://doi.org/10.1111/BJET.12933
5. Ifenthaler, D., Yau, J.Y.K.: Utilising learning analytics to support study success in higher education: a systematic review. Education Tech. Research Dev. **68**, 1961–1990 (2020). https://doi.org/10.1007/S11423-020-09788-Z
6. Ordoñez-Avila, R., Meza, J., Ventura, S.: Mining autonomous student patterns score on LMS within online higher education. PeerJ Comput Sci. **11**, e2855 (2025). https://doi.org/10.7717/PEERJ-CS.2855
7. Chang, W., et al.: Analysis of university students' behavior based on a fusion k-means clustering algorithm. Appl. Sci. **10**, 6566 (2020). https://doi.org/10.3390/APP10186566

8. Zhu, J., et al.: The impact of short videos on student performance in an online-flipped college engineering course. Humanit. Soc. Sci. Commun. **9**, 1–10 (2022). https://doi.org/10.1057/S41599-022-01355-6
9. Merceron, A., Yacef, K.: Educational data mining: a case study. In: International Conference on Artificial Intelligence in Education (2005)
10. Deeva, G., De Smedt, J., Saint-Pierre, C., Weber, R., De Weerdt, J.: Predicting student performance using sequence classification with time-based windows. Expert Syst. Appl. **209**, 118182 (2022). https://doi.org/10.1016/J.ESWA.2022.118182
11. Koyuncu, İ., Gelbal, S.: Comparison of data mining classification algorithms on educational data under different conditions. J. Meas. Eval. Educ. Psychol. **11**, 325–345 (2020). https://doi.org/10.21031/EPOD.696664
12. Batool, S., Rashid, J., Nisar, M.W., Kim, J., Kwon, H.Y., Hussain, A.: Educational data mining to predict students' academic performance: a survey study. Educ. Inf. Technol. (Dordr.) **28**, 905–971 (2023). https://doi.org/10.1007/S10639-022-11152-Y
13. Chen, J., Kaur, C., Singh, S.: A systematic review on deep learning in education: concepts, factors, models and measurements. J. Educ. Educ. Res. **7**, 125–129 (2024). https://doi.org/10.54097/GZK2YD38
14. Tsai, Y.-C.: Learner-centered analysis in educational metaverse environments: exploring value exchange systems through natural interaction and text mining. J. Metaverse **3**, 121–132 (2023). https://doi.org/10.57019/JMV.1302136
15. Habti, F.E. EL, Hiri, M., Chrayah, M., Bouzidi, A., Aknin, N.: Enhancing student performance prediction in e-learning ecosystems using machine learning techniques. Int. J. Inf. Educ.Technol. **15**, 301–311 (2025). https://doi.org/10.18178/IJIET.2025.15.2.2243
16. Lin, Y., Chen, H., Xia, W., Lin, F., Wang, Z., Liu, Y.: A comprehensive survey on deep learning techniques in educational data mining (2023). https://doi.org/10.48550/arXiv.2309.04761
17. Xiong, Z., et al.: A review of data mining in personalized education: current trends and future prospects (2024). https://doi.org/10.3868/s110-009-024-0004-9
18. Johnston, L.J., Griffin, J.E., Manolopoulou, I., Jendoubi, T.: Uncovering student engagement patterns in moodle with interpretable machine learning (2024). https://doi.org/10.48550/arXiv.2412.11826
19. Sales, A.C., Prihar, E.B., Gagnon-Bartsch, J.A., Heffernan, N.T.: Using auxiliary data to boost precision in the analysis of A/B tests on an online educational platform: new data and new results (2023). https://doi.org/10.48550/arXiv.2306.06273
20. Rabelo, A., Rodrigues, M.W., Nobre, C., Isotani, S., Zárate, L.: Educational data mining and learning analytics: a review of educational management in e-learning. Inf. Discov. Deliv. **52**, 149–163 (2024). https://doi.org/10.1108/IDD-10-2022-0099
21. Molla-Esparza, C., Gómez-Núñez, M.I., García-García, F.J.: Applications of learning analytics in the study of academic performance in higher education: a pilot-tested meta-review protocol. Int. J. Educ. Res. Open. **8**, 100433 (2025). https://doi.org/10.1016/J.IJEDRO.2024.100433
22. Al-Din, M.S.N., Al Abdulqader, H.A.: Students' academic performance prediction using educational data mining and machine learning: a systematic review. Int. J. Res. Innov. Soc. Sci. **VIII**, 1264–1291 (2024). https://doi.org/10.47772/IJRISS.2024.808095
23. Zhang, Y., Paquette, L.: Sequential pattern mining in educational data: the application context, potential, strengths, and limitations, pp. 219–254 (2023). https://doi.org/10.1007/978-981-99-0026-8_6
24. Durachman, Y., Bin Abdul Rahman, A.W.: Clustering student behavioral patterns: a data mining approach using k-means for analyzing study hours, attendance, and tutoring sessions in educational achievement. Artif. Intell. Learn. **1**, 35–53 (2025). https://doi.org/10.63913/AIL.V1I1.5

25. Mohamed Nafuri, A.F., Sani, N.S., Zainudin, N.F.A., Rahman, A.H.A., Aliff, M.: Clustering analysis for classifying student academic performance in higher education. Appl. Sci. **12**, 9467 (2022). https://doi.org/10.3390/APP12199467
26. Quinlan, J.R.: C4.5: Programs for Machine Learning. Morgan Kaufmann Publishers Inc., San Francisco (1993)
27. Wang, D.: Educational data mining: methods and applications. Appl. Comput. Eng. **16**, 205–209 (2023). https://doi.org/10.54254/2755-2721/16/20230892
28. Pan, Z., Biegley, L., Taylor, A., Zheng, H.: A systematic review of learning analytics: incorporated instructional interventions on learning management systems. J. Learn. Anal. **11**, 52–72 (2024). https://doi.org/10.18608/jla.2023.8093
29. Choque-Soto, V., Ibarra, W., Sosa-Jauregui, V.: Characterization of the dropout student profile using data mining techniques. Rev. Gestão Soc. Ambiental (2025). https://doi.org/10.24857/rgsa.v19n2-067
30. .Hoq, M., Brusilovsky, P., Akram, B.: Analysis of an explainable student performance prediction model in an introductory programming course. Int. Educ. Data Min. Soc. (2023). https://doi.org/10.5281/zenodo.8115693
31. Rezvani, S., Pourpanah, F., Lim, C.P., Wu, Q.M.J.: Methods for class-imbalanced learning with support vector machines: a review and an empirical evaluation. Soft Comput. **28**, 11873–11894 (2024). https://doi.org/10.1007/S00500-024-09931-5
32. Injadat, M., Lutfiyya, H., Shami, A., Moubayed, A.: Student engagement level in an e-learning environment: clustering using K-means. Am. J. Dist. Educ. **34**, 137–156 (2020). https://doi.org/10.1080/08923647.2020.1696140
33. Sujana, T., Astuti, R., Hamonangan, R., Prihartono, W.: Implementation of data mining using the K-means algorithm to group students based on academic performance. J. Artif. Intell. Eng. Appl. (JAIEA) (2025). https://doi.org/10.59934/jaiea.v4i2.936
34. Li, Z.: Research on English online teaching model based on association rules driven by big data. Int. J. High-Speed Electron. Syst. (2024). https://doi.org/10.1142/s0129156425400178
35. Xiao, B., Wang, T., Ma, W.: Student behavior data analysis based on association rule mining. Int. J. Comput. Intell. Syst. **15** (2022). https://doi.org/10.1007/s44196-022-00087-4
36. Yuan, Y.: Course design based on association rule mining in blended teaching of college English. J. Electr. Syst. (2024). https://doi.org/10.52783/jes.3102

Automated Surface Anomaly Detection Using 3D Point Clouds in Cultural Heritage: A Case Study from Palazzo Labriola, Basilicata, Italy

Carmen Fattore(✉), Arcangelo Priore, Sara Porcari, and Antonella Guida

Department for Humanistic, Scientific and Social Innovation (DIUSS), University of Basilicata, 75100 Matera, Italy
carmen.fattore@unibas.it

Abstract. This study presents a comprehensive, open-source methodology for the automatic classification of masonry pathologies in historical buildings using 3D point cloud data and supervised machine learning. The proposed pipeline integrates Terrestrial Laser Scanning (TLS) with a geometric feature-based analysis, followed by classification using a Random Forest algorithm executed in a cloud-based Python environment. The workflow was tested on Palazzo Labriola, a historic structure located in Tursi, Italy, characterized by diverse surface degradation phenomena. Point cloud preprocessing and feature extraction were performed using CloudCompare, focusing on curvature and point density as proxies for surface anomalies. A rule-based labeling strategy was used to generate training data, and classification results were visualized through color-coded outputs, facilitating expert interpretation. All operations were implemented within open-source frameworks, ensuring methodological transparency, computational accessibility, and cross-platform reproducibility. The results demonstrate the viability of the approach for supporting preventive conservation through scalable, automated diagnostics. By reducing dependency on manual inspection and commercial software, this workflow contributes to a more inclusive and standardized practice in digital heritage management. Future work will explore multimodal feature integration and broader applicability across architectural typologies.

Keywords: 3D point cloud analysis · Cultural Heritage · degradation detection

1 Introduction

The conservation and valorization of built cultural heritage has become an increasingly interdisciplinary field, engaging expertise from architecture, structural engineering, computer science, and heritage studies (Gil et al., 2024). Historic buildings, particularly those in masonry, are not only physical testimonies of historical architectural practices but also bearers of collective identity and intangible cultural values. Their exposure to atmospheric agents, seismic activity, biological colonization, and material aging makes them inherently vulnerable to progressive degradation processes (Yang et al., 2023). Timely identification of structural anomalies, surface pathologies, and material alterations is therefore essential to support preventive conservation and extend the life cycle of heritage assets (Pepe et al., 2022).

T. Guarda et al. (Eds.): ARTIIS 2025, CCIS 2789, pp. 475–488, 2026.
https://doi.org/10.1007/978-3-032-16758-3_36

Recent developments in 3D digital surveying, notably Terrestrial Laser Scanning (TLS) and Structure from Motion (SfM) photogrammetry, have enabled the generation of dense, high-resolution point clouds with sub-centimetric accuracy (Zhao et al., 2023). These data allow for detailed morphological and condition assessments. However, due to their inherently unstructured nature, point clouds are computationally intensive to analyze and often require extensive manual input for diagnosis and segmentation (Cotella, 2023; Lasorella et al., 2024).

To mitigate these limitations, researchers are increasingly applying Machine Learning (ML) and Artificial Intelligence (AI) techniques to automate point cloud interpretation in cultural heritage contexts (Gil et al., 2024; Yang et al., 2023). Among the algorithms available, Random Forests (RF) are frequently adopted due to their resilience to noise, ability to handle high-dimensional features, and generalization performance across complex datasets (Grilli & Remondino, 2020). When trained on geometric and radiometric features (e.g., curvature, roughness, RGB intensity), RF classifiers can detect and differentiate between pathology types such as cracks, erosion, and biological growth (Pepe et al., 2022).

Despite growing research interest, most studies focus on semantic segmentation for geometric modeling or HBIM (Heritage Building Information Modeling) reconstruction rather than direct pathology detection, which is critical for conservation and structural risk assessment (Moyano et al., 2021). Additionally, existing workflows often depend on proprietary software or are optimized for specific architectural typologies, limiting their reproducibility, modularity, and cross-case adaptability (Şentürk et al., 2024).

Moreover, several of the existing methodologies depend heavily on commercial software ecosystems or domain-specific toolchains, which can hinder reproducibility and limit methodological transparency. Some workflows may also lack modularity or adaptability, making it difficult to generalize their use across different case studies or heritage typologies (Midingoyi et al., 2020).

2 Methodology

This study introduces a comprehensive, open-source workflow for the automated classification of masonry pathologies in historic buildings, utilizing dense 3D point cloud data in conjunction with supervised machine learning techniques. The methodology aims to facilitate accurate, scalable, and reproducible diagnostics by bridging the gap between high-resolution geometric data acquisition and actionable condition assessment (Fattore et al., 2024). It does so by integrating established digital surveying techniques with accessible computational environments and algorithmic robustness (Pellerin Le Bas et al., 2024; Pepe et al., 2022).

The proposed pipeline is composed of four sequential stages: (i) acquisition of high-density 3D data using Terrestrial Laser Scanning (TLS) and/or Structure from Motion (SfM) photogrammetry, (ii) preprocessing and feature extraction through open-source tools, (iii) supervised classification of deterioration features using a Random Forest model, and (iv) visualization and evaluation of results. A key aspect of this methodology is its full implementation in open-access environments, ensuring both transparency and adaptability. Data processing begins with the cleaning and segmentation of the point cloud using CloudCompare, where key geometric and radiometric descriptors are computed. These include curvature, surface roughness, normal deviation, and where available, color and intensity features. The resulting feature set represents a rich spatial dataset capable of encoding textural and morphological cues associated with structural degradation.

To perform classification, the processed data is transferred into Google Colaboratory (Colab), a cloud-based Python environment that supports interactive code development and machine learning experimentation. Colab provides free GPU acceleration and seamless integration with widely used scientific libraries such as scikit-learn, enabling efficient model training and evaluation without the need for local high-performance computing infrastructure (Pham et al., 2023). This choice of environment not only democratizes access to advanced analytical tools but also enhances reproducibility, as the entire pipeline can be deployed, shared, and adapted via a single notebook interface.

The core analytical task involves training a Random Forest classifier on a subset of the point cloud manually labeled by domain experts. Pathological classes considered in this study include surface erosion, biological colonization, crack formation, and intact masonry (Pellerin Le Bas et al., 2024). The model is trained to learn relationships between the computed features and the corresponding labels, allowing it to generalize classification to the entire 3D dataset. This approach provides a practical and statistically robust framework for classifying deterioration phenomena that are often heterogeneous in appearance and distribution.

Once trained, the classifier is applied to the full point cloud, producing a spatially explicit map of predicted pathologies. These results are re-integrated into the 3D environment and visualized through color-coded rendering, facilitating intuitive interpretation and expert validation. The entire process, from raw data input to result visualization, occurs within an integrated and modular pipeline that is fully accessible to researchers, conservation professionals, and institutional stakeholders alike.

In contrast to many prior approaches that focus on object detection or architectural element segmentation for digital modeling or HBIM purposes, this work targets the less-explored domain of material pathology recognition (Zhao et al., 2023). Furthermore, unlike systems that depend on commercial software or fragmented toolchains, the proposed method offers a unified, open-source solution, which supports both scientific reproducibility and practical deployment in heritage diagnostics (Diara et al. 2018). By combining robust algorithmic performance with computational inclusivity, this methodology contributes meaningfully to ongoing efforts to digitalize and modernize conservation practices in the cultural heritage sector (Crisan et al., 2024; Medeiros e Sá et al., 2019).

2.1 Study Area

The suburb of Rabatana, the oldest nucleus of the city of Tursi in Basilicata, occupies a position that over time has assumed a strong strategic and symbolic value. This settlement, identified as the original nucleus of the city, is today an emblematic context in which historical stratifications, environmental vulnerabilities and morphological complexities are intertwined.

The urban conformation, compact and articulated, reflects a sedimentation process that spans epochs and civilisations: from the Byzantine phase, when Tursi was the capital of the third Catepanate of Italy (the Leukania), to the Lombard influences and the suggestive Islamic matrix evoked by the toponym 'Rabatana', attested from the 16th century onwards. This composite heritage, also read in the light of its function as a border between cultures, has helped to define the unique character of the site, making it a privileged laboratory for experimenting advanced knowledge and heritage management practices (Fonseca C.D., 2004).

The Rabatana thus becomes a system of complex relations between underground and above-ground architectures, between solids and voids, between material traces and immaterial memories. Precisely because of its paradigmatic value, this place has been the focus of systematic research aimed at the integrated cataloguing of the monumental and historical-artistic heritage, with the objective of developing replicable tools for other historical centres. The case of 'Palazzo Labriola', one of the most significant civil buildings in the urban tissue of the Rabatana (Fonseca C.D., 2004), fits into this scenario (Fig. 1). Distinguished by its eighteenth-nineteenth-century facies and remarkable spatial articulation, the building was chosen as the object of study for the elaboration of a digital methodological approach oriented to the sustainable management of historic buildings. The building thus becomes a concrete example of how it is possible, starting from in-depth and structured knowledge, to construct new forms of responsibility towards the architectural heritage, opening up prospects for planned maintenance and enhancement consistent with the values of the place.

2.2 Tools and Datasets Used

The processes performed, not taking into account the post-processing of the acquisitions to convert the data collected from proprietary to open formats, were run in open-source environments to validate the potential of this type of software and promote its validity and replicability in the scientific field. The software used in this case is CloudCompare (v.2.13.0).

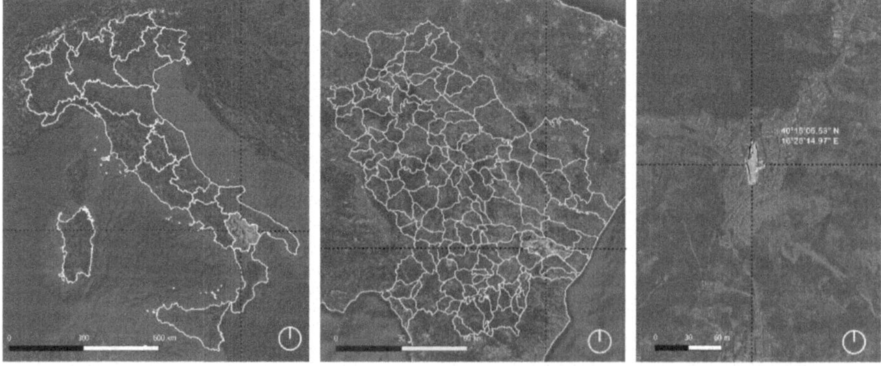

Fig. 1. Territorial overview of Palazzo Labriola, located in the province of Matera within the Basilicata region of Italy.

The instrument used for data acquisition is the ZEB Horizon RT. The specifications of the instrument are given below:

- Maximum range: 100 m
- Points per scan line: 1800
- Field of view: 360° * 2
- Scan rate: 300,000 points/s
- Scan range noise ±30 mm
- Frequency: 10 Hz
- Laser wavelength: 903 nm
- Horizontal angular resolution: 0.20°
- Protection Class: IP 54
- Power supply: 14.8 VDC ~ 1.5A
- Weight Scannerhead: 1.45 kg
- Weight Datalogger (inc. Battery): 1.40 kg.

In addition to acquiring lidar data, thanks to the integrated ZEB Vision, it was possible to acquire spherical photographs useful for subsequent point colouring processes. The total number of acquisitions was three: one overall (used as a reference for subsequent alignment processes) and two detailed ones on the South-West and North-East elevations respectively. The data exported by the instrument are in the proprietary '.geoslam' format, so it was necessary to import them into the Faro Connect software to post-process them, convert them into open formats and attribute to each point the colouring from the photos taken by the vision. The processing workflow in Faro involved several key steps. First, the '.geoslam' file was imported and the acquisition trajectory was identified, ensuring correct alignment of the points collected during the scan. A dense point cloud was then generated in '.laz' format—an open, compressed format that preserves data quality while reducing file size.

Subsequently, panoramic images captured by the Vision system were recognized and aligned to allow accurate projection of RGB values onto each point. The point cloud was then cleaned using specifically developed algorithms, designed to remove moving objects and produce a precise, static representation of the environment. Finally, the point cloud was colorized based on data from the Vision system.

This procedure was applied to all three scans. Each resulting point cloud was exported in '.las' format (Fig. 2).

The open-source software *CloudCompare* (v.2.13.0) was used to align the point clouds. After importing the individual clouds generated from different GeoSLAM scans, an initial manual alignment was performed using the "Rotation/Translation" tool, using the overall cloud as a reference. This step served as a prerequisite for the subsequent automatic alignment.

Following the manual roto-translation, the *Fine Registration (ICP)* algorithm was applied. For the first alignment, the parameters were set as follows:

- Number of iterations: 100
- Final overlap: 45%
- Random sampling limit: 1,000,000

Fig. 2. Colorized dense point cloud of Palazzo Labriola, produced by merging and post-processing the three ZEB Vision acquisitions in Faro Connect.

The same procedure was repeated for the second scan, using slightly different parameters:

- Number of iterations: 100
- Final overlap: 65%
- Random sampling limit: 1,000,000

Both alignments achieved a final Root Mean Square Error (RMS) of 0.009 m. The first scan is shown in blue and the second in yellow (see Fig. 3).

The operations described above were followed by a further phase of filtering and cleaning the clouds. The algorithm used for this process is the 'SOR Filter' with the following parameters:

- Number of points to use for mean distance estimation: 4
- Standard deviation multiplier threshold (nSigma): 1.00

After the following elaborations have been integrated a supervised pipeline for the automatic classification of surface degradation levels in 3D point clouds. The method is based on geometric feature extraction and a multiclass machine learning framework, segmented into four distinct phases: feature engineering and labeling, model training, predictive application, and spatial cluster analysis. To optimize computational efficiency, the merged point cloud, comprising data acquired from both terrestrial laser scanning and UAV-based photogrammetry (Fig. 4), was downsampled in CloudCompare using the 'Space' subsampling method. A minimum spacing threshold of 0.0123 m between points was applied, reducing the initial dataset from 12,806,045 to 8,463,901 points.

This resampling process preserved essential geometric detail while significantly decreasing processing load. The resulting point cloud was subsequently segmented into

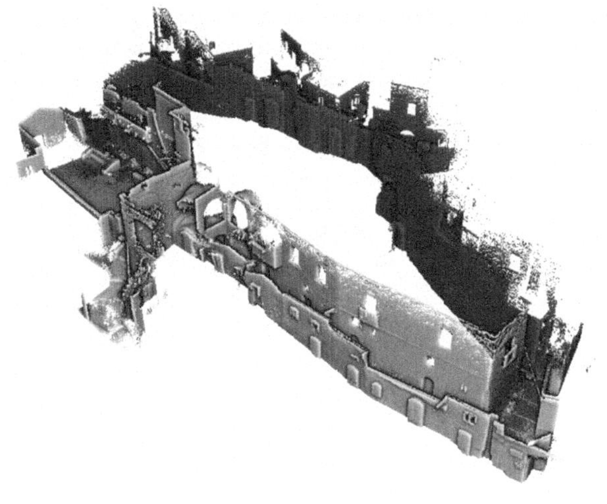

Fig. 3. Overlay of the first (blue) and second (yellow) ZEB Vision point clouds in CloudCompare after manual roto-translation and ICP fine registration (RMS = 0.009 m), highlighting their precise alignment and mutual overlap.

two distinct sections, corresponding to architectural elevations identified as Facade A and Facade B, for targeted analysis.

Fig. 4. Point cloud generated through photogrammetry from drone-based aerial survey of Palazzo Labriola

The initial step involves importing raw 3D point clouds in '.ply' format, typically generated via terrestrial laser scanning or photogrammetric reconstruction. Each point is described by its Cartesian coordinates (X, Y, Z), and, when available, color values (R, G, B). Surface normals are estimated using a local neighborhood of 30 nearest neighbors, and the neighborhood geometry is captured via a covariance analysis.

Two key geometric descriptors are computed per point:

- curvature: the ratio between the smallest eigenvalue and the sum of eigenvalues derived from the covariance matrix of the local neighborhood, indicating surface variation.
- point density: a measure of the local spatial concentration, defined as the number of neighbors divided by the Euclidean distance to their centroid.

A rule-based heuristic is then applied to assign each point to one of four degradation levels, based on percentile thresholds derived from the feature distributions (see Table 1).

Table 1. Heuristic rules for degradation classification.

Class	Curvature Condition	Density Condition
0 – Normal	Below 80th percentile	Above 20th percentile
1 – Light	80th–90th percentile	Above 10th percentile
2 – Moderate	90th–97th percentile	Above 5th percentile
3 – Severe	Above 97th percentile	Below 5th percentile

The outcome of this phase is a labeled dataset (in.csv format) and a colorized.ply file, where degradation classes are visually encoded (e.g., green for normal, yellow for light, orange for moderate and red for severe). This dual-format output facilitates both quantitative analysis and qualitative visual inspection.

To enable scalable application and reduce reliance on manually tuned thresholds, a Random Forest (RF) classifier is trained on the labeled data from first phase. The feature set includes curvature, density, and 3D coordinates (X, Y, Z). RGB values are excluded to ensure robustness across scans with varying lighting or coloring.

The dataset is split using an 80/20 stratified strategy to maintain class balance. A Random Forest classifier with 150 estimators is trained using the scikit-learn framework. Hyperparameters (e.g., tree depth, split criteria) are selected through internal validation. Performance is evaluated using: (i) accuracy; (ii) precision, recall and F1-score for each class; (iii) confusion matrix. The trained model is saved in.pkl format and exported along with visual performance summaries (.txt,.png) (see the Table 2). This step provides a reusable model for downstream inference.

Table 2. Classification performance of the Random Forest model applied to the labeled point cloud of Palazzo Labriola.

	Class	Precision	Recall	F1-Score	Support
Facade A	0 – Normal	1.00	1.00	1.00	556329
	1 – Light	1.00	1.00	1.00	138974
	2 – Moderate	1.00	1.00	1.00	90375
	3 – Severe	1.00	1.00	1.00	65721
	Accuracy			1.00	851399
	Macro	1.00	1.00	1.00	851399
	Weighted avg	1.00	1.00	1.00	851399
Facade B	0 – Normal	1.00	1.00	1.00	809315
	1 – Light	1.00	1.00	1.00	216229
	2 – Moderate	1.00	1.00	1.00	137813
	3 – Severe	1.00	1.00	1.00	99423
	Accuracy			1.00	1262780
	Macro	1.00	1.00	1.00	1262780
	Weighted avg	1.00	1.00	1.00	1262780

The trained Random Forest model is applied to previously unseen '.ply' files. The same pre-processing and feature extraction steps from phase 1 are conducted to ensure feature consistency. Each point is classified into one of the four degradation classes, and the results are stored in both tabular (.csv) and visual (.ply) formats. The point cloud output is colorized according to predicted class, allowing for immediate visual inspection of degradation severity across the surface (Fig. 5).

Fig. 5. Up classified point cloud of Facade A, below classified point cloud of Facade B, segmented according to categories defined by the Random Forest classification algorithm

3 Results and Discussion

The proposed methodology was validated through its application to the historical structure of Palazzo Labriola, a culturally and architecturally significant case study located in the Rabatana district of Tursi (Italy). This site, characterized by complex stratigraphy, exposed masonry, and various degradation typologies, served as an ideal testbed for evaluating the pipeline's diagnostic capacity in a real-world scenario. The point cloud dataset, acquired using a ZEB Horizon mobile LiDAR scanner with integrated RGB imagery from ZEB Vision, was processed through a fully open-source pipeline incorporating CloudCompare for data enrichment and Python-based Random Forest classification within Google Colaboratory.

The initial stage involved the computation of local geometric descriptors, specifically, surface curvature and point density, derived from the raw point cloud and used as proxies for morphological irregularities and surface fragmentation. These features were chosen for their low computational cost and their well-established sensitivity to deterioration patterns such as cracking, delamination, and erosion. A heuristic classification based on the percentile distribution of these features allowed the dataset to be labeled into four ordinal classes of degradation: normal, light, moderate, and severe. This manually curated ground truth served both as training input for the supervised classifier and as a benchmark for evaluating its performance.

The Random Forest algorithm, trained on an 80/20 split of the labeled dataset, achieved perfect classification scores across all metrics (accuracy, precision, recall, and F1-score = 1.00). While these results attest to the separability of the geometric classes under controlled conditions, they also prompt a critical reflection on the nature of the training data and the conditions of model generalizability. The uniformity of scanning conditions, the consistency in point density, and the clarity of geometric signatures in the dataset likely contributed to the model's high performance. In scenarios characterized by more diffuse or overlapping pathologies, or with input data from different sites or sensors, model robustness will need to be reassessed.

More importantly, the model was applied to a new scan of the same structure, acquired under different environmental conditions, yielding classification outputs that spatially coincided with known pathology zones observed during on-site inspections. The classifier was able to correctly highlight areas with notable surface disintegration—particularly at the base of exterior walls and within decorative elements of the façade—suggesting its potential for supporting early-stage risk mapping and targeted conservation.

From a methodological perspective, this result supports three key interpretations:

- geometric feature sufficiency: the successful classification using only curvature and density suggests that, in many cases, low-dimensional, geometry-driven models may be sufficient for capturing diagnostically relevant variations in masonry surfaces. This simplifies model training and deployment, particularly in resource-limited contexts.
- Labeling efficacy and interpretability: the rule-based labeling strategy, though simplistic, proved effective in providing initial training data. This underscores the value of semi-heuristic supervision in domains where ground truth is scarce or expert annotation is time-consuming. Importantly, it enables a balance between automation and interpretability.
- Operational scalability: the entire pipeline, from feature computation to classification and visualization, was executed using freely available tools. This reinforces the feasibility of deploying such workflows across diverse conservation contexts, including small institutions or local municipalities lacking advanced technical infrastructure.

Hence, while the current model demonstrates strong internal validity, its external validity, i.e., the extent to which it can be generalized across different buildings, materials, or climatic zones, remains to be evaluated. Addressing this will require training and testing on multi-site, multi-condition datasets, and possibly the incorporation of domain adaptation techniques or transfer learning strategies to enhance cross-context performance.

In sum, the results presented here not only validate the technical feasibility of the proposed method but also signal a broader methodological shift: from manual, qualitative survey practices to scalable, data-driven diagnostics that remain accessible, interpretable, and robust across conservation settings.

4 Conclusions

This research introduces and validates an open-source, machine learning–based pipeline for the automatic classification of surface degradation in historical masonry structures from 3D point cloud data. Through the integration of accessible digital surveying techniques, geometrically derived features, and robust supervised classification algorithms within a cloud-executed environment, the study contributes a replicable and operational methodology to the field of digital heritage diagnostics. The case study of Palazzo Labriola, a structurally complex and materially diverse site, demonstrated the pipeline's capacity to accurately identify and spatially map pathological conditions, such as cracking, erosion, and fragmentation, directly within a 3D spatial framework.

A key innovation of this work lies in the strategic use of open-source technologies, such as CloudCompare for data preprocessing and Google Colaboratory for machine learning computation. This decision ensures that the methodology remains accessible and the pipeline offers scalability and cross-platform compatibility, empowering a wider audience to implement automated diagnostics without the need for specialized hardware or proprietary software licenses. Equally significant is the methodological emphasis on interpretability and transparency. The use of the Random Forest algorithm allows for direct analysis of feature importance, facilitating expert trust in classification outputs. This is particularly important in heritage contexts where decision-making often involves interdisciplinary collaboration and requires traceable justifications for interventions. The output classification maps are natively compatible with standard 3D viewers and can be visually inspected within the point cloud environment, aligning with current best practices in conservation documentation.

The results achieved in this study highlight the pipeline's robustness and practical relevance. The model not only achieved high accuracy on curated test data but also demonstrated generalizability across different scan sessions of the same site, indicating resilience to acquisition variability. The identification of vulnerable zones on the structure, such as areas of increased surface curvature or density anomalies, provides actionable intelligence for preventive conservation planning, resource allocation, and risk mitigation. However, the approach is not without limitations. The reliance on geometric features alone, while promoting lighting independence and simplicity, may limit the classifier's sensitivity to degradation modes that are not geometrically distinctive (e.g., color changes due to biological colonization or salt efflorescence).

As the field of digital heritage continues to evolve, the integrative approach demonstrated here—merging algorithmic precision with practical usability—sets a precedent for future innovations aimed at embedding AI-driven diagnostics into the routine practices of heritage preservation.

Acknowledgments. This research was supported by Next Generation UE—NRRP "Tech4You Project" funds assigned to Basilicata University Spoke 4 (PP4.2.1—Materials, Architecture and Design: Open Knowledge and innovative digital tools for Cultural Heritage, Scientific Coordinator: Antonella Guida.

Author Contribution Conceptualization, A.P., C.F. and S.P.; methodology, C.F.; validation, A.P. and S.P.; formal analysis, C.F. and A.P.; investigation, S.P. and A.P.; resources, A.P. and S.P.; data curation, C.F.; writing-original draft preparation, C.F. and S.P.; writing-review and editing, A.P and C.F.; visualization, A.P. and C.F.; supervision, A.G.; project administration, A.G.; funding, A.G.

All authors have read and agreed to the published version of the manuscript.

References

Agustín-Hernández, L., Verdoscia, C., Tavolare, R.: A scan-to-BIM workflow proposal for cultural heritage. ISPRS Arch. (2023). https://doi.org/10.5194/isprs-archives-xlviii-m-2-2023-333-2023

Cotella, V. From 3D point clouds to HBIM (2023). https://doi.org/10.1016/j.autcon.2023.104936

Crisan, A., Pepe, M., Costantino, D., Herban, S.: From 3D point cloud to an intelligent model set for cultural heritage conservation. Heritage **7**(3), Article 68 (2024). https://doi.org/10.3390/heritage7030068

Diara, F., Rinaudo, F.: Open source HBIM for cultural heritage: a project proposal. ISPRS Arch. **XLII-2**, 303–309 (2018). https://doi.org/10.5194/ISPRS-ARCHIVES-XLII-2-303-2018

Fattore, C., Porcari, S., Priore, A., Porcari, V.D.: Non-invasive techniques for monitoring cultural heritage: change detection in dense point clouds at the san pietro barisano bell tower in Matera, Italy. Heritage **8**, 14 (2025). https://doi.org/10.3390/heritage8010014

Fonseca, C.D.: Tursi: La Rabatana. In Quaderni di Scienza della Conservazione, pp. 335–346. Fondazione Sassi, Matera (2004)

Gil, A., Arayici, Y., Kumar, B., Laing, R.: Machine and deep learning implementations for heritage BIM (2024). https://doi.org/10.1145/3649442

Grilli, E., Remondino, F.: Generalisation of ML for 3D heritage (2020). https://doi.org/10.3390/IJGI9060379

Lasorella, M., Cantatore, E., Rondinelli, M.F.L., Fatiguso, F.: A semi-automatic pipeline for the decay mapping and the state of conservation assessment of architectural heritage through point clouds. In: Guarda, T., Portela, F., Augusto, M.F. (eds.) ARTIIS 2024. CCIS, vol 2349, pp. 52–67. Springer, Cham (2025). https://doi.org/10.1007/978-3-031-83432-5_4

Medeiros e Sá, A., Ibañez Vila, A.B., Rodriguez Echavarria, K., Marroquim, R., Fonseca, V. L.: Accessible digitisation and visualisation of open cultural heritage assets. In: Eurographics Workshop on Graphics and Cultural Heritage (2019)

Midingoyi, C.A., et al.: Reuse of process-based models: automatic transformation into many programming languages and simulation platforms. Silico Plants **2**(1), diaa007 (2020). https://doi.org/10.1093/insilicoplants/diaa007

Moyano, León, J., Nieto-Julián, J.E., Bruno, S.: Semantic interpretation in HBIM workflows (2021). https://doi.org/10.1016/J.AUTCON.2021.103856

Phạm, T.M.H., Vũ, N.Q., Lê, T.N., Đoàn, T.H.N., Nguyễn, M.H.: Application of Random Forest and Google Colab for land cover classification. Tạp chí Khí tượng Thủy văn (2023). https://doi.org/10.36335/vnjhm.2023(756).29-41

Pellerin Le Bas, X., Froideval, L.O., Mouko, A., Conessa, C., Benoit, L., Perez, L.: Open-source software for 3D point cloud classification using random forest. Remote Sens. (2024). https://doi.org/10.3390/rs16162891

Pepe, M., Alfio, V.S., Costantino, D., Scaringi, D.: Point cloud classification using random forests in heritage contexts (2022). https://doi.org/10.1016/j.dib.2022.108250

Şentürk, H.S., Şimşek, C.F.: HBIM from 3D point clouds using AI (2024). https://doi.org/10.2339/politeknik.1503631

Yang, S., Hou, M., Li, S.: Three-dimensional point cloud semantic segmentation for cultural heritage: a comprehensive review. Remote Sens. **15**, 548 (2023). https://doi.org/10.3390/rs15030548

Zhao, J., Hua, X., Yang, J., Yin, L., Liu, Z., Wang, X.: A review of point cloud segmentation of architectural cultural heritage. ISPRS Ann. Photogramm. Remote Sens. Spatial Inf. Sci. **X-1/W1-2023**, 247–254 (2023). https://doi.org/10.5194/isprs-annals-X-1-W1-2023-247-2023

Evaluating Business Service Concepts for Generative AI from an Employee Perspective

Masaki Koizumi[1(✉)], Takumi Kato[2], and Kazuhiko Tsuda[3]

[1] NEC Corporation, 5-7-1 Shiba, Minato-ku, Tokyo 108-8001, Japan
masaki.koizumi.lab@gmail.com
[2] Meiji University, 1-1, Kanda Surugadai, Chiyoda-ku, Tokyo 101-8301, Japan
[3] University of Tsukuba, 3-29-1, Otsuka, Bukyo-ku, Tokyo 112-0012, Japan

Abstract. As generative AI is increasingly adopted, expectations for productivity gains are rising, and its applications across business domains are rapidly expanding. However, only a few studies have empirically examined generative AI from the employee perspective. A major barrier to its adoption is the fear that employees may be replaced by AI, highlighting the need for evidence-based strategies to enhance employee motivation. This study investigated how business service concepts related to generative AI influence employee motivation through a randomized controlled trial involving 1,000 non-managerial employees in the Japanese consumer goods manufacturing sector. Participants were randomly assigned to a control group that emphasized productivity or to one of four treatment groups, each highlighting a different concept: creativity, skill growth, work-life balance, or autonomy. The results revealed that only work-life balance—specifically, the idea of 'leaving work on time' due to reduced routine tasks by AI—significantly increased motivation compared to the control group ($p = 0.007$). These findings suggest that messages aligned with employees' values and concerns are more motivating than appeals based solely on managerial rationales such as efficiency or cost reduction. Thus, introducing generative AI should not be approached merely as a matter of technological innovation or management strategy, but as a communication challenge centred on employee engagement. Embedding values such as 'time', 'quality of life', and 'well-being' into the core of business service concepts is essential for driving successful transformation.

Keywords: Generative Artificial Intelligence · Employee Motivation · Internal Communication

1 Introduction

In recent years, the advancement of generative AI has led to structural transformations in corporate management, positioning its implementation as a core component of business strategy [1, 2]. The rapid proliferation of technologies such as ChatGPT has unlocked new business opportunities [3], accelerating its application across diverse domains, including business model redesign and marketing innovation [4, 5]. In particular, generative AI is increasingly being adopted in key operational areas—such as customer service, business

T. Guarda et al. (Eds.): ARTIIS 2025, CCIS 2789, pp. 489–502, 2026.
https://doi.org/10.1007/978-3-032-16758-3_37

operations, and back-office functions—where it is expected to enhance productivity and reduce costs [6, 7]. Furthermore, 91% of companies report that they expect productivity gains from generative AI adoption [8], and its implementation often assumes active use by frontline employees [9].

However, despite these developments, empirical studies that examine the acceptance of generative AI from the employee perspective remain limited. Existing research has primarily focused on managerial perspectives, such as institutional pressures, organisational characteristics, and ethical considerations, with accumulated knowledge on strategic preparedness and implementation frameworks [7, 9–11]. In contrast, a few studies have empirically explored how frontline employees perceive and make sense of generative AI in their daily tasks [12]. Furthermore, many business leaders identify human factors as the primary limitation to implementation [8], and only 16% of firms have established robust systems to support employee adoption of the technology [13]. This discrepancy between executive expectations and workplace realities presents a critical issue for future research and organizational practice.

Barriers to the acceptance of generative AI can be broadly categorized into two areas. First, employees often experience anxiety that their tasks may be automated. In the United States, approximately 30% of the jobs could be automated by generative AI by 2030 [6], and such projections have raised significant concerns in the workplace. This anxiety is especially pronounced among employees engaged in routine or repetitive tasks, contributing to AI adoption resistance [14–16].

Second, there is a notable mismatch between the internal messaging delivered by companies and the values held by employees. Many organizations tend to frame generative AI as a tool for enhancing operational efficiency or reducing labour costs; however, employees are often motivated by intrinsic factors such as a sense of purpose [17, 18], opportunities for skill development [19, 20], work-life balance [21, 22], and autonomy in decision-making [23, 24]. This misalignment may underlie psychological resistance toward AI implementation.

This study aimed to explore this cognitive gap between corporate leadership and employees and develop effective business service concepts that enhance acceptance of generative AI by employees in real-world settings. A randomized controlled trial (RCT) was conducted with non-managerial employees working in the Japanese consumer goods manufacturing sector to examine how different service concepts influence employee motivation.

The contribution of this study lies in its reframing of generative AI adoption—not merely as a question of technical feasibility or managerial strategy, but fundamentally as the alignment of the technology with employee values and intrinsic motivation. Communicating information is insufficient to facilitate workplace integration; therefore, conveying the purpose of adoption in a meaningful manner to employees is essential. Clarifying the conditions under which generative AI is accepted as a 'motivational technology' is key to ensuring its sustainable use in organizational contexts.

2 Literature Review and Hypothesis Development

Many companies emphasize technical readiness for generative AI from the perspective of productivity gains and cost reductions. However, empirical studies focusing on employees expected to use generative AI in their daily work are lacking. Particularly, the psychological processes and attitudinal changes that underlie employee acceptance remain underexplored [12].

Therefore, this study focused on the cognitive and motivational misalignment between corporate management and frontline employees to address this gap. It also sought to evaluate business service concepts that may foster greater acceptance of generative AI among employees.

2.1 Productivity

Corporate messaging regarding the introduction of generative AI has largely been framed from the managerial perspective. These messages often emphasize organisational rationales such as ‘operational efficiency’, ‘productivity improvement’, or ‘labour cost reduction’ [25, 26] portraying generative AI as a technology capable of complementing or even replacing intellectual labour [27]. However, such messages may not be well received by frontline employees. Particularly, concerns regarding potential displacement at their jobs can heighten anxiety and resistance toward adoption [14–16], thereby posing a significant psychological barrier to successful implementation.

2.2 Creativity

Many white-collar employees are overwhelmed by routine tasks, leaving minimal time to focus on strategic responsibilities such as planning and continuous improvement. The adoption of generative AI contributes to an emerging new way of working where standardized operations can be delegated to AI, enabling humans to concentrate on more creative and high-value tasks [28, 29]. Generative AI is increasingly functioning as a substitute for labour and a tool that complements and enhances human ideas and intuition [12, 30], accelerating creative processes such as writing, design, and programming support [29, 31]. Therefore, the following hypothesis was developed:

H1: Compared to a productivity-focused concept, a concept that emphasizes a shift toward creative work has a greater positive impact on employee motivation.

2.3 Skill Growth

In the past, reading, writing, and arithmetic were considered the foundational skills for all business professionals. However, with the advent of generative AI, this standard is undergoing a major transformation. Currently, the ability to effectively use AI to collect information and express ideas through language or visuals is emerging as a core competency in the new era [32]. As automation progresses, human judgment and creativity become increasingly valuable in relative terms [33], and generative AI catalyses unlocking those capabilities. In practice, employees who engage with generative AI can acquire specialized skills in areas such as design and programming, enabling them to become autonomous contributors of value [34, 35]. Thus, the following hypothesis was developed:

H2: Compared to a productivity-focused concept, a concept that emphasizes skill acquisition and professional growth has a greater positive impact on employee motivation.

2.4 Work-Life Balance

Generative AI is not merely a tool for improving productivity; it can also empower employees to regain control over their time. AI significantly reduces the time employees spend on day-to-day operations by automating repetitive routine tasks [36]. This shift challenges traditional work practices premised on long working hours and creates new employment styles that make leaving work on time a viable norm [37]. In the UK, full implementation of generative AI is estimated to reduce private-sector working hours by approximately 25% [38], drawing attention to the growing recognition that greater time autonomy is directly linked to employees' well-being and quality of life. Based on these considerations, the following hypothesis was developed:

H3: Compared to a productivity-focused concept, a concept that emphasizes improved work-life balance has a greater positive impact on employee motivation.

2.5 Autonomy

Generative AI lowers the barrier to specialized skills and enables employees to engage in more autonomous forms of work that involve direct value creation. Tasks such as design and programming, which previously required outsourcing, are now increasingly handled internally with the support of generative AI [29, 34, 35], allowing employees to take greater ownership of their output. This shift minimizes the need for complex coordination and approval processes, creating a work environment where employees can immerse themselves in production. Moreover, generative AI serves as an 'augmenting partner' that enhances human creativity and decision-making, thereby fostering discretionary behaviour and empowering employees to act with autonomy [39]. Therefore, the following hypothesis was developed:

H4: Compared to a productivity-focused concept, a concept that emphasizes enhanced autonomy has a greater positive impact on employee motivation.

3 Methodology

As Figs. 1, 2, 3, 4 and 5 illustrate, five internal message categories were developed: Productivity (P1), Creativity (P2), Skill Development (P3), Work-Life Balance (P4), and Autonomy (P5). These visuals were included to better simulate real workplace communication, allowing participants to imagine how receiving such messages might influence their work motivation.

An RCT was conducted to evaluate their effects. The RCT was implemented between 18 and 21 March 2025 in Japan aged 20–69. The survey was presented under the title 'Survey on Working Styles in Companies.'.

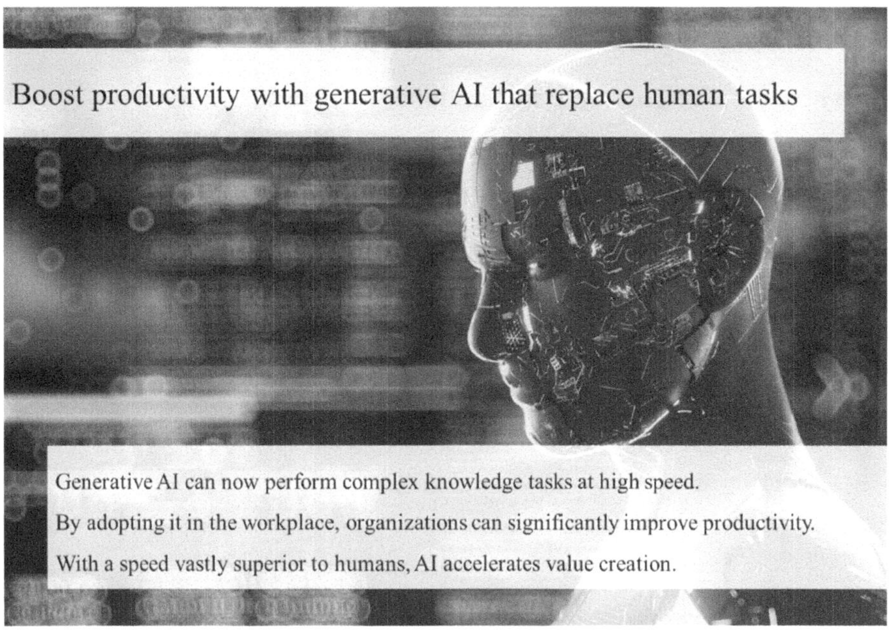

Fig. 1. Concept (Part 1): Productivity Framing

Fig. 2. Concept (Part 2): Creativity Framing

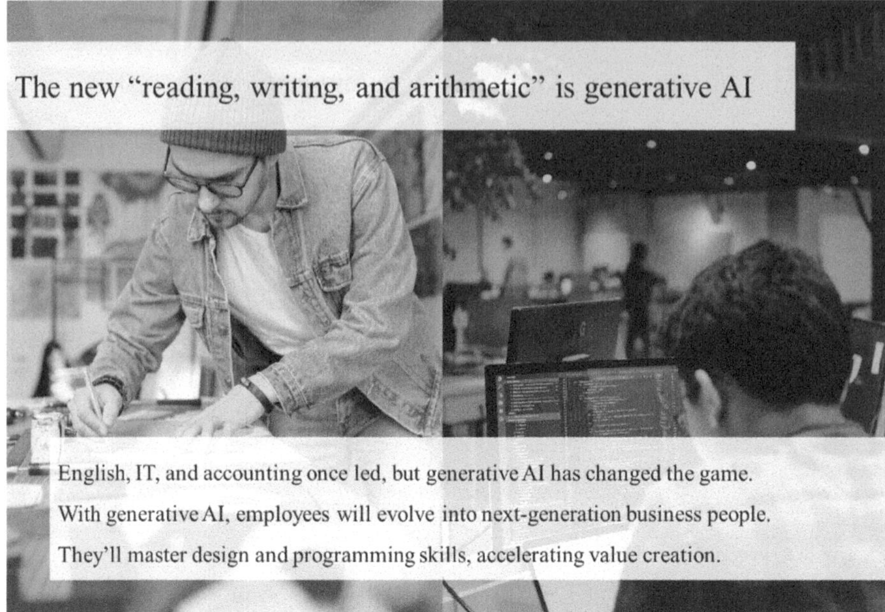

Fig. 3. Concept (Part 3): Skill Growth Framing

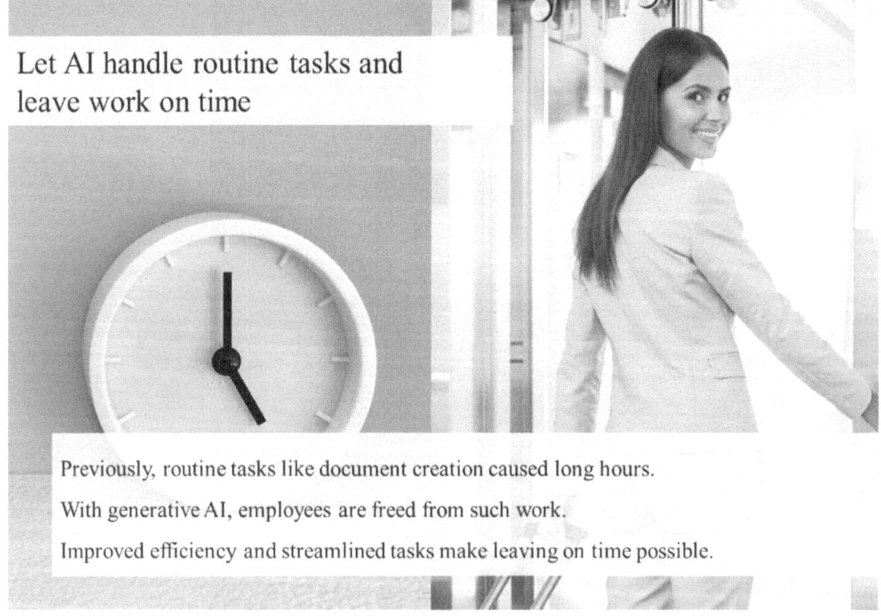

Fig. 4. Concept (Part 4): Work-Life Balance Framing

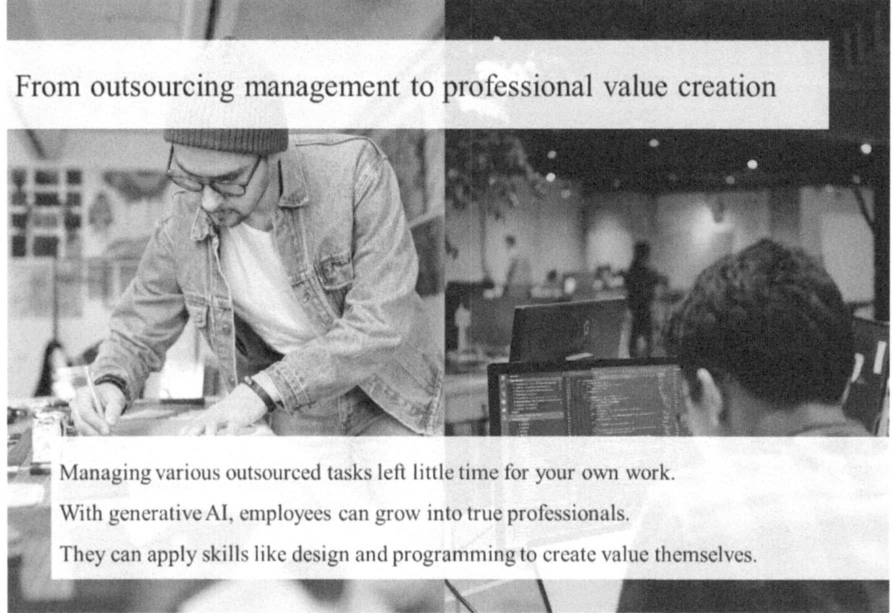

Fig. 5. Concept (Part 5): Autonomy Framing

Table 1 presents the demographic characteristics of the sample, confirming that the groups were reasonably balanced across sex and age to minimize sampling bias. Participants were 1,000 non-managerial employees aged 20–69 working in the consumer goods manufacturing industry, specifically in sectors such as food, beverages, toiletries, cosmetics, home appliances, and automobiles. They were recruited from an online research panel operated by Cross Marketing, Inc., a Japanese research company, and were randomly assigned to one of five groups (200 participants per group). Informed consent was obtained from all respondents prior to participation. The Productivity (P1) message served as the control condition, while the other four messages (P2–P5) served as treatment conditions.

Participants instructed as follows: 'You will now view an internal message regarding the organisational implementation of generative AI. Please respond based on how you would feel if this message were delivered at your current workplace.' Each group was then presented with one of the conceptual visuals in Figs. 1, 2, 3, 4 and 5 to better simulate real workplace communication.

After viewing the message, participants were asked, 'If your company were to introduce the generative AI described below, to what extent would your motivation at work increase?' Responses were recorded on a five-point Likert scale (e.g., 1 = Not at all motivated, 5 = Highly motivated). Following the top-two-box approach widely used in consumer and organizational behaviour research [40], responses of 4 or 5 were classified as 'motivated', and 1–3 as 'not motivated'.

A chi-square test was applied to the contingency table of group assignment × motivational response to evaluate statistical significance. When a significant difference was

Table 1. Respondents' demographic characteristics

Item	Categories	Number of Respondents	Composition Ratio
Sex	Male	457	45.70%
	Female	543	54.30%
Age	20s	200	20.00%
	30s	200	20.00%
	40s	200	20.00%
	50s	200	20.00%
	60s	200	20.00%
Number of Employees	1–100	287	28.70%
	101–500	221	22.10%
	501–1,000	118	11.80%
	1,001–5,000	125	12.50%
	5,001–10,000	66	6.60%
	10,000<	183	18.30%
Industry	Food	299	29.90%
	Beverage	46	4.60%
	Consumer	77	7.70%
	Electronics	101	10.10%
	Car	368	36.80%
	Others	109	10.90%

detected at 5%, a Kruskal–Wallis test with Holm correction was conducted to identify which treatment groups differed significantly from the control group.

4 Results and Discussions

4.1 Results

As in Fig. 6, the proportion of employees who reported increased motivation was highest for the Work-Life Balance (P4) message at 28.5%, followed by Autonomy (P5) at 24.5%, Skill Growth (P3) at 23.0%, Creativity (P2) at 20.0%, and Productivity (P1) at 15.5%. The bar chart visualizes these differences, with error bars representing the standard errors and annotated p-values for each comparison against the control condition (P1).

A chi-square test revealed a significant difference among the groups ($p = 0.027$). Further analysis was conducted using the Kruskal–Wallis test with Holm correction, indicating that the difference between Work-Life Balance (P4) and Productivity (P1) was significant ($p = 0.007$). In contrast, no significant differences were observed between Productivity (P1) and any of the other conditions: Creativity (P2, $p = 0.280$), Skill Growth (P3, $p = 0.143$), or Autonomy (P5, $p = 0.092$).

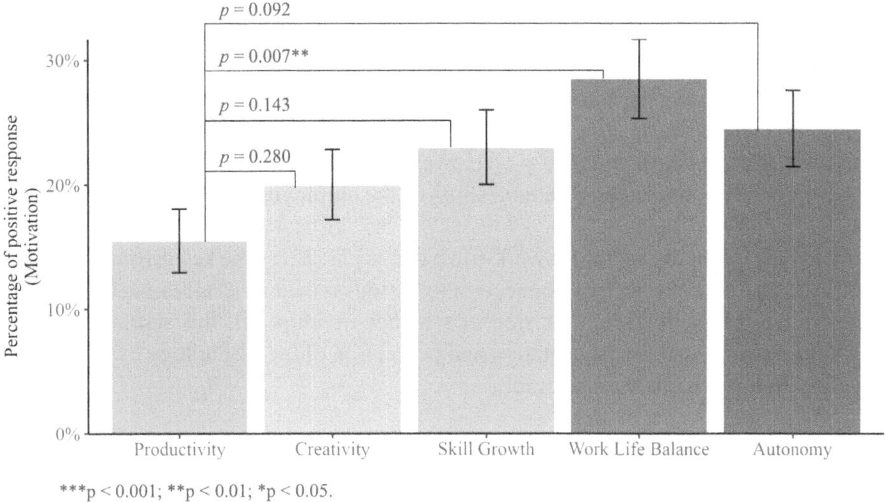

Fig. 6. Motivation evaluation results from the randomized controlled trials

These results provide statistical support only for Hypothesis H3 (the message emphasizing work-life balance and early departure from work); conversely, Hypotheses H1 (creativity), H2 (skill growth), and H4 (autonomy) were not supported.

4.2 Discussion

The support for Hypothesis H3 (messaging emphasizing work-life balance and early departure) can be attributed to the fact that 'visible outcomes' such as reduced working hours and improved task efficiency are intuitively and concretely perceived as benefits by employees [36]. Prior research has also revealed that improved work-life balance is strongly associated with increased motivation [38], aligning with the findings of this study. In addition, reduced routine tasks and time saved through generative AI may have contributed to a stronger sense of tangible improvement in the workplace [28, 37].

However, Hypotheses H1 (creativity), H2 (skill growth), and H4 (autonomy) were not supported. The lack of support for H1 may be due to the perception that, despite generative AI assisting with creativity, it may interfere with creative processes [12]. Particularly, the benefits of AI-driven creativity may not have been clearly communicated to employees, and more time may be required to fully recognize its effectiveness [30].

Regarding H2, skill development and career advancement are typically driven by long-term intrinsic motivation. Therefore, the short-term evaluation framework used in this study may not have adequately captured their perceived benefits [20].

Concerning H4, perceptions of autonomy vary with individual traits and job roles. Some employees may welcome increased autonomy; conversely, others may perceive it as an added burden or responsibility. This divergence in interpretation likely contributed to the lack of statistically significant effects.

4.3 Theoretical Implications

This study contributes to theory by introducing a novel perspective: the way generative AI is communicated internally shapes employee acceptance considerably. Prior research on generative AI adoption predominantly focused on organisational readiness from a managerial perspective [7, 9–11]. However, limited attention has been given to the psychological responses and attitudinal shifts of the employees who use the technology [9, 12].

This study explicitly identifies work-life balance [21, 22] as the key driver of intrinsic motivation and hypothesizes its connection to various business service concepts related to generative AI. Beyond the decision of whether to adopt AI, this research empirically demonstrates that the presentation and perception of the technology by employees influence their motivation considerably.

4.4 Practical Implications

This study offers three key practical implications. First, when designing internal business service concepts for generative AI adoption, aligning the communication with employee-centred values is essential. Traditional approaches that emphasize operational efficiency or cost reduction from a managerial perspective often do not resonate with frontline employees [8, 9]. The findings suggest that value framing rooted in employee concerns—such as time, quality of life, and well-being—elicits stronger motivational responses than those based on productivity or labour substitution.

Second, the message must be communicated tangibly and in a relatable manner. Benefits of generative AI adoption, such as 'leaving work on time' or 'being freed from repetitive tasks', should be presented as concrete workplace improvements. Prior research has revealed that visualizing such direct benefits effectively reduces resistance among employees with greater uncertainty or concern [36, 37].

Third, internal communication should be presented over time. This study indicates that messages emphasizing work-life balance are particularly effective in the early adoption phase, when prioritizing messages that reduce anxiety is important. As the implementation progresses, the presentation should shift toward developmental values such as skill enhancement and autonomy. This staged approach aligns with Herzberg's two-factor theory [41], which posits that hygiene factors (e.g., work-life balance) are more salient in early stages, while motivational factors (e.g., opportunities for creativity, skill development, and autonomy) gain importance as stability is established.

5 Conclusion and Limitations

This study examined the impact of business service concepts for generative AI on employee motivation. The findings demonstrate that, compared to conventional efficiency-oriented messages, those emphasizing work-life balance—such as 'being able to leave work on time'—elicited the highest motivational response. This suggests that employees prioritize tangible, daily benefits over abstract ideals. Particularly in the early implementation stages, message presentation based on tangible gains is more effective. The results highlight the importance of human-centred communication strategies in successfully adopting generative AI.

This study has some limitations. First, the data were collected at a single point in time, and employee responses to this emerging technology may evolve as adoption progresses and workplace norms shift. As familiarity with generative AI increases, employee concerns and values may also change [42]. Thus, longitudinal research is required to assess sustained impacts.

Second, this study was conducted solely in Japan, where cultural norms may influence the findings. Japan's traditional workplace culture, which is characterized by long working hours [43], may make work-life balance efforts, such as leaving work on time, particularly salient compared to other countries, especially as public attention to shorter working hours continues to grow. Therefore, cross-cultural validation is necessary.

Third, the analysis was limited to the consumer goods manufacturing sector and did not entirely account for individual-level variables such as job role, personality, or career stage. Therefore, future research should develop more targeted message frameworks based on demographic and occupational factors, as employee responses to generative AI likely vary across sectors.

These limitations highlight directions for further research to better understand how internal communication strategies can shape employee motivation in generative AI adoption.

Disclosure of Interests. The authors have no competing interests to declare that are relevant to the content of this article.

Note. Figures in this paper incorporate copyright-free materials obtained from Unsplash (https://unsplash.com/) and PhotoAC (https://www.photo-ac.com/). The source URLs for each image are given follows:

Figure 1 https://unsplash.com/photos/fMx5M3lg8oI

Figure 2 (left) https://unsplash.com/photos/1lGeOg6IULc; (right) https://unsplash.com/photos/mYZIWPQldVQ

Figure 3 and Figure 5 (left) https://unsplash.com/photos/bnoxUn-PDRE; (right) https://unsplash.com/photos/G1N9kDHqBrQ

Figure 4 (left) https://www.photo-ac.com/main/detail/29123542; (right) https://unsplash.com/photos/2TbTBE48dzk

References

1. Agrawal, A., Gans, J., Goldfarb, A.: ChatGPT and how AI disrupts industries. Harvard Bus. Rev. **12** (2022). https://hbr.org/2022/12/chatgpt-and-how-ai-disrupts-industries. Accessed 2 Aug 2025
2. Hatzius, J.: The potentially large effects of artificial intelligence on economic growth. Goldman Sachs (2023). https://static.poder360.com.br/2023/03/Global-Economics-Analyst_-The-Potentially-Large-Effects-of-Artificial-Intelligence-on-Economic-Growth-Briggs_Kodnani.pdf. Accessed 2 Aug 2025
3. Rotman, D.: ChatGPT is about to revolutionize the economy. We need to decide what that looks like. MIT Technology Review (2023). https://www.technologyreview.com/2023/03/25/1070275/chatgpt-revolutionize-economy-decide-what-looks-like/. Accessed 2 Aug 2025

4. Kanbach, D.K., Heiduk, L., Blueher, G., Schreiter, M., Lahmann, A.: The GenAI is out of the bottle: generative artificial intelligence from a business model innovation perspective. Rev. Manag. Sci. **18**(4), 1189–1220 (2024). https://doi.org/10.1007/s11846-023-00696-z
5. Cillo, P., Rubera, G.: Generative AI in innovation and marketing processes: a roadmap of research opportunities. J. Acad. Mark. Sci. 1–18 (2024). https://doi.org/10.1007/s11747-024-01044-7
6. Ellingrud, K., et al.: Generative AI and the future of work in America. McKinsey Global Institute (2023). https://www.mckinsey.com/mgi/our-research/generative-ai-and-the-future-of-work-in-america. Accessed 2 Aug 2025
7. Woolley, J.: Generative AI and business: a review and research agenda. Oxford Res. Encycl. Bus. Manage. (2024). https://doi.org/10.1093/acrefore/9780190224851.013.434
8. Dutt, D., Ammanath, B., Perricos, C., Sniderman, B.: The state of generative AI in the enterprise: now decides next. Deloitte AI Institute (2024). https://www2.deloitte.com/content/dam/Deloitte/us/Documents/consulting/us-state-of-gen-ai-report.pdf. Accessed 2 Aug 2025
9. Prasad Agrawal, K.: Towards adoption of generative AI in organizational settings. J. Comput. Inf. Syst. **64**(5), 636–651 (2024). https://doi.org/10.1080/08874417.2023.2240744
10. Al-kfairy, M., Mustafa, D., Kshetri, N., Insiew, M., Alfandi, O.: Ethical challenges and solutions of generative AI: an interdisciplinary perspective. Informatics **11**(3), 58 (2024). https://doi.org/10.3390/informatics11030058
11. Rana, N.P., Pillai, R., Sivathanu, B., Malik, N.: Assessing the nexus of generative AI adoption, ethical considerations and organizational performance. Technovation **135**, 103064 (2024). https://doi.org/10.1016/j.technovation.2024.103064
12. Budhwar, P., et al.: Human resource management in the age of generative artificial intelligence: perspectives and research directions on ChatGPT. Hum. Resour. Manag. J. **33**(3), 606–659 (2023). https://doi.org/10.1111/1748-8583.12524
13. KPMG LLP.: Generative AI in the workplace survey (2024). https://kpmg.com/us/en/media/news/gen-ai-survey-august-2024.html. Accessed 2 Aug 2025
14. Eloundou, T., Manning, S., Mishkin, P., Rock, D.: GPTs are GPTs: an early look at the labor market impact potential of large language models. arXiv (2023). https://doi.org/10.48550/arXiv.2303.10130
15. Li, J., Huang, J.S.: Dimensions of artificial intelligence anxiety based on the integrated fear acquisition theory. Technol. Soc. **63**, 101410 (2020)
16. Schwabe, H., Castellacci, F.: Automation, workers' skills and job satisfaction. PLoS ONE **15**(11), e0242929 (2020). https://doi.org/10.1371/journal.pone.0242929
17. Hu, H., Wang, C., Lan, Y., Wu, X.: Nurses' turnover intention, hope and career identity: the mediating role of job satisfaction. BMC Nurs. **21**(1), 43 (2022). https://doi.org/10.1186/s12912-022-00821-5
18. Peng, J., Zhang, J., Zheng, L., Guo, H., Miao, D., Fang, P.: Career calling and job satisfaction in army officers: a multiple mediating model analysis. Psychol. Rep. **123**(6), 2459–2478 (2020). https://doi.org/10.1177/0033294119862990
19. Kato, T., Yamamoto, S., Miyaji, A., Katsuki, S., Kataoka, C.: Which is more effective for job satisfaction, expert knowledge or career status through training? Differences between large enterprises and SMEs. J. Appl. Soc. Sci. **17**(1), 74–91 (2023). https://doi.org/10.1177/19367244221128553
20. Sesen, H., Ertan, S.S.: The effect of the employee perceived training on job satisfaction: the mediating role of workplace stress. Eur. J. Train. Dev. **46**(9), 953–973 (2022). https://doi.org/10.1108/EJTD-01-2021-0014
21. Bautista, J.R., et al.: Specific stressors relate to nurses' job satisfaction, perceived quality of care, and turnover intention. Int. J. Nurs. Pract. **26**(1), e12774 (2020). https://doi.org/10.1111/ijn.12774

22. Mas-Machuca, M., Berbegal-Mirabent, J., Alegre, I.: Work-life balance and its relationship with organizational pride and job satisfaction. J. Manag. Psychol. **31**(2), 586–602 (2016). https://doi.org/10.1108/JMP-09-2014-0272
23. Choi, J.: The mediating effect of positive psychological capital between autonomous work environment and self-directed behavior: evidence from South Korea. Hum. Resour. Dev. Int. **23**(1), 46–65 (2020). https://doi.org/10.1080/13678868.2019.1632094
24. Zhang, N., He, X.: Role stress, job autonomy, and burnout: the mediating effect of job satisfaction among social workers in China. J. Soc. Serv. Res. **48**(3), 365–375 (2022). https://doi.org/10.1080/01488376.2022.2048289
25. Singh, K., Chatterjee, S., Mariani, M.: Applications of generative AI and future organizational performance: the mediating role of explorative and exploitative innovation and the moderating role of ethical dilemmas and environmental dynamism. Technovation **133**, 103021 (2024). https://doi.org/10.1016/j.technovation.2024.103021
26. De Cremer, D., Kasparov, G.: AI should augment human intelligence, not replace it. Harv. Bus. Rev. **18**(1), 1–8 (2021). https://www.daviddecremer.com/wp-content/uploads/HBR2021_AI-Should-Augment-Human-Intelligence-Not-Replace-It.pdf. Accessed 2 Aug 2025
27. Alavi, M., Leidner, D., Mousavi, R.: Knowledge management perspective of generative artificial intelligence (GenAI). Alavi, Maryam, pp. 1–12 (2024). https://doi.org/10.17705/1jais.00859
28. Brynjolfsson, E., Li, D., Raymond, L.: Generative AI at work. Q. J. Econ. (2025). https://academic.oup.com/qje/article/140/2/889/7990658
29. Lee, H.K.: Rethinking creativity: creative industries, AI and everyday creativity. Media Cult. Soc. **44**(3), 601–612 (2022). https://doi.org/10.1177/01634437221077009
30. Heigl, R.: Generative artificial intelligence in creative contexts: a systematic review and future research agenda. Manag. Rev. Q. 1–38 (2025). https://doi.org/10.1007/s11301-025-00494-9
31. Palani, S., Ramos, G.: Evolving roles and workflows of creative practitioners in the age of generative AI. In: Proceedings of the 16th Conference on Creativity and Cognition, pp. 170–184 (2024). https://doi.org/10.1145/3635636.3656190
32. Tushar, H., Sooraksa, N.: Global employability skills in the 21st century workplace: a semi-systematic literature review. Heliyon **9**(11) (2023). https://doi.org/10.1016/j.heliyon.2023.e21023
33. Huang, M.H., Rust, R.T.: Artificial intelligence in service. J. Serv. Res. **21**(2), 155–172 (2018). https://doi.org/10.1177/1094670517752459
34. De Cremer, D., Bianzino, N.M., Falk, B.: How generative AI could disrupt creative work. Harv. Bus. Rev. **13** (2023). https://www.daviddecremer.com/wp-content/uploads/HBR2023_How-Generative-AI-Could-Disrupt-Creative-Work-1.pdf. Accessed 2 Aug 2025
35. Coutinho, M., Marques, L., Santos, A., Dahia, M., França, C., de Souza Santos, R.: The role of generative AI in software development productivity: a pilot case study. In: Proceedings of the1st ACM International Conference on AI-Powered Software, pp. 131–138 (2024). https://doi.org/10.1145/3664646.3664773
36. Noy, S., Zhang, W.: Experimental evidence on the productivity effects of generative artificial intelligence. Science **381**(6654), 187–192 (2023). https://doi.org/10.1126/science.adh2586
37. Dell'Acqua, F., et al.: Navigating the jagged technological frontier: field experimental evidence of the effects of AI on knowledge worker productivity and quality. Harvard Business School Technology & Operations Management Unit Working Paper (24-013) (2023). https://doi.org/10.2139/ssrn.4573321
38. Tony Blair Institute for Global Change.: The impact of AI on the labour market. Policy Rep. (2024). https://institute.global/insights/economic-prosperity/the-impact-of-ai-on-the-labour-market. Accessed 2 Aug 2025

39. Sack, D., et al.: GenAI doesn't just increase productivity. It expands capabilities. Boston Consulting Group (2024). https://www.bcg.com/publications/2024/gen-ai-increases-productivity-and-expands-capabilities. Accessed 2 Aug 2025
40. De Haan, E., Verhoef, P.C., Wiesel, T.: The predictive ability of different customer feedback metrics for retention. Int. J. Res. Mark. **32**(2), 195–206 (2015). https://doi.org/10.1016/j.ijresmar.2015.02.004
41. Mausner, B., Snyderman, B.B.: The Motivation to Work. Transaction Publishers (1993)
42. Kato, T.: Paralysis by inertia 'like' habit in social networking services: tendency to answer loyalty questions in marketing surveys. SAGE Open **13**(2), 1–15 (2023). https://doi.org/10.1177/21582440231174159
43. Nemoto, K.: Long working hours and the corporate gender divide in Japan. Gend. Work Org. **20**(5), 512–527 (2013). https://doi.org/10.1111/j.1468-0432.2012.00599.x

Information Retrieval System for the Automatic Generation of Scientific Abstracts with a Pre-trained Model

Diego Vallejo-Huanga[1,2](✉), Andrea Gonzalez[2], and Anthony Tandalla[2]

[1] IDEIAGEOCA Research Group, Universidad Politécnica Salesiana, Quito, Ecuador
dvallejoh@ups.edu.ec

[2] Department of Computer Science, Universidad Politécnica Salesiana, Quito, Ecuador
{agonzalez16,atandalla}@est.ups.edu.ec

Abstract. This article presents a web system for retrieving scientific articles, with a module for automatic generation of abstracts using the pre-trained GPT-2 model, which takes the title of a given scientific article as input. To improve the results of text generation, a fine-tuning was made to GPT-2 by re-training the model, with 6102 scientific articles retrieved with Europe PMC's RESTful API and using a set of keywords associated with computer science topics. The information retrieval system uses two similarity metrics, Jaccard and Cosine, to create a ranking of results according to the input of the query. These two similarity metrics were also used to measure the divergence between the original abstract and the one generated with the GPT-2 model. For the process of functional validation of the system, experiments were carried out with the keywords indexed in the list of lexemes for tuning the model. Two scientific articles were taken for each word. In addition, keywords outside the list were used, and 30 random experiments were carried out. The results showed a mean total similarity of 0.1064 and 0.2426 for the Jaccard and Cosine metrics. Although the results show a low level of similarity, it is essential to clarify that the original abstract of the article considered ground truth is a subjective text proposed by the authors. Therefore, this does not imply a system malfunction. Still, it shows that the methodology proposed in this article allows for the generation of coherent text with a small text string as input.

Keywords: Natural Language Processing · Artificial Intelligence · GPT-2 Model · Fine Tuning Model · Similarity Metrics

1 Introduction

The publication of scientific articles as an instrument for the dissemination of knowledge has made it possible to democratize science at different levels. In

This Work Was Supported by the IDEIAGEOCA Research Group of the Universidad Politécnica Salesiana in Quito, Ecuador.

T. Guarda et al. (Eds.): ARTIIS 2025, CCIS 2789, pp. 503–517, 2026.
https://doi.org/10.1007/978-3-032-16758-3_38

general, scientific papers have a structure that depends on compliance with specific guidelines imposed by each publisher, and that is due to the nature of the research process and the area of knowledge. However, most journals use the Introduction, Methods, Results, and Discussion (IMRaD) format, which provides a simple framework or template for researchers to develop scientific articles. This structure of the paper facilitates the readers' understanding and maintains a logical sequence in advance of the development of the investigation. The frequency of articles written using the IMRaD structure increased over time. From 1935 to 1955, the growth rate of IMRaD was 0 to 20%. However, from 1955 to 1975, the frequency of articles in this format quadrupled [5]. Currently, the widespread use of the IMRaD structure can be primarily attributed to the editors, who propose it to ensure that articles have a standard format. This format allows navigation between sections and facilitates the search for information and peer review in pre-established areas of the article.

Researchers are likely to perceive the structural features of the IMRaD format as significant advantages in a scientific article. Publishers typically request that scientific articles have a descriptive research title, an abstract of the content, and some keywords that will be indexed in a thesaurus. The abstract is a short description of the main ideas of the document to inform the reader about the article's content and the most relevant aspects [1,19]. The abstract is fundamental since it encompasses all the research proposed in a synthesized and punctual way [6]. Generating an automatic abstract paper requires models capable of producing coherent texts consistent with the corpus provided. Several studies are related to proposals for algorithms and processes for text generation. However, the approach has changed with the development of new paradigms within Artificial Intelligence (AI), and text generation is now more similar to what could be generated from human thought. In this context, the main objective of this paper is to develop a system capable of retrieving scientific articles and generating coherent abstracts from their titles. This system aims to assist researchers by automatically providing concise abstracts that align with the research's structure and purpose, and allow researchers to have a guide to define the essential points that should be covered in the research abstract, given a title.

Automatic generation of abstracts from titles allows for an initial assessment of the article's content without full access to the text, which can be restricted or time-consuming to review. This approach could improve the efficiency of the research process by helping researchers highlight the most critical topics that their scientific article should cover and capture key ideas. The ability to generate an abstract directly from a title has practical importance, especially in fields with a large volume of publications.

GPT is one of the pre-trained models developed by the OpenAI company, based on transformers that have shown high performance in various tasks such as machine translation, document generation, and parsing [14]. GPT-2 is an extension of GPT, with ten times more parameters and trained on ten times more data than its predecessor [9]. GPT-2 has a Deep Learning (DL) structure, can generate text from a previous one, and is a pre-trained model with 1.5 billion parameters. Depending on the size of the weight parameters of the neural network, GPT-2 models are classified into small (117 M parameters), medium (345 M parameters), and large (762 M parameters) pre-trained models [15]. Since the launch of GPT-2 in 2019, several studies and applications have been developed in various areas, the majority focusing on generating text, sentences, and dialogues. GPT-2 offers advantages over more advanced large language models (LLMs), making it a practical choice for specific applications. Its lower computational requirements allow it to run efficiently in resource-limited environments, making it well-suited for real-time applications and reducing operational costs. The extensive community support and documentation for GPT-2 further streamline its implementation and customization. Furthermore, GPT-2's outputs are often easier to interpret and control, thereby reducing the likelihood of excessive or irrelevant information, which is crucial in generating abstracts for scientific articles.

Our scientific article presents a web system called *Dolfin GO*, capable of retrieving information from scientific articles related to Machine Learning (ML), utilizing a RESTful API provided by the Open Access repository Europe PMC, which contains millions of biomedical research articles. Furthermore, the system allows for automatic real-time generation of an abstract from a title using GPT-2. Comparison using metrics, including Jaccard and Cosine, enables the measurement of precision or similarity between the text generated automatically by AI and the original text of the article written by a human being. The presented model aims to demonstrate the feasibility of automatically generating an abstract based on the title, as well as the convenience and precision of the results.

This study contributes to automated text generation and information retrieval by exploring and applying a fine-tuned GPT-2 model to generate abstracts from titles in the scientific literature, specifically addressing the need for efficient and accessible academic research. Although more advanced language models such as GPT-4 and the Retrieval-Augmented Generation (RAG) framework exist, our choice of GPT-2 is based on its proven ability to produce coherent summaries with lower computational requirements, making it suitable for more resource-constrained environments. Additionally, although Jaccard and cosine similarity metrics may be considered foundational, they provide reliable and interpretable measures of textual similarity, which are particularly useful in preliminary retrieval tasks. This approach balances computational efficiency with adequate performance, allowing us to assess the feasibility of abstract generation in a scalable format while laying a foundation for future iterations that may incorporate more advanced models as computational resources and use-case complexity increase.

1.1 Related Works

In the article by Mishra et al. [12], the text is generated and selected to produce the titles automatically. This process is executed in three modules. The process involves generating a group of specific titles, which undergo a heuristic-based selection process and are then refined by removing noise. The study proposes using a medium-sized GPT-2 transformative language model, trained on a dataset from the arXiv scientific article prepublication repository, and evaluated on two other datasets. For the final title selection, the similarity of Jaccard and Cosine is applied to the score, and the one with the most significant similarity is selected. Finally, results are evaluated using ROUGE and BLEU metrics, and human evaluations.

Harrag et al. [8] also propose the automatic generation of sentences with the GPT-2 Small-Arabic model to generate false sentences in Arabic. The deep fake system identifies the texts using a previously trained BERT model. The dataset comprises 3503 tweets, of which 1559 were selected based on content and verified to ensure a machine did not generate them. The dataset was expanded to 4196 tweets to improve the model. Different models based on Recurrent Neural Networks (RNN) word embeddings were compared for evaluation. The study mentions that it is the first approach to combine ARABERT and GPT-2 for detecting and classifying autogenerated texts in Arabic with an accuracy of up to 98%.

Kieuvongngam et al. [10] presented an application of the BERT and OpenAI GPT-2 models to perform a text summary based on the COVID-19 Open Research Dataset (CORD-19). The model provides complete and abstract information based on keywords extracted from the original articles. The research uses OpenAI GPT-2, previously trained to perform keyword mapping and generate a summary abstractly, while BERT is used for the unsupervised extractive summary. Finally, the results are evaluated using the ROUGE metric and a visual inspection score.

In the study [13], conducted in Japan at Keio University, the creation of news articles is presented using GPT-2 using the purchased news headline. The authors used tick (high-frequency transaction data) from the Japanese stock market and Reuters news from 2014 to 2016. The study evaluates news articles distributed to financial markets based on price fluctuation rates and predicts stock price fluctuations.

Some related works have explored the use of GPT-2 and similar models for generating and summarizing text, which are relevant to our task of abstract generation from titles. In [11], the authors investigated automatic title generation, which shares similarities with our study's aim to condense complex scientific content. Their work uses a GPT-2 model trained on scientific articles to generate titles. The generated titles are filtered through heuristic-based selection and refined by removing noise, with Jaccard and Cosine similarity measures applied to select the most relevant title. This study highlights the potential of GPT-2 in generating concise, meaningful content from scientific texts, similar to how our study aims to produce coherent abstracts from titles. Using Jaccard and Cosine metrics also aligns with our approach to evaluate text similarity.

In another related study, Harrag et al. [8] applied GPT-2 Small-Arabic to generate synthetic sentences in Arabic, focusing on detecting false or machine-generated sentences using a BERT-based deep fake detection system. While distinct in its goal of identifying deep fakes, this work demonstrates GPT-2's adaptability to specific languages and contexts, reinforcing the versatility of fine-tuning GPT-2 for particular tasks. This adaptability is relevant to our study, where a fine-tuned GPT-2 model generates abstracts in the scientific domain.

Kieuvongngam et al. [10] proposed a model that combines BERT and GPT-2 for automatic text summarization, based on the COVID-19 Open Research Dataset (CORD-19). GPT-2 generated abstract information, while BERT provided an extractive summary. This approach aligns with our work by employing GPT-2 in abstract generation; however, unlike Kieuvongngam et al., we utilize a single fine-tuned model for abstract creation, focusing on the title as the primary input. Their results, evaluated using ROUGE and visual inspection, emphasize the feasibility of automated summarization for scientific data, supporting the objectives of our study.

Finally, the work by Nishi et al. [13] explored using GPT-2 to create news articles based on financial data from the Japanese stock market, demonstrating its potential in generating coherent and relevant text from limited input (headlines). Though their focus was on financial news, this study further illustrates GPT-2's capability to produce content from brief prompts, analogous to generating abstracts from titles in our work.

Overall, these related studies demonstrate various applications of GPT-2 for generating concise textual content across domains. They establish the model's flexibility and feasibility for adapting it to abstract generation, providing a foundation upon which our study builds by applying GPT-2 specifically to generate scientific abstracts from titles.

2 Materials and Methods

2.1 Information Retrieval System

In our article, an Information Retrieval (IR) system has been designed to retrieve scientific documents related to AI and ML topics. The platform for information retrieval is Europe PMC [4]. This open scientific platform, developed by EMBL-EBI, allows access to worldwide publications and preprints from reliable sources. Europe PMC is a partner of the PubMed Central repository and offers a RESTful API that provides access to more than 33 million full-text publications or articles from various sources.

The Europe PMC API contains a module that allows you to search your publication database and returns relevance-ordered results in XML or JSON format according to the value indicated in the query parameter. In this investigation, the search module is used to retrieve a collection of documents according to the query entered by the user on the developed website. Each document is structured with various components and information; however, only the title, keywords, and abstract are used for the case study. These variables are the most relevant for calculating the similarities between the user's query and each document contained in the collection [3]. Then, a subset of documents containing these three parameters was selected to obtain a new collection of n documents.

2.2 Similarity Metrics for the IR System

Most scientific articles contain between three and ten keywords, the title between eight and ten tokens, and the abstract an average of 250 words. The title and keywords include a few tokens with a low probability of repetition. For these two elements, the Jaccard index is the metric used to calculate similarities between them and the entered query. On the other hand, the abstract has a higher number of tokens and is more likely to contain repeated words; therefore, a vector cosine model with Term Frequency-Inverse Document Frequency (TF-IDF) weighting was considered to measure the similarity between documents [17].

The Jaccard index measures the degree of similarity between the titles, T_n, and the query Q entered by the user in the n documents obtained from Europe PMC API. The same title methodology applies to the K_n keywords. Finally, the similarity between the original abstract of a specific document, A_i $(i = 1, 2, ..., n)$, and the abstract automatically generated by the GPT-2 model, $AGPT_i$ $(i = 1, 2, ..., n)$, used two similarity metrics; the first is the Jaccard coefficient. On the other hand, the Vector Space Model (VSM) converts text documents to vectors where each document is a point in the vector space [2]. VSM allows for calculating the degree of similarity concerning the papers in a collection, whose terms are weighted using a TF-IDF weighting system. Therefore, the vector cosine is the second similarity metric to calculate the divergence between the original abstract and the one generated by GPT-2. Furthermore, the VSM model is also used for the retrieval module, which compares the abstract A_n of the n documents obtained with the query Q of the user.

The similarity calculation for each element of the paper, the titles T_i, keywords K_i, and abstract A_i, results in three similarity matrices, which are unified by weighting each of the elements, according to their relevance [18]. The abstract is considered the element that provides the most information, while keywords provide more information than the title. For each variable, the established weights were 70%, 20%, and 10%, respectively. Thus, the total similarity of each document, S_i (D_i), is defined as:

$$S_i(D_i) = J_i(T_i) \cdot 0.10 + J_i(K_i) \cdot 0.20 + C_i(A_i) \cdot 0.7 \tag{1}$$

Although Jaccard and Cosine similarity provide a reliable and interpretable baseline for textual comparison, we acknowledge that they capture surface-level overlap rather than deep semantic coherence. More advanced metrics such as ROUGE, BLEU, METEOR, or BERTScore are often employed in abstractive summarization to evaluate semantic alignment. As the focus of this work is to demonstrate the feasibility of automatic abstract generation under resource constraints, we deliberately opted for lightweight measures. Nevertheless, the integration of semantic-oriented metrics remains an important direction for future work.

2.3 Fine-Tuning of GPT-2 Model

Since a model is required to generate scientific abstracts automatically in this work, it is possible to reuse the generic GPT-2 model and re-training through a fine-tuning process. Fine-tuning is a technique that enables the reuse of pre-trained models for a specific task, refining the model to perform a similar task based on the provided information. This technique improves the semantics of the original model, making it more relevant to a specific task and avoiding the need to create a new model. The fine-tuning of GPT-2 requires a dataset with relevant information to generate scientific abstracts. Then, some related keywords were considered in the context of computer science for information retrieval, so the automatically generated abstract has greater coherence when documents related to computer science are retrieved.

Keywords were extracted based on computing terms from organizations such as UNESCO, IEEE, and ACM. In total, 45 tokens and lexemes were obtained and can be consulted on the following open-source repository GitHub: https://github.com/atandalla/gpt2-pmc-app

For the GPT-2 model fine-tuning, four aspects related to the retraining process were considered. First, a dataset was created using information extracted from the Europe PMC repository, filtered by keywords, and considering only the abstracts of the articles as input. This approach allowed us to refine our model using the abstract of each recovered item. In total, 6,102 documents were recovered; however, for the refinement process, these scientific articles do not have abstracts. Second, the GPT-2 model tokenizer is downloaded from the official Hugging Face website. Third, classes are initialized *Trainer* for complete feature training and *TrainingArguments* to access customization points during training. In *TrainingArguments*, the hyperparameters to be used in the training process are defined: learning rate, number of training epochs, evaluation steps, and evaluation batch size. Finally, the model is trained with the new information and task characteristics that will be used later to generate the automatic abstract.

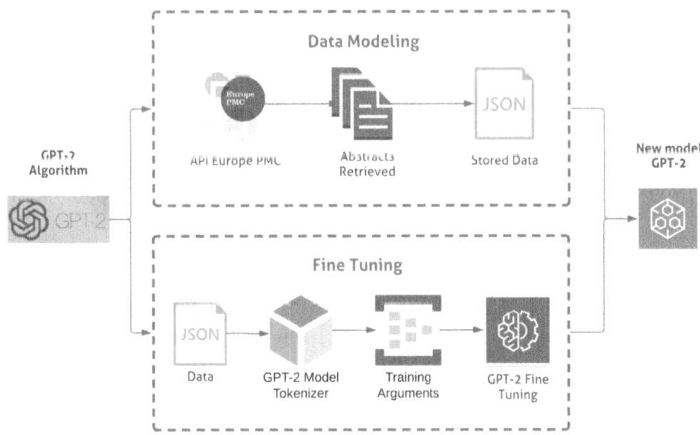

Fig. 1. Block diagram of the tuning process of the GPT-2 model.

Figure 1 represents the fine-tuning of the GPT-2 model, which is divided into two modules. The first module describes the data retrieval and storage process, and the second module represents the retraining of the GPT-2 model using the data stored in the first module. Finally, a new GPT-2 model is obtained as a result that will be used in the experimentation and calculation of the metrics of this scientific article.

The results generated with the IR system and the pre-trained GPT-2 model are presented in a web tool called *Dolfin Go*, available for unrestricted use in https://dolphingo.ideiageoca.org/. This tool allows for experimentation and automatic generation of abstracts in the context of computer science. Like this, *Dolfin Go* contains a text box where the user enters a query, and the system returns a set of documents related to the query. The user can view similar scientific articles and generate an abstract based on a selected title. It is also possible to visualize the calculated metrics to quantitatively assess the divergence between the abstract generated by the model and the original abstract.

2.4 Web System Design

The development of our website separated the presentation layer from the data access layer using the front-end and back-end, respectively. The front-end comprises the main search page, a results presentation page, and a section displaying the abstract generated by GPT-2 along with its similarity metrics. The back-end contains a service to retrieve information from the Europe PMC API. Processing information with ML returns the results to the front-end and a service that uses the GPT-2 model to generate abstracts.

Web System Back-End. The web application's ML modules were developed in Python version 3.8.10 and Flask 1.1.4. One API RESTful is a web software service using the HTTP protocol. This REpresentational State Transfer (REST) design principle establishes a one-to-one mapping between Create, Read, Update, and Delete (CRUD) operations and HTTP methods.

The API developed for this study uses the verb GET to meet the needs and requests required by the Web system. The petition GET */api/search/documents/<string:getquery>* searches documents by connecting to the Europe PMC API and returns results according to the context provided. Thus, this request receives the user's query *getquery* as an input parameter and sends it to the Europe PMC API, which returns n documents D_n, according to *getquery*. Of the retrieved document set, only those that contain the metadata title T_n, keywords K_n, and the abstract A_n are used. The similarity S between each document and the query is then calculated; and the result is stored in an array $S_i = [S_i(D_i), ... ,S_n(D_n)]$; $(i = 1 ... n)$. The vector cosine model with TF-IDF and Jaccard determines the similarity calculation.

The block diagram in Fig. 2 describes the request processing flow, which begins with the request on the website and then obtains the results through the Europe PMC API. The similarities are calculated, and the results are presented to the user on the website.

The petition GET */api/search/GPT2/<string:getquery2> /<string: abstract1>* of the API receives the document title, selected by the user on the

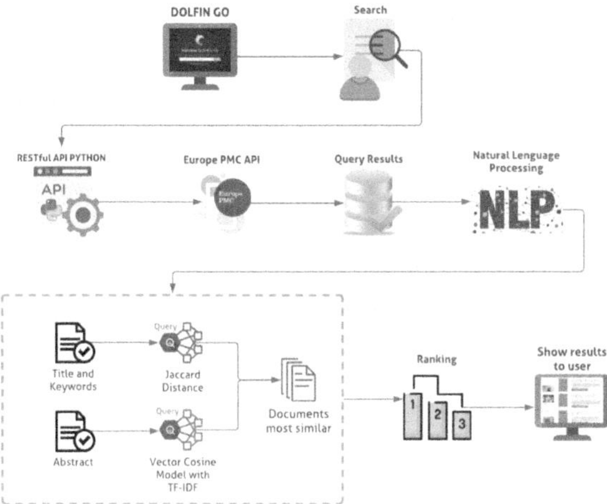

Fig. 2. Information retrieval process from a query made by the user and calculation of its similarity measure.

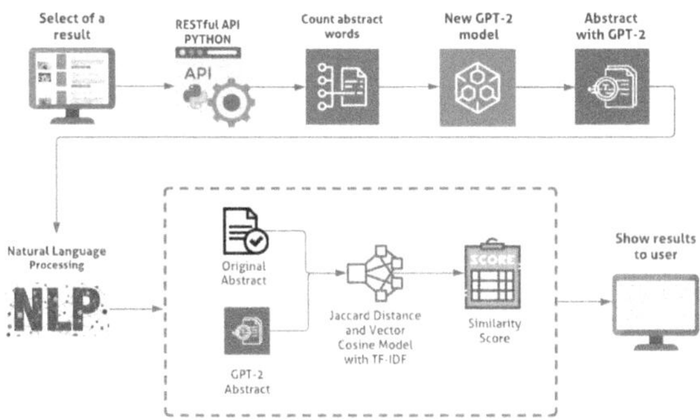

Fig. 3. Block diagram for the generation of an abstract with the fine-tuned GPT-2 model from the title of a document.

web interface, and stores it in $getquery2$ and abstract in $abstract1$. These parameters automatically obtain an abstract using the tuned GPT-2 model. Figure 3 shows the process of requesting and generating content on the website *Dolfin Go*.

Web System Front-End. The website *Dolfin Go* was developed in Node.js and Bootstrap, with three pages. On the main page, a section is presented to enter a query required by the user. This page contains a text box where the user will type the query to find related information.

Once the user enters the query and presses the button *Search*, the second page will be displayed, where the results are sorted by relevance in descending order according to the user's query. Each document in the results contains three buttons. The first function directs to the DOI of the retrieved article, the second retrieves similar articles, and the third automatically generates a summary with GPT-2.

Then, by pressing the button *Similar Articles*, three scientific articles related to the selected main title are displayed. This module's processing is done with the same logic developed to search for the results of a query. Therefore, instead of using the user's query, the title of the selected scientific article is used, and the first three articles of the ranking are created from the matrix of similarities calculated between each document.

On the other hand, by pressing the button *GPT2*, a third page is loaded where the original abstract of the selected document is presented together with the abstract generated with GPT-2 based on the title of the paper. In addition, the user is shown the number of words in each corpus. At the bottom of this page, the results of the similarity calculation of Jaccard and Vectorial Cosine are calculated between the original abstract and the abstract with GPT-2.

The source code of the web system and the text generation model are available in the GitHub repository: https://github.com/atandalla/gpt2-pmc-app.

3 Results and Discussions

The fine-tuned GPT-2 model does not generate an abstract with the same number of words as the original abstract, even though this parameter is specified in the model configuration. Therefore, it was necessary to find a metric that minimizes the difference between the number of tokens of the original abstract and the abstract generated by GPT-2. Therefore, ten randomized experiments were carried out, in which different articles of the IR system were selected, and the number of tokens of the original abstract, n_{A_i} and of the abstract generated by GPT-2, n_{AGPT2_i}. With these two scalar values, an index was generated, $r_p = n_{AGPT2_i}/n_{A_i}$, which expresses the differential portion between the two corpora. This index was calculated for the ten experiments, and a $\bar{r_p} = 0.76$ was obtained; therefore, the GPT-2 model was forced to generate 25% more words, roughly corresponding to the missing portion. These experiments are detailed in the Table 1.

In the process of experimentation, it was also observed that the abstract generated did not end with an endpoint, subtracting syntax and semantics from the textual corpus. A function was developed to correct this process by truncating the abstract at the nearest point. Consequently, the number of tokens increased, leading to an adjustment of the percentage of other words from 25% to 50%. In the experiments, as part of the system validation process, some of the exact keywords indexed in the token set were used to refine the model, and lexemes outside this set were included. The selected tokens were used as input parameters for the recovery system queries.

The first experiment generates an abstract when the RI system input receives tokens that have already been used to refine the model. Therefore, ten keywords were taken as input for this experiment, and a search was executed on the RI system. Two scientific articles are randomly selected for each keyword, and an

Table 1. Results of the abstract generation experiments to minimize the difference of words concerning the original

Titles of Scientific Articles	n_{A_i}	n_{AGPT2_i}	r_p
Recommendations for machine learning benchmarks in neuroimaging	164	128	0.78
Therapeutic Application of Machine learning in Psoriasis A Prisma Systemic Review	94	70	0.74
Machine learning approaches to explore digenic inheritance.	116	100	0.86
Utilizing Intensive Care Alarms for Machine Learning	80	63	0.78
Machine Learning on a Robotic Platform for the Design of Polymer-Protein Hybrids.	165	123	0.75
Anatomical prognosis after idiopathic macular hole surgery machine learning based prediction	266	188	0.71
Artificial intelligence in glaucoma	279	230	0.82
Artificial Intelligence in Echocardiography	84	50	0.6
Artificial Intelligence and Mechanical Circulatory Support	98	70	0.71
Artificial Intelligence in Undergraduate Medical Education	63	54	0.86

abstract is given to the GPT-2 model. The system returns the values of the similarity metrics of Jaccard and Cosine. As a result, 20 records are obtained that are detailed in Table 2.

On the other hand, the second experiment uses words that are not indexed in the dataset used to tune the GPT-2 model as input for the IR system search. Five computing-related keywords were entered for this experiment, as the model was refined with articles from this area. Similarly, the two similarity indices between the A_i and the $AGPT2_i$, for ten randomly selected scientific papers. Table 3 summarizes the results of this second experimentation process.

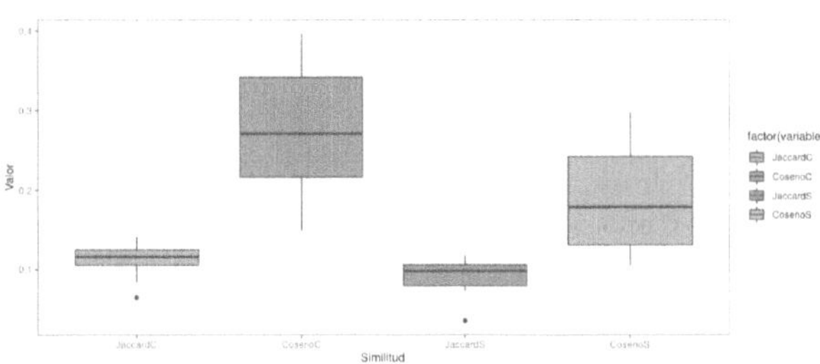

Fig. 4. Box-whisker plot for the two types of experiment.

The Fig. 4 allows us to observe the results of the values obtained for both similarity measures. In the case of the first group of experiments, the mean

Table 2. Similarity results between the A_i and $AGPT2_i$ for a search with indexed tokens in model tuning

Keywords	Original Title	J_i	C_i
Long Short Term Memory	Prediction of leachate quantity and quality from a landfill site by the long short-term memory model.	0.1111	0.396
Artificial Intelligence	Artificial intelligence for assessment of Stargardt macular atrophy.	0.1187	0.3637
Neural Networks	Operator compression with deep neural networks.	0.1157	0.3591
Intelligent Automation	Integrated Design of Financial Self-Service Terminal Based on Artificial Intelligence Voice Interaction.	0.1411	0.3518
Modeling and Simulation	An online participatory system for SWMM-based flood modeling and simulation.	0.0842	0.3507
Long Short Term Memory	Prediction of conotoxin type based on long short-term memory network.	0.1212	0.3379
Neural Networks	Deep neural networks and image classification in biological vision.	0.1259	0.3218
Support Vector Machines	Facial expression recognition using three-stage support vector machines.	0.1161	0.2966
Artificial Intelligence	Robotics and Artificial Intelligence in Endovascular Neurosurgery.	0.1411	0.2892
Supervised Learning	Generative Adversarial Training for Supervised and Semi-supervised Learning.	0.1231	0.275
Unsupervised Learning	Spatial position constraint for unsupervised learning of speech representations.	0.1419	0.2661
Support Vector Machines	Boosting support vector machines for cancer discrimination tasks.	0.1242	0.2305
Supervised Learning	Survey of Supervised Learning for Medical Image Processing.	0.1086	0.2263
Modeling and Simulation	Modeling and simulation of vagal afferent input of the cough reflex.	0.1017	0.225
Data Processing	Current data processing strategies for cryo-electron tomography and subtomogram averaging.	0.1085	0.2169
Unsupervised Learning	Unsupervised Learning for Hydrogen Breath Tests.	0.1417	0.2142
Deep Learning	Protein design via deep learning.	0.065	0.1874
Intelligent Automation	The impact of 5G on the evolution of intelligent automation and industry digitization.	0.0843	0.1747
Deep Learning	Deep learning in multimedia healthcare applications: a review.	0.0952	0.1719
Data Processing	General Strategies for Glycan Microarray Data Processing and Analysis.	0.1068	0.1491
Mean		0.113805	0.270195

Table 3. Results of similarity between A_i and $AGPT2_i$ for a search with nonindexed tokens in model tuning

Keywords	Original Title	J_i	C_i
Parallel Computing	Accelerating the discovery of space-time patterns of infectious diseases using parallel computing.	0.0959	0.2971
Business Intelligence	Modeling the prediction of business intelligence system effectiveness.	0.1069	0.2709
Ethical Computing	Ethics for integrating emerging technologies to contain COVID-19 in Zimbabwe.	0.0936	0.2572
Artificial Vision	Artificial vision support system (AVS(2)) for improved prosthetic vision.	0.1174	0.196
Distributed Systems	Emergent Bioanalogous Properties of Blockchain based Distributed Systems.	0.1139	0.182
Parallel Computing	Parallel computing in genomic research: advances and applications.	0.1024	0.1758
Ethical Computing	Legal and Ethical Consideration in Artificial Intelligence in Healthcare: Who Takes Responsibility?	0.0753	0.1359
Business Intelligence	ETL Framework for Real-Time Business Intelligence over Medical Imaging Repositories.	0.0731	0.1292
Artificial Vision	Artificial vision, white space and racial surveillance capitalism.	0.036	0.1247
Distributed Systems	How does mobility help distributed systems compute?	0.1005	0.1049
Mean		0.0915	0.18737

obtained was 0.1138 for the Jaccard similarity index and 0.2702 for Cosine. On the other hand, for the second group of experiments, the mean Jaccard similarity index was 0.09150 and 0.1874 in Cosine.

Although the relatively low average Cosine similarity (≈ 0.27) does not necessarily indicate a malfunction of the system. Abstracts written by human authors are inherently subjective and may highlight different aspects of a paper depending on the author's focus. Consequently, generated texts that diverge lexically from the original may still be coherent and contextually appropriate. This observation aligns with findings in previous studies (see [7] [16]) on abstractive summarization, where lexical overlap metrics often underestimate the actual quality of generated text. A more nuanced evaluation, including semantic metrics and human judgment, is left as future work.

A priori, it is expected that the first experiment will have a higher level of similarity than the second because it received input into the RI system, lexemes already used in the refinement of the GPT-2 model. The numerical results validate this hypothesis, as evidenced by the Jaccard metric in the first experiment, which shows an improvement in the level of similarity of 2.23%. For the cosine index, the improvement is 8.28%. Finally, the results also show that there is a difference between the two similarity metrics. It is essential to clarify that Cosine's similarity uses a system of weighting the terms and their occurrence. At the same time, Jaccard only evaluates the similarity in terms of the cardinality of the sets of tokens to compare.

4 Conclusions

Developing and implementing the information retrieval system for automatically generating scientific abstracts using a fine-tuned GPT-2 model demonstrates the potential of pre-trained models for specific tasks. The results showed that it is possible, through fine-tuning, to adapt the GPT-2 model to a particular need and to achieve coherent results based on a context. These levels of similarity are relative values since when calculating the similarity between the original abstract and the one generated with GPT-2, two texts generated with different methodologies are compared. The results of the experiments show that, although there is a divergence between the generated and original abstracts, the methodology provides a valid framework for generating contextual summaries with limited input data.

While this study has demonstrated the feasibility of generating abstracts from titles using a fine-tuned GPT-2 model, certain limitations remain. In particular, no human evaluation was conducted, and no expert-written abstracts were used as benchmarks for comparison. Future research should incorporate human judgments of coherence, readability, and relevance to complement automatic similarity scores. Additionally, the use of more sophisticated evaluation metrics could provide a more complete assessment of the semantic quality of generated abstracts.

References

1. Alexandrov, A.V., Hennerici, M.G.: Writing good abstracts. Cerebrovasc. Dis. **23**(4), 256–259 (2007)
2. Alodadi, M., Janeja, V.P.: Similarity in patient support forums using tf-idf and cosine similarity metrics. In: 2015 International Conference on Healthcare Informatics, pp. 521–522. IEEE (2015). https://doi.org/10.1109/ICHI.2015.99
3. Bani-Ahmad, S., Cakmak, A., Özsoyoglu, G., Al-Hamdani, A.: Evaluating publication similarity measures. IEEE Data Eng. Bull. **28**(4), 21–28 (2005)
4. Consortium, E.P.: Europe pmc: a full-text literature database for the life sciences and platform for innovation. Nucleic Acids Res. **43**(D1), D1042–D1048 (2015). https://europepmc.org/

5. Dixit, A.: The imrad format: a concise and clear way to present a scientific study. Indian J. Med. Specialities **2**(2) (2011)
6. El-Kassas, W.S., Salama, C.R., Rafea, A.A., Mohamed, H.K.: Automatic text summarization: a comprehensive survey. Expert Syst. Appl. **165**, 113679 (2021)
7. Graham, Y.: Re-evaluating automatic summarization with bleu and 192 shades of rouge. In: Proceedings of the 2015 Conference on Empirical Methods in Natural Language Processing, pp. 128–137 (2015)
8. Harrag, F., Debbah, M., Darwish, K., Abdelali, A.: Bert transformer model for detecting Arabic gpt2 auto-generated tweets (2021)
9. Irissappane, A.A., Yu, H., Shen, Y., Agrawal, A., Stanton, G.: Leveraging gpt-2 for classifying spam reviews with limited labeled data via adversarial training. arXiv preprint arXiv:2012.13400 (2020)
10. Kieuvongngam, V., Tan, B., Niu, Y.: Automatic text summarization of covid-19 medical research articles using bert and gpt-2 (2020)
11. Mishra, P., Diwan, C., Srinivasa, S., Srinivasaraghavan, G.: Automatic title generation for learning resources and pathways with pre-trained transformer models. Int. J. Semant. Comput. **15**(04), 487–510 (2021)
12. Mishra, P., Diwan, C., Srinivasa, S., Srinivasaraghavan, G.: Automatic title generation for text with pre-trained transformer language model, pp. 17–24 (2021). https://doi.org/10.1109/ICSC50631.2021.00009
13. Nishi, Y., Suge, A., Takahashi, H.: News articles evaluation analysis in automotive industry using gpt-2 and co-occurrence network, pp. 103–114 (2019)
14. Radford, A., Narasimhan, K., Salimans, T., Sutskever, I.: Improving language understanding by generative pre-training (2018)
15. Radford, A., et al.: Language models are unsupervised multitask learners. OpenAI blog **1**(8), 9 (2019)
16. Sul, J., Choi, Y.S.: Balancing lexical and semantic quality in abstractive summarization. In: Rogers, A., Boyd-Graber, J., Okazaki, N. (eds.) Proceedings of the 61st Annual Meeting of the Association for Computational Linguistics (Volume 2: Short Papers), pp. 637–647. Association for Computational Linguistics, Toronto, Canada (2023). https://doi.org/10.18653/v1/2023.acl-short.56,
17. Vallejo-Huanga, D., Morillo, P., Ferri, C.: Semi-supervised clustering algorithms for grouping scientific articles. Procedia Comput. Sci. **108**, 325–334 (2017). https://doi.org/10.1016/j.procs.2017.05.206. international Conference on Computational Science, ICCS 2017, 12-14 June 2017, Zurich, Switzerland
18. Vallejo Huanga, D.F., Morillo Alcívar, P.A., Ferri Ramírez, C.: ADoCS: automatic designer of conference schedules. In: Proceedings of the Software Demonstrations of the 15th Conference of the European Chapter of the Association for Computational Linguistics, pp. 41–44. Association for Computational Linguistics, Valencia (2017). https://aclanthology.org/E17-3011
19. Warren, E., Cobb, J., Nemeth, B.: The importance of writing a good abstract (2019)

Intelligent Monitoring and Analysis System for the Early Detection of Cardiovascular Anomalies Based on IoT and Deep Learning

Dominik Mendoza Ramos(✉), Cristina Vidal Falcon, and Abel Rosales Caururu

Universidad Peruana de Ciencias Aplicadas, Lima 15023, Peru
{u20201b980,u20211b952,PCSIABRO}@upc.edu.pe

Abstract. Cardiovascular diseases (CVDs) represent a leading factor in global mortality rates, posing substantial challenges for healthcare systems worldwide, presenting significant healthcare challenges in Metropolitan Lima. In Peru, delays and limited technology within the healthcare system hinder the early detection and timely treatment of CVDs, contributing to elevated mortality rates. This paper presents an "Intelligent Monitoring and Alert System" designed to address these gaps through a mobile alert application and an integrated web platform powered by deep learning and IoT-driven data collection. The system leverages a ResNet model to classify ECG data in real time, with Fog Computing ensuring rapid processing of metrics from sensors, such as the AD8232. Initial results demonstrate robust performance, achieving an AUC of 0.84 for ECG classification from a single-lead. The system has undergone validation according to GAMP 5 standards, along with usability testing conducted with healthcare professionals and received favorable usability ratings (4.53/5), with results demonstrating the system's effectiveness and utility.

Keywords: Cardiovascular Diseases · IoT · ResNet · Fog Computing · Deep Learning · ECG Classification · Healthcare System

1 Introduction

Cardiovascular diseases (CVDs) persist as a major worldwide health burden, maintaining their position as the primary contributor to global mortality [1]. As of 2021, CVDs were responsible for 20.5 million deaths globally, with more than 500 million individuals still suffering from these conditions [2].

In Peru, CVDs continue to represent a critical public health issue, being responsible for more than 30,000 fatalities in 2021, a reflection of the significant inefficiencies in the country's healthcare system [3]. Despite allocating 4% of GDP to healthcare, response times are still far from optimal [4]. In the EsSalud

T. Guarda et al. (Eds.): ARTIIS 2025, CCIS 2789, pp. 518–533, 2026.
https://doi.org/10.1007/978-3-032-16758-3_39

network, for instance, the average time from initial medical contact to ECG interpretation is approximately four hours. This far exceeds the recommended maximum of 10 min [5]. Moreover, the absence of emerging technologies, such as IoT and deep learning, further hinders the early and proactive detection of cardiovascular anomalies within hospital environments [6]. These delays and gaps in technological integration underscore the urgent need for more efficient, intelligent monitoring solutions to improve patient outcomes.

Several studies have proposed advanced IoT-based cardiovascular monitoring solutions achieving accuracies exceeding 98% in controlled environments [7–10]. However, a critical analysis of these approaches reveals significant deployment constraints for resource-limited healthcare settings such as Metropolitan Lima, where infrastructure limitations, economic barriers, and implementation complexities create a gap between technological capability and practical viability. These challenges, detailed in Sect. 2, needed a tailored approach that balances clinical effectiveness with deployment feasibility.

To bridge this gap between technological capability and practical implementation, we propose an intelligent monitoring and analysis system designed for the early detection of cardiovascular anomalies tailored for medical centers in Metropolitan Lima. The system integrates IoT technologies with deep learning, utilizing Fog Computing to enable real-time collection of vital health metrics. The detection of cardiovascular anomalies employs a one-dimensional Residual Neural Network (XResNet1D) architecture specially optimized for electrocardiographic signal analysis and classification, trained to identify heart failure, coronary artery disease, cardiomyopathy, and acute arrhythmias.

The rest of this manuscript is structured in the following manner: Sect. 2 reviews related work in IoT-based healthcare monitoring and deep learning models for ECG classification, providing critical analysis of existing solutions and their limitations for deployment in Metropolitan Lima healthcare settings. Section 3 presents our proposed model, including data acquisition, XResNet1D architecture, and the clinical monitoring system implementation. In Sect. 4, we describe our validation methodology using GAMP 5 standards and usability testing with healthcare professionals. Section 5 analyzes the experimental results and compares our approach with state-of-the-art methods. Finally, Sect. 6 provides the paper's conclusions and identifies possible avenues for subsequent research.

2 Related Work

2.1 IoT-Based Monitoring Solutions

Multiple IoT-based monitoring systems have been created to improve real-time cardiac healthcare monitoring [11–13], leveraging different sensors and computational methods. However, analysis of these approaches reveals deployment constraints for resource-limited healthcare settings such as Metropolitan Lima.

Mary et al. introduced the WISE system, utilizing Body Area Sensor Networks (BASN) to capture ECG data, which is processed through an Adaptive Deep Neural Network (ADNN), achieving a 98.1% classification accuracy for cardiac anomalies [11]. The system's BASN infrastructure requiring multiple interconnected wearable sensors presents implementation complexity exceeding typical resource-constrained healthcare capabilities.

Another solution by Rahman et al. combined IoT with fuzzy logic, using the NodeMCU ESP8266 microcontroller and ECG sensors. This setup achieved near-perfect accuracy for arrhythmia detection by applying multiple Butterworth filters for noise reduction and fuzzy inference for real-time classification [12]. However, the dependence on proprietary IoT-Blynk platform and complex fuzzy logic processing creates technical barriers for implementation in limited-resource environments.

Raheja and Manocha designed an IoT framework on the ThingSpeak platform, incorporating the AD8232 ECG sensor and the Triple Data Encryption Standard (3-DES) for secure ECG data transmission, reaching 99.12% accuracy with a CNN model [13]. Despite high accuracy, the system's dependence on commercial MATLAB/ThingSpeak licenses and complex encryption requirements may limit accessibility in cost-constrained healthcare settings.

Similarly, Islam et al. deployed a multi-sensor system with MAX30100, AD8232, and MLX90614 sensors, integrated with a NodeMCU ESP8266 microcontroller for real-time cardiac monitoring using a CNN model, achieving a classification accuracy of 98.2% [9]. The multi-sensor approach increases hardware complexity and maintenance requirements compared to single-sensor alternatives.

Rehman et al. focused on sudden cardiac death (SCD) risks with a wearable ECG sensor and smart gloves that transmit data to an edge computing node using Bluetooth [14]. The specialized hardware requirements and limited transmission range (27 m) present practical deployment challenges in diverse healthcare environments.

In an IoMT-based approach, Baseer et al. utilized ECG, heart rate, and blood pressure sensors connected to IoMT devices, integrating TabNet and CatBoost algorithms to predict coronary artery disease with an accuracy of 98% [15]. The DEEP-CARDIO system by Yashudas et al. employed an array of biosensors, including ECG, pressure, pulse, and glucose sensors, connected to an Arduino for data acquisition and transmission to a cloud platform. With a BiGRU model featuring attention layers, this system achieved 99.90% accuracy in cardiovascular condition classification [10]. Both approaches require multiple specialized sensors, increasing system complexity and technical expertise requirements.

Lastly, Utsha and Morshed's CardioHelp app combined the AD8232 sensor with edge-computing AI classifiers, specifically LSTM, to achieve a classification accuracy of 98.74%, supporting beat-by-beat ECG analysis for immediate intervention [16]. The hybrid fog-edge IoT architecture by Ramya and Ramamoorthy further enhanced real-time monitoring using ECG and pulse sensors, achieving low-latency data processing and high prediction accuracy through Q-DEM algorithms [17]. While demonstrating strong performance, these systems require high-end computational infrastructure and extensive technical expertise for deployment and maintenance.

2.2 Deep Learning Models

Several Deep Learning models have been applied to cardiovascular disease classification, yielding substantial improvements. However, critical analysis reveals significant deployment barriers for resource-constrained healthcare settings like Metropolitan Lima.

Early contributions include a hybrid 1D-CNN and Bi-LSTM model that demonstrated 99.41% accuracy in arrhythmia detection [20,22,23], though requiring complex multi-stage preprocessing (SWT + multiple filters) and dual-architecture expertise that exceeds typical resource-limited capabilities. A CNN-based classifier optimized with the Artificial Hummingbird algorithm achieved 98.87% accuracy [20], while a dual-attention LSTM-CNN model (DAC-LSTM) reached 94% accuracy on 12-lead ECG data [20], but both systems require multi-lead ECG infrastructure significantly more costly than single-lead alternatives. The InfusedHeart model integrating CNN, LSTM, and RNN achieved 93.38% accuracy in cardiac acoustic event classification [24], yet depends on specialized hardware (Eko digital stethoscope, four-channel amplifier) that presents acquisition and maintenance challenges in environments with limited medical device infrastructure.

Advanced architectures have further improved performance but introduced additional complexity barriers. A Grad-CAM technique applied to DenseNet and CNN models enhanced explainability in myocardial infarction detection, achieving 98.9% accuracy [25], though requiring 12-lead ECG systems and multi-model parallel implementation. Hybrid CNN-LSTM ensemble models reaching 99.89% accuracy [26,27] demand extensive training times (up to 38 min) and big data handling (123,998 ECG beats), while hybrid models with attention mechanisms and GRUs perform strongly in big data environments [21] but require Apache Hadoop distributed infrastructure unsuitable for fog computing scenarios.

Transformer-based models like CNN-DVIT and hART have made significant strides, improving arrhythmia detection and heart failure risk prediction [19,28]. However, CNN-DVIT requires 12-lead ECG with Vision Transformer complexity, while hART depends on longitudinal medical records spanning decades, which are unavailable in Lima's fragmented healthcare system (MINSA, EsSalud, private, regional entities). GAN-based Transformer networks achieved 94.69% accuracy [29,30], but the dual-architecture complexity (Transformer + GAN) presents stability and maintenance challenges. A BiGRU-based system for cardiovascular disease prediction via IoT reached 99.9% accuracy [10], though requiring multiple specialized sensors that increase hardware complexity.

Notably, ResNet-based models have demonstrated exceptional performance in ECG classification, with implementations achieving up to 92.5% AUC on the PTB-XL dataset [31]. Unlike the complex multi-architecture approaches mentioned above, ResNet's unified architecture aligns better with resource-constrained environments, providing a foundation for efficient single-lead ECG analysis suitable for fog computing deployment in settings like Metropolitan Lima.

3 Proposed Model

In this section, we introduce an Intelligent Monitoring and Alert System designed to support healthcare professionals in detecting cardiovascular anomalies. The system combines real-time ECG monitoring with IoT and deep learning capabilities, enabling prompt alerts and facilitating early intervention. Physiological data, including ECG signals and other vital metrics, are continuously collected using IoT sensors such as the MAX30102 and AD8232. A ResNet based model, optimized for real-time analysis through Fog Computing, classifies the data to identify potential anomalies. Subsequently, the system provides alert notifications to healthcare professionals via a dedicated web and mobile interface, named DeepKer, enhancing patient care and response times in resource-constrained environments (see Fig. 1).

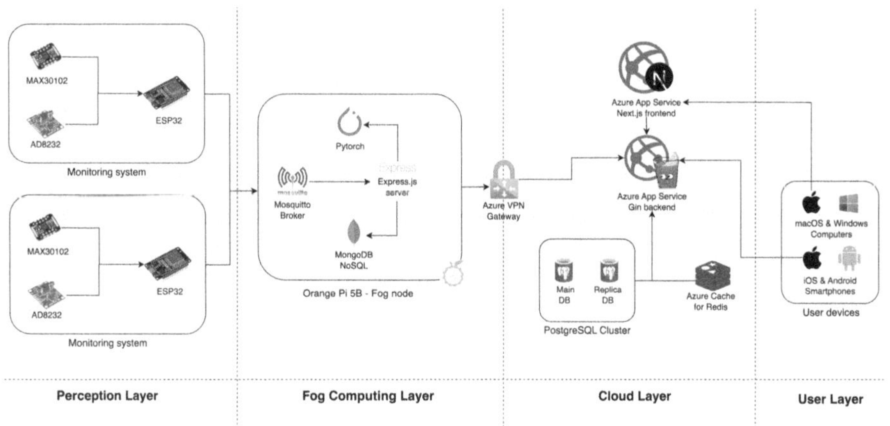

Fig. 1. DeepKer System Architecture for Intelligent Cardiovascular Monitoring Using IoT and Deep Learning for Early Anomaly Detection.

3.1 Data Acquisition

Data Collection. In the Perception Layer, physiological data from the patient is collected by a monitoring system composed of IoT sensors. Specifically, the MAX30102 sensor measures heart rate and blood oxygen levels, while the AD8232 records electrocardiogram (ECG) signals. For optimal data accuracy, the collection should take place in a low-noise environment with minimal interruptions, and preferably, the patient should remain still.

3.2 ECG Classification Using XResNet1D

Model Training. The model training procedure for our 1D ResNet architecture utilizes ECG signal information from the PTB-XL database, containing

21,837 12-lead ECG recordings gathered from 18,885 subjects, with each record lasting 10 s. It includes 71 ECG statements, categorized into diagnostic, form, and rhythm statements, annotated by up to two cardiologists [31]. While the data is available in both 500 Hz and 100 Hz formats, for our purposes, we will focus solely on the 100 Hz ECG data (Lead II) aligning the training with the specific data collected by our AD8232 sensor.

Proposed Architecture. Our XResNet1D model is designed for multi-label ECG classification, comprising 10,123,655 parameters. The architecture follows a deep residual network approach with four phases of residual blocks tailored for one-dimensional signal processing. The initial block comprises three convolutional layers incorporating BatchNorm1D and ReLU activation functions, progressively expanding feature representation from a single input channel [18]. The core comprises four ResNet blocks with a 4x expansion factor and kernel size of 5 for capturing complex ECG patterns. The feature extraction incorporates AdaptiveConcatPool1D, concatenating average and max pooling (producing 512 features), followed by a Flatten layer. The classification head includes BatchNorm1D, Dropout (0.5) to reduce overfitting [30], and Linear layers (512 → 128 → 5) with ReLU activation [18]. The output layer uses 5 units with implicit sigmoid activation for non-mutually exclusive class probabilities. The network undergoes training utilizing BCEWithLogitsLoss and the Adam optimization algorithm (learning rate: 0.001), with AUC as the primary performance metric. The complete architecture is illustrated in Fig. 2.

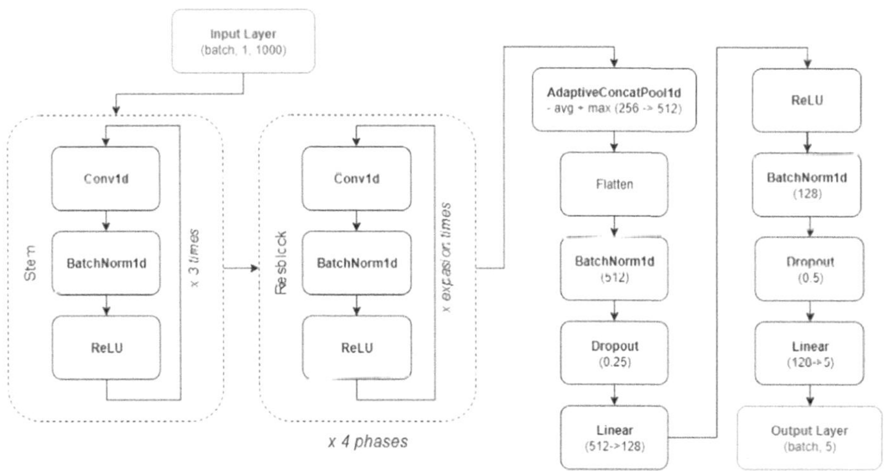

Fig. 2. XResNet1D Architecture for Multi-Label ECG Classification.

Inferences in Fog Computing Layer. In the Fog Computing Layer, the initial processing and inference of ECG data are conducted in proximity to the data source, facilitating real-time anomaly detection with minimal latency. Physiological data acquired via IoT sensors, including the MAX30102 (for heart rate and SpO_2) and AD8232 (for ECG), is transmitted via Wi-Fi protocol from the ESP32 microcontrollers to an Orange Pi 5B Plus computing unit. This node implements a non-relational MongoDB database for efficient time-series data storage.

The data is processed using PyTorch with implementation of our XResNet1D model for inference. This setup leverages the computational efficiency of the RK3588S octa-core ARM processor, ensuring prompt generation of critical insights. Only relevant information, such as detected anomalies, is forwarded to the frontend-also hosted within the Fog layer-to support swift decision-making. Simultaneously, the Fog server sends anomaly alerts to the Cloud layer for centralized management.

3.3 Clinical Monitoring System

The Clinical Monitoring System is engineered to deliver healthcare practitioners immediate access to patient information and notifications, supporting initiative-taking patient management. The system integrates various components across layers (Fog Computing, Cloud, and User) and is accessible through both web and mobile applications.

Cloud-Based Data Management. In the Cloud Layer, deployed on Azure, data and predictive results are securely transferred from the Fog Layer using a VPN gateway. This layer operates a backend server built with Go's Gin framework, which interacts with a PostgreSQL database cluster for safe data storage. The backend service supports comprehensive functionality including alert generation, patient filtering, user management, device administration, and real-time data synchronization. Running in a Docker container with sufficient capacity to handle predicted loads of up to 10 concurrent users, the system provides 24/7 access and ensures continuous monitoring capabilities for healthcare professionals.

User Interface. The User Layer enables medical professionals to interact with the Clinical Monitoring System through the DeepKer applications, accessible on both mobile and web platforms (see Fig. 3 and Fig. 4). These interfaces are designed to provide intuitive access to patient data, alerts, and system settings, streamlining clinical workflows.

The mobile application includes two primary modules: "Alerts", which serves as a centralized dashboard for viewing and managing real-time attended and unattended alerts, and "Account", which enables users to view personal and application information. The web application extends the functionality of the mobile app by incorporating additional modules: "Patients" for accessing detailed patient profiles and health records, "Devices" for managing IoT devices linked to patients, "User Guide" for system navigation, and "Administration" for managing user accounts and access.

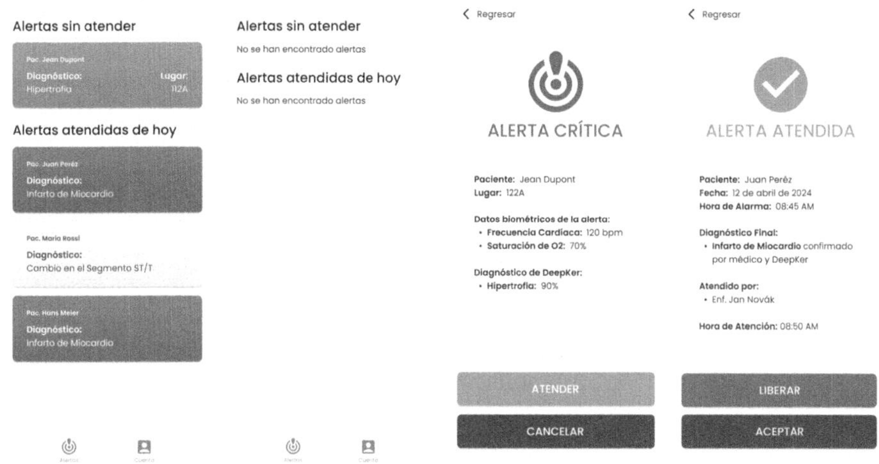

Fig. 3. Main user interfaces for DeepKer mobile application.

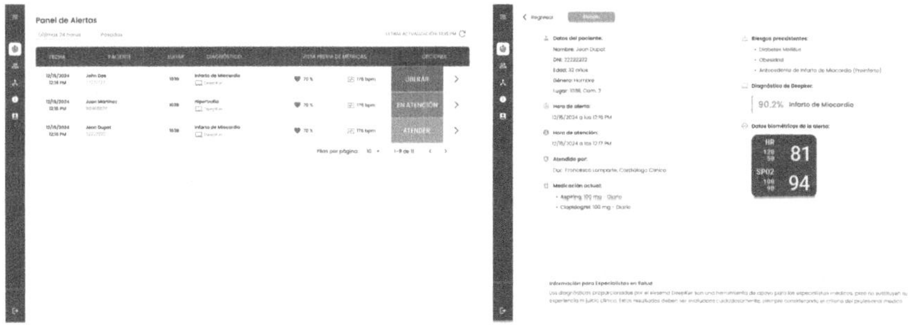

Fig. 4. Main user interfaces for DeepKer web application.

4 Validation

To validate the system, a two-phase approach was undertaken: system validation and usability evaluation. System validation, in collaboration with the pharmaceutical-focused organization "Gemba Group", followed Good Automated Manufacturing Practice (GAMP) 5 standards, which are widely accepted in healthcare and medical technology to ensure security, reliability, and regulatory compliance.

Usability validation involved 10 healthcare professionals from public and private institutions across Metropolitan Lima in a simulated clinical setting, focusing on device setup, alert response, and patient monitoring.

This dual approach allowed for a comprehensive validation of the system's security robustness and its usability from a medical professional's perspective, ensuring both compliance and practical effectiveness.

Table 1. Questionnaire for healthcare professionals.

Category	Question		Type
General Operations	Q1	What needs have you identified in your daily routine regarding the monitoring of patients' vital signs?	Open-ended
	Q2	Regarding the device, how easy do you find linking it to a patient?	Close-ended
	Q3	Regarding the alert, how simple was it to view and respond to the alert?	Close-ended
Usability	Q4	How relevant do you consider the use of advanced filters for patient search?	Close-ended
	Q5	How timely do you find the system's alerts in critical situations?	Close-ended
	Q6	Regarding receiving an alert on your phone, how useful do you find receiving an audible or visual alert to address an emergency?	Close-ended
Clinical Efficacy	Q7	Do you think the predictions provided by the DeepKer system could help in the early detection of cardiovascular abnormalities?	Close-ended
	Q8	How practical do you think the DeepKer system is for monitoring patients predisposed to cardiovascular abnormalities?	Close-ended

4.1 Experiment I - System Validation Using GAMP 5

To validate the system, we employed the GAMP 5 framework, which emphasizes a risk-based, iterative development approach that supports patient safety, data integrity, and product quality. This makes GAMP 5 a widely accepted standard for achieving FDA and other regulatory certifications [32,33].

In this phase, we collaborated with specialists from "Gemba Group", who conduct-ed an audit to assess the system's compliance with GAMP 5 standards as a Category 3 software, which includes non-configurable software used in regulated environments. Based on the audit findings, the specialists recommended a reduced validation approach focused on the system's core functions. To ensure compliance and system quality, a comprehensive validation framework was developed, encompassing a Risk Assessment, Validation Master Plan, and Validation Report. Following the validation tests, a final report was generated detailing the results.

4.2 Experiment II - Usability Evaluation with Medical Professionals

Usability validation was conducted with healthcare professionals from various institutions across Metropolitan Lima, Peru. A total of 10 participants were recruited for this qualitative evaluation using purposive sampling. This method was chosen to intentionally include professionals with different roles (5 doctors and 5 nurses) and work environments (from both public and private facilities) to gather a varied set of initial perspectives. The participants, aged 25 to 62, engaged in an evaluation held in a simulated clinical setting, which focused on device setup, alert response, patient monitoring, and user satisfaction. Each participant completed a structured session involving a questionnaire and a follow-up interview (see Table 1). Given the small sample size, the findings from this evaluation should be interpreted as exploratory insights intended for system refinement, not as conclusive or generalizable results.

The questionnaire, administered via Microsoft Forms during a live simulation of the platform, included eight questions organized into three categories. First, General Operations (Q1-Q2) covered participants' general monitoring needs and the task of linking a device. Second, Usability (Q3-Q5) tested the ease of interacting with alerts, the usefulness of search filters, and the alert system's timeliness. Lastly, Clinical Efficacy (Q6-Q8) assessed the practical value of mobile alerts, the system's predictive capabilities, and its overall suitability for monitoring at-risk patients. With the exception of the open-ended Q1, all questions were assessed using a 5-point Likert scale, where 1 indicated 'Strongly Disagree' and 5 indicated 'Strongly Agree' with the statement presented.

5 Results and Discussion

To evaluate the effectiveness of our trained XResNet1D architecture, we tested it on a separate validation dataset employing the Area Under the Receiver Operating Characteristic curve (AUC) measure. This metric proves especially useful for unbalanced ECG datasets since it assesses the model's capacity to differentiate between normal heart rhythms and diverse abnormalities independent of the chosen classification threshold.

Our model achieved an overall macro-average AUC of 0.847, demonstrating robust discriminative capability across the five diagnostic superclasses in the PTB-XL dataset. Figure 5 illustrates the ROC curves and corresponding AUC values for each diagnostic category.

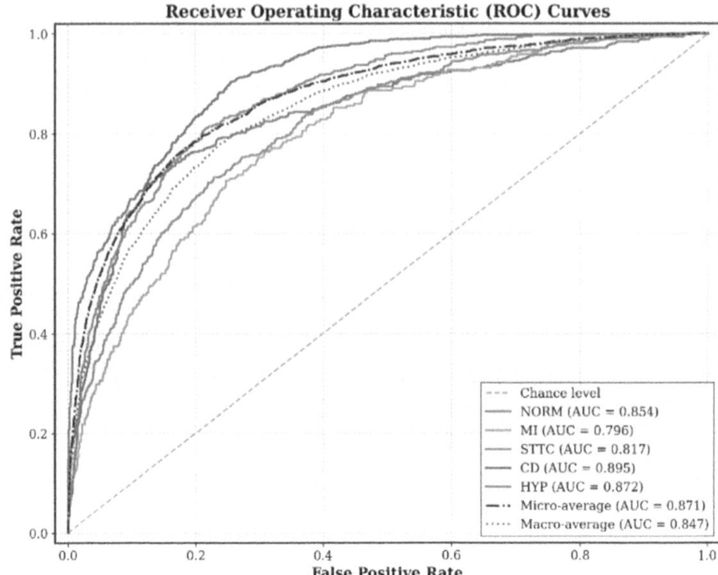

Fig. 5. ROC curves for the XResNet1D model across five diagnostic categories with micro and macro averages.

These results establish a solid foundation for our real-time ECG monitoring system. The strong performance in detecting Conduction Disturbances and Hypertrophy is particularly valuable for clinical applications, as these conditions often require prompt intervention. Future work will focus on improving classification accuracy for Myocardial Infarction, which remains challenging due to its complex manifestation in single-lead ECG signals.

5.1 Comparative Analysis

To position our XResNet1d model within the current research landscape, we performed a comparative evaluation against prominent ECG classification methodologies. Table 2 displays a performance assessment comparing our approach with various cutting-edge single-lead ECG analysis techniques, utilizing metrics derived from the thorough assessment [34].

Table 2. Comparative performance analysis of single lead ECG classification methods.

Method	AUC (%)
DenseCNN_Wang	82.7
SEresnet18	82.7
SEresnet34	82.9
CNN_Hannun	83.1
KD+FitNet	83.8
MVKT-ECG	84.3
DeepKer model	84.6

Our model achieves an AUC of 84.6%, outperforming all compared alternatives in this key discriminative metric. This superior performance can be attributed to two factors: our deep residual architecture's capacity to capture complex temporal ECG patterns, and our optimization approach focused on discriminative capability across multiple thresholds rather than at a single operating point. This design choice aligns with DeepKer's clinical application needs, where the ability to adjust sensitivity thresholds based on specific medical contexts is essential for effective monitoring [35]. These results validate our architectural decisions and demonstrate the system's potential for real-time cardiovascular classification in healthcare settings.

5.2 Expert Judgement

GAMP5 Evaluation. The Computerized System Validation (CSV) report documented that all primary system functionalities successfully passed the reduced validation process, with a data transmission time of approximately 2 s from the IoT device to the web monitoring platform. The system achieved passing results across all five critical areas tested: "User Access Management", "Alert Management", "Patient Management", "Device Integration", and "System Navigation and User Guidance". These comprehensive validation results confirm the system's compliance with GAMP 5 standards and its readiness for clinical implementation.

Usability for Medical Professionals. The high average scores (see Fig. 6) indicate a positive overall reception of the system. In the General Operations category, both nurses and doctors provided an average rating of 4.80 (SD $= \pm 0.45$), reflecting strong agreement on the system's ease of use. For the Usability category, the scores were 4.40 (SD $= \pm 0.63$) for doctors and 4.60 (SD $= \pm 0.63$) for nurses, showing high satisfaction with the alert features. Lastly, Clinical Efficacy category received average scores of 4.33 (SD $= \pm 0.98$) from doctors and 4.60 (SD $= \pm 0.51$) from nurses. While both groups responded positively overall, a notable divergence emerged in the Clinical Efficacy category. Nurses rated its efficacy with high consistency ($4.60, \mathrm{SD} = \pm 0.51$), whereas doctors' ratings were more varied and slightly lower ($4.33, \mathrm{SD} = \pm 0.98$). Interviews indicated this discrepancy reflects their professional roles: nurses focused on the system's immediate workflow efficiency, while the doctors' varied feedback was rooted in differing opinions on its diagnostic potential versus the need for more extensive clinical validation.

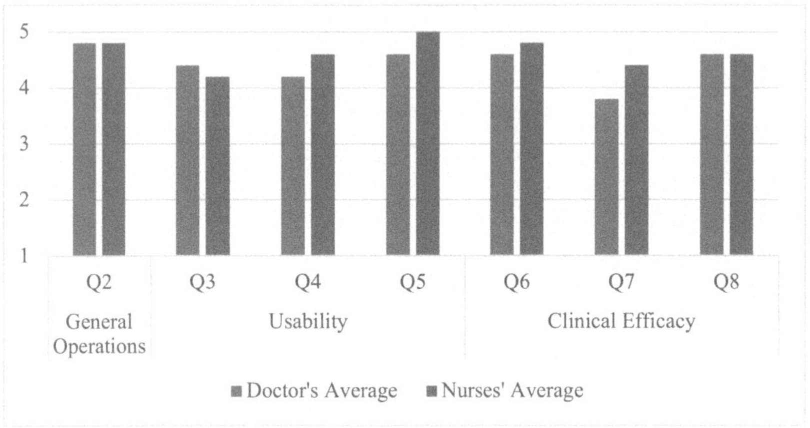

Fig. 6. Distribution of usability ratings from doctor and nursing personnel across system functionality.

6 Conclusions

This paper presented DeepKer, an intelligent system for classifying single-lead ECG data through a custom IoT device. The XResNet1D architecture achieved an AUC of 0.84, with successful GAMP 5 validation and positive usability ratings (4.53/5) from healthcare professionals. The system demonstrated effective IoT-Fog-Cloud integration with approximately 2-second data transmission latency.

Several limitations affect result interpretation and require acknowledgment. The performance variation across diagnostic categories (0.796 AUC for Myocardial Infarction versus 0.895 for Conduction Disturbances) and validation in simulated rather than real clinical environments indicate that performance metrics should be viewed as preliminary evidence. Furthermore, the single-lead ECG limitation, while addressing cost constraints in resource-limited settings, inherently reduces diagnostic capability compared to standard clinical practice, suggesting that our positive results represent preliminary rather than definitive validation for comprehensive cardiovascular monitoring.

However, these limitations primarily concern the specific classification model and sensor configuration rather than the overall system architecture. The validated software framework, including the alert management system, clinical interface, and IoT-Fog-Cloud integration, represents a reusable foundation that can accommodate improved sensors and enhanced models. The positive GAMP 5 compliance and usability validation demonstrate that the core infrastructure and workflow design are clinically viable, providing a scalable platform for future improvements.

For future work, conducting clinical trials with real patients and implementing multi-lead ECG capabilities would leverage this established foundation to achieve comprehensive cardiovascular monitoring in resource-constrained environments.

Disclosure of Interests. The authors have no competing interests to declare that are relevant to the content of this article.

References

1. World Health Organization. The top 10 causes of death (2024). https://www.who.int/news-room/fact-sheets/detail/the-top-10-causes-of-death. Accessed 3 Oct 2024
2. World Heart Federation. World Heart Report 2023: Confronting the World's Number One Killer. World Heart Federation (2023). https://world-heart-federation.org/wp-content/uploads/World-Heart-Report-2023.pdf. Accessed 4 Oct 2024
3. Institute for Health Metrics and Evaluation. GBD Compare (2023). https://vizhub.healthdata.org/gbd-compare/. Accessed 4 Oct 2024
4. Organización Panamericana de la Salud. Perfil de País - Perú | Salud en las Américas (2022). https://hia.paho.org/es/perfiles-de-pais/peru. Accessed 4 Oct 2024
5. Custodio-Sánchez, P., Miranda-Noé, D., López-Rojas, L.M., et al.: Proposal for initial management of uncomplicated ST elevation myocardial infarction in centers without percutaneous coronary intervention capacity in Peru. Archivos Peruanos de Cardiologia y Cirugia Cardiovascular **4**, 164–183 (2023). https://doi.org/10.47487/apcyccv.v4i4.335
6. Nancy, A.A., Ravindran, D., Raj Vincent, P.M.D., et al.: IoT-cloud-based smart healthcare monitoring system for heart disease prediction via deep learning. Electronics (Switzerland) **11** (2022). https://doi.org/10.3390/electronics11152292
7. Verma, P., Tiwari, R., Hong, W.C., et al.: FETCH: a deep learning-based fog computing and IoT integrated environment for healthcare monitoring and diagnosis. IEEE Access **10**, 12548–12563 (2022). https://doi.org/10.1109/ACCESS.2022.3143793
8. Sadad, T., Safran, M., Khan, I., et al.: Efficient classification of ECG images using a lightweight CNN with attention module and IoT. Sensors **23** (2023). https://doi.org/10.3390/s23187697
9. Islam, M.R., Kabir, M.M., Mridha, M.F., et al.: Deep learning-based IoT system for remote monitoring and early detection of health issues in real-time. Sensors **23** (2023). https://doi.org/10.3390/s23115204
10. Yashudas, A., Gupta, D., Prashant, G.C., et al.: DEEP-CARDIO: recommendation system for cardiovascular disease prediction using IOT network. IEEE Sens J. (2024). https://doi.org/10.1109/JSEN.2024.3373429
11. Mary, G.A.A., Sathyasri, B., Murali, K., et al.: Electrocardiogram signal classification in an IoT environment using an adaptive deep neural networks. Neural Comput. Appl. **35**, 15333–15342 (2023). https://doi.org/10.1007/s00521-023-08534-9

12. Rahman, M.Z., Akbar, M.A., Leiva, V., et al.: An intelligent health monitoring and diagnosis system based on the internet of things and fuzzy logic for cardiac arrhythmia COVID-19 patients. Comput. Biol. Med. **154** (2023). https://doi.org/10.1016/j.compbiomed.2023.106583
13. Raheja, N., Kumar Manocha, A.: An IoT enabled secured clinical health care framework for diagnosis of heart diseases. Biomed. Signal Process. Control **80** (2023). https://doi.org/10.1016/j.bspc.2022.104368
14. Rehman, S.U., Sadek, I., Huang, B., et al.: IoT-based emergency cardiac death risk rescue alert system. MethodsX **13** (2024). https://doi.org/10.1016/j.mex.2024.102834
15. Baseer, K.K., Sivakumar, K., Veeraiah, D., et al.: Healthcare diagnostics with an adaptive deep learning model integrated with the Internet of medical Things (IoMT) for predicting heart disease. Biomed. Signal Process. Control **92** (2024). https://doi.org/10.1016/j.bspc.2024.105988
16. Utsha, U.T., Morshed, B.I.: CardioHelp: a smartphone application for beat-by-beat ECG signal analysis for real-time cardiac disease detection using edge-computing AI classifiers. Smart Health **31** (2024). https://doi.org/10.1016/j.smhl.2024.100446
17. Ramya, R., Ramamoorthy, S.: Hybrid fog-edge-IoT architecture for real-time data monitoring. Int. J. Intell. Eng. Syst. **17**, 228–239 (2024). https://doi.org/10.22266/ijies2024.0229.22
18. Mohonta, S.C., Motin, M.A., Kumar, D.K.: Electrocardiogram based arrhythmia classification using wavelet transform with deep learning model. Sens. Biosensing. Res. **37** (2022). https://doi.org/10.1016/j.sbsr.2022.100502
19. Dong, Y., Zhang, M., Qiu, L., et al.: An arrhythmia classification model based on vision transformer with deformable attention. Micromachines (Basel) **14** (2023). https://doi.org/10.3390/mi14061155
20. Jin, Y., Li, Z., Qin, C., et al.: A novel attentional deep neural network-based assessment method for ECG quality. Biomed. Signal Process. Control **79** (2023). https://doi.org/10.1016/j.bspc.2022.104064
21. Rao, G.M., Ramesh, D., Sharma, V., et al.: AttGRU-HMSI: enhancing heart disease diagnosis using hybrid deep learning approach. Sci. Rep. **14** (2024). https://doi.org/10.1038/s41598-024-56931-4
22. Rahul, J., Sharma, L.D.: Automatic cardiac arrhythmia classification based on hybrid 1-D CNN and Bi-LSTM model. Biocybern. Biomed. Eng. **42**, 312–324 (2022). https://doi.org/10.1016/j.bbe.2022.02.006
23. Elyamani, H.A., Salem, M.A., Melgani, F., Yhiea, N.M.: Deep residual 2D convolutional neural network for cardiovascular disease classification. Sci. Rep. **14** (2024). https://doi.org/10.1038/s41598-024-72382-3
24. Pandya, S., Gadekallu, T.R., Reddy, P.K., et al.: InfusedHeart: a novel knowledge-infused learning framework for diagnosis of cardiovascular events. IEEE Trans. Comput. Soc. Syst. **11**, 3060—3069 (2024). https://doi.org/10.1109/TCSS.2022.3151643
25. Jahmunah, V., Ng, E.Y.K., Tan, R.S., et al.: Explainable detection of myocardial infarction using deep learning models with Grad-CAM technique on ECG signals. Comput. Biol. Med. **146** (2022). https://doi.org/10.1016/j.compbiomed.2022.105550
26. Rai, H.M., Chatterjee, K.: Hybrid CNN-LSTM deep learning model and ensemble technique for automatic detection of myocardial infarction using big ECG data (2021). https://doi.org/10.1007/s10489-021-02696-6/Published

27. Hasbullah, S., Mohd Zahid, M.S., Mandala, S.: Detection of myocardial infarction using hybrid models of convolutional neural network and recurrent neural network. BioMedInformatics **3**, 478—492 (2023). https://doi.org/10.3390/biomedinformatics3020033
28. Moroz, H., Li, Y., Marelli, A.: hART: deep learning-informed lifespan heart failure risk trajectories. Int. J. Med. Inform. **185** (2024). https://doi.org/10.1016/j.ijmedinf.2024.105384
29. Xia, Y., Xu, Y., Chen, P., et al.: Generative adversarial network with transformer generator for boosting ECG classification. Biomed. Signal Process. Control **80** (2023). https://doi.org/10.1016/j.bspc.2022.104276
30. Rahman, A.U., Alsenani, Y., Zafar, A., et al.: Enhancing heart disease prediction using a self-attention-based transformer model. Sci. Rep. **14** (2024). https://doi.org/10.1038/s41598-024-51184-7
31. Wagner, P., Strodthoff, N., Bousseljot, R.D., et al.: PTB-XL, a large publicly available electrocardiography dataset. Sci. Data **7** (2020). https://doi.org/10.1038/s41597-020-0495-6
32. Dong, Q.H., Vogel-Heuser, B., Neumann, E.M.: Including validation of process control systems' engineering into the technical debt classification. Forschung im Ingenieurwesen/Eng. Res. **88** (2024) . https://doi.org/10.1007/s10010-024-00742-6
33. Pedro, F., Veiga, F., Mascarenhas-Melo, F.: Impact of GAMP 5, data integrity and QbD on quality assurance in the pharmaceutical industry: How obvious is it? Drug Discov. Today **28**, 103759 (2023). https://doi.org/10.1016/J.DRUDIS.2023.103759
34. Qin, Y., Sun, L., Chen, H., et al.: MVKT-ECG: efficient single-lead ECG classification for multi-label arrhythmia by multi-view knowledge transferring. Comput. Biol. Med. **166** (2023). https://doi.org/10.1016/j.compbiomed.2023.107503
35. Śmigiel, S., Pałczyński, K., Ledziński, D.: ECG signal classification using deep learning techniques based on the PTB-XL dataset. Entropy **23** (2021). https://doi.org/10.3390/e23091121

AI Approach to Abstraction Process in Chilean Students of English as a Foreign Language

David Ruete[1], Margarita Aravena-Gaete[2], Scarlette Lepe[1], Edgardo Aragú[1], Carlos Cid[1], Pilar López-Lira[1], and Jean Paul Maidana[1,3(✉)]

[1] Universidad Andrés Bello, Viña del Mar, Chile
[2] Universidad Central, Santiago, Chile
[3] Instituto de Tecnología para la Innovación en Salud y Bienestar, Universidad Andrés Bello, Viña del Mar, Chile
jean.maidana@unab.cl

Abstract. This article explores the abstraction process in Chilean students studying English as a foreign language. The development of higher-order skills, including critical thinking and abstraction, is a fundamental objective in education. Abstraction, the ability to identify patterns and utilize information effectively, plays a pivotal role in this process. The study examines the correlation between second language learning and cognitive skill development, emphasizing the importance of English language education. It also delves into the impact of demographic factors like gender, age, school type, and parental education on students' abstraction skills. Results from descriptive analysis reveal that students generally perform better in perspective than in abstraction. Female students and older individuals demonstrate higher levels of abstraction, and private school students exhibit superior performance. First-generation university students tend to lag behind their peers. The classification analysis highlights the significance of using neural networks over K-Nearest Neighbors, especially Deep Neural Networks, in predicting. In conclusion, studying English as a foreign language can significantly enhance cognitive skills and critical thinking. The application of machine learning techniques improves the classification of abstraction. These findings have far-reaching implications for enhancing educational programs and promoting the development of abstraction skills in English as a foreign language students.

Keywords: thinking skills · second language · abstraction process

1 Introduction

In the realm of higher education, the quest to cultivate advanced cognitive skills within university students stands as a perennial challenge, faced not only by

T. Guarda et al. (Eds.): ARTIIS 2025, CCIS 2789, pp. 534–548, 2026.
https://doi.org/10.1007/978-3-032-16758-3_40

educational institutions within the domestic context but also resonating on the international stage. This ever-persistent challenge is particularly salient within the domain of English language teaching programs as a foreign language. These higher-order cognitive skills are progressively gaining prominence and recognition within the broader societal context [1].

The paramount goal underpinning the development of these advanced cognitive skills is to endow students with the essential tools needed to confront the intricacies and multifaceted challenges that may emerge within their academic and personal spheres [2]. Within the realm of these coveted cognitive abilities, critical thinking takes center stage, exemplifying a quintessential component of higher-order thinking skills that has, over the past decade, garnered widespread acknowledgment and acclaim within the field of education. Educators, in their continuous evolution, have come to a profound understanding of the central importance of fostering reasoning and thinking abilities among their students. This cognitive odyssey involves a panoply of cognitive activities that range from the probing of established convictions to the reevaluation of perspectives, the harboring of a healthy degree of skepticism, the art of making meaningful comparisons, the skill of critically assessing information, and the acumen to render sagacious judgments [3].

Critical thinking encompasses a complex cognitive process that hinges on the sagacious deployment of reason to judiciously discern the dichotomy between truth and falsehood. This cerebral dexterity isn't confined to the realms of the written word but extends its reach to the spoken discourse as well. Further illuminate that critical thinking and reasoning, in their integrated harmony, play a pivotal role in the manifestation of well-informed decisions and the successful resolution of intricate problems [4].

Guiding the educators and delineating the cognitive growth of students, Benjamin Bloom introduced the pioneering Bloom's Taxonomy in 1948 [5]. This paradigm has undergone subsequent iterations and refinements and stands as a pivotal scaffold for elucidating the cognitive skills that students must progressively accrue. This influential taxonomy, not only assists educators in elucidating explicit learning objectives but also plays a pivotal role in engendering the acquisition of specific cognitive skills. The taxonomy is organized into three distinct strata: lower-order cognitive skills, which encompass the capacities of remembering and understanding; middle-order cognitive skills that revolve around the application of knowledge; and higher-order cognitive skills, constituting the crowning tier that encapsulates the domains of analysis, evaluation, and creation. These higher-order cognitive skills, by virtue of their profound complexity, emerge as a focal point of emphasis within the domain of education.

In this tapestry of higher-order cognitive skills, abstraction emerges as a nuanced yet pivotal facet of the cognitive landscape. Abstraction, as a cognitive skill, thrusts students into the task of discerning patterns and the formulation of insightful responses to the stimuli that they encounter within their immediate environment. Mastering the art of abstraction entails equipping students with the capability to adroitly arrange and mobilize information, leading to an optimized cognitive process. It grants students the faculty to undertake cognitive shifts, enabling them to scrutinize multifaceted scenarios from diverse vantage points, ultimately facilitating the discernment of recurring patterns amidst the complexity of the world around them [5].

A growing body of empirical studies has unearthed a positive correlation between the pursuit of a second language and the development of a gamut of cognitive competencies. These encompass metalinguistic awareness, metacognitive proficiencies, cognitive flexibility, and abstract reasoning. Furthermore, it is noteworthy that advanced second-language learners have consistently demonstrated superior academic performance when compared to their monolingual counterparts [6]. These findings underscore the pivotal role of second-language acquisition in elevating cognitive abilities, within the spectrum of which abstraction occupies a central place.

As a quintessential higher-order cognitive skill, abstraction empowers students to forge connections, apprehend interrelationships, and broaden their cognitive horizons. This multifaceted skill bestows upon students the capability to scrutinize commonalities across diverse concepts and distinctions across myriad notions, ultimately furnishing them with a dynamic toolkit to confront novel challenges with heightened acumen and sagacity [7].

In the scholarly discourse delves into the multifaceted intricacies of abstraction, discerning two fundamental aspects intrinsic to this cognitive process. The first facet is the art of winnowing away superfluous information, a process that entails the distillation of the data to reveal its core essence. The second aspect is centered around the encapsulation of content through perceptive pattern recognition, a process that prompts the unearthing of connections and relationships, thereby furnishing an enriched cognitive landscape. It is evident that the meticulous application of this cognitive process, exerts a profound and transformative influence on students' faculties of reasoning, ultimately engendering a deeper coherence within their thought processes [1].

Within the context of higher education, aspirants for the vocation of educators, represented by students pursuing English pedagogy, stand at the crossroads of a compelling and ardent imperative. These aspiring educators must embark on a profound odyssey to cultivate their abstraction skills, thus equipping them to partake in judicious discourse across diverse educational scenarios and make informed, reflective, and sagacious decisions. In this educational tapestry, abstraction emerges as a cornerstone, interweaving its cognitive threads with other higher-order thinking skills, thereby crafting a potent and multifaceted foundation for educators [8].

In conclusion, by recognizing the paramount importance of critical thinking, discerning the profound influence of second language acquisition on cognitive development, and acknowledging the pivotal role played by abstraction in the pantheon of advanced thinking skills, educators and researchers are poised to take significant strides towards enhancing the quality of education. Their journey is inherently connected to the fervent development of multifaceted cognitive skills that are indispensable within today's dynamic, interconnected, and complex educational landscape. The introduction has shed light on the contextual underpinnings, thereby setting the stage for subsequent sections that delve into the scholarly milieu, the methodological landscape, and the nuanced findings related to the cultivation of abstraction among learners of English as a foreign language.

2 Related Works

Within the scholarly discourse, it becomes increasingly apparent that the acquisition of higher-order skills is intrinsically linked to the endeavor of second language acquisition, albeit with notable nuances and caveats. This interplay between second language learning and advanced cognitive competencies has attracted the attention of scholars and educators, ultimately birthing a tapestry of qualitative studies that illuminate the profound connections that underpin this relationship [5].

Benjelloun and El [5] underscore the integral role of the type of language activities and the intrinsic motivation exhibited by students in shaping the trajectory of their cognitive growth. Their qualitative explorations delve into the diverse dimensions of second language acquisition, acknowledging that the manner in which students engage with linguistic activities within the second language is instrumental in determining the extent to which higher-order cognitive skills are honed.

Furthermore, in this intricate tapestry of second language learning, Véliz and Véliz-Campos [9,10] emerge as prominent voices advocating for the infusion of critical thinking activities within English as a second language (L2) curricula. Their insights are rooted in the recognition that critical thinking, as a cognitive catalyst, not only augments linguistic proficiency but also propels learners into the realm of profound intellectual exploration. They propose comprehensive measures for the strategic realignment and redesign of study programs, elucidating the transformative potential of infusing such thinking within the academic continuum.

In the arena of educational programs, nuances in program design can profoundly shape the cognitive landscape of learners. Llinares and Evnitskaya [11] have diligently observed and documented the disparities that surface within study programs. It is evident that the configuration of educational programs, characterized by varied language exposure and meticulous content regulation, wields a profound influence on the outcomes related to higher-order thinking skills. Their qualitative investigations unearth a nexus between meticulous program design and the enhanced cultivation of these advanced cognitive capacities.

In the journey of exploring the connection between second language learning and higher-order cognitive skills, Sehic [6] offers intriguing insights. His study navigates the complex terrain of student performance within second language courses, endeavoring to discern the disparities that arise within this milieu. While his research might not reveal significant variances in the performance of students, it significantly elucidates the fascinating outcome that those who successfully pass these courses are often endowed with higher grades. This subtle yet noteworthy distinction underscores the relationship between language acquisition and cognitive development.

The capacity to think critically has, within the ambit of second language acquisition, been celebrated for its transformative influence on learners. Baranovska et al. [2] delve into the synergy that exists between English as a second language courses and the nurturing of critical thinking abilities. Their empirical findings paint a promising picture, revealing that a staggering 91% of students exhibit marked improvement in both their language acquisition skills and their cognitive competence. This enhancement spans across a spectrum of cognitive dimensions, encompassing differentiation, categorization, comparative analysis, estimation, critical examination, and synthesis of information.

Intriguingly, the realm of critical thinking extends its reach to the domain of writing proficiency in English as a second language, where profound interconnections have been illuminated. Soodmand et al. [12] and Ünaldı and Yüce [13] have undertaken a rigorous exploration of the intricate relationship that interlinks critical thinking, analytical prowess, and the evaluative capacities of students, ultimately discerning a significant correlation between these variables. Their research postulates that critical thinking, coupled with the ability to deeply analyze and rigorously evaluate information, emerges as a poignant predictor of writing proficiency within the English language.

Lastly, in this rich panorama of research, the imperative of evaluating the abstraction process within second language learning emerges as a focal point. Marzano et al. [14,15] and Beas et al. [16] have ventured to develop evaluative tools that are expressly rooted in the abstraction process. These innovative tools serve as a catalyst for conducting quantitative and innovative assessments of abstraction within the context of second language acquisition. Through these tools, educators, researchers, and scholars can delve deeper into the nuanced terrain of abstract thought, ultimately unearthing invaluable insights into the cognitive landscapes of learners.

In summary, the reviewed studies emphasize the importance of critical thinking and abstraction as core competencies in second language acquisition. However, divergences are evident in their methodological approaches, as some prioritize the explicit teaching of cognitive strategies, while others limit themselves to evaluating results without delving into the underlying processes. Furthermore, much of the literature comes from European and Asian contexts, with little evidence from Latin America, which represents a significant gap. In this context, the present research offers a novel approach by examining the abstraction process in Chilean students of English as a foreign language, integrating socio-educational variables and machine learning techniques to generate contextualized evidence. In sum, this background not only consolidates the relationship between second language acquisition and the development of higher-order cognitive skills but also establishes a critical framework that guides the methodological sections and findings presented in this work.

3 Methods

In this section, we will provide a comprehensive overview of the methodology employed in our study. We will detail the Abstraction Evaluation Test, designed and validated by Aravena-Gaete et al. [17], and explain its application to our sample, which consists of 81 students from the English Pedagogy program for Elementary and High School Teaching at the Universidad Nacional Andrés Bello. This sample includes a diverse representation of both male and female participants.

3.1 Instrument

The primary instrument used in our study is the Abstraction Evaluation Test, which was developed and rigorously validated by Aravena-Gaete et al. [17]. We selected this instrument based on its proven reliability and appropriateness for evaluating the abstraction skills of second language learners, aligning perfectly with the objectives of our research.

The Abstraction Evaluation Test features two key definitions of critical thinking, one as proposed by Paul and Elder [18] and the other by [19]. These definitions are commonly referenced in the literature and provide a solid theoretical foundation for our instrument. The test comprises a total of 14 questions, systematically organized into phases: three questions for each phase of the evaluation process. The only exception is the title proposal phase, which includes a single question. Responses to these questions are rated on a comprehensive scale ranging from 1 (deficient) to 4 (excellent). The final abstraction score is calculated as the simple average of these responses.

In addition to the core evaluation tool, we incorporated a set of demographic questions, which are pivotal for the subsequent descriptive, statistical, and classification analyses of our sample.

3.2 Descriptive Analysis Procedure

Our comprehensive analysis of the data obtained from the Abstraction Evaluation Test involves a meticulous and systematic process. The data is initially entered into a dedicated database to facilitate subsequent manipulation and analysis. This phase also includes data cleaning procedures to eliminate inaccuracies and inconsistencies, ensuring the accuracy and reliability of our dataset.

Within our analysis, we particularly focus on two significant aspects, Perspective and Abstraction. For Perspective, we consider the results of the analysis phase. In the case of Abstraction, we delve into a detailed assessment of synthesis (questions 1 to 3), question formulation, labeling, and title proposal (questions 4 to 13). All responses to these facets are consistently rated on the 1–4 scale, providing a robust basis for further analysis. Furthermore, the inclusion of demographic data enriches our understanding of the sample and facilitates more nuanced insights. Input variables from the test (see Eqs. 1 and 2):

- Time: Response time
- Age: Age of the participants
- Gender: Female and Male
- Semester: Semester enrolled in the program
- School type: Private, Subsidized, or Public
- First-generation university students
- Perspective/Synthesis evaluation: Questions 1 to 3
- Abstraction evaluation: Questions 4 to 13

The Output variables from model (see Eqs. 3 and 4):

- Perspective:

$$\overline{X_P} = \text{Average (Input Variables)} \tag{1}$$

$$\overline{X_P} = \begin{cases} \text{Deficient,} & 1 \leq \overline{X_P} < 2 \\ \text{Satisfactory,} & 2 \leq \overline{X_P} < 3 \\ \text{Good,} & 3 \leq \overline{X_P} < 3.5 \\ \text{Excellent,} & 3.5 \leq \overline{X_P} \leq 4 \end{cases} \tag{2}$$

- Abstraction:

$$\overline{X_{AB}} = \text{Average (Input Variables)} \tag{3}$$

$$\overline{X_{AB}} = \begin{cases} \text{Deficient,} & 1 \leq \overline{X_{AB}} < 2 \\ \text{Satisfactory,} & 2 \leq \overline{X_{AB}} < 3 \\ \text{Good,} & 3 \leq \overline{X_{AB}} < 3.5 \\ \text{Excellent,} & 3.5 \leq \overline{X_{AB}} \leq 4 \end{cases} \tag{4}$$

3.3 Classification Analysis Procedure

The classification analysis procedure constitutes a crucial component of our study. It involves the integration of demographic variables from the records into the evaluation of the test variables, adding depth and context to our analysis. For our research, we scrutinized records from 81 students and classified them into four distinct classes: Excellent (2.5%), Good (11.1%), Satisfactory (70.4%), and Defficient (16%).

To address the inherent class imbalance in our dataset, we implemented the well-established Random Oversampling technique, a prevalent approach in machine learning and data mining. This technique addresses the challenge of class imbalance by artificially increasing the number of records in the minority classes. As a result of this process, the number of records in each class was equalized, with a total of 228 records, comprising 57 records for each class.

Additionally, the models were carefully designed to minimize the risk of overfitting, incorporating cross-validation procedures and tuning of hyperparameters to ensure robust generalization.

In our pursuit of assessing the performance of machine learning algorithms, we conducted a series of 12 experiments. These experiments included five iterations with K-Nearest Neighbors (KNN) and seven with Neural Networks. To optimize the performance results, we fine-tuned the hyperparameters of these algorithms. For KNN, we explored varying numbers of neighbors (2, 6, and 10) and applied both the Minkowski metric and distance measures 1 (Manhattan) and 2 (Euclidean). In the case of Neural Networks, we examined configurations with 2 and 4 hidden layers, each featuring 128 and 64 neurons, along with batch sizes of 16 and 32.

It's important to note that the utilization of Random Oversampling can potentially lead to model overfitting. To mitigate this risk and ensure the generalizability of our results, we adopted the cross-validation technique. This method provided a structured approach to addressing class imbalance and assessing various machine learning algorithms on a balanced dataset. In summary, our methodological approach, anchored by the Abstraction Evaluation Test, is meticulously designed to comprehensively evaluate the abstraction skills of students in the context of second language learning. This approach encompasses a diverse and representative sample and leverages both descriptive and classification analyses to yield valuable insights into the factors influencing abstraction skills in second language learners.

4 Results

In this section, we present the results of our study, offering detailed insights into the descriptive analysis of students' performance in both Perspective and Abstraction. Additionally, we explore how demographic variables such as gender, age, school type, semester enrollment, and first-generation university status influence these skills. Furthermore, we delve into the classification analysis, which provides valuable findings regarding the performance of classification algorithms in assessing students' abstraction levels.

4.1 Descriptive Analysis

The descriptive analysis phase reveals valuable information about the students' performance in Perspective and Abstraction, shedding light on the influence of various demographic variables. It is evident that students generally excel in Perspective in comparison to Abstraction. This disparity can be attributed to Perspective being an initial phase in the Abstraction process. Despite this variation, the overall performance in both categories is noteworthy. Specifically, 79% of students exhibit some level of proficiency in Perspective, while 84% demonstrate development in Abstraction.

The distribution of Perspective and Abstraction levels by gender, as depicted in Fig. 1, demonstrates comparable results for Perspective. However, in the context of Abstraction, female students exhibit a notably higher level of development in this skill.of development in this skill.

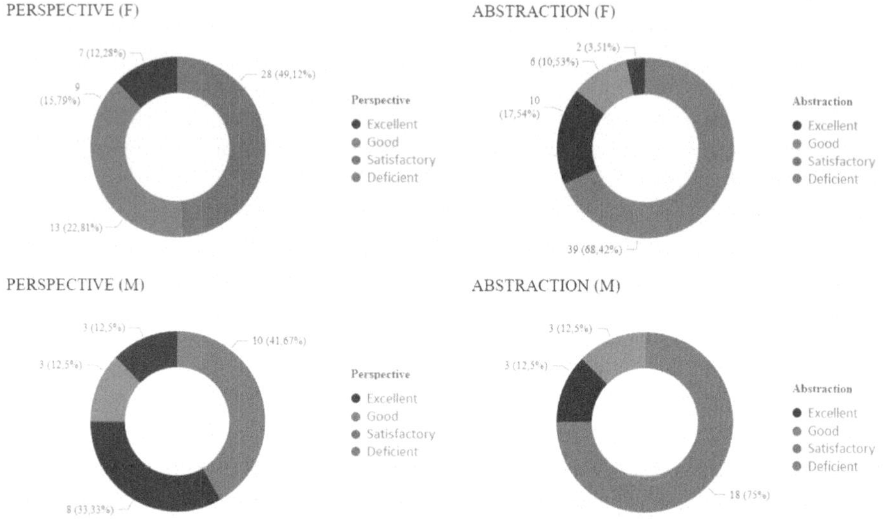

Fig. 1. Distribution of Perspective and Abstraction Levels by Gender.

When we examine the distribution of Perspective and Abstraction levels by age, we classify students into two age groups: 17 to 20 years and 20 to 30 years. While similar results are observed for Perspective across both age groups, the Abstraction analysis uncovers differences. Students between 17 and 20 years old display a 5.6% rate of optimal abstraction, while their counterparts between 21 and 38 years old demonstrate 0% optimal abstraction. Notably, students in the younger age group tend to struggle more with abstraction, with 22.2% falling into the deficient abstraction category, compared to 11.1% for those in the older age group.

Figure 2 presents the distribution of Perspective and Abstraction levels based on school type, categorizing students into Public, Subsidized, and Private institutions. In terms of Perspective, Subsidized and Private schools yield similar and favorable results, while Public school students exhibit deficient performance. Regarding Abstraction, Public and Subsidized schools achieve similar results, with a slight edge for Subsidized schools. Both groups demonstrate satisfactory results. Interestingly, students from Private schools perform exceptionally well in Abstraction, with all displaying some degree of abstraction proficiency.

Analyzing Perspective and Abstraction levels by the semester in which students are enrolled in their program, we notice a consistent pattern across both groups of students. Notably, students in the fifth to eighth semesters exhibit

Fig. 2. Distribution of Perspective and Abstraction Levels by School Type.

improvements in Perspective and Abstraction. This progression suggests that these skills tend to develop as students progress further in their academic programs.

Figure 3 illustrates the distribution of Perspective and Abstraction levels for first-generation university students compared to those with university-educated parents. It's apparent that first-generation students tend to achieve lower results. In the case of Perspective, 26.6% of first-generation students are classified as deficient, while this rate is 17% for other students. Concerning Abstraction, non-first-generation students exhibit a 4.3% rate of excellent classification, while this rate is 0% for first-generation students. Additionally, 26.5% of first-generation students fall into the deficient abstraction category, compared to 8.5% of students with university-educated parents.

These demographic results not only describe differences in student performance but also reveal patterns that reflect structural inequalities in the Chilean education system. The gaps observed between students from private and public schools, as well as between first-generation university students and those whose parents have higher education, suggest that the socio-educational context significantly influences the development of abstract thinking. Integrating these findings

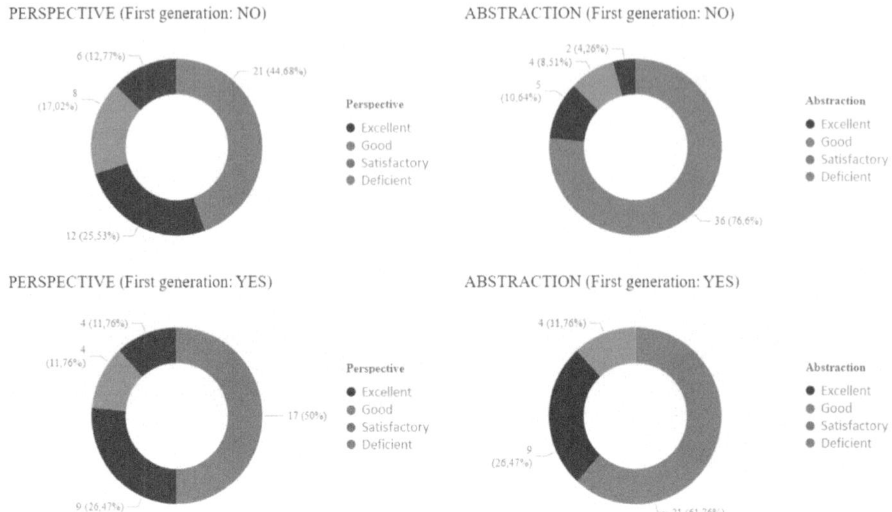

Fig. 3. Distribution of Perspective and Abstraction Levels for First-Generation University Students.

into the discussion of cognitive skills implies recognizing that strengthening critical and abstract thinking depends not only on foreign language teaching but also on conditions of access and cultural capital, reinforcing the need for more equitable educational policies.

4.2 Classification Analysis

Our study employed K-Nearest Neighbors (KNN) and Deep Neural Networks (DNN) algorithms to delve into the classification of the abstraction process in Chilean students learning English as a foreign language. These algorithms provided intriguing insights into their performance and classification capabilities.

KNN, known for its proximity-based methodology, displayed variability in performance with different configurations. The KNN model with 1 neighbor and the Manhattan metric (p=1) achieved the highest accuracy, standing at 91.3%. However, it's important to acknowledge that this model exhibited the highest loss, indicating potential overfitting issues.

KNN with 2 neighbors and the Manhattan metric also boasted high accuracy, hovering around 87%. Nevertheless, it was accompanied by a significant loss of 1.627, underscoring the sensitivity of KNN to hyperparameters and metrics. As the number of neighbors was increased to 10, and the Euclidean metric ($p = 2$) was applied, accuracy dropped to approximately 71.7% with a loss of 0.613. Neural networks, particularly those with 2 layers and 128-64 neurons, demonstrated consistent performance. When using the "adam" optimizer and the "sparse_categorical_crossentropy" loss function, these neural networks achieved accuracy rates of 82–84% with Kappa coefficients of 0.764–0.795, indicating their robustness in classifying abstraction.

Remarkably, extending the training epochs to 500, rather than 10, further enhanced neural network performance. This modification resulted in accuracy rates of up to 91% and a Kappa coefficient of 0.882. This emphasizes the significant impact of training duration on neural network performance.

The results underscore that neural networks, particularly Deep Neural Networks, provide a more stable and predictable performance in the classification of abstraction when compared to KNN. However, both methods encountered challenges in specific cases, highlighting the intricate nature of this problem. Moreover, these findings emphasize the influential role of factors such as gender, age, school type, and family background in the abstraction process among Chilean students. This information holds potential for enhancing educational programs in Chile and effectively addressing the development of abstraction skills among English as a foreign language students.

5 Discussion

The study's results offer a comprehensive overview of the intricate relationship between language education, cognitive skills development, and demographic factors. It is evident that achieving abstraction is a more intricate endeavor than acquiring perspective, aligning closely with the proposed abstraction process by [15] and [16]. This underscores the multifaceted nature of abstraction and its significance in the realm of cognitive development.

One of the key takeaways from the study is the positive correlation between age and curriculum advancement and its influence on students' cognitive skills. As students progress through their academic journey, their thinking skills, including perspective and abstraction, tend to naturally evolve and improve. This observation suggests that the university environment plays a vital role in fostering the development of these higher-order cognitive abilities over time.

Additionally, the study uncovers two crucial findings that bear significant implications for the Chilean education system. Firstly, the study emphasizes the existence of significant performance gaps between students who attended private schools and those from public or subsidized schools. The quality of education and available resources within these diverse school systems seems to exert a profound influence on students' abilities, particularly in the context of abstraction.

Secondly, the study highlights the pivotal role of parental educational background in students' cognitive skill development. First-generation university students, whose parents lack a university education, tend to achieve lower results in comparison to students from families with a university-educated background. This revelation underscores the far-reaching impact of familial and socioeconomic factors on educational outcomes and the need for targeted interventions to mitigate these disparities.

While the primary focus of the study was to assess students' abstraction skills, it becomes apparent that numerous variables interplay to influence the optimal development of abstraction in the participants. This complexity underlines the necessity of a holistic approach to education that considers various factors, including the quality of language instruction, curriculum design, and support systems.

The research findings affirm the positive correlation between the study of a second language, particularly English, and the development of cognitive skills like metalinguistic awareness, cognitive flexibility, and abstract reasoning. This underscores the fundamental role of English language education in nurturing higher-order thinking skills and highlights the potential of language education to act as a catalyst for broader cognitive development.

Moreover, the findings support the notion that studying a second language, especially English, can substantially enhance students' critical thinking abilities. The specific skills associated with critical thinking, such as differentiation, categorization, comparison, estimation, analysis, and synthesis of information, can be honed through a well-structured language education program.

The study's analysis of demographic variables offers valuable insights into the disparities and advantages that certain groups of students may experience. Gender, for instance, emerges as a significant factor, with female students demonstrating a higher level of abstraction compared to their male counterparts. This gender-related variation in cognitive skill development underscores the importance of fostering an inclusive and equitable learning environment.

The type of educational institution from which the participants originated also plays a pivotal role in students' cognitive skill development. The data reveals that the level of abstraction is higher in students who received education in private schools compared to those who attended public or subsidized schools. These disparities in educational outcomes suggest the need for more comprehensive and equitable educational policies.

Semester enrollment was another significant variable in the study's findings. The direct relationship between the level of abstraction in students and their progress in their academic journey suggests that universities should consider how to systematically integrate cognitive skill development into their curriculum. The study highlights that the more semesters a student has completed, the greater their capacity for abstraction, indicating that universities should focus on holistic and continuous student development.

The influence of parental educational level is evident in the findings. Students whose parents have a university education tend to exhibit a higher level of abstraction than students whose parents do not have higher education. This observation highlights the importance of promoting education not only within the student population but also within their families, ensuring that a culture of learning and cognitive development is fostered at home.

In addition to the descriptive analysis, classification experiments using machine learning algorithms, such as K-Nearest Neighbors (KNN) and Neural Networks (DNN), were conducted. These experiments added an innovative dimension to the study, offering insights into the potential of machine learning techniques in classifying abstraction skills.

The results indicate that neural networks, particularly Deep Neural Networks (DNN), displayed a more consistent and predictable performance in classifying abstraction compared to KNN. This observation emphasizes the potential of machine learning as a tool for understanding and classifying complex cognitive processes.

A crucial discovery from the classification experiments is the importance of the duration of training in the performance of neural networks. Increasing the number of training epochs to 500, as opposed to the initial 10, led to significant improvements in the performance of neural networks. This finding underscores the necessity of comprehensive and continuous training in the development of cognitive skills.

6 Conclusions

In summary, these findings offer a profound understanding of the multifaceted relationship between language education, cognitive skill development, and demographic factors. Studying English as a foreign language emerges as a significant factor in the development of cognitive skills and critical thinking in students. Furthermore, the application of machine learning techniques and the careful selection of algorithms hold the potential to enhance the classification of abstraction in the educational context.

These insights provide a valuable foundation for educational program improvements in Chile and beyond. By recognizing the importance of language education and cognitive skill development, policymakers and educators can work collaboratively to create inclusive and equitable learning environments that empower students to thrive. The study's comprehensive approach demonstrates the power of interdisciplinary research in reshaping educational paradigms and promoting cognitive development in students of English as a foreign language.

References

1. González-Murillo, L.A., Cárdenas-Galindo, J.A., Arellano-González, J.C.: Desarrollo de habilidades del pensamiento de orden superior a través de actitudes de desempeño. Revista electrónica anfei digital **6**, 1–9 (2017)
2. Baranovska, L., Morska, L., Simkova, I., Zasluzhena, A.: Enhancing critical thinking skills of future language scholars in pedagogical courses. Adv. Educ. **7**(14), 91–99 (2020). https://doi.org/10.20535/2410-8286.202382
3. Jaramillo-Naranjo, L.M., Puga-Peña, L.A.: El pensamiento lógico-abstracto como sustento para potenciar los procesos cognitivos en la educación. Colección de Filosofía de la Educación, **21**, 31–51 (2016). https://doi.org/10.17163/soph.n21.2016.01
4. Wing, J.M.: Computational thinking and thinking about computing. Philos. Trans. R. Soc. A: Math. Phys. Eng. Sci. *366*, 3717–3725 (2008). https://doi.org/10.1098/rsta.2008.0118
5. Benjelloun, M., El, K.: Bloom's taxonomy and Moroccan children's vocabulary and critical thinking skills development. Arab World English J. *10*(3), 342–352 (2019). https://doi.org/10.24093/awej/vol10no2.26

6. Sehic, S.: College-level second language courses and creative thinking skills: an ex post facto study. J. Lang. Learn. Teach. *1*(7), 119–142 (2017)
7. Murray, J.W.: Pensamiento y metacognición de orden superior en el aula de educación básica de primer año: Un estudio de caso sobre el uso de borradores codificados por colores. Open Rev. Educ. Res. *1*(1), 56–69 (2014). https://doi.org/10.1080/23265507.2014.964297
8. Rojas, J.: El pensamiento abstracto a partir de la interdisciplinariedad de las matemáticas. La educación matemática como herramienta en el desempeño profesional docente. Eco matemático, *8*(1), 51–53 (2016). https://doi.org/10.22463/17948231.1382
9. Veliz, L., Veliz-Campos, M.: An interrogation of the role of critical thinking in English language pedagogy in Chile. Teach. High. Educ. **24**(1), 47–62 (2019). https://doi.org/10.1080/13562517.2018.1456424
10. García, E.: El arte de preguntar para enseñar y aprender mejor. Byblios (2001)
11. Llinares, A., Evnitskaya, N.: Classroom interaction in CLIL programs: offering opportunities or fostering inequalities? TESOL Q. **55**(2), 366–397 (2021). https://doi.org/10.1002/tesq.607
12. Soodmand, A.H., Movassagh, H., Radi, A.H.: The interrelationship among critical thinking, writing an argumentative essay in an L2 and their subskills. Lang. Learn. J. **45**(4), 419–433 (2017). https://doi.org/10.1080/09571736.2017.1320420
13. Ünaldi, I., Yüce, E.: The relationship among vocabulary size, grammar proficiency, and critical thinking skills of adult language learners. Adult Learn. (2020). https://doi.org/10.1177/1045159520959
14. Marzano, R.J., Pickering, D.J.: Dimensiones del Aprendizaje. Manual para el maestro. ITESO (2005)
15. Marzano, R.J., et al.: Dimensiones del aprendizaje: Manual para el maestro. ITESO (2014)
16. Beas, F.J., Santa, C.V.J., Thomsen, Q.P., Utreras, G.S.: Enseñar a pensar para aprender mejor. Ediciones Universidad Católica Chile (2011)
17. Aravena-Gaete, M., Campos-Soto, M.N., Rodríguez-Jiménez, C.: Learning strategies at a higher taxonomic level in primary education students in the digital age. Sustainability **12**, 9877 (2020). https://doi.org/10.3390/su12239877
18. Paul, R., Elder, L.: La mini-guía para el pensamiento crítico, conceptos y herramientas. Fundación para el Pensamiento Crítico (2003)
19. Phan, H.P.: Critical thinking as a self-regulatory process component in teaching and learning. Psicothema **22**(2), 284–292 (2010)

Integrating Socio-Economic Characteristics and Marketing Analytics with Telecom Data for Sports Site Selection

Alexander Utkov[1](✉), Alexander Rozmanov[2], and Olga Selezneva[3]

[1] Graduate School of Management, St. Petersburg State University, St. Petersburg, Russia
st110964@gsom.spbu.ru
[2] Tyumen State University, Tyumen, Russia
[3] Politecnico di Milano, Milan, Italy
olga.selezneva@mail.polimi.it

Abstract. This study addresses the challenge of selecting optimal locations for new businesses, particularly in the sports industry, using geospatial and behavioral data. Despite the growing importance of location intelligence, practical applications of geospatial analysis in business strategy remain limited, especially when using telecom and urban data. The methodology involves integrating machine learning techniques such as K-means clustering, association rule learning, and SHAP-based feature interpretation to analyze location suitability. By applying these methods to geospatial data, including visitor patterns, infrastructure, and demographics, the study uncovers key factors influencing business success. This approach offers a more data-driven, accurate method for identifying optimal business locations, enhancing decision-making in site selection. The findings highlight the critical role of location in business strategies and provide actionable insights for improving site selection strategies in the sports industry.

Keywords: Geoanalytics · Machine Learning · Site Selection · Association Rule Mining · Clustering · SHAP

1 Introduction

The growing volume of geospatial data, fueled by the digital footprints users leave online and the advanced tracking capabilities of telecom networks, has created new opportunities for data-driven decision-making. Businesses and public institutions increasingly rely on geoanalytics to understand human mobility, consumer behavior, and spatial dynamics. This approach supports a wide range of applications, from urban planning to commercial site selection, by combining Geographic Information Systems (GIS) with Machine Learning (ML) to extract actionable insights from complex datasets.

Geospatial data (geodata) is becoming one of the most useful instruments for businesses to rely on. It facilitates the decision-making process and planning activities in any industry. Geodata is data that describes characteristics of the earth such as transportation networks, administrative boundaries, terrain models, aerial imagery, and coordinates of

T. Guarda et al. (Eds.): ARTIIS 2025, CCIS 2789, pp. 549–563, 2026.
https://doi.org/10.1007/978-3-032-16758-3_41

any objects on the map [1]. The development of geoanalytics is determined by the trend of point-by-point analysis of territories and population behavior patterns to make relevant strategic decisions for the development of city infrastructure, improving business decisions, solving social problems, as well as protecting the environment and natural resources.

According to MarketsandMarkets report [2], the global geoanalytics market is rapidly expanding, with projections estimating it will exceed $59 billion by 2029. Despite this growth, practical applications of geospatial analysis in business strategy remain limited, particularly in the domain of location intelligence. While many studies emphasize theoretical models, few demonstrate real-world implementations using actual telecom and urban data. This study addresses this gap by applying geospatial and behavioral data to predict optimal locations for opening new businesses using the sports industry as an example. By integrating mobility patterns, infrastructure data, population density, and other location-based variables, ML models can uncover key factors that influence commercial success. The sports industry serves as a test case due to its steadily increasing demand and spatially uneven supply, offering a representative context for validating geoanalytics-based site selection methods. In addition to that, our research combines multiple machine learning techniques such as clustering, association rule mining, and interpretable regression to provide a more comprehensive understanding of location dynamics. By incorporating behavioral features and interest-based visitor segments, we also identify new and previously underexplored factors that contribute to a location's attractiveness.

2 Theoretical Background

2.1 The Importance of Location for a Business

Owen and Daskin [3] stated that opening a new location is a long-term investment project. Therefore, it is important not only to evaluate location options carefully but also to consider uncertainty and assess various influencing factors over the long term [3]. Earlier, Drezner [4] highlighted that the study of location selection has a long history and spans multiple academic disciplines. This interdisciplinary nature underlines the complexity and significance of location decisions. Further, Shen and Yu [5] pointed out that the process of selecting a business location is a cross-functional task. It requires input from multiple departments, as such decisions are of strategic importance and may affect long-term performance. Jung and Jang [6] explored how geographic clustering varies by restaurant segment. They found that not only price but also proximity to a central business district (CBD) strongly influences customer behavior. For the case of fixed and equal prices, Hotelling's choice rule reduces to the proximity rule, e.g., customers patronize the closest facility [7]. Although the number of studies in this area remains limited due to data access challenges, the findings emphasize that location remains a key factor in a company's success.

2.2 Determination of Factors that Influence the Choice of the Location

Huff [8] proposed that floor area could serve as an important criterion. Later, Prosperi and Schuler [9] highlighted the role of price, and Schuler [10] expanded this list to include freshness, availability, convenience, quality of service, and parking. Timmermans [11] added variety of goods, price, and parking as relevant factors, while Drezner [12] suggested cleanliness, availability of preferred brands, higher product quality, and lower prices. Balbontin and Hensher [13] reviewed the main factors influencing location decisions and summarized the key studies in this field. Their research identified more than ten factors that can influence the choice of retail outlet locations. The most interesting ones are CBD location, distance to the CBD, accessibility to public transportation, safety, average rental price for a house, residential density, industry density, presence of a high school in the area, presence of a hospital in the area, parking facilities, number of workers employed in the area [13]. Willigers and Van Wee [14] showed that the presence of high-speed rail significantly increases the attractiveness of locations for office development in the Netherlands. Similarly, Weterings and Knoben [15] found that shorter distances to train stations positively influence business location decisions. These factors form the basis for building multi-factor models aimed at evaluating the attractiveness of specific locations.

2.3 Chosen Machine Learning Approaches for Site Selection

To solve the site selection problem, three machine learning approaches were applied: K-means clustering, association rule learning (ARL), and SHAP-based feature interpretation. Each was used to extract different types of insights from geospatial and urban data. ML allows adapting to large-scale calculations and improving the performance and accuracy for solving location problems [16]. Below is a brief description of how each algorithm works and its usefulness for business.

Cluster Analysis. K-means clustering was applied to divide the city into homogeneous zones based on location characteristics such as population density, accessibility, infrastructure, and business activity. Principal Component Analysis (PCA) was used beforehand to reduce the number of correlated variables and speed up computation. The resulting clusters helped identify areas with similar development potential and demand profiles.

Association Rule Learning. Association Rule Learning (specifically Apriori and FP-Growth algorithms) was used to detect combinations of features frequently present in high-potential zones. Different rules helped uncover spatial patterns linked to business success. These rules guided the selection of key factors for modeling and provided interpretable logic for decision-makers. Support measures how often a rule/characteristic is found in the database and denoted as a formula (1):

$$Support(A \rightarrow B) = \frac{Hexagons\ have\ both\ A\ and\ B\ characteristics}{Total\ Number\ of\ Hexagons} \tag{1}$$

Confidence signifies the likelihood of rule/characteristic B appear in dataset while rule/characteristic A is observed (2):

$$Confidence(A \rightarrow B) = \frac{Support(A \cup B)}{Support(A)} \tag{2}$$

Finally, lift compares the rule's frequency to that expected if A and B were independent (3):

$$Lift(A \rightarrow B) = \frac{Confidence(A \rightarrow B)}{Support(B)} \tag{3}$$

SHapley Additive exPlanations. SHAP values were used to explain predictions from tree-based models that ranked the attractiveness of specific locations. SHAP allowed for quantifying the influence of individual features—such as nearby competitors, green zones, or transport accessibility—on the predicted suitability of each site. This ensured that model outputs were transparent and actionable. Mathematically, the SHAP value for a feature i is given by the following formula (4):

$$\varphi_i = \sum_{S \subseteq N\{i\}} \frac{|S|!(|N| - |S| - 1)!}{|N|!} [\nu(S \cup \{i\}) - \upsilon(S)] \tag{4}$$

where:

S is subset of features excluding feature i.

N is the total number of features.

$\nu(S \cup \{i\})$ is the model prediction including feature i.

$\upsilon(S)$ is the model prediction excluding feature i.

3 Methodology

3.1 Overview

The research methodology includes the following stages:

Data Collection. The step involves reviewing data sources, which are relevant in terms of vital factors for business success. Later the open data is collected, stored, and merged with Tele2 internal sources into single dataset for modelling.

Data Analysis and Processing. After collecting the data, it is necessary to clean it and fill in any missing values or wrong values. Later all the data must be concatenated from different sources. Additionally, this stage involves processing the data to make it suitable for modelling and analyzing relationships between different variables.

Feature Engineering. This step involves identifying potential relationships within the data. It also includes creating new features or factors that may improve the modelling process.

ML Model Selection. Here, the focus is on establishing rules for modelling, methods for analyzing model quality, and outlining a plan for building models.

Model Validation. To validate models and assign scores to them the following metrics were used: The best-fitting regression was identified via R-squared (R2), followed by SHAP-based interpretation of the model. For cluster analysis, we used distortion score and the elbow criterion to choose k clusters. For association rule learning, we ranked rules using standard measures: support, confidence, and lift and pruned low-support/low-confidence rules.

R2 score represents the proportion of the variance in the target variable that is predictable from the independent variables group. Thus, this metric was specifically chosen, since the main goal is not to increase the predictive power of our models (for which Mean Absolute Error (MAE) could be suitable), but to show the factors that influence the variables that are important to us. The distortion score helps to determine the optimal number of clusters. It measures the sum of the squared distances between each data point and its nearest centroid (the center of a cluster). After plotting the distortion score against the number of clusters the «elbow method» was used to select an optimal number of clusters. The elbow method checks for a point where an increase in the number of clusters do not significantly reduce the distortion score.

Model Development. Finally, models are developed to evaluate location's attractiveness for sports industry based on geo and internal data for SPb. This includes evaluating model accuracy and quality, generating forecasts, and visualizing the results. The complete methodology, including the modeling, is presented in Fig. 1. Given the complexity and importance of the preparatory stages, the data collection and feature engineering processes are described separately in detail, as they form the foundation for all subsequent modeling efforts and play a crucial role in ensuring the reliability and interpretability of results.

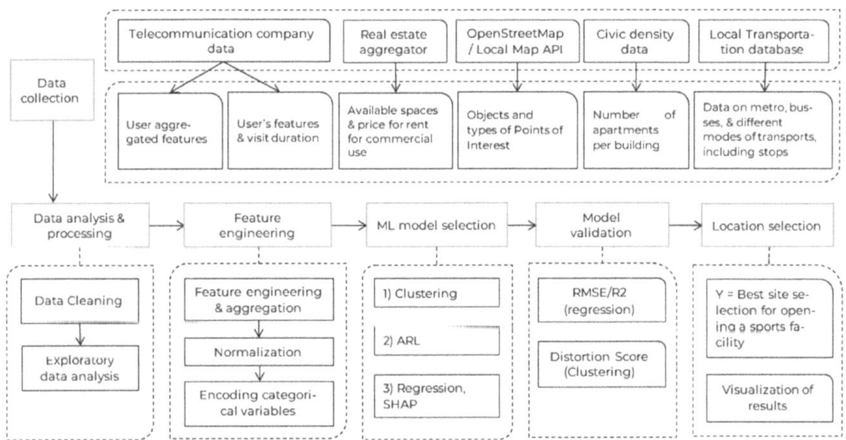

Fig. 1. Methodology for site selection

3.2 Data Collection

The telecommunications company provided two datasets: aggregated visitor data (age, income, gender, interests) at the hexagon level, and visit durations and individual interest features for the city of Saint Petersburg, which has a population of 5,600,044. The data spanned 3 weeks in March 2023. Each hexagon follows Uber's H3 system, wherein each hexagon has an approximate side length of 200 m, corresponding to an average area of 105,332 square meters. To improve location selection for sports facilities, external sources were also used. (1) OpenStreetMap and local map service for points of interest (cafes, educational institutions, etc.) and sports clubs. (2) Real estate aggregator for commercial property prices and space availability. (3) Local transportation database for roads, public transit, and related infrastructure. (4) Civic density data for data on the number of apartments per building.

3.3 Development of Features for Machine Learning

Based on the theoretical background, feature engineering was conducted along multiple dimensions. First, time-related features were derived by incorporating the start and end times of each visit record. Counts and shares of visits during morning, daytime, evening, and night intervals were computed, and visit durations were classified into short or long stays to yield counts and proportions per hexagon. Both mean and median visit lengths were also calculated for total and unique visitors. Second, the demographic characteristics of visitors such as income levels, age ranges, and gender were aggregated to represent the share of each group within a given hexagon. Visitor interests were similarly aggregated to capture the proportion of visitors with particular interests. Third, geo-related features were sourced from external datasets described in the Data Collection section.

To stabilize heavy-tailed distributions, count-type features were transformed using the log1p transformation. We distinguished structural zeros (e.g., no POIs) from missing values (source gaps), and computed shares relative to total visits and to unique visitors to separate overall foot traffic from audience composition. Prior to association rule mining, continuous features were discretized via quantile binning (KBins) with an explicit "Missing/Unknown" bin. To incorporate neighborhood effects, we computed H3 k-ring aggregates - statistics for areas with different diameters, spatial lags (means over adjacent cells), and distance-based accessibility measures. Which means distance to the nearest metro/fitness facility; distance-weighted counts with exponential decay. Points of interest counts were also converted to densities per square km and, where appropriate, per 1,000 residents.

By the end of the process, 63 time-related features, 98 features related to visitor interests and characteristics, and 111 geo features were generated, resulting in 272 features for the machine learning models. In contrast to previous studies that predominantly focus on traditional location attributes such as price, proximity to the CBD, or access to transportation, this study introduces and systematically integrates several novel behavioral and contextual factors that have not been extensively explored in existing location literature. Specifically, we include detailed temporal visit patterns, interest-based visitor segmentation, and mobility behavior proxies such as car-sharing and public transport usage. These variables capture the dynamic and behavioral aspects of location attractiveness, going beyond static infrastructural indicators. Furthermore, by computing each feature in both unique visitor and total visitor variants, we differentiate between broad foot traffic and targeted audience engagement. We argue that these behavioral and lifestyle dimensions provide richer explanatory power and offer more actionable insights for commercial location decisions.

4 Results

Due to the absence of direct revenue or profit data for specific organizations within SPb's hexagons, the analysis focused on the best available monetary-related features. In particular, the share of visits by representatives of the top salary group, the distribution of visits by time of day, and the number of sports establishments within a two-hexagon radius were used as a proxy for economic activity. The list of proxy features was discussed and approved with experts of the telecom company. In addition, other variables were tested for the proxy role. Nevertheless, they were not included in the final text of the article, as the results were less relevant and useful for business.

4.1 Association Rule Mining

For the share of unique visits from the highest income bracket ARL uncovered several notable patterns. Rules revealed that hexagons surrounded by cultural objects (such as museums, parks, and leisure amenities) within a four-hexagon radius tend to have a higher share of top earners. In contrast, an unexpectedly high interest in sportswear and footwear was linked to a lower share of rich visitors. Additionally, age-related rules indicated that areas with a significant presence of younger visitors (specifically, those in the 20–60th percentile) are more likely to exhibit higher proportions of top income individuals (Table 1).

Table 1. Top 5 rules by lift for richest income bracket high share unique visit

Antecedents	Consequents	Support	Confidence	Lift
Total Museums (Neighbour) [Low]	Salary Level 5 (Unique) [High]	0.130799	0.248416	1.145631
Age 20 (Unique) [High]	Salary Level 5 (Unique) [High]	0.107658	0.265451	1.106398
Total Parks of Culture & Leisure (Neighbour) [Low]	Salary Level 5 (Unique) [High]	0.065205	0.229276	1.066844
Sportswear & Floral (Unique) [Low]	Salary Level 5 (Unique) [High]	0.063046	0.209206	1.054322

Another set of ARL analyses focused on the proportion of visits during the evening at the lower end of the distribution. The rules indicated that lower daytime activity on Thursdays and Fridays strongly predicts minimal evening engagement. Longer daytime visit durations (especially visits lasting between 9–15 h or 15–20 h) correlate with low evening activity. Hexagons with shorter average and median visit durations tend to have reduced evening activity. Moreover, low night and weekday visits, as well as a lower surrounding population density, further support the pattern of minimal evening engagement (Table 2).

Table 2. Top 5 rules by lift for the low share of visits during the evening

Antecedents	Consequents	Support	Confidence	Lift
Friday Share [Low]	Evening Share [Low]	0.137828	0.738289	3.446593
Stay 9–15h Share [Low]	Evening Share [Low]	0.124334	0.621733	2.763883
Avg Duration (≥2h) [Low]	Morning Share [Low]	0.117103	0.588015	2.984657
Thursday Share [Low]	Morning Share [Low]	0.116505	0.508524	2.906222
Weekday Visits Share [Low]	Evening Share [Low]	0.112360	0.55652	2.782889

Overall, the ARL process yielded 12,416 distinct rules. A comprehensive list of the original features, along with their percentile breakdowns and the algorithms used for binarization, was delivered to the telecommunications company for further interpretation and decision support.

4.2 Regression Models and SHAP Values

Beyond association rules, regression models were used not for pure prediction but for interpreting the influence of various features on target variables. For that abstract we shed light on 2 target variables dependencies: the share of unique visits from the highest income group and the count of sports clubs within a two-hexagon radius. Before modeling, data standardization method was employed to ensure that all input features were on a comparable scale. A baseline Linear Regression model was first used, followed by experiments with a Random Forest Regressor and a Gradient Boosting Regressor. Model performance was evaluated using metrics such as R2, Mean Absolute Error (MAE), and Mean Absolute Percentage Error (MAPE).

SHAP (SHapley Additive exPlanations) values were used to interpret the outputs of our regression models. SHAP plot shows how each individual features (or independent variable) drive our model's target (or dependent variable). Target is share of unique visits from the highest income group in different areas. For each feature on the vertical axis, every dot corresponds to one hexagon SHAP value, its unique contribution to increasing or decreasing the predicted share of top-income visitors. The further a dot lies to the right, the more that feature increases the prediction; to the left it decreases it. Dot color encodes the feature's value in that zone (blue means low, red means high), so you can see, for example, whether high values of a feature tend to positively or negatively influence the target. For example, if you see many blue dots to the right of the centerline, it means that the smaller the feature value, the higher the target variable value (proportion of rich visitors in our case). A high share of car-sharing users among unique visitors and car owners was strongly connected with higher salary shares, indicating that areas with active mobility services tend to attract wealthier visitors. Additionally, increased proportions of individuals aged 40–60 (and those over 60) negatively affected the target, whereas a higher share of economically active visitors, particularly those in the 30–40 age group, showed a positive impact. Specific city districts with a lot of luxury real estate were positively associated with higher income levels. Lifestyle interests in healthy food, coffee, and elite sports also contributed positively. Moreover, metrics derived from the real estate aggregator such as the total and average property areas within a three-hexagon radius demonstrated a positive association, implying that areas with more active commercial real estate tend to support higher income bracket. Additional indicators, including population density and the availability of beauty and health amenities, further reinforced the model's predictions (Fig. 2).

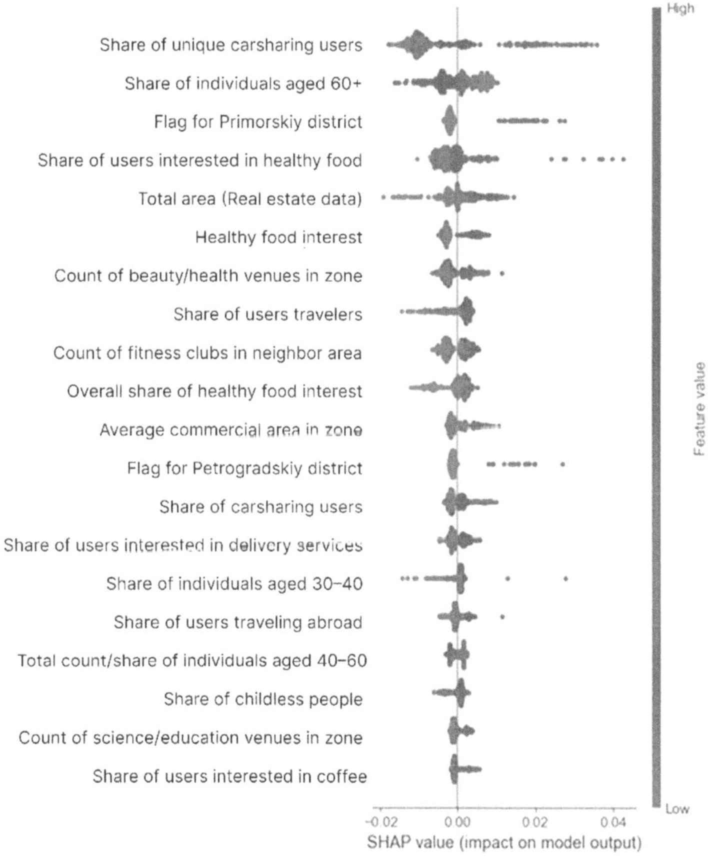

Fig. 2. SHAP values for the target variable: share of unique visits of the highest income group

Similarly, the SHAP analysis for the count of sports clubs within a two-hexagon radius target revealed that cultural and artistic amenities, such as venues for culture and art, strongly associated with the presence of fitness clubs. A higher concentration of mass media outlets and commercial property listings was connected with an increased number of fitness facilities. Conversely, a higher proportion of visits from older age groups was associated with fewer fitness clubs, potentially due to different leisure preferences. Other factors, including enhanced public transport accessibility (as indicated by the total metro count within a given radius) and the share of top income visitors, also emerged as significant predictors (Fig. 3).

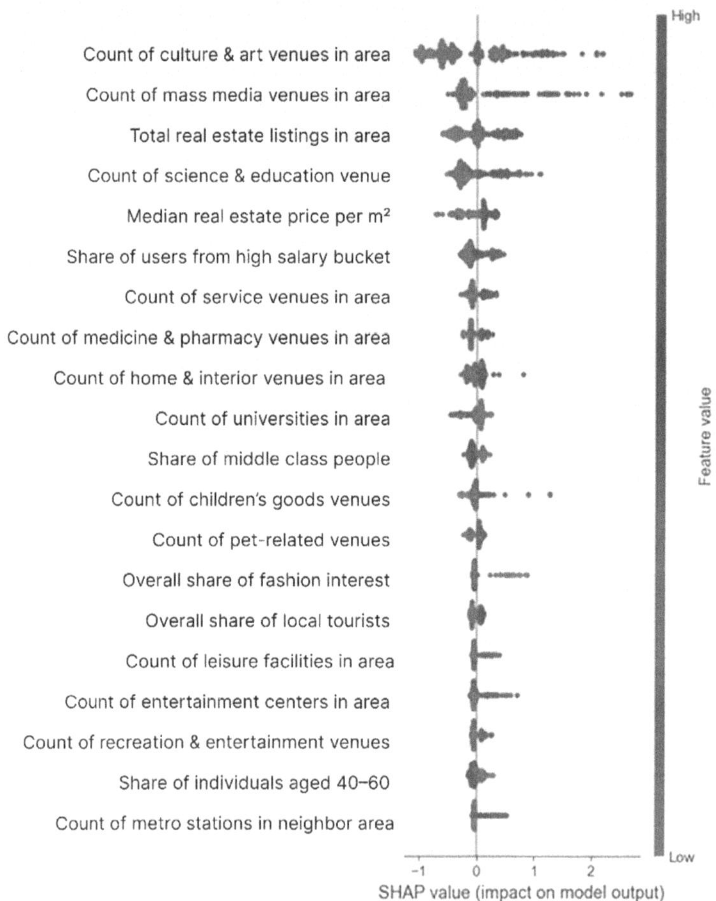

Fig. 3. SHAP values for the target variable: count of sports clubs within a two-hexagon radius

4.3 Cluster Analysis

To capture spatial heterogeneity and further understand location attractiveness, a cluster analysis was conducted using the k-means algorithm, preceded by Principal Component Analysis (PCA) to manage high-dimensional data. The optimal number of clusters was determined via the elbow method based on the distortion score. This process revealed five distinct clusters of hexagons in city, each characterized by unique socio-economic and infrastructural traits that are shown in Table 3 and visualized in Fig. 4.

Table 3. Cluster description

Cluster	Description	Size (hexagons)	Key Traits
0	Residential District	294	Balanced age groups, long stays, high share of overnight visits
1	Business Facilities	209	Low population density, daytime visits, 72% aged 30–60
2	City Center	216	High density of infrastructure, + 10% rental prices, mixed-use zones
3	Dormitories	441	Suburban areas, shorter stays (~5 h 12 m), high overnight activity
4	High Rental Cost Areas	175	High rents, metro proximity, likely commercial-heavy urban zones

The clustering results provide a clear geographic segmentation of city, revealing correlations with urban infrastructure, population density, and economic activity. This segmentation enables targeted decision-making by highlighting areas with distinct behavioral and socio-economic profiles.

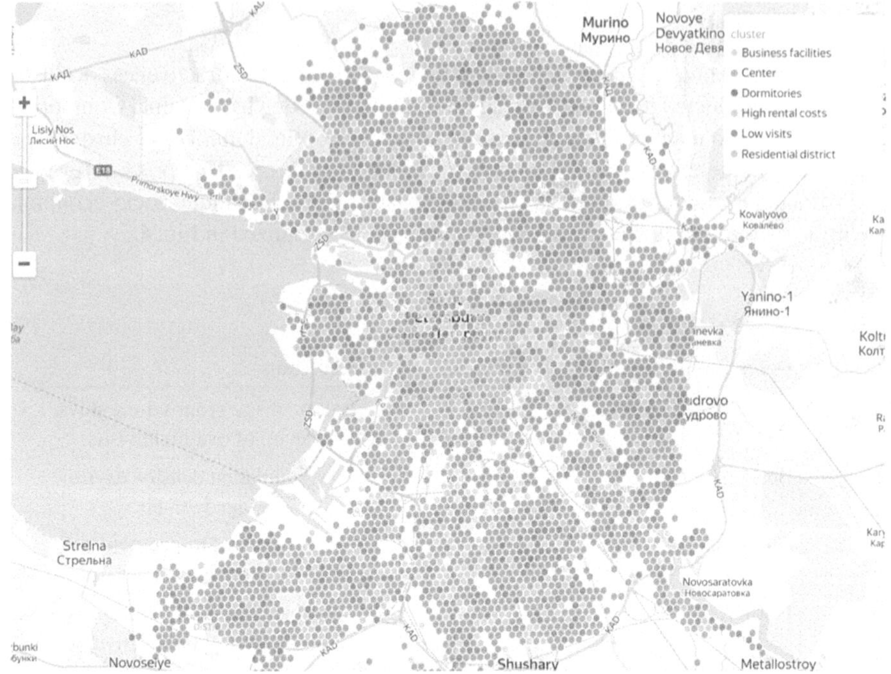

Fig. 4. Cluster visualization on the map

5 Discussion

The importance and potential of geospatial data is highlighted by its ability to provide detailed insights into locations. This data is crucial for making strategic decisions related to city infrastructure development, business improvement, and social problem-solving and environmental protection. This growth of geospatial analysis market reflects the increasing recognition of geospatial data as an indispensable resource for businesses and governments alike.

Despite recent progress in measuring business-location attractiveness, several gaps remain in the literature. Our results confirm and extend classic location theory: transport access and urban density remain salient, consistent with strategic and competitive models and gravity/Huff formulations [3, 7, 8], but behavioral and temporal signals, such as evening visit intensity, weekday profiles, and the share of high-income visitors, add meaningful explanatory power for site potential. Using interpretable ML, SHAP shows that hexagons with more nearby sports and health amenities and strong evening activity tend to have higher club density. In contrast, a higher share of older visitors in a hexagon is linked to fewer clubs. These patterns are in line with earlier studies showing that leisure-oriented businesses tend to cluster in city centers, while day-to-day services and convenience retail are more spread out [6]. Methodologically, our approach is consistent with hybrid designs that combine location models with machine learning and outperform single method baselines [16]. We extend this line by incorporating audience composition, mobility proxies such as public transport and car sharing, and interest-based segments. Each feature is computed in unique visitor and total visitor variants, which separates broad footfall from audience fit. In doing so, we turn firm and place specific drivers highlighted in the literature, including accessibility, neighborhood context, and behavioral pull factors, into measurable, decision ready variables rather than leaving them as unobserved heterogeneity [13]. Overall, grounding attractiveness in observed behavioral signals complements traditional distance and size based formulations and gives more actionable diagnostics for commercial site selection [3, 7, 8, 16]. Geoanalytics and ML techniques were used to assess the attractiveness of locations for business establishments, specifically focusing on the sports industry in SPb. The detailed feature engineering process, which included time-related features, visitor characteristics, and geo-related features, provided a comprehensive dataset that captured the complex dynamics of the modern world. Using this dataset, clustering techniques and advanced ML models such as ARL, regression models with SHAP values were applied to obtain useful insights.

The raw telecom datasets used in this study are proprietary and subject to contractual confidentiality; they cannot be shared publicly. All analysis code has been archived in a private GitHub repository and transferred to the data owner. To facilitate academic reproducibility, we can provide upon reasonable request the modeling code, configuration files, and scripts to retrieve and preprocess publicly available geospatial data (e.g., OpenStreetMap points of interest and public transport data).

Clustering analysis revealed 5 clusters that divided the hexagonal grid of SPb into 5 sectors with similar characteristics. Dormitory districts were identified, as well as the city center and districts with high business activity and high rental prices. These insights aid in making informed location decisions and contribute to a deeper understanding of urban dynamics, there-by supporting the growth and optimization of business operations in the city. The identification of 12 416 rules using ARL provides a granular understanding of how different features interact, offering a valuable tool for strategic planning. Despite the large number of rules, a methodology was found to select the most useful rules using filters and constraints. The experiments revealed meaningful patterns, such as the correlation between the proportion of high-income visitors and the presence of cultural facilities, and the relationship between fitness club density and surrounding infrastructure. The regression analysis, enhanced with SHAP values, explains the impact of various factors on key metrics like high-income visitor shares and fitness club presence, guiding targeted business initiatives. The most valuable relationships between important variables were identified.

The financial indicators of the proposed solutions were calculated, as well as the timeframe for their implementation. They were made based on the assumption that the proposed solution will be embedded in the existing Telecom company geo analytics platform. It was revealed that project payback period is 7 months, and it will bring a profit of approximately 7300 dollars per month since the implementation of the solution. According to telecom company representative's estimates, the implementation of the models will help increase the cost of a monthly subscription by 14% (Cluster analysis – 5%, ARL – 4%, Regression + SHAP – 5%).

Our framework's predictive power is limited by the absence of direct economic data, which force to rely on proxy metrics like high-income visitor proportions or the distribution of visits by time of day. While these proxies suggest relative market attractiveness, they cannot evaluate precise revenue streams, customer retention rates, and profitability margins. The research's temporal scope taking into account weeks of aggregated visitation. It fails to capture dynamic shifts such as holiday surges or weather-driven behavior changes. Furthermore, the exclusive examination of Saint Petersburg constrains external validity, as demographic composition, urban planning policies, and transportation networks differ across cities. Finally, while the hexagonal grid and selected features have balance between spatial detail and computational tractability, they omit unobserved variables such as local promotion campaigns or managerial quality of facilities. Those variables may meaningfully influence outcomes of research.

Future research should aim to integrate proprietary financial and operational indicators such as facility revenues and average annual attendance into the existing geoanalytics framework. By moving from proxy variables to actual economic metrics, predictive models of site profitability could achieve substantially higher accuracy. In parallel, the potential adoption of spatial-temporal deep learning modeling would allow researchers to capture seasonal trends and traffic spikes during holidays. Moreover, it is possible to add additional data sources, such as localized marketing campaign schedules, air quality indices, and noise levels, promises to enrich the feature set and sharpen predictions of location attractiveness. Validating this enhanced approach in other cities with diverse demographic and regulatory contexts would establish the generalizability of our findings.

The raw telecom datasets used in this study are proprietary and subject to contractual confidentiality; they cannot be shared publicly. All analysis code has been archived in a private GitHub repository and transferred to the data owner. To facilitate academic reproducibility, we can provide upon reasonable request the modeling code, configuration files, and scripts to retrieve and preprocess publicly available geospatial data (e.g., OpenStreetMap points of interest and public transport data).

6 Conclusion

In conclusion, this study demonstrates the potential of combining geoanalytics and machine learning for optimal business site selection. The application of clustering algorithms, association rule mining, and model interpretation techniques enabled the identification of key spatial and behavioral factors that influence optimal site location. By integrating telecom data, infrastructure characteristics, and audience profiles, the research offers a comprehensive approach to evaluating location attractiveness. The research insights benefit the telecommunications sector due to broader applications across various industries to optimize operations and enhance competitive advantage through advanced geoanalytics.

References

1. Mohtich, F.-E., Bensiali, S., Idri, A., El-Ayachi, M.: Geospatial data integration for intelligent transportation systems: how to leverage geospatial data to improve travel efficiency and

convenience through more accurate traffic forecasting in intelligent transportation systems. Afr. J. Land Policy Geospat. Sci. **6**(4), 683–692 (2023)

2. MarketsandMarkets: Geospatial Analytics Market by Software Type, Technology, Data Type, & Vertical – Global Forecast to 2029 (2025). https://www.marketsandmarkets.com/Market-Reports/geospatial-analytics-market-198354497.html. Accessed 19 June 2025
3. Owen, S.H., Daskin, M.S.: Strategic facility location: a review. Eur. J. Oper. Res. **111**(3), 423–447 (1998)
4. Drezner, Z.: Facility Location: A Survey of Applications and Methods. Springer, Berlin (1995)
5. Shen, C.Y., Yu, K.T.: A generalized fuzzy approach for strategic problems: the empirical study on facility location selection of authors' management consultation client as an example. Expert Syst. Appl. **36**(3), 4709–4716 (2009)
6. Jung, S.S., Jang, S.C.: To cluster or not to cluster?: understanding geographic clustering by restaurant segment. Int. J. Hosp. Manag. **77**, 448–457 (2019)
7. Drezner, Z., Eiselt, H.A.: Competitive location models: a review. Eur. J. Oper. Res. **316**(1), 5–18 (2024)
8. Huff, D.L.: Defining and estimating a trading area. J. Mark. **28**(3), 34–38 (1964)
9. Schuler, H.J., Prosperi, D.C.: A conjoint measurement model of consumer spatial behavior. J. Reg. Anal. Policy **7**(1), 122–134 (1977)
10. Schuler, H.J.: Grocery shopping choices: Individual preferences based on store attractiveness and distance. Environ. Behav. **13**(3), 331–347 (1981)
11. Timmermans, H.: Decompositional multiattribute preference models in spatial choice analysis: a review of some recent developments. Prog. Hum. Geogr. **8**(2), 189–221 (1984)
12. Drezner, T.: Locating a single new facility among existing unequally attractive facilities. J. Reg. Sci. **34**, 237–252 (1994)
13. Balbontin, C., Hensher, D.A.: Firm-specific and location-specific drivers of business location and relocation decisions. Transp. Rev. **39**(5), 569–588 (2019)
14. Willigers, J., van Wee, B.: High-speed rail and office location choices: a stated choice experiment for the Netherlands. J. Transp. Geogr. **19**(4), 745–754 (2011)
15. Weterings, A., Knoben, J.: Footloose: an analysis of the drivers of firm relocations over different distances. Pap. Reg. Sci. **92**(4), 791–810 (2013)
16. Wang, Y., Li, S., Zhang, X., Jiang, D., Hao, M., Zhou, R.: Site selection of digital signage in Beijing: a combination of machine learning and an empirical approach. ISPRS Int. J. Geo-Inf. **9**(4), 217 (2020)

Generative Artificial Intelligence as a Technological Resource to Strengthen the Teaching of Naval Doctrine

Wendy Esthela Wasbrum Tinoco[1], Margarita del Rocío Palma Samaniego[1](✉), Victor Danilo Lazo Alvarado[2], and Paola Nathaly Mantilla Carrera[1]

[1] Dpto. de Seguridad y Defensa, Universidad de Las Fuerzas Armadas, Espe, Quito, Ecuador
wewasbrun@espe.edu.ecm, mdpalma3@espe.edu.ec

[2] Dpto. Ciencias Exactas, Universidad de Las Fuerzas Armadas, Espe, Quito, Ecuador
vdlazo@espe.edu.ec

Abstract. This study aims to evaluate the potential use of generative artificial intelligence (GAI) to improve the teaching and learning of naval doctrine in the Ecuadorian Navy. The central problem lies in the limitations in accessing, updating, and systematizing doctrinal knowledge due to extensive and outdated formats, which affect the quality of learning and operational decision-making. The research adopts a quantitative, descriptive-explanatory approach, through structured Likert-type surveys administered digitally to student officers at the Naval War Academy between now and 2025, employing descriptive statistical techniques to identify perceptions and trends. The planned sample comprises between 40 and 50 officers in training, selected by purposive non-probability sampling. The aim is to determine the level of knowledge, willingness, and acceptance of GAI-based technologies, as well as to identify potential resistance or challenges to their integration. The results are expected to demonstrate a high level of acceptance and willingness to incorporate IAG tools into the doctrinal training process, reinforcing the potential of these technologies to facilitate access, understanding, and application of strategic and operational content. The findings will guide the implementation of technological strategies that enhance naval education, promoting a structural change in pedagogical methods and strengthening the preparation of officers for the challenges of the contemporary maritime environment.

Keywords: Generative Artificial Intelligence · Doctrine · Teaching · Technology · Acceptance

1 Introduction

Generative Artificial Intelligence (GAI) stands out as a transformative technology with significant potential in sectors such as defense and security. Its capabilities—processing vast information, generating coherent text, simulating dialogue, and supporting decisions—make it a strategic asset in military development (Wang, Li, & Chen, 2023; Center for Naval Analyses, 2023). In the Ecuadorian Navy, the gradual incorporation of GAI aligns with broader efforts in digitalization and modernization (Ecuadorian Navy, 2025).

T. Guarda et al. (Eds.): ARTIIS 2025, CCIS 2789, pp. 564–573, 2026.
https://doi.org/10.1007/978-3-032-16758-3_42

In technologically advanced nations like the United States, China, and NATO members, GAI has progressed from pilot projects to active use in training simulators, decision systems, and doctrinal analysis (Wang et al., 2023; DARPA, 2023). While Latin American countries such as Brazil and Chile have launched initial GAI initiatives, adoption remains limited by funding, infrastructure, and technological gaps (González & Pereira, 2022). Nonetheless, the Ecuadorian Navy has recognized the value of such tools to enhance instructional efficiency and doctrinal development (Ecuadorian Navy, 2020).

Naval doctrine provides the strategic foundation for officer training. Interactive tools—like doctrinal chatbots trained with manuals and field experiences—could transform how officers learn and apply doctrine at the Naval War Academy (Ecuadorian Navy, 2024; Hatata, 2022). These systems can provide instant, context-based access to content while capturing field insights that refine doctrine.

However, integrating GAI in military settings presents risks. Studies from RAND and the US Army War College (2023) highlight concerns such as data reliability, reduced decision-making autonomy, and overdependence on AI. Any implementation must include human oversight, validation protocols, and ethical safeguards (National Security Commission on AI, 2023).

This article explores how GAI, particularly doctrinal chatbots, could enhance naval officer training in Ecuador. It posits that these tools can improve both access to knowledge and the integration of operational experiences, strengthening a dynamic and adaptive doctrine.

2 State of the Art

Generative artificial intelligence (GAI) represents a significant evolution within the field of artificial intelligence, particularly in its ability to create new and contextualized content from large volumes of previously analyzed data. Its application has been widely documented in sectors such as marketing, healthcare, education, and, more recently, in security and defense (Wang, Li, & Chen, 2023). As modern conflicts and military preparedness require more dynamic and cognitively demanding responses, GAI is emerging as a key tool in the doctrinal and operational transformation of global armed forces.

One of the most relevant approaches in the application of IAG to the military sphere is its use as a support system for doctrinal learning. Military doctrine, understood as the set of principles and standards that guide the actions of the armed forces, requires constant updating and socialization. This has been enhanced by generative tools such as chatbots trained with doctrinal libraries, which facilitate immediate access to strategic and operational knowledge for military personnel in training (Hatata, 2022). Indeed, the use of conversational assistants allows for natural interaction with doctrinal texts, promoting more active, contextual, and adaptive learning.

Several studies have demonstrated the positive impact of these technologies in learning environments. Ahmed Hatata (2022), in his analysis of the adoption of chatbots in higher education, found that performance expectations, ease of use, and interaction with content significantly increased student acceptance. This model can be extrapolated to military educational environments, where doctrinal complexity requires new ways of accessing, understanding, and retaining knowledge.

At the international level, nations such as the United States, China, and NATO member states have begun developing generative AI systems specifically designed to strengthen military decision-making, optimize strategic planning, and automate doctrinal analysis. According to the RAND Corporation (2023), AGI has been used by the US military to generate operational scenarios, analyze tactical responses, and support officers in complex situations, all under strict validation and oversight conditions. The Defense Advanced Research Projects Agency (DARPA) has also promoted initiatives such as the "AI Next Campaign," which explores the use of generative systems to predict and simulate responses in conflict contexts (DARPA, 2023).

In the Chinese case, the Center for Naval Analyses (2023) reported that the People's Liberation Army is integrating generative models for training, doctrine analysis, and adaptive course of action generation, highlighting an interest in surpassing Western capabilities through autonomous technologies. These applications not only seek to gain operational efficiency but also to redefine doctrinal planning processes through artificial intelligence, raising the levels of precision and adaptability in volatile environments.

At the regional level, the panorama in Latin America shows incipient progress. Brazil has been a pioneer in projects integrating AI technologies in logistics and training environments, especially in the Brazilian Navy, where intelligent simulation platforms with conversational assistance have been developed for personnel training (González & Pereira, 2022). Chile, for its part, has included automation elements in the academic programs of its military academies, albeit with a more experimental approach. However, most Latin American countries face limitations related to technological infrastructure, financing for innovative projects, and technical training of personnel.

In the Ecuadorian context, the Ecuadorian Navy has taken important steps toward the digital transformation of its training and operational processes. According to the Doctrinal Map of the Ecuadorian Navy (2025), there is an institutional initiative to digitize and systematize fundamental doctrinal documents. Likewise, the Doctrine Generation Manual (2024) establishes the need to integrate operational experiences and lessons learned into doctrinal design, which opens the door to the use of IAG systems as mechanisms to efficiently collect, classify, and process strategic information.

However, the use of generative artificial intelligence in military contexts has also raised significant questions. One of the main ones is the reliability of the information these tools can generate. The RAND Corporation (2023) has warned that inadequate or unsupervised implementation can lead to doctrinal errors, tactical misinformation, or loss of control over the decision-making process. In agreement, the US Army War College (2023) emphasizes that the integration of GAI into military organizations requires a profound restructuring of decision-making systems, validation protocols, and lines of authority to avoid a technological dependence that compromises human judgment.

These concerns also relate to the ethical handling of information, cybersecurity, and doctrinal sovereignty. The National Security Commission on Artificial Intelligence (2023) has noted that generative algorithms must be aligned with the fundamental principles of transparency, human control, and strategic data protection. This is especially relevant in institutions like the Ecuadorian Navy, where national doctrines reflect not only technical considerations but also institutional values and principles that cannot be delegated to autonomous systems without adequate oversight.

In summary, the state of the art on generative artificial intelligence applied to the military environment shows an accelerated growth of initiatives, research, and projects in various latitudes, highlighting its transformative potential in doctrine, training, and strategic operations. However, its implementation requires not only technological resources but also a thorough institutional review to ensure the safe, ethical, and effective use of these tools. For the Ecuadorian Navy, the challenge lies in articulating emerging technological capabilities with its operational and doctrinal context, in order to enhance the development of its officers and strengthen its naval strategy from a robust, critical, and contextualized technological foundation.

2.1 Problem Statement

The operational and strategic environment in which the armed forces, including naval units, currently operate is determined by the rapid advancement of information technologies, the complexity of asymmetric conflicts, and the need for rapid and precise responses. In this context, the training and doctrinal development of military personnel require tools that enable flexible, up-to-date learning focused on the practical applicability of strategic and operational knowledge. However, in the Ecuadorian Navy, despite efforts to digitize processes and update doctrinal frameworks, significant limitations persist in the access, systematization, and updating of doctrinal knowledge among officers in training.

Currently, student officers face challenges in consulting and understanding doctrinal documents, which are often presented in lengthy, fragmented, or outdated formats. This situation directly impacts the quality of learning and operational decision-making, hindering the effective application of doctrine in real-life scenarios. Given this situation, there is a need to incorporate emerging technologies, such as generative artificial intelligence, that enable more dynamic and contextualized interaction with doctrinal content.

Despite the potential offered by tools such as chatbots trained with doctrinal manuals and operational experiences, their implementation in the Ecuadorian military training environment is still incipient and lacks clear guidelines. No institutional policies or methodological strategies have been developed to effectively integrate these technologies into teaching-learning processes. Therefore, the following research question arises: How can generative artificial intelligence support the study of naval doctrine for the development of naval officers in the Ecuadorian Navy? This question guides this study, which seeks to identify the opportunities and challenges involved in integrating generative artificial intelligence into doctrinal training, proposing mechanisms to optimize its use and contribute to a more effective, up-to-date, and accessible naval doctrine.

2.2 Justification

This research responds to the growing need for innovation in the Ecuadorian Navy's doctrinal training, in a global context where digital technologies are reshaping education and decision-making. GAI, particularly in the form of doctrinal chatbots, can address persistent issues such as fragmented content, limited access, and underutilized field experience.

By enabling faster, interactive access to operational and strategic information, GAI tools can significantly improve the learning process. They also support continuous learning and institutional knowledge retention, fostering an adaptable and feedback-driven doctrinal culture.

Strategically, this research aligns with the Navy's goals for digital transformation and doctrinal modernization. Academically, it contributes to the limited body of work on military education and technology in Latin America. Socially, it promotes a more competent, technologically literate naval force, essential for national security.

In sum, this research is timely, feasible, and strategically important for equipping the Ecuadorian Navy to meet contemporary challenges through the responsible integration of emerging technologies.

3 Methodology

This study is part of a descriptive-explanatory research project, as it seeks to characterize the potential use of generative artificial intelligence (GAI) in the doctrinal development process of naval officers, while also analyzing how its implementation can influence the improvement of doctrinal learning. This type of research allows us not only to describe the current perceptions of naval personnel regarding the use of emerging technologies, but also to establish relationships between variables such as access to knowledge, doctrinal applicability, and pedagogical innovation.

From an approach perspective, a quantitative approach is adopted, as the objective is to collect, process, and analyze numerical data obtained through structured surveys. This approach allows for the generation of measurable, comparable, and statistically representative results, facilitating the identification of trends, levels of acceptance, and priority areas for the integration of IAG into military educational processes.

Regarding the study population, it will be made up of student officers from the Naval War Academy (AGUENA) of the Ecuadorian Navy, who are enrolled in the Staff Program during the 2025 academic period. This population is relevant given that they are in a stage of professional development where access to and application of doctrine is key to the development of their strategic and operational skills.

For the sample, a non-probability, purposive sampling will be used, selecting student officers actively participating in training activities related to naval doctrine. The anticipated sample size is approximately 40 to 50 officers, which is representative considering the typical cohort size at AGUENA and provides sufficient information to establish patterns and conduct comparative analyses.

The data collection instrument will be a structured, ad hoc survey composed of closed-ended Likert-type questions (five levels) grouped into dimensions such as: level of knowledge about IAG, perception of its applicability in doctrinal study, willingness to use digital tools such as chatbots, and expectations regarding its implementation in naval training. The survey will be administered digitally using institutional online forms, ensuring the anonymity and confidentiality of participants.

The data obtained will be analyzed using descriptive statistical techniques (frequencies, percentages, and means), which will allow for the identification of general trends in officers' perceptions, as well as possible correlations between the variables investigated. These results will be used to draw conclusions about the viability, acceptance, and potential potential of generative artificial intelligence as a tool to support the teaching of naval doctrine in the Ecuadorian Navy.

4 Results

4.1 Survey Results

Table 1. I believe that generative artificial intelligence tools (such as chatbots) can facilitate the learning of naval doctrine.

Option	Frequency (f)	Percentage (%)
1. Totally disagree	1	2.2%
2. Disagree	3	6.7%
3. Neutral	6	13.3%
4. Agreed	20	44.4%
5. Totally agree	15	33.4%
Total	**45**	**100%**

The majority of respondents (77.8%) agree or strongly agree that the IAG facilitates doctrinal learning. Only 8.9% disagree. Positive perceptions are high, while neutrality (13.3%) reflects a minority that is not yet entirely convinced (Tables 1, 2).

Table 2. I would like to receive training on the use of generative artificial intelligence in the academic-military environment.

Option	Frequency (f)	Percentage (%)
1. Totally disagree	0	0%
2. Disagree	2	4.4%
3. Neutral	4	8.9%
4. Agreed	18	40.0%
5. Totally agree	21	46.7%
Total	**45**	**100%**

86.7% want to receive training on the use of IAG, while only 4.4% disagree. There were no "strongly disagree" responses. This reflects a strong willingness among naval personnel to pursue technological training to incorporate emerging tools into their training process (Table 3).

Table 3. The use of IAG would allow for more agile and practical access to doctrinal manuals.

Option	Frequency (f)	Percentage (%)
1. Totally disagree	1	2.2%
2. Disagree	2	4.4%
3. Neutral	5	11.1%
4. Agreed	22	48.9%
5. Totally agree	15	33.4%
Total	**45**	**100%**

82.3% believe that the IAG would facilitate practical access to doctrinal manuals. Only 6.6% disagree, and 11.1% remain neutral. These results confirm a widespread perception of the usefulness and concrete applicability of this technology in doctrinal consultation (Table 4).

Table 4. The inclusion of tools such as doctrinal chatbots would improve my academic performance

Option	Frequency (f)	Percentage (%)
1. Totally disagree	2	4.4%
2. Disagree	3	6.7%
3. Neutral	6	13.3%
4. Agreed	20	44.4%
5. Totally agree	14	31.2%
Total	**45**	**100%**

Nearly 75.6% believe that academic chatbots would improve their academic performance. A small percentage (11.1%) disagree, and 13.3% remain neutral. This suggests that officers recognize the positive impact of IAG on their learning, although some are still unclear (Table 5).

82.3% of officers are willing to incorporate IAG technologies into their doctrinal studies. Only 6.6% express disagreement. The high percentage of acceptance indicates a favorable institutional openness toward the digitalization of knowledge, with minimal resistance observed among participants.

4.2 General Analysis of Survey Results

The survey administered to 45 student officers at the Naval War Academy (AGUENA) reveals a strong and consistent level of acceptance and willingness to incorporate generative artificial intelligence (GAI) tools, such as doctrinal chatbots, into the doctrinal

Table 5. I am willing to incorporate IAG-based technologies into my doctrinal study activities.

Option	Frequency (f)	Percentage (%)
1. Totally disagree	1	2.2%
2. Disagree	2	4.4%
3. Neutral	5	11.1%
4. Agreed	21	46.7%
5. Totally agree	16	35.6%
Total	**45**	**100%**

learning process. Across the five items assessed using a Likert scale, the majority of respondents selected "Agree" or "Totally Agree" in support of GAI integration.

Specifically:

- 77.8% of participants believe GAI tools facilitate doctrinal learning.
- 86.7% express interest in receiving training in the use of GAI within academic-military contexts.
- 82.3% agree that GAI tools would improve access to doctrinal manuals and support their learning process.
- 75.6% feel that these tools would positively impact their academic performance.
- 82.3% are willing to incorporate GAI tools into their doctrinal studies.

These results suggest that GAI is viewed as a highly feasible and desirable enhancement to naval education, with most respondents recognizing its potential to improve the quality, accessibility, and efficiency of learning. Furthermore, the minimal level of disagreement and low neutrality rates (generally below 13%) indicate only limited skepticism or unfamiliarity with the technology.

Importantly, the strong interest in training (86.7%) suggests that the perceived value of GAI is coupled with an understanding that effective use requires specific competencies—highlighting the need for accompanying digital literacy initiatives and structured implementation strategies.

4.3 Comparative Feasibility Analysis

Despite the positive perception reflected in the survey, feasibility in the Ecuadorian context requires analysis from two complementary perspectives: technological infrastructure and institutional policy environment.

Compared to developed countries like the United States or China—where AI integration in defense is supported by robust digital infrastructure, cloud computing capabilities, and dedicated research funding—the Ecuadorian Navy faces several limitations:

Limited access to advanced hardware and cloud-based platforms may restrict the capacity to deploy large-scale GAI tools.

Network reliability and bandwidth constraints in some training facilities could affect real-time interactions with AI-driven systems such as chatbots.

There is a scarcity of specialized technical personnel (data scientists, AI engineers) within military education institutions to maintain or adapt generative models locally.

However, some strengths exist. The Navy's recent digitization efforts—such as the Doctrine Generation Manual (2024) and the Doctrinal Map (2025)—demonstrate a commitment to integrating digital tools. These initiatives can serve as a foundation for deploying scaled-down, cloud-hosted chatbot systems trained on official documents and accessible via secured institutional platforms.

From a policy standpoint, the Ecuadorian Navy has not yet established specific guidelines or protocols for the use of AI in training. In contrast, institutions such as the U.S. Department of Defense and NATO have developed formal strategies, ethical frameworks, and AI adoption roadmaps that define scope, accountability, and validation mechanisms.

The lack of defined policies in Ecuador presents both a barrier and an opportunity. Without regulation, implementation risks inconsistency or misuse. On the other hand, the current gap enables the formulation of customized, adaptive policies that consider the Navy's operational culture, national security priorities, and ethical expectations. These policies must address:

- Oversight and accountability protocols
- Data protection and doctrinal sovereignty
- Training standards for personnel interacting with AI tools

While the Ecuadorian Navy is technologically less equipped than its counterparts in major powers, the strong institutional will, coupled with high user acceptance and emerging doctrinal digitization efforts, supports a gradual and scalable implementation of GAI.

5 Conclusions

The integration of generative artificial intelligence tools, such as doctrinal chatbots, represents a viable alternative accepted by the majority of officers in training in the Ecuadorian Navy. The results show a broad consensus on their usefulness in facilitating learning and access to doctrinal content. This initial acceptance constitutes fertile ground for designing institutional technological implementation strategies that strengthen the educational process without replacing the critical role of human judgment in strategic decision-making.

There is a significant willingness among student officers to receive specific training in the use of tools based on generative artificial intelligence. This demonstrates that, beyond technological interest, there is a clear need to strengthen digital skills in the academic-military sphere. Therefore, the implementation of these technologies must be accompanied by training programs that allow users to properly leverage the potential of AI without becoming dependent on or misusing automated systems.

The survey results reflect that officers perceive that the IAG not only improves accessibility to doctrinal content but can also positively impact their academic performance. This perception indicates that the digitalization of doctrinal knowledge, through interactive systems, can become a catalyst for continuous learning improvement in naval training schools. This would strengthen learning autonomy, accelerate the access to key materials, and foster better doctrinal assimilation.

While a high level of acceptance is observed, there are still levels of neutrality and slight disagreements regarding the effectiveness of these technologies. This suggests that, although the majority of officers positively value the use of IAG, there are still segments that require greater awareness and empirical demonstration of their impact. Therefore, implementation should be gradual, with pilot phases that allow for building trust and validating their effectiveness within the institutional and cultural context of the Ecuadorian Navy.

Generative artificial intelligence has the potential to become a strategic tool for the doctrinal development of Ecuadorian naval officers. However, its integration should not be viewed as a simple technological modernization, but rather as a structural change in the way naval doctrine is taught, learned, and applied. Achieving this requires a clear institutional vision, a well-defined ethical framework, and sustained commitment from the military institution's academic, technological, and strategic stakeholders.

References

Ecuadorian Navy. Basic Doctrine of the Navy. Ecuadorian Navy (2020)

Ecuadorian Navy. Doctrine Generation Manual and Naval Library. Ecuadorian Navy (2024)

Ecuadorian Navy. Doctrinal Map. Ecuadorian Navy (2025)

Center for Naval Analyses. Generative AI for Enhanced Military Decision-Making (2023). https://www.cna.org/reports/2023

DARPA (Defense Advanced Research Projects Agency). Transforming Military Decision-Making with AI-Powered Systems (2023). https://www.darpa.mil/programs

González, R., Pereira, L.: Artificial intelligence in latin american defense: advances and challenges in the 21st century. Latin Am. J. Strategic Stud. **14**(2), 45–67 (2022)

Hatata, A.: Performance expectancy, effort expectancy, demographics, chatbot, behavioral intention. Int. J. High. Educ. Manage. (IJHEM) **8**(2) (2022)

National Security Commission on Artificial Intelligence. Risks and Ethical Implications of AI in Military Applications (2023). https://www.nscai.gov/reports

RAND Corporation. Exploring the Implications of Generative AI for Chinese Military Strategy (2023). https://www.rand.org/reports/2023

US Army War College. How Will the Structure of Military Organizations Evolve as Artificial Intelligence is Integrated? (2023). https://press.armywarcollege.edu/monographs/949

Wang, H., Li, J., Chen, X.: Artificial intelligence and military doctrine: global trends and applications. Int. J. Defense Technol. **9**(1), 89–110 (2023)

Comparison of 1:10 Scale Training Models for Track Detection

Bryan Betancourt-Ramírez[1], Rafael Reveles-Martínez[1,2], José G. Arceo-Olague[1], Erika P. Sánchez-Femat[1], Javier Saldívar-Pérez[1], Carlos E. Galván-Tejada[1], Luis C. Reveles-Gómez[1], Manuel A. Soto-Murillo[1], Antonio Martínez-Torteya[3], and José M. Celaya-Padilla[1(✉)]

[1] Unidad Académica de Ingeniería Eléctrica, Universidad Autónoma de Zacatecas, Jardín Juárez 147, Centro Histórico, 98000 Zacatecas, Mexico
jose.celaya@uaz.edu.mx

[2] Instituto Politécnico Nacional, Unidad Profesional Interdisciplinaria de Ingeniería Campus Zacatecas (UPIIZ), 98160 Zacatecas, Mexico

[3] Escuela de Ingeniería y Tecnologías, Universidad de Monterrey, 66238 San Pedro Garza García, Mexico

Abstract. Autonomous driving at scale represents a safe and efficient platform for research in vehicle perception and control. This study compares the performance of four machine learning algorithms (Logistic Regression, Random Forest, Support Vector Machine (SVM) and Artificial Neural Network (ANN)) in classifying track type (straight or curved) for an autonomous vehicle on a scale of 1:10. Using a dataset of 2,672 samples, consisting of front camera images and steering angle values, eight statistical features were extracted to train the models. These were evaluated using metrics such as accuracy (accuracy), sensitivity (recall), F1 score and area under the curve (AUC), employing feature selection methods such as RFE, LASSO and Boruta. The results showed that Random Forest performed the best (accuracy: 0.96, AUC: 0.99), followed closely by SVM and ANN, while feature selection did not significantly affect the results. The findings laid the groundwork for future research in dynamic and more diverse environments.

Keywords: Autonomous driving · Autonomous vehicles · Track detection · Binary classification · Random forest

1 Introduction

Autonomous driving is one of the most promising areas of modern engineering due to its potential to transform mobility by reducing human intervention in vehicle operation. This not only seeks to increase road safety, but also to improve transportation efficiency, reduce energy consumption, and facilitate accessibility in urban and rural environments. Its development integrates multiple disciplines such as artificial intelligence, computer vision, signal processing and control systems, making it a highly relevant field of study for applied research. The development of scaled autonomous vehicles represents a safe, economical and flexible

T. Guarda et al. (Eds.): ARTIIS 2025, CCIS 2789, pp. 574–589, 2026.
https://doi.org/10.1007/978-3-032-16758-3_43

alternative for experimentation. These vehicles allow the validation of perception and control algorithms in controlled environments, without the risks and logistical limitations that would be implied by doing so in full-size vehicles. In addition, their use facilitates the repetition of tests under similar conditions, which is fundamental to evaluate the performance of the proposed models. One of the key challenges in this context is the precise identification of the type of track the vehicle is driving on, as this information can be used to dynamically adjust control parameters such as speed. This scaled platform was used to collect real track data, which was then used to train and compare different machine learning algorithms to detect the type of track (straight or curved) on which the vehicle is driving. The ability to correctly interpret the environment is essential for safe and efficient navigation. In this work we propose the comparison of different machine learning algorithms: Logistic Regression, Random Forest, Support Vector Machine (SVM) and Artificial Neural Network (ANN), for the classification of the type of track in an autonomous car at 1:10 scale, using images obtained through a front camera.

The selected algorithms represent diverse approaches in supervised classification, allowing to explore their respective performances in terms of accuracy, robustness and inference time. The application is performed in a controlled environment that simulates real driving scenarios, allowing the effectiveness of each method to be evaluated under practical conditions. This study is part of a larger autonomous navigation architecture, in which track type recognition is a critical input for vehicle decision making and control. This work seeks to lay the groundwork for the autonomous car to adjust its speed according to the type of track detected. The idea is that, for example, if the car identifies a curve, it will automatically reduce its speed to avoid going off the road. This is achieved by integrating the detection system with a PID controller [15,16], which regulates the speed precisely. Implementing this type of intelligence in autonomous vehicles, even on a small scale, is essential to improve their performance and bring them closer to a behavior more similar to that of a human driver. Furthermore, this approach may be useful for future applications in real vehicles, contributing to the development of safer and more efficient driving systems, this article is organized as follows: Sect. 2 presents related work and advances in clue detection. Section 3 details the methodology used, including data collection, feature extraction, and variable selection. Section 4 presents the results obtained from the comparison of machine learning models. Section 5 includes a discussion of the results. Finally, Sect. 6 presents the conclusions of this study and future lines of research.

2 Related Work

In recent years, several approaches have been developed to improve perception and decision making in autonomous vehicles, many of which complement the objective of this study.

In 2018 [2], a convolutional neural network (CNN) specialized in curved trajectory detection was developed. The model achieved an accuracy of 80–90%

and was designed with an emphasis on computational efficiency, which makes it suitable for scaled vehicles with limited resources. In addition, this same work stands out for applying neuroevolution techniques to optimize the architecture and weights of the neural networks, thus reducing latency and improving system performance in real time.

In 2022, a systematic review of the perception systems for autonomous vehicles based on deep learning was presented, highlighting the importance of multisensor fusion. This combination, especially between visual and steering angle data, has been shown to significantly improve curve detection and vehicle stability in real scenarios [14].

3 Methods and Materials

Figure 1 illustrates the overall methodology used in this study for track type classification.

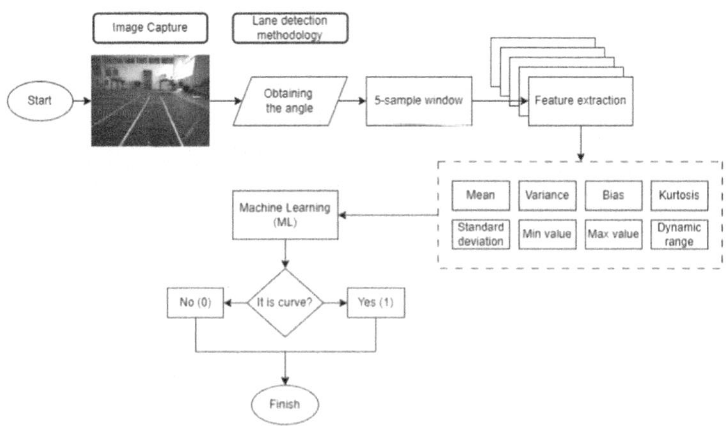

Fig. 1. Track detection methodology, own creation.

The diagram illustrates the complete process followed to address the problem of track classification (curved and straight) in autonomous vehicles in 1:10 scale. It starts with the vehicle, from which data are collected, by capturing images and obtaining the angle by lane detection [15]. These data are then subjected to a preprocessing that includes cleaning and normalization tasks to subsequently carry out the feature extraction, where representative variables of the track type detection are selected. Once this is done, the data is trained on four classification models: Random Forest (RF), Logistic Regression (LR), Support Vector Machine (SVM) and Artificial Neural Network (ANN). The performance of the four models is then evaluated using key metrics such as area under the curve (AUC), Recall, F1-score and accuracy (ACC).

To perform track type detection, the first step was the construction of a specific dataset. This set was formed from samples collected directly by the vehicle during its circulation on a test track. Two key elements were recorded for each sample: an image captured by the car's front camera and the value of the steering angle corresponding to the moment when the image was taken. The relationship between both data made it possible to establish a label for each sample, indicating whether the vehicle was traveling on a straight section or on a curve. In this way, a labeled dataset was generated that served as input to train and evaluate the different machine learning algorithms used in this study.

A 1:10 scale autonomous vehicle, designed and built specifically for research and testing tasks in controlled environments, was used for data collection. The vehicle chassis is based on a commercial model of a radio-controlled car, to which various electronic components and sensors were integrated to enable its autonomous operation. The vehicle's perception system consists of a front-mounted Intel RealSense D435i camera that captures real-time images of the environment. This camera combines RGB vision and depth, allowing detailed visual information to be generated for tasks such as lane detection and track type analysis. For data processing and decision making, the vehicle is equipped with a high-performance Intel NUC computer, which executes the perception, classification and control algorithms. In addition, a PID control system is used to regulate the vehicle's speed and direction based on the intelligent system's decisions [16]. The vehicle also has servomotors that allow autonomous steering and acceleration. The entire system is powered by a rechargeable Li-Po battery, which provides enough autonomy to perform complete runs on test tracks [15]. The assembled 1:10 scale autonomous vehicle is shown in Fig. 2.

Fig. 2. 1:10 vehicle assembly, own creation.

3.1 Data Collection

The dataset used in this study is composed of a total of 2,672 samples. Each sample includes two main columns: "Frame", which corresponds to the image captured by the vehicle camera, and "Angle", which represents the value of the steering angle recorded at that instant. To facilitate the training of the classification algorithms, these samples were manually labeled in two categories: 0 to represent straight stretches and 1 for curves. Table 1 shows a fragment of the dataset obtained during data collection.

Table 1. Dataset for track classification.

Frame	Angle	Label
frame_00000.png	87.42815939	0
frame_00001.png	87.56335175	0
frame_00002.png	86.88769139	0
frame_00003.png	88.37502364	0
frame_00004.png	87.96908576	0
⋮	⋮	⋮
frame_02671.png	79.42124106	0

Lane detection, fundamental to the operation of the autonomous vehicle, is described in detail in a previous paper [16]. Since this component is part of the overall system, but not the main focus of the present study, only a general diagram summarizing the key stages of the process is presented in this section, with the objective of providing the reader with an overview of the perception system used.

Figure 3 shows a simplified diagram of the implemented lane detection methodology, which includes stages such as image acquisition, preprocessing, lane segmentation and direction angle calculation.

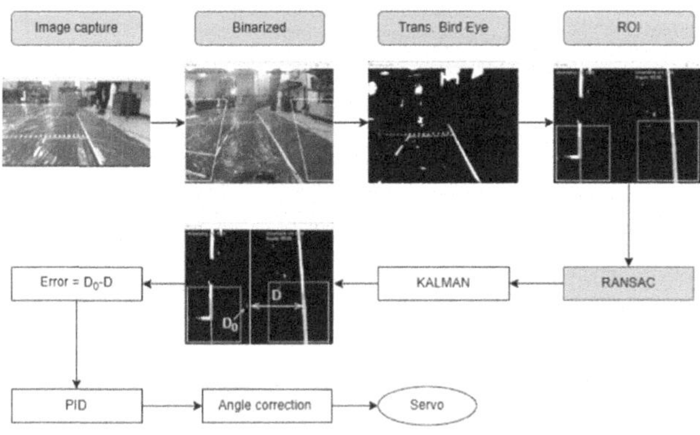

Fig. 3. Lane detection methodology, own creation.

The collection of this data was carried out while the autonomous car was driving around the official track used in the Mexican Robotics Tournament (TMR) shown in Fig. 4, which ensures that the dataset reflects real and diverse conditions of the competition environment [15].

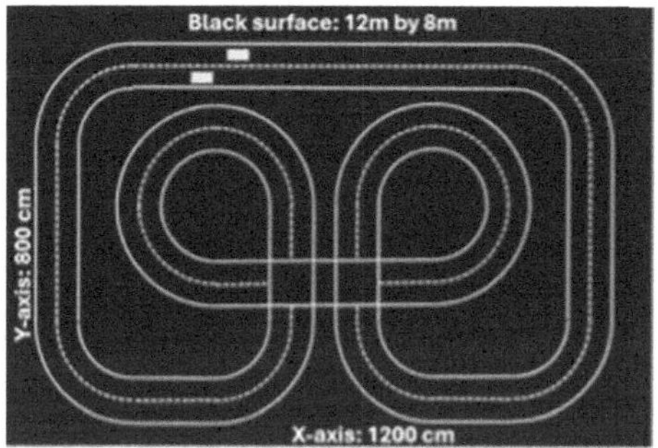

Fig. 4. Official TMR track [15].

3.2 Feature Extraction

Based on previous work [4], it was decided to adopt an approach focused on the use of machine learning algorithms to classify the track type. To capture the temporal context of driving, a sliding window technique was implemented. Specifically, a window of five consecutive samples was employed, allowing the data to be analyzed sequentially and generating new, more informative instances for the models. In order to improve the interpretation of the original data and provide the models with more relevant information, a feature extraction process was performed. In total, eight features derived from the main columns of the original data set (image and angle) were obtained, which are described in detail in Table 2.

Table 2. Extracted features.

Feature	Formula
Mean	$\bar{x} = \frac{1}{n}\sum_{i-1}^{n} X_i$
Variance	$\sigma^2 = \frac{\sum_{i=1}^{n}(X_i - \bar{X})^2}{N}$
Skewness	$\gamma_1 = \frac{\frac{1}{n}\sum_{i=1}^{n}(x_i-\bar{x})^3}{\left[\frac{1}{n-1}\sum_{i=1}^{n}(x_i-\bar{x})^2\right]^{3/2}}$
Kurtosis	$K = \frac{\sum_{i=1}^{N}(X_i - \bar{X})^4}{Ns^4} - 3$
Standard Deviation	$\sigma = \sqrt{\sigma^2}$
Min value	$X_{\max} = \max\{X_1, \ldots, X_n\}$
Max value	$X_{\min} = \min\{X_1, \ldots, X_n\}$
Dynamic range	$DR = X_n - \min\{X_1, \ldots, X_n\}$

From Table 2, X_i is the i-th row of the signal value in the 5-sample window being processed.

As a result of this process, the total number of samples was reduced from 2,672 to 534 composite records, each representing a sequence that was used to determine whether the vehicle was on a straight section or a curve. An excerpt from this dataset is shown in Table 3.

Table 3. Dataset after feature selection.

Mean	Variance	Skewness	Kurtosis	Std. dev.	Max	Min	Dyn. R	Label
87.6446	0.3162	−0.0232	−1.7481	0.5623	88.3750	86.8876	1.4873	0
88.5914	0.0896	1.60E-08	−1.9119	0.2993	88.9701	88.2127	0.7574	0
88.7698	0.6669	−0.3002	−2.1020	0.8166	89.5381	87.6985	1.8396	0
87.7256	0.1133	−0.8019	−1.2699	0.3366	87.9690	87.1578	0.8112	0
87.6446	0.3162	−0.0232	−1.7481	0.5623	88.3750	86.8876	1.4873	0
⋮	⋮	⋮	⋮	⋮	⋮	⋮	⋮	⋮
87.2396	1.1932	0.4535	−1.6429	1.0923	88.9165	86.2128	2.7036	0

3.3 Feature Selection

Feature selection is an important step in identifying the most relevant variables in a dataset. Multiple methods were evaluated for the feature selection stage, including algorithms based on univariate scoring (SelectKBest), statistical relevance (VarianceThreshold, Correlation-based feature selection), linear models (Lasso), envelopes (RFE, RFECV), and tree-based methods such as Permutation Feature Importance and Boruta. Figure 5 shows a visual summary of the result of these methods applied on the eight features extracted from the original dataset. Based on these consistent results, it was concluded that it was not necessary to eliminate any variable, as all features contributed relevant information to the model. This also allows preserving the richness of the dataset and potentially improving the generalization of the applied machine learning algorithms.

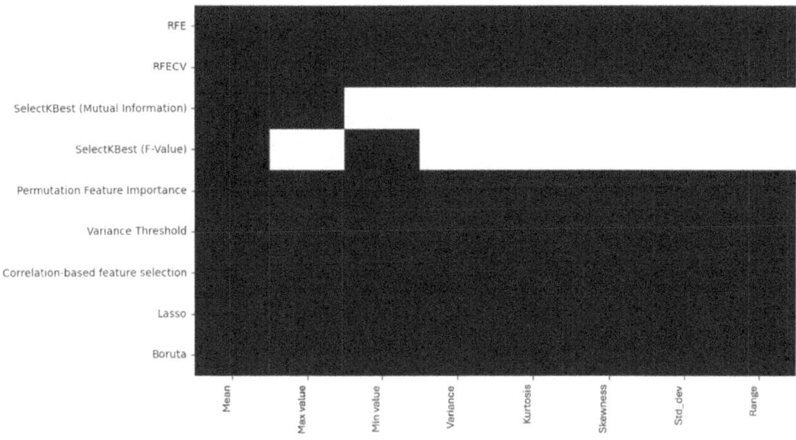

Fig. 5. Feature selection.

Among all the approaches evaluated, we chose to retain all the characteristics, since the RFE, Lasso and Boruta methods (recognized for their ability to select relevant attributes in a robust manner) identified all the variables as significant. Specifically:

Recursive Feature Elimination (RFE). It selects features recursively by eliminating less important features based on a base model (e.g., a Logistic Regression or a decision tree). That all variables have been retained suggests that each contributes value to the performance of the classification model [5].

Lasso (Least Absolute Shrinkage and Selection Operator). LASSO (Least Absolute Shrinkage and Selection Operator) regression applies a penalty based on the L_1 rule on the regression coefficients. This technique favors automatic variable selection by reducing some coefficients to exactly zero, which makes it a useful tool to obtain partial and more interpretable models.

On the other hand, the L_2 penalty, used in Ridge regression, minimizes the sum of the residuals by imposing a constraint on the L_2 norm of the coefficients. Although this technique improves model performance by reducing variance, it fails to eliminate predictors, since it retains all non-zero coefficients.

An alternative that combines both approaches is the Elastic Net method, which incorporates the L_1 and L_2 penalties simultaneously. Its penalty function is expressed as follows:

$$\hat{\beta}_{(\text{elastic-net})} = \arg\min_{\beta} \left\{ \|y - X\beta\|_2^2 + \lambda_2 \|\beta\|^2 + \lambda_1 \|\beta\|_1 \right\} \tag{1}$$

where X is the data matrix, and λ_1 and λ_2 are the regularization hyperparameters. Another way to represent this penalty is:

$$P_\alpha(\beta) = \sum_{j=1}^{p} [(1-\alpha)\beta_j^2 + \alpha|\beta_j|] \tag{2}$$

Here, parameter α controls the type of regularization: if $\alpha = 0$, the model behaves like Ridge; if $\alpha = 1$, like LASSO. By combining both penalties, Elastic Net allows to obtain sparse models, preserving useful regularization properties [12].

Boruta. Boruta is a wrapper method based on Random Forest that selects relevant variables by comparing them with artificial variables called shadows. These are created by randomizing the original variables to break their relationship with the response. Then, the model evaluates the importance of all variables (original and shadow) using Z scores. Variables that significantly exceed the maximum Z value of the shadow variables (MZSA) are considered important, while those that do not are discarded. Thus, Boruta allows to identify features with statistically significant relevance [13].

3.4 Model Construction

For this research, as already mentioned, one of its objectives is to model algorithms that can be able to efficiently predict the type of track being traveled, i.e., whether it is curved or straight. Four models were made, which were based on detecting curves, where the classes were determined from the angle obtained, based on the visual support provided by the image captured from the column frame, where generally an angle less than 80° meant that the vehicle was in a curve (class 1), otherwise it was in a straight section (class 0), although this was not necessarily the case, so it was based entirely on the image to determine the classification. Using the aforementioned feature selection methods, the best ones to work with were determined. In this way, binomial Logistic Regression, Random Forest, SVM and ANN models were trained, and cross-validated with 5-folds, with 80% training data and 20% test data.

Random Forest. Random Forest is a very common learning algorithm that uses a technique known as ensemble. It consists of building multiple decision trees and combining their predictions to obtain a more robust and accurate result. The main idea behind Random Forest is that the combination of several weak models (decision trees) can generate a strong model. This is a model that performs successive partitions of the feature space, making decisions based on binary questions (e.g., "Is age greater than 25 years"). For a training set T, the algorithm generates N decision trees $(T_1, T_2, ..., T_N)$, and the final prediction is the mode (in classification) or the average (in regression) of the predictions of each tree. Table 3 presents the decision tree formulas for both classification and regression [3,8,11] (Table 4).

Table 4. Formulas for Random Forest model.

Feature	Formula
Classification	$\hat{y} = mode(T_1(x), T_2(x), ..., T_N(x))$
Regression	$\hat{y} = \frac{1}{N}\sum_{i=1}^{N} T_i(x)$

Logistic Regression. Another training model for this research was Logistic Regression. This statistical tool is useful when we have a dichotomous variable, that is, when our study requires a prediction of values, for example, between 0 and 1. This is a classification model. Its objective is to predict the probability that an instance belongs to a particular class. It is defined by a sigmoid function, which transforms the linear predictions of the model into a probability between 0 and 1:

$$F(x) = \frac{1}{1 + e^{-x}} \tag{3}$$

where $F(x)$ is the probability that a drop exists; x is a linear combination of the input variables of the form $\beta 0 + \beta 1x1 + ... + \beta nxn$ [6,7].

Support Vector Machine (SVM). Support Vector Machines (SVM) are a machine learning method widely used in data classification, due to their ability to find optimal decision boundaries between different classes. They are also known as kernel machines, as they can use kernel functions to transform data and allow separation into higher dimensional spaces. SVMs are commonly implemented in C to achieve efficient execution, using fast optimization algorithms to solve the classification problem. From a mathematical point of view, an SVM seeks to find the optimal hyperplane that separates two classes in the feature space with the largest possible margin [9,10].

$$H(x) = w^T x + b \tag{4}$$

where w is a vector of coefficients perpendicular to the hyperplane, b is the skewness and x is a vector with the input data.

Artificial Neural Network (ANN). Artificial Neural Networks (ANNs) are computational models inspired by the human brain. They consist of interconnected artificial neurons linked by weights that represent the strength of the connections. Each unit processes information through weighted inputs, an activation function, and a single output.

An ANN is defined by its transfer function, learning rule, and the way its neurons are connected. The basic unit mimics the behavior of a biological neuron: it receives inputs, applies weights, combines them, and passes the result through a function (commonly the sigmoid function) to produce an output [1].

The net input value to a neuron is the sum of the values arriving to it, weighted by the weight of the connections, plus the skewness.

$$x = \sum_{i=1}^{n} x_i w_i + b \tag{5}$$

It is usually represented as the matrix product

$$x = XW + b \tag{6}$$

An activation function (g) is usually applied to this value, which transforms it into what is known as the activation value a, which is what finally comes out of the neuron.

$$a = g(x) = g(XW + b) \tag{7}$$

The specific architecture of the implemented ANN is shown in Fig. 6 and follows a feed-forward topology with 3 dense layers: The input layer, corresponding to the 8 extracted features; two hidden layers, where the first dense layer has 64 neurons and ReLU activation, followed by a Dropout layer (rate=0. 3) for regularization and to reduce overfitting during training, and the second dense layer which has 32 neurons and ReLU activation and uses the same Dropout as the previous layer; and the output dense layer, which has 1 neuron and uses the sigmoid activation function.

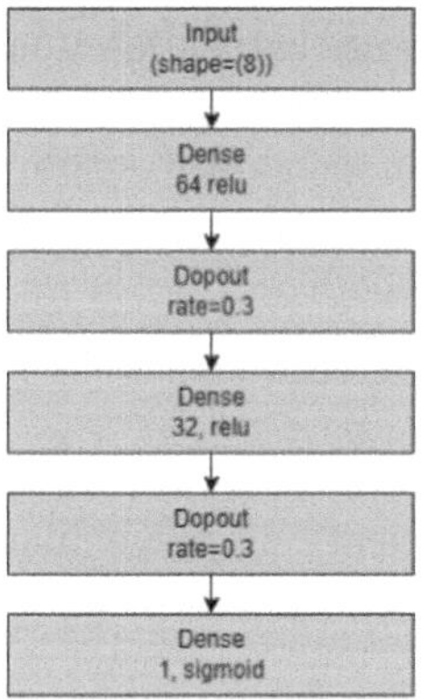

Fig. 6. ANN diagram for binary classification, own creation.

4 Results

Table 5 presents the performance results obtained by the four classification models evaluated: Random Forest, Logistic Regression, SVM and Artificial Neural Network (ANN), using three different feature selection methods: RFE (Recursive Feature Elimination), LASSO and BORUTA. Metrics analyzed include AUC, Recall, F1-score and Accuracy.

Table 5. Results of evaluated models.

Model	Method of selection	AUC	Recall	F1-score	Accuracy
Random Forest	RFE	0.99	0.97	0.94	0.96
	LASSO	0.99	0.97	0.94	0.96
	BORUTA	0.99	0.97	0.94	0.96
Logistic Regression	RFE	0.98	0.91	0.91	0.94
	LASSO	0.98	0.91	0.91	0.94
	BORUTA	0.98	0.91	0.91	0.94
SVM	RFE	0.99	0.94	0.92	0.95
	LASSO	0.99	0.94	0.92	0.95
	BORUTA	0.99	0.94	0.92	0.95
ANN	RFE	0.98	0.97	0.94	0.96
	LASSO	0.98	0.97	0.94	0.96
	BORUTA	0.98	0.97	0.94	0.96

Overall, Random Forest is observed to be the best overall performing model, achieving AUC, Recall, F1-score and Accuracy values of up to 0.99, 0.97, 0.94 and 0.96, respectively, consistently across the three selection methods. This suggests that such a model is highly robust against the feature reduction method used. Figure 7 shows the ROC curve and the confusion matrix where the results can be seen.

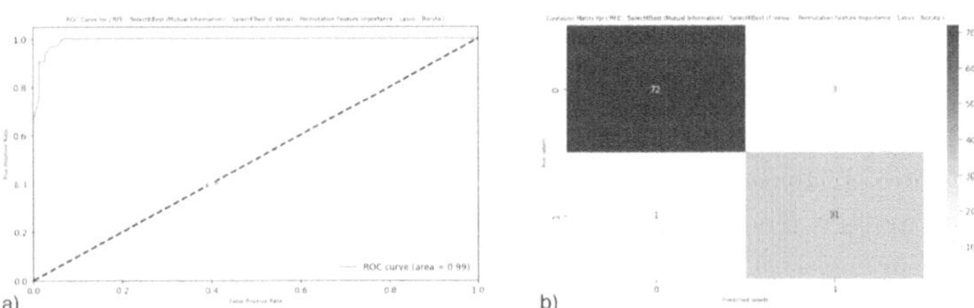

Fig. 7. a) Random Forest ROC curve and b) Confusion matrix.

Logistic Regression showed slightly lower performance, especially in Recall and F1-score, with values in the range of 0.91 to 0.94. Despite this, it maintains an acceptable accuracy (0.94) and an AUC around 0.98. Figure 8 shows the results obtained from the ROC curve and the confusion matrix.

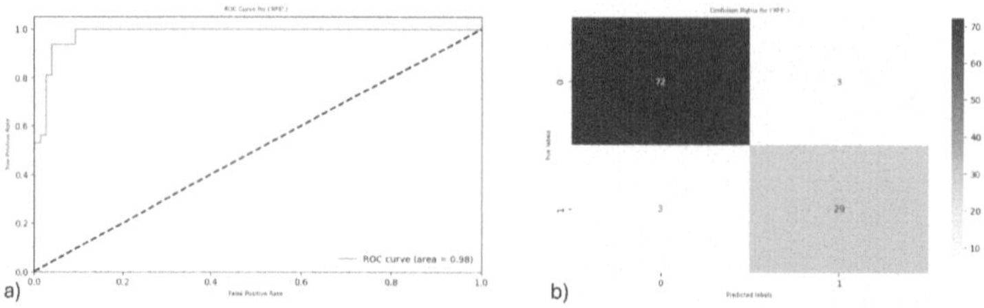

Fig. 8. a) Logistic Regression ROC curve and b) Confusion matrix.

For its part, the SVM model achieved comparable performance to Random Forest, with maximum AUC values of 0.99, and Recall and F1-score metrics of up to 0.94 and 0.92 respectively, regardless of the selection method applied. This demonstrates a good ability of the model to generalize to the classification task. Figure 9 shows the roc curve and confusion matrix of the results obtained from SVM.

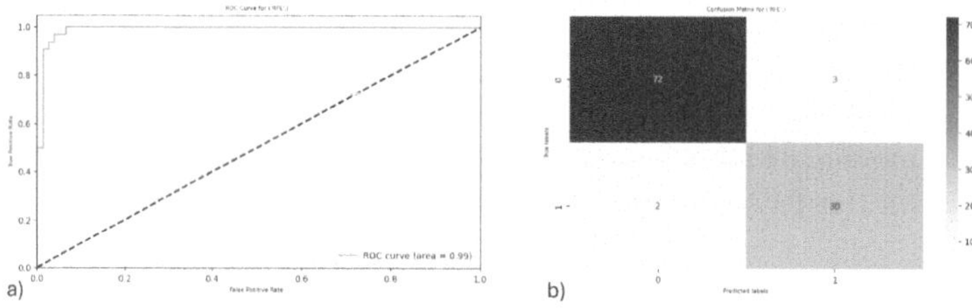

Fig. 9. a) SVM ROC curve and b) Confusion matrix.

Finally, the artificial neural network (ANN) obtained competitive results, standing out with a Recall and F1-score of up to 0.97 and 0.94, and an Accuracy of 0.96 in some cases. Although it did not outperform Random Forest, it showed solid and stable performance. Figure 10 shows the roc curve and confusion matrix of the ANN results.

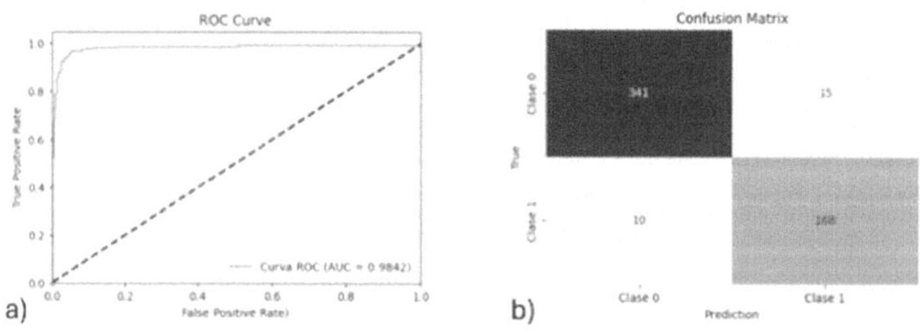

Fig. 10. a) ANN ROC curve and b)Confusion matrix.

5 Discussion

The results obtained indicate that all the models evaluated were able to classify with high accuracy the type of track (straight or curved), even using different feature selection methods. The similarity between the results suggests that the features extracted from the dataset are robust and discriminative, which is an important advantage in real-time applications such as autonomous navigation.

In particular, the Random Forest model showed slightly better performance than the rest, maintaining high and consistent values in all evaluated metrics (AUC, Recall, F1-score and Accuracy) regardless of the selection method used. This stability positions it as an ideal candidate for embedded system implementations, where reliability is critical.

Logistic regression and SVM also offered competitive performance, although with a slightly higher sensitivity to the selection method. The artificial neural network (ANN) obtained similar results, especially in terms of Recall and F1-score, making it a viable alternative, especially if infrastructure with network computing capacity is available.

An additional finding is that the feature selection methods (RFE, LASSO and BORUTA) did not generate significant variations in the results. This can be interpreted as an indication that the original feature set already contained enough relevant information for classification, allowing for a reduction in preprocessing complexity without sacrificing performance.

One of the main contributions of this study is its potential application in automatic vehicle speed regulation, by integrating this classification with a PID controller. This will allow the car to reduce its speed when facing curves, thus increasing safety and navigation control. The low latency and high accuracy of the selected models make their implementation feasible in real time, even in scale vehicles with limited computational resources.

6 Conclusion

This study compared four machine learning algorithms Logistic Regression, Random Forest, Support Vector Machine (SVM) and Artificial Neural Network (ANN)-for the task of track type classification on a 1:10 scale autonomous vehicle. Among the evaluated models, Random Forest stood out as the most efficient and robust, achieving the best results in all the analyzed metrics. Furthermore, the feature selection methods (RFE, LASSO and Boruta) had minimal impact on classifier performance, suggesting that the original feature set was sufficiently informative and well constructed.

This study demonstrates the feasibility of classifying track type on a 1:10 scale platform. However, it is important to consider its limitations. The relatively small database, collected on a single track type, could affect the models' ability to generalize in more complex environments. Furthermore, the analysis did not include an evaluation of algorithm latency, a crucial metric for real-time applications. The successful integration of these models into a detection and control loop, through a PID controller, reinforces their practical potential for achieving adaptive vehicle behavior in real time.

As future work, we propose to address these limitations by integrating the models into embedded systems, evaluating them under more complex environments, and exploring deep learning architectures such as convolutional neural networks (CNNs) that could eliminate the need for manual feature extraction and improve the robustness of the system in different scenarios.

References

1. Agatonovic-Kustrin, S., Beresford, R.: Basic concepts of artificial neural network (ANN) modeling and its application in pharmaceutical research. J. Pharm. Biomed. Anal. **22**(5), 717–727 (2000). https://doi.org/10.1016/S0731-7085(99)00272-1
2. Balasriram, K., Manimozhi, M.: Curve path detection in autonomous vehicle using deep learning. Preprints (2018). https://doi.org/10.20944/preprints201805.0326.v1. https://www.preprints.org/manuscript/201805.0326/v1
3. Breiman, L.: Random forests. Mach. Learn. **45**(1), 5–32 (2001). https://doi.org/10.1023/A:1010933404324
4. Celaya-Padilla, J.M., et al.: Speed bump detection using accelerometric features: a genetic algorithm approach. Sensors **18**(2), 443 (2018). https://doi.org/10.3390/s18020443
5. Darst, B.F., Malecki, K.C., Engelman, C.D.: Using recursive feature elimination in random forest to account for correlated variables in high dimensional data. BMC Genet. **19**(Suppl 1), 65 (2018). https://doi.org/10.1186/s12863-018-0633-8
6. Friedman, J., Hastie, T., Tibshirani, R.: The Elements of Statistical Learning: Data Mining, Inference, and Prediction, 2nd edn. Springer Series in Statistics. Springer, New York (2009)
7. Hosmer, D.W., Lemeshow, S., Sturdivant, R.X.: Applied Logistic Regression, 3rd edn. Wiley Series in Probability and Statistics. Wiley, Hoboken (2013)
8. James, G., Witten, D., Hastie, T., Tibshirani, R.: An Introduction to Statistical Learning: with Applications in R. Springer Texts in Statistics, 1 edn. Springer, New York (2013). https://doi.org/10.1007/978-1-4614-7138-7
9. Jorge Botana, G.D.: Máquinas de vector soporte. Universidad Complutense de Madrid, repositorio Docta Complutense (2023). https://hdl.handle.net/20.500.14352/87527, apuntes de docencia del Máster en Metodología de las Ciencias del Comportamiento y de la Salud
10. Kecman, V.: Support vector machines – an introduction. In: Wang, L. (ed.) Support Vector Machines: Theory and Applications. Studies in Fuzziness and Soft Computing, vol. 177, pp. 1–47. Springer, Heidelberg (2005). https://doi.org/10.1007/10984697_1
11. Liaw, A., Wiener, M.: Classification and regression by `randomForest`. R News **2**(3), 18–22 (2002). https://CRAN.R-project.org/doc/Rnews/
12. Maeda-Gutiérrez, V., et al.: Risk-profile and feature selection comparison in diabetic retinopathy. J. Personal. Med. **11**(12), 1327 (2021). https://doi.org/10.3390/jpm11121327
13. Maeda-Gutiérrez, V., et al.: Evaluating feature selection methods for accurate diagnosis of diabetic kidney disease. Biomedicines **12**(12), 2858 (2024). https://doi.org/10.3390/biomedicines12122858

14. Pavel, M.I., Tan, S.Y., Abdullah, A.: Vision-based autonomous vehicle systems based on deep learning: a systematic literature review. Appl. Sci. **12**(14), 6831 (2022). https://doi.org/10.3390/app12146831
15. Quezada-Villalobos, A.C., et al.: Lane direction by implementing random sampling. Algorithms (2024, in press)
16. Reveles-Martínez, R., et al.: Data-driven autonomous system for lane keeping in a 1:10 scale vehicle for autonomous driving. In: Proceedings of the Mexican Robotics Tournament 2024 (2024)

Performance Indicator of Academic Achievement Based on the Development of Generic Competencies from Challenge-Based Learning

Samara Romero Caballero(✉), Andrés Rodríguez Toscano, and Liliana Canquiz Rincón

Universidad de la Costa CUC, Barranquilla, Colombia
{sromero10,arodrigu83,lcanquiz}@cuc.edu.co

Abstract. This research analyzes the development of generic competencies and learning outcomes through the implementation of Challenge-Based Learning (CBL) in a higher education institution. This research aims to identify a performance indicator of academic **achievement** based on the development of generic competencies. Professional training requires the solid development of transversal and higher-order skills that facilitate efficient performance in changing work contexts. It is essential that higher education prioritize innovation, creativity, relational skills, and, especially, the meaningful appropriation of knowledge, as well as comprehensive training in important competencies for life and work. This research identified a performance indicator of academic achievement based on the development of key generic competencies. This allows for balanced planning and relevant teaching strategies for classroom management for the development of generic and specific competencies through the implementation of CBL. In addition, important findings related to behaviorism are shown in certain ranges of competency performance. In summary, the results show that the institutional CBL strategy must be intentionally planned, considering behavioral effects that do not prevent the decline of these competencies.

Keywords: Challenge-based learning · Performance indicators · Academic performance · Generic competencies · Classroom management planning

1 Introduction

Universities and higher education centers around the world are increasingly focused on creating educational environments that favor the learning of their students, implementing various methodologies and teaching approaches [1].

The objective is for future professionals to be able to apply the acquired knowledge in real situations, proposing solutions to different problems in the environment [2]. In this context, the strengthening of generic competencies has taken on a central role as a key factor in the training process [3].

T. Guarda et al. (Eds.): ARTIIS 2025, CCIS 2789, pp. 590–601, 2026.
https://doi.org/10.1007/978-3-032-16758-3_44

Consequently, for the planning and creation of these training environments, active experiences play a fundamental role. Therefore, in the university field, challenge-based learning (CBL) emerges from experiential learning as a holistic and integrated approach to learning that combines experience, cognition, and behavior [4], under the premise that students acquire knowledge in a more significant way when they participate in situations similar to those they will face in real life, in these scenarios, students experience both achievements and failures, make risky decisions, manage uncertainty [5] and even behaviorism arises in them, especially in those students who present low academic performance but increase their generic skills, this behavior can be explained as an adaptive response to the reinforcement system of the educational environment.

According to operant conditioning, proposed by [6], people tend to repeat actions that have been positively rewarded. In this sense, strengthening generic competencies such as self-regulation, critical thinking, and problem-solving skills can be considered behaviors adopted to achieve a specific goal, such as passing a course.

Therefore, CBL seeks to connect students interests with relevant educational experiences, thus providing practical value to the teaching process [7]. This is confirmed by [8], who were able to establish that evaluation, success, and performance rates are higher among university students with active methodologies such as CBL. In this way, professionals in training can see how their learning outcomes impact reality. However, a good number of new professionals continue to have difficulties in applying what they have learned to the work context, which implies important skills such as critical and systemic thinking [9] that are developed from teaching methods or methodologies that improve said learning and its relevance in the business [10, 11]. In this sense, from a practical point of view, systemic thinking drives future professionals towards the design, execution and evaluation of the projects developed and their dynamic impact on the performance of the activity linked to sustainable development [12].

In this context, CBL represents a disruptive transformation in the substantive function of teaching in higher education. Its main characteristic is that pedagogical activity ceases to focus exclusively on the teacher and the transmission of content, as occurs in traditional approaches, because the focus shifts toward the context and its demands. This requires autonomy and self-efficacy on the part of students, since these competencies are directly associated with academic performance and act as a mediating variable of motivation, facilitating self-regulation and commitment mechanisms in students, as demonstrated through structural models [13].

This implies planning lessons not in an improvised but intentional manner, based on the indicators to be evaluated and the goals to be achieved, because classroom management planning constitutes an essential element of the educational act, since it involves meticulously anticipating and structuring objectives, indicators, content, methods, and evaluation, with the purpose of addressing the diversity of the student body and promoting meaningful learning environments [14]. Hence the importance of defining an academic performance indicator based on the development of generic competencies.

In addition to the above, pedagogical activity in the European context [15], together with other research, highlights that the design, planning, and execution of activities aimed at strengthening metacognition in students not only favors self-regulation processes linked to critical thinking, but also provides teachers with tools to regulate their own pedagogical intervention. This is because these activities offer continuous feedback on the level of development of students critical thinking and reasoning, allowing teaching strategies to be adjusted in a more relevant and timely manner [16].

Thus, Challenge-Based Learning, aimed at strengthening generic competencies, highlights the implementation of teaching strategies that increase student motivation to achieve learning objectives [17]. However, this approach demands the development of multiple skills, including self-regulation of learning and an active disposition towards autonomy using appropriate methods and resources [18]. In this order of ideas, the elements that influence the effectiveness of CBL have acquired increasing relevance, consolidating itself as an emerging line of research with broad potential for application in different areas of knowledge.

The work of [19], shows how this pedagogical approach can be adapted and generate positive impacts in diverse disciplinary contexts. From this perspective, several of the aforementioned studies agree that active methodologies promote the development of generic competencies and that there is a correlation between these competencies and professional performance [20].

However, critical areas for improvement are also identified, especially regarding the strengthening of communication, linguistic, and collaborative work skills, the lack of which constitutes a significant gap for the advancement of knowledge from contemporary research practice [8] and the simple behaviorism mediated between academic performance and performance in generic competencies.

Likewise, based on a review of the main theoretical frameworks in the field of pedagogy in Latin America, various studies have identified that fostering student motivation is a key element not only for ensuring the acquisition of knowledge, but also for fostering transformations in their social and professional environments. Furthermore, a positive self-concept regarding one's abilities is, in one way or another, related to students motivation for learning [21] Thus, several recent studies confirm that academic self-efficacy and self-esteem act as mediators between student motivation and performance.

For example, [22] demonstrated that the positive effect of autonomous learning management on academic performance was significant only when students had a strong belief in their own efficacy. This finding underscores the importance of strengthening academic confidence as a cornerstone of pedagogical strategies that integrate motivation, generic competencies, and learning outcomes.

Therefore, self-efficacy, understood according to [23] as the belief in one's ability to organize and execute the actions necessary to achieve specific objectives, constitutes a determining factor in the learning process. This perception directly influences how students face academic challenges, regulate their effort, and persistence in the face of difficulties. In the context of the development of generic competencies, self-efficacy acts as an internal driving force that drives students to take on a greater commitment to improving skills such as critical thinking, self-regulation, and collaborative work.

In this sense, as they experience progress in their performance, the achievements they obtain reinforce their belief in personal efficacy, generating a positive cycle of motivation and performance. This positive feedback not only improves their academic performance but also strengthens their resilience to failure and their willingness to adopt active methodologies such as challenge-based learning. The development of generic competencies takes on a central role, as these skills help shape attitudes oriented toward building a more just and sustainable society [24].

Thus, these competencies highlight the need to promote them regardless of the profession, which is why [25] propose that the development of generic competencies requires pedagogical approaches and methodological strategies that contextualize knowledge and allow solving environmental challenges and include technological tools as part of innovation. However, student autonomy also implies the ability to plan their actions, assume an active and committed role in learning, and build deep and meaningful understandings [26].

This is confirmed by [27], who emphasize the importance of planning and creating classroom conditions that foster self-reflection, as this enhances the ability to make informed decisions. However, this development is not possible without the presence of an engaged teacher who intentionally plans classroom management and designs and implements teaching and assessment strategies specifically geared toward strengthening these competencies [28].

These conditions are also related to the way generic competencies are assessed in higher education. This process must include moments in which students integrate and apply their knowledge in an articulated manner based on clear performance indicators and preferably in real-life contexts, with the aim of strengthening the authenticity of the assessment [29]. In this scientific context, certain key competencies have been identified that require greater attention, such as the command of a second language and the development of communication skills, considered relevant areas for improvement.

These elements, such as strategies, evaluation, and content, are part of the curriculum. From the curricular design, universities must define precise indicators and specific strategies aimed at developing learning. In this case, these are linked to generic competencies, since these constitute an essential condition that must be materialized in pedagogical practices within the classroom [29]. Another important aspect when delving deeper into this research topic revolves around the prioritization and equivalences of the generic competencies to be developed in university students.

On the other hand, in the Latin American context, the most frequently identified competencies are ethical commitment, teamwork, the ability to learn and adapt to new situations, and oral and written communication [11]. In this sense, student learning is favored by the implementation of active methodological strategies. However, this development is limited by critical factors, such as the limited practical applicability of the content, insufficient training of teaching staff to plan educational activities with student-centered methodologies, as well as by the personal conditions of the students, including immaturity and lack of motivation [11].

In contrast to the above, the least developed generic skills in this context are creativity, capacity for abstraction, reasoning and analysis, decision-making, autonomous learning and motivation, which are essential for the training process of professionals [30]. Therefore, there is a need for specific pedagogical routes to be planned at the higher education level for working on these skills, establishing efficient hierarchies and also including digital skills [15].

Therefore, the objective of this research is to analyze the development of generic competencies and performance in learning outcomes from the implementation of Challenge-Based Learning in a higher education institution to identify a performance indicator of academic achievement based on the development of generic competencies that allows establishing adequate planning of classroom management, because the preparation of professionals demands the solid development of transversal and higher-order skills that facilitate their efficient performance in changing work contexts.

2 Methodology

To analyze the development of generic competencies and academic performance in the advanced courses taken by students in the final semesters of the different programs using the challenge-based learning (CBL) pedagogical approach, with a view to identifying a performance indicator of academic achievement based on the development of generic competencies. Initially, data on academic performance and generic competencies were collected from a cohort of 476 higher education students who took the generic competency assessment test at the end of the academic year. The variables analyzed were:

- Independent variable: Performance on generic competencies (scale 0 to 5).
- Dependent variable: Academic performance measured through a composite indicator.

To construct the composite indicator, academic performance was adjusted for generic competencies using a quotient to observe relative dispersion. This quotient was interpreted as a measure or indicator of academic performance based on the development of generic competencies. The indicator equation is shown below:

$$\mathrm{PI} = \mathrm{AA}/\mathrm{GC} \tag{1}$$

where:

PI: Performance indicator of academic achievement based on the development of actual generic competencies.

AA: Actual academic achievement

GC: Actual performance in generic competencies

To theoretically model the relationship between both variables, a fourth-degree polynomial regression model was applied. The choice of model was justified by the nonlinearity of the distribution, the high coefficient of determination, and the need to capture inflections in the behavior of the data. A polynomial regression model of the form:

$$y = a_4x^4 + a_3x^3 + a_2x^2 + a_1x + a_0 \tag{2}$$

where:

y: academic performance indicator based on the development of generic theoretical competencies

x: Performance in generic competencies

The coefficients were estimated using least squares.

To evaluate the model, the coefficient of determination (R2) was determined. To do this, the observed data were represented using a scatter plot, and the curve of the academic performance indicator was superimposed on the development of theoretical generic competencies, allowing for the identification of patterns of concentration and dispersion.

Furthermore, to calculate the relative variation of the theoretical indicator (y), data ranging from 0 to 5 in the development of generic competencies were generated to replace them in the equation (y). This allows the calculation of the performance indicator to be compared with the value of the previous interval for each performance interval to determine when changes are not significant and to conduct analyses based on this. The formula for percentage relative change is shown below:

$$\text{Relative change } (\%) = \left(\frac{y_n - y_n - 1}{y_n - 1}\right) \times 100 \tag{3}$$

where:

y_n : is the theoretical performance indicator of academic achievement based on the current development of generic competencies.

y_{n-1}: is the theoretical performance indicator of academic performance based on the development of the previous generic competencies.

The resulting percentage change values were plotted against performance on generic competencies, producing a smooth curve illustrating the dynamics of the relative impact of academic performance versus competency levels.

3 Results and Discussion

The results and discussions of the research are presented below. Figure 1 shows the academic performance indicator based on the development of generic competencies.

This figure shows a clear inverse and nonlinear relationship between generic competency and the academic achievement/generic competency ratio, modeled using a fourth-degree polynomial regression with a coefficient of determination R^2 of 0.8585. This indicates that the model explains approximately 85.85% of the variance observed in the academic achievement indicator based on performance in generic competencies. This validates a significant and nonlinear relationship, indicating a strong fit between the model and the data.

The general trend shows that, as performance in generic competencies increases, the ratio decreases rapidly at first and then stabilizes, suggesting that students with lower generic competencies show greater variability and lower relative academic efficiency. Visually, there is a high dispersion at low levels of competency and a progressive concentration of the data as this improves, which can be interpreted as a reduction in the variance of relative achievement.

Likewise, potential outliers are identified at the lower end of the competency scale, associated with the academic performance indicator based on the development of high generic competencies, which may require individual analysis. This trend implies that strengthening generic competencies, especially at the lower levels, could translate into

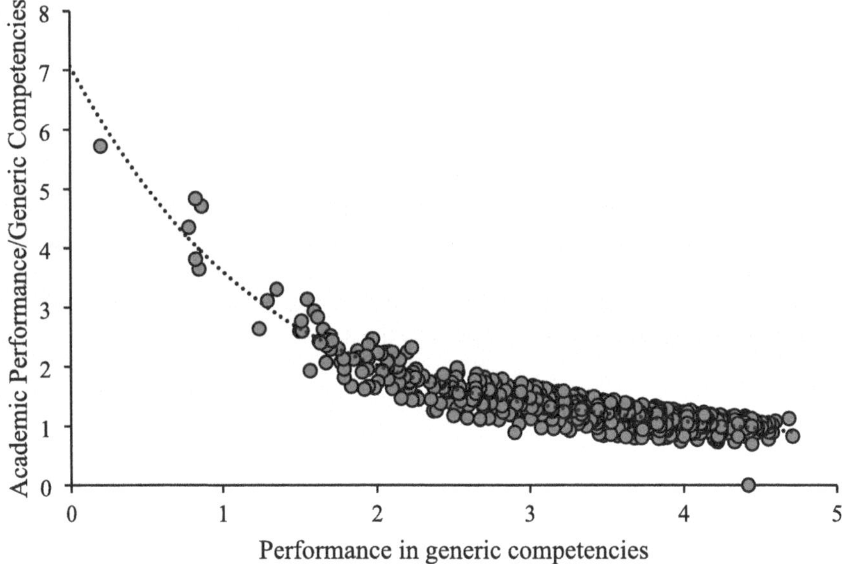

Fig. 1. Performance indicator of academic achievement and generic competencies

a significant improvement in the efficiency of academic performance, providing a valuable input for educational decision-making aimed at equity and quality in classroom management planning.

Figure 2 shows the relative change in the theoretical performance indicator of academic achievement based on the development of generic competencies.

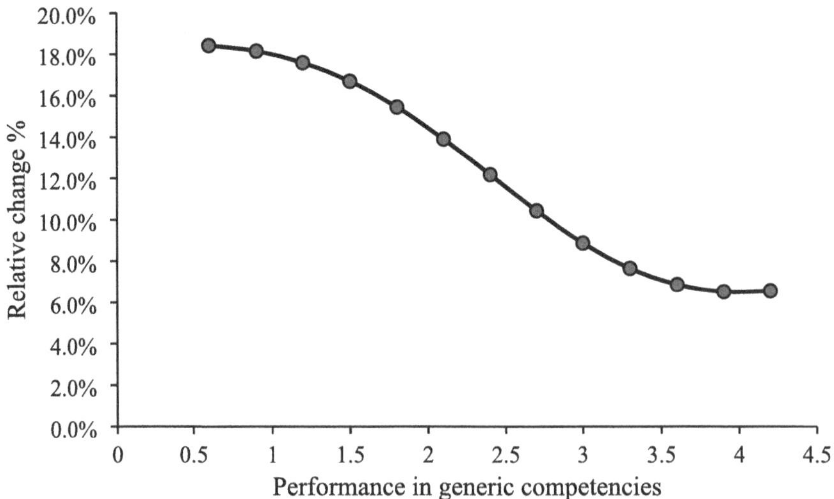

Fig. 2. Relative change in the performance indicator

Figure 2 shows how the percentage relative change systematically decreases with increasing generic competency: from values close to 18% at low levels to stabilizing below 6% at a competency value close to 3.5. This progressive decline in relative change suggests that marginal improvements in generic competency have increasingly smaller impacts on relative performance, evidencing a phenomenon of diminishing returns. Overall, the data support the hypothesis that strengthening generic competencies is more critical and produces greater positive effects in the lower reaches of academic performance. This is a key argument for focusing differential pedagogical and didactic strategies on those facing larger performance gaps.

By integrating both figures, it can be stated that there is a consistent inverse relationship between generic competency and relative academic performance. This threshold, empirically identified as a turning point where the performance/competency ratio begins to stabilize and marginal effects decrease, represents an optimal level of competency development at which students demonstrate greater relative academic efficiency. In this context, if teachers plan their classroom management with challenge-based learning strategies so that their students' generic competencies reach a maximum of 3.6, this can lead to students progressively improving their academic performance.

The fact that students with low academic performance in advanced subjects began to show greater interest in achieving higher scores in developing generic competencies, since these tests were administered at the end of the academic year, may be associated with a behaviorist logic: they seek positive reinforcement, for example, good grades or recognition, which increases the frequency of successful behaviors. According to behaviorism, specifically [6], operant conditioning, each reinforced behavior is more likely to be repeated. In this case, the student identifies that by demonstrating improved generic competencies. For example, study skills, organization, or problem-solving, hey receive rewards (grades, praise), which strengthens these behaviors. Similarly, negative reinforcement, such as avoiding extra tasks or reprimands when improving results, also promotes the repetition of these efficient behaviors.

On the other hand, although traditional behaviorism focuses on stimuli and responses, it is now clear that students also build self concept: they are driven by the need to protect their self-esteem. According to [31], the theory of self-worth suggests that low-achieving students adopt strategies such as self-handicapping or enhancing generic skills to avoid the stigma of failure. Thus, by improving skills, they seek to build an internal (and social) narrative of being competent, minimizing the likelihood of being evaluated as incapable.

Therefore, self-efficacy, according to [23] also plays a key role. Although it comes from cognitive behaviorism, the response reinforces that, by experiencing improvements in skills, the student builds confidence, which generates a virtuous cycle: greater effort → more reinforcements → greater self-efficacy → greater motivation. This phenomenon is supported by recent studies that indicate that self-efficacy mediates the relationship between motivation and academic performance, for example, in a sample of 659 doctoral students in China, it was identified that academic motivation influences performance not only directly, but also through its impact on self-efficacy, and the latter has a significant mediating effect on academic performance [32].

In summary, from a behaviorist perspective, low-achieving students increase their efforts to improve generic skills because they associate these efforts with positive reinforcement and a reduction in negative stimuli, while simultaneously building and protecting their academic self-efficacy and self-esteem. These combined components form the psychopedagogical basis of their behavior.

From a behaviorist perspective, the behavior of students who exhibit low academic performance but increase their generic skills can be explained as an adaptive response to the reinforcement system of the educational environment. According to [33] operant conditioning, individuals repeat behaviors that have been positively reinforced. In this case, improving generic skills such as self-regulation, critical thinking, or problem-solving becomes an observable strategy for achieving a desired outcome: passing the course.

This behavior is shaped by the educational system, which reinforces it with grades, passing grades, teacher recognition, or grade advancement. When a student perceives that improving their competency brings them closer to achieving the goal (passing the course), this behavior is strengthened and tends to be repeated. Furthermore, if previous poor performance has led to negative consequences (failing, sanctions, social disapproval), the effort to increase competency can also be motivated by negative reinforcement: avoiding punishment or unpleasant experiences. Both forms of reinforcement (positive and negative) are fundamental within the behaviorist paradigm.

Additionally, based on the theory of self-worth [22], students protect their self-esteem by redirecting their efforts toward areas where they can demonstrate achievement, even if their overall academic performance has not been optimal. Increasing competencies allows for the construction of a narrative of personal progress and reinforces the perception of self-efficacy, a concept developed by [23]. Academic self-efficacythe belief in one's ability to achieve specific educational goals, is a powerful motivator for persistence, even after experiences of failure.

Finally, recent empirical studies have confirmed that strengthening generic competencies acts as a protective factor against low performance, improving students' ability to face demanding academic tasks, adapt to active methodologies and achieve passing criteria for the subjects. This is connected with a study carried out with nursing students that demonstrated significant improvements in critical thinking, problem-solving and communication skills after implementing active learning strategies, showing that these skills strengthen students' ability to face demanding tasks and improve their academic performance [34].

4 Conclusions and Recommendation

Students with lower academic performance tend to respond positively to educational reinforcement, developing generic competencies as an adaptive strategy, in a cycle influenced by positive and negative reinforcement, according to the principles of Skinner's operant conditioning, since there is an inverse, significant, and nonlinear relationship between the development of generic competencies and relative academic performance. This pattern was effectively modeled using a fourth-degree polynomial regression, with a high level of fit ($R^2 = 0.8585$), which empirically validates that, at lower levels of generic competency, academic efficiency is more compromised.

On the other hand, the greatest positive effects of strengthening generic competencies are evident in the lower segments of academic performance. In these cases, improvements in competencies are associated with substantial percentage changes in relative academic performance, indicating greater sensitivity to change and justifying prioritizing pedagogical interventions at these levels.

Thus, observed academic behavior is mediated by psychological factors such as academic self-efficacy and self-esteem, suggesting that generic competencies not only impact performance but also emotional well-being and student persistence.

The data support the idea that strengthening generic competencies acts as a protective factor against low performance, improving students ability to tackle demanding tasks and adapt to active methodologies, especially in environments that promote autonomous and collaborative learning.

In this sense, if teachers strategically plan their classroom instruction by incorporating a challenge-based learning (CBL) approach, specifically geared toward progressively strengthening generic competencies to levels close to 3.6 (on a scale of 1 to 5), a significant and sustained impact on students' academic performance can be generated.

Therefore, the systematic implementation of CBL with clear competency goals can be a key pedagogical tool for improving overall student performance, especially in contexts requiring innovative training responses focused on comprehensive development.

By reaching a maximum level of generic competency development of 3.6, students not only acquire better cognitive and attitudinal tools to successfully tackle complex tasks, but also narrow the academic performance gaps that often occur at lower levels of competency, thus promoting greater equity in learning outcomes.

In this regard, it is recommended to design differentiated pedagogical strategies, focusing especially on low-performing students, since evidence suggests that the impact of competency strengthening is more significant in these groups. Therefore, it is important to establish minimum and structured standards for working on generic competencies, defining variables such as the number of hours, type of challenge, and number of competencies addressed, in order to ensure a more efficient and measurable pedagogical implementation.

Furthermore, it is pertinent to include formative assessments focused on self-efficacy, which allow students to visualize their progress in developing competencies, strengthening motivation and confidence in their own learning process.

Thus, future longitudinal and multivariate research is suggested to explore the cumulative effects of the development of generic competencies in different academic contexts and their interaction with variables such as gender, field of study, and teaching modality. Furthermore, research can establish how the performance indicator of academic efficiency achievement changes based on the actual development of generic competencies, versus the timing of the administration of tests to measure these competencies during the academic period; therefore, at the higher education level, the development of generic competencies is essential as a cross-cutting axis in institutional policies for educational quality, ensuring that they are recognized, evaluated, and systematically provided feedback in all subjects and programs.

Finally, this study could be expanded to a larger sample in other academic contexts at universities (other semesters, other universities, other cultures, etc.) in order to further counter or strengthen the argued conclusions. Future research could encompass a global scope with actions to improve generic competencies and academic performance.

References

1. Morales Salas, R.E., Veytia Bucheli, M.V.B.G.: Metodologías activas que mejoran el aprendizaje en la Educación Superior. Univ. Tarraconensis Rev. Ciències l Educ. 93–111 (2022)
2. Gleason Rodríguez, M.A., Rubio, J.E.: Implementación del aprendizaje experiencial en la universidad, sus beneficios en el alumnado y el rol docente. Rev. Educ. 264–282 (2020)
3. Soto-Araya, M., Baños, J.E., Pérez, J., Moyano, E.: Competencias transversales: una revisión de las mallas curriculares de la carrera de odontología en Chile. Int. J. Odontostomatol. **15**(4), 928–937 (2021)
4. Tecnológico de Monterrey. Aprendizaje Basado En Retos. México (2018)
5. Mora Gutiérrez, J.P.: Aprendizaje Basado en Retos en Lingüística, asignatura de primero del Grado de Filología Hispánica. In: Ciclos Mejor. en el aula. Año 2019. Exp. innovación docente la Univ. Sevilla, pp. 1402–1428 (2020)
6. Skinner, B.F.A.A.K.: Aboutbehaviorism (1957)
7. Portuguez Castro, M., Gómez Zermeño, M.G.: Challenge based learning: Innovative pedagogy for sustainability through e-learning in higher education. Sustain. **12**(10) (2020)
8. López-Fraile, L.A., Agüero, M.M., Jiménez-García, E.: Effect of challenge-based learning on academic performance rates in communication degree programs at the European University of Madrid. Form. Univ. **14**(5), 65–74 (2021)
9. Rueda Lizarazo, H., Canós-Darós, L., Santandreu Mascarell, C., Guijarro, E.: Competencias socioemocionales de pensamiento crítico y resolución de problemas en la formación universitaria. Prax. Pedag. **23**(35), 232–256 (2023)
10. Felipe Afonso, M.I., García, L.A., Castro Sánchez, J.J.: Cognitive learning strategies and study control strategies and their relationship with academic performance in psychology students at the University of La Laguna. Rev. Investig. Educ. **18**(3), 304–315 (2020)
11. Illesca Pretty, M., Barraza Tello, A., Alejandro Antonio, H.D., Godoy Pozo, J.: Competencias genéricas: opinión de estudiantes de la carrera de Nutrición y Dietética, Universidad de Atacama-Chile. Arch. Médico Camagüey **26** (2022)
12. Marcos-Sánchez, R., Ferrández, D., Morón, C.: Systems thinking for sustainability education in building and business administration and management degrees. Sustain. **14**(19), 1–20 (2022)
13. Meng, Q., Zhang, Q.: The influence of academic self-efficacy on university students' academic performance: the mediating effect of academic engagement. Sustain. **15**(7) (2023)
14. Cifuentes Garzón, J.E.: Planeación de clases en el marco de la enseñanza para la comprensión con metodología de Lesson Study. Plumilla Educ. 39–67 (2021)
15. Tura, L.V., Bargallo, C.M., Prat, B.O.: A didactic proposal for the development of critical thinking in the high school science classroom. Rev. Eureka **20**(1), 130201–130214 (2023)
16. Torres, A.D., Vera, M.G., Llamocca, M.Á.J.: "Efecto de un programa de estrategias metacognitivas sobre el pensamiento crítico de los estudiantes de primaria. Horizontes. Rev. Investig. Ciencias Educ. **9**(36), 69–84 (2025)
17. Sanchez Cuevas, M., Pérez Restovic, R., Fernández, J.A.: Aprendizaje basado en retos: propuesta educativa para la transformación social. Rev. Int. Aprendiz. **5**(2), 117–126 (2019)

18. Sinche Villa, D.A., Quizhpe Cueva, J.L., del C. Alvarado Jaramillo, E., Granda Medina, M.N.: Aprendizaje basado en retos para el desarrollo de competencias matemáticas en la educación básica superior. LATAM Rev. Latinoam. Ciencias Soc. Human. **4**(6) (2023)
19. Caballero, S.R., Rincón, L.C., Rodríguez, A., Pérez, A.V., Gómez, G.M.: Challenge-based learning and design thinking in higher education: institutional strategies for linking experiential learning, innovation, and academic performance. Innov. Educ. Teach. Int. 1–18 (2024)
20. Rohanai, R., Daud, K.A.M., Omar, N.H., Ismail, M.E., Sulaiman, A.: Concept of Correlation between active learning and employability skills in TVET. Online J. TVET Pract. **5**(1) (2020)
21. Muñoz Guevara, L.A.: Autoeficacia académica y competencias genéricas en estudiantes de Educación de una universidad nacional de Lima. Rev. Investig. Psicol. **25**(1), 23–39 (2022)
22. Zhao, Z., Ren, P., Yang, Q.: Student self-management, academic achievement: exploring the mediating role of self-efficacy and the moderating influence of gender—insights from a survey conducted in 3 Universities in America. J. Integr. Soc. Sci. Humanit. 1–12 (2023)
23. Bandura, A.: Self-efficacy: The exercise of control. W H Freema (1997)
24. Riquelme Hernández, C., Osses Paredes, G., Iturra Tapi, C.: Experiencias innovadoras y desarrollo socio-educativo, Asociación. Madrid (2019)
25. Gillate, I., Castrillo, J., Luna, U., Ibañez-Etxeberria, A.: Controversial issues and apps for developing social and civic competence. analysis of the effectiveness of Project 1936 in the initial teacher training. Rev. Psicodidact. **28**(1), 51–58 (2023)
26. Rosale Herrera, L.G., Peraza Treviño, R.: Competencias genéricas para el fortalecimiento del aprendizaje en la educación superior de la Región Occidente de México. Rev. Educ. Tecnol. **13**(1), 1–15 (2020)
27. Cabrera Lanzo, N., Fernández-Ferrer, M., Maina, M.F., Sangrà, A.: Design of a self-assessment proposal for the development of student self-regulation in higher education. RIED-Rev. Iberoam. Educ. Dist. **26**(1), 223–244 (2023)
28. Gallego Henao, A.M., Cardona Ocampo, J.E., Botero Bedoya, S.M., García Jiménez, M.D., Ramírez Arroyave, R.D.: Competencias genéricas y específicas, un análisis desde la perspectiva docente en una institución de educación superior. In: Triangulaciones entre gestión educativa, pedagógica y comunitaria, Fondo Editorial Universidad Católica Luis Amigó, pp. 50–63 (2025)
29. Ojeda-Nahuelcura, R., Carter Thuillier, B., López-Pastor, V., Fuentes-Nieto, T., Gallardo-Fuentes, F.: Assessment of generic competences in physical education teachers. Retos **43**, 521–532 (2021)
30. Pesantez, R., López, Z., Paz, K.: El desarrollo de las competencias generales en jóvenes universitarios para el emprendimiento sustentable. Rev. Conrado **17**(82), 402–410 (2021)
31. Covington, M.V.: Self-worth theory of achievement motivation: new insights and directions. Educ. Psychol. **58**(2), 87–101 (2023)
32. Guo, H., Zhou, Z., Ma, F., Chen, X.: Doctoral students' academic performance: the mediating role of academic motivation, academic buoyancy, and academic self-efficacy. Heliyon **10**(12) (2024)
33. Skinner, B.F.: About behaviorism (1974)
34. Chan, C.W.H., Tang, F.W.K., Chow, K.M., Wong, C.L.: Enhancing generic capabilities and metacognitive awareness of first-year nursing students using active learning strategy. BMC Nurs. **20**(1) (2021)

Author Index

T. Guarda et al. (Eds.): ARTIIS 2025, CCIS 2789, pp. 603–605, 2026.
https://doi.org/10.1007/978-3-032-16758-3

The manufacturer's authorised representative in the EU is Springer Nature Customer Service Centre GmbH, Europaplatz 3, 69115 Heidelberg, Germany. If you have any concerns regarding our products, please contact ProductSafety@springernature.com

Printed and bound by CPI Group (UK) Ltd, Croydon, CR0 4YY
07/07/2026
02160906-0017